LEGAL RESOLUTION OF NUCLEAR NON-PROLIFERATION DISPUTES

How viable is the resolution of nuclear non-proliferation disputes through the International Court of Justice and international arbitration? James Fry examines the compromissory clauses in the IAEA Statute, IAEA safeguards agreements and the Convention on the Physical Protection of Nuclear Material that give jurisdiction to these fora and analyzes recent jurisprudence to demonstrate how legal resolution can handle such politically sensitive disputes. In sum, legal resolution of nuclear non-proliferation disputes represents an option that States and commentators have all too often ignored. The impartiality and procedural safeguards of legal resolution should make it an acceptable option for target States and the international community, especially vis-à-vis the procedural shortcomings and general heavy-handedness of Security Council involvement under the UN Charter Chapter VII.

JAMES D. FRY is Assistant Professor of Law at the University of Hong Kong Faculty of Law, where he is also Director of the LL.M. program, Deputy Director of the Japan and Korea program and Warden of Lee Shan Kee Hall.

This publication has been made possible by a generous grant from the Research Grants Council of the Hong Kong Special Administrative Region, China (Project No HKU 744310H).

LEGAL RESOLUTION OF NUCLEAR NON-PROLIFERATION DISPUTES

JAMES D. FRY

CAMBRIDGE
UNIVERSITY PRESS

CAMBRIDGE
UNIVERSITY PRESS

University Printing House, Cambridge CB2 8BS, United Kingdom

Published in the United States of America by Cambridge University Press, New York

Cambridge University Press is part of the University of Cambridge.

It furthers the University's mission by disseminating knowledge in the pursuit of education, learning, and research at the highest international levels of excellence.

www.cambridge.org
Information on this title: www.cambridge.org/9781107041295

First published 2013

Printed in the United Kingdom by CPI Group Ltd, Croydon CR0 4YY

A catalogue record for this publication is available from the British Library

Library of Congress Cataloguing in Publication data
Fry, James D., 1975–
Legal resolution of nuclear non-proliferation disputes / James D. Fry.
pages cm
ISBN 978-1-107-04129-5
1. Nuclear nonproliferation 2. Dispute resolution (Law) 3. Diplomatic negotiations in international disputes. I. Title.
KZ5675.F79 2013
341.7′34–dc23
2013013388

ISBN 978-1-107-04129-5 Hardback

Optimus Parentibus

CONTENTS

PART I

Introduction

1

Foundational elements of the study

1.1 The problem and solution

In a dramatic exchange within the Security Council during the 1962 Cuban missile crisis, US ambassador to the UN Adlai Stevenson asked USSR ambassador to the UN Valerian Zorin point-blank whether the USSR had placed in Cuba missiles capable of carrying out a nuclear attack on the United States, to which Zorin sneered that he was not in a courtroom and that he did not appreciate being interrogated as if in a courtroom.[1] Stevenson retorted that Zorin was in the "courtroom of world opinion" and that he was prepared to provide evidence of such missiles as if in a courtroom, after which he presented evidence of intelligence photographs of the missile sites in courtroom-like fashion.[2] Apart from its rhetorical value, was there any significance to Stevenson's reference to the Security Council as a courtroom and to his procedural formalism? Some commentators assert that fairness and legitimacy depend partly on the procedures followed during a decision-making process, with legal resolution providing a better quality process vis-à-vis that of the Security Council on account of legal resolution's structural impartiality and due-process safeguards.[3] A desire on the part of Stevenson to improve the perceived fairness and legitimacy of those proceedings conceivably could have been the reason behind his words and actions in this case. Regardless, this suggests that problems with resolving nuclear non-proliferation disputes could arise partly out of shortcomings in the process, with the procedures of legal resolution improving on those shortcomings, thus presumably increasing the chances that the disputant State(s) respect the final determination. At the

1 See Robert F. Kennedy, Thirteen Days: A Memoir of the Cuban Missile Crisis 53–54 (2nd edn, 1971).

2 Ibid.

3 See ch. 5.3 *infra*; see also Thomas M. Franck, Fairness in International Law and Institutions 7–8, 218–244, 316–349 (1995).

same time, Zorin's response reflects the relatively common notion that legal resolution is inappropriate with politically sensitive disputes.[4] This study attempts to reconcile these two conflicting notions in exploring the possibility of legal resolution of nuclear non-proliferation disputes. Given how the International Court of Justice (ICJ) and international arbitral tribunals can find jurisdiction through compromissory clauses in nuclear non-proliferation agreements and the favorable jurisprudence on justiciability, legal resolution represents an option for States trying to resolve their nuclear non-proliferation disputes. Given the destructive potential of war, especially nuclear war, and the shortcomings of the Security Council's decision-making process when it comes to its Chapter VII measures, States should see legal resolution as a somewhat attractive option in terms of the procedural fairness it provides. This study represents an invitation to States to further consider legal resolution as an option with nuclear non-proliferation disputes.

The nuclear non-proliferation regime is one of the most important treaty regimes in existence, inasmuch as nuclear weapons possess the capability to end modern civilization as we know it. This regime also seems to be one of the most fragile, with any one State's noncompliance having the potential to unravel the entire regime.[5] Combine this fragility with the relative regularity of noncompliance (although at times minor),[6] and it is not difficult to see international peace and security as

[4] See ch. 6.5 *infra*.

[5] See generally Lewis A. Dunn, *The Collapse of the NPT: What If?*, in BEYOND 1995: THE FUTURE OF THE NPT REGIME 27 (JOSEPH F. PILAT and ROBERT E. PENDLEY ed., 1990); Giorgio Franceschini, *Assessing the Nuclear Non-proliferation Regime: What Are the Loopholes? What Are the Challenges?*, in EUROPE FACING NUCLEAR WEAPONS CHALLENGES 155 (GRÉGORY BOUTHERIN ed., 2008); JAMES F. KEELEY, *Compliance and the Non-proliferation Treaty: Developments in Safeguards and Supply Controls*, in TREATY COMPLIANCE: SOME CONCERNS AND REMEDIES 21, 22 (Canadian Council on International Law ed., 1998); Joseph F. Pilat and Charles W. Nakhleh, *A Treaty Reborn? The NPT after Extension*, in THE NUCLEAR NON-PROLIFERATION REGIME 41, 51–52 (RAJU G. C. THOMAS ed., 1998).

[6] See, e.g., Richard L. Williamson, Jr., *Hard Law, Soft Law, and Non-law in Multilateral Arms Control: Some Compliance Hypotheses*, 4 CHI. J. INT'L L. 59, 69–70 (2003) (asserting that compliance with arms control and disarmament treaties might be impossible or unimportant at times, but noting that such noncompliance might be tolerable because these States might not have any nuclear program or intentions to develop one); Barry Kellman, *International Consensus and States Non-parties*, in FUTURE LEGAL RESTRAINTS ON ARMS PROLIFERATION 151, 167–168 (JULIE DAHLITZ ed., 1996) (asserting that limited bureaucratic resources might make it impossible for some States to comply with reporting requirements contained in nuclear non-proliferation agreements); GLORIA DUFFY, *Arms Control Treaty Compliance*, in 1 ENCYCLOPEDIA OF ARMS CONTROL AND DISARMAMENT 279, 289 (Richard Dean Burns ed., 1993) (seeing

being in a very precarious situation indeed.[7] A glance at the newspapers from the past two decades reveals that international peace and security actually have been in such a precarious situation for some time now, with the alleged nuclear proliferation efforts of India, Pakistan, Iraq, Iran, and North Korea grabbing countless headlines. As if the situation were not precarious enough, certain States have threatened war – even nuclear war – against these allegedly noncompliant States,[8] thus escalating tensions even further. Certain commentators have tried to develop new

as inevitable disputes arising over the control of weapons such as nuclear weapons); Antonia Handler Chayes and Abram Chayes, *From Law Enforcement to Dispute Settlement: A New Approach to Arms Control Verification and Compliance*, 14 INT'L SEC. 147, 163 (1990) (asserting that disputes over the meaning and application of the rules of complex regulatory regimes such as that relating to nuclear non-proliferation are "an inevitable feature of life" under that regime); Joseph D. Douglass, Jr., WHY THE SOVIETS VIOLATE ARMS CONTROL TREATIES (1988) (exploring the alleged violations by the USSR).

[7] See, e.g., LOUIS RENÉ BERES, APOCALYPSE: NUCLEAR CATASTROPHE IN WORLD POLITICS (1977); BEFORE IT'S TOO LATE: THE CHALLENGE OF NUCLEAR DISARMAMENT (PAUL ABRECHT and NINAN KOSHY ed., 1983); KATHLEEN C. BAILEY, DOOMSDAY WEAPONS IN THE HANDS OF MANY: THE ARMS CONTROL CHALLENGE OF THE 90S (1991); LISL MARBURG GOODMAN AND LEE ANN HOFF, OMNICIDE: THE NUCLEAR DILEMMA (1990); GEORGE H. HAMPSCH, PREVENTING NUCLEAR GENOCIDE (1988); BERTRAND RUSSELL, HAS MAN A FUTURE? (1961); LAWRENCE S. WITTNER, ONE WORLD OR NONE: A HISTORY OF THE WORLD NUCLEAR DISARMAMENT MOVEMENT THROUGH 1953 (1993); AT THE NUCLEAR PRECIPICE: CATASTROPHE OR TRANSFORMATION? (RICHARD FALK and DAVID KRIEGER ed., 2008).

[8] The Bush Administration made clear in its 2001 Nuclear Posture Review Report that the United States would use force, including nuclear weapons, to "dissuade adversaries from undertaking military programs or operations that could threaten U.S. interests or those of allies and friends." U.S. DEP'T OF DEF., NUCLEAR POSTURE REVIEW REPORT, Dec. 31, 2001, at 9. The Obama administration has taken a step back from this bellicose position. With regard specifically to alleged noncompliance with nuclear non-proliferation norms, commentators have heralded the Obama administration's recent push to bring real progress through multilateral co-operation as providing "new ideas" for "old worries," *Old Worry, New Ideas*, THE ECONOMIST, April 17–23, 2010, at 55, yet the proposals surprisingly lack significant substance, at least in terms of trying to engage with Iran and North Korea in a meaningful dialogue. In fact, the United States' repeated promise not to use nuclear weapons against non-nuclear-weapon States that comply with the NPT, made in the 2010 Nuclear Posture Review, seems more antagonistic than reassuring. See U.S. DEP'T OF DEF., NUCLEAR POSTURE REVIEW REPORT, April 2010, at viii, ix, 15, 17, 46 ("declaring that the United States will not use or threaten to use nuclear weapons against non-nuclear weapons states that are party to the NPT and in compliance with their nuclear non-proliferation obligations"); see also Barack Obama, *Renewing American Leadership*, FOR. AFF., July/Aug. 2007, at 8–9 (refusing to take "the military option off the table" with supposed nuclear proliferators Iran and North Korea). Apparently such lightly veiled threats of nuclear attack are not new. See CHARLES MOXLEY, NUCLEAR WEAPONS AND INTERNATIONAL LAW IN THE POST-COLD

rules of international law that would allow the unilateral use of force against would-be proliferators, which has not helped the situation.[9] In an apparent attempt to alleviate tensions and resolve the matter, the Security Council occasionally has intervened. However, the Security Council's heavy-handed method of imposing and enforcing obligations through its UN Charter Chapter VII powers might have exacerbated the situation, arguably leading some target States to further recalcitrance. The stage is set to explore new alternatives that might help avoid war over these kinds of disputes. As Albert Einstein once said, "The unleashed power of the atom has changed everything save our modes of thinking, and we thus drift toward unparalleled catastrophe." Nobel laureate and former director-general of the IAEA Mohamed ElBaradei concludes his recent book by asserting, "The final reason not to lose faith that diplomacy and dialogue can prevail as the strategy for dealing with nuclear crises is based on a point of logic: the alternative is unacceptable."[10] The "alternative" to diplomatic resolution that ElBaradei referred to was nuclear war.[11] This study emphasizes a third alternative distinct from diplomatic resolution and nuclear war – a new "mode of thinking" with nuclear non-proliferation disputes – by proposing legal resolution as an option, especially in the face of war, on the one hand, and coercive Security Council measures, on the other. The cover art of this book captures the essence of its thesis, with Roman general Gaius Marius disarming the soldier that had been sent to kill him through his legal authority, as opposed to his physical strength.

War World 515–520 (2000) (asserting that the United States "explicitly threatened to use nuclear weapons on at least five occasions during the Cold War, including in Korea in 1950–1953, Suez in 1956, Lebanon in 1958, Cuba in 1962, and the Middle East in 1973, and after the Cold War in Iraq during the Gulf War); Robert S. McNamara, Argument without End: In Search of Answers to the Vietnam Tragedy (1999) (mentioning the threat of using nuclear weapons in Vietnam).

9 See, e.g., Matthew C. Waxman, *The Use of Force against States that Might Have Weapons of Mass Destruction*, 31 Mich. J. Int'l L. 1 (2009); Cody Coombs, *Blue Morning-Glories in the Sky: Correcting Sanctions to Enforce Nuclear Nonproliferation in Iran*, 19 Ind. Int'l & Comp. L. Rev. 419, 457–458 (2009) (advocating the formation of a coalition of nations to enforce nuclear non-proliferation norms outside the NPT and outside the UN system); Matthew Lund, *The Eighty Percent and Twenty Percent Solutions to Nuclear Proliferation*, 2009 BYU L. Rev. 741 (2009) (same).

10 Mohamed ElBaradei, The Age of Deception: Nuclear Diplomacy in Treacherous Times 321 (2011).

11 See ibid. See also D. M. Edwards, *International Legal Aspects of Safeguards and the Non-proliferation of Nuclear Weapons*, 33 Int'l & Comp. L.Q. 1, 22 (1984) (calling for individuals to "keep searching for ways of reducing the fears and insecurity which States feel and which may encourage them to consider the nuclear option seriously").

Likewise, the legal authority of the ICJ and international arbitral tribunals might be a crucial element in helping resolve nuclear non-proliferation disputes, as opposed to the realpolitik of the Security Council and war.

Admittedly, this study is not unique in asserting that legal resolution can become a more attractive option in the face of coercive action.[12] Nor is this study unique in believing that all disputes can be peacefully resolved, with the determining factor being finding the right method of resolution and the appropriate incentives for those particular actors in that particular situation.[13] This study is highly unique, however, in its application of these ideas to arguably the most politically sensitive disputes. In an era that some commentators characterize with the belief that even the most difficult problems can be solved,[14] the time is now ripe to test that notion with regard to legal resolution of nuclear non-proliferation disputes, thereby pushing the current boundaries of the legal literature. To be clear, while previous studies have explored *how* to interpret nuclear non-proliferation agreements,[15] this study explores *who* should be allowed to interpret such agreements, or, to be more specific, whether the ICJ and international arbitral tribunals ought to be given the opportunity to resolve disputes over these agreements before the Security Council gets involved with its Chapter VII powers.

1.2 Outline

This study is divided into four parts broken into seven chapters. Part I provides this relatively short introduction to the study (Chapter 1), as well as an introduction to the nuclear non-proliferation regime and an introduction to international dispute settlement generally (Chapter 2), all of which sets the foundation and framework for the substance of the study. Part II (comprising Chapter 3) elaborates on the problem alluded to in the preceding section with regard to Security Council involvement

[12] See, e.g., Richard B. Bilder, *Judicial Procedures Relating to the Use of Force*, 31 VA. J. INT'L L. 249, 268 (1991).

[13] See, e.g., Manfred Lachs, *The Law and the Settlement of International Disputes*, in DISPUTE SETTLEMENT THROUGH THE UNITED NATIONS 283, 286 (K. VENKATA RAMAN ed., 1977).

[14] See *A $300 Idea that Is Priceless*, THE ECONOMIST, April 30, 2011, at 66 (asserting that this is an era when the dominant belief is that even the most difficult problems can be solved).

[15] See, e.g., DANIEL H. JOYNER, INTERPRETING THE NUCLEAR NON-PROLIFERATION TREATY (2011) (providing an in-depth analysis of the Nuclear Non-proliferation Treaty in light of the Vienna Convention on the Law of Treaties).

with nuclear non-proliferation disputes under UN Charter Chapter VII. Indeed, States and the international community might prefer to use force when trying to remove the nuclear-weapon capabilities of allegedly noncompliant and recalcitrant States; alternatively, they might prefer to create a strong incentive for those States by using coercive language in Security Council decisions, or even imposing enforcement measures such as sanctions and the authorization of force.[16] The dangers of war are obvious, especially when nuclear weapons are involved.[17] This is particularly true when the notorious three fallacies of nuclear war are allowed to increase the chances of nuclear war happening: "1. That nuclear war is not *really* going to happen *or, if so, then only to other people*. 2. That nothing can be done to prevent nuclear war *except, perhaps, by someone else* . . . 3. That nuclear war can be averted by further armament, *unyielding threats etc.*"[18] Instead of focusing on war, however, Part II focuses on the more subtle dangers of Security Council involvement in terms of the perceived flaws in the Security Council's procedures in adopting its Chapter VII measures.

Chapter 3 undertakes a comprehensive analysis of Security Council involvement, under Chapter VII, with nuclear non-proliferation disputes, including those disputes involving India, Pakistan, Iraq, Iran, and North Korea. Critics will be quick to assert that many, if not all, of those problems over nuclear non-proliferation are policy oriented and that policy-oriented solutions, not legal solutions, are needed in order to resolve these policy-oriented tensions. In other words, critics will argue that these are the exact situations where the ICJ and international arbitral tribunals cannot get involved, but where the Security Council should have, and does have, exclusive competence vis-à-vis the ICJ and international arbitral tribunals as the entity charged with maintaining international peace and security. One example of a policy-related problem is the West's policy of not allowing Iran to develop its civilian

16 See Kellman, *supra* note 6, at 169.

17 See B.V.A. Röling, *International Law, Nuclear Weapons, Arms Control and Disarmament*, in NUCLEAR WEAPONS AND LAW 181, 183 (ARTHUR SELWYN MILLER and MARTIN FEINRIDER ed., 1984) (asserting every war may eventually involve nuclear war). The obviousness of the dangers of nuclear war has not stopped some commentators from spelling out the dangers. See, e.g., J. Carson Mark, *Consequences of Nuclear War*, in THE DANGERS OF NUCLEAR WAR 7 (FRANKLYN GRIFFITHS and JOHN C. POLANYI ed., 1979); Marshal Costa Gomez, *Nuclear Arms and the Danger of an Atomic War*, in 2 TOWARDS A NUCLEAR WEAPON-FREE AND NON-VIOLENT WORLD (1990).

18 See JULIE DAHLITZ, NUCLEAR ARMS CONTROL 7 (1983) (emphasis in original).

nuclear program, notwithstanding Iran's "inalienable" right to do so, as alluded to in Article IV(1) of the Nuclear Non-Proliferation Treaty (NPT), as explained in Chapter 3.2.6 below. However, underlying such policy issues are legal ones, in the form of legally enforceable rights and obligations – for example, whether Iran actually has an inalienable legal right to develop its civilian nuclear program, and, if so, the scope of that right. Policy-oriented disputes that the Security Council and other political bodies should handle over legal resolution involve issues where no legally enforceable rights or obligations exist, such as with the argument of non-nuclear-weapon States that nuclear-weapon States are in violation of NPT Article VI for not relinquishing their nuclear weapons, where the norms in Article VI are overwhelmingly softened with phrases such as "undertakes to pursue" such negotiations to eventually stop the nuclear arms race "at an early date."[19] States and organizations that want to limit Iran's options when it comes to a civilian nuclear program are free to make policy arguments why Iran should not be allowed to develop its civilian nuclear program. However, these policy arguments do not strip the dispute of its underlying legal components, in the form of Iran's legal rights under the NPT. Chapter 6.4 below on treaty interpretation elaborates on this example of how the ICJ or an international arbitral tribunal could interpret such legal rights, with reference to previous cases that have interpreted similar language. At the same time, it is important to note how this study does not focus specifically on the actual nuclear non-proliferation disputes involving India, Pakistan, Iraq, Iran, and North Korea discussed in Chapter 3, at least when it comes to providing an example of how legal resolution would resolve one of these sensitive disputes, since the Security Council already has suspended many of their treaty rights through the adoption of conflicting obligations under UN Charter Chapter VII. If legal resolution had a stronger tradition of reviewing Security Council resolutions, then legal resolution might have remained more of a viable option with these particular disputes. Therefore, this study is geared more towards encouraging disputants of nuclear non-proliferation disputes *in the future* to invoke legal resolution, wherever the option exists, before the situation rises to the level of endangering international peace and security and the Security Council suspends treaty rights that the ICJ or an international arbitral tribunal might be well suited to interpret. Chapter 5.2.3 below attempts to identify when

[19] See Treaty on the Non-proliferation of Nuclear Weapons, Art. VI, July 1, 1968, 729 U.N. T.S. 161 (extended May 11, 1995, 34 I.L.M. 959).

the option of legal resolution might exist in the future and the present, with Chapter 6.4 exploring the possibility of legal resolution of issues involving China's building of two nuclear power plants for Pakistan. Despite the relatively forward-looking orientation of this study, Chapter 3 nevertheless provides ample examples throughout of how the ICJ or an international arbitral tribunal might have interpreted the rights and obligations of these States under the relevant nuclear non-proliferation agreements had the Security Council *not* intervened with its Chapter VII powers in those situations, which intervention suspended many of those rights and imposed its interpretation of those obligations. For example, as Chapter 3 below points out in numerous places, many of the Security Council's interpretations of nuclear non-proliferation agreements run counter to at least one of the principal pillars of the nuclear non-proliferation regime, namely the peaceful use of nuclear energy,[20] which presumably the ICJ or an international arbitral tribunal would not have done when interpreting these provisions "in good faith in accordance with the ordinary meaning to be given to the terms of the treaty in their context and in the light of its object and purpose," as explained in Chapter 3.1.3 below.

With these problems in mind, Part III focuses on whether legal resolution is a viable option with such nuclear non-proliferation disputes. Part III starts with Chapter 4, painting the historical picture of legal resolution handling military-related disputes, which can be seen as having a similar degree of sensitivity as nuclear non-proliferation disputes. These examples show both how States have entrusted to legal resolution politically sensitive disputes and how the ICJ and international arbitral tribunals regularly have felt that they have the analytical tools to decide such sensitive disputes. When it comes to the "viability" of legal resolution, viability is believed to be determined if, on a balance of the probabilities, the ICJ or international arbitral tribunal will be able to satisfy itself that it has the requisite jurisdiction over the dispute (discussed in Chapter 5) and that it has the tools to properly address the matter (discussed in Chapter 6). While nuclear non-proliferation disputes conceivably involve a State's vital interests, this factor is seen as no longer a significant barrier to justiciability. Moreover, both disputants need not agree to legal resolution after the dispute has arisen in

[20] See, e.g., ch. 3.2.3.8, *infra* (discussing how Security Council Resolution 707 suspended Iraq's right to develop nuclear energy for peaceful purposes); ch. 3.2.6., *infra* (discussing how Security Council Resolution 1696 suspended Iran's "enrichment-related and reprocessing activities, including research and development, to be verified by the IAEA . . ."). See also Joyner, *supra* note 15, at 1–2, 35–75 (noting how nuclear-weapon States interpret the NPT in such a way as to ignore this "pillar" of the NPT).

order for the ICJ or an international arbitral tribunal to move forward, because pre-existing compromissory clauses in key nuclear non-proliferation agreements provide these fora with the requisite jurisdiction. Whether disputants choose to give effect to these pre-existing compromissory clauses or to provide their consent to legal resolution through some other method depends on their calculations as to whether such acts further their *sui generis* interests. This study does not pretend to be able to anticipate all of the factors that might go into that calculus or the relative weight to be given to each factor. Instead, it is designed to help States and concerned individuals think through some of the key advantages and disadvantages of legal resolution, thereby fueling future debate that might be needed for States to actually rely on legal resolution in these situations.

Part IV is made up of a lone, concluding chapter (Chapter 7), which provides concluding remarks aimed at tying all of the chapters together. To foreshadow here that ending, it must be admitted up front that legal resolution is not the panacea to the world's problems, especially with nuclear non-proliferation disputes. However, States and the international community need to consider that the target State must be willing to accept the outcome of resolution efforts if friction ultimately is to be mitigated, if not eliminated. As with all compliance systems, whether domestic or international, success with the nuclear non-proliferation regime depends on the voluntary compliance of its member States, not on the forceful imposition of the system's obligations.[21] As explained in Chapter 5.3 below, the procedural safeguards and relative impartiality of legal fora improve the chances of such voluntary compliance with the ultimate outcome of resolution efforts because of the perceived fairness of the process. This study provides these parties with the opportunity to consider this particular option. Just as international law became relevant to the discussions over the legality of nuclear weapons in "professional and policy-planning circles" in the 1980s,[22] as well as to the debates in the 1990s surrounding the ICJ's *Legality of the Threat or Use of Nuclear Weapons* advisory opinion, this study argues that the time has arrived for legal resolution to become relevant to the discussions on how to resolve nuclear non-proliferation disputes.

[21] See James F. Keeley, *Compliance and the Non-proliferation Treaty: Developments in Safeguards and Supply Controls*, in TREATY COMPLIANCE: SOME CONCERNS AND REMEDIES 21, 22–23 (Canadian Council on International Law ed., 1998).

[22] See Richard Falk, *Toward a Legal Regime for Nuclear Weapons*, in NUCLEAR WEAPONS AND LAW 107, 111 (ARTHUR SELWYN MILLER and MARTIN FEINRIDER ed., 1984).

1.3 Methodology

As is clear from the preceding sections, the dominant characteristic of this study's structure is its orientation towards defending a thesis – that legal resolution is a viable option with nuclear non-proliferation disputes. Each chapter within this study is geared towards defending that thesis, which acts as the golden thread to bring coherence to its various parts. At the same time, each chapter has its own sub-thesis that fits within the overarching thesis, which likewise gives coherence to each chapter. This study supports this overarching thesis and these related sub-theses through critical legal analysis of primary and secondary sources found mostly in the international law literature on international dispute settlement, UN law, and the broader area of disarmament and arms control (as opposed to just nuclear non-proliferation), with occasional consideration of relevant material in related fields. By "critical legal analysis," this study means an approach that focuses on providing careful judgment of the relevant thinking contained in the literature on any particular topic, not simply taking the literature at face value or citing material just for the information it provides,[23] thus hopefully demonstrating higher-order cognitive skills, according to Bloom's taxonomy.[24] The study has a distinct revisionist tone throughout, inasmuch as it criticizes earlier commentators for having overlooked or mischaracterized much of the nuclear non-proliferation regime as unsuitable for legal resolution and other related matters, although such criticism in no way is meant to show disrespect to the commentators who have made this analysis possible.

In undertaking this critical legal analysis, this study adopts a markedly qualitative approach. Such a qualitative methodology limits the types of generalizations that can be made. Indeed, this methodology provides the study with strong internal validity, but it also brings with it weaker external validity, which prevents broader application of the conclusions to legal resolution of politically sensitive disputes of other types, such as international environmental disputes or territorial disputes. Even though nuclear non-proliferation disputes might be considered the most controversial disputes to face the ICJ and international arbitral tribunals, one must resist the urge to extend the observations and

[23] See generally MARIO BUNGE AND KARL R. POPPER, THE CRITICAL APPROACH TO SCIENCE AND PHILOSOPHY (1964).

[24] See generally B. S. BLOOM, TAXONOMY OF EDUCATIONAL OBJECTIVES: THE COGNITIVE DOMAIN (1956).

conclusions made in this study to other topics that do not fall under the exact focus here. Nevertheless, it is not that nuclear non-proliferation disputes are uniquely suited for legal resolution. On the contrary, these disputes are unique in how high the stakes are for the disputants and the world. In completely calm times, it might be better to resolve these types of disputes through diplomatic forms of resolution, such as negotiation and mediation, where the parties have the most control over the proceedings and the ultimate solution. However, the elevated likelihood of hostilities and the destructive capability of these weapons arguably justify consideration of less optimal methods of resolution of these disputes – the fitting of square pegs into round holes, so to speak.

As alluded to in the introduction above, there are many contemporary examples of States allegedly violating nuclear non-proliferation norms, primary among which are the alleged activities of Iran and North Korea. While this study certainly grew out of a fascination with these particular disputes, it sees legal resolution as being more appropriate to disputes where the Security Council has not yet intervened under its Chapter VII powers, as noted at 1.2 above. As the Security Council already has intervened in most contemporary nuclear non-proliferation disputes, the study's focus falls on future disputes. This study falls short of saying that there should be (or that there must be) a first for legal resolution of these disputes. The point is merely that States, commentators, and the international community should not conclude that legal resolution cannot be used with these disputes merely because it has not been used in the past, nor should they read too much into the lack of case law in this area as meaning that case law cannot develop over time. Admittedly, Max Weber has a point about the power of habit in the international arena:

> It cannot be overstressed that the mere habituation to a mode of action, the instinct to preserve this habituation, and, much more so, tradition, have a formidable influence in favor of a habituated legal order, even when such an order originally derives from legal enactment. This influence is more powerful than any reflection on impending means of coercion or other consequences . . .[25]

[25] Max Weber, *The Economy and Social Norms*, in 2 Economy and Society: An Outline of Interpretive Sociology 311, 327 (Guenther Roth and Claus Wittich ed., 1978).

This study ultimately aims to help States, commentators and the international community reconsider this habit of disfavoring legal resolution of such politically sensitive disputes.

Finally, a few words must be said about the general approach of this study as reflected in its organization. Critics will note that the analysis of legal resolution does not start until Part III. However, Part II, on Security Council involvement under Chapter VII, is important in setting up the problems that legal resolution is capable of improving. Therefore, these parts should not be read out of order. In particular, procedural shortcomings and general heavy-handedness make Security Council involvement a less-than-ideal option for attempting to resolve nuclear non-proliferation disputes in such a way that target States feel that they can accept and carry out the final determination. In other words, Part II provides a real referent against which to compare the more theoretical arguments about legal resolution of these disputes. States that fear Security Council involvement with their own emergent nuclear non-proliferation disputes might look at these examples and see how the Security Council arguably ran roughshod over those States' interests when adopting its Chapter VII measures, thus creating a strong impetus for these States to seriously consider legal resolution of their emerging disputes, where such an option exists. As explained in Chapters 5 and 6 of this study, such an option exists primarily under the arbitration clause of IAEA safeguards agreements, through the compromissory clause in the IAEA Statute, and through a *compromis*. These options influence the intended audience of this study, as explained in the following section.

1.4 Audience

A few words must be said about this study's target audience. With its efforts to fill a theoretical gap in the international law literature dealing with international dispute settlement and nuclear non-proliferation, the most obvious audience is international law academics who specialize in these areas. However, more important for its potential to impact international relations, this study also targets decision-makers (both lawyers and policy-makers) in the following four groups of States:

(1) all States with an IAEA safeguards agreement that fear unfair treatment by the Security Council, reminding them of the option of international arbitration under those safeguards agreements with disputes other than those where the IAEA Board of Governors has

determined that it cannot confirm that nuclear material has not been diverted;

(2) all member States of the IAEA Statute that have a dispute over that treaty, reminding them of the option of legal resolution provided there, assuming the failure of negotiations and barring an agreement on another mode of settlement, as provided by IAEA Statute Article XVII(A); and

(3) all States and the international community, reminding them of the merits of legal resolution so that they consider:
   (a) agreeing to *compromis* once nuclear non-proliferation disputes arise or start to arise;
   (b) agreeing to compromissory clauses in future nuclear non-proliferation agreements that provide a right to resolve disputes through legal resolution;
   (c) amending existing nuclear non-proliferation agreements to provide a right to resolve disputes through legal resolution; and
   (d) removing reservations in unilateral declarations that would otherwise give the ICJ jurisdiction over such disputes.

This study acknowledges that relatively weaker States likely will be more attracted to the option of legal resolution of nuclear non-proliferation disputes than stronger States, as is typical with dispute resolution where power asymmetries exist between disputants.[26] Admittedly, stronger States might be attracted to the option of legal resolution in general where they find themselves part of a group of States with a weaker position,[27] or when they have disputes with other, stronger States,[28] but this is unlikely to be the case with nuclear non-proliferation disputes where the stronger, nuclear-weapon States possess a disproportionate amount of power and discretion under the current regime. Therefore, this study anticipates weaker States having greater interest in the arguments of this study, although the study has the decision-makers of *all States* as its target audience.

Whether any of the results mentioned above are realized depends entirely on the political will of the States involved, as is typical with

[26] See Louis B. Sohn, *The Role of Arbitration in Recent International Multilateral Treaties*, 23 VA. J. INT'L L. 171, 171–172 (1982–1983).

[27] See ibid.

[28] See LILLIAN L. RANDOLPH, THIRD-PARTY SETTLEMENT OF DISPUTES IN THEORY AND PRACTICE 176 (1973). But see MAURICE BERTRAND, THE UNITED NATIONS: PAST, PRESENT AND FUTURE 175–176 (1994).

international law.[29] This study, nevertheless, aims to spark debate among (and within) these States and within the international community as a whole with these particular ends in mind, with the firm belief that States and the international community should be open to all options, especially where the threat of war and coercive Security Council measures exist. Such a sensitive situation calls for originality of thinking and exploration of ideas that some might consider controversial, both of which this study provides in ample portions.

The broader public and experts in other subfields of international relations should find some interest in this study, inasmuch as nuclear non-proliferation disputes feature prominently in contemporary mass-media markets and in those fields. The audience, nevertheless, is assumed to have some knowledge of UN law and the law relating to nuclear non-proliferation, as well as some knowledge of the history and politics surrounding the activities of alleged proliferators in contemporary times. This assumption enables the analysis to focus on the heart of the issues with only a minimal amount of background and description, which the lay reader can find in other studies. An unfortunate, although necessary, by-product of this approach is that the broader public and experts in other fields might not fully appreciate the analysis on account of paradigmatic and other differences between this field and theirs.

1.5 Originality of this study

Besides the combination of unique theses and theoretical elements alluded to above, this study is distinct from other studies in four ways. First, most, if not all, other studies do not take seriously the possibility of legal resolution of nuclear non-proliferation disputes. The introduction to Part III reviews the legal literature on the nuclear non-proliferation regime in particular and arms control in general as it relates to legal resolution, and shows exactly how this study is unique in its focus on legal resolution of such disputes. Second, this study is unique in its comprehensive analysis of the Security Council's involvement, under its Chapter VII powers, with nuclear non-proliferation (Chapter 3). Third, although commentators already have provided detailed analysis

[29] See generally Richard von Weiszäcker, *All Depends on Member States*, in PAIX, DÉVELOPPEMENT, DÉMOCRATIE: BOUTROS BOUTROS-GHALI AMICORUM DISCIPULORUMQUE LIBER 827 (GEORGES ABI-SAAB et al. ed., 1999).

of the relationship between the Security Council and the ICJ,[30] demonstrably no other study on *nuclear non-proliferation* compares legal resolution with Security Council resolution of disputes in this particular area. Those studies that mention both in the context of dispute resolution do so in passing,[31] or alternatively in discussing how the ICJ might play a role in reviewing Security Council decisions.[32] Moreover, no other study focuses on the negative aspects of Security Council resolution of nuclear non-proliferation disputes and then uses these perceived flaws to emphasize the attractiveness of legal resolution as an alternative. Finally, as its lengthy bibliography attests, this study casts as wide a net as possible in reviewing secondary material, and as a result it provides a snapshot of a significant portion of the relevant legal literature as it relates to the central thesis at hand. The goal of casting such a wide net is not to rely on this literature as authority, but rather to identify the limits of the literature before pushing those limits. In all four of these ways, this study contributes to the legal literature in particular, with the ultimate hope of a trickle-down effect on the management of international relations in this area. In sum, this study presents a fresh perspective on a variety of widely held beliefs about (1) the involvement of the Security Council with nuclear non-proliferation disputes under its Chapter VII powers; (2) the potential role of legal resolution of nuclear non-proliferation disputes; (3) the relationship between the Security Council and legal resolution when it comes to nuclear non-proliferation

[30] See Vera Gowlland-Debbas, *The Relationship between the International Court of Justice and the Security Council in the Light of the Lockerbie Case*, 88 AM. J. INT'L L. 643, 649 (1994); DOMINGO E. ACEVEDO, *Disputes under Consideration by the UN Security Council or Regional Bodies*, in THE INTERNATIONAL COURT OF JUSTICE AT A CROSSROADS 242 (LORI F. DAMROSCH ed., 1987); Malcolm N. Shaw, *The Security Council and the International Court of Justice: Judicial Drift and Judicial Function*, in THE INTERNATIONAL COURT OF JUSTICE: ITS FUTURE ROLE AFTER FIFTY YEARS 219 (A. S. MULLER, D. RAIC, and J. M. THURANSKY ed., 1997).

[31] See Ajmal Mian, *The Challenge of Nuclear Proliferation Control in South Asia*, in FUTURE LEGAL RESTRAINTS ON ARMS PROLIFERATION 187, 198 (JULIE DAHLITZ ed., 1996) (mentions in passing, in the conclusion, how legal resolution, combined with robust Security Council enforcement of legal resolution's decisions, is necessary for meaningful enforcement of arms control treaties, without providing further analysis); Dahlitz, *supra* note 18, at 109; Alyn Ware, *Rule of Force or Rule of Law? Legal Responses to Nuclear Threats from Terrorism, Proliferation, and War*, 2 SEATTLE J. SOC. JUST. 243, 263 (2003) (listing the different entities that can have a role in dealing with nuclear threats, including the Security Council and the ICJ, without providing further analysis).

[32] See, e.g., DANIEL H. JOYNER, INTERNATIONAL LAW AND THE PROLIFERATION OF WEAPONS OF MASS DESTRUCTION 218–225, 228–242 (2009).

disputes; and (4) nuclear non-proliferation law, international dispute settlement, and UN law generally.

With these foundational matters in mind, the following chapter proceeds with the introduction by providing key definitions, delimitations, and disclaimers with regard to the nuclear non-proliferation regime and international dispute settlement. All of these introductory points are essential to fully understanding the substantive chapters of this study and the main thesis of this study – that legal resolution is a valid option with regard to nuclear non-proliferation. Again, this is not to say that legal resolution is the panacea to the world's problems or even the panacea to nuclear non-proliferation disputes. Instead, it portrays legal resolution as one option among many – an option that States and academia all too often have ignored. This study aims to remedy that situation.

2

Definitions, delimitations and disclaimers of the study

French abstract artist Robert Delaunay lamented how definitions frighten him, although he went on to acknowledge that we almost always are forced to provide them. Likewise, this study acknowledges the need for definitions in identifying for the reader the exact parameters of its subject matter, and so this chapter provides those necessary definitions. At the same time, the study acknowledges that definitions often are a source of contention, as British lawyer Frederick Pollock has observed: "It is odd how learned persons fail to see that new terms and definitions are apt to mean new doubts and litigation." This study tries hard not to provide "new" definitions for the concepts of "nuclear non-proliferation," "international dispute settlement," or "legal resolution," but one presumably cannot help but stray a little when contextualizing them. Therefore, it seems only prudent for this chapter to couple a discussion of key definitions with delimitations and disclaimers in an effort to minimize possible "doubts and litigation" that may result from any of these definitions.

As is apparent from its title, this study focuses on legal resolution of nuclear non-proliferation disputes. Such a focus has three basic elements: "legal resolution," "nuclear non-proliferation," and "dispute." The definition of "dispute" in the legal sense is inextricably linked to justiciability, and so a detailed explanation of that term is reserved for Chapter 6, which concerns justiciability. It is sufficient to say here that, for the purposes of this study up to Chapter 6, a "dispute" involves a disagreement between two or more States over some fact or law to the point of direct contention. This chapter focuses on defining the other two concepts – "nuclear non-proliferation" and "legal resolution" – with a definition of "international dispute settlement" being needed inasmuch as "legal resolution" represents one of its branches.

While this chapter could have been combined with the preceding one, it ultimately was allowed to stand on its own so as not to clutter Chapter 1 and otherwise detract from that chapter's properly foundational nature. Nevertheless, this chapter remains introductory in that it explains the common elements found throughout the rest of this study. Other definitions, delimitations, and disclaimers that are relevant to particular chapters and not to the study as a whole are provided in those chapters, rather than here.

2.1 The nuclear non-proliferation regime

The advent of nuclear weapons in the 1940s sparked a number of initiatives to curb their proliferation, such as the Baruch Plan[1] and the Atoms for Peace program, in which the United States proposed to provide research facilities, training, and even fissionable material in exchange for safeguards to entrench its status as sole nuclear-weapon State, especially in light of the USSR's efforts to develop its own nuclear weapons.[2] However, calls for creating a nuclear non-proliferation regime per se began in earnest in the early 1960s in response to French nuclear tests and a belief that China was close to developing its own nuclear weapons, which culminated in a UN General Assembly resolution calling for the establishment of such a regime.[3] What resulted was the nuclear non-proliferation regime that exists today, which essentially freezes the number of nuclear-weapon States at five – China, France, the Russian Federation, the United Kingdom, and the United States. The

[1] See Bernard M. Baruch, Statement of the United States Policy on Control of Atomic Energy to the United Nations Atomic Energy Commission (June 14, 1946); UN GAOR 8th Sess. Plenary Meetings. Vol. 1, 470th meeting, December 8, 1953, at 450 (proposed in response to the Soviet Union's successful test of a nuclear weapon in 1953).

[2] See Thomas Graham, Jr. and Damien J. LaVera, Cornerstones of Security: Arms Control Treaties in the Nuclear Era 2 (2003) (discussing the Atoms for Peace program, among other developments during the nuclear era); Joseph F. Pilat, Atoms for Peace: A Future after Fifty Years? (2007). For a review of the history of these initiatives and the history leading up to the NPT, see Joseph I. Lieberman, The Scorpion and the Tarantula: The Struggle to Control Atomic Weapons 1945–1949 (1970); George Bunn, *The Nuclear Nonproliferation Treaty: History and Current Problems*, Arms Control Today 1, 1–4 (Dec. 2003).

[3] See Prevention on the Wider Dissemination of Nuclear Weapons, G.A. Res. 1665, UN GAOR, 16th Sess., Supp. No. 17, at 5, UN Doc. A/5100 (Dec. 4, 1961); Geoffrey S. Carlson, *An Offer They Can't Refuse? The Security Council Tells North Korea to Re-sign the Nuclear Non-proliferation Treaty*, 46 Colum. J. Transnat'l L. 420, 423 (2008) (citing this resolution). See also John Woodliffe, *Nuclear Weapons and Non-proliferation: The Legal Aspects*, in Nuclear Weapons and International Law 84, 87 (Istvan Pogany ed., 1987).

rest appear destined to be non-nuclear-weapon States, barring an amendment to or an overly creative interpretation of the NPT.[4] In short, the nuclear non-proliferation regime is designed to stop these non-nuclear-weapon States from becoming nuclear-weapon States, through a combination of reporting and verification.[5]

By "non-proliferation," this study means "the prevention of an increase in something," with the *Oxford English Dictionary* making specific reference to the Nuclear Non-proliferation Treaty.[6] The legal literature on the nuclear non-proliferation regime typically breaks down the types of proliferation into "horizontal" proliferation, or the sharing of nuclear-related material, knowledge, and technology *between* States, and "vertical" proliferation, or the organic development of nuclear-related material, knowledge, and technology *within* a State.[7] Interestingly, the first drafts of the NPT framed it as a purely horizontal non-proliferation regime, although vertical non-proliferation and nuclear disarmament were added to the final draft under pressure from non-nuclear-weapon States,[8] in addition to promises of transfer of nuclear technology for peaceful purposes.[9] Some commentators assert

[4] See, e.g., David S. Jonas, *Variations on Non-Nuclear: May the "Final Four" Join the Nuclear Nonproliferation Treaty as Non-nuclear Weapon States while Retaining Their Nuclear Weapons?*, 2005 MICH. ST. L. REV. 417 (2005) (paradoxically calling for the creative interpretation of the NPT to allow the creation of a third classification of State in order to include the remaining States within the regime – non-nuclear-weapon States that possess nuclear weapons).

[5] See generally IAN BELLANY, CURBING THE SPREAD OF NUCLEAR WEAPONS (2005) (explaining the basics of the nuclear non-proliferation regime); GARY T. GARDNER, NUCLEAR NONPROLIFERATION: A PRIMER (1994) (same); LAWRENCE SCHEINMAN, THE INTERNATIONAL ATOMIC ENERGY AGENCY AND WORLD NUCLEAR ORDER (1987) (same); James M. Acton, *The Problem with Nuclear Mind Reading*, SURVIVAL 119, 119 (Feb. 2009) (emphasizing the importance of IAEA verification in determining intent of the State); EPHRAIM ASCULAI, VERIFICATION REVISITED: THE NUCLEAR CASE (2002) (providing a nice overview of NPT verification mechanisms).

[6] "Non-proliferation," OXFORD ENGLISH DICTIONARY (3rd edn, 2003, online version, March 2011). The term has no discernible legal significance.

[7] See, e.g., DANIEL JOYNER, INTERNATIONAL LAW AND THE PROLIFERATION OF WEAPONS OF MASS DESTRUCTION xiv–xv (2009).

[8] See Miguel Marin Bosch, *The Non-proliferation Treaty and Its Future*, in INTERNATIONAL LAW, THE INTERNATIONAL COURT OF JUSTICE AND NUCLEAR WEAPONS 375, 377 (LAURENCE BOISSON DE CHAZOURNES and PHILIPPE SANDS ed., 1999).

[9] See NAMIRA NEGM, TRANSFER OF NUCLEAR TECHNOLOGY UNDER INTERNATIONAL LAW: CASE STUDY OF IRAQ, IRAN AND ISRAEL (2009). Some commentators see the ability of non-nuclear-weapon States to develop nuclear energy

that the NPT as a horizontal non-proliferation regime has "probably run its course," inasmuch as most States are party to the NPT and proliferation between States poses a limited risk, at least compared to vertical proliferation within a State.[10] However, as long as nuclear weapons and nuclear-weapon-related knowledge exist, this study views both types of proliferation as a genuine threat.

A "regime" involves the "principles, norms, rules and decision-making procedures around which actors' expectations converge in a given area of international relations."[11] These types of regimes are important for fostering co-operation between States inasmuch as the regime's principles, norms, rules, and decision-making procedures create a common set of expectations concerning their behavior, which help foster trust between members of the regime.[12] Such trust between States is particularly important with regard to nuclear non-proliferation. As David Koplow eloquently puts it, referring to "disarmament" in an article on nuclear non-proliferation,

> international law is more than just an ephemeral debating point. In disarmament, as in other salient aspects of international life, law has meaning and impact. It guides behaviors, shapes expectations, undergirds notions of appropriateness and legitimacy, and, in the extreme, provides at least an imperfect collective format for redress of violations and other grievances. In the area of arms non-proliferation, in particular, law can be one of the sinews that bind the community of nations, contributing valuably to the overall effort to retard the spread of dangerous weaponry.[13]

As explored in detail in Chapter 5.3.2.1 below, relying on the rule of law and submitting disputes to legal resolution gives States the image of

for peaceful purposes under the NPT as the main problem with the nuclear non-proliferation regime. See generally Amir Azaran, *NPT, Where Art Thou? The Nonproliferation Treaty and Bargaining: Iran as a Case Study*, 6 Chi. J. Int'l L. 415 (2005); Natasha Bajema and Mary Beth Nikitin, *Assessing Nuclear Maturity: Determining Which States Should Have Access to What Nuclear Technology*, 28 Fletcher F. World Aff. 157 (2004) (same).

10 Bosch, *supra* note 8, at 382–383.

11 Stephen D. Krasner, *Structural Causes and Regime Consequences: Regimes as Intervening Variables*, in International Regimes 1, 2 (S. D. Krasner ed., 1983).

12 See Lea Brilmayer, *Transforming International Politics: An American Role for the Post Cold War World*, 64 U. Cin. L. Rev. 119, 125 (1995). See generally Stephan Haggard and Beth A. Simmons, *Theories of International Regimes*, 41 Int'l Org. 491 (1987).

13 David A. Koplow, *The Jurisprudence of Non-proliferation: Taking International Law Seriously*, 2 Transnat'l L & Contemp. Probs. 357, 358 (1992).

being willing to abide by their promises and the confidence to be held to those promises by binding third-party resolution.[14] In the long run, this creates greater trust between States, which can decrease the costs of interacting with each other by decreasing uncertainty,[15] and adds much-needed stability to international relations in general.

The following subsection defines the treaties that make up the nuclear non-proliferation regime and the key terms associated with those treaties, primary among which is "nuclear weapons."

2.1.1 Treaties comprising the regime

There is considerable debate over where the principles, norms, rules, and decision-making procedures of the nuclear non-proliferation regime come from. Some commentators take a narrow approach. This includes commentators who see the Nuclear Non-proliferation Treaty (NPT) as containing the entirety of the nuclear non-proliferation regime.[16] The NPT certainly is the cornerstone of the nuclear non-proliferation

[14] See Jan Paulsson, *Avoiding Unintended Consequences*, in APPEALS MECHANISM IN INTERNATIONAL INVESTMENT DISPUTES 241, 245 (KARL P. SAUVANT and MICHAEL CHISWICK-PATTERSON ed., 2008).

[15] See ibid.

[16] See, e.g., Matthew Liles, *Did Kim Jong-Il Break the Law? A Case Study on How North Korea Highlights the Flaws of the Non-proliferation Regime*, 33 N.C. J. INT'L L. & COM. REG. 103, 111–112 (2007); Erik Raines, *North Korea: Analyzing the "New" Nuclear Threat*, 12 CARDOZO J. INT'L & COMP. L. 349, 354 (2004) (but noting that the Agreed Framework "advance[s] the goals of the international nuclear non-proliferation regime," although not expressly including it within that regime); Michael J. Brenner, *Renewing the Non-proliferation Regime: A Multilateral Approach*, in ARMS CONTROL: THE MULTILATERAL ALTERNATIVE 145 (Edward C. Luck ed., 1983). A little broader scope to this narrow approach would include not only the NPT but also the IAEA Statute and the IAEA safeguards agreements. See Susan Carmody, *Balancing Collective Security and National Security: Does the United Nations have the Right to Inspect North Korea's Nuclear Facilities?*, 18 FORDHAM INT'L L.J. 229, 230–231 (1994); Michael Spies, *Iran and the Limits of the Nuclear Non-proliferation Regime*, 22 AM. U. INT'L L. REV. 401, 411 (2007); Monica J. Washington, *The Practice of Peer Review in the International Nuclear Safety Regime*, 72 N.Y.U.L. REV. 430, 432 n. 5 (1997) (referring explicitly to the NPT and safeguards in the regime, with implicit reference to the IAEA Statute); David S. Jonas and Christopher Swift, *Reformulating the Nuclear Nonproliferation Regime: Al-Qaeda, Global Terrorism, and the Rogue State Paradigm*, 13 UCLA J. INT'L L. & FOR. AFF. 337, 347–348 (2008) (same). See also Perla Carvalho-Soto, *Mexican Perspectives on Nuclear Disarmament*, 31 CASE W. RES. J. INT'L L. 647, 647–648 (1999) (limiting the regime to the NPT and the CTBT).

regime, as the Security Council has identified,[17] and provides the most symbolic strength for nuclear non-proliferation.[18] Indeed, even though the International Atomic Energy Agency (IAEA) Statute was adopted in 1957, it was not until the NPT's entry into force in 1968 that the modern safeguards system was established, with the IAEA assuming its key role of supervision within that system.[19] However, this study considers it impossible that the NPT constitutes the entire nuclear non-proliferation regime inasmuch as the NPT itself envisions other treaties outside the NPT as playing a key role in nuclear non-proliferation, such as the IAEA Statute and the IAEA safeguards agreements, to which NPT Article III(1) refers.[20] It is no mystery that the IAEA, with its Statute and safeguards agreements, is crucial in implementing the NPT and the nuclear non-proliferation regime, as the Security Council and others have recognized.[21] NPT Article III(1) expressly ties all three elements together by

[17] S. C. Res. 1887, preamb. ¶ 6, UN Doc. S/RES/1887 (Sept. 24, 2009) ("Underlining that the NPT remains the cornerstone of the nuclear non-proliferation regime and the essential foundation for the pursuit of nuclear disarmament and for the peaceful uses of nuclear energy"); see also David A. Koplow, *Parsing Good Faith: Has the United States Violated Article VI of the Nuclear Non-proliferation Treaty?*, WIS. L. REV. 301, 308 (1993); Zachary S. Davis, *The NPT: Coping with the Best and Worst Cases*, in THE NUCLEAR NON-PROLIFERATION REGIME 140, 140 (RAJU G. C. THOMAS ed., 1998) (referring to the NPT as the "corner-stone of the non-proliferation regime," but not saying what else makes up that regime); Woodliffe, *supra* note 3, at 84 (referring to the NPT as the "cornerstone" of non-proliferation).

[18] See Gary J. Meise, *Securing the Strength of the Renewed NPT: China, the Linchpin "Middle Kingdom"*, 30 VAND. J. TRANSNAT'L L. 539, 549–550 (1997); GARDNER, *supra* note 5, at 53–54 (cited in Meise).

[19] See GUIDO DEN DEKKER, THE LAW OF ARMS CONTROL: INTERNATIONAL SUPERVISION AND ENFORCEMENT 144 (2001).

[20] See Treaty on the Non-proliferation of Nuclear Weapons, Art. III(1), July 1, 1968, 21 U. S.T 483, 492, 729 U.N.T.S 483, 489 (entered into force March 5, 1970, extended May 11, 1995) (hereinafter NPT). This assumes that these commentators do not see there being multiple nuclear non-proliferation regimes, as Burns Weston and Christopher Ford assert. See Burns H. Weston, *Law and Alternative Security: Toward a Nuclear Weapons-Free World*, 75 IOWA L. REV. 1077, 1084 (1990); Christopher A. Ford, *The Nonproliferation Bestiary: A Typology and Analysis of Nonproliferation Regimes*, 39 N.Y.U. J. INT'L L. & POL. 937 (2007). These other commentators, however, do not show signs of holding such a view.

[21] See S. C. Res. 487, ¶ 3, UN Doc. S/RES/487 (June 19, 1981); S. C. Res. 825, preamb. ¶ 3, UN Doc. S/RES/825 (May 11, 1993). See generally DAVID FISCHER, HISTORY OF THE INTERNATIONAL ATOMIC ENERGY AGENCY: THE FIRST FORTY YEARS (1997) (describing the creation and history of the IAEA); Hans Blix, *The Role of the IAEA in the Development of International Law*, 58 NORDIC J. INT'L L. 231 (1989); D. M. EDWARDS, *International Legal Aspects of Safeguards and the Non-proliferation of Nuclear Weapons*, 33 INT'L & COMP. L.Q. 1 (1984); Claudio Grossman, *Supervision*

referring to all three in requiring States parties to the NPT to "accept safeguards, as set forth in an agreement to be negotiated and concluded with the International Atomic Energy Agency in accordance with the Statute of the International Atomic Energy Agency and the Agency's safeguards system."[22] In other words, by becoming a member of the NPT, a State automatically has the obligation to become a member of the IAEA Statute and to enter into a safeguards agreement with the IAEA.[23] In short, this triumvirate forms the bedrock of the nuclear non-proliferation regime.

The essential obligations of the nuclear non-proliferation regime are found in NPT Article II and require non-nuclear-weapon States

> not to receive the transfer from any transferor whatsoever of nuclear weapons or other nuclear explosive devices or of control over such weapons or explosive devices directly, or indirectly; not to manufacture or otherwise acquire nuclear weapons or other nuclear explosive devices; and not to seek or receive any assistance in the manufacture of nuclear weapons or other nuclear explosive devices.[24]

The essential task of the IAEA within this nuclear non-proliferation regime is the "verification of the fulfillment of [States parties'] obligations assumed under this Treaty with a view to preventing diversion of nuclear energy from peaceful uses to nuclear weapons or other nuclear explosive devices,"[25] with the IAEA Statute governing the institutional functioning of the IAEA and the IAEA safeguards agreements governing the bilateral, legal relationship between the IAEA and the States. In return, non-nuclear-weapon States get assistance in developing their peaceful uses of nuclear energy under NPT Article IV(2) and IAEA Statute Articles II, III(A), VIII, and XI, as well as the security assurances of nuclear-weapon States under Security Council Resolutions 255 and 984, as explained in Chapter 3.2.1 below.

Despite the express design of the NPT to give the NPT, the IAEA Statute and the IAEA safeguards agreements a crucial role with the nuclear non-proliferation regime, some commentators nevertheless take a much broader approach to defining the nuclear non-proliferation regime. Orde Kittrie lists within the nuclear non-proliferation regime the

within the International Atomic Energy Agency, in SUPERVISORY MECHANISMS IN INTERNATIONAL ECONOMIC ORGANIZATIONS 489 (P. VAN DIJK ed., 1984).

22 NPT, *supra* note 20, Art. III(1).

23 Interestingly, however, by becoming a member of just the IAEA Statute, as in the case of Israel, no obligation arises for it also to join the NPT.

24 NPT, *supra* note 20, Art. II. 25 Ibid., Art. III(1).

NPT, the Convention on the Physical Protection of Nuclear Material, the Partial Test Ban Treaty, and the regional nuclear-weapon-free zones in Southeast Asia, Africa, and Latin America.[26] For whatever reason, Kittrie does not expressly include the IAEA Statute or the IAEA safeguards agreements within the regime, although these presumably are implicitly included inasmuch as he discusses them in the body of his study. Gary Meise lists the Limited Test Ban Treaty, the Outer Space Treaty, the NPT, and the Latin America nuclear-weapon-free zone as part of the nuclear non-proliferation regime, though he notes that the NPT is the backbone of the nuclear non-proliferation regime that has the most symbolic strength for non-proliferation.[27] Similar to Kittrie, Meise also implicitly includes the IAEA Statute and the IAEA safeguards agreements in the nuclear non-proliferation regime.[28] The same would appear to be true of Benoît Pélopidas, who includes within the nuclear non-proliferation regime the NPT, the Comprehensive Test Ban Treaty, and the Additional Protocol of the IAEA,[29] and Sharon Squassoni and her co-authors, who include the NPT, the regional nuclear-weapon-free zones, and the Convention on the Physical Protection of Nuclear Material.[30] David Sloss includes within the nuclear non-proliferation regime the NPT, the Convention on the Physical Protection of Nuclear Material, and the regional nuclear-weapon-free zones in Latin America and the South Pacific, with IAEA safeguards agreements (and implicitly the IAEA Statute) as key elements of the regime.[31] Richard Williamson takes perhaps the broadest approach, starting with the NPT as the "centerpiece" of this regime, and the Latin American regional nuclear-weapon-free zone as "the most significant" of the "several other bilateral or regional treaty arrangements which support the same general norms"

[26] See Orde F. Kittrie, *Averting Catastrophe: Why the Nuclear Nonproliferation Treaty Is Losing Its Deterrence Capacity and How to Restore It*, 28 MICH. J. INT'L L. 337, 346–347 (2007).

[27] See Meise, *supra* note 18, at 549–550; GARDNER, *supra* note 5, at 53–54.

[28] See Meise, *supra* note 18, at 550–551.

[29] See Benoît Pélopidas, *Comparative and Prospective Looks at the EU Non-proliferation Policy*, in EUROPE FACING NUCLEAR WEAPONS CHALLENGES 181, 183 (GRÉGORY BOUTHERIN ed., 2008).

[30] See SHARON A. SQUASSONI ET AL., PROLIFERATION CONTROL REGIMES: BACKGROUND AND STATUS 14–15 (2002).

[31] See David Sloss, *It's Not Broken, So Don't Fix It: The International Atomic Energy Agency Safeguards System and the Nuclear Nonproliferation Treaty*, 35 VA. J. INT'L L. 841, 844 n. 17 (1995).

as the NPT.[32] Other treaties that he mentions as being part of this regime are the Convention on the Physical Protection of Nuclear Materials, the regional nuclear-weapon-free zones in the South Pacific and Africa (which regional treaty was merely a possibility at the time of his writing), the IAEA Statute, the IAEA safeguards agreements, and "subsidiary arrangements and facility attachments which draw their legal authority from the safeguards agreement itself," as well such regional treaties as the Treaty Establishing the European Atomic Energy Community (EURATOM) and that which created the Brazilian–Argentine Agency for Accounting and Control of Nuclear Material.[33] Given this debate over defining the nuclear non-proliferation regime, it is somewhat surprising that a number of commentators feel able to focus entire studies on the nuclear non-proliferation *regime* without defining exactly where the norms for this regime come from, although they note that the NPT is one of multiple sources of norms for that regime.[34]

The closest thing to a common denominator among all of these views of the nuclear non-proliferation regime would be the inclusion of the NPT, the IAEA Statute, and the IAEA safeguards agreements, which make up the core of the nuclear non-proliferation regime. These treaties

[32] See Richard L. Williamson Jr., *Law and the H-Bomb: Strengthening the Nonproliferation Regime to Impede Advanced Proliferation*, 28 Cornell Int'l L.J. 71, 117–119 (1995).

[33] Ibid., at 117–121.

[34] See, e.g., Patricia Hewitson, *Nonproliferation and Reduction of Nuclear Weapons: Risks of Weakening the Multilateral Nuclear Nonproliferation Norm*, 21 Berkeley J. Int'l L. 405, 406 (2003) (stating that the "global regime [is] underpinned by the Nuclear Non-proliferation Treaty," but not saying what other treaties make up the rest of the regime); Jonas, *supra* note 4, at 418–419 (asserting that accession to the NPT is not enough to participate in the "entire spectrum of the nuclear non-proliferation regime," without listing the other treaties making up this regime); Benjamin Wastler, *Having Its Yellowcake and Eating It Too: How the NSG Waiver for India Threatens to Undermine the Nuclear Nonproliferation Regime*, 33 B.C. Int'l & Comp. L. Rev. 201, 202 (2010) (referring to the NPT as the "linchpin of the nuclear nonproliferation regime," but without mentioning what other treaties make up that regime); Sepehr Shahshahani, *Politics under the Cover of Law: Can International Law Help Resolve the Iran Nuclear Crisis?*, 25 B.U. Int'l L.J. 369, 382–383, 408 (2007) (same); Council on Foreign Relations, Issue Brief: The Global Nuclear Nonproliferation Regime, www.cfr.org/publication/18984/ (referring to the NPT as the "core component of the global nonproliferation regime," but not mentioning what the other components to the regime are); Raven Winters, *Preventing Repeat Offenders: North Korea's Withdrawal and the Need for Revisions to the Nuclear Non-proliferation Treaty*, 38 Vand. J. Transnat'l L. 1499, 1503 (2005) (identifying the NPT as the "backbone of the nuclear nonproliferation regime," but without noting what the other elements of the regime are).

are the main treaties upon which this study focuses. Nevertheless, while this study does not exclude the possibility that other treaties make up part of the nuclear non-proliferation regime, the NPT, the IAEA Statute and the IAEA safeguards agreements do form the central core. In the end, however, this study is not about *how* the ICJ or international arbitral tribunals should interpret any of these treaties, as it will be for that forum to choose between the competing interpretations. Instead, this study focuses on the more general notion of legal resolution of disputes in this area, whatever the exact substance of those disputes and the resolution of those disputes might be. As a result, this study does not provide exhaustive background analysis of the treaties making up the nuclear non-proliferation regime, instead providing only what is required to make any given point.

This subsection has explained the sources of law that one would look to in deciding the content of the norms of the nuclear non-proliferation regime. Given the references in these treaties to "nuclear weapons," the task remains of providing an appropriate definition, which is the topic of the following subsection.

2.1.2 Nuclear weapons

Commentators consistently characterize nuclear weapons as the bane of international peace and security, as did the introduction to this study. On numerous occasions, all of which are discussed in Chapter 3 below, the Security Council itself has explicitly linked nuclear weapons and their proliferation to a threat to international peace and security.[35] Despite all the talk of nuclear weapons, few, if any, authoritative sources provide a clear definition of "nuclear weapons." None of the treaties identified as falling squarely within the nuclear non-proliferation regime – the NPT, the IAEA Statute, and the IAEA safeguards agreements – define "nuclear weapons." This is somewhat surprising for the NPT, inasmuch as it uses the phrase on numerous occasions. After all, "nuclear weapons" is in its official title – Treaty on the Non-proliferation of *Nuclear Weapons*. Admittedly, the NPT defines a "nuclear-weapon State" as "one which has manufactured and exploded a nuclear weapon or other nuclear explosive device prior to January 1, 1967,"[36] but it leaves out a

[35] See, e.g., S. C. Res. 825, preamb. ¶ 2, UN Doc. S/RES/825 (May 11, 1993); S.C. Res. 1887, preamb. ¶ 4, UN Doc. S/RES/1887 (Sept. 24, 2009).
[36] NPT, *supra* note 20, Art. IX(3).

definition of "nuclear weapon" or anything that resembles such a definition. The same is true with the IAEA safeguards agreements, which consistently refer to nuclear weapons.[37] The lack of a definition in the IAEA Statute is less surprising inasmuch as it does not refer to "nuclear weapons," in part because it focuses on the IAEA's institutional functions instead of on the substantive obligations of States or the IAEA's operational functions.[38]

Looking outside the treaties of the narrowly defined nuclear non-proliferation regime, one can find a legal definition in the Treaty of Tlatelolco and the Treaty of Rarotonga, which create regional nuclear-weapon-free zones in South America and Africa respectively. The Treaty of Tlatelolco provides the following definition:

> For the purposes of this Treaty, a nuclear weapon is any device which is capable of releasing nuclear energy in an uncontrolled manner and which has a group of characteristics that are appropriate for use for warlike purposes. An instrument that may be used for the transport or propulsion of the device is not included in this definition if it is separable from the device and not an indivisible part thereof.[39]

The Treaty of Rarotonga provides the following definition:

> For the purposes of this Treaty and its Protocols . . . "nuclear explosive device" means any nuclear weapon or other explosive device capable of releasing nuclear energy, irrespective of the purpose for which it could be used. The term includes such a weapon or device in unassembled and partly assembled forms, but does not include the means of transport or delivery of such a weapon or device if separable from and not an indivisible part of it . . .

Three aspects of these definitions stand out. First, these definitions contain circularity in using part of the term being defined ("nuclear") – presumably a cardinal sin of lexicography. Second, the definition of the Treaty of Tlatelolco refers to an ambiguous "group of characteristics that are appropriate for use for warlike purposes" without elaborating or even

37 International Atomic Energy Agency, *The Structure and Content of Agreements between the Agency and States Required in Connection with the Treaty on the Non-proliferation of Nuclear Weapons*, IAEA Doc. INFCIRC/153 (June 1972) (hereinafter IAEA Model Safeguards Agreement).

38 See Chittharanjan F. Amerasinghe, Principles of the Institutional Law of International Organizations 163–172 (2nd edn, 2005) (explaining the differences between institutional and operational functions and acts).

39 Treaty for the Prohibition of Nuclear Weapons in Latin America, Art. 5, Feb. 14, 1967, 22 U.S.T. 762, 634 U.N.T.S. 762 (hereinafter Treaty of Tlatelolco).

suggesting what those exact characteristics might be. Nevertheless, it provides more specificity than the Treaty of Rarotonga because it qualifies the release of nuclear energy as being "in an uncontrolled manner," whereas the Treaty of Rarotonga broadly refers to "explosive device[s] capable of releasing nuclear energy, irrespective of the purpose for which it could be used." Finally, both definitions exclude the delivery systems for nuclear weapons or other explosive devices, which undoubtedly reflects heated debates during the conventional conferences. Despite their perceived flaws, these definitions represent the best legal definitions of "nuclear weapons" in existence, with the other treaties that relate to nuclear weapons providing no definition at all. In other words, these other treaties that lack a formal definition would appear to adopt a common-usage definition of "nuclear weapons." Given the lack of specificity in the nuclear-weapon-related treaties that actually provide some semblance of a definition, these other treaties that use a common-usage definition presumably are no worse off for the lack of an express definition.

By "nuclear weapons," this study means weapons that "operate by atomic fission, that is a process which disintegrates the atomic nucleus of a heavy metal such as uranium or plutonium," as well as those that "operate by atomic fusion, that is the combination of two light atoms, deuterium and tritium, which are both isotopes of hydrogen," both of which "release [a] vast amounts of energy."[40] This is similar to the one the ICJ adopted in the *Legality of the Threat or Use of Nuclear Weapons* advisory opinion as "explosive devices whose energy results from the fusion or fission of the atom,"[41] although the ICJ's definition is not as developed. Some commentators try to establish threshold amounts of resources for such devices,[42] although this seems futile inasmuch as thresholds are bound to change as related technologies improve over time and the weapon's characteristics change with that changing technology. A strict distinction between nuclear material and nuclear weapons would seem artificial inasmuch as it is use of nuclear material in weapon form that this regime is designed to regulate. Therefore,

[40] François Bugnion, *The International Committee of the Red Cross and Nuclear Weapons: From Hiroshima to the Dawn of the 21st Century*, 859 Int'l Rev. Red Cross 511, 518 (2005).

[41] See Legality of the Threat or Use of Nuclear Weapons, Advisory Opinion, 1996 ICJ Rep. 226, 243 (July 8).

[42] See Julie Dahlitz, Nuclear Arms Control 178 (1983).

this study sees control over nuclear material as just as important as control over nuclear weapons inasmuch as the material makes the weapon.[43]

Critics conceivably might argue that disputes over nuclear material and nuclear weapons do not deserve special treatment that is different from disputes involving conventional weapons, inasmuch as they are sufficiently similar. Indeed, the power of nuclear weapons is measured in terms of an equivalent conventional explosion. For example, the power of the Hiroshima fifteen-kiloton bomb was equivalent to 15,000 tons of TNT.[44] In that regard, nuclear detonations of the same magnitude as conventional ones are no more powerful than conventional ones, contrary to assertions of some analysts.[45] Arguing the contrary is like saying a pound of lead weighs more than a pound of feathers. The fact that a nuclear weapon requires less mass to create an equivalent blast as a conventional weapon does not necessarily make it more powerful.[46] Take, for example, thermobaric bombs such as the BLU-118/B warhead that can be mounted on a GBU-28 laser-guided bomb, which incorporates high temperature with devastating pressure waves.[47] Called "the Big Ones" by the US Department of Defense because they weigh 5,000 pounds, these bombs can penetrate meters of reinforced concrete using the BLU-113 or the BLU-118/B conventional warhead.[48] US forces used the first thermobaric bomb in combat during Operation Anaconda against an Al Qaeda cave complex in Afghanistan.[49] Their effectiveness

[43] See JAN KOLASA, DISARMAMENT AND ARMS CONTROL AGREEMENTS: A STUDY ON PROCEDURAL AND INSTITUTIONAL LAW 13 (1995).

[44] See Williamson, *supra* note 32, at 97.

[45] See U.S. DEPT. OF DEF. & ENERGY RESEARCH AND DEVELOPMENT ADMINISTRATION, THE EFFECTS OF NUCLEAR WEAPONS ¶ 1.02 (SAMUEL GLASSTONE and PHILIP J. DOLAN ed., 3rd edn, 1977); Susan W. Brenner and Marc D. Goodman, *In Defense of Cyberterrorism: An Argument for Anticipating Cyber-Attacks*, U. ILL. J.L. TECH. & POL'Y 1, 5–6 n. 12 (2002).

[46] See U.S. DEPT. OF DEF. & ENERGY RESEARCH AND DEVELOPMENT ADMINISTRATION, *supra* note 45. Nonetheless, it does make delivery of destructive energy much easier, which in turn makes nuclear weapons particularly dangerous to civilization as we know it. See Final Doc. SSDI, A/RES/S-10/2, at 4–5; Dahlitz, *supra* note 42, at 32.

[47] See MIR BAHMANYAR, AFGHANISTAN CAVE COMPLEXES 1979–2004: MOUNTAIN STRONGHOLDS OF THE MUJAHIDEEN, TALIBAN AND AL QAEDA 23 (2004).

[48] See Michel Chossudovsky, *"Tactical Nuclear Weapons" against Afghanistan?*, Centre for Research on Globalisation (CRG) (Dec. 5, 2001), at www.globalresearch.ca/articles/CHO112C.html (last visited May 27, 2011).

[49] See Bahmanyar, *supra* note 47, at 23.

against such targets is classified. Nonetheless, these conventional detonations are not unlike nuclear ones in that their released energy increases the temperature and pressure so that surrounding materials are changed into compressed gases of a very high temperature, which creates a shock wave in ground or water, and a blast wave in the air.[50] This shock or blast wave is the primary source of destruction of these weapons,[51] which both conventional and nuclear weapons exhibit.

Even though a conventional detonation may be comparable in size, the number of casualties from a nuclear blast can be much greater in terms of long-term effects.[52] The main difference between nuclear and conventional weapons that creates this difference in casualties does not lie in the amount of energy released but in the way the energy is released: a nuclear detonation results from "the energy released by reactions involving atomic nuclei, either fission or fusion or both."[53] This unique method of energy release creates two destructive components not typically observed in conventional detonations: radiation and poisonous gases. The ICJ in the *Legality of the Threat or Use of Nuclear Weapons* advisory opinion focused on radiation as the unique characteristic distinguishing nuclear weapons from other weapons, which renders nuclear weapons "potentially catastrophic" in that their "destructive power ... cannot be contained in either space or time" and has "the potential to destroy all civilization and the entire ecosystem of the planet."[54] This radiation takes the form of thermal radiation in the intense heat and light released, which can burn skin and ordinary materials in a large area.[55] Radiation also comes from the penetrating but invisible rays of the "initial nuclear radiation" and their residue.[56] According to the ICJ, the radiation from nuclear weapons "would affect health, agriculture,

[50] See U.S. Dept. of Def. & Energy Research and Development Administration, *supra* note 45.
[51] See ibid.
[52] See Guy B. Roberts, *The Counterproliferation Self-Help Paradigm: A Legal Regime for Enforcing the Norm Prohibiting the Proliferation of Weapons of Mass Destruction*, 27 Denv. J. Int'l L. & Pol'y 483, 483 n. 2 (1999).
[53] Ctr. for Def. & Int'l Sec. Studies, Devil's Brews in Details: Nuclear Weapons, at www.cdiss.org/nw.htm (last visited May 27, 2011).
[54] See Legality of the Threat or Use of Nuclear Weapons, Advisory Opinion, 1996 ICJ Rep. 226, 243 (July 8).
[55] See U.S. Dept. of Def. & Energy Research and Development Administration, *supra* note 45.
[56] Ibid.

natural resources and demography over a very wide area," and would pose "a serious danger to future generations."[57] Indeed, radiation causes injuries as serious as or worse than those induced by poison.[58] As the Solomon Islands asserted in its written statement to the Court in the *Legality of the Threat or Use of Nuclear Weapons* advisory opinion, this type of radiation has a similar effect on living matter as genotoxic poison in that it causes serious genetic risks to all those directly exposed to it, including fetuses.[59] The ICJ apparently considered these characteristics of nuclear weapons, as well as their indiscriminate nature,[60] as the Solomon Islands requested, though the weight the ICJ gave to these factors in reaching its ultimate decision remains unclear.[61] Not only does the radiation from nuclear weapons act like poison, but nuclear weapons themselves actually create poisonous and asphyxiating gases.[62] Even US president Kennedy acknowledged this in a public address in 1963.[63] Conventional weapons, no matter their size, lack the initial and residual radiation of nuclear weapons, as well as the inherent poisoning properties of weapons that have long-term effects on the exposed population. These unique physical characteristics pose particular problems for the international community over and above those posed by conventional weapons, which justifies their separate treatment in this study.

[57] See Legality of the Threat or Use of Nuclear Weapons, Advisory Opinion, 1996 ICJ Rep. 226, 243–244 (July 8).

[58] See, e.g., Richard Falk et al., Nuclear Weapons and International Law 22, 26 (1981); Nagendra Singh and Edward McWhinney, Nuclear Weapons and Contemporary International Law 124–125 (2nd rev. edn, 1989); Georg Schwarzenberger, The Legality of Nuclear Weapons 38 (1958).

[59] See Solomon Islands, Written Observations on the Request by the General Assembly for an Advisory Opinion, ¶¶ 3.64–70, reprinted in 7 Crim. L.F. 299 (1996).

[60] See Legality of the Threat or Use of Nuclear Weapons, Advisory Opinion, 1996 ICJ Rep. 226 (July 8), ¶¶ 34–36.

[61] See Edda Kristjansdottir, *The Legality of the Threat or Use of Nuclear Weapons under Current International Law: The Arguments behind the World Court's Advisory Opinion*, 30 N.Y.U. J. Int'l L. & Pol. 291, 347 (1998).

[62] See, e.g., Ian Brownlie, *Some Legal Aspects of the Use of Nuclear Weapons*, 14 Int'l & Comp. L.Q. 437, 441–444 (1965).

[63] See John F. Kennedy, *Commencement Address at American University (June 10, 1963)*, in "Let the Word Go Forth": The Speeches, Statements, and Writings of John F. Kennedy 1947–1963 282 (1988), at www.jfk.library.org/j061063.htm ("[War] makes no sense in an age when the deadly poisons produced by a nuclear exchange would be carried by wind and water and soil and seed to the far corners of the globe and to generations yet unborn").

2.2 Focus on legal resolution

In addition to the focus on the nuclear non-proliferation regime, this study focuses on *legal resolution* of disputes over the norms of that regime. By "legal resolution," or its synonym "international adjudication," this study means attempts at resolution through the binding decision of a third party that necessarily bases its decision on law.[64] This definition has two important elements – that the decisions are binding and that they are rendered through the application of law, both of which this subsection discusses. Before doing so, however, it is important to take a step back and explain the broader framework of international dispute settlement and where legal resolution fits within the whole.

2.2.1 Variety in dispute settlement mechanisms

The history of international dispute settlement starts with the birth of the modern State system through the Peace of Westphalia in 1648.[65] Certainly, legal resolution existed before 1648, as the examples in Chapter 4.2 show. However, legal resolution's place in the inter-State system was secured in the Peace of Westphalia, which referred to international arbitration as an appropriate method of resolving disputes between these nascent States.[66] Arbitration exhibited advanced procedures in resolving hostilities compared to the other methods of settlement existent at that time.[67] Admittedly, most disputes sent to international arbitration today that involve a State are oriented towards investment and commerce, partially due to the burgeoning docket of the World Bank's International Centre for Settlement of Investment Disputes and the proliferation of bilateral investment treaties (BITs), where States have given certain rights to investors to bring claims to international arbitration on their own behalf, as opposed to through their State and espousing their claims in diplomatic protection.[68]

[64] See John G. Merrills, International Dispute Settlement 91 (4th edn, 2005).

[65] See Mary Ellen O'Connell, International Dispute Resolution 3, 7 (2006).

[66] See ibid. [67] See ibid., at 7–8.

[68] See John Collier and Vaughan Lowe, The Settlement of Disputes in International Law: Institutions and Procedures 7 (1999); Stephan W. Schill, *System-Building in Investment Treaty Arbitration and Lawmaking*, 12 German L.J. 1083, 1083–1084 (2011) (discussing the proliferation of BITs and investment arbitration, as well as its impact on the system).

However, this does not mean that more politically sensitive disputes involving military-related matters cannot be sent to legal resolution, as Part III shows. Indeed, as explained there, recent ICJ disputes have tended to be more politically sensitive in nature. When the alternative is armed conflict or other coercive measures such as Security Council resolution, States would be (and are) well advised to give legal resolution a try with such politically sensitive disputes. After all, the key requirement under the UN Charter Article 2(3) is that States resolve their disputes through peaceful means, regardless of exactly which mechanism is used. This section explains in detail the various mechanisms that can be used in peacefully resolving international disputes.

International dispute settlement refers to the broad topic of public international law that deals with the peaceful resolution of disputes involving one or more States.[69] The "peaceful" element is key, obviating the use of force in resolving conflicts, which some commentators see as the "commonest method of resolving conflict."[70] UN Charter Article 33(1) provides a list of peaceful methods of international dispute settlement:

> The parties to any dispute, the continuance of which is likely to endanger the maintenance of international peace and security, shall, first of all, seek a solution by negotiation, enquiry, mediation, conciliation, arbitration, judicial settlement, resort to regional agencies or arrangements, or other peaceful means of their own choice.[71]

[69] See JOHN O'BRIEN, INTERNATIONAL LAW 633–671 (2001); ALINA KACZOROWSKA, PUBLIC INTERNATIONAL LAW 615–686 (4th edn, 2010); J.-MAURICE ARBOUR, DROIT INTERNATIONAL PUBLIC 515–553 (3rd edn, 1997); JEAN COMBACAU and SERGE SUR, DROIT INTERNATIONAL PUBLIC 551–610 (6th edn, 2004); EMMANUEL DECAUX, DROIT INTERNATIONAL PUBLIC 237–278 (5th edn, 2006); DENIS ALLAND, DROIT INTERNATIONAL PUBLIC 447–520 (2000); PIERRE-MARIE DUPUY, DROIT INTERNATIONAL PUBLIC 535–638 (6th edn, 2002); DAVID RUZIÉ, DROIT INTERNATIONAL PUBLIC 178–203 (19th edn, 2008); RAYMOND RANJEVA and CHARLES CADOUX, DROIT INTERNATIONAL PUBLIC 225–259 (1992); CLAUDE EMANUELLI, DROIT INTERNATIONAL PUBLIC 603–648 (2nd edn, 2004). For the journals devoted to international dispute settlement, see JOURNAL OF INTERNATIONAL DISPUTE SETTLEMENT (Oxford University Press); LAW AND PRACTICE OF INTERNATIONAL COURTS AND TRIBUNALS (Brill).

[70] See Kosta Tsipis, *Foreword*, in C. MOXLEY, NUCLEAR WEAPONS AND INTERNATIONAL LAW IN THE POST-COLD WAR WORLD i, xix (2000) ("A weapon is a device, a tool used in combat, the commonest method for resolving conflict").

[71] UN Charter Art. 33(1); see also G.A. Res. 37/10, Annex, UN Doc. A/RES/37/10/Annex (Nov. 15, 1982) (Manila Declaration on the Peaceful Settlement of International Disputes reaffirming Art. 33(1), inter alia, in an effort to enhance the United Nation's effectiveness in the peaceful settlement of international disputes).

Notably, this is not an exhaustive list, as States are free to choose other methods such as consultation or the possibility of receiving prior consent, which operate in combination with the principle of international estoppel, both of which are valid methods of international dispute settlement.[72] Nor does this list of methods of international dispute settlement establish a hierarchy between them.[73] Instead, States are free to choose whatever method or methods of resolution they prefer, so long as they are seeking to resolve their disputes peacefully, assuming they do not have an express requirement upon them to resolve their disputes in a particular manner. Article 33 makes this point abundantly clear with its last phrase, "or other peaceful means of their own choice." The ICJ reaffirmed this point that States are free to choose whatever method of resolution they want in its judgment in the 1998 *Fisheries Jurisdiction* case between Spain and Canada.[74] Therefore, these methods of dispute settlement ought to be seen as possible tools available to States, not as a required progression up the ladder to legal resolution. For example, States are free to jump right to legal resolution or to remain in conciliation if they so choose. An obvious exception would be where there is a compromissory clause in the underlying treaty and one of the disputants invokes that clause; then the options become somewhat limited in terms of remaining exclusively within the realm of nonlegal methods of resolution. Moreover, disputants also can try multiple methods of resolution at the same time, with a few exceptions, which point

[72] See generally Merrills, *supra* note 64; Christian Tomuschat, *Article 33*, in THE CHARTER OF THE UNITED NATIONS: A COMMENTARY 583, 583–585 (BRUNO SIMMA ed., 2002). See generally Hans Blix, *The Principles of Peaceful Settlement of Disputes*, in THE LEGAL PRINCIPLES GOVERNING FRIENDLY RELATIONS AND CO-OPERATION AMONG STATES 44 (MOHAMMED K. NAWAZ et al. ed., 1966).

[73] See COLLIER and LOWE, *supra* note 68, at 7 ("The various forms of settlement procedure are not stages through which the parties must progress, any more than a garage mechanic 'progresses' through the spanners, hammers, screwdrivers and other tools at his disposal. They are alternatives, from which the parties involved choose the procedure most likely to yield a satisfactory result"); Tomuschat, *supra* note 72, at 583–585. But see M. Scott Garrison, *Sovereignty of Aves Island: An Argument against Compulsory, Standardized Arbitration of Maritime Boundary Disputes Subject to Review by the International Court of Justice*, 38 U. MIAMI INTER-AM. L. REV. 185, 214–215 (2006) (asserting that UN Charter Article 33 creates a hierarchy of dispute settlement mechanisms that gives priority to diplomatic methods of resolution over legal).

[74] See *Fisheries Jurisdiction Case (Spain v. Canada)*, 1998 ICJ Rep. 434, 456 (Dec. 4) ("Any resultant disputes are required to be resolved by peaceful means, the choice of which, pursuant to Article 33 of the Charter, is left to the parties").

becomes particularly important when this study discusses the complementary functionality of different methods of dispute settlement. In particular, the continuing process of negotiation does not itself hinder the ICJ's involvement in a case, assuming the ICJ has the necessary jurisdiction over the dispute,[75] just as the involvement of the ICJ should not hinder the parties' attempts at finding a negotiated settlement.

Notwithstanding the non-exhaustive nature of Article 33(1), there is some order to it. The methods of peaceful dispute settlement generally are divided into two categories: legal resolution and diplomatic resolution, or rather legal and nonlegal resolution. Legal resolution generally involves the methods of arbitration and judicial settlement listed in Article 33(1). These two broad categories of legal and diplomatic resolution are similar in that they both are based on State consent.[76] Legal resolution generally is distinct from nonlegal resolution in two ways. First, as the name implies, decisions of legal resolution are made by the application of international law by the judge or arbitrator, typically the standard sources of international law reflected in ICJ Statute Article 38 (1).[77] ICJ Statute Article 38(2) does allow "the Court to decide a case *ex aequo et bono*, if the parties agree thereto."[78] However, no disputants have mutually agreed that the ICJ can disregard the law in reaching its

[75] See *Aegean Sea Continental Shelf (Greece v. Turkey)*, 1978 ICJ Rep. 3, 12–13 (Dec. 19).

[76] Some commentators distinguish international arbitration from ICJ resolution in that States are not obliged to consent to an arbitral tribunal's jurisdiction or to its decision. See Eric A. Posner and John C. Yoo, *Judicial Independence in International Tribunals*, 93 CAL. L. REV. 1, 9 (2005). However, this does not make any sense because an international arbitral tribunal cannot exist without the consent of the disputants. A single consent, such as that in an arbitration clause, is sufficient to give a tribunal jurisdiction over the dispute, assuming that that tribunal stays within the limitations of its jurisdiction. See CHITTHARANJAN F. AMERASINGHE, JURISDICTION OF INTERNATIONAL TRIBUNALS 77 (2003); Hazel Fox, *States and the Undertaking to Arbitrate*, 37 INT'L & COMP. L.Q. 1, 4–5 (1988). Moreover, one fundamental characteristic of arbitration is that it is binding, as explained below.

[77] See ICJ Statute, Art. 38(1). See also Hideharu Onuma, *The ICJ: An Emperor without Clothes? International Conflict Resolution, Article 38 of the ICJ Statute and the Sources of International Law*, in LIBER AMICORUM JUDGE SHIGERU ODA 191 (NISUKE ANDO et al. ed., 2002); Jonathan I. Charney, *International Lawmaking: Article 38 of the ICJ Statute Reconsidered*, in NEW TRENDS IN INTERNATIONAL LAWMAKING: INTERNATIONAL "LEGISLATION" IN THE PUBLIC INTEREST 171 (JOST DELBRÜCK ed., 1997). Please note that disputants that elect to use arbitration to resolve the dispute can designate the applicable law, with international law being the applicable law with such a designation. See D. H. N. Johnson, *International Arbitration Back in Favour?*, 34 Y.B. WORLD AFF. 305, 306 (1980).

[78] ICJ Statute Art. 38(2).

decision *ex aequo et bono*, although the ICJ has asserted that it can apply a type of *ex aequo et bono* in applying the law to a unique set of facts in a particular case.[79] Disputes that are resolved through nonlegal methods of settlement typically are settled without the application of law.[80] For example, when resolving disputes, political entities such as the Security Council look at the political issues of the dispute and are able to make their decisions with politics (and other nonlegal factors) in mind.[81] The UN Charter itself provides the Security Council this flexibility inasmuch as it says that the Security Council has the freedom to "recommend such terms of settlement as it may consider appropriate,"[82] which would not necessarily involve legal considerations. At the same time, UN Charter Article 36(3) encourages the Security Council to "take into consideration that legal disputes should as a general rule be referred by the parties to the International Court of Justice in accordance with the provisions of the Statute of the Court."[83] However, there is nothing in UN Charter Chapter VI that prohibits the Security Council from getting involved in resolving these legal disputes with its regular political methods when the

[79] See *Case Concerning the Frontier Dispute (Burkina Faso/Mali)*, 1986 ICJ Rep. 554, 567–568 (Dec. 22); Michael Akehurst, *Equity and General Principles of Law*, 25 Int'l & Comp. L.Q. 801, 801–802 (1976) (referring to equity infra legem being common in ICJ jurisprudence); Prosper Weil, *L'équité dans la jurisprudence de la Cour internationale de justice: Un mystère en voie de disparition?*, in Fifty Years of the International Court of Justice: Essays in Honour of Sir Robert Jennings 121 (A. Vaughan Lowe and Colin Warbrick ed., 1996); C. Wilfred Jenks, The Prospects of International Arbitration 316–427 (1964). After all, what is there to stop judges from basing their decisions on hunches. See generally Joseph C. Hutcheson, Jr., *The Judgment Intuitive: The Function of the "Hunch" in Judicial Decision*, 14 Cornell L.Q. 274 (1929).

[80] See Merrills, *supra* note 64, at 80–81, 86, 90–95, 104–105; Hans-Jürgen Schlochauer, *Arbitration*, in 1 Encyclopedia of Public International Law 215, 224–225 (Rudolf Bernhardt ed., 1992); *International Law Commission Draft Articles on Arbitral Procedure*, [1953] 2 Y.B. Int'l L. Comm'n 201, UN Doc. A/CN.4/SER.A/1953/Add.1. Some commentators refer to something they call "auto-adjudication" in the context of nuclear non-proliferation disputes. See Dahlitz, *supra* note 42, at 161. However, this seems to be an oxymoron, inasmuch as adjudication by definition involves the involvement of a third party in reaching a decision through the application of law. What Dahlitz is referring to seems to be more like auto-interpretation of obligations, which must be distinguished from adjudication.

[81] See Vera Gowlland-Debbas, *The Relationship between the International Court of Justice and the Security Council in the Light of the Lockerbie Case*, 88 Am. J. Int'l L. 643, 654 (1994).

[82] UN Charter, Art. 37(2); see also Gowlland-Debbas, *supra* note 81, at 654.

[83] UN Charter Art. 36(3).

disputants refuse to refer the matter to the ICJ. In the instances where the disputants exercise their sovereignty and send a dispute to legal resolution, it is this sovereignty that typically requires international law to be the applicable law, inasmuch as States generally are immune from the municipal laws of other States, unless, of course, the disputants exercise that sovereignty to designate another body of applicable law.[84]

Second, the decisions of legal resolution are binding, whereas the decisions of the nonlegal methods of resolution typically are not binding. Lawyers generally tend to believe that you can overcome distrust between disputants by adopting binding dispute settlement mechanisms that create legal obligations on the parties.[85] It is the dispositive nature of legal resolution that makes it an attractive option for many States – as reflected in ICJ Article 60, which states that its decisions are "final and without appeal" – who then are free to proceed to address other issues.[86] The ICJ's decisions have so much legal and moral weight to them that States that see themselves as having lost a case typically cannot challenge that decision in the political realm once it has been rendered,[87] thus supporting the notion that the rendering of a decision ends the dispute. A key exception where States have agreed to nonlegal methods of resolution to bind them is with the Security Council, which can bind disputants by its Chapter VII decisions in accordance with UN Charter Article 25: "The Members of the United Nations agree to accept and carry out the decisions of the Security Council in accordance with the

[84] See *Report of the International Law Commission to the General Assembly*, 13 UN GAOR Supp. (No 9), UN Doc. A/3859 (1958), reprinted in [1958] 2 Y.B. INT'L L. COMM'N 78, 84, Arts. 8, 10 and 12, UN Doc. A/CN.4/117 (hereinafter 1958 ILC Report) (Art. 10 providing that the tribunal is to apply the standard sources of international law in the absence of agreement between the parties as to the applicable law); COLLIER and LOWE, *supra* note 68, at 33; MAURO RUBINO-SAMMARTANO, INTERNATIONAL ARBITRATION LAW AND PRACTICE 133–44, 157–158 (2nd edn, 2001); MALCOLM N. SHAW, INTERNATIONAL LAW 739 n. 143 (4th edn, 1997) (citing the *Nottebohm* case, 1953 ICJ Rep. 111, 119).

[85] See LOUIS B. SOHN, ADJUDICATION AND ENFORCEMENT IN ARMS CONTROL 365–366 (1960).

[86] Richard B. Bilder, *International Dispute Settlement and the Role of International Adjudication*, in THE INTERNATIONAL COURT OF JUSTICE AT A CROSSROADS 155, 163 (LORI F. DAMROSCH ed., 1987); Andreas Zimmermann and Tobias Thienel, *Article 60*, in THE STATUTE OF THE INTERNATIONAL COURT OF JUSTICE: A COMMENTARY 1275, 1276–1277 (ANDREAS ZIMMERMANN et al. ed., 2006).

[87] See Max Sørensen, *The I.C.J.: Its Role in Contemporary International Relations*, 14 INT'L ORG. 261, 274–275 (1960); CONSTANZE SCHULTE, COMPLIANCE WITH DECISIONS OF THE INTERNATIONAL COURT OF JUSTICE 403 (2004).

present Charter."[88] According to UN Charter Article 103, these decisions trump conflicting obligations: "In the event of a conflict between the obligations of the Members of the United Nations under the present Charter and their obligations under any other international agreement, their obligations under the present Charter shall prevail."[89] Other international organizations and organs of international organizations have the ability to bind States by their decisions, such as the Economic Community of Central African States,[90] the European Free Trade Association,[91] the Organisation of Eastern Caribbean States,[92] the International Grains Council,[93] Norden,[94] the World Health Organization,[95] and the International Cocoa Organization.[96] However,

[88] UN Charter, Art. 25. See generally Jost Delbrück, *Article 25*, in THE CHARTER OF THE UNITED NATIONS: A COMMENTARY 452 (BRUNO SIMMA ed., 2002).

[89] UN Charter, Art. 103. See generally Rudolf Bernhardt, *Article 103*, in The Charter of the United Nations: A Commentary 1292 (BRUNO SIMMA ed., 2002).

[90] Treaty Establishing the Economic Community of Central African States, Art. 11(2), Oct. 18, 1983, entered into force Dec. 18, 1984, at http://www.iss.co.za/AF/RegOrg/unity_-to_union/pdfs/eccas/eccastreaty.pdf ("Decisions shall be binding on the Member States and institutions of the Community, except for the Court of Justice").

[91] Convention establishing the European Free Trade Association, Jan. 4, 1960 (entered into force May 3, 1960), Art. 43(4) ("In exercising its responsibility under this Article, the Council may take decisions, which shall be binding on all Member States, and may make recommendations to Member States").

[92] Treaty establishing the Organisation of Eastern Caribbean States (Treaty of Basseterre), July 18, 1981, Art. 6(5), at http://www.oecs.org/Documents/treaties/oecs_treaty.pdf ("Such decisions by the Authority shall be binding on all Member States and on all institutions of the Organization and effect shall be given to any such decisions provided that it is within the sovereign competence of Member States to implement them").

[93] Grains Trade Convention 1995, Dec. 7, 1994, entered into force July 1, 1995, Art. 14(2), at http://www.igc.org.uk/en/downloads/brochure/iga1995.pdf ("Without prejudice to the complete liberty of action of any member in the determination and administration of its agricultural and price policies, each member undertakes to accept as binding all decisions of the Council under the provisions of this Convention").

[94] Treaty of Cooperation between Denmark, Finland, Iceland, Norway and Sweden (the Helsinki Treaty), March 23, 1962, entered into force July 1, 1962, as amended in 1971, 1974, 1983, 1985, 1991, 1993 and 1995), Art. 63, available at www.norden.org/avtal/helsingfors/uk/helsinki_agreement.pdf ("The decisions of the Council of Ministers are binding on each country").

[95] See Constitution of the World Health Organization, July 22, 1946, entered into force April 7, 1948, Art. 20, available at http://apps.who.int/gb/bd/PDF/bd47/EN/constitution-en.pdf ("Each Member undertakes that it will, within eighteen months after the adoption by the Health Assembly of a convention or agreement, take action relative to the acceptance of such convention or agreement").

[96] International Cocoa Agreement 2001, March 13, 2001 (came into force Oct. 1, 2003), Art. 12(4), at http://www.icco.org/pdf/agree01english.pdf ("Members undertake to accept as binding all decisions of the Council under the provisions of this Agreement").

none of these organizations has such purview over security-related matters as the Security Council enjoys.[97]

In concluding this section, it must be noted that this study focuses on a legal approach to dispute resolution, inasmuch as it focuses on the rules and procedures for dispute resolution, both throughout the duration of the process and at the end of the process.[98] From this perspective, the dispute ends when there is a negotiated settlement or when a court or tribunal renders a binding judgment.[99] As Lon Fuller notes, the purpose of the legal approach to dispute settlement is to determine the just result by giving effect to the law,[100] not necessarily to bring about peace. It is important to note that obviously nonlegal methods of resolution are involved with international dispute settlement, as is contained in the subfield of international dispute settlement typically known as "diplomatic resolution," which tends not to rely on the application of law to resolve the dispute.[101] The assertion that international dispute settlement is a "legal approach" is merely to juxtapose it with the international-relations approach to dispute resolution, otherwise known as conflict prevention or conflict resolution, which focuses on the

[97] Critics might be tempted to point to the European Union as the exception here, with its shared competence over security and military matters with member States under Art. 4(2) of Part I of the consolidated version of the Treaty on the Functioning of the European Union. However, this study sees the European Union more as a supranational entity that impacts the daily lives of its citizens, much like the federal government of the United States, Germany, or Canada, than as an international organization like the United Nations. See Ingolf Pernice, *The Treaty of Lisbon: Multilevel Constitutionalism in Action*, 15 COLUM. J. EUR. L. 349, 358 (2009); Stuart E. Eizenstat, *U.S. Relations with the European Union and the Changing Europe*, 9 EMORY INT'L L. REV. 1, 2–3 (1995) (asserting that "the EU is not an international organization like the UN," although also acknowledging that it is not a decentralized nation-state like Canada, the United States and others); Oliver Gerstenberg, *Denationalization and the Very Idea of Democratic Constitutionalism: The Case of the European Community*, 14 RATIO JURIS 298 (2001).

[98] See O'CONNELL, *supra* note 65, at 5.

[99] See Richard B. Bilder, *An Overview of International Dispute Settlement*, 1 EMORY J. INT'L DIS. RESOL. 1, pt VII (1986); ICJ Statute, Art. 60 ("The judgment is final and without appeal").

[100] See Glenn S. Koppel, *Reflections on the "Chimera" of a Uniform Code of State Civil Procedure: The Virtue of Vision in Procedural Reform*, 58 DEPAUL L. REV. 971, 1006 (2009), quoting Lon L. Fuller, *The Needs of American Legal Philosophy*, in THE PRINCIPLES OF SOCIAL ORDER 249, 263 (Kenneth I. Winston ed., 1981).

[101] See COLLIER and LOWE, *supra* note 68, at 5–7, 19–31; MERRILLS, *supra* note 64, at 1–89; Charles Manga Fombad, *Consultation and Negotiation in the Pacific Settlement of International Disputes*, 1 AF. J. INT'L & COMP. L. 707 (1989).

effectiveness of dispute resolution mechanisms and asks such questions as why disputants obey or disobey a particular judicial outcome.[102] Under the international-relations approach, commentators cannot fathom how the ICJ or international arbitral tribunals can create sufficient sanctions for recalcitrant States to get them to comply with their decisions.[103] For the most part, such questions fall outside the scope of this study because of the desire here to focus on legal matters. Besides, practice has shown that implementation of ICJ and international arbitral decisions is less of a problem than international-relations commentators make it out to be, with States typically preferring voluntary implementation over the political costs associated with refusal.[104] In this regard, this study is quite Kelsenian in that it attempts to divorce law from politics and focus on the former as its own discipline.[105] While law and politics interrelate,[106] they nevertheless were created as separate fields and remain largely distinct,[107] and will be treated as such. Again, as explained in Chapter 6.5 below, there likely is no harm in international judges and arbitrators being aware of the larger context of the matters placed before them, and counsel for the parties certainly will do their very best to ensure that these decision-makers are fully aware of the potential impact of their decision, thus making it virtually impossible for them to remain ignorant of the wider political ramifications for very long.[108] However, the rule of law requires that these considerations not dictate the outcome of these legal proceedings, as explained in Chapter 5.3 below.

[102] See O'Connell, *supra* note 65, at 5.

[103] See Tom Ginsburg and Richard H. McAdams, *Adjudicating in Anarchy: An Expressive Theory of International Dispute Resolution*, 45 Wm and Mary L. Rev. 1229, 1328 (2004).

[104] See Merrills, *supra* note 64, at 106; John Merrills, *The Means of Dispute Settlement*, in International Law 529, 541 (Malcolm Evans ed., 2003); Colter Paulson, *Compliance with Final Judgments of the International Court of Justice since 1987*, 98 Am. J. Int'l L. 434 (2004); Schulte, *supra* note 87 (showing that, apart from a few limited incidents in the 1970s, States generally have complied with ICJ decisions).

[105] See generally Hans Kelsen, Pure Theory of Law (trans. Max Knight, 1967).

[106] See, e.g., Louis Henkin et al., eds., International Law: Cases and Materials 1 (3rd edn, 1993) (asserting "law is politics").

[107] See O'Connell, *supra* note 65, at 5.

[108] See Robert Jennings, *International Courts and International Politics*, in Contemporary Issues in International Law 13, 24 (David Freestone et al. ed., 2002).

2.2.2 *Legal resolution in this study*

With this understanding of how legal resolution fits within the larger framework of international dispute settlement now in place, it is important to define legal resolution for the purposes of this study. Legal resolution generally involves three methods of resolution: proceedings before an international arbitral tribunal, before a general international court, and before a specialized international court.[109] As alluded to in the preceding subsection and explained in detail in Chapter 5.3.1, all of these fora reach their decisions through the application of law. By "general international court," this study means the International Court of Justice, as it is the only entity that fits in this category. This study does not focus on any of the seventeen or so specialized international courts that currently exist,[110] because none exist at this time that specifically handle nuclear non-proliferation disputes. However, this is not to say that the option of establishing a specialized court to handle disputes of these types is not an attractive one, as others have argued elsewhere.[111] In particular, this study is delimited by not including quasi-legal resolution by the WTO Dispute Settlement Mechanism, which might be used to resolve disputes concerning trade in nuclear material or nuclear-weapon-related goods and services. Instead, such disputes are most likely to be addressed, if at all, at the International Court of Justice or in international arbitral tribunals, on account of their general jurisdiction, which lacks a geographic or substantive limitation, as do the other international courts and tribunals that currently exist. As Part III explains, these fora are sufficiently equipped to handle these types of disputes.

It is common for the literature on legal resolution to combine ICJ resolution with legal resolution by international arbitration in providing

[109] See SOHN, *supra* note 85, at 366; MERRILLS, *supra* note 64, at 316; Rosalyn Higgins, *The Desirability of Third-Party Adjudication: Conventional Wisdom or Continuing Truth?*, in INTERNATIONAL ORGANIZATION: LAW IN MOVEMENT 37, 38 (J. E. S. FAWCETT and ROSALYN HIGGINS ed., 1974).

[110] See Cesare P. R. Romano, *The Proliferation of International Judicial Bodies: The Pieces of the Puzzle*, 31 NYU J. INT'L L & POL. 709, 711–723 (1999) (exhaustively listing all of the international courts in existence today); Rama Mani, *Peaceful Settlement of Disputes and Conflict Prevention*, in THE OXFORD HANDBOOK ON THE UNITED NATIONS 300, 306 (THOMAS G. WEISS and SAM DAWS ed., 2007).

[111] See T. DUPUY and G. HAMMERMAN (eds.), A DOCUMENTARY HISTORY OF ARMS CONTROL AND DISARMAMENT 29 (1973) (referring to Jeremy Bentham's proposals to create a court to resolve arms-related disputes, which presumably would have included nuclear-weapon disputes if nuclear weapons had existed at that time).

their analyses and conclusions,[112] and this study does the same. These two are handled together because they are closely connected, with the practice of legal resolution before an international court coming from the tradition of international arbitration,[113] the shift in predominance from legal resolution before an international arbitral tribunal to legal resolution before an international court occurring in the interwar period with the creation of the PCIJ.[114] Admittedly there are differences between the ICJ and international arbitral tribunals, such as the way the decision-makers are selected and the permanency of the forum.[115] Some commentators even venture to say that one is better than the other

[112] See generally Hersch Lauterpacht, The Function of Law in the International Community 381 (1933) (combining the analysis of the PCIJ and international arbitration); John L. Simpson and Hazel Fox, International Arbitration: Law and Practice (1959) (combining the analysis of the PCIJ, ICJ and international arbitration); C. Wilfred Jenks, The Prospects of International Adjudication (1964) (same, but calling it all international arbitration). But see Richard Bilder, *Adjudication: International Arbitration Tribunals and Courts*, in Peacemaking in International Conflict: Methods and Techniques 155 (I. William Zartman and J. Lewis Rasmussen ed., 1997) (comparing and contrasting adjudication before the ICJ and international arbitral tribunals); Robert Y. Jennings, *The Differences between Conducting a Case in the ICJ and in an Ad Hoc Tribunal: An Inside View*, in Liber Amicorum Judge Shigeru Oda 893 (N. Ando et al. ed., 2002) (same).

[113] See Merrills, *supra* note 64, at 91; Sohn, *supra* note 85, at 366; Louis B. Sohn, *Settlement of Disputes Relating to the Interpretation and Application of Treaties*, 150 Rec. des cours 195, 206 (1976).

[114] See Leland M. Goodrich and Anne P. Simons, The United Nations and the Maintenance of International Peace and Security 322 (1955).

[115] See, e.g., Louis B. Sohn, *The Future of Dispute Settlement*, in The Structure and Process of International Law 1121, 1125 (R. St. J. Macdonald and Douglas M. Johnston ed., 1986). Some commentators assert that the disputants enjoy greater control over the proceedings when before the ICJ than before international arbitral tribunals. See Robert Jennings, *The Role of the International Court of Justice* 68 Brit. Y.B. Int'l L. 1 (1997); Georges Abi-Saab, *The International Court as a World Court*, in Fifty years of the International Court of Justice 3 (Vaughan Lowe and Malgosia Fitzmaurice ed., 1996). However, this seems counterintuitive. After all, parties to an international arbitration have the ability to choose the arbitrators, either by direct appointment or through a designated appointing authority. See *Int'l Law Commission Draft Articles on Arbitral Procedure*, [1953] 2 Y.B. Int'l L. Comm'n 201, UN Doc. A/CN.4/SER.A/1953/Add.1. In international arbitration, it is standard for the disputants to choose two-thirds of the arbitrators for a multi-member tribunal, with those arbitrators then selecting one or several arbitrators, depending on the specifics of the arbitration agreement. However, this difference makes a negligible difference inasmuch as all judges and arbitrators are required to remain impartial, regardless of the way they were selected.

with respect to nuclear non-proliferation disputes,[116] although this study prefers to focus on the differences between legal resolution and Security Council resolution, not between adjudication by the ICJ and by international arbitral tribunals, because they both contain the essential element of the application of law by an impartial third-party decision-maker.[117] Besides, any time-saving benefits in having a pre-established forum in the ICJ vis-à-vis an ad hoc arbitral forum are relatively minor in this context inasmuch as the compromissory clauses that provide for international arbitration are reasonably clear on how the arbitral tribunal is to be established, such that it will not take long to establish the tribunal. If that were not the case, then using the pre-established ICJ would hold greater benefit for the parties, assuming they want a reasonably quick process.

When it comes to international arbitration, it must be acknowledged that there are several different kinds. By "international arbitration" and "international arbitral tribunal," this study means the public international law variety, not the private international law variety. Arbitral proceedings between States fall within the field of public international arbitration, whereas transnational proceedings that involve private entities fall within private international arbitration.[118] Whether or not a dispute involving an international organization is considered public international arbitration likely will depend on the nature of the dispute. For example, international organizations regularly designate arbitration as the preferred dispute settlement mechanism in their procurement contracts,[119] as well as in resolving tort claims after they have arisen.[120] The International Atomic Energy Agency (IAEA) is no exception when it comes to dispute settlement provisions in its agreements with contractors and in resolving such disputes in practice, though there are few

[116] See Edwin J. Nazario, *The Potential Role of Arbitration in the Nuclear Non-proliferation Treaty Regime*, 10 Am. Rev. Int'l Arb. 139, 148–149 (1999) (favoring arbitration over the ICJ with disputes over the NPT because of the ability to select arbitrators, to keep the proceedings confidential and to otherwise maintain better control over the proceedings).

[117] See Nejib Jibril, *The Binding Dilemma: From Bakassi to Badme – Making States Comply with Territorial Decisions of International Judicial Bodies*, 19 Am. U. Int'l L. Rev. 633, 644–646 (2004) (noting this similarity after discussing the differences).

[118] See Alan Redfern et al., Law and Practice of International Commercial Arbitration 55 (4th edn, 2004); Merrills, *supra* note 64, at 100–101.

[119] See August Reinisch, *Developing Human Rights and Humanitarian Law Accountability of the Security Council for the Imposition of Economic Sanctions*, 95 Am. J. Int'l L. 851, 867 (2001).

[120] See Charles H. Brower II, *International Immunities: Some Dissident Views on the Role of Municipal Courts*, 41 Va. J. Int'l L. 1, 78–80 (2000).

details of such proceedings in the public domain.[121] Disputes involving a private party will imply private international arbitration, just as when States enter into commercial contracts with private entities. However, where the other side in the dispute is a State, then it will imply public international arbitration. Given that international organizations have international legal personality and are established under international law as opposed to municipal law,[122] it makes considerable sense to include these types of disputes within the realm of public international arbitration. It is not often that international organizations are obliged to rely on international arbitration to resolve their disputes with States, as provided in the IAEA safeguards agreements discussed in Chapter 6.2 below. Nonetheless, the Permanent Court of Arbitration (PCA) has seen fit to establish optional arbitration rules for where disputes arise between an international organization and a State, or between two international organizations. Although Article 1 of these optional rules requires the international organization and the State to have agreed in writing to their disputes being resolved under these particular rules,[123] these rules are nonetheless helpful in showing how the United Nations Commission on International Trade Law (UNCITRAL) Arbitration Rules, which were designed for use in ad hoc arbitrations, also provide adequate procedures for resolving disputes between such entities.[124]

Finally, it must be noted that this study does not focus on adjudication before national courts. There is the possibility that nuclear non-proliferation disputes would involve crimes of a universal-jurisdiction nature that can be prosecuted in domestic courts and under the framework of criminal

[121] See Paul C. Szasz, The Law and Practices of the International Atomic Energy Agency 938–949 (1970).

[122] See Henry G. Schermers and Niels M. Blokker, International Institutional Law 27–37 (3rd rev. edn, 2003); see also Permanent Court of Arbitration, Permanent Court of Arbitration Optional Rules for Arbitration Involving International Organizations and States, July 1, 1996, Art. 33(1), available at http://www.pca-cpa.org/upload/files/IGO2ENG.pdf (last visited May 29, 2011). In addition, commentators consider states and international organizations equivalent when determining the international and public nature of a dispute. See Amerasinghe, *supra* note 76, at 4–8; Karl-Heinz Böckstiegel, *States in the International Arbitral Process*, in Contemporary Problems in International Arbitration 40, 40 (Julian D. M. Lew ed., 1986).

[123] See Permanent Court of Arbitration Optional Rules, *supra* note 122, Art. 1.

[124] See Permanent Court of Arbitration, Introduction to the PCA Optional Rules for Arbitration Involving International Organizations and States 97 (1996), at http://www.pca-cpa.org/upload/files/IGO2ENG.pdf; see also Shaw, *supra* note 84, at 742.

law, as well as municipal civil proceedings and inquiries.[125] Some studies focus on the role of domestic courts in handling such matters.[126] Indeed, the 1955 *Shimoda* case, where five Japanese victims of the atomic bombs on Hiroshima and Nagasaki sued the Japanese government in the District Court of Tokyo for waiving all claims against the Allied Powers for actions relating to the war in Article 19(a) of the peace treaty that ended the war in the Pacific theater, shows how domestic courts can be involved with disputes relating to nuclear weapons.[127] However, these domestic possibilities for adjudication fall outside the scope of this study, which instead focuses exclusively on the legal resolution of nuclear non-proliferation disputes on the international level.

2.3 Pragmatism over utopianism

With this foundation and definitional framework in place, the stage is set for critics to attempt to cut the legs out from under this study by attacking its core assumptions and paradigms. This section attempts to pre-empt some of those critics by emphasizing the point that this study focuses on the *pragmatic* resolution of disputes, as opposed to holding legal resolution out as the panacea for all the world's ills. This study's focus on legal resolution does not mean that it should be seen as part of what David Kennedy has referred to as the "contemporary internationalist sensibility" of young international lawyers – a type of idealistic naivety that hangs its hopes on the international as opposed to the domestic in addressing the world's problems.[128] These individuals

[125] See generally Françoise Hampson and Hilaire McCoubrey, *Evidence in Cases Involving Proliferation Issues*, in FUTURE LEGAL RESTRAINTS ON ARMS PROLIFERATION 273, 285–289 (JULIE DAHLITZ ed., 1996).

[126] See, e.g., Peter Weiss, *Nuclear War in the Courts*, in NUCLEAR WEAPONS, THE PEACE MOVEMENT AND THE LAW 178 (JOHN DWAR et al. ed., 1986).

[127] See generally *Shimoda* case, 1964 JAPANESE ANN. INT'L L. 212 (1964) (providing a translation of the decision); Richard A. Falk, *The Shimoda Case: A Legal Appraisal of the Atomic Attacks upon Hiroshima and Nagasaki*, 59 AM. J. INT'L L. 759 (1965); MARGARET E. GOUIN, NUCLEAR LAW: THE APPLICATION OF CANADIAN AND RELATED INTERNATIONAL PUBLIC LAW PRINCIPLES TO THE OBLIGATIONS OF CANADA IN RELATION TO NUCLEAR WEAPONS 6–7 (1989) (discussing the *Shimoda* case). See also ibid., 6–21 (discussing other domestic cases dealing with the legality of nuclear weapons in the United Kingdom, West Germany, Belgium, the Netherlands, and Canada).

[128] David W. Kennedy, *A New World Order: Yesterday, Today, and Tomorrow*, 4 TRANSNAT'L L. & CONTEMP. PROBS. 329, 332 (1994). See also Jan Klabbers, *The*

would include international lawyers who might try to regulate all aspects of international life through legal methods, including legal internationalists from the early 1900s.[129] Such international utopianism is not unlike that of Philip Noel-Baker, who believes that international peace "will only come from . . . the submission of all legal conflicts to the International Court [of Justice]," including weapon-related conflicts.[130] This study emphatically rejects such an extreme preference for legal resolution of virtually all matters. Just as Robert Jennings asserts, commentators look too often to international courts and tribunals with unrealistic expectations of how they can save the world from war and spend too little time trying to improve the "political decision-making machinery" at the heart of international dispute resolution.[131] However, when it comes to nuclear non-proliferation disputes, too little attention is given to the possibility of legal resolution, even among international lawyers, to the point where it seems necessary to remind the world that legal resolution remains a viable option for such disputes. As Richard Bilder has asserted, "Even if adjudication is not a panacea for problems of world order, it makes sense to do all that we can to strengthen and encourage the greater use of judicial institutions, and to improve their ability to respond in flexible ways to nations' dispute-settlement needs."[132] This study believes that legal resolution is an important mechanism for dispute settlement, which States and the international community should remember in an effort to maximize the options available to them.

This section particularly anticipates the criticism that diplomatic resolution should trump legal resolution of such sensitive disputes as

Life and Times of the Law of International Organizations, 70 Nordic J. Int'l L. 287, 288 (2001) (describing the international project as "the idea that everything international is wonderful precisely because it is international"); Quincy Wright, *Arbitration as a Symbol of Internationalism*, in International Trade Arbitration 3, 7 (M. Domke ed., 1958); Bilder, *supra* note 86, at 177–178 (asserting that "international adjudication symbolizes the rule of law in international affairs").

129 See Donald W. Greig, *The Interpretation of Treaties and Article IV.2 of the Nuclear Non-proliferation Treaty*, 6 Aust. YB Int'l L. 77, 116 (1974); Henry Richard and Edouard Descamps, Arbitration: Two Views 6–7 (1971).

130 See Philip Noel-Baker, The Arms Race: A Programme for World Disarmament 563 (1958).

131 Robert Jennings, Presentation on the Contributions of the Court to the Resolution of International Tensions, Proceedings of the ICJ/UNITAR Colloquium to Celebrate the 50th Anniversary of the Court, *reprinted in* Increasing the Effectiveness of the International Court of Justice 78, 79 (Connie Peck and Roy S. Lee ed., 1997).

132 Bilder, *supra* note 86, at 176.

those relating to nuclear non-proliferation. It is difficult to argue against the merits of resolving any dispute with a negotiated settlement. This study emphatically does not dismiss the merits of negotiation or other diplomatic methods of resolution, which notably need not end with the commencement or conclusion of the adjudicative process. However, this study believes that any approach that places all eggs in the proverbial basket of negotiation is myopic, in that it can create the vain hope that success is just around the corner, and that all that is needed is more time and effort, when in reality negotiation may not be enough for real progress with the dispute.[133] Francis Vallat refers to the phenomenon of "stalemate disputes" where "neither side is prepared to accept the other side's view as to the form of an ultimate settlement" and "[b]oth sides prefer to continue with the status quo in the hope that ultimately a solution acceptable to it will be found."[134] Situations such as those involving nuclear non-proliferation disputes are particularly prone to such a scenario, where it is difficult to differentiate between situations that pose a legitimate threat to peace and security and those that are an intermediate step towards the peaceful settlement of that dispute.[135] Taking other steps towards resolution while negotiations and other diplomatic methods of resolution are under way can help avoid such a dilemma.

Along with this pragmatism come certain features, including a somewhat cautious approach to the subject in two ways. First, the sensitive nature of nuclear non-proliferation disputes would seem to require such a cautious approach. As Ian Brownlie comments in the introduction to his discussion of the justiciability of highly political disputes, published in 1967, a cautious approach is warranted where the "inherent character of the subject-matter hardly admits of dogmatic treatment."[136] Oscar Schachter believed that the justiciability of politically sensitive disputes involving the use of force is "a delicate and complex problem on which

[133] See Vik Kanwar, *Two Crises of Confidence: Securing Non-proliferation and the Rule of Law through Security Council Resolutions*, 35 Ohio N.U.L. Rev. 171, 211 (2009) (noting the confusion in the non-proliferation context of knowing whether a situation poses a threat to peace and security or whether it is an intermediate step towards the peaceful settlement of that dispute).

[134] See Francis Vallat, *Foreword*, in Humphrey Waldock, International Disputes: The Legal Aspects i, vii, xii (1972).

[135] See Kanwar, *supra* note 133, at 211.

[136] Ian Brownlie, *The Justiciability of Disputes and Issues in International Relations*, 42 British Y.B. Int'l L. 123, 123 (1967).

reasonable persons can well differ,"[137] which would be equally true of nuclear non-proliferation disputes, if not more so. While this study maintains a clear thesis throughout, the subject matter of the study makes a large degree of humility not only advisable but essential.

In addition, a cautious approach is warranted where one option is being explored among many options. International law acknowledges that States have an endless number of options at their disposal in resolving their disputes. As explained in the preceding subsection, although UN Charter Article 33 lists seven peaceful methods of dispute resolution – "negotiation, enquiry, mediation, conciliation, arbitration, judicial settlement, resort to regional agencies or arrangements" – it nonetheless is careful to reserve for States "other peaceful means of their own choice." This last phrase creates an endless number of possible permutations, which justifies caution when comparing methods of resolution. Moreover, international law provides States with another layer of flexibility by giving them the option of refraining from settling their disputes.[138] Leaving persistent disputes alone might be a viable option with many areas of international relations,[139] thus preserving for disputants freedom of action and allowing them to avoid the risk of decisions going against their interests.[140] Presumably this would be the preferred option for recalcitrant States such as Iran and North Korea,[141] if they could get away with it. However, from the perspective of the international community, ignoring such disputes would not seem to be the prudent course, as they could fester and develop into nuclear war. Indeed, it must be kept in mind that "undue prolongation of disputes"

[137] Oscar Schachter, *Disputes Involving the Use of Force*, in THE INTERNATIONAL COURT OF JUSTICE AT A CROSSROADS 223, 239 (LORI F. DAMROSCH ed., 1987).

[138] See IAN BROWNLIE, PRINCIPLES OF PUBLIC INTERNATIONAL LAW (4th edn, 1990) ("There is no obligation in general international law to settle disputes, and procedures for settlement by formal and legal procedures rest on the consent of the parties").

[139] See generally Manfred Lachs, *The Law and the Settlement of International Disputes*, in DISPUTE SETTLEMENT THROUGH THE UNITED NATIONS 283, 288 (K. VENKATA RAMAN ed., 1977) (acknowledging that issues occasionally are "left in abeyance").

[140] See Jonathan I. Charney, *Disputes Implicating the Institutional Credibility of the Court: Problems of Non-appearance, Non-participation, and Non-performance*, in THE INTERNATIONAL COURT OF JUSTICE AT A CROSSROADS 288, 303 (LORI F. DAMROSCH ed., 1998).

[141] See John R. Crook, *Continuing U.S. and Multilateral Efforts to Curb Iran's Nuclear Program*, 102 AM. J. INT'L L. 187, 189 (2008) (reporting how Iran's president Mahmoud Ahmadinejad told the UN General Assembly in September 2008 that Iran saw as "closed" any dispute over its alleged enrichment activities).

can "increase and exaggerate international differences and tensions,"[142] thereby poisoning international relations and increasing the likelihood of armed conflict.

This study hopes to encourage the resolution of these types of disputes by presenting another option, namely legal resolution. In light of the lingering possibility of war and the problems inherent with Security Council involvement under Chapter VII, as explained in the following part, legal resolution should be seen as a relatively attractive option.

[142] Vallat, *supra* note 134, at vii, viii.

PART II

Security Council involvement with nuclear non-proliferation disputes under UN Charter Chapter VII*

* A version of parts of this part originally appeared in the MICHIGAN JOURNAL OF INTERNATIONAL LAW. See James D. Fry, *Dionysian Disarmament: Security Council WMD Disarmament and Arms Control Measures and Their Legal Implications*, 29 MICHIGAN JOURNAL OF INTERNATIONAL LAW 197–292 (2008).

3

Exploring potential problems with Security Council involvement

3.1 Introduction

The seventeenth-century English lawyer and philosopher Francis Bacon famously quipped, "The remedy is worse than the disease." Just as dosage often distinguishes poison from cure, Security Council involvement under Chapter VII with nuclear non-proliferation disputes can have a positive or a negative impact, depending both on the level of involvement and, more importantly, on the type of involvement. This chapter focuses on the ways in which the Security Council imposes obligations on States in the realm of nuclear non-proliferation through its UN Charter Chapter VII powers and uses inferior procedural safeguards in doing so. This chapter posits that the coercive element, combined with the Security Council's inadequate procedural safeguards, differentiates poison from cure in this context.

A considerable number of commentators assert that the Security Council cannot impose such obligations on States in this general area without their express consent.[1] The examples in this chapter undermine that assertion. These commentators are not without solid support, given how the International Court of Justice (ICJ) declared the following in its 1986 *Nicaragua* judgment:

1 See, e.g., Francis O. Wilcox and Carl M. Marcy, Proposals for Changes in the United Nations 182 (1955); Dimitris Bourantonis and Marios Evriviades, *New Directions in Disarmament*, in The United Nations in the New World Order: The World Organization at Fifty 154, 156 (Dimitris Bourantonis and Jarrod Wiener ed., 1995); Jorge Castañeda, Legal Effects of United Nations Resolutions 58–60 (trans. Alba Amoia, 1969); Erwin Dahinden, *The Future of Arms Control Law: Towards a New Regulatory Approach and New Regulatory Techniques*, 10 J. Conflict & Security L. 263, 272 (2005); Guido den Dekker, *The Effectiveness of International Supervision in Arms Control Law*, 9 J. Conflict & Security L. 315, 317 (2004); Jozef Goldblat, *The Role of the United Nations in Arms Control: An Assessment*, in The United Nations and the Maintenance of International Peace and Security 369 (UN Institute for Training and Research ed., 1987).

> in international law there are no rules, other than such rules as may be accepted by the State concerned, by treaty or otherwise, whereby the level of armaments of a sovereign State can be limited, and this principle is valid for all States *without exception.*[2]

The important part of this quote is the requirement that States *accept* the rules that are designed to limit their armaments. Inclusion of the phrase "without exception" emphasizes the strength of this rule in the eyes of the ICJ, which should warrant a conservative approach when doubts arise as to whether the State has provided its consent to the rules in question. Where UN members are the target of Security Council measures, it is possible to find the target State's consent to whatever the Security Council decides through that State's original consent to the UN Charter. However, this does not necessarily mean that there are absolutely no flaws in that State's consent, as alluded to later in this introduction, in the following section, and throughout this chapter. However, the principal flaw that this chapter focuses on is the Security Council's procedural shortcomings in failing to provide target States with adequate due-process safeguards.

Although there are many ways in which the regulation of arms can be seen as coercive in the UN context, this chapter focuses on just one: the coercive measures taken by the Security Council to combat nuclear proliferation through its distinct powers provided by Chapter VII. These measures can take the form of nonmilitary and military coercive measures under UN Charter Articles 41 and 42 respectively. Chapter 3.1.4 below analyzes these provisions of the UN Charter. The Security Council has adopted such measures in the context of nuclear non-proliferation through the following resolutions:

- Resolution 487, which called upon Israel "to place its nuclear facilities under the safeguards of the International Atomic Energy Agency" (IAEA) even though its safeguards agreement was extremely limited and Israel was not a party to the NPT;[3]
- Resolution 687 and related resolutions, which required Iraq to submit to an extensive inspection regime that related to its nuclear weapons program, among other WMD programs;[4]

[2] *Military and Paramilitary Activities (Nicaragua v. US)*, 1986 ICJ 14, 135 (June 27) (emphasis added).

[3] S.C. Res. 487, ¶ 5, UN Doc. S/RES/487 (June 19, 1981).

[4] S.C. Res. 687, UN Doc. S/RES/687 (April 3, 1991).

- Resolution 825, which called upon North Korea to "honour its non-proliferation obligations under the [NPT] and comply with its safeguards agreement with the IAEA";[5]
- Resolution 1540, which imposed certain obligations on all States in the context of nuclear terrorism;[6]
- Resolutions 1695 and 1718, which required North Korea to abide by the NPT and the IAEA safeguards agreement, even though it had withdrawn from these instruments, and Resolution 1874, which called upon North Korea to abide by the Comprehensive Nuclear Test Ban Treaty;[7]
- Resolutions 1696 and 1737, which called upon Iran to abide by its Additional Protocol with the IAEA, even though Iran had not yet ratified it,[8] and Resolutions 1747, 1803, and 1835, which expanded the sanctions on Iran and States that violate these sanctions against Iran;[9] and
- Resolution 1887, which called upon all States to comply with the NPT, the Comprehensive Test Ban Treaty (CTBT), and IAEA Additional Protocols.[10]

As explained in Chapter 3.1.4 below, all of these resolutions can be considered as creating binding obligations on certain States (typically the target State) on account of the fact that they refer either directly or indirectly to Chapter VII. Admittedly, Resolutions 1540 and 1887 differ from the other resolutions cited above in that they impose obligations on all States in more of a legislative manner, whereas the others target specific States and disputes. This chapter includes Resolutions 1540 and 1887 in an effort to be exhaustive in analyzing all Security Council resolutions adopted under Chapter VII that relate to nuclear non-proliferation, especially those that create coercive obligations. Critics might be perfectly correct in noting how these legislative resolutions fall outside the express powers of the Security Council under Chapter VII,

[5] S.C. Res. 825, ¶ 2, UN Doc. S/RES/825 (May 11, 1993).

[6] S.C. Res. 1540, UN Doc. S/RES/1540 (April 28, 2004).

[7] S.C. Res. 1695, ¶ 6, UN Doc. S/RES/1695 (July 15, 2006); S.C. Res. 1718, ¶ 4, UN Doc. S/RES/1718 (Oct. 14, 2006); S.C. Res. 1874, ¶ 29, UN Doc. S/RES/1874 (June 12, 2009).

[8] S.C. Res. 1696, ¶ 6, UN Doc. S/RES/1696 (July 31, 2006); S.C. Res. 1737, ¶ 8, UN Doc. S/RES/1737 (Dec. 23, 2006).

[9] See S.C. Res. 1747, UN Doc. S/RES/1747 (March 14, 2007); S.C. Res. 1803, preamb. ¶ 4, UN Doc. S/RES/1803 (March 3, 2008); S.C. Res. 1835, ¶ 4, UN Doc. S/RES/1835 (Sept. 27, 2008).

[10] See S.C. Res. 1887, ¶¶ 4, 7 15(b), UN Doc. S/RES/1887 (Sept. 24, 2009).

which appears to have been designed to respond to particular situations, as is made clear in the language "the *existence* of any threat to the peace, breach of the peace, or act of aggression" of UN Charter Article 39 and as discussed in Chapter 3.2.4 below,[11] rather than being designed to *prevent* possible threats to peace, breaches of the peace, or acts of aggression in the distant future. Despite the accuracy of this observation, this has not stopped the Security Council from adopting resolutions of these types in this context. Without a better mechanism for challenging a Security Council resolution as falling outside its powers, this study takes these resolutions at face value and assumes, *arguendo*, they were adopted within the Security Council's powers. Moreover, notwithstanding the language of Article 39 dealing with "existing" threats, *prevention* of future disputes is an important part of international dispute settlement, as the United Nations Conference on Trade and Development has shown by its recent focus on dispute *prevention*,[12] with these more legislative resolutions from the Security Council helping to prevent future disputes by extending the coverage in certain nuclear non-proliferation agreements to activities of non-State actors and by extending obligations in certain agreements to nonmembers of those agreements, as explained in Chapters 3.2.5 and 3.2.7 below.

Two other Security Council resolutions relate to nuclear non-proliferation, although they fall short of creating coercive obligations. Resolutions 255 and 984, which provided assurances to non-nuclear-weapon States that enabled their co-operation in the Treaty on the Non-proliferation of Nuclear Weapons (NPT)[13] negotiations in 1968 and in the negotiations to extend the NPT indefinitely in 1995,[14] lack a reference to Chapter VII or other aspects that might enable them to be classified as establishing coercive measures. Therefore, at the most, these resolutions can be seen as establishing binding obligations in the area of nuclear non-proliferation, not coercive ones. Nevertheless, this chapter discusses these resolutions for the sake of exhaustiveness and

[11] UN Charter, Art. 39 (emphasis added).

[12] See, e.g., *United Nations Conference on Trade and Development, Investor–State Disputes: Prevention and Alternatives to Arbitration*, proceedings of symposium held on 29 March 2010, UN Doc. UNCTAD/WEB/DIAE/IA/2010/8 (2010).

[13] See generally Treaty on the Non-proliferation of Nuclear Weapons, opened for signature July 1, 1968, 21 U.S.T. 483, 729 U.N.T.S. 161 (extended May 11, 1995, 34 I.L.M. 959) (hereinafter NPT).

[14] S.C. Res. 255, UN Doc. S/RES/255 (June 19, 1968); S.C. Res. 984, UN Doc. S/RES/984 (April 11, 1995).

also to suggest to the reader how resolutions with merely binding obligations might differ from coercive ones.

Despite the key language in these resolutions that involves the Security Council's Chapter VII powers in the realm of nuclear non-proliferation, the resolutions create a number of potential problems:

- by requiring States to join nuclear non-proliferation agreements;
- by requiring States to abide by certain nuclear non-proliferation agreements that are not already binding on those States;
- by requiring States to abide by obligations that resemble modified nuclear non-proliferation agreement provisions;
- by requiring States to abide by certain nuclear non-proliferation obligations not contained in treaties; and
- by recalling pre-existing nuclear non-proliferation agreement obligations on States, thereby incorporating them into the UN law framework and modifying the nature of the obligations in doing so, since a State cannot withdraw from a Security Council resolution, for example.

Commentators who recommend strengthening the nuclear non-proliferation regime through Security Council measures under Chapter VII, such as the ones listed above, overlook these potential problems.[15] This study gives these problems their due consideration when analyzing the legal implications for each resolution.

3.1.1 *Structure of this chapter*

This chapter is divided into four sections. This brief introduction and a conclusion constitute sections 1 and 4. Section 2 explains how to interpret Security Council resolutions, since a significant portion of this chapter involves such interpretation. Section 3 provides the bulk of the chapter's analysis as it systematically analyzes the various ways in which the Security Council has imposed coercive measures on States in this area. The legal implications of each are addressed as they arise within each set of Security Council resolutions.

[15] See generally Orde F. Kittrie, *Averting Catastrophe: Why the Nuclear Proliferation Treaty Is Losing Its Deterrence Capacity and How to Restore It*, 28 MICH. J. INT'L L. 337 (2007); Allen S. Weiner, *The Use of Force and Contemporary Security Threats: Old Medicine for New Ills*, 59 STAN. L. REV. 415 (2006).

3.1.2 Disclaimers for this chapter

Three disclaimers are appropriate for this particular chapter. First, the limited number of cases in which the Security Council has imposed obligations on States does not allow one to conclude definitively that the Security Council has a particular pattern of behavior in this area. Second, this chapter focuses on the coercive obligations on the target States to abide by certain norms that they were not otherwise obliged to abide by before the Security Council's imposition, and fits within the broader debate over coercion in international law.[16] Third, the qualitative methodology adopted in this study limits its ability to say whether there is a definitive causal link between the coercive obligations that the Security Council imposes and any tangible results on the ground. What is more important than causality here is the notion that the Security Council's practice of imposing obligations expands what constitutes "collective security" beyond the traditional definition, which ranges from responding to breaches of the peace to responding to the mere possession of certain weapons.[17] Such an expansion is not unlike those observed with grave breaches of human rights and international humanitarian law that have broadened the scope of acts that can trigger a collective security response under Chapter VII.[18]

[16] See, e.g., Christian Tomuschat, *Obligations Arising for States without or against their Will*, 241 Rec. des cours 195 (1993-IV).

[17] See M. V. Naidu, Collective Security and the United Nations 17 (1975) (reflecting the traditional conception of collective security in terms of "actual or potential breach[es] . . . of security"). But see ibid., at 92–93 (noting that, since its early days, the ambiguity of the "collective security" concept has permitted expansive readings that have "been used to rationalize aggressive alliances, to identify regional alliances, to support bloc antagonisms of the Cold War, to describe economic and diplomatic sanctions, to define pacific settlement methods, to explain the security scheme envisaged in the UN Charter and to justify the so-called UN peacekeeping methods").

[18] See Vera Gowlland-Debbas, *The Limits of Unilateral Enforcement of Community Objectives in the Framework of UN Peace Maintenance*, 11 Eur. J. Int'l L. 361, 365 (2000); Georges Abi-Saab, *The Security Council Legibus Solutus On the Legislative Forays of the Council*, in International Law and the Quest for its Implementation: Liber Amicorum Vera Gowlland-Debbas 23, 26–27 (Laurence Boisson de Chazournes and Marcelo Kohen ed., 2010) (explaining how John Major of the UK declared on behalf of the Security Council's presidency in 1992 that the Security Council would expand its interpretation of "threats to the peace" to include "systemic threats" such as threats to the environment and threats from refugee problems).

3.1.3 *Methods of interpreting Security Council resolutions*

Since most of this chapter involves the interpretation of Security Council resolutions dealing with nuclear non-proliferation, an explanation must be provided for the method of interpretation that this chapter applies to these resolutions. Chapters 5 and 6 involve interpretation of various treaties, so some of the points made here will apply there. The primary guide for interpretation on the international level is the Vienna Convention on the Law of Treaties (VCLT). VCLT Article 31(1) provides: "A treaty shall be interpreted in good faith in accordance with the ordinary meaning to be given to the terms of the treaty in their context and in the light of its object and purpose."[19] Some commentators elevate this paragraph to the status of a formal or general rule of interpretation,[20] while others consider this paragraph as providing clear guidelines for interpretation.[21] Yet others complain that the VCLT's provisions on interpretation are too strict.[22] Regardless of whether one calls this a rule or a guideline, it is anything but clear and certainly not strict. Indeed, VCLT Article 31(1) appears to have been drafted so as to simultaneously represent four somewhat distinct schools of treaty interpretation. Ian Sinclair acknowledges that Article 31(1) reflects several distinct schools at the same time, though he seems to contradict himself by asserting "broadly speaking" that its language gives preference to the textual approach.[23] This subsection asserts that one can find aspects of four distinct schools within Article 31(1), which have the following basic characteristics:

[19] Vienna Convention on the Law of Treaties, Art. 31(1), May 23, 1969, 1155 U.N.T.S. 331, 8 I.L.M. 679 (hereinafter VCLT).

[20] See, e.g., JAN KLABBERS, AN INTRODUCTION TO INTERNATIONAL INSTITUTIONAL LAW 86 (2nd edn, 2009) (referring to it as a "general rule"); Jochen Abr. Frowein, *Unilateral Interpretation of Security Council Resolutions: A Threat to Collective Security*, in LIBER AMICORUM GUNTHER JAENICKE 97, 99 (VOLKMAR GOTZ et al. ed., 1998).

[21] See, e.g., Dale E. McNiel, *The NAFTA Panel Decision on Canadian Tariff-Rate Quotas: Imagining a Tariffying Bargain*, 22 YALE J. INT'L L. 345, 374 (1997).

[22] See generally TETSUO SATO, EVOLVING CONSTITUTIONS OF INTERNATIONAL ORGANIZATIONS: A CRITICAL ANALYSIS OF THE INTERPRETATIVE FRAMEWORK OF THE CONSTITUENT INSTRUMENTS OF INTERNATIONAL ORGANIZATIONS (1996).

[23] See Ian M. Sinclair, *Vienna Conference on the Law of Treaties*, 19 INT'L & COMP. L.Q. 47, 61, 64–65 (1970). Perhaps a VCLT article on interpreting the articles that deal with interpretation might have been useful, although that is doubtful. These provisions on interpretation likely were intended to be ambiguous.

- "good faith," which is a community interest-based interpretation (in its broadest sense, the antithesis of the textual approach);
- "ordinary meaning," which represents the consent-based, textualist interpretation, because it looks at the language actually used in the text;
- "in their context," which, according to the rest of Article 31, looks at the extrinsic circumstances surrounding the text in a way that reinforces the subjective intentions of the parties; and
- "in light of its object and purpose," which represents a teleological approach to interpretation by looking at the instrument being interpreted as a whole.[24]

Regardless of the exact number of approaches contained in VCLT Article 31, the multifaceted, perhaps even schizophrenic, nature of Article 31(1) explains why tribunals and parties of all stripes can – and do – point to VCLT Article 31(1) to support the interpretive method that best suits their needs. It is difficult to imagine that the International Law Commission intended all of these interpretive schools to be used simultaneously when it drafted VCLT Article 31(1), given that a textual approach and an approach that looks more at the subjective intent of the parties appear diametrically opposed to one another.[25] In short, Article 31(1) seems to provide no absolute guidance on interpretation, but instead leaves the door open for States to push for, and decision-makers to adopt, whichever method of interpretation leads to the desired result.[26]

One way to reconcile these different approaches to interpretation is to see them as different "elements" of a "single process" of interpretation, as Michael Wood has asserted.[27] Indeed, some tribunals have tried to use

[24] See Francis G. Jacobs, *Varieties of Approach to Treaty Interpretation: With Special Reference to the Draft Convention on the Law of Treaties before the Vienna Diplomatic Conference*, 18 INT'L & COMP. L.Q. 318 (1969) (discussing these categories, though not in the exact same terms used here). Blaine Sloan adds a fifth way of interpreting treaties, which he calls "subjective (intention of the parties)." Blaine Sloan, *The United Nations Charter as a Constitution*, 1 PACE Y.B. INT'L L. 61, 95–98 (1989). However, this approach is not expressly reflected in VCLT Art. 31.

[25] See Jacobs, *supra* note 24, at 319.

[26] As José Alvarez explains, the broad approach of VCLT Article 31(1) opens up interpretation of legal instruments by international courts and tribunals to manipulation. See JOSÉ E. ALVAREZ, INTERNATIONAL ORGANIZATIONS AS LAW-MAKERS 87–92 (2005). See also Gerald Fitzmaurice, *Vae Victis or Woe to the Negotiators! Your Treaty or Our "Interpretation" of It?*, in THE LAW OF TREATIES 281 (SCOTT DAVIDSON ed., 2004).

[27] See Michael C. Wood, *The Interpretation of Security Council Resolutions*, 2 MAX PLANCK Y.B.UNL. 73, 88–93 (1998).

multiple elements in the same interpretive process, although their effectiveness is somewhat suspect. For example, the international arbitral tribunal in *SGS Société Générale de Surveillance SA v. Republic of the Philippines* relied first on the ordinary meaning of "disputes with respect to investments," then used as support the teleological approach by looking at the purpose of the treaty and the meaning of other provisions in that same treaty vis-à-vis the language being interpreted, as well as a contextual approach by looking at how "investments are characteristically entered into."[28] Still, how these different approaches interrelate and how to reconcile their contradictions when interpreting a single legal instrument remain undertheorized, even though there is a large body of literature on how to interpret treaties in general, which this study sees as somewhat inadequate inasmuch as it does not explain how to reconcile the different approaches to interpretation. Lumping all approaches into one and ignoring their internal contradictions is one possible way to get rid of the issue, which option is not unlike Philip Allott's modern doctrine of international law – a theory that Martti Koskenniemi characterizes as a hotchpotch of approaches "in happy confusion."[29] VCLT Article 31(2) could be seen as reflecting this hotchpotch approach, since it includes within the context of the text *the text itself* – which seems counterintuitive – as well as several other elements:

> The context for the purpose of the interpretation of a treaty shall comprise, *in addition to the text*, including its preamble and annexes:
>
> (a) any agreement relating to the treaty which was made between all the parties in connection with the conclusion of the treaty;
> (b) any instrument which was made by one or more parties in connection with the conclusion of the treaty and accepted by the other parties as an instrument related to the treaty.[30]

Along with agreements and instruments recognized by the parties, as alluded to in Article 31(2), Article 31(3) notes two elements for

[28] *SGS Société générale de surveillance SA v. Republic of the Philippines*, 8 ICSID 515, 554–555 (W. Bank) (Jan. 29, 2004).

[29] See MARTTI KOSKENNIEMI, FROM APOLOGY TO UTOPIA: THE STRUCTURE OF INTERNATIONAL LEGAL ARGUMENT 66 (2006) ("Modern doctrine, as Philip Allott has shown, uses a mixture of positivistic and naturalistic, consensualistic and non-consensualistic, teleological, practical, political, logical and factual arguments in happy confusion, unaware of its internal contradictions"); Martti Koskenniemi, *The Politics of International Law*, 1 EUR. J. INT'L L. 4, 12 (1990) (same).

[30] VCLT, Art. 31(2) (emphasis added).

consideration by the interpreter that would not be considered part of the context:

> There shall be taken into account, together with the context:
>
> (a) any subsequent agreement between the parties regarding the interpretation of the treaty or the application of its provisions;
> (b) any subsequent practice in the application of the treaty which establishes the agreement of the parties regarding its interpretation;
> (c) any relevant rules of international law applicable in the relations between the parties.

Nevertheless, inasmuch as they are to be "taken into account, together with the context," when interpreting a legal instrument and inasmuch as there is no express hierarchy among all of these elements,[31] the legal significance of these elements in Article 31(3) seems no different from the contextual elements enumerated in Article 31(2). In sum, when interpreting a treaty, the interpreter needs to take into account the ordinary meaning of the text, the surrounding textual elements, the teleological elements of the instrument, related community norms, any subsequent agreements or practice that give meaning to the language in question, and any other rules of international law, all without any hierarchy between these different elements. Considering all of these elements concurrently when interpreting a treaty seems like quite a Herculean task, even with the simplest treaty provisions.

VCLT Article 32 provides that, where the meaning of the treaty is "ambiguous or obscure, or leads to a result which is manifestly absurd or unreasonable," one *may* look beyond all of the myriad elements in Article 31 to the "supplementary means of interpretation, including the preparatory work of the treaty and the circumstances of its conclusion."[32] The question becomes, under what circumstances could a guileless interpreter conceivably conclude there is *absolutely* no ambiguity, obscurity, or absurdity from all of these elements operating at once, thus removing as an option the supplementary means of interpretation under Article 32? The large number of elements to consider suggests that the situations where supplementary means of interpretation are irrelevant will be extremely limited. Moreover, inasmuch as Ludwig Wittgenstein's theory of linguistic meaning postulates that all

[31] See JOHN DUGARD et al., INTERNATIONAL LAW: A SOUTH AFRICAN PERSPECTIVE 418 (3rd edn, 2005) (discussing how there is no hierarchy among these VCLT elements).
[32] VCLT, Art. 32.

language is indeterminate at its core,[33] it seems highly unlikely that such ambiguity, obscurity, and absurdity will not result from an analysis of the text and its context, let alone the other elements mentioned in VCLT Article 31, which add another layer of ambiguity, obscurity, and absurdity. Therefore, it seems an obvious point that supplementary means of interpretation may be referred to on virtually all occasions when interpreting a treaty under the Vienna Convention on the Law of Treaties, and may just be the determining factor of the meaning of any given treaty provision. Just as Ian Sinclair saw, the main dilemma with interpreting legal instruments may turn out to be whether to involve the preparatory work itself,[34] regardless of the interpretive wrinkles the other contextual and non-contextual elements provide. At a minimum, it seems relatively safe to characterize treaty interpretation under VCLT Articles 31 and 32 as vague. Nonetheless, what is perfectly clear about these provisions is that treaty interpretation involves much more than just looking for the ordinary meaning of the text, as recent commentators on treaty interpretation appear inclined to do.[35] Reflecting the sophistication in VCLT Articles 31 and 32, this study's analysis of treaties is done in as sophisticated a manner as possible.

With all of this analysis of the VCLT in mind, the question now becomes whether VCLT Articles 31 and 32 apply to the interpretation of Security Council resolutions. VCLT Article 2(1)(a) defines what it means by "treaty": "'treaty' means an international agreement concluded between States in written form and governed by international law, whether embodied in a single instrument or in two or more related

[33] See generally LUDWIG WITTGENSTEIN, TRACTATUS LOGICO-PHILOSOPHICUS (trans. C. K. Ogden, 1992) (1922) (arguing that the ambiguity inherent in language is the source of disagreement).

[34] See Sinclair, *supra* note 23, at 61.

[35] See, e.g., ALEXANDER ORAKHELASHVILI, THE INTERPRETATION OF ACTS AND RULES IN PUBLIC INTERNATIONAL LAW (2008); RICHARD GARDINER, TREATY INTERPRETATION (2008); ROBERT KOLB, INTERPRÉTATION ET CRÉATION DU DROIT INTERNATIONAL: ESQUISSE D'UNE HERMÉNEUTIQUE JURIDIQUE MODERNE POUR LE DROIT INTERNATIONAL PUBLIC (2006). This does not necessarily mean that the interpreter cannot rely on what it sees as the plain and ordinary meaning of the text, as the ICJ recently did in its 2011 *Application of the International Convention on the Elimination of All Forms of Racial Discrimination* advisory opinion (*Georgia v. Russian Federation*), Preliminary Objections, General List No. 140, April 1, 2011, at 48–54. Instead, the point that this section is making is that the plain and ordinary meaning might not be able to be objectively determined, no matter how convinced the interpreter is that the text leads to only one possible interpretation.

instruments and whatever its particular designation."[36] Admittedly, Security Council resolutions lack several of the standard characteristics of treaties, such as States parties,[37] although States are involved in the adoption of Security Council resolutions.[38] Some commentators assert that resolutions such as those of the Security Council fall under treaty law because they are adopted under powers provided by an international treaty,[39] though this would seem to be a highly controversial assertion.[40] Indeed, if not for any other reason, a distinction must be made between treaties and instruments adopted by international organizations with a treaty at their foundation, or else *all* resolutions of international organizations would become equivalent to treaties, which seems like an untenable position.[41]

Even if Security Council resolutions are not treaties per se, the argument still remains that they should be interpreted in the same manner as treaties. There are no clear guidelines or rules under international law for how to interpret Security Council resolutions in particular. There is the general notion of auto-interpretation (or the right of each State to interpret the law for themselves), which flows from a positivistic, decentralized view of international law and often is seen as the default rule for international law.[42] This study sees international law as a *centralized* system of rules and principles, in which auto-interpretation seems

[36] VCLT, Art. 2(1)(a).

[37] See Maarten Bos, A Methodology of International Law 177 (1984); Michael Byers, *Agreeing to Disagree: Security Council Resolution 1441 and International Ambiguity*, 10 Global Governance 165, 176 (2004) ("Security Council resolutions . . . resemble executive orders more than contracts, and the interpretive rules that apply to them might therefore be somewhat different"); Hugh Thirlway, *The Law and Procedure of the International Court of Justice 1960–1989*, 67 British Y.B. Int'l L. 27, 29 (1996).

[38] UN Charter, Art. 27 (providing the voting mechanism for the Security Council).

[39] See, e.g., Renata Sonnenfeld, Resolutions of the United Nations Security Council 7 (trans. Tomasz Dobrowolski, 1988) (citing Polish legal scholars such as Bierzanek and Nahlik, who make this assertion).

[40] See, e.g., Frowein, *supra* note 20, at 99 ("It should not be automatically assumed that Security Council resolutions be interpreted in all respect [*sic*] in the same way as treaties").

[41] See generally Castañeda, *supra* note 1; Obed Y. Asamoah, The Legal Significance of the Declarations of the General Assembly of the United Nations (1966).

[42] See generally Gunther Teubner, Law as an Autopoietic System (trans. Anne Bankowska and Ruth Adler, 1993); Leo Gross, 1 Essays on International Law and Organization 383–386 (1984); Joel P. Trachtman, *The Jurisdiction of the World Trade Organization: Remarks by Joel P. Trachtman*, 98 ASIL Proc. 139, 140 (2004) (discussing auto-interpretation as the default rule for international law).

anathema to that centralized system. Without a better alternative, it seems only too logical to use the method of interpreting treaties for interpreting Security Council resolutions, *mutatis mutandis*. After all, what is most important in interpreting Security Council resolutions would be the same as with interpreting treaties, namely that the method of interpretation is designed to give effect to the Security Council's intentions, as Michael Wood has noted with Security Council resolutions.[43]

As alluded to earlier, some commentators assert that the textual approach to interpretation is the main method of treaty interpretation.[44] Others seem to make this same assertion when it comes to interpreting Security Council resolutions.[45] These commentators are not without some support. Perhaps the best example would be the order of April 14, 1992, on provisional measures in the *Questions of Interpretation and Application of the 1971 Montreal Convention Arising from the Aerial Incident at Lockerbie* case ("*Lockerbie*" case), where, after quoting large portions of Security Council Resolutions 731 and 748, the ICJ held that the disputants were obliged to abide by the resolutions under UN Charter Articles 25 and 103 (regardless of what potentially conflicting treaty obligations required), with the court simply taking the language of the resolutions at face value.[46] More recently, in its 2011 *Application of the International Convention on the Elimination of All Forms of Racial Discrimination* judgment on preliminary objections, the ICJ strictly limited its analysis of the CERD Convention to the ordinary meaning of the text, mentioning other methods of interpretation only in *obiter dicta*.[47] However, in practice, the ICJ often has looked past the ordinary meaning of treaties and has provided a sophisticated interpretation of the text in light of various contextual and non-contextual elements, such

[43] See Wood, *supra* note 27, at 95.

[44] See, e.g., Orakhelashvili, *supra* note 35; Kolb, *supra* note 35.

[45] See, e.g., Jules Lobel and Michael Ratner, *Bypassing the Security Council: Ambiguous Authorizations to Use Force, Cease-Fires and the Iraqi Inspection Regime*, 93 Am. J. Int'l L. 124, 137–138 (1999) (implying that unambiguous language governs).

[46] See *Questions of Interpretation and Application of the 1971 Montreal Convention arising from the Aerial Incident at Lockerbie (Libya v. UK)*, Order on Provisional Measures, 1992 ICJ Rep. 3, 11–16 (Order of April 14); *Questions of Interpretation and Application of the 1971 Montreal Convention arising from the Aerial Incident at Lockerbie (Libya v. US)*, Order on Provisional Measures, 1992 ICJ Rep. 114, 122–127 (Order of April 14).

[47] See *Application of the International Convention on the Elimination of All Forms of Racial Discrimination (Georgia v. Russian Federation)*, Preliminary Objections, General List No 140, April 1, 2011, at 48–55.

as those mentioned above. The ICJ typically is not clear exactly what other elements it is focusing on in reaching its preferred interpretation, although what is clear is that it is relying on elements other than the text itself.

A recurrent theme in the ICJ is that the text should not be slavishly followed. Judge Alvarez first expressed this sentiment in his dissenting opinion to the 1950 *Second Admissions* advisory opinion:

> The text must not be slavishly followed. If necessary, it must be vivified so as to harmonize it with the new conditions of international life. When the wording of a text seems clear, that is not sufficient reason for following it literally, without taking into account the consequences of its application. Multilateral treaties are not drafted with the help of a dictionary, and their wording is often the result of a compromise which influences the terms used in the text ... [I]t must be recognized that even the clear provisions of a treaty must not be given effect, or must receive appropriate interpretation, when, as a result of modifications in international life, their application would lead to manifest injustice or to results contrary to the aims of the institution. For, otherwise, marked discrepancies would result between the written text and the reality; and that would be inadmissible.[48]

Other dissenting judges have expressed a similar approach to interpretation, such as Judge Weeramantry in the 1996 *Legality of the Use by a State of Nuclear Weapons in Armed Conflict* advisory opinion, where he argued in favor of a broad interpretation of the World Health Organization's constitution that looked at the spirit of the treaty, as opposed to the letter, which supposedly should have allowed it to request the advisory opinion with the questions posed.[49]

Such a sophisticated approach to interpretation certainly is not limited to dissenting opinions. For example, the ICJ began to avoid slavishly following the text of treaties when interpreting them in its 1949 *Reparations* advisory opinion. There, the ICJ was asked whether the United Nations had standing on the international level to bring a claim against a State when Israeli extremists assassinated UN diplomat Count Folke Bernadotte, whom the UN had dispatched to Palestine in 1948 to broker a peace between the Jewish and Arab communities vying

[48] See, e.g., *Competence of the General Assembly for the Admission of a State to the United Nations*, Advisory Opinion, 1950 ICJ Rep. 4, 17 (March 3) (J. Alvarez, dissenting).

[49] See *Legality of the Use by a State of Nuclear Weapons in Armed Conflict*, Advisory Opinion, 1996 ICJ Rep. 66, 147–149 (July 8).

for power after British withdrawal.[50] In the UN's struggle to establish respect for itself and protection for its agents, the ICJ seemed to work hard to interpret the UN Charter in such a way as to allow the United Nations to have sufficient international legal personality to bring claims to protect its rights, even where the text of the UN Charter could not be interpreted in such a way as to allow such an ability. The ICJ acknowledged that the UN Charter limits the United Nations to its "delegated and enumerated powers," one of which was not the ability to assert reparation claims.[51] Nevertheless, the ICJ concluded that the "Members [of the UN] . . . have clothed it with the competence required to enable [its] functions to be effectively discharged,"[52] and that the United Nations must be "an international person" capable of bringing such claims if it is to perform its functions.[53] This approach to interpretation, which did not base itself on the face of the text, frustrated textualists such as Judge Green Hackworth, who wrote a lively dissent.[54] Nevertheless, this and other opinions gave birth to the twin doctrines of functional necessity and implied powers, which allowed the United Nations and international organizations the flexibility needed to evolve beyond the face of their constitutive treaties to meet new challenges as they arise, as has been articulated by Michel Virally and others.[55] It falls outside the scope of this study to provide the details of those doctrines and the myriad cases supporting them.[56] Rather, it will suffice to mention a few opinions where the ICJ used these other elements to reach a

[50] See generally KATI MARTON, A DEATH IN JERUSALEM (1994); see also Roger S. Clark, *The Laws of Armed Conflict and the Use or Threat of Use of Nuclear Weapons*, 7 CRIM. L. F. 265, 274–275 (1996).

[51] See *Reparations for Injuries Suffered in the Service of the United Nations*, Advisory Opinion, 1949 ICJ 174, 178.

[52] Ibid., at 179. [53] Ibid. (the word "[a]ccordingly" indicating relationship).

[54] See ibid., at 196 (J. Hackworth, dissent).

[55] See generally Michel Virally, *La notion de function dans la théorie de l'organisation internationale*, in MÉLANGES OFFERTS À CHARLES ROUSSEAU: LA COMMUNAUTÉ INTERNATIONALE 277 (1974); PETER H. F. BEKKER, THE LEGAL POSITION OF INTERGOVERNMENTAL ORGANIZATIONS: A FUNCTIONAL NECESSITY ANALYSIS OF THEIR LEGAL STATUS AND IMMUNITIES (1994); BERNARD ROUYER-HAMERAY, LES COMPÉTENCES IMPLICITES DES ORGANISATIONS INTERNATIONALES (1962); Jerzy Makarczyk, *The International Court of Justice on the Implied Powers of International Organizations*, in ESSAYS IN INTERNATIONAL LAW IN HONOUR OF JUDGE MANFRED LACHS 501 (Jerzy Makarczyk ed., 1984).

[56] Please note that there has been ample criticism of the doctrine of functional necessity, including the view that it provides weak limitations on the implied powers of the international organizations, and that the implied powers must be to accomplish an explicitly stated power and not just a general purpose of the constitutive instrument. See,

meaning for the treaty language that differed from its more obvious meaning on the face of the treaty.

Besides the *Reparations* advisory opinion, the first opinion to be mentioned here is the 1962 *Certain Expenses* advisory opinion, where the General Assembly asked the ICJ to determine whether expenses for two UN peace operations in the Middle East and the Congo that the General Assembly had authorized were "expenses of the Organization" to be borne by UN members as apportioned by the General Assembly, in accordance with UN Charter Article 17(2).[57] UN Charter Article 17(2) reads: "The expenses of the Organization shall be borne by the Members as apportioned by the General Assembly." In determining what the "expenses" of the United Nations were under Article 17(2), the ICJ looked at it from a number of perspectives, first looking at the language of the paragraphs surrounding the paragraph in question (namely paragraphs 1 and 3 of Article 17), the *travaux préparatoires* for all of these provisions, and the General Assembly's practice in relation to all of these provisions when it came to the expenses that were to be included in the organization's budget and whether those expenses were limited to administrative ones.[58] Indeed, Article 17(3) referred to "administrative budgets," and a textual approach to interpretation might have led to the application of "administrative" there to Article 17(2) in its reference to expenses. However, the ICJ instead looked at General Assembly practice from 1947 to 1961 when it included in its budget expenses "unforeseen and extraordinary expenses," and the ICJ concluded from this practice that the expenses referred to in Article 17 were of a general variety that could include UN peace operations.[59] This advisory opinion suggests how the ICJ can give priority to State practice and other elements over purely textual analysis when interpreting treaty provisions.

Other advisory opinions similarly look past the face of the text to other contextual and non-contextual elements of the provisions in

e.g., Michael Bothe, *Les limites des pouvoirs du Conseil de sécurité*, in THE DEVELOPMENT OF THE ROLE OF THE SECURITY COUNCIL 67, 74–75 (RENE-JEAN DUPUY ed., 1993); Vera Gowlland-Debbas, *The Relationship between the International Court of Justice and the Security Council in the Light of the Lockerbie Case*, 88 AM. J. INT'L L. 643, 665 (1994) (noting this same point); Bardo Fassbender, *The United Nations Charter as Constitution of the International Community*, 36 COLUM. J. TRANSNAT'L L. 529, 596 (1998) (noting the fear that a lack of meaningful limits on the United Nations might make it become a type of Leviathan).

57 *Certain Expenses of the United Nations (Article 17, Paragraph 12, of the Charter)*, Advisory Opinion, 1962 ICJ Rep. 151, 152–153 (July 20).

58 See ibid., at 156–165. 59 Ibid., at 160–161.

question. In the *Second Admissions* advisory opinion, the General Assembly asked the ICJ whether UN Charter Article 4(2) allowed the General Assembly to decide on the admission of a State to the United Nations where the Security Council had not recommended admission.[60] Article 4(2) states: "The admission of any such state to membership in the United Nations will be effected by a decision of the General Assembly *upon the recommendation* of the Security Council."[61] The fundamental issue was whether the Security Council's failure to reach a decision could be seen as a negative recommendation, but a recommendation nonetheless, thus enabling the General Assembly to proceed to make its own decision on admission. The ICJ looked past the more obvious meaning of "recommendation" as being optional when it concluded that the Security Council's recommendation was mandatory before the General Assembly could proceed to its decision on admission.[62] More recently, in the 2010 *Kosovo* advisory opinion, where the General Assembly asked the ICJ to determine whether Kosovo had declared its independence in accordance with international law, the ICJ adopted a much more sophisticated approach to interpreting Security Council resolutions than merely focusing on the face of the resolution.[63] The Security Council had set out in Resolution 1244 the general principles that would govern the political solution to the Kosovo crisis of the late 1990s, including the end of violence in Kosovo and the establishment of a UN administration in Kosovo,[64] and so the interpretation of this resolution was central to the ICJ's efforts to respond to the General Assembly's question. As the ICJ explained generally in the *Kosovo* advisory opinion,

> The interpretation of Security Council resolutions may require the Court to analyse statements by representatives of members of the Security Council made at the time of their adoption, other resolutions of the Security Council on the same issue, as well as the subsequent practice

60 See *Competence of the General Assembly for the Admission of a State to the United Nations*, Advisory Opinion, 1950 ICJ Rep. 4, 5 (March 3).
61 UN Charter, Art. 4(2) (emphasis added).
62 See *Competence of the General Assembly for the Admission of a State to the United Nations*, Advisory Opinion, 1950 ICJ Rep. 4, 8–10 (March 3).
63 See generally *Accordance with International Law of the Unilateral Declaration of Independence in Respect of Kosovo*, Advisory Opinion, ICJ General List No 141, July 22, 2010 (hereinafter Kosovo advisory opinion). See also S.C. Res. 1244, UN Doc. S/RES/1244 (June 10, 1999).
64 See S.C. Res. 1244, *supra* note 63, ¶¶ 9–11, annex 2.

of relevant United Nations organs and of States affected by those given resolutions.[65]

The ICJ started its analysis by looking at Resolution 1244 in its entirety, which included interpreting it in light of the principles for political solution of the Kosovo crisis contained in two annexes to the resolution.[66] The ICJ then cited the object and purpose of the resolution – which it saw as "establish[ing] a temporary, exceptional legal régime which, save to the extent that it expressly preserved it, superseded the Serbian legal order and which aimed at the stabilization of Kosovo, and that it was designed to do so on an interim basis" – in helping to decide whether the declaration was in accordance with Resolution 1244.[67] In light of these contextual considerations, the ICJ determined that Security Council Resolution 1244 did not show an intent on the part of the Security Council to prohibit that particular declaration of independence by the Assembly of Kosovo, nor did the resolution decide on any final-status issues such as independence.[68] Yet again, these advisory opinions show that one should not rely too heavily on the facial meaning of the legal instrument being interpreted in order to determine its legal effect, but rather should take a more sophisticated approach in looking at the context of that language and at such extraneous aspects as practice. That said, this does not mean that the textualist approach to interpretation is not a valid school on its own.

The ICJ has adopted a similarly sophisticated approach to interpreting UN Security Council resolutions that goes beyond the face of the resolution's language, in particular to determine whether a Security Council resolution might be considered a binding Chapter VII resolution even though that resolution does not mention Chapter VII. A key example is the 1971 *Namibia* advisory opinion, where the Security Council asked the ICJ, "What are the legal consequences for States of the continued presence of South Africa in Namibia notwithstanding Security Council resolution 276 (1970)?"[69] Answering this question involved a determination of the legal effect of certain provisions of Security Council resolutions, which discussion is particularly relevant to this study. In the relevant portion of the opinion, the ICJ asserted that

65 See Kosovo advisory opinion, *supra* note 63, at 34–35. 66 See ibid., at 35.

67 Ibid., at 35–36. 68 See ibid., at 36–42.

69 *Legal Consequences for States of the Continued Presence of South Africa in Namibia (South-West Africa) Notwithstanding Security Council Resolution 276 (1970)*, Advisory Opinion, 1971 ICJ Rep. 16, 17 (June 21).

related resolutions can have "a combined and a cumulative effect," and so you must look at all of the related resolutions that were incorporated through reference when interpreting one resolution – there, Resolutions 264 (1969) and 269 (1969), in addition to key Resolution 276 (1970).[70] In deciding whether these resolutions were adopted under UN Charter Article 25 and were binding on States, the ICJ looked to aspects in addition to the resolution's text, since Resolution 276 did not specifically refer to Article 25:

> It emerges from the communications bringing the matter to the Security Council's attention, from the discussions held and particularly from the text of the resolutions themselves, that the Security Council, when it adopted these resolutions, was acting in the exercise of what it deemed to be its primary responsibility, the maintenance of peace and security, which, under the Charter, embraces situations which might lead to a breach of the peace.[71]

In particular, the ICJ saw as important the pre-resolution discussions leading up to its adoption and the language of all of the related resolutions in interpreting any one resolution. The ICJ also looked at the preamble and the surrounding provisions of these related resolutions to find whether the Security Council had the intent to create binding obligations on States through these resolutions. To be specific, the ICJ looked at the seriousness of the circumstances to which the Security Council was responding and focused on how the Security Council, in the preamble of Resolution 264, talked about being "*Mindful* of the grave consequences of South Africa's continued occupation of Namibia," and on the Security Council's declaration in paragraph 4 that "the actions of the Government of South Africa [that are] designed to destroy the national unity and territorial integrity of Namibia through the establishment of Bantustans are contrary to the provisions of the United Nations Charter."[72] The ICJ further focused on *how* the Security Council determined in Resolutions 269 and 276 that the occupation of Namibia by South Africa negatively impacted the UN's authority.[73] In short, the ICJ looked at all the related resolutions and the discussions leading up to the adoption of these resolutions to determine whether Resolution 276 was designed to be binding on States.

As to determining the legal effect of paragraph 2 of Resolution 276, the ICJ again showed a willingness to look beyond the face of the provision,

[70] See ibid., at 51. [71] Ibid., at 51–52. [72] Ibid., at 52 (emphasis in original).
[73] See ibid.

with the text merely being the starting point of the analysis.[74] Paragraph 2 of Resolution 276 reads: "*Declares* that the continued presence of the South African authorities in Namibia is illegal and that consequently all acts taken by the Government of South Africa on behalf of or concerning Namibia after the termination of the Mandate are illegal and invalid."[75] In responding to the argument of some States that this and other language of these resolutions was merely exhortatory rather than mandatory, the ICJ stated, "The language of a resolution of the Security Council should be carefully analysed before a conclusion can be made as to its binding effect," and that it would consider "the terms of the resolution to be interpreted, the discussions leading to it, the Charter provisions invoked and, in general, *all circumstances* that might assist in determining the legal consequences of the resolution of the Security Council."[76] This reference to "all circumstances" suggests that the ICJ takes the most expansive approach possible in interpreting Security Council resolutions, not unlike the modern approach to treaty interpretation alluded to earlier.

In applying this rule to the Security Council resolutions at issue in the *Namibia* advisory opinion, the ICJ focused on the preamble of Resolution 269 that referred to Article 25: "*Mindful* of its responsibility to take necessary action to secure strict compliance with the obligations entered into by States Members of the United Nations under the provisions of Article 25 of the Charter of the United Nations."[77] In light of this preambular language in one of the *related* resolutions, the ICJ concluded that the norms in the *related* resolutions were "adopted in conformity with the purposes and principle of the Charter and in accordance with its Articles 24 and 25," and therefore were all binding on all UN member States, notwithstanding the supposedly hortatory language in any of these resolutions.[78] This part of the *Namibia* advisory opinion stands as a prime example of the extent to which the ICJ will use its broad powers of interpretation to give binding effect to a provision in a Security Council resolution whose face does not obviously provide for such an effect.

As explained in the following section, this part of the *Namibia* advisory opinion is particularly helpful in determining the legal effect of

[74] Ibid., at 52.
[75] S.C. Res. 276, UN Doc. S/RES/276, ¶ 2 (July 29, 1970) (emphasis in original).
[76] *Legal Consequences for States of the Continued Presence of South Africa in Namibia (South-West Africa) Notwithstanding Security Council Resolution 276 (1970)*, Advisory Opinion, 1971 ICJ Rep. 16, 53 (June 21) (emphasis added).
[77] See ibid., at 53. [78] Ibid., at 53.

Security Council resolutions that might not contain an express reference to Chapter VII but where a related resolution contains such an express reference.

3.1.4 Binding resolutions of the Security Council

The binding nature of certain Security Council resolutions derives from several sources, primary among which are UN Charter Articles 25 and 103. UN Charter Article 25 provides: "The Members of the United Nations agree to accept and carry out the decisions of the Security Council in accordance with the present Charter."[79] In cases in which Security Council decisions conflict with other State obligations, UN Charter Article 103 makes it clear that Security Council decisions trump those other obligations: "In the event of a conflict between the obligations of the Members of the United Nations under the present Charter and their obligations under any other international agreement, their obligations under the present Charter shall prevail."[80] The ICJ has confirmed the supremacy of Security Council resolutions over conflicting treaty obligations in its *Nicaragua* and *Lockerbie* cases, although, as explained below, the Security Council cannot divest a court or tribunal of its jurisdiction once it has been established.[81] The framers of the UN Charter drafted these articles to give the Security Council the power to bind member States, a power that the Council of the League of Nations lacked, which led to its overall weakness and ultimately to the League of Nations' demise.[82]

In addition to UN Charter Articles 25 and 103, it is the involvement of certain provisions of Chapter VII – in particular Articles 41 and 42 – and the implicit, if not explicit, threat of enforcement measures in response to noncompliance with Security Council decisions that give Security

[79] UN Charter, Art. 25. See generally Jost Delbrück, *Article 25*, in THE CHARTER OF THE UNITED NATIONS: A COMMENTARY 452 (BRUNO SIMMA ed., 2002).

[80] UN Charter Art. 103. See generally Rudolf Bernhardt, *Article 103*, IN THE CHARTER OF THE UNITED NATIONS: A COMMENTARY 1292 (BRUNO SIMMA ed., 2002).

[81] See *Military and Paramilitary Activities (Nicaragua v. US)*, 1986 ICJ Rep. 14, 440 (June 27); *Questions of Interpretation and Application of 1971 Montreal Convention Arising from Aerial Incident at Lockerbie (Libya v. US)*, 1992 ICJ Rep. 114, 124, 138, 140 (the later two pin cites referring to the separate opinions of Judges Lachs and Shahabuddeen).

[82] See DAVID SCHWEIGMAN, THE AUTHORITY OF THE SECURITY COUNCIL UNDER CHAPTER VII OF THE UN CHARTER: LEGAL LIMITS AND THE ROLE OF THE INTERNATIONAL COURT OF JUSTICE 31–32 (2001).

Council decisions their real coercive power.[83] As one commentator puts it, Security Council coercion is a case of "forced order maintained by threat of sanctions."[84] Although there are numerous usages of the term "coercion," including "violence, compulsion, punishment, force, [and] interference,"[85] this chapter refers to a broader type of coercion more in the sense of *compulsion* as envisioned by St Thomas Aquinas, Immanuel Kant, and especially John Stuart Mill, which involves involuntariness without necessarily involving the use of force, even though the threat of the use of force must be present, as is the case with Security Council Chapter VII resolutions. Although Hans Kelsen spoke of coercion primarily as a physical force,[86] some of his writings indicate a definition of coercion with a lower threshold, similar to the one proposed above: "[Sanctions] are coercive in so far as they are to be taken even *against the will of the subject* to whom they are applied, *if necessary* by the employment of force."[87] Contemporary philosophical discussions on coercion, starting with Robert Nozick in 1969, focus almost exclusively on one agent *compelling* another agent through conditional threats, though no use of force actually is applied.[88] As Joshua Meltzer asserts, "Any form of coercion reduces the normative quality of State consent."[89] In sum, coercive action can be as simple as a shift from persuasion to

[83] See *Legal Consequences for States of the Continued Presence of South Africa in Namibia (South-West Africa) Notwithstanding Security Council Resolution 276 (1970)*, Advisory Opinion, 1971 ICJ Rep. 16, 52–53 (June 21).

[84] Shigeyoshi Ozaki, *International Law and Coercion*, 27 Japanese Annual of Int'l L. 12, 20 (1984); see also Christopher C. Joyner, *Collective Sanctions as Peaceful Coercion: Lessons from the United Nations Experience*, 16 Austl. Y.B. Int'l L. 241, 242 (1995).

[85] See Scott Anderson, *Coercion*, in Stanford Encyclopedia of Philosophy, Feb. 2006, http://plato.stanford.edu/entries/coercion (last visited Dec. 28, 2010).

[86] See, e.g., Hans Kelsen, Pure Theory of Law 1–69 (trans. Max Knight, 1967); Hans Kelsen, Law and Peace in International Relations 48–81 (1952); Hans Kelsen, Introduction to the Problems of Legal Theory (1932) 108 (trans. Bonnie Litschewski Paulson and Stanley Paulson, 1992). See also Charles Leben, *Hans Kelsen and the Advancement of International Law*, 9 Eur. J. Int'l L. 287, 288 (1998); Clemens Japloner, *Kelsen and His Circle: The Viennese Years*, 9 Eur. J. Int'l L. 368, 372 (1998).

[87] Hans Kelsen, *Sanctions in International Law under the Charter of the United Nations*, 31 Iowa L. Rev. 499, 499 (1946) (emphasis added).

[88] See Anderson, *supra* note 85 (citing Robert Nozick, *Coercion*, in Philosophy, Science, and Method: Essays in Honor of Ernest Nagel 440, 441–445 (Sidney Morgenbesser et al. ed., 1969)).

[89] Joshua Meltzer, *State Sovereignty and the Legitimacy of the WTO*, 26 U. Pa. J. Int'l Econ. L. 693, 707 (2005).

pressure with the threat of force in trying to compel a State to act or refrain from acting,[90] with the main difference between persuasion and pressure roughly being the reliance on logical reasoning in the former and the tangible threat of force in the latter. As a general rule, the United Nations operates mainly in the realm of persuasion, not coercion.[91] Indeed, the UN Charter was designed to foster inter-State co-operation in solving common problems,[92] including nuclear non-proliferation problems. However, this does not mean that the United Nations cannot and does not exercise coercive powers. On the contrary, this is a main function of the Security Council under certain provisions of UN Charter Chapter VII.

UN Charter Articles 41 and 42 provide the Security Council with a wide array of coercive options to enforce obligations and give the Security Council maximum discretion to choose the appropriate measures to bring about the desired impact:

> Article 41. The Security Council may decide what *measures not involving the use of armed force* are to be employed to give effect to its decisions, and it may call upon the Members of the United Nations to apply such measures. These may include complete or partial interruption of economic relations and of rail, sea, air, postal, telegraphic, radio, and other means of communication, and the severance of diplomatic relations.
>
> Article 42. Should the Security Council consider that measures provided for in Article 41 would be inadequate or have proved to be inadequate, *it may take such action by air, sea, or land forces* as may be necessary to maintain or restore international peace and security. Such action may include demonstrations, blockade, and other operations by air, sea, or land forces of Members of the United Nations.[93]

[90] See GUIDO DEN DEKKER, THE LAW OF ARMS CONTROL: INTERNATIONAL SUPERVISION AND ENFORCEMENT 130 (2001) ("Only in cases of complete failure of these attempts [to comply with warning that their acts violate the treaty that] will supervision result in coercive action, substituting persuasion by pressure").

[91] See QUINCY WRIGHT, INTERNATIONAL LAW AND THE UNITED NATIONS 77 (1960).

[92] See LELAND M. GOODRICH et al., CHARTER OF THE UNITED NATIONS: COMMENTARY AND DOCUMENTS 35 (1969).

[93] UN Charter, Arts. 41–42 (emphasis added). See generally Jochen Abr. Frowein and Nico Krisch, *Article 41*, in THE CHARTER OF THE UNITED NATIONS: A COMMENTARY 735 (BRUNO SIMMA ed., 2002); Jochen Abr. Frowein and Nico Krisch, *Article 42*, in THE CHARTER OF THE UNITED NATIONS: A COMMENTARY 748 (BRUNO SIMMA ed., 2002); Lori F. Damrosch, *Enforcing International Law through Non-forcible Measures*, 269 REC. DES COURS 191 (1997); JEAN COMBACAU, LE POUVOIR DE SANCTION DE L'O.N.U. (1974); VERA GOWLAND-DEBBAS, COLLECTIVE RESPONSES TO

Although Article 42 makes it clear that the Security Council must at least contemplate nonmilitary force before military force, the Security Council can authorize the wide range of coercive measures without first *trying* nonmilitary measures.[94] When the Security Council adopts a resolution under Chapter VII, its coerciveness would not be lessened if it did not enact actual sanctions, as the mere threat of sanctions through the mention of Chapter VII should be sufficient. As Max Weber asserted, "This apparatus [of coercion] must also possess such power that there is in fact a *significant probability* that the norm will be respected because of the possibility of recourse to such legal coercion."[95] It is the real *possibility* of recourse to coercive measures – namely sanctions under Articles 41 and 42 – that makes a Security Council Chapter VII resolution coercive. The Security Council's signal to target States through these resolutions that their actions are unacceptable to the international community provides a type of psychological, social, and moral coercion,[96] which might not be present if a State chose to impose its will through unilateral action, even if the multilateral and unilateral reasoning and results are identical. Commentators have acknowledged that these less traditional types of coercion are applicable in the context of the Security Council trying to regulate arms through its Chapter VII powers, including nuclear weapons.[97]

Having set out that explicit or implicit reference to Chapter VII and the establishment of sanctions are key determinants of whether particular Security Council resolutions have a coercive nature, this study turns its attention to the Security Council resolutions listed in the introduction to Chapter 3 to answer whether they contain these elements. Apart from

ILLEGAL ACTS IN INTERNATIONAL LAW: UNITED NATIONS ACTION IN THE QUESTION OF SOUTHERN RHODESIA (1990); Vera Gowlland-Debbas, *Security Council Enforcement Action and Issues of State Responsibility*, 43 INT'L COMP. L.Q. 55 (1994); GORGIO GAJA, *Use of Force Made or Authorized by the United Nations*, in THE UNITED NATIONS AT AGE FIFTY 39 (CHRISTIAN TOMUSCHAT ed., 1995); CHRISTINE GRAY, INTERNATIONAL LAW AND THE USE OF FORCE (2nd edn, 2004).

94 See Frowein and Krisch, *Article 42*, *supra* note 93, at 753–754.

95 MAX WEBER, ON LAW IN ECONOMY AND SOCIETY 314 (G. ROTH AND C. WITTICH ed., 1968).

96 See Alexander Thompson, *Coercion through IOs: The Security Council and the Logic of Information Transmission*, 60 INT'L ORG. 1, 2 (2006); Eiichi Fukatsu, *Coercion and the Theory of Sanctions in International Law*, in THE STRUCTURE AND PROCESS OF INTERNATIONAL LAW: ESSAYS IN LEGAL PHILOSOPHY DOCTRINE AND THEORY 1187, 1188–1190 (R. ST. J. MACDONALD and DOUGLAS M. JOHNSTON ed., 1983).

97 See RAMESH THAKUR, THE UNITED NATIONS, PEACE AND SECURITY: FROM COLLECTIVE SECURITY TO THE RESPONSIBILITY TO PROTECT 168 (2006).

Resolutions 487 (dealing with Israel in 1981), 825 (dealing with North Korea in 1993), 1695 (dealing with North Korea in 2006), 1835 (dealing with Iran in 2008), and 1887 (dealing with nuclear non-proliferation generally), each of the other resolutions expressly refers to UN Charter Chapter VII in responding to a threat of the peace.[98] Resolutions 1718, 1737, 1747, 1803, and 1874 expressly refer to Article 41,[99] which widely is considered as creating coercive enforcement measures on the target State or States.[100] Resolutions 687 and 1540 only refer to Chapter VII, not to Article 41 or Article 42 per se, but such a reference can be implied in light of the strong sanctions regimes established by those resolutions.[101] Such explicit and implicit reference to Articles 41 and 42 removes any guesswork over whether these resolutions were intended to be coercive in nature. Those Chapter VII resolutions that also provide actual sanctions on the target State or States – namely Resolutions 687, 1695, 1696, 1718, 1737, 1747, 1803, and 1874 – have an equally clear coercive nature to them,[102] although, again, the express adoption of sanctions is not crucial for these resolutions to be deemed coercive.

[98] See S.C. Res. 687, preamb. ¶ 26, UN Doc. S/RES/687 (April 3, 1991); S.C. Res. 1540, preamb. ¶ 16, UN Doc. S/RES/1540 (April 28, 2004); S.C. Res. 1718, preamb. ¶ 10, UN Doc. S/RES/1718 (Oct. 14, 2006); S.C. Res. 1874, preamb. ¶ 10, UN Doc. S/RES/1874 (June 12, 2009); S.C. Res. 1696, preamb. ¶ 10, UN Doc. S/RES/1696 (July 31, 2006); S.C. Res. 1737, preamb. ¶ 10, UN Doc. S/RES/1737 (Dec. 23, 2006); S.C. Res. 1747, preamb. ¶ 10, UN Doc. S/RES/1747 (March 14, 2007); S.C. Res. 1803, preamb. ¶ 13, UN Doc. S/RES/1803 (March 3, 2008).

[99] See S.C. Res. 1718, preamb. ¶ 10, UN Doc. S/RES/1718 (Oct. 14, 2006); S.C. Res. 1737, preamb. ¶ 10, UN Doc. S/RES/1737 (Dec. 23, 2006); S.C. Res. 1747, preamb. ¶ 10, UN Doc. S/RES/1747 (March 14, 2007); S.C. Res. 1803, preamb. ¶ 13, UN Doc. S/RES/1803 (March 3, 2008); S.C. Res. 1874, preamb. ¶ 10, UN Doc. S/RES/1874 (June 12, 2009).

[100] See Frowein and Krisch, *Article 41*, *supra* note 93, at 739; James Crawford, *The Relationship between Sanctions and Countermeasures*, in UNITED NATIONS SANCTIONS AND INTERNATIONAL LAW 57 (VERA GOWLLAND-DEBBAS ed., 2001).

[101] See S.C. Res. 687, preamb. ¶ 26, UN Doc. S/RES/687 (April 3, 1991); S.C. Res. 1540, preamb. ¶ 16, UN Doc. S/RES/1540 (April 28, 2004).

[102] See, e.g., S.C. Res. 687, ¶ 4, UN Doc. S/RES/687 (April 3, 1991) (authorizing States to take "all necessary measures" to guarantee the international boundary of Kuwait); S.C. Res. 1695, ¶¶ 3–4, UN Doc. S/RES/1695 (July 15, 2006) (requiring States to prevent missile-related technology from getting to North Korea); S.C. Res. 1696, ¶ 5, UN Doc. S/RES/1696 (July 31, 2006) ("*Calls upon* all States . . . to exercise vigilance and prevent the transfer of any items, materials, goods and technology that could contribute to Iran's enrichment-related and reprocessing activities") (original emphasis); S.C. Res. 1718, ¶ 8, UN Doc. S/RES/1718 (Oct. 14, 2006) (requiring States to prevent the transfer to North Korea of certain materiel and luxury goods, inter alia); S.C. Res. 1737, ¶¶ 3–9, 12–16, 18–19 UN Doc. S/RES/1737 (Dec. 23, 2006) (establishing a range of different sanctions and a Security Council Sanctions Committee to help curtail Iran's trade in

Admittedly, one of these Chapter VII resolutions – namely Resolution 1696 – refers to Article 40 of Chapter VII,[103] which involves provisional measures to "prevent an aggravation of the situation."[104] Such reference to being "provisional" does not necessarily mean that measures contained in those resolutions are merely recommendatory, as allowing such measures to have binding effects is the only way to avoid making Article 40 superfluous in light of the Security Council's power to give recommendations for nonbinding cease-fires under UN Charter Chapter VI.[105] Moreover, State practice supports the notion that Article 40 resolutions can be binding.[106] Whether Article 40 resolutions create binding obligations depends on the language used in those resolutions and other contextual aspects such as the creation of clear sanctions on the target State through the resolution. Although Resolution 1696 could contain more forceful language in creating sanctions on Iran, it nevertheless seems to create such sanctions when it "[*c*]*alls upon* all States . . . to exercise vigilance and prevent the transfer of any items, materials, goods and technology that could contribute to Iran's enrichment-related and reprocessing activities."[107] The implication of sanctions becomes clearer when this text is read in light of the similar language used in the *Namibia* advisory opinion, discussed above, thereby suggesting how Resolution 1696 could have binding aspects to it notwithstanding its reference to UN Charter Article 40.

As explained above with the *Namibia* advisory opinion, even if the resolution at issue does not contain an express reference to Chapter VII (namely Resolutions 487, 825, 1695, and 1887, as alluded to above), or an express reference to Article 41 or 42 (namely Resolution 1696), such a reference nevertheless can be read into the resolution at issue through incorporation if a related resolution makes such a

and development of nuclear-weapon-related equipment and technology, among other things); S.C. Res. 1747, ¶¶ 4–5, UN Doc. S/RES/1747 (March 14, 2007) (extending the sanctions in Resolution 1737 against Iran); S.C. Res. 1803, ¶¶ 5–8, 12, 14, UN Doc. S/RES/1803 (March 3, 2008) (same); S.C. Res. 1874, ¶¶ 9–10, 14–17, UN Doc. S/RES/1874 (June 12, 2009) (expanding the list of sanctioned items against North Korea from Resolution 1718).

103 See S.C. Res. 1696, preamb. ¶ 10, UN Doc. S/RES/1696 (July 31, 2006).

104 See ibid.; UN Charter, Art. 40.

105 See Jochen Abr. Frowein and Nico Krisch, *Article 40*, in The Charter of the United Nations: A Commentary 729, 734 (Bruno Simma ed., 2002).

106 See ibid. (citing the practice surrounding Security Council Resolution 54 involving the cease-fire in Palestine and Resolution 598 involving the cease-fire between Iran and Iraq in 1987).

107 S.C. Res. 1696, ¶ 5, UN Doc. S/RES/1696 (July 31, 2006).

reference. With Resolution 1696, assuming, *arguendo*, one is not convinced of its coercive nature from its creation of sanctions, later resolutions (including Resolution 1737) expressly refer to both Resolution 1696 and Article 41,[108] thereby bringing Resolution 1696 into the Article 41 framework, in light of the reasoning in the *Namibia* advisory opinion.

With regard to Resolutions 825 and 1695, dealing with North Korea, both are referred to and incorporated by reference in Resolutions 1718 and 1874, which expressly refer to Chapter VII and create sanctions on North Korea.[109] Therefore, it is relatively easy to see the norms created in Resolutions 825 and 1695 as having a coercive nature, especially under the reasoning of the *Namibia* advisory opinion provided above.[110] Even if this were not the case (i.e., even if Resolution 1718 did not refer to Chapter VII and incorporate Resolution 825 by reference), Resolution 825 still perhaps has enough in it to imply that the Security Council adopted it under Chapter VII, where the Security Council "reaffirm[ed] the crucial contribution which progress in non-proliferation can make to the maintenance of international peace and security."[111] Likewise, Resolution 1695 refers to the Security Council "[*a*]*cting* under its special responsibility for the maintenance of international peace and security,"[112] which can be seen as equivalent to saying it is acting under Chapter VII inasmuch as it is under Chapter VII that the Security Council derives such "special responsibility."

Similar to Resolutions 825 and 1695, Resolutions 1835 (dealing with Iran in 2008) and 1887 (supporting the nuclear non-proliferation regime in a more general manner) do not refer to Chapter VII. While no other Chapter VII resolutions incorporate Resolution 1887 by reference, Resolution 1887 itself incorporates several Chapter VII resolutions by reference, including Resolutions 1540, 1696, 1718, 1737, 1747, 1803, and 1874.[113] Likewise, Resolution 1835 incorporates several Chapter VII resolutions by reference, including Resolutions 1696, 1737, 1747, and 1803.[114] This is somewhat different from the *Namibia* advisory opinion,

[108] S.C. Res. 1737, preamb. ¶¶ 1 and 10, UN Doc. S/RES/1737 (Dec. 23, 2006).

[109] S.C. Res. 1718, preamb. ¶ 1, ¶¶ 8, 10, UN Doc. S/RES/1718 (Oct. 14, 2006); S.C. Res. 1874, preamb. ¶ 10, ¶ 1, 9–10, 14–17, 23–25, UN Doc. S/RES/1874 (June 12, 2009).

[110] See *Legal Consequences for States of the Continued Presence of South Africa in Namibia (South-West Africa) Notwithstanding Security Council Resolution 276 (1970)*, Advisory Opinion, 1971 ICJ Rep. 16, 53 (June 21).

[111] S.C. Res. 825, preamb. ¶ 3, UN Doc. S/RES/825 (May 11, 1993).

[112] S.C. Res. 1695, preamb. ¶ 13, UN Doc. S/RES/1695 (July 15, 2006).

[113] See S.C. Res. 1887, ¶¶ 15, 16, 24, UN Doc. S/RES/1887 (Sept. 24, 2009).

[114] S.C. Res. 1835, ¶ 1, UN Doc. S/RES/1835 (Sept. 27, 2008).

inasmuch as there the resolutions without a Chapter VII reference were later incorporated *into* Chapter VII resolutions, and here the resolution without a Chapter VII reference *incorporated* Chapter VII resolutions. However, this distinction should not make much of a difference inasmuch as related resolutions still should have "a combined and a cumulative effect," as the ICJ said in the *Namibia* advisory opinion,[115] regardless of when the Chapter VII resolution was incorporated by reference. There is little else in Resolution 1835 that would suggest that it was adopted under Chapter VII. Resolution 1887 provides some other grounds to argue that the Security Council implicitly adopted it under Chapter VII, such as its reaffirmation that "proliferation of weapons of mass destruction, and their means of delivery, constitutes a threat to international peace and security," as well its noting that it was "[*g*]*ravely concerned* about the threat of nuclear terrorism."[116] However, the Security Council expressly reserves to itself in the future the ability to "determine if [a situation of noncompliance with non-proliferation obligations] constitutes a threat to international peace and security."[117] Such an assertion means that the Security Council had not, at that point, made a determination, suggesting that this resolution perhaps would not be a Chapter VII resolution but for the incorporation by reference of other Chapter VII resolutions.

Resolution 487, which condemned Israel's attack on Iraq's nuclear installation, also does not expressly refer to Chapter VII. Unlike Resolutions 825, 1695, and 1887, no other Chapter VII resolution incorporates Resolution 487 by reference and Resolution 487 does not incorporate another Chapter VII resolution by reference. Nevertheless, the Security Council implicitly adopted Resolution 487 under Chapter VII by acknowledging in preambular paragraph 8 its deep concern regarding the "danger to international peace and security created by the premeditated Israeli air attack on Iraqi nuclear installations."[118] This language goes beyond the threshold language for Chapter VI resolutions – "*likely to endanger* the maintenance of international peace and security" – as provided by UN Charter Articles 33(1) and 34.[119] Operative paragraph 1

[115] *Legal Consequences for States of the Continued Presence of South Africa in Namibia (South-West Africa) Notwithstanding Security Council Resolution 276 (1970)*, Advisory Opinion, 1971 ICJ Rep. 16, 51 (June 21).

[116] S.C. Res. 1887, preamb. ¶¶ 4, 18, UN Doc. S/RES/1887 (Sept. 24, 2009).

[117] Ibid., ¶ 1. [118] S.C. Res. 487, preamb. ¶ 8, UN Doc. S/RES/487 (June 19, 1981).

[119] UN Charter, Arts. 33(1) and 34.

of Resolution 487 was even clearer in framing this resolution as a Chapter VII resolution when it "[s]*trongly condemn*[*ed*] the military attack by Israel *in clear violation of the Charter of the United Nations* and the norms of international conduct."[120] Israel could not simultaneously have clearly violated the UN Charter and avoided threatening international peace and security, thus making it clear that the Security Council implicitly adopted Resolution 487 under Chapter VII.

All of this context becomes particularly relevant when trying to determine the legal effect of certain provisions within these Chapter VII resolutions that start with apparently hortatory language, such as "calls upon." The remainder of this section explores the legal significance of the phrase "calls upon" as a signal in Security Council resolutions in creating coercive obligations on States. Such an analysis is crucial to this study inasmuch as many of the nuclear non-proliferation resolutions discussed in this chapter contain this language.

As a disclaimer, one ought to resist the urge to categorically define any phrase in a vacuum without any consideration of various contextual and non-contextual elements, as the ICJ warned in its *Namibia* advisory opinion. However, when talking about Chapter VII resolutions, the general thinking when it comes to "calls upon" is that it will have coercive meaning.[121] Again, this approach is supported by the ICJ's *Namibia* advisory opinion. There, in interpreting Resolution 276 and its legal effect in relation to South Africa's occupation of Namibia, the ICJ noted how paragraph 3 of Resolution 264 "[c]*alls upon* South Africa to withdraw its administration from Namibia immediately," how paragraph 5 of Resolution 269 "[c]*alls upon* the Government of South Africa to withdraw its administration from the Territory immediately and in any case before 4 October 1969," and how paragraph 5 of Resolution 276 "[c]*alls upon* all States, particularly those which have economic and other interests in Namibia, to refrain from any dealings with the Government of South Africa which are inconsistent with operative paragraph 2 of this resolution."[122] As explained in the preceding section, the ICJ declared

[120] S.C. Res. 487, ¶ 1, UN Doc. S/RES/487 (June 19, 1981) (emphasis added).

[121] See, e.g., John P. Grant, *Beyond the Montreal Convention*, 36 Case W. Res. J. Int'l L. 453, 470 (2004) ("'Calls upon' is hardly the language of obligation, but it is not that far short, particularly in a resolution expressly adopted under Chapter VII of the Charter").

[122] *Legal Consequences for States of the Continued Presence of South Africa in Namibia (South-West Africa) Notwithstanding Security Council Resolution 276 (1970)*, Advisory Opinion, 1971 ICJ Rep. 16, 51 (June 21).

binding on all UN member States the norms contained in these provisions with a "calls upon" signal – in particular, that South Africa had to withdraw its administration of Namibia and that all States had to work to bring this about on account of its illegality[123] – because of the language in the preamble of Resolution 269 that the Security Council was "[*m*]*indful* of its responsibility to take necessary action to secure strict compliance with the obligations entered into by States Members of the United Nations under the provisions of Article 25 of the Charter of the United Nations."[124] In light of the reasoning in this advisory opinion, the "calls upon" provisions in the Chapter VII resolutions dealing with nuclear non-proliferation discussed later in this chapter can be seen as coercive measures, primarily because target States would see them as coercive measures on account of the reference to Chapter VII (at least somewhere in the related resolutions) and the inclusion of sanctions in most instances.

If one were to take a belt-and-suspenders approach to determining the coercive nature of the obligations contained in provisions with the "calls upon" signal, one could find ample evidence in the broader language of the resolution and related resolutions, in the discussions leading up to the adoption of the resolution, and, in short, in "*all circumstances* that might assist in determining the legal consequences of the resolution of the Security Council," as the ICJ asserted in its *Namibia* advisory opinion.[125] In particular, the United States acknowledged this when US ambassador to the United Nations John Bolton included the two paragraphs of Resolution 1696 that start with "calls upon" (paragraphs 1 and 5) in the list of mandatory obligations of that resolution for Iran and all UN member States.[126] US ambassador Alejandro Wolff similarly asserted that the three provisions of Resolution 1737 involving Iran that begin with "calls upon" are among that resolution's *requirements* on Iran and member States, and concluded as follows:

> [Resolution 1737] compels all United Nations Member States to take all measures necessary to deny Iran equipment, technology, technical assistance, and financial assistance that would contribute to Iran's

[123] See ibid., at 58 (providing the conclusions of the ICJ in relation to the question asked).

[124] See ibid., at 53. [125] Ibid. (emphasis added).

[126] UN SCOR, 61st Sess., 5500th mtg., at 3, UN Doc. S/PV.5500 (Jul. 31, 2006) (hereinafter UN Doc. S/PV.5500); UN SCOR, 61st Sess., 5612th mtg., at 2, UN Doc. S/PV.5612 (Dec. 23, 2006) (hereinafter UN Doc. S/PV.5612).

> enrichment, reprocessing, heavy water or nuclear-weapon delivery programmes. It is clear on this and not open to interpretation. We will insist on absolute adherence to its requirements.[127]

The United Kingdom similarly asserted that Iran had an obligation to take the steps required by the IAEA, in accordance with the provision of the Additional Protocol, before the August 31 deadline established by paragraph 7 of Resolution 1696. This obligation appears to have been established by paragraph 1 of Resolution 1696, which begins with "calls upon."[128] Likewise, France asserted that individuals involved in Iran's nuclear and missile programs would be prohibited from traveling due to the travel restrictions placed upon them by paragraph 10 of Resolution 1737, which starts with the signal "calls upon."[129] Finally, after the Security Council adopted Resolution 1737, Japan noted, "In defiance of resolution 1696 (2006), Iran has refused to take any steps *required* of it to comply with the measures set out by the [IAEA] and the Security Council."[130] This requirement to comply with the IAEA measures was imposed by paragraph 1 of Resolution 1696, which begins with the signal "calls upon." Notwithstanding all of these acknowledgments of the coerciveness of "calls upon" provisions, it is the direct or indirect reference to Chapter VII and the establishment of sanctions that speaks loudest in showing that these provisions contain coercive measures.

Critics might argue that the coercive nature of "calls upon" provisions in such resolutions might be diminished if those resolutions have a legislative nature – for example, those "calls upon" provisions that refer to norms that apply to *all States*. Indeed, nonmembers of the United Nations have not consented to the UN Charter and therefore ought not to be bound by Security Council resolutions, or so the argument would go.[131] However,

[127] See UN Doc. S/PV.5612, *supra* note 126, at 3–4. [128] Ibid., at 5.
[129] See ibid., at 6. [130] Ibid. (emphasis added).
[131] See, e.g., Jean-Pierre Puissochet, *The Court of Justice and International Action by the European Community: The Example of the Embargo against the Former Yugoslavia*, 20 Fordham Int'l L.J. 1557, 1568–1569 (1997). Please note, however, that there is some practice to suggest that perhaps States might consider themselves bound by Security Council Chapter VII resolutions. For example, under the counterterrorism regime of Resolution 1373, nonmember States Cook Islands and Niue both filed reports, even though they are States and presumably are not directly bound by Security Council decisions. See Chairman of the Counter-terrorism Committee, Letter Dated 2 January 2002 from the Chairman of the Security Council Committee Established Pursuant to Resolution 1373 (2001) Concerning Counter-terrorism, at 3–4, addressed to the President of the Security Council, UN Doc. S/2002/7 (Jan. 2, 2002) (for Niue); Chairman of the Counter-terrorism Committee, Letter Dated 28 December 2001

the ICJ in its 1971 *Namibia* advisory opinion seemed to think that the "calls upon" provisions in Resolution 276 have binding effect on nonmember States, in particular where it declared South Africa's occupation of Namibia *erga omnes* illegal and subsequently called upon "all States, particularly those which have economic and other interests in Namibia, to refrain from any dealings with the Government of South Africa" that could be deemed invalid on account of South Africa's illegal occupation of Namibia.[132] Thus we see that the legislative nature of resolutions might not have as much influence over the legal effect of "calls upon" provisions as some might expect. This point becomes particularly relevant when analyzing Security Council Resolutions 1540 and 1887, below, which are more legislative in nature than the rest of the nuclear non-proliferation resolutions discussed in this chapter. At the same time, it must be recognized that the *erga omnes* nature of the obligations that South Africa was violating in Namibia might be the true source of the binding effect on nonmembers, not the "calls upon" language of Resolution 276, in which case these critics have a valid point. Regardless, a review of the *travaux préparatoires* for this resolution suggests that it is difficult to conclude whether it was the UN Charter or the *erga omnes* nature of those obligations that convinced the Security Council to call upon all States in that particular situation.

This section has provided a basic understanding of what this chapter means by the coercive measures of the Security Council, thereby enabling the reader to understand better the problems that can arise from heavy-handed Security Council actions in the realm of nuclear non-proliferation disputes, as explained in the remainder of this part of the book. In particular, the following section lays out the exact ways in which the Security Council has been involved with coercive measures in the realm of nuclear non-proliferation from its inception until recent times, all of which have serious legal implications.

from the Chairman of the Security Council Committee Established Pursuant to Resolution 1373 (2001) Concerning Counter-terrorism, at 3–5, addressed to the President of the Security Council, UN Doc. S/2001/1324 (Dec. 31, 2001) (for the Cook Islands).

132 See *Legal Consequences for States of the Continued Presence of South Africa in Namibia (South-West Africa) Notwithstanding Security Council Resolution 276 (1970)*, Advisory Opinion, 1971 ICJ Rep. 16, 56 (June 21) (citing S.C. Res. 276, UN Doc. S/RES/276, ¶¶ 2, 5 (July 29, 1970)).

3.2 Security Council Chapter VII measures

Some commentators think that the Security Council was not involved in the area of nuclear non-proliferation before its involvement in Iraq in 1990–1991.[133] Commentators before Iraq share this same brand of skepticism, saying that animosity between the United States and the Soviet Union during the Cold War stopped the Security Council from getting involved in this area.[134] A relatively sophisticated analysis of Security Council activities during the Cold War asserts that "[d]uring four decades of Cold War, the Security Council never grappled seriously with the threats posed ... by weapons of mass destruction,"[135] which includes matters related to nuclear weapons. Since that analysis mentions two of the seven incidents discussed in this section (Resolution 255 involving NPT assurances and Resolution 487 involving Israel's 1981 attack on an Iraqi nuclear complex),[136] it would reveal that that commentator believes the Security Council "never grappled seriously" with either of those incidents, despite the extensive debates contained in the Security Council verbatim record and the strong, yet nuanced, language adopted in both resolutions. Other analysis of the Security Council's post-Cold War disarmament and arms control activities is similarly skeptical, asserting that the Security Council had been "little involved in actual questions of disarmament and monitoring of WMD" since the 1992 statement by the Security Council that "the proliferation of all weapons of mass destruction constitutes a threat to international peace

[133] See Sven Bernhard Gareis and Johannes Varwick, The United Nations: An Introduction (2005, trans. Lindsay P. Cohn, first published 2003); Rolf Ekeus, *The Iraqi Experience and the Future of Nuclear Nonproliferation*, Wash. Q. 67 (Autumn 1992), 68; Dorinda G. Dallmeyer, *The Future Role of the United Nations in Disarmament: Learning from the Iraq Experience*, in Adapting the United Nations to a Postmodern Era: Lessons Learned 129, 136 (W. Andy Knight ed., 2001).

[134] See Jozef Goldblat, *The Role of the United Nations in Arms Control: An Assessment*, 7 Arms Control 115, 123, 129 (1986) (asserting that the Security Council's role in disarmament "has been reduced to almost nothing"); Richard Hiscocks, The Security Council: A Study in Adolescence 36 (1974); Alf Ross, The United Nations: Peace and Progress 297 (1966) (asserting that the Security Council stopped playing a role in UN discussions on disarmament after 1950 when the Soviet Union left the Commission on Conventional Armaments).

[135] Edward C. Luck, The UN Security Council: Practice and Promise 95 (2006).

[136] See ibid., at 96–97 n. 21.

and security."[137] Here, the author's citation of Resolution 825 involving North Korea indicates that he believes that this instance represented only "little" involvement. Some commentators overlook the very possibility that the Security Council can impose arms limitations on States,[138] while others even point to a long-established practice of discussing WMD matters outside the Security Council – a practice that supposedly is so entrenched that WMD matters are seen as having been removed from the Security Council's competence altogether.[139] The bulk of this section challenges the notion that the Security Council has not been significantly involved in nuclear non-proliferation through its coercive measures or otherwise lacks the tools to make a meaningful contribution in this area. However, as the analysis of the legal implications for each shows, one could make a plausible argument that many of these measures cross the line between cure and poison.

3.2.1 *Resolutions 255 and 984: establishing security assurances*

Resolution 255 is the first instance of the Security Council imposing nuclear non-proliferation obligations on an entity through one of its resolutions. The norms contained in this resolution and in Resolution 984 were not typical binding resolutions, inasmuch as they did not involve enforcement or create obligations for States. Interestingly, the first entity targeted by a binding Security Council obligation in this realm was the Security Council itself. States that made specific, unilateral security assurances at the time of Resolution 255 also may be bound to uphold these assurances under the principle of international estoppel. Before discussing the potential legal obligations of the Security Council

[137] Pascal Teixeira, The Security Council at the Dawn of the Twenty-First Century 81 (2003) (citing the president of the Security Council, Note by the President of the Security Council, UN Doc. S/23500 (Jan. 31, 1992)).

[138] See Goldblat, *supra* note 134, at 115; Castañeda, *supra* note 1, at 58; H. G. Nicholas, The United Nations as a Political Institution 27 (5th edn, 1975) (asserting that the Security Council cannot "impose a decision, but only to preserve the peace," though failing to discuss whether it can impose a decision to preserve the peace, which seems obvious under UN Charter Article 25).

[139] See Daniel S. Cheever, *The UN and Disarmament*, in The United Nations: International Organization and Administration 479, 488 (Maurice Waters ed., 1967) ("The Security Council may be quickly disposed of since it has played scarcely any role in disarmament discussions despite the Charter's mandate that it should formulate plans 'for the establishment of a system for the regulation of armaments'"); Maurice Bertrand, The United Nations: Past, Present and Future 95 (1994).

and the permanent members that made unilateral security assurances in the context of Resolution 255, the following subsection provides a brief analysis of Resolution 255 itself.

3.2.1.1 Positive security assurances of Resolution 255

Resolution 255 is unique among the resolutions discussed in this section in that the obligation does not arise from a decision that binds a State through Article 25 or Chapter VII. Its third preambular paragraph states: "*Bearing in mind* that any aggression accompanied by the use of nuclear weapons would endanger the peace and security of all States."[140] This is far from an assertion that international peace and security had been threatened by the underlying events. Nor do any of the signals within the three operative paragraphs support the notion that the Security Council had decided anything that could bind a State under Article 25 or Chapter VII. Rather, Resolution 255 is the result of non-nuclear-weapon States seeking security assurances from the nuclear-weapon States before agreeing to the terms of the NPT.[141]

Even before the NPT negotiations began, non-nuclear-weapon States were pushing hard for adequate security assurances from nuclear-weapon States.[142] During the NPT negotiations, non-nuclear-weapon States believed that they would be vulnerable to nuclear attack from States falling outside the NPT regime if they relinquished their ability to develop their own nuclear-weapon capabilities.[143] Moreover, the NPT on its face reflected a considerable imbalance between the rights and obligations of the non-nuclear-weapon States vis-à-vis those of the nuclear-weapon States,[144] as well as somewhat legitimizing possession of nuclear weapons by nuclear-weapon States by failing to provide hard disarmament obligations for those States.[145] Despite the best efforts of

140 S.C. Res. 255, preamb. ¶ 3, UN Doc. S/RES/255 (June 19, 1968) (original emphasis).

141 Ibid. ¶¶ 1–3.

142 See THOMAS GRAHAM Jr., DISARMAMENT SKETCHES: THREE DECADES OF ARMS CONTROL AND INTERNATIONAL LAW 283 (2002).

143 See ANDREW BOYD, FIFTEEN MEN ON A POWDER KEG: A HISTORY OF THE UN SECURITY COUNCIL 336 (1971).

144 See Bourantonis and Evriviades, *supra* note 1, at 161.

145 See THAKUR, *supra* note 97, at 171 (arguing that the NPT created a significant amount of fear and uncertainty concerning potential proliferation by allowing non-nuclear-weapon States to develop and use nuclear energy for peaceful purposes). Furthermore, the NPT does not prescribe a way of handling those States not party to the NPT regime.

the non-nuclear-weapon States to get some security assurances during the NPT negotiations from nuclear-weapon States that would appear clearly within the NPT, the United States, the United Kingdom, and the Soviet Union were determined to address this issue in the United Nations and not within the NPT itself.[146] As a result, these three States made a joint request to the Security Council on June 12, 1968, to meet in order to decide whether to give security assurances to the non-nuclear-weapon States of the nascent NPT regime.[147] At that meeting, these States presented a draft resolution that was designed to reassure non-nuclear-weapon States that the Security Council would come to their aid if they were attacked with or threatened with attack by nuclear weapons.[148] This draft resolution eventually became Resolution 255.

Resolution 255 provides only positive security assurances to the non-nuclear-weapon States. Positive assurances involve the promise from a nuclear-weapon State that it will come to the aid of a non-nuclear-weapon State party to the NPT that finds itself the victim of a nuclear attack.[149] Paragraph 1 of Resolution 255

> [*r*]*ecognizes* that aggression with nuclear weapons or the threat of such aggression against a non-nuclear-weapon State would create a situation in which the Security Council, and above all its nuclear-weapon State permanent members, would have to act immediately in accordance with their obligations under the United Nations Charter . . .[150]

This provision essentially re-emphasizes the Security Council's – and especially its permanent members' – intentions to act immediately under the powers provided by the UN Charter in the case of a use or threatened use of nuclear weapons. Such immediate acts on the Security Council level could include both military and nonmilitary sanctions under Articles 41 and 42 of the UN Charter. For the individual permanent members, such acts could include immediate efforts to get the Security Council involved by raising the matter within the Security Council, as well as to participate in a collective self-defense response under Article

146 See Jean du Preez, *Security Assurances against the Use or Threat of Use of Nuclear Weapons: Is Progress Possible at the NPT Prepcom?*, James Martin Center for Nonproliferation Studies (Monterey Institute for International Studies, Monterey, CA), April 24, 2003, http://cns.miis.edu/research/npt/nptsec.htm.

147 See Boyd, *supra* note 143, at 335–336. 148 Ibid.

149 See Bourantonis and Evriviades, *supra* note 1, at 161.

150 S.C. Res. 255, ¶ 1, UN Doc. S/RES/255 (June 19, 1968).

51 during the time it takes the Security Council to take action. Paragraph 2 of Resolution 255

> [*w*]*elcomes* the intention expressed by certain States that they will provide or support immediate assistance, in accordance with the Charter, to any non-nuclear-weapon State Party to the Treaty on the Non-Proliferation of Nuclear Weapons that is a victim of an act or an object of a threat of aggression in which nuclear weapons are used . . .[151]

This paragraph refers to more concrete measures that certain permanent members of the Security Council were prepared to take in response to the use or threatened use of nuclear weapons against a non-nuclear-weapon State.

To learn exactly what these States indicated as their intentions, one must look to the statements made by the United States, the United Kingdom, and the Soviet Union on June 17, 1968, in combination with this resolution. In fact, these three statements were the same, the most relevant parts being a *declaration* in the fifth paragraph and a *reaffirmation* in the sixth of each statement:

> Aggression with nuclear weapons or the threat of such aggression against a non-nuclear-weapon State would create a qualitatively new situation in which the nuclear-weapon States which are permanent members of the United Nations Security Council would have to act immediately through the Security Council to take the measures necessary to counter such aggression or remove the threat of aggression in accordance with the United Nations Charter, which calls for taking "effective collective measures for the prevention and removal of threats to the peace, and for the suppression of acts of aggression or other breaches of the peace." Therefore, any State which commits aggression accompanied by the use of nuclear weapons or threatens such aggression must be aware that its actions will be countered effectively by measures to be taken in accordance with the United Nations Charter to suppress the aggression or remove the threat of aggression . . .
>
> [That particular State] reaffirms its intention, as a permanent member of the United Nations Security Council, to seek immediate Security Council action to provide assistance, in accordance with the Charter, to any non-nuclear weapon State, party to the Treaty on the Non-Proliferation of Nuclear Weapons, that is a victim of an act of aggression or an object of a threat of aggression in which nuclear weapons are used.[152]

[151] Ibid., ¶ 2.

[152] See generally UN SCOR, 23rd Sess., 1430th mtg., at 5–8, UN Doc. S/PV.1430 (June 17, 1968) (hereinafter UN Doc. S/PV.1430).

According to these statements, these assurances were to come into force at the same time as would the Security Council resolution concerning safeguards for non-nuclear-weapon States.[153] Notably, these assurances are no more than the assurance provided in paragraph 1 of Resolution 255 that they will act immediately through the Security Council to counter the aggression or to remove the threat of aggression.[154] Essentially, the assurance is that they will *try* to get the Security Council to act, though if it is unable to act – either because of another State's veto or because the draft resolution lacks a sufficient number of affirmative votes to pass – then their obligation will have been met. This is not a strong assurance for the non-nuclear-weapon States, though it is not completely vacuous, since the UN Charter does not otherwise oblige permanent members to *act* immediately in response to a threat or an attack. Regardless, these assurances prove to have been sufficient to convince non-nuclear-weapon States to consent to the NPT and the obligations contained therein.

Critics will question the significance of Resolution 255. Jozef Goldblat has asserted that the security assurances under Resolution 255 were empty because they did no more than reaffirm the obligation of UN member States to assist States that find themselves the victims of aggression.[155] However, there is no such positive obligation under the UN Charter. Article 51 recognizes the "inherent right of individual and collective self-defence" in responding to an armed attack, although this does not create a positive obligation on member States to come to the aid of other States if attacked.[156] Article 48 requires member States to carry out the Security Council's decisions in maintaining international peace and security, although only at the Security Council's express authorization of their involvement.[157] Therefore, Goldblat places too much

[153] See generally ibid. [154] See S.C. Res. 255, ¶ 1, UN Doc. S/RES/255 (June 19, 1968).

[155] See Jozef Goldblat, NPT and the Security of NNWS, No First Use of Nuclear Weapons, Working Paper for the Pugwash Meeting No. 279, Nov. 15–17, 2002, available at http://www.pugwash.org/reports/nw/goldblat.htm (last visited Dec. 29, 2010) (asserting that the positive assurances of Resolution 255 "were clearly insufficient, as they merely reaffirmed the duty of UN Members to provide assistance to a country which has been aggressed, irrespective of the type of weapon used in aggression").

[156] UN Charter, Art. 51. See also Albrecht Randelzhofer, *Article 51*, in The Charter of the United Nations: A Commentary 788, 802–803 (Bruno Simma ed., 2002); Jost Delbrück, *Collective Self-Defence*, in Encyclopedia of Public International Law 646, 656 (1992).

[157] See UN Charter, Art. 48. See also Brun-Otto Bryde and August Reinisch, *Article 48*, in The Charter of the United Nations: A Commentary 776 (Bruno Simma ed., 2002).

significance on the language "in accordance with the UN Charter," thus inappropriately robbing Resolution 255 of what little legal significance it actually provides victim States.

3.2.1.2 Positive security assurances of Resolution 984

In negotiating the NPT's indefinite extension, the same positive security assurances were reasserted in Resolution 984 as appeared in Resolution 255, although Resolution 984 was sponsored by all five permanent members of the Security Council, while Resolution 255 was jointly sponsored by only the United States, the United Kingdom, and the Soviet Union.[158] Commentators characterize the negotiations over the extension as being "a surprisingly smooth process,"[159] and one cannot help but see these positive security assurances in Resolution 984 as playing a crucial role. NPT Article X(2) provides:

> Twenty five years after the entry into force of the Treaty, a conference shall be convened to decide whether the Treaty shall continue in force indefinitely, or shall be extended for an additional fixed period or periods. This decision shall be taken by a majority of the Parties to the Treaty.[160]

Since the NPT entered into force on March 5, 1970, it became necessary in 1995 for the nuclear-weapon States to begin canvassing non-nuclear-weapon States for their support, just as they did when the NPT was being negotiated in 1968. Resolution 984 is similar to Resolution 255 in that it attempts to soften the difficulties that non-nuclear-weapon States might have with the NPT, primary among which is the discrimination between nuclear-weapon States and non-nuclear-weapon States.

Resolution 984 repeats much of Resolution 255 and other arrangements provided for in the UN Charter. The second operative paragraph of Resolution 984 repeats the essence of the first operative paragraph of Resolution 255, which deals with the positive security assurance that the nuclear-weapon States and the Security Council will "act immediately in accordance with the relevant provisions of the Charter of the United Nations, in the event that such States are the victim of an act of, or object of a threat of, aggression in which nuclear weapons are used."[161] The fifth

[158] UN SCOR, 50th Sess., 3514th mtg, UN Doc. S/PV.3514 (April 11, 1995).

[159] Miguel Marin Bosch, *The Non-proliferation Treaty and Its Future*, in INTERNATIONAL LAW, THE INTERNATIONAL COURT OF JUSTICE AND NUCLEAR WEAPONS 375, 380 (LAURENCE BOISSON DE CHAZOURNES and PHILIPPE SANDS ed., 1999).

[160] NPT, *supra* note 13, Art. X(2).

[161] S.C. Res. 984, ¶ 2, UN Doc. S/RES/984 (April 11, 1995).

and ninth operative paragraphs of Resolution 984 essentially repeat the third operative paragraph of Resolution 255, which reaffirms Article 51 and the ability of States to take individual or collective self-defense measures if an armed attack occurs. Resolution 984 is somewhat more detailed in specifying that the assistance from States can include "technical, medical, scientific, or humanitarian assistance,"[162] although this addition is relatively meaningless inasmuch as States always are free to assist other States in such a dire situation as a nuclear attack. The third paragraph of Resolution 984 repeats the essence of UN Charter Article 35(1), and, in part

> [*r*]*ecognizes further* that, in case of aggression with nuclear weapons or the threat of such aggression against a non-nuclear-weapon State Party to the [NPT], any State may bring the matter immediately to the attention of the Security Council to enable the Council to take urgent action to provide assistance, in accordance with the Charter, to the State victim of an act of, or object of a threat of, such aggression . . .[163]

Some might see this portion of the third paragraph as creating a new right for all States to bring the use or threat of use of nuclear weapons to the attention of the Security Council, although it is unclear how this is any different from the power provided to all UN member States under Article 35(1) to bring any situation that is likely to endanger the maintenance of international peace and security to the attention of the Security Council.[164]

Resolution 984 provides new obligations in the second portion of paragraph 3, which

> *recognizes also* that the nuclear-weapon State permanent members of the Security Council will bring the matter immediately to the attention of the Council and seek Council action to provide, in accordance with the Charter, the necessary assistance to the State victim . . .[165]

This paragraph is a new obligation on the permanent members of the Security Council because nowhere within the UN Charter are permanent members required to bring any situation to the attention of the Security Council – other than when they take measures in the exercise of the right of self-defense under Article 51 – or to seek Security Council action on any particular issue. Even though Article 39 *requires* the Security Council to "determine the existence of any threat to the peace, breach

[162] Ibid., ¶¶ 5, 9. [163] Ibid., ¶ 3. [164] See UN Charter, Art. 35, ¶ 1.
[165] S.C. Res. 984, ¶ 3, UN Doc. S/RES/984 (April 11, 1995).

of the peace, or act of aggression,"[166] Articles 41 and 42 are permissive in saying what types of action the Security Council "*may*" take.[167] Article 51 provides that States may act in self-defense "if an armed attack occurs against a Member of the United Nations, until the Security Council has taken measures necessary to maintain international peace and security,"[168] but nothing in the UN Charter requires the Security Council to take such action. Therefore, again, this is not an insignificant obligation on the permanent members of the Security Council to bring the situation to the attention of the Security Council and to seek Security Council action. Both France and Russia are under the same obligation due to unilateral declarations that were referred to in Resolution 984.[169]

3.2.1.3 Negative security assurances of the unilateral statements

Both Resolution 255 and Resolution 984 lack any explicit reference to negative security assurances. For such assurances, non-nuclear-weapon States must look to the statements of the permanent members of the Security Council that were incorporated into Resolution 984 by reference.[170] A review of these statements makes it seem that the United States, the United Kingdom, France, and Russia all worked together in coming up with a common negative security assurance:

> [The particular State] will not use nuclear weapons against non-nuclear-weapon States parties to the Treaty on the Non-Proliferation of Nuclear Weapons, except in the case of an invasion or any other attack on [the particular State], its territory, its armed forces or other troops, its allies or on a State towards which it has a security commitment, carried out or sustained by such a non-nuclear-weapon State in association or alliance with a nuclear-weapon State.[171]

[166] UN Charter, Art. 39. [167] UN Charter, Arts. 41–42. [168] UN Charter, Art. 51.

[169] Letter dated 6 April 1995 from the Permanent Representative of France to the United Nations addressed to the Secretary-General, UN SCOR, 50th Sess., UN Doc. S/1995/264 (April 6, 1995) (hereinafter Letter from the Permanent Representative of France); Letter dated 6 April 1995 from the Permanent Representative of the Russian Federation to the United Nations addressed to the Secretary-General, UN SCOR, 50th Sess., UN Doc. S/1995/261 (April 6, 1995) (hereinafter Letter from the Permanent Representative of the Russian Federation). Such redundancy does not affect their obligations under Resolution 984.

[170] S.C. Res. 984, *supra* note 14, ¶ 1.

[171] Letter from the Permanent Representative of the Russian Federation, *supra* note 169; *accord* Letter dated 6 April 1995 from the Permanent Representative of the United Kingdom of Great Britain and Northern Ireland to the United Nations addressed to the

The only variations are that the United States and United Kingdom left out the comma before "except," Russia failed to capitalize "Parties" in "State Parties," the United Kingdom referred to "its dependent territories" instead of "its territory," the United States referred to "its territories," France referred to "or against its allies" instead of just "its allies," and the United States added an extra comma after "its allies." Needless to say, these variations are relatively insignificant. China's statement was much shorter in terms of providing a negative security assurance: "China undertakes not to be the first to use nuclear weapons at any time or under any circumstances," which can be seen as a strong no-first-use policy.[172] Still, as is explained in greater depth below, none of these statements contain wording that is sufficiently unconditional or that shows an intent to be bound. Thus, these negative security assurances are not legally binding. Although the bulk of the positive security assurances within these statements also are not legally binding, small portions of two of them are.

3.2.1.4 International estoppel and security assurances

In order for the principle of international estoppel to apply to any given situation, the entity being estopped must have voluntarily and publicly made an unambiguous statement that another entity detrimentally relies on in good faith.[173] It must be noted that this unilateral declaration from a State is only one of several preconditions for the doctrine of international estoppel to apply, with other elements including the lack of ambiguity and detrimental reliance, so they should not be seen as one and the same thing. The 1974 ICJ *Nuclear Tests* case is useful in understanding how this principle can work in international practice. In 1973, New Zealand and Australia brought cases against France relating to its testing of nuclear devices in the South Pacific. After the claims had been brought, the French president declared that France would no longer test

Secretary-General, UN SCOR, 50th Sess., UN Doc. S/1995/262 (April 6, 1995) (hereinafter Letter from the Permanent Representative of the United Kingdom); Letter dated 6 April 1995 from the Chargé d'affaires a.i. of the Permanent Mission of the United States of America to the United Nations addressed to the Secretary-General, UN SCOR, 50th Sess., UN Doc. S/1995/263 (April 6, 1995) (hereinafter Letter from the Chargé d'affaires); Letter from the Permanent Representative of France, *supra* note 169.

172 See Letter dated 6 April 1995 from the Permanent Representative of China to the United Nations addressed to the Secretary-General, UN SCOR, 50th Sess., at 2, UN Doc. S/1995/265 (April 6, 1995) (hereinafter Letter from the Permanent Representative of China).

173 See IAN BROWNLIE, PRINCIPLES OF PUBLIC INTERNATIONAL LAW 646 (5th edn, 1998).

nuclear devices there. The ICJ said that such a declaration created international legal obligations on the State, as the following excerpt illustrates:

> It is well recognized that declarations made by way of unilateral acts concerning legal or factual situations, may have the effect of creating legal obligations. Declarations of this kind may be, and often are, very specific. When it is the intention of the State making the declaration that it should become bound according to its terms, that intention confers on the declaration the character of a legal undertaking, the State being thenceforth legally required to follow a course of conduct consistent with the declaration. An undertaking of this kind, if given publicly, and with an intent to be bound, even though not made within the context of international negotiations, is binding. In these circumstances, nothing in the nature of a quid pro quo, nor any subsequent acceptance of the declaration, nor even any reply or reaction from other States, is required for the declaration to take effect, since such a requirement would be inconsistent with the strictly unilateral nature of the juridical act by which the pronouncement by the State was made . . . When States make statements by which their freedom of action is to be limited, a restrictive interpretation is called for.[174]

Thus, for a unilateral statement to be legally binding under the principle of international estoppel, it must be (1) made in public, (2) with the intention of being bound, and (3) without conditions.

The remainder of this subsection reviews these three elements, Resolutions 255 and 984, and the relevant unilateral statements of the permanent members of the Security Council. The public nature of these resolutions and statements containing the security assurances of the Security Council and its permanent members easily fulfills the public element for international estoppel. The fact that the statements were incorporated by reference into the resolutions, as opposed to being made entirely outside the United Nations context, shows the desire of the assurers to give those receiving the assurance added security that they meant what they were saying.

With regard to the intention to be bound, the Security Council's intent to be bound derives from the lack of equivocation in both Resolution 255 and Resolution 984. Whereas States are legally bound by decisions of the Security Council under Article 25, the Security Council will be bound by its pronouncements that use obligatory language such as "shall," "will,"

[174] *Nuclear Tests (N.Z. v. Fr.)*, 1974 ICJ Rep. 457, 472–473 (Dec. 20); *Nuclear Tests (Austl. v. Fr.)*, 1974 ICJ Rep. 253, 267 (Dec. 20).

and "would," and that are sufficiently clear on their face to warrant good-faith reliance by States. Concerning the Security Council's security assurance in Resolution 255, the first operative paragraph's obligatory language ("*would create* a situation in which the Security Council … *would have to* act immediately") reflects such an intent to be bound and contains no conditions.[175] This conclusion would have been different had the Security Council used such optional language as "*could* have to" or "*might* have to." The very design of these resolutions was to elicit the reliance of the non-nuclear-weapon States on these assurances so that they would agree to the NPT and to the indeterminate extension of the NPT. It would seem considerably disingenuous for the Security Council or anyone else to assert after the fact that the Security Council was not creating a binding obligation. Admittedly, the exact actions that the Security Council was to take were not spelled out, although this should not be seen as a condition for action, but rather a prudent attempt to preserve the discretion of the Security Council in deciding how to tailor its response to the hypothetical nuclear attack envisioned in the resolution.

The permanent members of the Security Council also made unilateral security assurances to the non-nuclear-weapon States in trying to convince them to agree to the NPT and to extend the NPT indefinitely, so it too would seem somewhat disingenuous for them to claim now that they were not actually giving any real assurances at all. As is common with legal matters, the devil proves to be in the details, so to speak. Indeed, one must look at the exact wording that the permanent members used in their statements to see if they showed a genuine, unconditional intent to be bound. One could try to surmise that the permanent members actually provided no such assurances in the language of paragraph 2 of Resolution 255 and paragraph 7 of Resolution 984, which state that the permanent members had expressed "the *intention* … that they will provide or support immediate assistance,"[176] with "intention" raising a considerable number of red flags. Nonetheless, a thorough review of their statements indicates that at least Russia and France provided a sufficiently clear and unconditional intent to be bound for them to be

[175] Operative Paragraph 2 of Resolution 984 has the obligatory "will act immediately" in place of Resolution 255's "would have to act immediately," although the legal significance of having established an intention to be bound is the same.

[176] S.C. Res. 255, ¶ 2, UN Doc. S/RES/255 (June 19, 1968); S.C. Res. 984, ¶ 7, UN Doc. S/RES/984 (April 11, 1995).

estopped from later claiming that they had absolutely no obligations, although the bulk of their so-called assurances would not be legally binding. The positive security assurances of the Soviet Union, the United Kingdom, and the United States contain an intent to be bound to "act immediately through the Security Council" to respond to the aggression or threat of aggression, although they did not show an intention to be bound to have any particular results flowing from that initial commitment to move within the Security Council.[177]

As noted above in the preceding subsection, the United States, the United Kingdom, France, and Russia all made essentially the same negative security assurances in connection with Resolution 984. These statements, however, contain considerable conditions: the assurances apply except where there has been an invasion or other attack on the State, its allies, or a State that it had a security arrangement with, and when the attack was carried out with the aggressor having an association or alliance with a nuclear-weapon State.[178] These conditions seem sufficiently large to absolve these States of any legally binding obligations under these statements except in the most narrow of circumstances, even though each statement used the obligatory language "will." Noticeably, China's statement was the only one that unconditionally stated the following: "China undertakes not to be the first to use nuclear weapons at any time or under any circumstances."[179] China somewhat redundantly asserted in the paragraph directly following that "China undertakes not to use or threaten to use nuclear weapons against non-nuclear-weapon States or nuclear weapon-free zones at any time or under any circumstances."[180] Both of these statements by China would not appear to be legally binding due to the phrases "China *undertakes* not to," which is considerably different from China assuring that it flatly *would not* be the first to use nuclear weapons. No other part of China's unilateral statement shows an intent on the part of China to create an

[177] See generally U.N. SCOR, 23rd Sess., 1430th mtg., at 2–5, UN Doc. S/PV.1430 (June 17, 1968).

[178] See Letter from the Permanent Representative of the Russian Federation, *supra* note 171, at 3; Letter from the Permanent Representative of the United Kingdom, *supra* note 171, at 3 (adding that the beneficiary of the assurance must not be "in material breach of its own non-proliferation obligations under the [NPT]"); Letter from the Chargé d'affaires, *supra* note 171, at 2; Letter from the Permanent Representative of France, *supra* note 169.

[179] Letter from the Permanent Representative of China, *supra* note 172.

[180] Ibid.

unambiguously binding obligation that another State could rely upon in good faith to their detriment.

Concerning the positive security assurances from the other permanent members of the Security Council, only Russia and France showed an intent to be bound by unconditional assurances on a small portion of the assurances that they provided, which would indicate that they will be estopped from claiming that they do not have such legal obligations. Russia refrains from saying that it will act immediately beyond bringing the matter to the attention of the Security Council.[181] As noted already, Resolution 984 already obliged the permanent members to bring such matters to the attention of the Security Council. With regard to other actions, Russia merely says that it "will seek to ensure that they provide, in accordance with the Charter, necessary assistance to the State that is a victim of such an act of aggression or that is threatened by such aggression."[182] "Seeking to ensure" is different from "ensuring," and would indicate an unwillingness to be legally bound to carry out that particular task. Nonetheless, as already mentioned, being bound to bring the matter to the attention of the Security Council is a new obligation, and is not an insignificant development. France makes the same assurance as Russia – although France uses the word "pledges" – that it "will immediately inform the Security Council." However, France goes a step further than Russia by saying that it will "act within the Council to ensure that the latter takes immediate steps to provide, in accordance with the Charter, necessary assistance to any State which is the victim of such an act or threat of aggression,"[183] as opposed to merely seeking to ensure that the Security Council provides the necessary assistance. Thus, Russia and France might be held responsible under these unilateral statements if they fail to report immediately the use or threatened use of a nuclear weapon to the Security Council, with France being obliged to take some acts within the Security Council that would constitute ensuring that it gives the necessary assistance to the victim State, whether that means proposing a draft resolution or calling for an emergency meeting of the Security Council.

The other permanent members of the Security Council seem to create no legally binding obligations through their unilateral assurances to the

[181] Letter from the Permanent Representative of the Russian Federation, *supra* note 171, at 2 ("[T]he nuclear Powers which are permanent members of the Security Council will immediately bring the matter to the attention of the Council").

[182] Ibid. [183] Letter from the Permanent Representative of France, *supra* note 169, at 3.

non-nuclear-weapon States. The United Kingdom refrains from asserting that it will bring the matter to the Security Council, as Russia and France assured, but it does assert that it will "seek immediate Security Council action to provide assistance,"[184] which is roughly as vague as Russia's "seek to ensure." The statement of the United States seems closest to the assurances provided by Resolution 984 to the non-nuclear-weapon States, namely that the "nuclear-weapon-State permanent members of the United Nations Security Council would have to act immediately through the Security Council ... to take the measures necessary to counter such aggression or to remove the threat of aggression," and that the United States has the "intention to provide or support immediate assistance, in accordance with the Charter, to any non-nuclear-weapon State Party to the [NPT] that is a victim" of the use or threat of use of a nuclear weapon.[185] The phrase "intention to provide or support immediate assistance" does not mean "promises to provide or support immediate assistance," which would appear to enable the United States to avoid the creation of a legally binding obligation. All of this technical analysis aside, the principle of international estoppel opens up the possibility that both the Security Council and the permanent members that make certain security assurances will be held responsible if they fail to live up to these commitments.

3.2.1.5 Legal nature of these assurances

Resolutions 255 and 984 raise several interesting legal issues, three of which are discussed below. An issue arises over the legal status of these resolutions and unilateral statements. Some commentators have asserted that these security assurances have become an integral part of the commitments of the nuclear-weapon States party to the NPT, although without providing sufficient explanation as to how this might occur.[186] It would make sense to read the NPT along with the security assurances provided to non-nuclear-weapon States through the Security Council resolutions and unilateral statements discussed above, because it is there – and not in the NPT – that non-nuclear States have the positive assurance that nuclear-weapon States and the Security Council will come to their aid if attacked or threatened with an attack with a nuclear

[184] Letter from the Permanent Representative of the United Kingdom, *supra* note 171, at 4.
[185] Letter from the Chargé d'affaires, *supra* note 171, at 2–3.
[186] See Bourantonis and Evriviades, *supra* note 1, at 161.

weapon. Chapter 3.1.3 above analyzed VCLT Articles 31(2) and 31(3) and some of the contextual and non-contextual elements that can be used in interpreting a treaty. VCLT Article 31(2)(b) could be particularly relevant in deciding whether these unilateral declarations could be useful in interpreting the NPT. VCLT Article 31(2)(b) includes within the context to be considered when interpreting a treaty "any instrument which was made by one or more parties in connection with the conclusion of the treaty and accepted by the other parties as an instrument related to the treaty."[187] These unilateral declarations clearly satisfy two of the four elements of VCLT Article 31(2)(b): (1) these unilateral declarations are instruments; and (2) they were made by a party to the NPT. These unilateral declarations can satisfy the other two elements, although one also could raise issues with these other two elements if necessary. Even though the unilateral declarations were incorporated into Resolution 984 by reference, and not incorporated directly into the NPT by reference, it seems obvious that they were made in connection with the conclusion of the treaty because non-nuclear-weapon States were requiring the security assurance that these unilateral declarations were presumed to provide. As to whether the other parties accepted them as "an instrument related to the treaty,"[188] again, non-nuclear-weapon States can be presumed to have accepted them as they stand to benefit from such instruments.[189] Even those States that had the greatest interest in keeping these unilateral declarations separate from the NPT – namely the nuclear-weapon States – repeatedly referred to the NPT within their declarations, as if explicitly tying them together.[190] One declaration went so far as to explicitly tie them together: "parties to the Treaty on the Non-Proliferation of Nuclear Weapons must be in compliance with *these* undertakings [contained in the unilateral declaration] in order to be eligible for any benefits of adherence to the Treaty."[191] Therefore, it would appear that these unilateral declarations could be included as context in interpreting the NPT. One might also come to the same

[187] VCLT, *supra* note 19, Art. 31(2)(b). [188] See ibid., Art. 31(2)(b).

[189] See Letter from the Permanent Representative of France, *supra* note 169, annex ¶ 8 (France noting that non-nuclear-weapon States are the ones that benefit from these security assurances).

[190] See Letter from the Chargé d'affaires, *supra* note 171; Letter dated 6 April 1995 from the Permanent Representative of the United Kingdom, *supra* note 171; Letter from the Permanent Representative of the Russian Federation, *supra* note 171; Letter from the Permanent Representative of France, *supra* note 169; Letter from the Permanent Representative of China, *supra* note 172.

[191] Letter from the Chargé d'affaires, supra note 171, ¶ 2 (emphasis added).

conclusion by relying on VCLT Article 31(3), which provides that an interpreter can consider subsequent agreements or subsequent practice that shows the agreement of the parties, or other relevant rules of international law applicable to the parties. In the end, an interpreter of a treaty need not be overly legalistic in determining what elements to consider, inasmuch as the ICJ in the *Namibia* advisory opinion broadly declared that an interpreter can consider, "in general, *all circumstances* that might assist in determining the legal consequences of the resolution of the Security Council,"[192] which presumably could include these unilateral declarations, regardless of whether they perfectly satisfy all of the elements of any particular provision of VCLT Article 31(2) or (3).

Allowing an interpreter of the NPT to rely on these unilateral declarations conceivably would mean that these unilateral declarations became an integral part of the NPT. There is some precedent for such integration of unilateral declarations into a treaty, such as with the letters from then US president Carter to then Egyptian president Sadat and then Israeli prime minister Begin in relation to the 1979 Israel–Egypt Peace Treaty, in which the United States unilaterally guaranteed compliance with the treaty by asserting that it would "take such other action as it may deem appropriate and helpful to achieve compliance with the Treaty."[193] These letters have been seen as an integral part of the 1979 Israel–Egypt Peace Treaty.[194] The significance of such integration is the creation of the expectation that you should not look at one without the other.

3.2.1.6 Binding permanent members of the Security Council

Perhaps a more interesting legal issue is whether permanent members of the Security Council can be bound by Security Council resolutions. The United Nations seems to have been designed so that no actions can be taken against the interests of the permanent members of the Security Council due to their veto power over all substantive matters under UN Charter Article 27(3).[195] Still, this does not mean that the permanent members cannot vote for a resolution that imposes certain obligations on

192 Ibid., at 53 (emphasis added).

193 Letters from President Carter to Prime Minister Begin and President Sadat, March 26, 1979, 32 UST 2146, 2148.

194 See, e.g., Anthony Lewis, Editorial, *A Cloud No Bigger*, NY Times, March 25, 1982, at A31 (discussing how Egypt wanted to rely on this letter in calling on the US to ensure the appropriate withdrawals took place in accordance with the Peace Treaty).

195 See UN Charter, Art. 27(3).

themselves just as it imposes obligations on other States. After all, Article 25 requires *all* States – not just non-permanent members – to "accept and carry out the decisions of the Security Council."[196]

If this is indeed the case, why then would the permanent members of the Security Council consent to have their options limited in the future in such a sensitive area as the nuclear non-proliferation regime, with the possibility of legal repercussions arising from the violation of such obligations? Indeed, it is rational for these powerful States to bind themselves in order to reassure other powerful States and the rest of the international community that they will not be dominated, thus lowering the costs of maintaining international peace and security.[197] Such self-binding measures as those contained in Resolutions 255 and 984, along with the accompanying unilateral statements from the permanent members of the Security Council, are a strong example of what Eric Myjer calls the "juridification" of arms control and disarmament norms, which is "the process whereby States are willing to bind themselves, either legally or politically, via arrangements of a legal nature."[198] The placing of nuclear non-proliferation obligations on other States, as discussed throughout the remainder of this subsection, also would be an example of this type of juridification. Before moving on to discuss these examples of juridification, it is interesting to note that the self-binding of permanent members referred to in this subsection undermines the notion espoused by some commentators that the permanent members lack real commitment to nuclear non-proliferation because they have been unwilling to commit themselves to nuclear disarmament.[199] Obviously more can be done by permanent members of the Security Council to promote nuclear disarmament among themselves, although any legally binding obligation is better than none at all from the perspective of trying to promote nuclear non-proliferation.

[196] Ibid., Art. 25.

[197] See Thompson, *supra* note 96, at 4 (citing G. John Ikenberry, After Victory: Institutions, Strategic Restraint, and the Rebuilding of Order after Major Wars (2001)).

[198] Eric P. J. Myjer, *The Law of Arms-Control and International Supervision*, 3 Leiden J. Int'l L. (Special Issue) 99, 99 (1990).

[199] See John B. Rhinelander, *Limitations and Safeguards in Arms Control Agreements*, in Law and Force in the New International Order 247, 254–255 (Lori F. Damrosch and David J. Scheffer ed., 1991).

3.2.1.7 Binding the Security Council

As noted above, paragraph 1 of Resolution 255 and paragraph 2 of Resolution 984 oblige the Security Council to take immediate action if a non-nuclear-weapon State is ever attacked or threatened with attack by nuclear weapons. The question arises whether international organizations and their organs can have such obligations placed upon them. The ICJ advisory opinion concerning the *Interpretation of the Agreement of 25 March 1951 between the World Health Organization (WHO) and Egypt* made it clear that international organizations – in particular, the United Nations – are subjects of international law and can be bound by general rules of international law.[200] Logically, if such entities have obligations, then they must also have the possibility of violating those obligations, and face the consequences – responsibility or accountability, whichever term you prefer – that subsequently flow from such violations.

In 2009, the International Law Commission (ILC) came out with sixty-six draft articles on the responsibility of international organizations, which States and international organizations were supposed to comment on by January 1, 2011.[201] One noteworthy issue that arose during the ILC's work in 2005 was the question what law would apply to an international organization with respect to determining its responsibility or accountability.[202] Article 9(1) of the draft articles makes clear that an international organization breaches an international obligation "when an act of that international organization is not in conformity with what is required of it by that obligation, regardless of its origin and character."[203] The last phrase, "regardless of its origin and character," indicates that an international organization conceivably can be held responsible for a breach of an obligation it created for itself in one of its own resolutions. The commentary to Article 9(1) supports this assertion, where it discusses the "rules of the organization" and indicates that

[200] See *Interpretation of the Agreement of 25 March 1951 between the WHO and Egypt*, Advisory Opinion, 1980 ICJ Rep. 73, 89–90 (Dec. 20).

[201] See Official Records of the General Assembly, Sixty-fourth session, Supplement No.10 (A/64/10), ¶¶ 48–51.

[202] See Special Rapporteur, *Third Report on Responsibility of International Organizations*, at 3–9, delivered to the International Law Commission, UN Doc. A/CN.4/553 (May 13, 2005) (hereinafter Third Report).

[203] See Official Records of the General Assembly, Sixty-fourth session, Supplement No.10 (A/64/10), at 21.

> most obligations [of international organizations] are likely to arise from the rules of the organization, which are defined in article 2, subparagraph (b), of the present articles as meaning "in particular, the constituent instruments, decisions, resolutions and other acts of the organization adopted in accordance with those instruments, and established practice of the organization."[204]

Here, the source of the obligation is specific, a Security Council resolution binding the Security Council itself, which conceivably would involve the breach of an international obligation if the Security Council did not follow the obligation it created for itself.

Holding the Security Council responsible for the breach of such international obligations, nevertheless, remains quite a theoretical concept, since there currently is no effective way for a State to hold the Security Council to these obligations. Sometimes the United Nations allows itself to be sued, as with the UN administration in East Timor (UNTAET) being a defendant in such cases as the Takeshi Kashiwagi case in Dili District Court, which related to his illegal detention there,[205] and as with the United Nations allowing claims review boards in their status-of-forces agreements with host States concerning damages caused by UN peace operations of a private-law nature.[206] Even then, it is difficult to determine exactly how the United Nations' acts – or failures to act – give rise to certain levels of accountability. Nonetheless, these practical difficulties do not change the fact that the Security Council may incur responsibility for violations of these obligations from a formalist perspective.

204 See ibid., at 78. See generally G. Balladore Pallieri, *Le droit interne des organisations internationales*, 127 Rec. des cours 1 (1969-II) (discussing the broad concept of the "rules of the organization" and how it is a part of international law, as cited in the commentary); Nguyen Quoc Dinh, Patrick Daillier and Alain Pellet, Droit international public 567–577 (7th edn, 2002) (same).

205 See Carla Bongiorno, *A Culture of Impunity: Applying International Human Rights Law to the United Nations in East Timor*, 33 Colum. Hum. Rts. L. Rev. 623, 666–676 (2002) (discussing the complicated civil case brought by Takeshi Kashiwagi against UNTAET, inter alia, for illegal detention).

206 See Daphna Shraga, *U.N. Peacekeeping Operations: Applicability of International Humanitarian Law and Responsibility for Operations-Related Damage*, 94 Am. J. Int'l L. 406, 409–412 (2000) (citing, inter alia, Model Status of Forces Agreement, ¶ 51, UN Doc. A/45/594 (1990), although acknowledging that the number of third-party claims has remained low since the inception of these claims review boards in 1957 with the United Nations Emergency Force in Egypt). See generally Mahnoush H. Arsanjani, *Claims against International Organizations: Quis Custodiet Ipsos Custodes*, 7 Yale J. World Public Order 131 (1981).

3.2.2 *Resolution 487 and Israel's attack on Iraq*

The second example of the Security Council's imposition of nuclear nonproliferation obligations is Resolution 487, which involved Israel's 1981 attack on Iraq's nuclear complex at Tuwaitha (also known as Osirak).[207] Interestingly, Iraq alleged in a Security Council meeting directly following this 1981 attack that Israel had tried to destroy that same complex on September 27, 1980, and that it had warned the Security Council then that Israel was going to attack that same reactor again.[208] Israel conceded that it was responsible for this 1981 attack, although it claimed that it was an act of self-preservation due to the fear of nuclear obliteration by a nuclear-armed Iraq.[209] Israel claimed that Iraq was developing nuclear weapons in an underground laboratory under the nuclear reactor there. IAEA director-general Sigvard Eklund asserted before the Security Council that the IAEA inspectorate had been satisfied with Iraq's accounting for all nuclear material through its safeguards inspections and that it had been aware of a vault under the reactor at that complex, but that it was for maintenance purposes and could not have been the site for producing plutonium and other weaponization efforts.[210] Eklund noted that Israel's attack on the Osirak nuclear complex could be classified as an attack on the IAEA's safeguards system, and he characterized it as a "matter of grave concern to the IAEA."[211]

On the same day as those statements by the IAEA director-general, June 19, 1981, the Security Council unanimously adopted Resolution 487, which "[s]trongly condemn[ed] the military attack by Israel in clear violation of the Charter of the United Nations and the norms of international conduct."[212] In addition, the Security Council "[*c*]*all*[*ed*] *upon* Israel urgently to place its nuclear facilities under the safeguards of the International Atomic Energy

207 S.C. Res. 487, UN Doc. S/RES/487 (June 19, 1981). See generally TIMOTHY L. H. MCCORMACK, SELF-DEFENSE IN INTERNATIONAL LAW: THE ISRAELI RAID ON THE IRAQI NUCLEAR REACTOR (1997).

208 UN SCOR, 36th Sess., 2280th mtg., at 3, 7, UN Doc. S/PV.2280 (June 12, 1981).

209 Ibid., at 8–12; see also GRAY, *supra* note 93 (discussing Israel's claim of anticipatory self-defense).

210 UN SCOR, 36th Sess., 2288th mtg., at 2–3, UN Doc. S/PV.2288 and Corr. 1 (June 19, 1981); see also GRAY, *supra* note 93, at 133 (citing the IAEA's statement that there was no evidence that Iraq planned to use the nuclear reactors for developing nuclear weapons).

211 UN SCOR, 36th Sess., 2288th mtg., at 3, UN Doc. S/PV.2288 and Corr. 1 (June 19, 1981).

212 S.C. Res. 487, ¶ 1, UN Doc. S/RES/487 (June 19, 1981).

Agency."[213] Calling upon Israel urgently to place its nuclear facilities under IAEA supervision was seen as an essential element in managing the threat coming from Israel,[214] as the Security Council had concluded that Israel's armed attack "constituted a serious threat to the IAEA safeguards system and the nuclear nonproliferation system."[215]

The question arises concerning what it means to place facilities under the IAEA's safeguards in this context. According to the IAEA, "Safeguards are activities by which the IAEA can verify that a State is living up to its international commitments not to use nuclear programmes for nuclear-weapons purposes."[216] NPT Article III(1) requires non-nuclear-weapon States "to accept safeguards, as set forth in an agreement to be negotiated" at a later date, in accordance with the IAEA Statute.[217] The interesting aspect of Resolution 486 is that Israel has never been a party to the NPT, even though it became a member of the IAEA in 1957.[218] Some safeguards apply to Israel's activities because it is party to the IAEA Statute and has a safeguards agreement with the IAEA that covers some minor facilities.[219] However, the IAEA has no treaty-based authority to scrutinize Israel's most significant nuclear activities because Israel's safeguards agreement does not cover these and because it is not a party to the NPT.[220] As a result, the IAEA has asserted that States that have not become a party to the NPT, including

[213] Ibid. ¶ 5 (original emphasis). But see W. Thomas Mallison and Sally V. Mallison, *The Israeli Aerial Attack of June 7, 1981, upon the Iraqi Nuclear Reactor: Aggression or Self-Defense?*, 15 Vand. J. Transnat'l L. 417, 440 (1982) (stating that the Security Council did not impose mandatory sanctions on Israel).

[214] UN SCOR, 36th Sess., 2288th mtg., at 13, UN Doc. S/PV.2288 and Corr. 1 (June 19, 1981) (noting a statement by Uganda's representative that this was why it supported the resolution, although it wished that the Security Council had invoked the provisions of Chapter VII).

[215] See ibid., at 15. But see ibid., at 13 (reporting that the German Democratic Republic read this Resolution as not requiring Israel to stop nuclear collaboration); ibid., at 14 (noting that Tunisia seemed to interpret this resolution as not requiring Israel to stop its nuclear weapon development).

[216] International Atomic Energy Agency, IAEA Factsheets and Frequently Asked Questions, at www.iaea.org/Publications/Factsheets/English/sg_overview.html (last visited Dec. 28, 2010).

[217] See NPT, *supra* note 13, Art. III(1).

[218] The same is true for India and Pakistan.

[219] See Louis René Beres, *Israel, Iran and Preemption: Choosing the Least Unattractive Option under International Law*, 14 Dick. J. Int'l L. 187, 200 (1996).

[220] See Uranium Information Centre (UIC), Safeguards to Prevent Nuclear Proliferation, Briefing Paper 5 (Oct. 2007), available at www.uic.com.au/nip05.htm (last visited May 26, 2011); Anthony D'Amato, *Israel's Air Strike upon the Iraqi Nuclear Reactor*, 77 Am. J. Int'l L. 584, 587 (1983).

Israel, Pakistan, and India, are "under no Treaty obligations and have few or no obligations to the IAEA under safeguards agreements."[221] Although Israel could accept new agreements allowing the IAEA to implement safeguards with respect to Israel's declared facilities (based on INFCIRC/66 guidelines for the IAEA's safeguards system, for example[222]), it would still need Israel's consent and would not cover special inspections normally covered by Additional Protocols.[223]

Even if Israel placed its nuclear facilities under IAEA safeguards, as required by Resolution 487, the IAEA would have no yardstick against which to measure Israel's compliance, since the NPT creates many of the international obligations on States in this realm, such as the obligations to prevent proliferation, seek nuclear disarmament, and promote peaceful nuclear energy use, while the IAEA Statute creates the basic mechanisms through which it can verify compliance with those obligations.[224] As Guido den Dekker points out, the IAEA inspection regime established under the IAEA Statute cannot begin until after States parties to the NPT have made their initial declarations and the IAEA has conducted its initial inspections.[225] Therefore, in order for the Security Council's pronouncement to have full meaning with regard to Israel, the Security Council would need to impose at least some of the NPT's obligations on Israel. For example, by requiring Israel to place its facilities under IAEA safeguards, the Security Council must classify Israel as a non-nuclear-weapon State under the NPT regime, since nuclear-weapon States do not have an obligation under the IAEA Statute to accept such safeguards. While such a classification is called for by the NPT, given the cut-off date of January 1, 1967, to become a nuclear-weapon State, in accordance with NPT Article IX(3), it is difficult to accept this classification of Israel inasmuch as it is widely known that Israel possesses nuclear weapons.

Moreover, the Security Council's actions could be seen as imposing the NPT obligations of non-nuclear-weapon States on Israel. This interpretation

221 IAEA, *Safeguards in Israel*, IAEA InfoLog, March 2005, available at www.iaea.org/blog/Infolog/?p=3 (last visited May 26, 2011).

222 See IAEA, *The Agency's Safeguards System (1965, as Provisionally Extended in 1966 and 1968)*, IAEA Doc. INFCIRC/66/Rev.2 (Sept. 16, 1968), available at www.iaea.org/Publications/Documents/Infcircs/Others/inf66r2.shtml (last visited May 25, 2011).

223 See Barry Kellman and David S. Gualtieri, *Barricading the Nuclear Window: A Legal Regime to Curtail Nuclear Smuggling*, 1996 U. Ill. L. Rev. 667, 706 n. 167 (1996).

224 IAEA, *Safeguards in Israel*, *supra* note 221; Dekker, *supra* note 90, at 81.

225 See Dekker, *supra* note 90, at 82. However, it is unclear what provisions Dekker relies upon in reaching this conclusion.

of Resolution 487 is confirmed by the subsequent General Assembly resolutions in 1984 and 1985 that noted, in a negative manner, how Israel had not adhered to the NPT, as required,[226] even though nothing had expressly required Israel to adhere to the NPT before then. Indeed, without such an interpretation of Resolution 487, requiring Israel to place its facilities under IAEA safeguards would have little meaning, again, due to the lack of a yardstick against which to assess Israel's compliance and a lack in required reporting by Israel. Hence, this arguably is the first example of the Security Council imposing portions of a nuclear non-proliferation agreement on a State and is something that the Security Council seems to have been fond of doing since the end of the Cold War.

3.2.3 *The 1991 Gulf War and Resolution 687*

The 1991 Gulf War was important for international relations and the United Nations for several reasons. For example, the Gulf War marked the clear end of the Cold War, in that the Soviet Union relinquished support of a key client State with the hope of saving its core union.[227] This newfound co-operation from the Soviet Union enabled a return to the UN system as its framers had intended at its creation, with a strong emphasis on collective security coming at the direction of the Security Council. More important for this study, the 1991 Gulf War and one of its related Security Council resolutions – Resolution 687 – provides another example of the Security Council imposing nuclear non-proliferation obligations on a State.

Some commentators assert it was the Iraqi invasion of Kuwait that forced the Security Council to get involved to a greater extent with WMD proliferation issues, including the proliferation of nuclear weapons.[228] However, it was not the invasion itself but rather Iraq's alleged possession of WMD and a nascent nuclear weapons program that spurred such involvement, not to mention its use of WMD against its enemy during the Iran–Iraq War. Iraq's invasion of Kuwait demonstrated clearly to the world how dangerous Iraq could be to the maintenance of international peace and security, a menace that would be intolerable if it were to use

[226] G.A. Res. 39/14, UN Doc. A/RES/39/14 (Nov. 16, 1984); G.A. Res. 40/6, UN Doc. A/RES/40/6 (Nov. 1, 1985).

[227] See Martin McCauley, Russia, America and the Cold War, 1949–1991 81–87 (2nd edn, 2004).

[228] See Luck, *supra* note 135, at 99.

WMD on a large scale or to lend its WMD to terrorists. Despite the limited international protests that resulted from such use during the Iran–Iraq War, those atrocities likely were foremost in the minds of Coalition commanders and troops before they went into Iraq in Operation Desert Storm.[229] Whereas the initial objectives – and resolutions – prior to the actual invasion were the ouster of Iraq from Kuwait and the restoration of the Kuwaiti government, as opposed to the elimination of Iraq's WMD, including nuclear weapons,[230] the overall objectives quickly expanded to reducing Iraq's ability to threaten its neighbors and to destroying Iraq's WMD programs once the air campaign began to raise fears of WMD attacks in the near future.[231] In short, it was clear towards the end of the Gulf War in 1991 that a strong disarmament (including nuclear-weapon disarmament) component would be involved in the postwar rebuilding of Iraq.[232]

3.2.3.1 Cease-fire agreement on the ground

To begin, a thumbnail sketch of the relevant facts of the 1991 Gulf War might be useful. Iraq invaded Kuwait on August 2, 1990, which led to a string of Security Council resolutions that climaxed with Resolution 678 and its authorization of member States to "use all necessary means to uphold and implement resolution 660 (1990) and all subsequent relevant resolutions and to restore international peace and security in the area"[233] if Iraq did not leave Kuwait by January 15, 1991. Language such as "all necessary means" within a Chapter VII decision of the Security Council is commonly interpreted as an authorization to use force.[234]

[229] See JAMES S. SUTTERLIN, THE UNITED NATIONS AND THE MAINTENANCE OF INTERNATIONAL SECURITY: A CHALLENGE TO BE MET 105 (2003).

[230] See LUCK, *supra* note 135, at 99.

[231] See William H. Lewis and Christopher C. Joyner, *Proliferation of Unconventional Weapons: The Case for Coercive Arms Control*, 10 COMP. STRATEGY 299, 299–301 (1991).

[232] See ibid.

[233] S.C. Res. 660, ¶ 2, UN Doc. S/RES/660 (Aug. 2, 1990) (condemning Iraq's invasion of Kuwait and demanding that "Iraq withdraw immediately and unconditionally all its forces to the positions in which they were located on 1 August 1990"); S.C. Res. 678, ¶ 2, UN Doc. S/RES/678 (Nov. 29, 1990).

[234] For more information on the various types of language the Security Council employs when authorizing the use of force, see generally James D. Fry, *The UN Security Council and the Law of Armed Conflict: Amity or Enmity?*, 38 GEO. WASH. INT'L L. REV. 327, 336–339 (2006) (exploring the consistencies among the interpretations of varying "necessary means" provisions among resolutions, which generally imply the authorization of the use of force).

Iraq did not comply with Resolution 678, and US-led Coalition forces began Operation Desert Storm on January 17, 1991, to liberate Kuwait. This successful operation liberated Kuwait on February 27, 1991, pushed on to Baghdad, and captured some 86,000 Iraqi prisoners of war, all in approximately forty-two days, with only the last hundred hours consisting of actual ground combat.[235] This overwhelming success – for the Coalition, that is – set off a cascade of events, including the unilateral suspension of the fighting by President George H.W. Bush on February 28, 1991, and the formalization of a cease-fire agreement on March 3, 1991, between the commander of Coalition forces, General Norman Schwarzkopf, and the deputy chief of staff of the Iraqi Ministry of Defense, Lieutenant General Sultan Hashim Ahmad al-Jabburi.[236] This agreement did not contain any provisions on disarmament, but rather expressly allowed Iraq to fly military helicopters in the cease-fire zone, and provided for a demarcation line and the repatriation of prisoners of war.[237] Such a concession on allowing Iraq to fly military helicopters is not only the opposite of a disarmament or an arms control measure, but it was a considerable mistake in retrospect, given that Iraq had requested the use of its helicopter gunships to help move personnel and materiel but instead used them to kill 50,000 to 80,000 Kurds and Shias who were involved in an uprising against the Saddam Hussein regime at that time.[238] One must look to Resolutions 686 and 687 for any express mention of disarmament or arms control obligations placed on Iraq.

3.2.3.2 Nuclear disarmament obligations of Resolution 687

The new strength in Security Council disarmament and arms control resolutions in the post-Cold War era began with Resolution 687, which was the first resolution in which the Security Council adopted measures requiring the destruction of a State's WMD and WMD programs, and

[235] See David M. Morriss, *From War to Peace: A Study of Cease-Fire Agreements and the Evolving Role of the United Nations*, 36 Va. J. Int'l L. 801, 890 (1996).

[236] Andru E. Wall, *The Legal Case for Invading Iraq and Toppling Hussein*, 32 Isr. Y.B. Hum. Rts. 165, 178–179 (2002); Ben Rooney, *Coalition Faces Problem in Knowing When War Is Over*, Daily Telegraph, Sept. 4, 2003, available at http://www.telegraph.co.uk/news/main/jhtmxml=/news/2003/04/09/wirq409.xml; Morriss, *supra* note 235, at 888–97; Christopher Greenwood, *New World Order or Old? The Invasion of Kuwait and the Rule of Law*, 55 Modern L. Rev. 153, 153 (1992).

[237] See Wall, *supra* note 236, at 178–179.

[238] See Norman G. Printer Jr., *Establishing an International Criminal Tribunal for Iraq: The Time Is Now*, 36 UWLA L. Rev. 27, 38 (2005); Kenneth M. Pollack, The Threatening Storm: The Case for Invading Iraq 48–51 (2002).

provided for an extensive inspection and monitoring regime to prevent the re-establishment of those WMD and WMD programs.[239] As illustrated below, the disarmament of Iraq envisioned in Resolution 687 is not unlike the disarmament of Germany after the First World War in terms of the magnitude and punitive nature of the disarmament measures.[240] All of these provisions can be seen in light of preambular paragraph 15 of Resolution 687: "*Concerned* by reports in the hands of Member States that Iraq has attempted to acquire materials for a nuclear-weapons programme contrary to its obligations under the Treaty on the Non-Proliferation of Nuclear Weapons of 1 July 1968." Part C of Resolution 687 addresses Iraq's disarmament, and requires, inter alia, the following from Iraq:

- the unconditional "destruction, removal, or rendering harmless, under international supervision," of its WMD materials and facilities, including its ballistic missiles with a range greater than 150 kilometers;
- that Iraq provide detailed reports to the UN Secretary-General and the IAEA director-general of Iraq's inventories of such WMD, WMD facilities, and missiles, including their locations, amounts, and types;
- that Iraq unconditionally "undertake not to use, develop, construct, or acquire" any of the items it is being required to destroy and report on; and
- that Iraq unconditionally accept urgent on-site inspections to verify the capabilities mentioned in Iraq's declarations and other locations chosen by the Special Commission created for that purpose.[241]

All of these demands were significant disarmament commitments for Iraq and were new obligations inasmuch as they did not exist before this time in any other legal instrument. Admittedly, the requirement that Iraq report its inventories of WMD and related capacities is similar to that required by paragraph 3(d) of Resolution 686, although here the reference to Iraq's WMD program included its nuclear-weapon program, in addition to requiring Iraq to report on WMD throughout *all of Iraq* in Resolution 687, not just those in Kuwait and the parts of Iraq

[239] See Pascal Teixeira de Silva, Weapons of Mass Destruction: The Iraqi Case, in The UN Security Council: From the Cold War to the 21st Century 205, 205 (David Malone ed., 2004); Dallmeyer, *supra* note 133, at 129–130.

[240] See Max Hilaire, United Nations Law and the Security Council 213 (2005).

[241] See S.C. Res. 687, ¶ 8–10, 12, UN Doc. S/RES/687 (April 3, 1991) (original emphasis).

where Coalition forces were located, as was required by Resolution 686. In essence, Resolution 687 required that Iraq give up all of its WMD capabilities or have such capabilities removed, which is quite broad in scope. In paragraph 14, Resolution 687 goes even further than this by pulling the wider Middle East into this resolution and stating the goal of establishing a WMD-free zone for the whole of the Middle East. Again, these provisions relating to WMD include nuclear weapons. Resolution 687 was truly a revolutionary resolution from a nuclear-weapon disarmament and arms control perspective.

3.2.3.3 UNSCOM and UNMOVIC under Resolution 687

In addition to Resolution 687 requiring Iraq to surrender its WMD and WMD programs, the resolution called for the UN Secretary-General to establish a plan for the United Nations Special Commission (UNSCOM), in connection with the IAEA, to conduct on-site inspections of Iraq's WMD-related facilities.[242] Paragraph 13 of Resolution 687 referred to the need for Security Council approval of this plan.[243] The UN Secretary-General submitted the plan for disarming Iraq on April 18, 1991, pursuant to paragraph 9(b)(i) of Resolution 687, which proposed that UNSCOM be established as soon as possible in order to begin implementation of Resolution 687, and in particular the destruction or removal of biological and chemical weapons, ballistic missiles, and nuclear-weapons capabilities, as well as to provide future compliance and operations support.[244] In addition to a staff of twenty to twenty-five people, UNSCOM would be supplemented by technical experts to assist with its responsibilities.[245] The UN Secretary-General also submitted the IAEA's plan for disarming Iraq of its nuclear capabilities on May 17, 1991, which proposed that all nuclear-weapons-usable materials be removed from Iraq for destruction, since they could not be destroyed in Iraq, and that nuclear-weapon research and production facilities be decommissioned.[246] Unlike the Secretary-General's plan of April 18, paragraph 13 of this May 17 plan referred to the "plan being approved

[242] See ibid., ¶¶ 9(b), 13.

[243] See S.C. Res. 687, ¶ 13, UN Doc. S/RES/687 (April 3, 1991).

[244] See Secretary-General, Report of the Secretary-General, Implementation of paragraph 9 (b)(i) of Security Council Resolution 687 (1991), UN Doc. S/2250, 1–2 (April 18, 1991).

[245] See Secretary-General, *Report of the Secretary-General, Implementation of paragraph 9 (b)(i) of Security Council Resolution* 687 (1991), UN Doc. S/2250, 2 (April 18, 1991).

[246] See Note by the Secretary-General transmitting the IAEA's Plan, UN Doc. S/22615, 3–4 (May 17, 1991).

by the Council," which it did on June 17, 1991, through Resolution 699 (a Chapter VII resolution). Resolution 699 confirmed that UNSCOM and the IAEA had the authority to act under Part C of Resolution 687 to destroy, remove, and render harmless Iraq's WMD and WMD capabilities,[247] asked for biannual reports from the Secretary-General,[248] and encouraged maximum assistance "in cash and in kind" from UN member States to make sure that Part C of Resolution 687 was implemented effectively and quickly, although it also decided that Iraq ultimately was to carry the full financial burden of implementing Part C.[249]

Although the Security Council did not approve the IAEA's plan until June 17, UNSCOM and the IAEA apparently began their work disarming Iraq of its WMD in May 1991 (just one month after the Security Council adopted Resolution 687).[250] UNSCOM's and the IAEA's desire to get to work before getting the Security Council's approval was not surprising, given that it was to carry out the disarmament plan provided by the Secretary-General and the IAEA director-general "within forty-five days following approval by the Council."[251] This short time frame reflects the somewhat unrealistic expectations of the Security Council when it adopted Resolution 687.

Despite these unrealistic expectations, it still is somewhat troubling from a legal perspective that UNSCOM and the IAEA began removing Iraq's nuclear capabilities before receiving express authorization from the Security Council, as Resolution 687 apparently required. When it became clear that Iraq's declarations had been incomplete and that Iraq was not complying with its obligations to disclose its WMD and WMD capabilities,[252] it became clear that UNSCOM would not be able to carry

[247] See S.C. Res. 699, ¶ 2, UN Doc. S/RES/699 (June 17, 1991). [248] See ibid., ¶ 3.

[249] See ibid., ¶ 4.

[250] Note by the Secretary-General transmitting the IAEA's Plan, UN Doc. S/22615, at 3 (May 17, 1991). See also Trevor Findlay, *Lessons of UNSCOM and UNMOVIC for WMD Non-proliferation, Arms Control and Disarmament*, in ARMS CONTROL AFTER IRAQ: NORMATIVE AND OPERATIONAL CHALLENGES 140, 141–142 (WAHEGURU PAL SINGH SIDHU and RAMESH THAKUR ed., 2006).

[251] S.C. Res. 687, ¶ 13, UN Doc. S/RES/687 (April 3, 1991).

[252] See Secretary-General, Letter dated 26 June 1991 from the Secretary-General Addressed to the President of the Security Council, at 2–3, UN Doc. S/22739 (June 26, 1991); Secretary-General, Letter dated 28 June 1991 from the Secretary-General Addressed to the President of the Security Council, at 2, UN Doc. S/22743 (June 28, 1991); Secretary-General, Letter dated 12 July 1991 from the Director-General of the International Atomic Energy Agency Addressed to the Secretary-General, at 9–14, UN Doc.S/22788 (July 15, 1991); Secretary-General, Letter dated 25 July 1991 from the

out this plan in the given amount of time, and so UNSCOM and the IAEA began to focus on identifying the gaps and finding the undeclared items. Iraq began to be completely unco-operative in June 1991, when it refused access to two sites suspected of being part of its nuclear-weapons program and even attacked UNSCOM inspectors to stop them inspecting and, later, retrieving confiscated documents.[253]

Despite Iraq's lack of co-operation, UNSCOM pressed forward in unearthing Iraq's WMD activities through its reliance on clever tactics to avoid tipping Iraq off as to where it was headed.[254] With tremendous personnel support from all over the world and technological capabilities given to it by willing Western governments,[255] it took UNSCOM approximately six months of operations to conclude in its reports to the Security Council that "[t]he elements of misinformation, concealment, lack of cooperation, and violation of the privileges and immunities of the Special Commission and IAEA have not created any trust in Iraq's intentions."[256] The Security Council acknowledged the fact that Iraq was noncompliant with Part C of Resolution 687 and noncompliant with its safeguards agreement with the IAEA in violation of the NPT in its Resolution 707 of August 15, 1991,[257] and again demanded Iraq's compliance with Resolution 687, including allowing UNSCOM and the IAEA teams "immediate, unconditional, and unrestricted access to any and all areas, facilities, equipment, records, and means of transportation which they wish to inspect."[258] These efforts to apply considerable pressure to Iraq to get it to comply had no discernible impact. In an effort to improve the inspection regime and to apply yet greater pressure to Iraq, the Security Council updated the inspection plan with Resolution 715, enabling UNSCOM to inspect facilities of all types and to remove

Director-General of the International Atomic Energy Agency Addressed to the Secretary-General, at 5–11, UN Doc. S/22837 (July 25, 1991).

253 See Findlay, *supra* note 250, at 142.

254 See Tsutsomu Kono, *Role in Addressing WMD Issues: Assessment and Outlook*, in ARMS CONTROL AFTER IRAQ: NORMATIVE AND OPERATIONAL CHALLENGES 83, 103 (WAHEGURU PAL SINGH SIDHU and RAMESH THAKUR ed., 2006); Findlay, *supra* note 250, at 142–143.

255 See Findlay, *supra* note 250, at 141–42; Dallmeyer, *supra* note 133, at 131 (discussing how "the nuclear inspection team which was detained in 1991 in the car park was composed of thirty-seven people from twenty-two countries including Morocco, Egypt, and Syria, notions previously not at the forefront of arms control verification").

256 Secretary-General, *Report of the Sixth IAEA Inspection Team, delivered to the Security Council*, UN Doc. S/23122 (Oct. 8, 1991).

257 See S.C. Res. 707, ¶¶ 1–2, UN Doc. S/RES/707 (Aug. 15, 1991).

258 Ibid., ¶ 3(a)–(b).

anything of interest during these inspections, among other powers provided for in a plan developed by the UN Secretary-General.[259]

Security Council resolutions were relatively silent on UNSCOM's inspections of Iraq after Resolution 715 until June 1996, when Iraq refused access to UNSCOM yet again, which led the Security Council to declare in Resolution 1060 that Iraq had violated its disarmament obligations under Resolution 687 and that it must grant "immediate, unconditional, and unrestricted access" to the inspectors of all sites.[260] A similar situation occurred a year later, and the Security Council responded in the same manner in Resolution 1115, but threatened an escalation of sanctions,[261] although without significant impact. Without these inspections, the Security Council was unable to know how much of a threat Iraqi WMD posed, although it was believed that Iraq still had such capabilities.[262] The Security Council repeated these threats four months later in Resolution 1134,[263] and actually imposed greater sanctions in the form of travel bans on Iraqi officials.[264] Without Iraq's cooperation, the burden of proving that Iraq did not have WMD seems to have inappropriately shifted from Iraq to the Security Council.[265] In an effort to shift the burden back to Iraq, the Security Council threatened further military action if Iraq refused to comply with inspectors. Resolution 1154 required Iraq to give "immediate, unconditional, and unrestricted access to the Special Commission and the IAEA."[266] Resolution 1205 strongly condemned "the decision by Iraq of 31 October 1998 to cease cooperation with the Special Commission as a flagrant violation of resolution 687 (1991) and other relevant resolutions," and required that it rescind immediately and unconditionally the decision of October 31, 1998, as well as the decision of August 5, 1998, to "suspend cooperation with the Special Commission and to maintain restrictions on the work of the IAEA and that Iraq provide

259 See S.C. Res. 715, ¶ 1, UN Doc. S/RES/715 (Oct. 11, 1991).

260 S.C. Res. 1060, ¶¶ 1–2, UN Doc. S/RES/1060 (June 12, 1996).

261 See S.C. Res. 1115, ¶¶ 2–6, UN Doc. S/RES/1115 (June 21, 1997).

262 See Sutterlin, *supra* note 229, at 106.

263 See S.C. Res. 1134, ¶¶ 1–6, UN Doc. S/RES/1134 (Oct. 23, 1997).

264 See S.C. Res. 1137, ¶ 4, UN Doc. S/RES/1137 (Nov. 12, 1997).

265 See Kono, *supra* note 254, at 92–93. This flip-flopping of burdens of proof ultimately led to confusion over the Coalition's authority in Iraq and the questionable move to seek reauthorization for the use of force in Iraq in 2002, which the Security Council failed to provide in its Resolution 1441.

266 S.C. Res. 1154, ¶ 3, UN Doc. S/RES/1154 (March 2, 1998).

immediate, complete, and unconditional cooperation with the Special Commission and the IAEA."[267]

This led to the joint US–UK action Operation Desert Fox from December 16 to 19, 1998, which involved a four-day air campaign that included as many cruise missiles as were used during the entire 1991 Gulf War.[268] Operation Desert Fox was not expressly authorized by the Security Council, although it arguably was in response to Iraq's violation of an earlier Security Council resolution.[269] As one commentator asserts, Operation Desert Fox was designed to harm Iraq's WMD capabilities, not to bring Iraq into compliance with Security Council resolutions,[270] although the latter likely was a desired result as well. After nearly two years of inspectors not having access to Iraq, the Security Council dissolved UNSCOM and replaced it with the United Nations Monitoring, Verification, and Inspection Commission (UNMOVIC) in Resolution 1284.[271] Unlike Resolution 687, which had been adopted quickly under somewhat unrealistic expectations, the Security Council had the time to craft UNMOVIC in such a way so as to incorporate the lessons it had learned with UNSCOM. Like UNSCOM, UNMOVIC was a subsidiary organ of the Security Council (accountable solely to the Security Council) with responsibility for verifying Iraq's compliance with Resolution 687, although it also had the tasks of addressing the unresolved WMD disarmament issues and of identifying other sites in Iraq to include within the monitoring and verification regime, among other things.[272] UNMOVIC was given a stronger ability to avoid the barriers that Iraq put in its way in that Resolution 1284 required Iraq to give UNMOVIC teams "immediate, unconditional, and unrestricted access to any and all areas, facilities, equipment, records, and means of transport which they wish to inspect,"[273] without such limitations as presidential sites and a requirement of advance notice that had plagued UNSCOM. In terms of practice, UNMOVIC was an improvement on UNSCOM in that it learned from UNSCOM's mistakes.[274] Whereas

[267] S.C. Res. 1205, ¶¶ 1–2, UN Doc. S/RES/1205 (Nov. 5, 1998).

[268] See Gray, *supra* note 93, at 266.

[269] See Sean M. Condron, *Justification for Unilateral Action in Response to the Iraqi Threat: A Critical Analysis of Operation Desert Fox*, 161 Mil. L. Rev. 115, 178 (1999).

[270] See Kono, *supra* note 254, at 94.

[271] See S.C. Res. 1284, UN Doc. S/RES/1284 (Dec. 17, 1999).

[272] See ibid., ¶ 2.

[273] Ibid., ¶ 4.

[274] See Findlay, *supra* note 250, at 156 (noting UNSCOM's early practice of dynamiting chemical weapons in open pits and other practices that led to the exposure of inspectors to harmful chemical agents).

UNSCOM and UNMOVIC relied heavily on intelligence from certain States to learn about Iraq's WMD, Hans Blix, the head of UNMOVIC, made sure that this was one-way intelligence sharing with UNMOVIC by requiring UNMOVIC staff to be UN civil servants subject to the requirements of UN Charter Article 100, which addresses staff independence and greatly improved UNMOVIC's perceived impartiality and, hence, legitimacy.[275] Blix even made sure that his staff members received the appropriate training to make them sensitive to Iraqi culture, history, and religion, among other things.[276] Nevertheless, Iraq refused to co-operate with UNMOVIC until 2002, when the United States and the United Kingdom again began to increase their military presence in the Gulf region. During this military buildup, the Security Council adopted Resolution 1441, which not only deplored Iraq's failure to comply with its past disarmament obligations and requirements to report its WMD programs,[277] but required, among other things, renewed commitment to comply with these obligations as well as a renewed obligation on Iraq to allow UNMOVIC to inspect all sites, including presidential palaces, and to suspend Iraq's ground and aerial movement.[278]

Despite the strengthened mandate of UNMOVIC, several Western States – in particular, the United States, the United Kingdom, and Spain (the Coalition States) – believed that Iraq still was successfully concealing its WMD capabilities from inspectors,[279] and believed that Saddam Hussein showed no intention of complying with UNMOVIC or the IAEA, as initial reports had indicated.[280] However, later reports from UNMOVIC and the IAEA stated that their monitoring operations were being implemented smoothly and with the full co-operation of the Iraqi

[275] See Hans Blix, Disarming Iraq 49 (2004); Kono, *supra* note 254, at 92–93; Newton R. Bowles, The Diplomacy of Hope: The United Nations Since the Cold War 162 (2004); Lewis and Joyner, *supra* note 231, at 299–301.

[276] See Blix, *supra* note 275, at 51–52.

[277] See S.C. Res. 1441, preamb. ¶¶ 1, 6–9, UN Doc. S/RES/1441 (Nov. 8, 2002).

[278] See ibid., preamb. ¶¶ 2–7, UN Doc. S/RES/1441 (Nov. 8, 2002).

[279] Interestingly, the belief that Iraq had been able to conceal its biological weapons program from inspectors for so long had a significant impact on the negotiations for a protocol to strengthen the Biological Weapons Convention, although Iraq was later found to have no biological weapons program. See Patricia Lewis, *Why We Got It Wrong: Attempting to Unravel the Truth of Bioweapons in Iraq*, in Arms Control after Iraq: Normative and Operational Challenges 160, 160–166 (Waheguru Pal Singh Sidhu and Ramesh Thakur ed., 2006).

[280] See Sutterlin, *supra* note 229, at 106; Gray, *supra* note 93, at 272.

government, though the inspections still were difficult.[281] Indeed, before the invasion, Saddam Hussein opened Iraq's doors to inspectors without any conditions and asserted that it had made a complete declaration of its WMD programs.[282] However, it appeared to be too little too late. Indeed, the list of unresolved disarmament issues reported to the Security Council under Resolution 1284 suggested that UNMOVIC was having considerable problems in Iraq.[283] Moreover, inspections did not uncover WMD, the existence of which largely was taken as a given by the Coalition States. Therefore, the Coalition States decided that there was sufficient justification for a military invasion to forcefully remove Iraq's WMD permanently, which these States carried out in March 2003.[284] After the invasion, the Security Council unanimously adopted Resolution 1483, which called for international verification that Iraq had ceased its WMD programs.[285] As time has told, Iraq seems to have ceased its WMD programs before the invasion, thus making the main rationale for the invasion meritless, assuming, *arguendo*, that it had any merit to begin with. UNMOVIC suspended inspections with the invasion in 2003. The Security Council terminated UNMOVIC's mandate in 2007.[286] Termination of the most intrusive disarmament regime to date was relatively unceremonious. Although Iraq had tried to frustrate UNSCOM's and UNMOVIC's activities at nearly every step, save at the very end, these entities were quite successful in removing Iraq's WMD capabilities.[287] This success can be credited to the Security Council's control of these entities, which, along with the help of strong leadership of UNSCOM and UNMOVIC, enabled them largely to avoid the meddling of outside entities such as other States, the IAEA

[281] See Kono, *supra* note 254, at 104–105; THAKUR, *supra* note 97, at 168 (claiming that the UNSCOM and UNMOVIC inspections were a success); BOWLES, *supra* note 275, at 162 (asserting, among other things, that Hans Blix told the Security Council that UNMOVIC could finish inspections of Iraq within a few months); GRAY, *supra* note 93, at 272 (arguing that, after some initial delays, Iraq began to co-operate more fully in February 2003).

[282] See BOWLES, *supra* note 275, at 162; Findlay, *supra* note 250, at 147–148.

[283] See Kono, *supra* note 254, at 94.

[284] See generally BOWLES, *supra* note 275, at 11–12; SUTTERLIN, *supra* note 229, at 106. But see GRAY, *supra* note 93, at 192 (asserting that the United Kingdom's purpose in invading Iraq in 2003 was to disarm Iraq of its WMD, although the United States' purpose was regime change).

[285] See S.C. Res. 1483, ¶ 11, UN Doc. S/RES/1483 (May 22, 2003).

[286] See S.C. Res. 1762, ¶ 1, UN Doc. S/RES/1762 (June 29, 2007).

[287] See SUTTERLIN, *supra* note 229, at 99 (asserting that Iraq's disarmament was a notable achievement by the United Nations); Findlay, *supra* note 250, at 150–151.

Board of Governors, and the UN Secretariat.[288] It remains to be seen whether UNSCOM and UNMOVIC will be useful models for coercive disarmament activities in the future. Some commentators believe that they will,[289] while others do not.[290] Those in the latter group formed this opinion before the Security Council adopted strong disarmament resolutions against Iran and North Korea, as can be seen simply by comparing the dates of publication of those resolutions and those opinions. In reality, these resolutions have gone beyond those regarding Iraq in many ways, such as the clear imposition of *treaty* obligations on these States. Before delving into those later resolutions, the following subsection examines several of the pressing legal issues that arose from the coercive measures that the Security Council took against Iraq.

3.2.3.4 Iraq's acceptance of Resolution 687

The resolutions involved with the WMD disarmament of Iraq raise the most pressing legal issues of any of the resolutions discussed in this chapter. The four main legal issues discussed here are: Iraq's acceptance of Resolution 687, UNSCOM's strength, due-process concerns with Security Council proceedings, and Security Council imposition of treaty obligations on States.

A major question that arises when discussing the disarmament measures under Security Council Resolution 687 is whether Iraq's acceptance of Resolution 687 constitutes consent, and so renders the case not one of coercion by the Security Council. Indeed, Iraq accepted, though quite grudgingly, the cease-fire terms of Resolution 687 on April 6, 1991,[291] as required by paragraph 33 of that resolution, which stated that the cease-fire would become effective "upon official notification by Iraq to the Secretary-General and to the Security Council of its acceptance."[292]

It is important to note that Iraq technically was obliged to accept Resolution 687 as a member of the United Nations, in accordance with Article 25, which states that States are bound to "accept and carry out the

[288] See Findlay, *supra* note 250, at 150–152; Ekeus, *supra* note 133, at 67, 71.

[289] See, e.g., Kono, *supra* note 254, at 91.

[290] See, e.g., SUTTERLIN, *supra* note 229, at 107.

[291] See Identical Letters dated 6 April 1991 from the Permanent Representative of Iraq to the United Nations addressed respectively to the Secretary-General and the President of the Security Council, at 7, UN Doc. S/22456 (April 6, 1991).

[292] S.C. Res. 687, ¶ 33, UN Doc. S/RES/687 (April 3, 1991).

decisions of the Security Council,"[293] thus suggesting that Iraq's acceptance under paragraph 33 of Resolution 687 was unnecessary for Resolution 687 to come into effect. Nonetheless, Iraq's acceptance of the demands of the coercer (here, the Security Council) does not diminish the coercive nature of those demands, just as an unruly bar patron's decision to leave the bar under the threat of the bouncer's violence in a way makes the patron's decision to leave no more voluntary than had the bouncer actually used force to come to the same result.[294]

3.2.3.5 UNSCOM's strength

What stands out in Iraq's WMD disarmament saga is the broad authority the Security Council gave UNSCOM and UNMOVIC to inspect and disarm Iraq. The Security Council initially had considerable assurances that Iraq would co-operate in this endeavor, including Iraq's express acceptance of the terms of Resolution 687. Once it became clear that Iraq would not co-operate, however, the Security Council and UNSCOM were forced to decide how far they were willing to go to compel Iraq to comply with Resolution 687. What resulted was a gradual ratcheting up of coercive measures against Iraq based on the imposition of obligations under Resolution 687. Resolution 1441, of course, represents the outer limit of what the Security Council was willing to do to disarm Iraq at that time. In Resolution 1441, the Security Council refrained from expressly authorizing the use of force against Iraq for a second time, but it also did not expressly end the ability to use force under Resolutions 678, 686 and 687. All of these resolutions and efforts to disarm Iraq seem rather devoid of Iraqi consent. However, Iraq gave its consent to future Security Council actions when it joined the United Nations, and gave up an expectation of freedom from interference when it chose to develop WMD in violation of WMD norms and when it chose to invade its neighbor.[295] The Security Council was perfectly within its administrative

[293] UN Charter, Art. 25; see generally Sonnenfeld, *supra* note 39, at 120–144 (1988) (discussing the legal effects of Security Council resolutions under UN Charter Art. 25). See also UN Charter, Art. 48(1) ("The action required to carry out the decisions of the Security Council for the maintenance of international peace and security shall be taken by all the Members of the United Nations or by some of them, as the Security Council may determine").

[294] See Anderson, *supra* note 85.

[295] See Harald Müller, *Dealing with WMD Crises: The Role of the United Nations in Compliance Politics*, in ARMS CONTROL AFTER IRAQ: NORMATIVE AND OPERATIONAL CHALLENGES 114, 128 (WAHEGURU PAL SINGH SIDHU and RAMESH THAKUR ed., 2006) (asserting that Iraq was in trouble with the Security

powers, provided under UN Charter Article 29, to establish a subsidiary body tasked to disarm a target under a Chapter VII mandate.[296] The Security Council's choice to use this power within the disarmament and arms control context marked a shift away from nuclear *regulation* to a stronger focus on nuclear *enforcement* in the post-Cold War era.[297]

These enforcement decisions are made without consulting – at least openly – any other entities, including the UN Secretary-General or the ICJ, regarding the existence of an actual violation,[298] and are adopted as powerful Chapter VII resolutions that signal to the target State that military force backs up these decisions. As explained in the subsections below, the Security Council's imposition of stiff nuclear non-proliferation obligations on Iran and North Korea in this same manner signals that the Security Council's emphasis on nuclear disarmament *enforcement* with supposed non-nuclear-weapon States is a trend that likely will stay.

3.2.3.6 Due-process concerns with Security Council proceedings

Given the failure to discover WMD in Iraq after the 2003 invasion, serious questions have arisen as to what types of due-process safeguards can be put in place in order for the international community to avoid making such important decisions based on weak evidence. For example, one would expect that States that lodge complaints with the Security Council must provide some evidence to support their claims,[299] or that the Security Council must find evidence elsewhere upon which to satisfy its presumed burdens of proof and evidence in providing a fair

Council not for violations of a WMD treaty obligation but for breaching disarmament and arms control obligations under Resolution 687). However, the Security Council's imposition of obligations through Resolution 687 stemmed from Iraq's suspected covert development of nuclear weapons in violation of its NPT obligations prior to Resolution 687, which the Security Council confirmed was a violation of the NPT in Resolution 707.

[296] See THAKUR, *supra* note 97, at 168. [297] See Dallmeyer, *supra* note 133, at 136.

[298] See Lewis and Joyner, *supra* note 231, at 309 (calling for the Security Council and the UN Secretary-General to work in concert to impose coercive arms control measures on alleged violators of WMD non-proliferation norms); ALLAN GOTLIEB, DISARMAMENT AND INTERNATIONAL LAW: A STUDY OF THE ROLE OF LAW IN THE DISARMAMENT PROCESS 39 (1965) (discussing a US proposal that the ICJ should have jurisdiction over all disputes concerning the interpretation and application of the disarmament treaty).

[299] See JOZEF GOLDBLAT, ARMS CONTROL: A GUIDE TO NEGOTIATIONS AND AGREEMENTS 209 (1994).

proceeding.[300] If the theory is correct that multilateral decision-making provides greater legitimacy over unilateral decision-making in the context of non-proliferation,[301] one would hope that part of that legitimacy would derive from greater procedural safeguards within that multilateral process, even though that multilateral process might not be required to provide such procedural safeguards.

Despite such seemingly reasonable expectations, Security Council decision-making procedures are not known for their due-process safeguards, and it might even be too much to expect a political body such as the Security Council to provide due-process safeguards. After all, in responding to a General Assembly request to interpret UN Charter Article 4(1) to see whether political organs (in particular the Security Council) could consider other factors than those listed in Article 4(1) in deciding on States' UN membership applications,[302] the ICJ declared in its 1948 *Conditions of Admission of a State to Membership in the United Nations* advisory opinion that political organs such as the Security Council are "entitled to base their arguments and their vote upon political considerations."[303] However, the ICJ went on to say that such political organs are not "emancipated from all duty to respect the law."[304] In particular, the ICJ determined that these political organs must consider the conditions provided in Article 4(1) when deciding on a membership application, and essentially required the political organ to decide similar cases in a similar way when the law provides for some limitations on the organ's power.[305] In short, the Security Council is bound to abide by certain limitations on its powers, thus providing the possibility of due process for target States inasmuch as the UN Charter

[300] See generally Karel Wellens, *The UN Security Council and New Threats to the Peace: Back to the Future*, 8 J. Conflict & Sec. L. 15 (2003) (discussing the Security Council's burdens of proof and evidence when determining threats to the peace); Nicolas Angelet, *International Law Limits to the Security Council*, in United Nations Sanctions and International Law 71 (Vera Gowlland-Debbas ed., 2001) (same); Erika de Wet, The Chapter VII Powers of the United Nations Security Council 352–353 (2004).

[301] See G. John Ikenberry, *America's Imperial Ambition*, For. Aff., Oct./Sept. 2002, at 56.

[302] See *Conditions of Admission of a State to Membership in the United Nations*, Advisory Opinion, 1948 ICJ Rep. 57, 58 (May 28).

[303] Ibid., at 85. [304] Ibid.

[305] See ibid. But see Abi-Saab, *supra* note 18, at 28 (noting how the Security Council has "inconsistent treatment of like situations").

and the Security Council's Provisional Rules of Procedure provide for such process.

According to the Security Council's Provisional Rules of Procedure, the Security Council is to meet in public. However, informal consultations generally are held in private, which would appear to be where most of the actual decision-making occurs.[306] Concerning the Security Council meetings, UN Charter Article 31 provides nonmembers of the Security Council that are specially affected by questions before the Security Council with the *possibility* of "participat[ing], without vote, in the discussion of any question brought before the Security Council,"[307] while Article 32 *requires* that nonmembers of the Security Council that are "a party to a dispute under consideration by the Security Council" be allowed to "participate, without vote, in the discussion relating to the dispute."[308] To make the distinction clear, Article 31 involves permissive language with States that are specially affected by the discussions, while Article 32 involves mandatory language in requiring that actual disputant States be allowed to participate in the discussions on the dispute.[309] This general arrangement was designed to appease smaller States that wanted reassurances they would be able to participate in Security Council discussions that specially affected them, with the distinction between Articles 31 and 32 being a type of compromise with the larger States.[310] However, how it works is that States that are merely specially affected by a resolution have no right to be invited to participate in the debates, there being only limited options for these States formally to object to the Security Council's decision-making process.[311]

[306] See Sydney D. Bailey, The Procedure of the UN Security Council 53–54, 60–75 (1975); Loie Feuerie, *Informal Consultation: A Mechanism in Security Council Decision-Making*, 18 NYU J. Int'l L & Pol. 267 (1985).

[307] UN Charter, Art. 31. [308] UN Charter, Art. 32.

[309] See *Legal Consequences for States of the Continued Presence of South Africa in Namibia (South-West Africa) Notwithstanding Security Council Resolution* 276 (1970), Advisory Opinion, 1971 ICJ Rep. 16, 22 (June 21).

[310] See Rudolf Dolzer, *Article 31*, in The Charter of the United Nations: A Commentary 573, 573–580 (Bruno Simma ed., 2002) (explaining the distinction between Articles 31 and 32); Rudolf Dolzer, *Article 32*, in The Charter of the United Nations: A Commentary 580, 580–582 (Bruno Simma ed., 2002) (same); R. B. Russel and J. E. Muther, A History of the United Nations Charter 651–653 (1958).

[311] See Nicholas Angelet, *Protest against Security Council Decisions*, in International Law: Theory and Practice: Essays in Honour of Eric Suy 277 (Karel Wellens ed., 1998).

States have expressed a variety of frustrations with Articles 31 and 32 in the context of being invited to participate in Security Council discussions. Certain States have been frustrated by the Security Council's refusal to invite them to discussions when they see themselves as being specially affected, such as India in the lead-up to Resolution 1172.[312] Such frustration can be expected where the UN Charter fails to define key phrases like "specially affected."[313] Even if a State is invited into the proceedings, however, there is no guarantee that it will be allowed an opportunity to be heard *before* the Security Council votes on the resolution that creates significant obligations on that State, as Iran complained regarding Resolution 1696.[314] Indeed, there are two barriers to these provisions providing a considerable degree of protection for target States: first, such States must be *invited* by the Security Council, and second, the Security Council is free to refer to the questions and disputes under its consideration under Articles 31 and 32 as "issues," "concerns," "matters," or any other euphemism that would relieve the Security Council of having to decide whether to extend an invitation, or instead assert that the *party* to the dispute is not a State at all.[315] The ICJ noted in its 1971 *Namibia* advisory opinion that the Security Council's

[312] The Permanent Representative of India to the United Nations, Letter dated 4 June 1998 from the Permanent Representative of India to the United Nations Addressed to the President of the Security Council, at 1, UN Doc. S/1998/464 (June 4, 1998) (reporting that India complained, during the debates leading up to the adoption of Resolution 1172, that the Security Council "disregarded [Article 31] by not giving India an opportunity to participate in the discussions on this draft," thus showing how the Security Council "is neither open nor transparent"). But see UN SCOR, 2666th mtg., at 2–5, UN Doc. S/PV.2666 (Feb. 24, 1986) (noting that the president of the Security Council made it clear that some States that were not necessarily welcome during the debates over Iraq's use of chemical weapons against Iran were nonetheless allowed to participate).

[313] See Dolzer, *Article 31*, *supra* note 310, at 576–577.

[314] See UN Doc. S/PV.5500, *supra* note 126, at 2 (reporting that Iran complained that the president of the Security Council did not allow it to address the Council before the vote for Resolution 1696, even though it had requested such an opportunity on several occasions, thus reflecting "the degree of the Council's transparency and fairness that it has adopted a presidential statement and a resolution without even allowing the views of the concerned party to be heard").

[315] But see Dolzer, *Article 31*, *supra* note 310, at 577–578 (asserting that a State party to a dispute has the *right* to participate under Article 31, although it shows signs of confusing the role of permissive and obligatory language when relying on Rule 37 of the Provisional Rules of Procedure for support of that right and that Rule merely states that non-members *may* be invited to participate by the Security Council, thus putting the State on a "weak legal foundation").

classification of the question of Namibia as a *situation* on its agenda, as opposed to a dispute, led to South Africa's inability to demand to be allowed to participate in the discussions under UN Charter Article 32.[316] There, the ICJ required South Africa to object to that classification when the Security Council made it and refused to allow it to be reclassified through the adjudicative process.[317]

Assuming, *arguendo*, that such States are liberally granted the ability to participate actively in Security Council debates, they have neither the right to a reasoned decision from the Security Council that can stand up to scrutiny nor the possibility of appeal,[318] among other standard due-process safeguards. Nevertheless, critics could reasonably argue that the Security Council is becoming more conscious of due-process considerations. For example, the Security Council demonstrated its understanding of the significance of due process when it established the ICTY and ICTR as subsidiary bodies and gave accused individuals such rights as the right to be present for the trial,[319] in accordance with Article 14(3)(d) of the International Covenant on Civil and Political Rights.[320] Although Security Council Resolutions 1267 and 1373 showed serious deficiencies in terms of due process, in that they required States to adopt sanctions

316 See *Legal Consequences for States of the Continued Presence of South Africa in Namibia (South-West Africa) Notwithstanding Security Council Resolution* 276 (1970), Advisory Opinion, 1971 ICJ Rep. 16, 22 (June 21).

317 See ibid., at 22–23 (June 21).

318 See *Request for Indication of Provisional Measures, Concerning Questions of Interpretation and Application of 1971 Montreal Convention Arising from Aerial Incident at Lockerbie (Libya v. US)*, Provisional Measures, 1992 ICJ Rep. 114, 124; see also Frederic L. Kirgis, Jr., *The Security Council's First Fifty Years*, 89 AM. J. INT'L L. 506, 527 (1995) (claiming that no judicial review is available, and thus the Security Council is left alone to decide how far to stretch the United Nation's purposes and principles). Please note that this was written before the *Lockerbie* case. But see Thomas M. Franck, *The "Powers of Appreciation": Who Is the Ultimate Guardian of UN Legality*, 86 AM. J. INT'L L. 519, 521–522 (1992) (comparing the *Lockerbie* case with the US Supreme Court case *Marbury v. Madison*, and suggesting that *Lockerbie* might also establish judicial review on the international level); John Dugard, *Judicial Review of Sanctions*, in UNITED NATIONS SANCTIONS AND INTERNATIONAL LAW 83, 87 (VERA GOWLLAND-DEBBAS ed., 2001) (citing ICJ and ICTY review as examples).

319 See Statute of the International Criminal Tribunal for the Former Yugoslavia, S.C. Res. 827, Art. 21(4), UN Doc. S/RES/827 (May 27, 1993); Statute of the International Criminal Tribunal for Rwanda, S.C. Res. 955, UN Doc. S/RES/955/Annex Art. 20(4)(d) (Nov. 8, 1994).

320 International Covenant on Civil and Political Rights, Art. 14(3)(d), Dec. 16, 1966, 999 U.N.T.S. 171.

against suspected terrorists "without delay,"[321] these deficiencies gradually have been improved. Such an improvement is likely due to the pressure that European Union member States and Switzerland placed on the Security Council to establish a delisting process for those who found themselves on the lists of terrorists maintained by the 1267 Committee;[322] a delisting procedure was not included in Resolution 1526 but eventually was included in Resolution 1730.[323] Despite this evidence of consciousness of due-process safeguards, alleged violations of nuclear non-proliferation obligations by such States as Iran and North Korea are not likely to inspire the Security Council to protect their due-process rights in the same way as those of *individuals* before the international criminal tribunals or on Security Council committee terrorist lists, if one can indeed say that these individuals' due-process rights have been protected.

As with Iraq's alleged WMD in 2002, there was no meaningful examination of the evidence that US Secretary of State Colin Powell presented

[321] See S.C. Res. 1373, ¶ 1(c), UN Doc. S/RES/1373 (Sept. 28, 2001) ("Freeze *without delay* funds" (emphasis added)); S.C. Res. 1267, ¶ 2, UN Doc. S/RES/1267 (Oct. 15, 1999) ("Demands that the Taliban turn over Usama bin Laden *without further delay*" (emphasis added)); see also S.C. Res. 1526, ¶ 1(a), UN Doc. S/RES/1526 (Jan. 30, 2004) ("Freeze *without delay* funds" (emphasis added)). See generally Peter Gutherie, *Security Council Sanctions and the Protection of Individual Rights*, 60 NYU Annual Survey of American Law 491 (2004) (discussing the due-process problems with the Security Council's listing process of suspected terrorists); Watson Institute for International Studies, *Strengthening Targeted Sanctions through Fair and Clear Procedures*, White Paper, March 30, 2006, *available at* watsoninstitute.org/pub/Strenthening_Targeted_Sanctions.pdf (last visited June 9, 2011) (same).

[322] See Richard Ryan, Permanent Representative of Ireland to the United Nations, Statement on Behalf of European Union, UN SCOR, 59th Sess., 4892nd mtg., at 23–24, UN Doc. S/PV.4892 (Jan. 14, 2004); Pierre Helg, Deputy Permanent Representative of Switzerland to the United Nations, ibid., at 28.

[323] See S.C. Res. 1526, UN Doc. S/SER/1526 (Jan. 30, 2004); S.C. Res. 1730, UN Doc. S/RES/1730/Annex (Dec. 19, 2006). These procedures appear to have been modeled after the delisting procedures established by the Resolution 1267 Committee in November 2006, in which the entity on the list can petition its government of residence or citizenship to review the case. That government then approaches the government that initially put the entity on the list in order to consider the justifications for removal. Either government can request that the Committee remove the entity from the list, which can occur by consensus of the Committee members or by a decision of the Security Council. See Security Council 1267 Committee, Guidelines of the Security Council Committee Established Pursuant to Resolution 1267 (1999) for the Conduct of Its Work, Nov. 7, 2002, as amended Nov. 29, 2006, at 7, available at http://www.un.org/Docs/sc/committees/1267/1267_guidelines.pdf (last visited Dec. 28, 2010). However, Resolution 1730 also provides listed entities the possibility of submitting delisting requests through the UN Secretariat. See S.C. Res. 1730, UN Doc. S/RES/1730/Annex (Dec. 19, 2006).

to the Security Council during a special meeting on February 5, 2003. Secretary Powell presented the US case for invading Iraq to other foreign ministers for over an hour, and the other foreign ministers merely read their prepared speeches after Secretary Powell had finished his presentation.[324] Where such sensitive topics as nuclear non-proliferation and the possibility of invading another State that allegedly possesses nuclear capabilities is involved, one would hope that the standard of proof would be sufficiently high to avoid reliance on questionable evidence to make such a key determination. Perhaps clear and convincing evidence would be the most appropriate standard in cases in which military action is threatened, while non-military sanctions might be authorized on a lesser standard, such as a preponderance of the evidence.[325] Possible reliance on classified information provided by national intelligence services further exacerbates the hypothetical problem of the Security Council's meeting evidentiary standards.[326] Information provided by national intelligence services is politically problematic because spying typically is prohibited under national laws, while international law does not expressly prohibit it,[327] so criminal-law arguments relating to "fruit of the poison tree" seem apropos. From an evidentiary and human rights perspective, such information ought to be viewed with considerable suspicion where it and the provider of that particular of the information cannot be subjected to rigorous cross-examination.[328] At a minimum, the Security Council might want to establish some procedural rules for admitting evidence under its powers provided by UN Charter Article 30. For example, the Security Council might allow evidence from treaty bodies, but require certain corroboration of evidence provided by national intelligence networks,[329] at least where military action is proposed. Reports

324 See Müller, *supra* note 295, at 128. 325 See Wellens, *supra* note 300, at 23.

326 See Simon Chesterman, Shared Secrets: Intelligence and Collective Security 47–54 (2006).

327 See John Norton Moore et al. (eds.), National Security Law 433 (1990).

328 See, e.g., International Covenant on Civil and Political Rights, Art. 14, Dec. 16, 1966, 999 U.N.T.S. 171 (providing a right to cross-examination); Charter of the International Military Tribunal Annexed to the London Agreement for the Prosecution and Punishment of the Major War Criminals of the European Axis, Art. 16(e), Aug. 8, 1945, 82 U.N.T.S. 280 (same); Statute of the International Tribunal for the Prosecution of Persons Responsible for Serious Violations of International Humanitarian Law Committed in the Territory of the Former Yugoslavia Since 1991, Art. 21(4)(e), annexed to Report of the Secretary-General Pursuant to Paragraph 2 of Security Council Resolution 808 (1993), U.N. SCOR, 48th Sess., UN Doc. S/25704 (1993) (same).

329 See Müller, *supra* note 295, at 133.

suggest that the reason such corroboration has not been provided in the past was in order to "protect intelligence sources,"[330] and there are no indications in the public record to suggest that this practice has changed. Even if such corroboration were to be provided, the question still remains whether one can trust the information provided by national intelligence networks without adequate examination of that particular evidence. As one commentator controversially noted in 1999 about the Security Council's reliance on national intelligence networks, "The result of the American hijacking of the UN's intelligence activities was that Saddam survived but UNSCOM did not,"[331] suggesting perhaps that the evidence from national intelligence sources was unreliable, at least at that time. This study does not necessarily condone that assertion, but it nevertheless adheres to the general rule that evidence provided by experts who cannot be rigorously cross-examined should not be relied upon, especially in such sensitive situations where the use of force is involved.

In addition, a procedure of advocacy might also be useful where one State would act as impartial prosecutor and the other as defense counsel, which is largely what already happens informally, and with the target State having a *right* to participate in the deliberations.[332] The Security Council might also place considerable weight on determining a target State's intent, much like a criminal judge or jury would be asked to do, which could be done by calling in an expert group to assess the evidence and by calling neighboring States as so-called witnesses.[333] With all of this information, the Security Council would be in a better position to craft its response specifically to the intents of the target State and the magnitude of the threat.

[330] Letter from the Permanent Representative of the United Kingdom of Great Britain and Northern Ireland to the United Nations addressed to the President of the Security Council, ¶ 3, UN Doc. S/2001/949 (Oct. 8, 2001). See also Kirgis, *supra* note 318, at 516 (asserting that the US could provide evidence to the Security Council that Libya sponsored terrorism, but in such a way so as to "protect intelligence sources"); John Quigley, *The United Nations Security Council: Promethean Protector or Helpless Hostage?*, 35 Tex. Int'l L.J. 129, 140 (2000) (describing instances where the Security Council has relied exclusively on evidence provided by national intelligence networks); Simon Chesterman, *UNaccountable The United Nations, Emergency Powers, and the Rule of Law*, 42 Vand. J. Transnat'l L. 1509, 1519 (2009) (characterizing the freezing of terrorist assets as "preventive acts based on secret intelligence [that] look more like a form of punitive confiscation unsupported by evidence").

[331] Seymour M. Hersh, *Saddam's Best Friend*, New Yorker, April 5, 1999, at 32.

[332] See Müller, *supra* note 295, at 133.

[333] See ibid., at 121, 133–134.

While the Security Council is a political body and not a court of law, and could conceivably act without any significant evidence as support,[334] such baseless action would forfeit whatever legitimacy the Security Council has were such arbitrariness to be made public. As Inger Österdahl notes,

> It is not illegal on the part of the Security Council to be arbitrary, but if it becomes apparent that its choice of situations in which to intervene is arbitrary, both in the sense that some situations are intervened in but not others presenting the same characteristics, and that the situations in which the Council does intervene are very different from one another and the Council does not convincingly or consistently show in its resolutions why it intervenes in these situations, or precisely what makes these situations worthy of Security Council consideration, then the decisions and the possible follow-up action of the Security Council risk losing a large measure of legitimacy.[335]

Again, this essentially is what the ICJ stated in its 1948 *Conditions of Admission of a State to Membership in the United Nations* advisory opinion, as analyzed above. By adding these types of due-process safeguards, the Security Council would run less of a risk of relying on incorrect evidence and losing legitimacy, as could have occurred had it authorized the use of force in Resolution 1441 based on Secretary Powell's presentation of US evidence for going to war with Iraq.

3.2.3.7 Reiterating treaty obligations

There is the legal question whether Resolution 687 imposed *treaty* obligations on Iraq. Paragraph 7 of Resolution 687 invited Iraq to ratify the Biological Weapons Convention (BWC),[336] as well as to reaffirm its obligations under the 1925 Geneva Gas Protocol and the NPT.[337] The reaffirmation of Iraq's obligations under the NPT through this Chapter VII resolution causes problems by bringing these pre-existing

[334] See Vera Gowlland-Debbas, *The Limits of Unilateral Enforcement of Community Objectives in the Framework of UN Peace Maintenance*, 11 EUR. J. INT'L L. 361, 364 (2000) (asserting that "the violation [of international law] becom[es] therefore a constitutent element of the threat to, or breach of, the peace"). However, a violation of international law is not necessarily needed for the Security Council to find a threat to the peace.

[335] INGER ÖSTERDAHL, THREAT TO THE PEACE: THE INTERPRETATION BY THE SECURITY COUNCIL OF ARTICLE 39 OF THE UN CHARTER 103–110 (1998).

[336] See Convention on the Prohibition of the Development, Production and Stockpiling of Bacteriological (Biological) and Toxin Weapons and on Their Destruction (BWC), April 10, 1972, 26.1 U.S.T. 583, 1015 U.N.T.S. 163.

[337] See S.C. Res. 687, ¶¶ 7, 11, UN Doc. S/RES/687 (April 3, 1991).

obligations within the UN legal framework. In other words, if a State breaches a nuclear non-proliferation obligation, there likely are a host of countermeasures under the treaty and under the international law of State responsibility (which falls outside the treaty) that the other parties can take to encourage compliance.[338] When the Security Council requires States to abide by the same obligations as already required by a treaty, it opens up another, parallel, avenue through which to compel compliance with the international obligation: by the Security Council imposing sanctions for violating Article 25, which requires States to accept and carry out the Security Council's decisions. This raises the question whether it matters that the Security Council brings these obligations within the UN legal framework. Resolution 232 of 1966 suggests that there is a particular set of sanctions for violating Security Council decisions when it states that "failure or refusal by any of them to implement the present resolution shall constitute a violation of Article 25 of the United Nations Charter."[339] In reality, there does not appear to be a difference between the sanctions the Security Council will apply to a violation of Article 25 and a sanction in response to a "regular" threat to international peace and security. Indeed, as Alfred Rubin notes, no provision in the UN Charter specifies the measures to be taken when a State violates Article 25, and so the moral–political order seems to be left to decide the appropriate sanctions on its own.[340] This point notwithstanding, incorporation into UN law could be significant as treaties typically allow States to withdraw from their obligations, and when

[338] See generally Draft Articles on State Responsibility, Arts. 50–51, G.A. Res. 56/83, U.N. GAOR, 56th Sess., Supp. No. 10, UN Doc. A/RES/56/10 (Dec. 12, 2001) (providing the rules on countermeasures); David J. Bederman, *Counterintuiting Countermeasures*, 96 Am. J. Int'l L. 817, 827 (2002); Oscar Schachter, *International Law in Theory and Practice*, 178 Rec. des cours 185–186 (1982-V); N. Jansen Calamita, *Sanctions, Countermeasures, and the Iranian Nuclear Issue*, 42 Vand. J. Transnat'l L. 1393 (2009) (discussing the relationship between Security Council non-forcible coercive measures and countermeasures in the case of Iran).

[339] S.C. Res. 232, ¶ 3, UN Doc. S/RES/232 (Dec. 16, 1966).

[340] See Alfred P. Rubin, *Secession and Self-Determination: A Legal, Moral, and Political Analysis*, 36 Stan. J. Int'l L. 253, 257 n. 17 (2000). Please note, however, that some commentators have argued persuasively that violators of Security Council-created sanctions should have the same measures imposed on them under Article 25. See, e.g., Jeremy P. Carver, *Making Financial Sanctions Work: Preconditions for Successful Implementation of Sanctions by the Implementing State* (Expert Seminar on Targeting UN Financial Sanctions, Paper for Working Group 1, 1998), available at http://www.seco.admin.ch/themen/00513/00620/00639/00641/index.htmllang=en (last visited May 24, 2011).

treaties do not have such a provision, Article 56 of the Vienna Convention on the Law of Treaties will provide the ability to withdraw, assuming that it can be established that the treaty parties meant to admit the possibility of withdrawal and that the right to withdraw can be implied from the treaty's nature.[341] However, there is no obvious ability to withdraw from Security Council resolutions. Therefore, when the Security Council incorporates treaty obligations into the UN legal framework by reiterating them in a Security Council resolution, it becomes even clearer that these treaty obligations bind the parties.

Critics arguing against the significance of reiterating treaty obligations within Security Council resolutions could try to adopt ad hoc ICJ Judge Ahmed Sadek El-Kosheri's argument in the ICJ *Lockerbie* case. There, Judge El-Kosheri asserted in his dissent that States do not have to obey Security Council decisions that have no basis in the Charter, because Article 25 requires States to obey Council decisions "in accordance with the present Charter,"[342] and treaty obligations do not have a basis in the Charter. However, this is a weak argument because nothing in the UN Charter stops the Security Council from incorporating non-UN documents into its decisions. On the contrary, the Security Council regularly incorporates non-UN documents into its decisions by reference to these documents, just as Resolutions 255 and 984 with regard to the NPT and various security assurances to non-nuclear-weapon States incorporated the unilateral statements of permanent members of the Security Council. Such decisions will be adopted in accordance with the UN Charter where the Security Council invokes the correct phrasing contained in Article 39 to unlock its Chapter VII powers.

3.2.3.8 Suspending Iraq's NPT rights

Some commentators assert that Resolution 687 altered Iraq's treaty rights under the NPT. NPT Article IV(1) acknowledges the "inalienable right of all the Parties to the Treaty to develop research, production and use of nuclear energy for peaceful purposes without discrimination and in conformity with articles I and II of this Treaty."[343] NPT Article IV(2) allows States parties "to facilitate, and

[341] See VCLT, *supra* note 19, Art. 56.

[342] *Questions of Interpretation and Application of the 1971 Montreal Convention arising from the Aerial Incident at Lockerbie (Libya v. US)*, 1992 ICJ Rep. 199, 206–207 (J. El-Kosheri, dissenting opinion).

[343] NPT, *supra* note 13, Art. IV(1).

have the right to participate in, the fullest possible exchange of equipment, materials and scientific and technological information for the peaceful uses of nuclear energy."[344] Dorinda Dallmeyer asserts that the Security Council did not allow such civilian use when it adopted Resolution 687 due to the distrust Iraq created by developing a nuclear weapons program while party to the NPT.[345] However, paragraph 12 of Resolution 687 only requires Iraq "not to acquire or develop nuclear weapons or nuclear-weapon-usable material or any subsystems or components or any research, development, support or manufacturing facilities related to the above."[346] In support of the idea that Iraq was still free to develop nuclear energy for peaceful purposes, paragraph 13 of Resolution 687 calls for the IAEA director-general, through the UN Secretary-General and UNSCOM, to come up with a plan to monitor and verify Iraq's compliance with the nuclear aspects of this resolution, "including an inventory of all nuclear material in Iraq subject to the Agency's verification and inspections to confirm that Agency safeguards cover all relevant nuclear activities in Iraq."[347] That same paragraph referred to Iraq's "rights and obligations" under the NPT.[348] The Security Council likely would not have used this language if it were simultaneously suspending Iraq's ability to develop its peaceful use of nuclear energy, even though there admittedly is a fine line between developing nuclear energy for peaceful and for aggressive purposes.[349]

Instead of Resolution 687, however, paragraph 3(f) of Resolution 707 interfered with Iraq's NPT rights to develop nuclear energy for peaceful purposes, because it required Iraq to

> [h]alt all nuclear activities of any kind, except for use of isotopes for medical, agricultural or industrial purposes, until the Council determines that Iraq is in full compliance with the present resolution and with paragraphs 12 and 13 of Resolution 687 (1991) and the Agency determines that Iraq is in full compliance with its safeguards agreement with the Agency . . .[350]

Therefore, it is true that the Security Council coercively removed Iraq's NPT right to develop nuclear energy for peaceful purposes. Not only

[344] Ibid. Art. IV(2). [345] See Dallmeyer, *supra* note 133, at 136.
[346] S.C. Res. 687, ¶ 12, UN Doc. S/RES/687 (April 3, 1991). [347] Ibid., ¶ 13. [348] Ibid.
[349] See THAKUR, *supra* note 97, at 172 ("For nuclear energy for peaceful purposes can be pursued legitimately to the point of being a screwdriver away from a weapons capability").
[350] S.C. Res. 707, ¶ 3(f), UN Doc. S/RES/707 (Aug. 15, 1991).

this, but paragraph 4 of Resolution 707 also divested Iraq of its ownership rights in the WMD and WMD-related materials that UNSCOM "destroyed, removed, or rendered harmless," which property conceivably had a value of many millions of dollars.[351] Such divestiture of treaty-based and contract-based rights should cause target States to seek other options than Security Council resolution, where available.

3.2.4 *India, Pakistan, and Resolution 1172*

India and Pakistan have had nuclear ambitions since the 1960s, when China was developing its own nuclear weapons. India appears to have tested a nuclear device in 1974 in what some refer to as the "Smiling Buddha" tests in the Rajasthan Desert,[352] which led Pakistan to begin its own nuclear development program. Pakistan tested an intermediate-range nuclear missile in April 1998 that it had named after a twelfth-century Muslim warrior responsible for having conquered a part of India, which prompted India to conduct five underground nuclear tests the following month.[353] Pakistan responded with five nuclear tests of its own just two weeks later.[354] Pakistan's provocation in 1998 is somewhat surprising, given that Pakistan had prided itself on being a leader in nuclear non-proliferation issues in South Asia before it tested its nuclear device in 1998,[355] and even asserted that it offered a bilateral test ban with India that India rejected,[356] only to change its approach when it appeared that the testing of its own nuclear devices was needed in order to defend itself and to deter aggression.[357]

India and Pakistan's nuclear tests in 1998 took most of the world by surprise. Prophetically, before India's nuclear tests in 1996, Thakur pointed out that "[f]aced with U.S.-led United Nations coercion, an isolated, sullen, and resentful India is more likely to respond with an open nuclear programme, including a . . . series of nuclear tests."[358] The initial response from the Security Council was a statement by its

[351] Ibid., ¶ 4.
[352] See *India and Pakistan: Tense Neighbours*, BBC News, Dec. 16, 2001, at www.news.bbc.co.uk/1/hi/world/south_asia/102201.stm (last visited May 25, 2011).
[353] See ibid. [354] See ibid.
[355] See Letter from Ahmad Kamal, Permanent Representative of Pakistan to the United Nations, to the Secretary-General, United Nations (May 29, 1998), at 2, UN Doc. A/52/920 (June 1, 1998).
[356] See ibid., at 8. [357] See ibid., at 2.
[358] Thakur, *supra* note 97, 163 (quoting Ramesh Thakur, *Nuclear India Needs Coaxing, Not Coercion*, Austl., Sept. 6, 1996).

president, reiterating the special statement that had been made by all Security Council member heads of State on January 31, 1992, that the "proliferation of all weapons of mass destruction constitutes a threat to international peace and security."[359] Resolution 1172 was adopted three weeks later, on June 6, 1998, and not only "[*c*]*ondemn*[*ed*] the nuclear tests,"[360] but also "[*d*]*emand*[*ed*] that India and Pakistan refrain from further nuclear tests. . . ."[361] Interestingly, the foreign ministers of the permanent members of the Security Council apparently "called on both countries to refrain from carrying out new nuclear tests" and "appealed to [them] to adhere to the Nuclear-Test-Ban Treaty and to the Treaty on the Non-Proliferation of Nuclear Weapons" on June 4, 1998.[362] Therefore, in the intervening two days before the resolution was adopted on June 6, somehow the statement rose to the level of a *demand*, which reflects a clear imposition of obligations on India and Pakistan.

Particularly relevant is that neither India nor Pakistan had committed to the NPT or the CTBT, so the Security Council imposed an element of those treaties on these States. One element is in CTBT Article I, which requires States parties "not to carry out any nuclear weapon test explosion or any other nuclear explosion, and to prohibit and prevent any such nuclear explosion at any place under its jurisdiction or control."[363] Another element is in NPT Article II, which requires non-nuclear-weapon States parties "not to manufacture or otherwise acquire nuclear weapons or other nuclear explosive devices," with nuclear tests such as these being an integral part of manufacturing nuclear weapons. Slovenia – one of the four sponsors of the draft resolution that became Resolution 1172 – acknowledged that India and Pakistan "legitimately argue[d] that they ha[d] not violated any of their treaty obligations," which made it

[359] Provisional Verbatim Record of the Three Thousand and Forty-Sixth Meeting, UN SCOR 47th Sess., 3046th mtg., at 145, UN Doc. S/PV.3046 (Jan. 31, 1992).

[360] S.C. Res. 1172, ¶ 1, UN Doc. S/RES/1172 (June 6, 1998) (original emphasis).

[361] Ibid., ¶ 3 (original emphasis).

[362] UN SCOR, 53d Sess., 3890th mtg., at 5, UN Doc. S/PV.3890 (June 6, 1998) (hereinafter UN Doc. S/PV.3890); Letter dated 5 June 1998 from the Permanent Representatives of China, France, the Russian Federation, the United Kingdom of Great Britain and Northern Ireland and the United States of America to the United Nations to the President of the Security Council, UN Doc. S/1998/473 (June 5, 1998) ("India and Pakistan should therefore stop all further such tests ... To reinforce security and stability in the region and more widely, the Five strongly believe that India and Pakistan should adhere to the [CTBT] immediately and unconditionally, thereby facilitating its early entry into force").

[363] Comprehensive Nuclear Test Ban Treaty, Art. 1(1), opened for signature Sept. 24, 1996, S. Treaty Doc. No. 105–28, 35 I.L.M. 1439 (not in force).

necessary for the Security Council to create an obligation that India and Pakistan refrain from future nuclear testing so that they legally could be held responsible if they were to continue their testing.[364] In light of this statement, at least one sponsor of Resolution 1172 saw this resolution as expressly creating treaty-type obligations for India and Pakistan. Notably, the Security Council did not impose the entirety of the CTBT on India and Pakistan, in the way that Resolution 1737 required North Korea to abide by the NPT. Nevertheless, Resolution 1172 clearly imposed a portion of the CTBT on both India and Pakistan. The ultimate result was not that India and Pakistan joined the CTBT or NPT, as some States had hoped.[365] Instead, India and Pakistan both declared a moratorium on nuclear tests,[366] which essentially gave effect to the requirement imposed by paragraph 3. India apparently expressed its willingness to convert this so-called unilateral moratorium into a formal obligation,[367] although in this India was too late, since Resolution 1172 already had done so.

Paragraph 7 of Resolution 1172 imposes a less formal obligation on India and Pakistan. The Security Council

> [*c*]*all*[*ed*] *upon* India and Pakistan immediately to stop their nuclear weapon development programmes, to refrain from weaponization or from the deployment of nuclear weapons, to cease development of ballistic missiles capable of delivering nuclear weapons and any further production of fissile material for nuclear weapons, to confirm their policies not to export equipment, materials or technology that could contribute to weapons of mass destruction or missiles capable of delivering them and to undertake appropriate commitments in that regard ...[368]

This provision imposes more than just some of the CTBT and NPT commitments on States not party to these treaties, and also limits their ability to develop certain ballistic missiles and to engage in certain types of trades. Neither India nor Pakistan had entered treaties that impose

364 See U.N. SCOR, 53d Sess., 3890th mtg., at 6, UN Doc. S/PV.3890 (June 6, 1998).
365 See ibid., at 3, 9, 13.
366 See Secretary-General, Letter dated 8 July 1998 from the Secretary-General addressed to the President of the Security Council, ¶ 7, UN Doc. S/1998/619 (July 9, 1998).
367 Ibid.; Permanent Representative of India to the United Nations, Letter dated 9 June 1998 from the Permanent Representative of India to the United Nations addressed to the President of the Security Council, UN Doc. S/1998/489 (June 10, 1998).
368 S.C. Res. 1172, ¶ 7, UN Doc. S/RES/1172 (June 6, 1998) (original emphasis).

these obligations on them, so this resolution imposes new disarmament and arms control limitations on these two States.

To come to the conclusion that paragraph 7 imposes obligations on India and Pakistan, it is necessary to recall the analysis of "calls upon" provided in Chapter 3.1.4 above. Despite the theoretical generalizations there, States ascribed varying levels of significance to this signal during the debates on Resolution 1172. At one end of the spectrum, China saw Resolution 1172 as demanding "in explicit terms" that India and Pakistan adhere to the CTBT and the NPT,[369] not just to the provision of the CTBT that prohibits nuclear testing, thus indicating that China sees the language "calls upon" in paragraph 7 as imposing a binding obligation. At the other end of that spectrum, Costa Rica saw Resolution 1172 as "a *vehement and vigorous appeal* to India and Pakistan to cease immediately the development of nuclear weapons and, as soon as possible, to accede unconditionally to the Treaty on the Non-Proliferation of Nuclear Weapons and the Comprehensive Nuclear-Test-Ban Treaty."[370] Use of the word "appeal" indicates Costa Rica's belief that the "calls upon" language of Resolution 1172 does not contain coercive measures. Just like Japan, Brazil, and the European Union,[371] Costa Rica's statement reflects the idea that Resolution 1172 was designed to push India and Pakistan into joining the CTBT and the NPT.[372] Others that fall between these two poles show signs of confusion. France, for example, asserts that India and Pakistan "*must* also display restraint and demonstrate, by acting in according with the Security Council's *requests*, their willingness to commit themselves to this path [of peace by giving up their nuclear weapon development programmes],"[373] thus reflecting a slight paradox that India and Pakistan are *bound* to exercise their *choice* in a particular manner, which makes little sense. One could interpret the US statement as reflecting a belief that these provisions were merely recommendatory. It stated that the intent was to "convince them it is in their own national security interests to do what the international community is *urging* them to do," which was to sign and ratify the CTBT immediately and without

[369] UN Doc. S/PV.3890, *supra* note 362, at 12. [370] Ibid., at 7 (emphasis added).

[371] Ibid., at 3 (reporting that Japan hoped that the imposition of this obligation on India and Pakistan under the Security Council resolution would "urge them to become parties to the NPT and the CTBT without delay and without conditions"); see also ibid., at 9 (reporting that Brazil called for India and Pakistan to join the CTBT); ibid., at 13 (noting that the European Union, through the United Kingdom, urged India and Pakistan to join the CTBT).

[372] See ibid., at 7. [373] Ibid., at 11 (emphasis added).

conditions.[374] However, Resolution 1172 is not being construed here as implying an obligation to join the CTBT, but rather as imposing certain CTBT and NPT provisions on India and Pakistan without them being members of the CTBT or the NPT, but with the ultimate, implicit hope that they would join the CTBT and the NPT.

Perhaps even more interesting than the imposition of the obligations in paragraph 7, the second half of paragraph 3 of Resolution 1172 imposed on *all States* obligations that were of the same nature as those imposed on India and Pakistan in the first half of that paragraph.[375] Indeed, the second half of paragraph 3 "in this context *calls upon* all States not to carry out any nuclear weapon test explosion or any other nuclear explosion in accordance with the provisions of the Comprehensive Nuclear Test Ban Treaty."[376] This provision arguably imposes obligations on all States to abide by Article I of the CTBT, which requires States parties "not to carry out any nuclear weapon test explosion or any other nuclear explosion."[377] Just as some States had hoped that the imposition of the CTBT obligations on India and Pakistan would lead them to join the CTBT, there is some evidence in the verbatim record that at least France hoped that the imposition of an obligation on all States to refrain from testing their nuclear weapons would lead to them joining the CTBT "without delay and without conditions."[378] Gambia was another State that supported this resolution because it "reiterate[d] its firm conviction that nuclear disarmament is an obligation of all States without exception."[379] The same was true for Slovenia, which emphasized the "importance of universal adherence to the NPT and the CTBT, which are essential foundations for the pursuit of nuclear disarmament."[380] Such language in the resolution likely was a concession that the permanent members of the Security Council had to give during their canvassing efforts to secure the support needed to adopt this resolution.

Before discussing the particular language in Resolution 1172, however, it is important to note one general Security Council policy that Resolution 1172 seemed to establish. During the debates on Resolution 1172, Costa Rica asserted that, with this resolution condemning India's and Pakistan's tests, the Security Council established a "substantive policy of condemning test explosions of nuclear weapons as well as any other type of nuclear

[374] See ibid., at 8 (original emphasis).
[375] See S.C. Res. 1172, ¶ 3, UN Doc. S/RES/1172 (June 6, 1998).
[376] Ibid. (original emphasis). [377] CTBT, *supra* note 363, Art. I.
[378] UN Doc. S/PV.3890, *supra* note 362, at 10. Interestingly, France has signed but not yet ratified the CTBT.
[379] Ibid. [380] Ibid., at 6.

explosion, in accordance with the provisions of the Comprehensive Nuclear-Test-Ban Treaty."[381] Such a policy would complement the policy that all WMD proliferation issues, including nuclear ones, create a threat to international peace and security, as was first established by the 1992 statement of the president of the Security Council[382] and reaffirmed by the first preambular paragraph of Resolution 1540.[383] The response of the Security Council to Iran and North Korea in 2006, as explained below, emphasizes the veracity of Costa Rica's assertion. This policy of condemning all nuclear explosions does not absolve the Security Council of the need to weigh the facts on a case-by-case basis before condemning such tests, or otherwise establish a default rule that Security Council members can rely on in condemning future actions. Nevertheless, States that plan on testing nuclear weapons can expect a strong condemnation from the Security Council, unless the State is a permanent member of the Security Council, in which case the condemnation will have to come in the form of international public opinion. This is exactly what France experienced in 1973, when it tested its nuclear weapons in the South Pacific, until it agreed to move its testing underground, and again when French president Jacques Chirac announced in 1995 that France would yet again test its nuclear weapons in the South Pacific. Although there have not been overt nuclear tests since 1998 in India and Pakistan, the Security Council's strength in condemning the recent activities of Iran and North Korea indicates that this policy of condemning all nuclear explosions still remains, and perhaps even exists in an intensified form.

The main legal issue arising from this resolution – apart from the legal significance of "calls upon" – deals with the ability of the Security Council to impose treaty-based obligations on all States. The CTBT has not even entered into force for those States that have signed and ratified it, yet the Security Council seems to be imposing the substance of its provisions on States nonetheless. The principal question is whether this resolution actually imposes obligations on all States, assuming that "calls upon" reflects a decision of the Security Council, as asserted in Chapter 3.1.4 above. In particular, does "in this context" in paragraph 3 qualify this Security Council decision to the point where it has little meaning outside India's and Pakistan's tests? If this were the case, it essentially would read all meaning out of the requirement that all States

[381] Ibid., at 7.

[382] See President of the Security Council, Note by the President of the Security Council, UN Doc. S/23500 (Jan. 31, 1992).

[383] See S.C. Res. 1540, preamb. ¶ 1, UN Doc. S/RES/1540 (April 28, 2004).

refrain from carrying out nuclear tests, since only India and Pakistan had independently tested nuclear devices in 1998. Therefore, this interpretation would not seem appropriate.

This language of Resolution 1172 that creates norms for "all States" raises issues relating to whether the Security Council can act as a global legislature. By "legislature," this study adopts the definition proffered by Georges Abi-Saab: "[T]he creation of prospective, general and abstract rules of conduct that bind all the subjects of the legal system in the unlimited future."[384] Commentators have hotly debated in the past decade whether the Security Council has been acting as a global legislature and whether such acts are *ultra vires*, primarily in the context of the Security Council's adoption of Resolutions 1373 and 1540 in the international fight against terrorism.[385] In particular, these resolutions were seen as revolutionary because they required States to act in a way other than to discipline a particular State.[386] For example, Reuven Young states that Resolution 1373 was "the first use of Chapter VII powers to

[384] See Abi-Saab, *supra* note 18, at 26–27 (distinguishing this type of legislation from a more internal variety, such as when the Security Council adopts its own rules of procedure). Please note that Abi-Saab appears to be the only one who attempts to provide a clear definition of "legislation" among the commentators on the Security Council as a global legislature.

[385] See, e.g., ibid.; Sumon Dantiki, *Power through Process: An Administrative Law Framework for United Nations Legislative Resolutions*, 40 Geo. J. Int'l L. 655 (2009); Ian Johnstone, *The Security Council as Legislature*, in The UN Security Council and the Politics of International Authority 80 (Bruce Cronin and Ian Hurd ed., 2008); Stefan Talmon, *The Security Council as World Legislature*, 99 Am. J. Int'l L. 175 (2005); Axel Marschik, *The Security Council as World Legislator Theory, Practice and Consequences of an Expanding World Power*, IILJ Working Paper No. 2005–18; Eric Rosand, *The Security Council as "Global Legislator": Ultra Vires or Ultra Innovative?*, 28 Fordham Int'l L.J. 542 (2005); Matthew Happold, *Security Council Resolution 1373 and the Constitution of the United Nations*, 16 Leiden J. Int'l L. 593 (2003); Paul C. Szasz, *The Security Council Starts Legislating*, 96 Am. J. Int'l L. 901, 901–902 (2002); Karl Doehring, *Unlawful Resolutions of the Security Council and Their Legal Consequences*, 1 Max Planck Y.B. UN L. 91 (1997). However, the ability of the United Nations to legislate is not a new topic. See, e.g., Edward Yemin, Legislative Powers in the United Nations and Specialized Agencies (1969).

[386] See, e.g., Reuven Young, *Defining Terrorism: The Evolution of Terrorism as a Legal Concept in International Law and Its Influence on Definitions in Domestic Legislation*, 29 B.C. Int'l & Comp. L. Rev. 23, 43–44 (2006) (placing particular emphasis on this language to suggest that this resolution marks the beginning of a new legislative role for the Security Council); Eric Rosand, *Security Council Resolution 1373, The Counter-terrorism Committee, and the Fight against Terrorism*, 97 Am. J. Int'l L. 333, 334 (2003) (asserting that such a resolution as 1373, which creates uniform obligations on all UN members, is "an unprecedented step for the Security Council to take"); Szasz, *supra* note 385, at 901–902.

order states to take or refrain from specific actions other than when disciplining a specific country."[387] Similarly, Cardenas sees Resolution 1373 as "'[breaking] new ground' by using, for the first time ever, the Council's Chapter VII powers to direct all Member States to take steps to do or refrain from doing what it mandates, in a general context not directly related to disciplining any individual country or particular non-state actor."[388] What these commentators fail to recognize is that a number of earlier Chapter VII resolutions use the same type of language – namely "all States" – within their operative paragraphs.[389] Some of the resolutions that impose obligations on "all States" before Resolution 1373 involve nuclear weapons. Resolution 687 dealing with the First Gulf War provides the following language with regard to Iraq's nuclear-weapons program:

> *Decides* that, in accordance with resolution 661 (1990) and subsequent related resolutions and until a further decision is taken by the Security Council, *all States* shall continue to prevent the sale or supply, or the promotion or facilitation of such sale or supply, to Iraq by their nationals, or from their territories or using their flag vessels or aircraft, of:
>
> (a) Arms and related materiel of all types, specifically including the sale or transfer through other means of all forms of conventional military equipment, including for paramilitary forces, and spare parts and components and their means of production, for such equipment;
> (b) Items specified and defined in paragraphs 8 and 12 above not otherwise covered above;
> (c) Technology under licensing or other transfer arrangements used in the production, utilization or stockpiling of items specified in subparagraphs (a) and (b) above;
> (d) Personnel or materials for training or technical support services relating to the design, development, manufacture, use, maintenance or support of items specified in subparagraphs (a) and (b) above[.][390]

It will be noted that the above provision makes an internal reference to paragraphs 8 to 12 of the same resolution. Both paragraphs 11 and 12 deal with nuclear weapons, with paragraph 11 of Resolution 687 dealing with

[387] See Young, *supra* note 386, at 42.

[388] Emilio J. Cardenas, *The United Nations Security Council's Quest for Effectiveness*, 25 Mich. J. Int'l L. 1341, 1341 (2004) (citing Szasz, *supra* note 385, at 901).

[389] See, e.g., S.C. Res. 1267, ¶¶ 3–4, UN Doc. S/RES/1267 (Oct. 15, 1999); S.C. Res. 748, ¶¶ 3–6, UN Doc. S/RES/748 (March 31, 1992); S.C. Res. 687, ¶ 24, UN Doc. S/RES/687 (April 3, 1991).

[390] Res 687, ¶ 24, UN Doc. S/RES/687 (April 3, 1991) (emphasis added).

the Security Council's invitation to Iraq to "reaffirm unconditionally its obligations under the Treaty on the Non-Proliferation of Nuclear Weapons of 1 July 1968," and paragraph 12 requiring Iraq to

> unconditionally agree not to acquire or develop nuclear weapons or nuclear-weapons-usable material or any subsystems or components or any research, development, support or manufacturing facilities related to the above; to submit to the Secretary-General and the Director-General of the International Atomic Energy Agency within fifteen days of the adoption of the present resolution a declaration of the locations, amounts, and types of all items specified above; to place all of its nuclear-weapons-usable materials under the exclusive control, for custody and removal, of the International Atomic Energy Agency, with the assistance and cooperation of the Special Commission as provided for in the plan of the Secretary-General discussed in paragraph 9 (b) above; to accept, in accordance with the arrangements provided for in paragraph 13 below, urgent on-site inspection and the destruction, removal or rendering harmless as appropriate of all items specified above; and to accept the plan discussed in paragraph 13 below for the future ongoing monitoring and verification of its compliance with these undertakings[.][391]

Therefore, paragraph 24 of Resolution 687 required all States to take steps to frustrate Iraq's efforts to develop nuclear weapons. This resolution appears to be the first resolution that imposed obligations on all States in the context of nuclear non-proliferation. However, these obligations targeted a particular State (namely Iraq and its proliferation efforts), so it seems reasonable to conclude that Resolution 687 did not involve Security Council legislation, as defined above. This honor would appear to fall to Resolution 1172, inasmuch as it imposes obligations on all States in a general context and without focusing on the disciplining of one particular State, at least not in those provisions that impose a general obligation on all States. Despite any perceived problems with the Security Council legislating in theory,[392] the Security Council nevertheless has seen fit to adopt such resolutions. In the absence of clear avenues for judicial review of such decisions, the legality of these

391 Res 687, ¶¶ 11–12, UN Doc. S/RES/687 (April 3, 1991).

392 See, e.g., Abi-Saab, *supra* note 18, at 28–44 (arguing that the Security Council does not have the express power to legislate inasmuch as the UN Charter creates specific and circumscribed powers for the Security Council).

legislative resolutions remains debated and debatable.[393] It falls outside the scope of this study to rehash those arguments in reaching a definitive conclusion on that issue.

To summarize, Resolution 1172 requires all States to comply with Article I of the CTBT. This language marks the beginning of a universalism movement for nuclear non-proliferation law, where all States – even non-parties to these treaties – appear to have had obligations placed on them by the Security Council. The resolutions dealing with North Korea and Iran, discussed in the following two sections, strengthen this general trend as well. Therefore, the discussion provided in this section will be applicable there.

3.2.5 *North Korea and various Security Council resolutions*

This subsection addressing North Korea is important for several reasons, including providing further evidence of the Security Council's pattern of imposing treaty obligations on States that violate nuclear non-proliferation norms and the pattern of emphasizing coercive enforcement of these norms, all through inadequate procedures from the perspective of

393 See generally Lorraine Finlay, *Between a Rock and a Hard Place: The Kadi Decision and Judicial Review of Security Council Resolutions*, 18 Tulane J. Int'l & Comp. L. 477 (2009); Pasquale De Sena and Maria Vitucci, *The European Courts and the Security Council: Between Dedoublement Fonctionnel and Balancing of Values*, 20 Eur. J. Int'l L. 193 (2009); Kamrul Hossain, *Legality of Security Council Action: Does the ICJ Move to Take up the Challenge of Judicial Review*, 5 Rev. Int'l L. & Pol 133 (2009); Mark Angehr, *The International Court of Justice's Advisory Jurisdiction and the Review of Security Council and General Assembly Resolutions*, 103 Nw. Univ. L. Rev. 1007 (2009); James Crawford, *Marbury v. Madison at the International Level*, 36 GW Int'l L. Rev. 505, 513 (2004); Babback Sabahi, *The ICJ's Authority to Invalidate Security Council Decisions under Chapter VII: Legal Romanticism or the Rule of Law*, 17 N.Y. Int'l L. Rev. 1 (2004); Georg Nolte, *The Limits of the Security Council's Powers and Its Functions in the International Legal System: Some Reflections*, in The Role of Law in International Politics 315 (Michael Byers ed., 2000); Bernd Martenczuk, *The Security Council, the International Court and Judicial Review*, 10 Eur. J. Int'l L. 517 (1999); Gabriël Oosthuizen, *Playing the Devil's Advocate: The UN Security Council Is Unbound by Law*, 12 Leiden J. Int'l L. 549 (1999); Dapo Akande, *The International Court of Justice and the Security Council: Is There Room for Judicial Control of Decisions of the Political Organs of the United Nations*, 46 Int'l & Comp. L.Q. 309 (1997); Jose Alvarez, *Judging the Security Council*, 90 Am. J. Int'l L. 1 (1996); Ken Roberts, *Second-Guessing the Security Council: The International Court of Justice and Its Powers of Judicial Review*, 7 Pace Int'l L. Rev. 281 (1995); Mohammed Bedjaoui, The New World Order and the Security Council: Testing the Legality of Its Acts (1994); Geoffrey Watson, *Constitutionalism, Judicial Review and the World Court*, 34 Harv. Int'l L.J. 1 (1993).

target States. In addition, this subsection demonstrates a relatively new willingness on the part of the Security Council to impose obligations on States that have – or are believed to have – nuclear weapons. This is significant because some commentators saw the Security Council as being rarely involved in nuclear non-proliferation issues, and, when it did get involved, as too weak on cases of alleged noncompliance, such as in 1993 when the Security Council left resolution of North Korea's attempt to leave the NPT to bilateral negotiations led by the United States.[394] Moreover, before the resolutions against North Korea that are discussed in this section were adopted, commentators thought that the different priorities of the permanent members of the Security Council concerning nuclear non-proliferation would make it difficult for the Security Council to take action against States protected by a so-called veto umbrella of a permanent member.[395] However, as with the measures taken against North Korea that are discussed in this section, the permanent members of the Security Council – especially China – have shown a surprising willingness to reassess alliances and take coercive measures against former client States when nuclear non-proliferation issues are involved.

North Korea has had a long and shaky relationship with the rest of the international community when it comes to its nuclear non-proliferation activities.[396] As explained below, the primary legal issue that the international community struggles with now, however, is whether North Korea can leave the NPT regime. NPT Article X(1) provides States with the ability to withdraw from the NPT:

[394] See Müller, *supra* note 295, at 127, 129; Berhanykun Andemicael, *Nuclear Verification in North Korea and Iran*, in SWORDS INTO PLOWSHARES: BUILDING PEACE THROUGH THE UNITED NATIONS 123, 131 (ROY S. LEE ed., 2006).

[395] See Kono, *supra* note 254, at 106; see also Müller, *supra* note 295, at 129 ("Politics and national idiosyncrasies repeatedly got in the way of fair and appropriate decision-making on WMD non-compliance"); THAKUR, *supra* note 97, at 168 ("Pyongyang has yet to face any consequences for its serial brinksmanship, hiding safely behind P5 disagreement on any appropriate policy response").

[396] See generally Bruce Cumings, *Nuclear Imbalance of Terror: The American Surveillance Regime and North Korea's Nuclear Programme*, in THE NUCLEAR NON-PROLIFERATION REGIME 207 (RAJU G. C. THOMAS ed., 1998); JAMES L. SCHOFF et al., NUCLEAR MATTERS IN NORTH KOREA: BUILDING A MULTILATERAL RESPONSE FOR FUTURE STABILITY IN NORTHEAST ASIA (2008); JASPER BECK, ROGUE REGIME: KIM JONG IL AND THE LOOMING THREAT OF NORTH KOREA (2005) (providing a journalistic perspective on North Korea's ambitions to development of nuclear weapons).

> Each Party shall in exercising its national sovereignty have the right to withdraw from the Treaty if it decides that extraordinary events, related to the subject matter of this Treaty, have jeopardized the supreme interests of its country. It shall give notice of such withdrawal to all other Parties to the Treaty and to the United Nations Security Council three months in advance. Such notice shall include a statement of the extraordinary events it regards as having jeopardized its supreme interests.[397]

North Korea agreed to a safeguards agreement with the IAEA in 1992, apparently in response to the US removal of its tactical nuclear weapons from South Korea.[398] Article 26 of that safeguards agreement states the following: "This Agreement shall remain in force as long as the Democratic People's Republic of Korea is party to [the NPT]."[399] In light of these two provisions, North Korea's obligations would cease if it ever withdrew from the NPT. The following paragraphs discuss the difficulties that have arisen over North Korea's efforts to withdraw.

North Korea began its efforts to develop peaceful nuclear energy in the 1980s with Soviet assistance, which led North Korea to join the NPT in 1985.[400] North Korea allowed six inspections of its nuclear facilities before denying access to two facilities based on the assertion that they were conventional military facilities.[401] Suspicions quickly arose over North Korea's production of plutonium due to the fact that the IAEA found an inconsistency between what it reported and what the IAEA found in an analysis of North Korea's nuclear waste.[402] Resenting the allegations of wrongdoing, North Korea announced its withdrawal from the NPT on March 12, 1993.[403] The IAEA Board of Governors referred North Korea to the Security Council on April 1, 1993, after "*find*[*ing*] that the DPRK is in non-compliance with its obligations under its

397 NPT, *supra* note 13, Art. X(1). 398 See Andemicael, *supra* note 394, at 127.

399 Agreement of January 30, 1992, between the Government of the Democratic People's Republic of Korea and the International Atomic Energy Agency for the Application of Safeguards in Connection with the Treaty on the Non-proliferation of Nuclear Weapons Art. 26, INFCIRC/403 (May 1992).

400 See Andemicael, *supra* note 394, at 127.

401 See, e.g., UN SCOR, 48th Sess., 3212th mtg., at 53, UN Doc. S/PV.3212 (May 11, 1993) (noting that the United Kingdom mentioned these inspections) (hereinafter UN Doc. S/PV.3212); John F. Murphy, *Force and Arms*, in 1 United Nations Legal Order 247, 314–315 (Oscar Schachter and Christopher Joyner ed., 1995).

402 Andemicael, *supra* note 394, at 127; David B. Thomson, A Guide to the Nuclear Arms Control Treaties 103–104 (2001) (providing a detailed story of North Korea's efforts to develop its nuclear capabilities).

403 See generally Dekker, *supra* note 1, at 298.

Safeguards Agreement with the Agency" and "[*f*]*urther find*[*ing*], pursuant to Article 19 of the Agreement, that the Agency is not able to verify that there has been no diversion of nuclear material required to be safeguarded under the terms of the Safeguards Agreement to nuclear weapons or other nuclear explosive devices."[404] Meanwhile, the depositories of the NPT – Russia, the United States, and the United Kingdom – challenged North Korea's reasons for withdrawal,[405] while the Security Council refrained from challenging these reasons.[406] Instead, the Security Council in Resolution 825 "call[ed] upon [North Korea] to honour its non-proliferation obligations under the Treaty and comply with its safeguards agreement with the IAEA as specified by the IAEA Board of Governors' resolution of 25 February 1993."[407] Given the analysis of "calls upon" provided in Chapter 3.1.4 above, this is not an insignificant measure that the Security Council took in imposing the obligations of the NPT and the safeguards agreement on North Korea.[408] In fact, the United Kingdom even asserted that North Korea remains bound by its safeguards agreement despite its attempts to withdraw from the NPT.[409] Although North Korea claimed in the Security Council

[404] *Report by the Director General on the Implementation of the Resolution Adopted by the Board on 25 February 1993 (Gov/2636) and of the Agreement between the Agency and the Democratic People's Republic of Korea for the Application of Safeguards in Connection with the Treaty on the Non-proliferation of Nuclear Weapons* (INFCIRC/403), IAEA Doc. Gov/2645, ¶¶ 1, 2, 4 (April 1, 1993) (original emphasis). See also Murphy, *supra* note 401, at 315. It should be noted that such a requirement to report to the Security Council ensures that the Security Council stays abreast of situations in this sensitive area as they develop. This requirement on the Board to report to the Security Council should not be seen as a limitation on the Security Council's powers when it comes to situations involving nuclear non-proliferation, inasmuch as its powers derive from Chapter VII of the UN Charter and not the IAEA Statute. Still, it is interesting to note how the IAEA Statute expressly involves the Security Council there and in Article III(B)(4), thus recognizing how nuclear non-proliferation relates to the maintenance of international peace and security.

[405] See, e.g., UN Doc. S/PV.3212, *supra* note 401, at 54.

[406] See S.C. Res. 825, preamb. ¶ 7, UN Doc. S/RES/825 (May 11, 1993) (noting, however, that the depositories challenged North Korea's stated reasons for withdrawing from the NPT); see also Müller, *supra* note 295, at 127 (noting that certain permanent members likely were reluctant to challenge North Korea's reasons for withdrawing because they did not want to establish a precedent and later be challenged when they themselves decide to withdraw from a treaty).

[407] S.C. Res. 825, ¶ 2, UN Doc. S/RES/825 (May 11, 1993); see also ibid., preamb. ¶ 6.

[408] But see SUTTERLIN, *supra* note 229, at 107 (asserting that Resolution 825 contained only "admonitory" language).

[409] See UN Doc. S/PV.3212, *supra* note 401, at 54.

debates that it had acted legally by withdrawing from the NPT,[410] the members of the Security Council were clearly of a different opinion.[411]

On the day before the ninety-day notification period was to expire under NPT Article X(1),[412] North Korea suspended its withdrawal after agreeing with the United States on the points that would later become the US–North Korea Agreed Framework, in which North Korea committed to freeze its nuclear reactors and reprocessing plants in exchange for needed economic assistance, including two nuclear reactors that did not pose a threat to the nuclear non-proliferation regime and fuel oil pending the construction of those reactors.[413] In the years following this agreement, the United States failed to provide all of the promised assistance and continued to criticize North Korea. North Korea announced its withdrawal from the NPT again in 2003, though this time it declared "an automatic and immediate effectuation of its withdrawal from the NPT."[414] Significant debate has arisen over whether this withdrawal was valid because North Korea failed to wait the requisite ninety days after notification.[415] However, all of these commentators fail to remember that North Korea simply had suspended its withdrawal from the NPT in 1993, thus suggesting that North Korea had waited more than the required time before officially withdrawing.[416]

Regardless, there was confusion in the Security Council over whether North Korea had withdrawn from the NPT. In preambular paragraph 10

410 See, e.g., ibid., at 7, 36. 411 See generally ibid.

412 See Douglas Jehl, *North Korea Says It Won't Pull Out of Arms Pact Now*, N.Y. Times, June 12, 1993, at A11.

413 See, e.g., Christophe Carle, *Arms Control in Reluctant Installments: Iraq and North Korea, Arms Control and Disarmament Cluster* 1999–2000, Occasional Paper Series No. 9, 3 (2000).

414 *North Korea: Statement On Pullout*, N.Y. Times, Jan. 11, 2003, at A7 ("Systematically violating the D.P.R.K.–U.S. Agreed Framework, the U.S. brought up another 'nuclear suspicion' and stopped the supply of heavy oil, reducing the Agreed Framework to a dead document").

415 See, e.g., Christopher Le Mon, *Did North Korea's Nuclear Test Violate International Law?*, Opinio Juris, Oct. 9, 2006, at www.opiniojuris.org/posts/1160382356.shtml (last visited May 25, 2011); Frederic L. Kirgis, *North Korea's Withdrawal from the Nuclear Nonproliferation Treaty*, ASIL Insights, January 2003, available at http://www.asil.org/insights/insigh96.htm (last visited May 25, 2011).

416 The purpose of this section is not to assess the legality of North Korea's actions. Although it is inappropriate to separate these two incidents, quite a few commentators see North Korea's withdrawal efforts in 2003 in isolation from the 1993 withdrawal efforts. Thus they would take issue with North Korea's allegedly faulty withdrawal in 2003 without the requisite notification. See, e.g., Teixeira, *supra* note 137, at 84; Thakur, *supra* note 97, at 171; Sutterlin, *supra* note 229, at 107.

of Resolution 1695, adopted in response to its test of ballistic missiles capable of delivering its nuclear weapons and North Korea's withdrawal from the NPT, the Security Council expressly "[*d*]*eplor*[*ed*] [North Korea's] announcement of withdrawal from the [NPT] and its stated pursuit of nuclear weapons in spite of its treaty on Non-Proliferation of Nuclear Weapons and [IAEA] safeguards obligations."[417] Use of the word "announcement" in "announcement of withdrawal" is interesting, as it suggests a distinction between this and an actual withdrawal. Operative paragraph 6 of Resolution 1695 also strongly urged North Korea to "return at an early date to the Treaty on Non-Proliferation of Nuclear Weapons and International Atomic Energy Agency safeguards."[418]

Despite the question whether North Korea validly left the NPT, Resolution 1718 makes it clear that North Korea still has obligations under the NPT. Resolution 1718 was adopted just five days after North Korea detonated a one-kiloton nuclear device underground that registered 4.2 on the Richter scale.[419] Therefore, one gets a sense of greater urgency when reading Resolution 1718 vis-à-vis Resolution 1695. In particular, preambular paragraph 3

> [e]xpress[es the Security Council's] gravest concern at the claim by the DPRK that it has conducted a test of a nuclear weapon on 9 October 2006, and at the challenge such a test constitutes to the Treaty on the Non-Proliferation of Nuclear Weapons and to international efforts aimed at strengthening the global regime of non-proliferation of nuclear weapons, and the danger it poses to peace and stability in the region and beyond . . .[420]

As a result of this "gravest concern," operative paragraph 6 of Resolution 1718 obliges North Korea to abide by the NPT and its safeguards agreement:

> [*The Security Council d*]*ecides* that [North Korea] shall abandon all nuclear weapons and existing nuclear programmes in a complete, verifiable and irreversible manner, shall act strictly in accordance with the obligations applicable to parties under the Treaty on the

417 S.C. Res. 1695, ¶ 10, UN Doc. S/RES/1695 (July 15, 2006) (original emphasis).
418 Ibid., ¶ 6.
419 See David E. Sanger, *North Korea Says It Tested a Nuclear Device Underground*, N.Y. Times, Oct. 9, 2006, at A1.
420 S.C. Res. 1718, preamb. ¶ 3, UN Doc. S/RES/1718 (Oct. 14, 2006).

> Non-Proliferation of Nuclear Weapons and the terms and conditions of its [IAEA] Safeguards Agreement . . .[421]

Not only did this resolution force North Korea back to the NPT and the safeguards agreement,[422] which, in theory, it previously had been allowed to withdraw from, but the resolution extended North Korea's obligations beyond the obligations it had under the NPT and the safeguards agreement.

On May 25, 2009, North Korea again conducted an underground test of a nuclear weapon, which again surprised the international community.[423] The Security Council responded by adopting Resolution 1874, which called this test a violation of Resolution 1718,[424] castigated North Korea for this challenge to the NPT and "the international efforts aimed at strengthening the global regime of non-proliferation of nuclear weapons,"[425] and reiterated the obligation from Resolution 1718 that it refrain from conducting further nuclear tests.[426] In addition, it required North Korea to "retract its announcement of withdrawal from the NPT" and "return at an early date to the NPT and the [IAEA] safeguards." As if this were not clear enough, Resolution 1874 required North Korea to

> abandon all nuclear weapons and existing nuclear programs in a complete, verifiable and irreversible manner and immediately cease all related activities . . . act strictly in accordance with the obligations applicable to parties under the NPT and the terms and conditions of the IAEA Safeguards Agreement (IAEA INFCIRC/403) and . . . provide the IAEA transparency measures extending beyond these requirements, including such access to individuals, documentation, equipment and facilities as may be required and deemed necessary by the IAEA.[427]

This is in addition to reiterating the already existing obligations under Resolution 1718,[428] as well as requiring various implementing measures from member States, such as requiring them to carefully inspect North

421 Ibid., ¶ 6 (original emphasis).

422 See Geoffrey S. Carlson, *An Offer They Can't Refuse? The Security Council Tells North Korea to Re-sign the Nuclear Non-proliferation Treaty*, 46 Colum. J. Transnat'l L. 420 (2008).

423 See Choe Sang-Hun, *North Korea Says it Tested Nuclear Device*, N.Y. Times, May 26, 2009, at A1. See also *Indications of Another Missile Test*, N.Y. Times, May 31, 2009, at 8A (reporting how North Korea tested an intercontinental ballistic missile six days after this nuclear test).

424 See S.C. Res. 1874, preamb. ¶ 3, ¶ 1, UN Doc. S/RES/1874 (June 12, 2009).

425 Ibid., preamb. ¶ 3. 426 See ibid., ¶ 2. 427 Ibid., ¶ 8. 428 See ibid., ¶¶ 9–10.

Korean ships.[429] In terms of new nuclear non-proliferation obligations, Resolution 1874 called upon North Korea to join the Comprehensive Nuclear Test Ban Treaty.[430] At the time of writing, North Korea appears to continue its recalcitrance – notwithstanding all of these coercive measures from the Security Council – by shielding its nuclear program from IAEA scrutiny, by opening new enrichment facilities, and by asserting that Libya's foolishness in abandoning its own program in 2003 left it vulnerable to NATO airstrikes in 2011.[431] While one might dismiss out of hand North Korea's ridicule of Libya, it is not difficult to imagine other would-be proliferators taking note of Libya's situation.

On September 24, 2009, after reaffirming the recent Security Council resolutions involving the nuclear activities of Iran and North Korea, the Security Council adopted Resolution 1887, which emphasized that allegations of noncompliance with nuclear non-proliferation agreements would continue to be brought to the Security Council's attention.[432] Interestingly, Resolution 1887 specifically called upon "State Parties" to the NPT to comply with their NPT obligations, but then called upon "all States that are not Parties to the NPT to accede to the Treaty as non-nuclear-weapon States so as to achieve its universality at an early date, and pending their accession to the Treaty, to adhere to its terms."[433] As a tip of the hat to the criticism that non-nuclear-weapon States levy against the NPT's apparent bias in favor of nuclear-weapon States, Resolution 1887 called upon NPT parties to work towards nuclear arms reduction and disarmament, as well as general and complete disarmament, as indicated in NPT Article VI.[434] Resolution 1887 then went on to call upon "all States to refrain from conducting a nuclear test explosion and to sign and ratify the Comprehensive Nuclear Test Ban Treaty (CTBT), thereby bringing the treaty into force at an early date."[435] Finally, Resolution 1887 reiterated the obligation on non-nuclear-weapon States under the NPT to enter safeguards agreements with the IAEA,[436] but went a step further by calling upon "all States to sign, ratify and implement an additional protocol, which together with comprehensive safeguards agreements constitute essential elements of the IAEA safeguards system."[437] In short, Resolution 1887 extends many of the

[429] See ibid., ¶¶ 12–22. [430] See ibid., ¶ 29.

[431] See, e.g., Mark McDonald, *North Korea Sees Nuclear Error by Libya*, N.Y. Times, March 25, 2011, at A12.

[432] See S.C. Res. 1887, ¶ 1, UN Doc. S/RES/1887 (Sept. 24, 2009). [433] Ibid., ¶ 4.

[434] See ibid., ¶ 5. [435] Ibid., ¶ 7. [436] See ibid., ¶ 15(a). [437] Ibid., ¶ 15(b).

nuclear non-proliferation obligations, in an unprecedented manner, to States that did not otherwise have these obligations – obligations of the NPT, the CTBT and the IAEA Additional Protocol. The following subsections explore the legal implications of these obligations that the Security Council created.

3.2.5.1 Imposing treaty obligations on North Korea

The main legal issue that arises here, again, is the Security Council's ability to impose treaty obligations on North Korea. Similar to the case with India and Pakistan, as noted above in Chapter 3.2.4, Resolution 1874 created obligations on North Korea to join the Comprehensive Nuclear Test Ban Treaty,[438] and the analysis provided in Chapter 3.2.4 applies here. With regard to the NPT and North Korea, the Security Council seems to concede that North Korea successfully withdrew from the NPT. Yet Resolution 1718 requires North Korea to return to the NPT, thus imposing an entire international treaty on a non-party (or former party) to that treaty. Resolution 1718 also extends North Korea's obligations beyond the obligations it had had under the NPT and the safeguards agreement in at least two ways. First, whereas States can withdraw from treaties either according to specific treaty provisions, such as NPT Article X, or according to VCLT Article 56,[439] no mechanism currently exists for allowing withdrawal from Security Council resolutions, some of which make North Korea's NPT obligations different from the obligations of other States parties to the NPT.

Second, Resolution 1718 strips North Korea of one of its so-called inalienable rights, similar to what happened with Iraq, as explained in Chapter 3.2.3.8 above. Under NPT Article IV(1), States have the "inalienable right" to "develop research, production and use of nuclear energy for peaceful purposes without discrimination and in conformity with Articles I and II of this Treaty."[440] At least three Security Council Chapter VII resolutions reaffirm this inalienable right.[441] Such

[438] See S.C. Res. 1874, ¶ 29, UN Doc. S/RES/1874 (June 12, 2009).

[439] See VCLT, *supra* note 19, Art. 56.

[440] NPT, *supra* note 13, Art. IV(1).

[441] S.C. Res. 487, ¶ 4, UN Doc. S/RES/487 (June 19, 1981) ("[T]he Security Council *fully recognizes* the inalienable sovereign right of Iraq and all other States, especially the developing countries, to establish programmes of technological and nuclear development to develop their economy and industry for peaceful purposes in accordance with their present and future needs and consistent with the internationally accepted objectives of preventing nuclear-weapons proliferation"); S.C. Res. 1696, preamb. ¶ 2, UN Doc. S/RES/1696 (July 31, 2006) ("*Reaffirming* its commitment to the Treaty on the

references to these so-called inalienable rights by the Security Council conceivably could even stop the Security Council from changing its tune in the face of overwhelming pressure from key Western States to essentially rewrite NPT Article IV(1) and deny North Korea these rights. However, paragraph 6 of Resolution 1718, with its reference to "existing nuclear programmes," as opposed to "existing nuclear-weapons programmes" or its equivalent,[442] makes it seem as though North Korea was required to give up even its programs to develop nuclear energy for peaceful purposes, assuming it had such programs. Admittedly, this is not the first time that the Security Council has, in effect, stripped a State of its inalienable right to nuclear energy for peaceful purposes, as it had done this with Iraq through Resolution 707.[443] Admittedly, there is a fine line between development for peaceful purposes and development for aggressive purposes,[444] and the Security Council has the power to override conflicting treaty obligations under Article 103. Nonetheless, this stripping of North Korea's ability to develop its nuclear energy for peaceful purposes goes against what the Security Council has said on at least three other occasions and against what is provided for in NPT Article IV, and should be troubling for those who care about such rights under the nuclear non-proliferation regime. After all, the ability to develop – and indeed the promise of assistance with developing – nuclear energy for peaceful purposes is the key carrot held out by the nuclear non-proliferation regime to encourage non-nuclear-weapon States to comply, and to continue to comply, with the obligations of that regime. If certain States – Iraq, North Korea, and Iran, as explained below – can be denied their "inalienable rights" to develop nuclear energy for peaceful purposes, other non-nuclear-weapon States likely are taking notice and getting the message that such rights might not be inalienable after all. It is not inconceivable that such a denial of rights could lead to the entire unraveling of the nuclear non-proliferation regime over time, given that a major incentive to participate has thus been denigrated.

Non-proliferation of Nuclear Weapons, and recalling the right of States Party, in conformity with Articles I and II of that Treaty, to develop research, production and use of nuclear energy for peaceful purposes without discrimination"); S.C. Res. 1737, preamb. ¶ 2, UN Doc. S/RES/1737 (Dec. 23, 2006).

[442] S.C. Res. 1718, ¶ 6, UN Doc. S/RES 1718 (Oct. 14, 2008).

[443] See S.C. Res. 707, ¶ 3(f), UN Doc. S/RES/ 707 (Aug. 15, 1991).

[444] See THAKUR, *supra* note 97, at 172.

3.2.5.2 Imposing treaty obligations on all States parties

The other aspect to notice about Resolution 1718 is that the Security Council "*underlines* the need for all States Parties to the Treaty on the Non-Proliferation of Nuclear Weapons to continue to comply with their Treaty obligations."[445] Although "underlines" is softer than "decides," "demands," or even "calls upon," it can nonetheless be read as constituting a Security Council decision to be followed in accordance with Article 25, especially in light of Resolution 1718 being a Chapter VII resolution that creates coercive sanctions.[446] The Security Council's intent in that resolution is clear: to interfere with the ability of States to withdraw from the NPT in the future, thus modifying the obligations of all parties to the treaty. While the UN Charter's allowance of broad discretion to the Security Council to decide what constitutes a threat to the peace means that it can stop North Korea from leaving the NPT,[447] it is an entirely separate matter to interfere in the ability of all States parties to withdraw from the NPT, especially those members of the NPT who are not UN members, as explained in Chapter 3.1.4 above concerning how the Security Council occasionally imposes obligations on all States in a legislative capacity. Moreover, Resolution 1887's imposition of the NPT, CTBT, and IAEA Additional Protocol obligations to all States perhaps best demonstrates the Security Council's willingness to adopt sweeping measures that create treaty-like obligations for all States without their having expressly consented to these agreements.

3.2.6 *Iran and various Security Council resolutions*

Unlike North Korea, Iran seems to have been in compliance with the legal obligations created by the NPT and its safeguards agreement for many years before allegedly acting in violation of them in the new millennium.[448] Problems began to arise in 2003 with what the IAEA called a general policy of concealment by Iran.[449] Iran's sudden change

[445] S.C. Res. 1718, ¶ 4, UN Doc. S/RES/1718 (Oct. 14, 2008) (emphasis added).

[446] See ch. 3.1.4., *supra*. [447] See Kirgis, *supra* note 415.

[448] See Andemicael, *supra* note 394, at 128–29; Haleh Vaziri, *Iran's Nuclear Quest: Motivations and Consequences*, in THE NUCLEAR NON-PROLIFERATION REGIME 310 (RAJU G. C. THOMAS ed., 1998) (discussing Iran's earlier nuclear ambitions); Shahram Chubin, Iran's Nuclear Ambitions (2006) (asserting that Iran aims to become a regional hegemon through the development of nuclear weapons).

[449] See generally Steven E. Miller, *Proliferation Gamesmanship: Iran and the Politics of Nuclear Confrontation*, 57 SYRACUSE L. REV. 551, 551–560 (2007) (discussing Iran's poor behavior since 2003).

in 2003 could have flowed from its sense of strategic vulnerability, with significant US forces on both sides of it in Iraq and Afghanistan and with India and Pakistan as nuclear neighbors, coupled with US support of Israel and the classification by the US in 2002 of Iran as a member of the "Axis of Evil" along with North Korea and Iraq.[450] Regardless of Iran's reasoning, the Security Council imposed sanctions and obligations on Iran as a result of its concerns over Iran's nuclear program, which concerns arose from IAEA reports and resolutions that raised these issues, including the fear of militarization of its nuclear program on account of the inability of the IAEA to confirm that nuclear material had not been diverted.[451] Despite these fears, the IAEA has not alleged that Iran actually has diverted nuclear material for a military purpose, that Iran has broken an agreement concerning an IAEA project, or that its acts constitute safety or health violations, thus suggesting that the fears concerning Iran's activities might be exaggerated.[452] In such a situation, relying on legal resolution to confirm rights and obligations might be a particularly attractive option, at least before the Security Council gets involved with its coercive measures under Chapter VII.

Notwithstanding the IAEA's reluctance or inability to claim breach, the Security Council demanded in Resolution 1696 that Iran "suspend all enrichment-related and reprocessing activities, including research and development, to be verified by the IAEA."[453] There was general consensus

450 See Andemicael, *supra* note 394, at 128–129.

451 See S.C. Res. 1696, UN Doc. S/RES/1696 (July 31, 2006). Some commentators complain that it took too long for the Security Council to take action against Iran after the IAEA determined that Iran had violated its Safeguards Agreement. See Müller, *supra* note 295, at 129. However, the Security Council moves deliberately and carefully before imposing such disarmament and arms control measures.

452 See generally IAEA Board of Governors, *Implementation of the NPT Safeguards Agreement in the Islamic Republic of Iran*, IAEA Doc. Gov/2006/14 (Feb. 4, 2006); see also Yaël Ronen, The Iran Nuclear Issue 16–29 (2010) (noting that the IAEA merely expresses concern that Iran might have non-peaceful purposes for its nuclear-energy activities, but no hard evidence that material was diverted, rather that Iran had not fully complied with its reporting requirements in 2003, which Iran claims was inadvertent and that other States make similar failures without similar consequences); Michael Spies, *Iran and the Limits of the Nuclear Non-proliferation Regime*, 22 Am. U. Int'l L. Rev. 401, 424–435 (2007) (discussing the IAEA and Iran's nuclear activities); Saira Khan, Iran and Nuclear Weapons: Protracted Conflict and Proliferation (2010) (uncertain of Iran's nuclear ambitions); Sverre Lodgaard, *Iran's Uncertain Nuclear Ambitions*, in Nuclear Proliferation and International Security 96 (Morten Bremer Mærli and Sverre Lodgaard ed., 2007) (same); Emmanuel Decaux, Droit international public 292–293 (5th edn, 2006).

453 S.C. Res. 1696, ¶ 2, UN Doc. S/RES/1696 (July 31, 2006).

among the permanent members of the Security Council that this provision created mandatory obligations for Iran,[454] which is clear from the language of Resolution 1696. This imposition is a clear suspension of Iran's rights and obligations under the Iran–IAEA Safeguards Agreement, in particular Article 37, which allows Iran a certain amount of natural and depleted uranium with a certain level of enrichment.[455] In addition, NPT Article IV provides Iran with an inalienable right to develop its nuclear energy capabilities for peaceful purposes, a right that Iran often has emphasized but that others have questioned due to the fact that Iran's large oil reserves remove the credible civilian need for such development.[456]

Even more crucial language in Resolution 1696 is in paragraph 6, in which the Security Council "*call*[*ed*] *upon* Iran to act in accordance with the provisions of the Additional Protocol and to implement without delay all transparency measures as the IAEA may request in support of its ongoing investigations."[457] Again, the legal significance of "calls upon" discussed in Chapter 3.1.4 above is relevant here. The conclusion that "calls upon" creates binding obligations for the target State is even more persuasive here, where representatives of permanent members – most notably Ambassador Bolton of the United States and Ambassador Emyr Jones Parry of the United Kingdom – asserted during debate on the resolution that these provisions of Resolution 1696 that have the signal "calls upon" create part of the mandatory obligations of that resolution.[458] The United States implied this same point with respect to the

[454] UN Doc. S/PV.5500, *supra* note 126, at 4–7; see also Letter dated 25 July 2006 from the Permanent Representative of France to the United Nations Addressed to the President of the Security Council, at 1–2, UN Doc. S/2006/572 (July 26, 2006) (noting that it was the permanent members' purpose to impose such a mandatory obligation on Iran when it sought to adopt a resolution in this case).

[455] Agreement between Iran and the Agency for the Application of Safeguards in Connection with the Treaty on the Non-proliferation of Nuclear Weapons, Art. 37, Dec. 13, 1974, INFCIRC/214, available at http://www.iaea.org/Publications/Documents/Infcircs/Others/infcirc214.pdf.

[456] See Andemicael, *supra* note 394, at 126; see also UN Doc. S/PV.5612, *supra* note 126, at 6 (providing France's Permanent Representative Jean-Marc De La Sablière's assertions on this matter).

[457] S.C. Res. 1696, ¶ 6, UN Doc. S/RES/1696 (July 31, 2006) (original emphasis).

[458] See UN Doc. S/PV.5500, *supra* note 126, at 3–4; ibid., at 4 (recording that the United Kingdom asserts that Iran had an obligation to take the steps required by the IAEA, in accordance with the provision of the Additional Protocol, before the August 31, 2006 deadline established by Resolution 1696, ¶ 7, the obligation of which appears to have been established by Resolution 1696, ¶ 1, which began with "calls upon").

"calls upon" provisions of Resolution 1737.[459] This particular provision of Resolution 1696 is interesting because, while Iran joined the NPT in 1970 and agreed to a safeguards agreement that entered into force on May 15, 1974, it signed on December 18, 2003, but did not ratify, an Additional Protocol with the IAEA.[460] Iran apparently signed it in response to US allegations that it was developing nuclear weapons, and it wanted to show that its "activities are peaceful."[461] This Additional Protocol would have allowed unscheduled inspections of Iranian facilities, although the Protocol never entered into force because Iran never ratified it. While Iran followed the Additional Protocol starting in 2003 and apparently allowed the IAEA considerable access under this Additional Protocol in order for it to conduct robust inspections[462] (over 2,000 inspector-days of scrutiny between then and 2006), it changed its mind when the IAEA took up the issue of whether Iran had violated certain of its international obligations at the beginning of 2006.[463] This eventually led to the IAEA Board of Governors referring the situation in Iran to the Security Council in 2006.[464] IAEA referral is the process by which the Board of Governors seeks to inform the Security Council of particular situations under its purview. There are three provisions within the IAEA Statute that relate specifically to referral to

[459] UN Doc. S/PV.5612, *supra* note 126, at 2 (recording the United States' implication that the provisions that start with the signal "calls upon" are among the requirements of this draft resolution).

[460] See International Atomic Energy Agency, *Safeguards and Verification*, at www.iaea.org/OurWork/SV/Safeguards/sg_protocol.html (last visited Dec. 28, 2010) (listing the dates that certain States have signed and ratified Additional Protocols to their IAEA Safeguards Agreements).

[461] *Iran Agrees to Nuclear Checks*, China Daily, Dec. 19, 2003, at 1, available at http://www.chinadaily.com.cn/en/doc/2003-12/19/content_291677.htm; *Iran to Agree to Nuclear Inspection Protocol*, White House Bull., Dec. 17, 2003, at 1.

[462] UN Doc. S/PV.5500, *supra* note 126, at 9 (showing a statement by Iran that it allowed "2,000 inspector-days of scrutiny over the past three years; the signing of the Additional Protocol on 18 December 2003 and its immediate implementation until 6 February 2006; the submission of more than 1,000 pages of declaration [*sic*] under the Additional Protocol; allowing over 53 instances of complementary access to different sites across the country; and permitting inspectors to investigate baseless allegations by taking the unprecedented step of providing repeated access to military sites").

[463] See Steven R. Weisman, *Iran Hints at Compromise on Nuclear Inspections*, N.Y. Times, Feb. 18, 2006, at A3.

[464] See, e.g., Elaine Sciolino and William J. Broad, *Atomic Agency Sees Possible Link Of Military to Iran Nuclear Work*, N.Y. Times, Feb. 1, 2006, at A1; Glenn Kessler, *Diplomats Press Iran on Nuclear Activities*, Wash. Post, March 31, 2006, at 1.

the Security Council. IAEA Statute Article XII(C) provides, "The Board shall report the non-compliance to all members and to the Security Council and General Assembly of the United Nations."[465] This provision in the IAEA Statute is relevant to NPT Article III(1) because NPT Article III(1) requires States parties

> to accept safeguards, as set forth in an agreement to be negotiated and concluded with the International Atomic Energy Agency in accordance with the Statute of the International Atomic Energy Agency and the Agencys [*sic*] safeguards system, for the exclusive purpose of verification of the fulfillment of its obligations assumed under this Treaty with a view to preventing diversion of nuclear energy from peaceful uses to nuclear weapons or other nuclear explosive devices.

IAEA Statute Article XII is part of the portion of the IAEA Statute dealing with monitoring of these Agency safeguards. In addition, IAEA Statute Article III(B)(4) and (5) requires the IAEA to "notify the Security Council, as the organ bearing the main responsibility for the maintenance of international peace and security" if "there should arise questions that are within the competence of the Security Council" and to "[s]ubmit reports to the Economic and Social Council and other organs of the United Nations on matters within the competence of these organs," respectively. In short, these provisions appear to repeat the same substantive requirement of referral to the Security Council, although the term used in Article III(B)(4) is "notify" and the terms in Articles XII(C) and XVI(B)(2) are "report" and "submission of reports." Regardless of the exact provision under which the IAEA Board of Governors acts, it is considered referral to the Security Council.

Without the IAEA referral and the Security Council's subsequent involvement under Chapter VII, Iran should have been allowed to reject the Additional Protocol because it had not consented to the creation of any obligations under the Additional Protocol by ratifying that legally binding instrument. Certain obligations do arise after signing, as indicated in Article 18(a) of the VCLT, including "refrain[ing] from acts which would defeat the object and purpose of a treaty," as discussed in Chapter 5.2.3.3 below.[466] However, this obligation continues until the State "shall have made its intention clear not to become a party to the treaty."[467] The infamous US "unsigning" of the Rome Statute demonstrates that States can release themselves from this obligation once they

[465] IAEA Statute, Art. XII(C). [466] VCLT, *supra* note 19, Art. 18. [467] Ibid., Art. 18(a).

express that they have no intention of ratifying the instrument.[468] Iran's parliament declared that it would not ratify the Additional Protocol in 2004.[469] Despite this explicit unwillingness on the part of Iran to ratify the Additional Protocol, the United States has pushed for universal adherence to the principles reflected in the Additional Protocols, regardless of ratification and the general need for consent under VCLT Article 14.[470] Ironically, the United States has signed but not yet ratified its own Additional Protocol with the IAEA.[471] In addition, the IAEA Board of Governors has been calling on Iran to follow the spirit of the Additional Protocol since well before the adoption of these resolutions in September 2003,[472] suggesting that the Board perhaps has been looking beyond actual legal obligations in making its determinations.

The Security Council called upon Iran to abide by the Additional Protocol in paragraph 6 of Resolution 1696.[473] While actual Additional Protocols between the IAEA and NPT members are confidential and vary between States, the IAEA adopted a model Additional Protocol on May 15, 1997, which requires the State to provide certain nuclear-related information under Articles 2 and 3, and to give access to certain sites under conditions specified under Articles 4 and 5, inter alia.[474] This analysis assumes that the IAEA–Iran Additional Protocol resembles the Model Additional Protocol, which is a relatively safe assumption, given how the IAEA closely followed the Model Safeguards Agreement when concluding safeguards agreements with member States, as explained in Chapter 5.2.3.2 below. The Security Council required Iran to carry out all transparency measures the IAEA requested, which obligation is contained in Article 2(c) of the Model Additional Protocol, stating, "Upon request by the Agency, [the State] shall provide amplifications or

468 See generally Edward T. Swaine, *Unsigning*, 55 STAN. L. REV. 2061 (2003).

469 See Nazila Fathi, *Iran Rebuffs UN Agency On Atom Issue*, N.Y. TIMES, Sept. 20, 2004, at A15.

470 See VCLT, *supra* note 19, Art. 14. But see, e.g., KOSKENNIEMI, *supra* note 29, 270–291 (1989) (arguing against the need for consent for international obligations to be established).

471 See IAEA, *Strengthened Safeguards System: Status of Additional Protocols*, at www.iaea.org/OurWork/SV/Safeguards/sg_protocol.html (last visited May 25, 2011) (listing that the United States signed its Additional Protocol on June 12, 1998, but that it has not yet entered into force, which means that it has not yet been ratified).

472 See Andemicael, *supra* note 394, at 132.

473 S.C. Res. 1696, ¶ 6, UN Doc. S/RES/1696 (July 31, 2006).

474 Model Protocol Additional to the Agreement(s) between State(s) and the International Atomic Energy Agency for the Application of Safeguards (Additional Protocol), Arts. 2–5, available at www.iaea.org/Publications/Documents/Infcircs/1997/infcirc540c.pdf (last visited Dec. 28, 2010).

clarifications of any information it has provided under this Article, in so far as relevant for the purpose of safeguards."[475] Again, Iran did not have this obligation before, since it did not ratify its Additional Protocol and the IAEA Statute does not provide the IAEA with such broad powers to request this type of information. Indeed, the IAEA's safeguard powers under Article XII of the IAEA Statute include the ability "to examine the design of specialized equipment and facilities . . . to require the observance of any health and safety measures . . . to call for and receive progress reports," and to obtain and verify the accounting a State provides of its fissionable materials.[476] None of the IAEA's enumerated powers involves the ability to demand whatever transparency measures it chooses. Granted, Article XII(c) allows the Board of Governors to "call upon the recipient State or States to remedy forthwith any noncompliance which it finds to have occurred,"[477] though this falls short of having to provide all information the IAEA demands.

About five months later, on December 23, 2006, the Security Council adopted Resolution 1737, this time under UN Charter Article 41, instead of Article 40, under which Resolution 1696 had been adopted.[478] As explained in Chapter 3.1.4 above, resolutions adopted under Articles 40, 41, and 42 all can have binding force as coercive measures, although Article 41 resolutions have a clearer coercive nature than Article 40 resolutions. Paragraph 2 of Resolution 1737 repeated paragraph 2 of Resolution 1696, suspending "all enrichment-related and reprocessing activities, including research and development," and added that Iran also must suspend "work on all heavy water-related projects, including the construction of a research reactor moderated by heavy water, also to be verified by the IAEA."[479] These provisions clearly imposed binding nuclear non-proliferation obligations on Iran, although the resolutions imposed other obligations as well.[480] In particular, Resolution 1737 went beyond Resolution 1696's requirement for Iran to abide by the

475 Ibid., Art. 2(c).

476 See Statute of the International Atomic Energy Agency Arts. XII(1)–(4), Oct. 26, 1956, available at www.iaea.org/About/statute_text.html (last visited May 26, 2011).

477 Ibid., Arts. XII(c).

478 See S.C. Res. 1737, preamb. ¶ 10, UN Doc. S/RES/1737 (Dec. 23, 2006); S.C. Res. 1696, preamb. ¶ 10, UN Doc. S/RES/1696 (July 31, 2006).

479 Ibid., ¶ 2.

480 Ibid. Sixteen of Resolution 1737's twenty-five paragraphs begin with the signal "[d]ecides," which is considerable in light of other Chapter VII resolutions. However, all except paragraph 2 deal with obligations on all States to ensure that Iran lacks the materials and other support needed to develop nuclear weapons.

Additional Protocol, and instead "*call*[*ed*] *upon* Iran to ratify promptly the Additional Protocol."[481] As noted above, some permanent members of the Security Council implied during the debate over this resolution that "calls upon" provisions of Resolution 1737 make up part of the mandatory obligations that the resolution imposed on Iran,[482] and this study is inclined to agree.

Almost three months later, on March 14, 2007, the Security Council adopted Resolution 1747, in which it responded to Iran's failure to comply with Resolutions 1696 and 1737 by ratcheting up the sanctions on Iran by expanding the list of sanctioned Iranian individuals and entities,[483] prohibiting Iran from any trade in arms and related materiel,[484] and calling upon States not to enter into new financial relations with Iran except for humanitarian and development purposes.[485] These measures are in addition to calling on States to remain vigilant in restricting the travel of Iranians involved with Iran's nuclear activities,[486] as well as with restricting Iran's trade in arms.[487] Therefore, while Resolution 1747 clearly supports the earlier Resolutions 1696 and 1737, Resolution 1747 itself imposes no new nuclear non-proliferation obligations. Nearly a year later, the Security Council adopted Resolution 1803 on March 3, 2008, in response to the IAEA's continued determination that Iran had not terminated its enrichment and reprocessing activities of nuclear material, co-operated with the IAEA under the Additional Protocol that Resolution 1737 had imposed on it, or otherwise complied with those earlier resolutions.[488] Resolution 1803 further ratcheted up the sanctions on Iran for its recalcitrance by expanding the list of sanctioned Iranian individuals, entities, and items,[489] and calling on States to inspect cargo to and from Iran,[490] in addition to calling on States to remain vigilant with the sanctions against Iran. Again, Resolution 1803 did not require any new nuclear non-proliferation obligations than those imposed by earlier resolutions. Over six months later, the Security Council adopted Resolution 1835 on September 27, 2008, calling upon Iran to comply with its earlier obligations, without

[481] Ibid., ¶ 8 (original emphasis).

[482] UN Doc. S/PV.5612, *supra* note 126, at 2 (reporting that the United States implied that the provisions that start with the signal "calls upon" are among the requirements of this draft resolution).

[483] See S.C. Res. 1747, ¶ 4, UN Doc. S/RES/1747 (March 14, 2007). [484] Ibid., ¶ 5.

[485] Ibid., ¶ 7. [486] Ibid., ¶ 2. [487] Ibid., ¶ 6.

[488] See S.C. Res. 1803, preamb. ¶ 4, UN Doc. S/RES/1803 (March 3, 2008).

[489] See ibid., ¶¶ 3, 7–8. [490] See ibid., ¶ 11.

requiring anything further.[491] However, the Security Council adopted Resolution 1929 on June 9, 2010, again in response to the IAEA's numerous reports that Iran had not suspended its enrichment and reprocessing activities of nuclear material, had not co-operated with the IAEA through its Additional Protocol, and had not complied with the earlier resolutions of the Security Council,[492] but also noted its "serious concern that Iran has constructed an enrichment facility at Qom in breach of its obligations to suspend all enrichment-related activities" and "serious concern that Iran has enriched uranium to 20 per cent."[493] Resolution 1929 reiterated many of the obligations in earlier resolutions, including complying with its safeguards agreement, but extended the sanctions on Iranian individuals and entities, as well as clarifying the inspection and sanction expectations on member States, inter alia.[494] Thus we see how the Security Council gradually can ratchet up the strictness of the sanctions against a State in response to its continuing recalcitrance by expanding the scope of the applicability of the sanctions through repetitive resolutions. At the time of writing, Iran appears to continue its recalcitrance – notwithstanding these coercive Security Council measures – by allegedly redoubling its efforts at enriching uranium and showing interest in triggering technology for nuclear weapons.[495]

The legal issues raised in these resolutions relating to Resolutions 1696 and 1737 are similar to many of those raised in the other resolutions, especially the significance of "calls upon" and the ability of the Security Council to impose treaty obligations on States. In particular, that these resolutions require Iran to abide by its Additional Protocol is similar to those resolutions requiring North Korea to return to the NPT and the obligations of its safeguards agreement. Just as with those resolutions on North Korea, the permanent members of the Security Council acted in this coercive manner not only to maintain international peace and security but also to support the IAEA's activities in this area.[496] This

[491] See S.C. Res. 1835, ¶ 4, UN Doc. S/RES/1835 (Sept. 27, 2008).

[492] See S.C. Res. 1929, preamb. ¶ 4, UN Doc. S/RES/1929 (June 9, 2010).

[493] Ibid., preamb. ¶¶ 7–9. [494] See ibid., ¶¶ 1–24.

[495] See, e.g., David E. Sanger and William J. Broad, *Watchdog Finds Evidence that Iran Worked on Nuclear Triggers*, N.Y. Times, May 25, 2011, at A4 (it is unclear from the report when Iran supposedly developed this technology); David E. Sanger and William J. Broad, *Iran Says It Will Speed up Uranium Enrichment*, N.Y. Times, June 9, 2011, at A14.

[496] See UN Doc. S/PV.5612, *supra* note 126, at 2 (reporting that Russia noted this as its "main thrust" in supporting Resolution 1737).

stands as another example of the extent to which the Security Council is willing to create new nuclear non-proliferation obligations that somewhat resemble treaty obligations, and is not just an example of the Security Council trying to get a State to comply with its already existing obligations, as some commentators assert.[497] In addition, it shows the Security Council's willingness to act coercively in removing nuclear-weapon capabilities from States, despite commentary to the contrary.[498] Iran understandably has claimed a violation of its sovereignty as a result.[499] In such a situation, it is conceivable that Iran might benefit from relying on legal resolution for a determination of its rights and obligations, as explained in Part III of this study. That is to say, this would have been an ideal option before the Security Council had become involved.

3.2.7 WMD terrorism and Resolution 1540

The last resolution to be discussed in this part is Resolution 1540 and its impact on the Security Council's WMD counterterrorism efforts, including the nuclear non-proliferation regime. The September 11, 2001, terrorist attacks intensified the international community's attitude towards combating international terrorism and marked the shift of international terrorism from an "issue of ongoing concern" for the General Assembly to one that threatened international peace and security sufficiently to engage the Security Council in a meaningful way.[500] The intensity of the international community's efforts towards curbing terrorism has overflowed into the international community's WMD counterproliferation efforts, which includes nuclear non-proliferation. The fear of the destruction that could result if terrorists were to use such devastating weapons as nuclear weapons drives much of the recent multilateral activity in this area.[501] The link between WMD and

[497] See Andemicael, *supra* note 394, at 123–124.
[498] See Sutterlin, *supra* note 229, at 101.
[499] See, e.g., Elaine Sciolino, *Threats Rattle at Nuclear Meeting on Iran*, N.Y. Times, March 9, 2006, at A6.
[500] See Young, *supra* note 386, at 34; Rosand, *supra* note 386, at 333 (calling the Security Council's "deep involvement in the United Nation's counterterrorism effort" following September 11 a "new development").
[501] See generally Graham T. Allison, Nuclear Terrorism: The Ultimate Preventable Catastrophe (2004); Michael A. Levi, On Nuclear Terrorism (2007); Charles D. Ferguson, Preventing Catastrophic Nuclear Terrorism (2006).

terrorism was strengthened by President George W. Bush's 2002 State of the Union address, in which he combined the war against terrorism with a war against the members of the "Axis of Evil," which he asserted might pass WMD on to terrorist groups if they were allowed to develop their WMD capabilities. This link was further strengthened in the 2002 National Security Strategy of the United States.[502] Not surprisingly, in 2004, the United Nations High-Level Panel on Threats, Challenges, and Change (the High-Level Panel) saw WMD terrorism as a major threat to the international community.[503] While the Obama administration has retired the notion of "Axis of Evil," it nonetheless continues the close scrutiny of Iran and North Korea that intensified with that notion.

For some commentators, the only solution in responding to the heightened threat is for the Security Council to get involved in imposing obligations on States to take certain measures to stop WMD from getting into the hands of terrorists.[504] These commentators assert that the terrorism-related conventions adopted before September 11 provide the legal basis for action, although they do not state exactly what action should occur in case of violation, which would be left up to the Security Council to decide.[505] While it is true that these conventions are largely silent on what measures are to be taken in case of violation, they are clear about some of the preventive measures that States are to take prior to such a violation. Indeed, nine – and arguably ten – of the twelve conventions that deal with certain acts of terrorism before September 11 require some form of criminalization by the States parties. This seems to be the same approach that the Security Council has taken with Resolution 1540 in preventing WMD terrorism. Indeed, some might

[502] See Gray, *supra* note 93, at 176.

[503] See Report of the Secretary-General's High-Level Panel on Threats, Challenges and Change, *A More Secure World: Our Shared Responsibility*, at 19–21, 38–49, UN Doc. A/59/565 (Dec. 2, 2004).

[504] See e.g. Sutterlin, *supra* note 229, at 108.

[505] See ibid., at 110. These terrorism-related conventions that were adopted before September 11 include the Convention for the Suppression of Unlawful Seizure of Aircraft, the Convention for the Suppression of Unlawful Acts against the Safety of Civil Aviation, the United Nations Convention on the Prevention and Punishment of Crimes against Internationally Protected Persons, the International Convention against the Taking of Hostages, the Convention for the Suppression of Unlawful Acts against the Safety of Maritime Navigation, the International Convention for the Suppression of Terrorist Bombings, the International Convention for the Suppression of the Financing of Terrorism, the Convention on the Marking of Plastic Explosives for the Purpose of Detection, and the Convention on Offences and Certain Other Acts Committed on Board Aircraft.

say that the area of disarmament and arms control has entered a criminalization phase with the adoption of Resolution 1540, something that Bernard Baruch proposed in 1946 and Abram Chayes advocated in 1985,[506] but which had not been realized with regard to nuclear non-proliferation norms until Resolution 1540.

The threats coming from WMD terrorism are perceived to be so tremendous that the Security Council had to impose obligations on States through Resolution 1540 to try to deal with that threat, with Resolution 1810 encouraging States to comply with or continue their compliance with the obligations of Resolution 1540.[507] The question becomes whether these obligations constitute new obligations that are not covered by the WMD non-proliferation norms, especially the NPT, given how this study focuses on nuclear non-proliferation. Again, even if new obligations are not involved, and what is considered is rather the incorporation of treaty obligations into the UN law framework through a Security Council resolution, this would not be insignificant in itself, in that it would add Article 25 sanctions to the sanctions envisioned under the respective multilateral treaties, as explained in Chapter 3.1.4 above. The literature indicates that the main purpose of Resolution 1540 is to apply these treaties to non-parties in their entirety.[508] However, this interpretation of Resolution 1540 runs contrary to the plain meaning of paragraph 5 of that resolution, which makes it clear that "none of the obligations set forth in this resolution shall be interpreted so as to conflict with or alter the rights and obligations of State Parties to the [NPT, Chemical Weapons Convention (CWC), and BWC]."[509] In other words, Resolution 1540 does not touch the NPT, CWC, or BWC either by modifying them or by changing their membership, but rather *adds* to the obligations that States already have – or do not have, in the case of non-parties to these treaties – without these new obligations being *treaty* obligations per se. This interpretation of paragraph 5 is emphasized by the reference in paragraph 8(b), in which the Security Council "[c]alls

[506] See Abram Chayes, Arms Control Agreements 4 (1985); Statement of the United States Policy on Control of Atomic Energy as Presented by Bernard M. Baruch, Esq., to the United Nations Atomic Energy Commission (June 14, 1946). See also Note, *Legal Models of Arms Control: Past, Present, and Future*, 100 Harv. L. Rev. 1326, 1327 (1987) (discussing this aspect of the Baruch Plan).

[507] See S.C. Res. 1810, preamb. ¶ 4, ¶¶ 1–5, UN Doc. S/RES/1810 (April 25, 2008).

[508] See, e.g., Lisa Tabassi, *A Note on UN Security Council Resolution* 1540 (2004), 64 CBW Conventions Bull. 12, 12–13 (June 2004).

[509] S.C. Res. 1540, ¶ 5, UN Doc. S/RES/1540 (April 28, 2004).

upon all States . . . [t]o adopt national rules and regulations, where it has not yet been done, to ensure compliance with *their* commitments under the [NPT, CWC, and BWC]."[510] Had Resolution 1540 extended the NPT, CWC, and BWC themselves to non-parties, then paragraph 8(b) more likely would have replaced "their commitments" with "the commitments," because "their" emphasizes that the particular commitments might be different for different States.

In terms of new obligations that Resolution 1540 imposes on States, the resolution potentially creates at least three new obligations with its emphasis on non-State actors, on States adopting legislation, and on preventing trafficking and brokering. Paragraph 1 of Resolution 1540 requires all States to "refrain from providing any form of support to non-State actors that attempt to develop, acquire, manufacture, possess, transport, transfer or use *nuclear*, chemical or biological weapons and their means of delivery."[511] Paragraph 2 requires all States to

> adopt and enforce appropriate effective laws which prohibit any non-State actor to manufacture, acquire, possess, develop, transport, transfer or use *nuclear*, chemical or biological weapons and their means of delivery, in particular for terrorist purposes, as well as attempts to engage in any of the foregoing activities, participate in them as an accomplice, assist or finance them . . .[512]

Paragraph 3 states that the Security Council

> [*d*]*ecide*[*d*] also that all States shall take and enforce effective measures to establish domestic controls to prevent the proliferation of nuclear, chemical, or biological weapons and their means of delivery, including by establishing appropriate controls over related materials and to this end shall:
>
> a. Develop and maintain appropriate effective measures to account for and secure such items in production, use, storage or transport;
> b. Develop and maintain appropriate effective physical protection measures;
> c. Develop and maintain appropriate effective border controls and law enforcement efforts to detect, deter, prevent and combat, including through international cooperation when necessary, the illicit trafficking and brokering in such items in accordance with their national legal authorities and legislation and consistent with international law;
> d. Establish, develop, review and maintain appropriate effective national export and trans-shipment controls over such items, including appropriate laws and regulations to control export, transit, trans-shipment

[510] Ibid., ¶ 8(b) (emphasis added). [511] Ibid., ¶ 1 (emphasis added). [512] Ibid., ¶ 2.

> and re-export and controls on providing funds and services related to such export and transshipment such as financing, and transporting that would contribute to proliferation, as well as establishing end-user controls; and establishing and enforcing appropriate criminal or civil penalties for violations of such export control laws and regulations . . .[513]

The following three sections compare these three paragraphs with the provisions of the NPT, with an eye towards determining whether Resolution 1540 creates any new obligations. In short, there are three types of obligations that Resolution 1540 imposes on all States: an emphasis on non-State actors, an obligation to adopt legislation, and the requirement that all States incorporate into their legislation supply-side measures against nuclear non-proliferation.

3.2.7.1 New obligations concerning non-State actors

Compared to the other points in this section, this is a relatively minor one. The NPT lacks any reference to non-State actors, notwithstanding whatever obligations other WMD conventions impose on non-State actors. NPT Article III(1) does provide that safeguards "shall be applied on all source or special fissionable material in all peaceful nuclear activities within the territory of such State, under its jurisdiction, or carried out under its control anywhere."[514] However, this seems more like an obligation on the IAEA in implementing the safeguards agreements than an obligation on States to control the activities of non-State actors.

3.2.7.2 New obligations concerning legislation

The second type of obligation that Resolution 1540 contains involves the requirement for States to adopt legislation against persons who engage in particular activities. It is interesting to note how such an obligation is not unlike what a majority of the terrorism-related conventions have required of their member States.[515] This requirement to adopt legislation under Resolution 1540, as well as these terrorism-related conventions,

[513] Ibid., ¶ 3. [514] NPT, *supra* note 13, Art. III(1).

[515] For more information on how terrorism-related conventions have required legislation criminalizing certain terrorist activities and groups, see generally James D. Fry, *The Swindle of Fragmented Criminalization: Continuing Piecemeal Responses to International Terrorism and Al Qaeda*, 43 New England L. Rev. 377 (2009).

targets terrorist organizations that operate within domestic settings. Domestic legislation is essential to prosecuting and deterring such entities because there is no widely recognized international crime of terrorism yet.

It is important to first assess whether the NPT requires States to adopt legislation, and if so, what types of legislation they must adopt. The NPT contains no requirement – and no semblance of a requirement – that member States adopt legislation against persons who violate any of its provisions. Nonetheless, NPT Article III(4) requires non-nuclear-weapon States parties to "conclude agreements with the International Atomic Energy Agency to meet the requirements of this Article either individually or together with other States in accordance with the Statute of the International Atomic Energy Agency."[516] Out of the 162 States that the IAEA reports as having a safeguards agreement in force, seventy-seven of those States have publicized their safeguards agreement on the IAEA's website, and the Former Yugoslav Republic of Macedonia accepted the conditions of the Model Safeguards Agreement.[517] A review of these agreements for seventy-eight States shows that not one contains a requirement that the State adopt legislation against persons who violate the provisions of the NPT or the IAEA safeguards agreement. Nor does the IAEA Model Safeguards Agreement contain such a requirement, and nor do any other nuclear non-proliferation agreements, for that matter. Thus it is relatively safe to conclude that nothing at least in the core of the nuclear non-proliferation regime requires States to adopt legislation against particular acts that are in violation of the NPT, the IAEA safeguards agreements, or other related obligations.

In contrast, Resolution 1540, in paragraphs 2 and 3(d), requires States to adopt legislation against certain types of activity. Paragraph 2 of Resolution 1540 establishes the need for States to "adopt and enforce appropriate effective *laws*" against non-State actors who make or possess WMD and try to engage in such activities, or who act as accomplices, assistants, or financiers of such activities.[518] In addition, Paragraph 3(d) of Resolution 1540 requires States to

[516] NPT, *supra* note 13, Art. III(4).

[517] See Agreement For the Application of Safeguards in Connection with the Treaty on the Non-proliferation of Nuclear Weapons: An Agreement by Exchange of Letters with the Former Yugoslav Republic of Macedonia in Connection with the Treaty on the Non-proliferation of Nuclear Weapons, Maced.–IAEA, Oct. 4–Oct. 10, 2000, INFCIRC/610 (May 22, 2002).

[518] See S.C. Res. 1540, ¶ 2, UN Doc. S/RES/1540 (April 28, 2004) (emphasis added).

> [e]stablish, develop, review and maintain appropriate effective national export and trans-shipment controls over such items, including appropriate laws and regulations to control export, transit, trans-shipment and re-export and controls on providing funds and services related to such export and trans-shipment such as financing, and transporting that would contribute to proliferation, as well as establishing end-user controls; and establishing and enforcing appropriate criminal or civil penalties for violations of such export control laws and regulations . . .[519]

The obligation to adopt laws is clear. In sum, Resolution 1540 requires all States to adopt legislation criminalizing the manufacturing, acquisition, possession, development, transportation, transferring, or using of WMD; attempts to do any of these; and any participation in these activities as an accomplice, assistant, or financier.[520] By so doing, Resolution 1540 creates a minimum standard for all States, regardless of their obligations under the NPT, among other nuclear non-proliferation agreements.

3.2.7.3 New obligations in preventing trade in nuclear weapons and material

The third type of relevant obligation that Resolution 1540 contains is the obligation on States to legislate against persons who act as illicit traffickers or brokers of WMD, or who in any way assist in the acquisition or manufacturing of WMD. Paragraphs 3(c) and (d) of Resolution 1540 address trade in WMD, although it is paragraph 2 that has the broadest scope in this context. As already noted above, paragraph 2 requires States to adopt laws against non-State actors who make or possess WMD; who try to engage in such activities; or who are accomplices, assistants, or financiers of such activities.[521] Such accomplices, assistants, and financiers conceivably would be involved in the trade and transfer of such WMD. Paragraph 3(d), quoted above, clarifies that States are required to adopt "national export and trans-shipment controls" over WMD trade.[522] Paragraph 3(c) further requires that all States combat the "illicit trafficking and brokering" of WMD, whatever that might

[519] Ibid., ¶ 3(d).

[520] At the time of writing, 124 States had reported to the 1540 Committee legislation that they were in compliance with the requirements of Resolution 1540. See 1540 Committee Legislative Database, at http://disarmament2.un.org/Committee1540/list-legdb.html (last visited Dec. 28, 2010).

[521] See S.C. Res. 1540, ¶ 2, UN Doc. S/RES/1540 (April 28, 2004).

[522] Ibid., ¶ 3(d).

mean.[523] Use of the qualifier "illicit" suggests that States do not need to take and enforce effective measures to combat *non-illicit* trafficking and brokering of WMD, if this is possible. Similar to the analysis of Resolution 3(d) provided above, this language supports the notion that trade in WMD is not entirely prohibited by Resolution 1540 but instead is subject to a minimum standard for all States.

What is particularly interesting about paragraph 3(c) of Resolution 1540 in the context of nuclear non-proliferation is that it shifts focus from the demand side of nuclear non-proliferation to the supply side. Supply-side measures are defined as those "intended to restrict the military capabilities of Third World countries [and other States] by denying them access to technologies and materials likely to produce weapons of mass destruction," and demand-side restraints are defined as those "intended to eliminate or temper political and economic disputes that might serve as catalysts for armed conflict."[524] In comparison with other WMD treaties, the CWC and the BWC contain both types of obligations. CWC Article I(1)(a) requires States "never under any circumstances ... [t]o develop, produce, otherwise acquire, stockpile or retain chemical weapons, or transfer, directly or indirectly, chemical weapons to anyone,"[525] and Article I(1)(d) requires States "never under any circumstances ... [t]o assist, encourage or induce, in any way, anyone to engage in any activity prohibited to a State Party under this Convention."[526] Likewise, BWC Article I requires States "never in any circumstances to develop, produce, stockpile or otherwise acquire or retain [biological and toxin weapons]," with Article III requiring States "not to transfer to any recipient whatsoever, directly or indirectly, and not in any way to assist, encourage, or induce any State, group of States or international organizations to manufacture or otherwise acquire any of the agents, toxins, weapons, equipment or means of delivery specified in article I of the Convention." The NPT, however, involves demand-side non-proliferation obligations for all but the five nuclear-weapon States. Article II states,

> Each non-nuclear-weapon State Party to the Treaty undertakes not to receive the transfer from any transferor whatsoever of nuclear weapons

[523] Ibid., ¶ 3(c). [524] Lewis and Joyner, *supra* note 231, at 301.

[525] Convention on the Prohibition of the Development, Production, Stockpiling and Use of Chemical Weapons and on Their Destruction (CWC), Art. I(1)(a), Jan. 13, 1993, 1974 U.N.T.S. 45 (1997).

[526] Ibid., Art. I(1)(d).

> or other nuclear explosive devices or of control over such weapons or explosive devices directly, or indirectly; not to manufacture or otherwise acquire nuclear weapons or other nuclear explosive devices; and not to seek or receive any assistance in the manufacture of nuclear weapons or other nuclear explosive devices.[527]

This provision says that they cannot receive, make, or have assistance in making nuclear weapons or other nuclear explosive devices, which are clearly demand-side measures. At the same time, the NPT says absolutely nothing about these States giving or helping others to get or make nuclear weapons or other nuclear explosive devices, which would be supply-side measures. The assumption is that non-nuclear-weapon States are unable to provide such assistance because it is the nuclear-weapon States that have a monopoly on these materials and information, and have their own supply-side non-proliferation obligations provided by NPT Article I. Admittedly, the IAEA maintains an Illicit Trafficking Database with the assistance of approximately eighty States,[528] although involvement is voluntary and does not constitute a treaty obligation.

In sum, paragraph 3(c) of Resolution 1540 introduces new supply-side measures to the nuclear non-proliferation regime. Resolution 1540 imposes such supply-side nuclear non-proliferation measures on all States, regardless of their prior nuclear non-proliferation commitments.

3.2.7.4 Shifting to supply-side non-proliferation measures through imposition

Resolution 1540 raises many of the same issues that the earlier resolutions have raised, such as the ability of the Security Council to impose treaty-type obligations on States. In addition to these common points, it is interesting to note how the Security Council occasionally has replaced the cumbersome treaty negotiating process with the quick establishment of rules through its legislating those rules for all States.[529] This appears to be what happened in Resolution 1540. Indeed, it would have taken years

[527] NPT, *supra* note 13, Art. II.

[528] See Tariq Rauf and Jan Lodding, *UNSCR 1540 and the Role of the IAEA*, IN GLOBAL NON-PROLIFERATION AND COUNTER-TERRORISM: THE IMPACT OF UNSCR 1540 86, 92 (OLIVIA BOSCH and PETER VAN HAM ed., 2007).

[529] See Georg Nolte, *Lawmaking through the UN Security Council: A Comment on Erika de Wet's Contribution*, in DEVELOPMENTS OF INTERNATIONAL LAW IN TREATY MAKING 237, 241 (RÜDIGER WOLFRUM and VOLKER RÖBEN ed., 2005) (discussing this ability of the Security Council in the context of Resolution 1373 and its counter-terrorism efforts).

for States to shift to an emphasis on supply-side measures through perhaps renegotiating the NPT or commencing the negotiations for a new instrument. However, the Security Council achieved this through approximately one hour of formal debate within the Security Council and a unanimous vote of only fifteen members of the international community.[530] Nevertheless, as the principal agent of the international community,[531] the Security Council's circumvention of the treaty negotiating process shows a level of commitment by the international community to the adoption of effective measures regardless of consent. Unfortunately, the imposition of such supply-side controls in such a heavy-handed manner, such as in Resolution 1540, is not guaranteed to lead to tangible results, as dual-use technology is becoming so advanced that key items are bound to evade the best efforts at detection and inspection.[532] In an ideal world, the most effective way to combat nuclear proliferation would involve the slow persuasion of States through diplomatic negotiations to give up their demand for nuclear weapons, although such negotiations often take too much time and lead to relatively unpredictable results.[533] The Security Council is not powerless to impact the demand side of the equation. For example, a clear Security Council commitment that it will authorize the use of force against a State that deploys or threatens to deploy nuclear weapons would help to create the environment necessary to convince a State that they can give up their nuclear ambitions. In the end, a combination of supply-side and demand-side measures likely will be necessary to combat nuclear proliferation effectively, as the High-Level Panel concluded in 2004.[534]

States obviously will be less eager to comply with resolutions that lack their preferred amendments or counter their interests. States and civil

[530] See UN SCOR Provisional Verbatim Record, 59th Sess., 4956th mtg., at 2, UN Doc. S/PV.4956 (April 28, 2004). Presumably the real negotiating happened in small circles behind closed doors.

[531] See Ian Sinclair, *State Crimes Implementation Problems: Who Reacts?*, in INTERNATIONAL CRIMES OF STATE 256, 256–257 (JOSEPH H. H. WEILER et al. ed., 1989); Antti Korkeakivi, *Consequences of "Higher" International Law: Evaluating Crimes of State and* Erga Omnes, 2 J. INT'L LEGAL STUD. 81, 102–103 (1996); Richard Butler, *The Evolving Role of the UN and Disarmament*, in THE FUTURE OF DISARMAMENT 176, 190 (United Nations ed., 1998); Bardo Fassbender, *The UN Security Council and International Terrorism*, in ENFORCING INTERNATIONAL LAW NORMS AGAINST TERRORISM 83, 100 (ANDREA BIANCHI ed., 2004).

[532] See Dallmeyer, *supra* note 133, at 137.

[533] See Lewis and Joyner, *supra* note 231, at 301, 304.

[534] See High-Level Panel Report, *supra* note 503; see also THAKUR, *supra* note 97, at 177.

society invariably will complain that such heavy-handed imposition of obligations is undemocratic and contrary to the Security Council's mandate in the UN Charter, which does not expressly enable it to act as a global legislature.[535] Such critics must not forget the considerable discretion and power to bind that States gave to the Security Council when they joined the United Nations, which discretion is provided by Articles 25 and 103, as well as by Chapter VII. Nevertheless, the Security Council's activities take on a more coercive feel when it acts under the UN Charter as opposed to the relevant treaty provisions of the nuclear non-proliferation regime laid out in the following chapter, inasmuch as it becomes more difficult to argue that the target State has consented to the measures taken against them.

3.3 Conclusion for this part

Nobel Peace Prize Laureate and disarmament advocate Arthur Henderson asserted after the First World War that "[i]t has become impossible to give up the enterprise of disarmament without abandoning the whole great adventure of building up a collective peace system." Whereas Henderson saw the collective security system as needing disarmament, in the intervening decades the system has evolved to the point where the realization of disarmament and arms control – including nuclear non-proliferation efforts – actually needs encouragement from the Security Council (the hub of the modern collective security system) for there to be real progress in certain situations. This chapter has explored a variety of ways that the Security Council has imposed nuclear non-proliferation obligations on States. The resolutions referred to in Chapter 3.2.1 above, dealing with the security assurances relating to the NPT and resolutions relating to Israel, act as evidence of what was possible during the Cold War when the United States and the Soviet Union were in agreement. The Security Council's importance in the non-proliferation discourse seems to vary, depending on how well the permanent members of the Security Council co-operate.[536] Just as the end of the Cold War brought a new era of co-operation, with the United States and the Soviet Union reaching nuclear non-proliferation agreements

[535] See also THAKUR, *supra* note 97, at 169.

[536] See HERNANE TAVARES DE SÁ, THE PLAY WITHIN THE PLAY: THE INSIDE STORY OF THE UN 9 (1966).

both within and outside the United Nations system,[537] partial détente between the United States and the Soviet Union at certain times throughout the Cold War made possible the resolutions that the Security Council adopted during the Cold War.

Starting with Resolution 255, the ability of these two superpowers to agree to give security assurances to non-nuclear-weapon States was truly remarkable. However, before concluding that this was an anomaly in an otherwise cantankerous half-century of relations between the United States and the Soviet Union, it is interesting to note how some historians identify two Cold Wars as having followed the Second World War,[538] with Resolution 255 having occurred during that inter-Cold War period.

Resolution 487, dealing with Israel, stands as another example of the way in which the Security Council was able to impose obligations during the Cold War when the United States and the Soviet Union were in agreement. Here, agreement was possible in condemning a US client State – namely Israel – because the United States thought that Israel had violated the UN Charter by not exhausting the peaceful means of resolution that had been available to it,[539] and that the IAEA should be "respected by all nations."[540] The Soviet Union emphasized the need to respond strongly to Israel's attack in order to preserve the IAEA safeguards system and the nuclear non-proliferation system.[541] Admittedly, members of the Security Council had varying reasons for opposing Israel's actions against Iraq – with some States focused more on the IAEA's determination that there was no evidence that Iraq was going to use the reactors to develop nuclear weapons, while others were opposed to Israel's brand of anticipatory self-defense – although they all agreed that a relatively strong response against Israel was in order. However, it

[537] See Bourantonis and Evriviades, *supra* note 1, at 155; Ekeus, *supra* note 133, at 67 (noting, for example, the Treaty on Intermediate-Range and Shorter-Range Missiles, the Treaty on Conventional Forces in Europe, the Strategic Arms Reduction Treaties I and II, the CWC, and Security Council Resolution 687 regarding the disarmament of Iraq).

[538] See generally MARTIN MCCAULEY, RUSSIA, AMERICA AND THE COLD WAR, 1949–1991 81–87 (2nd edn, 2004); Matthew Leitner, HEI Lecture, *The First Cold War: The Battle for Europe*, May 8, 2006.

[539] See GRAY, *supra* note 93, at 133.

[540] UN SCOR, 36th Sess., 2288th mtg., at 4, UN Doc. S/PV.2288 (June 19, 1981).

[541] See ibid., at 15. But see ibid., at 13–14 (noting that the German Democratic Republic read this resolution as not requiring Israel to stop nuclear collaboration); see ibid., at 14.

was the US–Soviet agreement on this general matter that made Resolution 487 possible.

The rapprochement between the United States and the Soviet Union (and later the Russian Federation) that ended the Cold War made agreement within the Security Council far easier than before, which led to an increase in the number and strength of resolutions imposing nuclear non-proliferation obligations on States. Barring the deterioration of relations between the United States and Russia (or any other permanent members of the Security Council), it is likely that the Security Council will continue to impose nuclear non-proliferation measures on States through its Chapter VII powers when issues of supposed non-compliance arise. Such reliance on coercive measures by the Security Council can help put pressure on States to comply with nuclear non-proliferation norms.[542] Although admittedly not all violations of nuclear non-proliferation norms are equally threatening,[543] the Security Council has been quite clear that any violation of nuclear non-proliferation norms is a threat to international peace and security.[544] The first preambular paragraph of Resolution 1540 affirmed that WMD proliferation, including nuclear proliferation, is a threat to international peace and security,[545] thus warranting greater coercive measures in this field by the Security Council in the future. That WMD proliferation prima facie equates to a threat to international peace and security has been a groundbreaking change in this field inasmuch as it signaled the Security Council's ongoing commitment to combating WMD proliferation with all the force it has at its disposal. Just as Clark Eichelberger called in 1955 for "universal enforceable disarmament" through collective security,[546] this newfound willingness of the Security Council to use its Chapter VII powers to respond to WMD proliferation issues, including nuclear proliferation issues, reflects the possibility of this becoming a reality. In light of the resolutions discussed above, especially the resolutions against Iran

542 See THAKUR, *supra* note 97, at 168.

543 LOUIS B. SOHN (ed.), CASES ON UNITED NATIONS LAW 994–995 (1st edn, 1956) (stating that "it is [a] fact that many breaches of [arms limitation treaties] are of a minor, unintentional or technical character"). But see WRIGHT, *supra* note 91, at 122 (implying that all violations of disarmament agreement constitute a threat to international peace and security by not specifying that there might be minor violations that do not constitute such a threat).

544 The President of the Security Council, *Note by the President of the Security Council*, *supra* note 137, at 4; see Ekeus, *supra* note 133, at 68.

545 S.C. Res. 1540, ¶ 1, UN Doc. S/RES/1540 (April 28, 2004).

546 CLARK M. EICHELBERGER, UN: THE FIRST TEN YEARS 52–53 (1955).

and North Korea, the Security Council is well on its way to fulfilling a role as creator and enforcer of such non-proliferation norms.

However, this is not necessarily a positive development, as some critics might argue, saying that more Security Council involvement diminishes the need for involvement of international courts and tribunals. This study responds by emphasizing the *quality* over the *quantity* of that involvement, especially from the perspective of the target State, whose co-operation with and approval of the resolution process with that particular dispute possibly makes a meaningful difference in the realization of international peace and security in that situation. As this chapter has shown and as Chapter 5.3 below emphasizes, the Security Council's activities with regard to nuclear non-proliferation might have negative legal implications on States and the international community, at least vis-à-vis legal resolution, even though the Security Council may have designed them to have a positive impact on international peace and security. In particular, the Security Council's imposition of nuclear non-proliferation obligations is seen as causing problems in at least five ways:

- by requiring States to join nuclear non-proliferation agreements;
- by requiring States to abide by certain nuclear non-proliferation agreements that are not already binding on those States;
- by requiring States to abide by obligations that resemble modified nuclear non-proliferation agreement provisions;
- by requiring States to abide by certain nuclear non-proliferation obligations not contained in treaties; and
- by recalling pre-existing nuclear non-proliferation agreement obligations on States, thereby incorporating them into the UN law framework and modifying the nature of those obligations in doing so, since a State cannot withdraw from a Security Council resolution, for example.

Ironically, by imposing obligations on States in an effort to uphold various agreements of the nuclear non-proliferation regime, it may be undermining the very regime it struggles to support by suspending States' rights under this regime and otherwise impacting their sovereignty. Although the Security Council acts in a lawful manner under its UN Charter Chapter VII powers when doing so, the Security Council must consider that the legality and optimality of its actions are not necessarily the same, especially when such a sensitive regime as that involving nuclear non-proliferation is concerned. To borrow a saying among climbers, "One who is poised on the edge of a cliff is wise to define progress as a step backward." The Security Council might want to consider whether its heavy-handed measures, in the absence of adequate due-process safeguards, actually cause more problems than they cure. To remind the reader, those problems could include the target State's refusal to accept the outcome due to the perceived flaws in the process, and the possible escalation of the dispute as a result of the target State's gaining a stronger us-versus-them fortress mentality, both of which are potential problems noted in the introductory portion of this study. However, recognizing that the Security Council will do what it will do under its broad Chapter VII powers, the following part of this book turns to a legal option that exists in the hands of would-be target States – namely legal resolution of their nuclear non-proliferation disputes.

PART III

Legal resolution and nuclear non-proliferation disputes*

* A version of parts of this part originally appeared in the *Stanford Journal of International Law*. See James D. Fry, Arbitrating Arms Control Disputes, 44 *Stanford Journal of International Law* 359–420 (2008).

INTRODUCTION

"Be careful: they have arms, and no alternatives," warned Polish author Ryszard Kapuscinski. When coercive measures loom and a State feels that the international community intends to isolate it, having the option of an impartial third party to resolve all or part of the underlying dispute through settled procedures and through the application of law might, in certain situations, be just what is needed. The preceding part of this study explained some of the problems that arise from Security Council involvement with nuclear non-proliferation disputes under its Chapter VII powers. This part proposes legal resolution as a viable alternative to Security Council involvement under Chapter VII, which the target State may be able to rely upon in avoiding problems of these types, in addition to the more obvious problems associated with war. To be clear, this study presents legal resolution of nuclear non-proliferation disputes as a viable *alternative* to Security Council involvement with nascent disputes that have not yet reached the level of endangering international peace and security. This study does not portray legal resolution as fulfilling a *complementary* role to Security Council involvement under Chapter VII with these types of disputes because they fulfill roughly parallel functions in dealing with the rights and obligations of States – legal resolution interpreting States' rights and obligations and the Security Council creating new rights and obligations and suspending old ones using its Chapter VII powers.[1] This is not to say that legal resolution never can fulfill a function complementary to that of the Security Council, inasmuch as legal resolution potentially can handle all types of nuclear non-proliferation disputes, including minor ones of a very technical nature, with Security Council involvement being reserved for the more politically sensitive matters. With the Security Council's ability

[1] See Vera Gowlland-Debbas, *The Relationship between the International Court of Justice and the Security Council in the Light of the Lockerbie Case*, 88 Am. J. Int'l L. 643, 658–659 (1994) (discussing "parallel functionalism" between the ICJ and the Security Council).

to suspend conflicting treaty obligations and the lack of a strong tradition in judicial review of Security Council resolutions, it becomes increasingly difficult to envision a way for these two methods of resolution to be complementary, apart from the type of situation where the Security Council gets involved at the request of one of the parties to the dispute to "give effect to the judgment" of the International Court of Justice, as provided for by UN Charter Article 94(2),[2] or where armed conflict occurs in relation to a dispute after the commencement of legal proceedings but before the conclusion of those proceedings.[3]

This part pushes the envelope of the legal literature on account of the fact that contemporary commentators tend to dismiss legal resolution of nuclear non-proliferation disputes. Many studies talk of the need for new alternatives with nuclear non-proliferation disputes and, in that context, may discuss improving conflict resolution generally, but they make no significant mention of legal resolution,[4] despite the fact that they tend to canvass quite creative alternatives, such as having political leaders

[2] See UN Charter, Art. 94(2).

[3] See Shilan Shah-Davis, *Conclusion*, in INTERNATIONAL LAW AND ARMED CONFLICT: CHALLENGES IN THE 21ST CENTURY 425, 428–429 (NOËLLE QUÉNIVET and SHILAN SHAH-DAVIS ed., 2010).

[4] See generally JOHAN GALTUNG, THERE ARE ALTERNATIVES! FOUR ROADS TO PEACE AND SECURITY 40–80 (1984); WILLIAM EPSTEIN and BERNARD T. FELD (eds.), NEW DIRECTIONS IN DISARMAMENT (1974); T. T. POULOSE, THE FUTURE OF NUCLEAR ARMS CONTROL (1987); Harold A. Feiveson and Theodore B. Taylor, *Alternative Strategies for International Control of Nuclear Power*, in NUCLEAR PROLIFERATION: MOTIVATIONS, CAPABILITIES, AND STRATEGIES FOR CONTROL 123 (TED GREENWOOD et al. ed., 1974) (proposing new ideas with nuclear arms control); DAVID C. GOMPERT et al. (eds.), NUCLEAR WEAPONS AND WORLD POLITICS: ALTERNATIVES FOR THE FUTURE (1974) (same); BURNS H. WESTON (ed.), TOWARD NUCLEAR DISARMAMENT AND GLOBAL SECURITY: A SEARCH FOR ALTERNATIVES (1984) (same); HILLIARD RODERICK and ULLA MAGNUSSON (eds.), AVOIDING INADVERTENT WAR: CRISIS MANAGEMENT (1983) (discussing different means of crisis management when nuclear war is threatened, but not mentioning the option of legal resolution); ANDREW C. GOLDBERG et al. (eds.), AVOIDING THE BRINK: THEORY AND PRACTICE IN CRISIS MANAGEMENT (1990) (same); RICHARD NED LEBOW, NUCLEAR CRISIS MANAGEMENT: A DANGEROUS ILLUSION (1987) (same); JEFFREY LAURENTI and CARL ROBICHAUD (eds.), BREAKING THE NUCLEAR IMPASSE: NEW PROSPECTS FOR SECURITY AGAINST WEAPONS THREATS (2007); WILLIAM C. POTTER and GAUKHAR MUKHATZHANOVA (eds.), FORECASTING NUCLEAR PROLIFERATION IN THE 21ST CENTURY: THE ROLE OF THEORY (2010). But see Arthur Larson, *The Role of Law in Building Peace*, in PREVENTING WORLD WAR III: SOME PROPOSALS 332 (QUINCY WRIGHT et al. ed., 1962) (in a book that addresses nuclear non-proliferation disputes in part, a chapter that tentatively explores the possibility of legal resolution of politically sensitive disputes, though without itself mentioning nuclear non-proliferation disputes per se).

submit to lie-detector tests when making policy statements concerning their nuclear-weapon programs.[5] Some commentators see the need for new *legal* solutions to problems relating to nuclear non-proliferation disputes,[6] although again they do not talk about legal resolution in particular, let alone focus on it. The titles of some studies hold out the hope that they will address legal resolution of nuclear non-proliferation disputes, such as David Koplow's article "The Jurisprudence of Non-proliferation: Taking International Law Seriously," though his usage of the term "jurisprudence" has nothing to do with adjudication, but instead relates broadly to legal matters such as the development of treaties, customary international law, and disarmament institutions that relate to non-proliferation of weapons generally.[7]

Those commentators who mention legal resolution in the context of nuclear non-proliferation tend to do so in passing, sometimes with an ironic note that these issues receive little scholarly attention,[8] or tend to

[5] See Ralph W. Gerard, *Truth Detection*, in PREVENTING WORLD WAR III: SOME PROPOSALS 52 (GINCY WRIGHT et al. ed., 1962).

[6] See Barry Kellman, *International Consensus and States Non-parties*, in FUTURE LEGAL RESTRAINTS ON ARMS PROLIFERATION 151, 174 (JULIE DAHLITZ ed., 1996).

[7] See generally David A. Koplow, *The Jurisprudence of Non-proliferation: Taking International Law Seriously*, 2 TRANSNAT'L L & CONTEMP. PROBS. 357 (1992). See also Alyn Ware, *Rule of Force or Rule of Law? Legal Responses to Nuclear Threats from Terrorism, Proliferation, and War*, 2 SEATTLE J. SOC. JUST. 243 (2004) (referring to the possibility of "legal responses" to nuclear proliferation, without mentioning legal resolution); Eric Yong-Joong Lee, *The Six-Party Talks and the North Korean Nuclear Dispute Resolution under the IAEA Safeguards Regime*, 5 ASIAN-PACIFIC L. & POL'Y J. 101 (2004) (focusing on dispute resolution under the IAEA Safeguards Regime without acknowledging the express role of legal resolution there); Serge Sur, *A Legal Approach to Verification in Disarmament or Arms Limitation* 8 (UNIDIR, Research Paper No. 1, 1988); Arsalan M. Sulemna, *Bargaining in the Shadow of Violence: The NPT, IAEA, and Nuclear Non-proliferation Negotiations*, 26 BERKELEY J. INT'L L. 206 (2008) (referring to the nuclear non-proliferation regime throughout as a "dispute system," presumably meaning a "dispute settlement system," without recognizing legal resolution's role therein).

[8] See Burns H. Weston, *Lawyers and the Search for Alternatives to Nuclear Deterrence*, 54 U. CIN. L. REV. 451, 460 (1985) (listing legal resolution along with many of the other methods of resolution mentioned in UN Charter Art. 33 in the context of trying to enhance dispute resolution mechanisms as a viable alternative if nuclear disarmament is not to be realized); Matthew Liles, *Did Kim Jong-Il Break the Law? A Case Study on How North Korea Highlights the Flaws of the Non-proliferation Regime*, 33 N.C.J. INT'L L. & COM. REG. 103, 138 (2007) (mentioning how the ICJ can handle disputes over interpretation of the IAEA Statute under IAEA Statute Art. XVII(A)); Kellman, *supra* note 6, at 159 (ironically asking the question, "Will international tribunals have competence over arms control offences?" and then acknowledging that these types of question have

dismiss the possibility without explaining why.[9] This typically is done after conducting a somewhat superficial review of the dispute settlement provisions in related treaties.[10] These commentators barely even mention expanding the involvement of legal resolution in the very sections where they address ways to improve the disarmament and arms control regime in the future.[11] Those commentators who do mention expanding the involvement of legal resolution in this context go no further than briefly referring to it in a wishful manner.[12] Their haste in downplaying

"received scant scholarly attention" before moving on to other topics without providing any more analysis).

9 See Françoise Hampson and Hilaire McCoubrey, *Evidence in Cases Involving Proliferation Issues*, in FUTURE LEGAL RESTRAINTS ON ARMS PROLIFERATION 273, 289 (JULIE DAHLITZ ed., 1996); John B. Rhinelander, *Limitations and Safeguards in Arms Control Agreements*, in LAW AND FORCE IN THE NEW INTERNATIONAL ORDER 247, 250, 255 (LORI F. DAMROSCH and DAVID J. SCHEFFER ed., 1991); JAN KOLASA, DISARMAMENT AND ARMS CONTROL AGREEMENTS: A STUDY ON PROCEDURAL AND INSTITUTIONAL LAW 52, 64 (1995) (noting the role of the ICJ (but not international arbitration) with some arms control and disarmament treaties, but concluding the chapter with a generalization that "a definite tendency towards the regulation of disputes, arising out of the process of implementation of disarmament and arms control treaties, through political rather than judicial means may be identified"); Julie Dahlitz, NUCLEAR ARMS CONTROL 119 (1983) (recognizing the possibility of ICJ involvement in resolving nuclear non-proliferation disputes but dismissing the possibility for international arbitration, without explaining why).

10 See generally KOLASA, *supra* note 9, at 51–61 (providing, in a chapter on procedural clauses within disarmament and arms control treaties, a section on dispute settlement, although essentially all he does is walk the reader through the various dispute settlement and interpretation provisions in the various treaties, with little theoretical development of the possibility of legal resolution of disputes over these treaties); GÖRAN LYSÉN, THE INTERNATIONAL REGULATION OF ARMAMENTS: THE LAW OF DISARMAMENT 216–217 (1990) (devoting a single page of his book THE LAW OF DISARMAMENT to the ways that treaties make reference to the ICJ with regard to dealing with disputes, with the clear emphasis being on diplomatic methods of resolution and no other discussion of the possibility of legal resolution being made in the rest of the book); GUIDO DEN DEKKER, THE LAW OF ARMS CONTROL: INTERNATIONAL SUPERVISION AND ENFORCEMENT 203–208, 72, 114, 109, 134 (2001) (walking the reader through the dispute settlement provisions of various arms control treaties in six pages of a section on dispute settlement, the first cited here, but nonetheless dismissing the role of legal resolution of these types of dispute); ibid., at 71, 134 (confusingly noting a few instances where international adjudication has been involved with weapon-related matters but immediately forgetting these instances when he refers to the "absence of involvement of the [international] judiciary in arms control matters" and states that "no arms control agreement establishes a judicial body for the purpose of settling disputes relating to the treaty").

11 See LYSÉN, *supra* note 10, at 218–19, 224 (1990) (mentioning the possible establishment of the International Disarmament Organization, the International Satellite Monitoring Agency and other bilateral verification bodies for the United States and Russia).

12 See John H. McNeill, *Commentary on Dispute Resolution Mechanisms in Arms Control Agreements*, in LAW AND FORCE IN THE NEW INTERNATIONAL ORDER 258, 260–261 (LORI F. DAMROSCH and DAVID J. SCHEFFER ed., 1991); Vejay Lalla, *The Effectiveness of*

the role of legal resolution within these treaties is emblematic of their disparaging attitude towards legal resolution.

Of those commentators who provide reasons for rejecting legal resolution in this context, the main reasons are (1) that nuclear non-proliferation disputes are too politically sensitive for legal resolution, (2) that legal resolution can exacerbate tensions, (3) that legal resolution is principally a means for States to harass other States or to file protests against the political process, (4) that legal resolution is too inflexible and slow for such important disputes, (5) that disputants lose too much control by submitting these important disputes to legal resolution, (6) that there are too many gaps in the law relating to nuclear non-proliferation for legal resolution to render a valid decision, (7) that legal resolution is too biased, and (8) that legal resolution is too unpredictable for such important disputes. In an effort to convince States and the international community to give legal resolution due consideration with nuclear non-proliferation disputes when the alternatives are war or coercive Security Council measures, Chapter 5.3 sets out and responds to all of these criticisms except the first, which Chapter 6 responds to in detail. As those portions show, none of these criticisms pose the level of difficulty for legal resolution that these commentators envision.

A few exceptions exist where the commentator does take somewhat seriously the involvement of legal resolution concerning nuclear weapons. There are an inordinate number of legal studies – dating back to the first works on the legal issues surrounding nuclear weapons – that focus exclusively on the legality of nuclear weapons from the perspective of the

the Comprehensive Test Ban Treaty on Nuclear Weapons Proliferation: A Review of Nuclear Non-proliferation Treaties and the Impact of the Indian and Pakistani Nuclear Tests on the Non-proliferation Regime, 8 CARDOZO J. INT'L & COMP. L. 103, 124 (2000) (declaring, internal citations omitted, "Although international law is generally designed to prevent disputes and promote arbitration, it should play a more controlling role where there is a dispute between two parties to a nuclear non-proliferation treaty," though doing little to discuss the matter further to help their wish become a reality); Edwin J. Nazario, *The Potential Role of Arbitration in the Nuclear Non-proliferation Treaty Regime*, 10 AM. REV. INT'L ARB. 139, 154 (1999); Susan Carmody, *Balancing Collective Security and National Sovereignty: Does the United Nations have the Right to Inspect North Korea's Nuclear Facilities?*, 18 FORDHAM INT'L L.J. 229 (1994); Gerald T. McLaughlin, *Remembering the Bay of Pigs: Using Letters of Credit to Facilitate the Resolution of International Disputes*, 32 GA. J. INT'L & COMP. L. 743, 768–769 (2004) (proposing a creative way to get compromissory clauses involved with weapons-related disputes, suggesting that States might try to sneak compromissory clauses into certain situations by providing letters of credit to recalcitrant States if they promise to give up their WMD ambitions, though without acknowledging that compromissory clauses already exist in treaties of these types).

laws of war, the law relating to the use of force, international environmental law, or international human rights law, with an implicit or explicit eye towards involving the ICJ in making a determination of legality of nuclear weapons.[13] Many of these works seem to be an extension of the ban-the-bomb peace movement. However, none of

[13] See, e.g., Ellery Stowell, *The Law of War and the Atomic Bomb*, 39 AM. J. INT'L L. 784 (1945); Elbert D. Thomas, *Atomic Bombs in International Society*, 39 AM. J. INT'L L. 736 (1945); Elbert D. Thomas, *Atomic Warfare and International Law*, 40 AM. J. INT'L L. 84 (1946); J. SPAIGHT, THE ATOMIC PROBLEM (1948); R. E. Charlier, *Questions juridiques soulevées par l'évolution de la science atomique*, 91 REC. DES COURS 354 (1957); GEORG SCHWARZENBERGER, THE LEGALITY OF NUCLEAR WEAPONS (1958); MORRIS GREENSPAN, THE MODERN LAW OF LAND WARFARE 368–378 (1959); A. Euler, *Légalité ou illégalité des armes nucléaires*, 2 REC. DE LA SOCIÉTÉ INTERNATIONALE DE DROIT PÉNAL MILITAIRE ET DE DROIT DE LA GUERRE 93 (1963); Henri Meyrowitz, *Les juristes devant l'arme nucléaire*, 1963 RGDIP 820, 844, 852 (1963); STEFAN GLASER, L'ARME NUCLÉAIRE À LA LUMIÈRE DU DROIT INTERNATIONAL (1964); Ian Brownlie, *Some Legal Aspects of the Use of Nuclear Weapons*, 14 INT'L & COMP. L.Q. 437 (1965); Fred Bright, *Nuclear Weapons as a Lawful Means of Warfare*, 30 MIL. L. REV. 1 (1965); F. von der Heydte, *Le problème que pose l'existence des armes de destruction massive et la distinction entre les objectifs militaries et non militaries en général*, 52(2) ANNUAIRE DE L'INSTITUT DE DROIT INTERNATIONAL 88 (1967); W. Thomas Mallison, *The Laws of War and Juridical Control of Weapons of Mass Destruction in General and Limited War*, 36 G.W. L. REV. 308 (1968); M. THEE (ed.), ARMAMENTS AND DISARMAMENT IN THE NUCLEAR AGE (1976) (arguing that there needs to be more international humanitarian law to regulate nuclear weapons); B. V. A. ROLING AND O. SUKOVIC, THE LAW OF WAR AND DUBIOUS WEAPONS (1976); P. Bretton, *Le problème des "méthodes et moyens de guerre ou de combat" dans les Protocoles additionnels aux Conventions de Genève du 12 août 1949*, 82 RGDIP 32 (1978); Henri Meyrowitz, *La stratégie nucléaire et le Protocole additionnel aux Conventions de Genève de 1949*, 83 RGDIP 905 (1979); RICHARD FALK et al., NUCLEAR WEAPONS AND INTERNATIONAL LAW (1981); Richard Bilder, *Distinguishing Human Rights and Humanitarian Law: The Issue of Nuclear Weapons*, 31 AM. UNIV. L. REV. 959 (1982); Amynmohamed Sajoo, *Human Rights Perspectives on the Arms Race*, 28 MCGILL L. REV. 628 (1982); Edward Cummings, *The Role of Humanitarian Law*, 9 BROOKLYN J. INT'L L. 269 (1983); Ved Nanda, *Nuclear Weapons and the Right to Peace under International Law*, 9 BROOKLYN J. INT'L L. 283 (1983); Simone Courteix, *La contrôle de la prolifération des armes nucléaires*, 28 MCGILL L.J. 591 (1983); Elliott L. Meyrowitz, *The Laws of War and Nuclear Weapons*, in NUCLEAR WEAPONS AND LAW 19 (ARTHUR SELWYN MILLER and MARTIN FEINRIDER ed., 1984); Eric David, *À propos de certaines justifications théoriques à l'emploi de l'arme nucléaire*, in STUDIES AND ESSAYS ON INTERNATIONAL HUMANITARIAN LAW AND RED CROSS PRINCIPLES IN HONOUR OF JEAN PICTET 325 (CHRISTOPHE SWINARSKI ed., 1984); John Norton Moore, *Nuclear Weapons and the Law: Enhancing Strategic Stability*, in NUCLEAR WEAPONS AND LAW 51 (ARTHUR SELWYN MILLER and MARTIN FEINRIDER ed., 1984) (responding to Meyrowitz's arguments); Harry H. Almond Jr., *Deterrence and a Policy-Oriented Perspective on the Legality of Nuclear Weapons*, in NUCLEAR WEAPONS AND LAW 57 (ARTHUR SELWYN MILLER and MARTIN FEINRIDER ed.,

them deals with nuclear non-proliferation disputes per se. Numerous legal studies since 1996 follow the same logic that focuses on bodies of law outside that relating specifically to nuclear non-proliferation, as they review the ICJ's *Legality of Nuclear Weapons* advisory opinion, though their arguments exhibit minimal, if any, applicability to the broader notion that legal resolution can resolve actual nuclear non-proliferation disputes.[14] These studies' lack of focus on the law relating to nuclear non-proliferation per se is not surprising, given

1984); Richard Falk, *Toward a Legal Regime for Nuclear Weapons*, in NUCLEAR WEAPONS AND LAW 107 (ARTHUR SELWYN MILLER and MARTIN FEINRIDER ed., 1984); W. Michael Reisman, *Deterrence and International Law*, in NUCLEAR WEAPONS AND LAW 129 (ARTHUR SELWYN MILLER and MARTIN FEINRIDER ed., 1984); Burns H. Weston, *Nuclear Weapons versus International Law: A Contextual Reassessment*, in NUCLEAR WEAPONS AND LAW 133 (ARTHUR SELWYN MILLER and MARTIN FEINRIDER ed., 1984); B. V. A. Röling, *International Law, Nuclear Weapons, Arms Control and Disarmament*, in NUCLEAR WEAPONS AND LAW 181 (ARTHUR SELWYN MILLER and MARTIN FEINRIDER ed., 1984); Frank P. Grad, *Consequences of Nuclear Weapons Use as Viewed by an Environmental Lawyer*, in NUCLEAR WEAPONS AND LAW 387 (ARTHUR SELWYN MILLER and MARTIN FEINRIDER ed., 1984); Burns H. Weston, *Nuclear Weapons and International Law: Prolegomenon to General Illegality*, 4 N.Y. L. SCH'L J. INT'L & COMP. L. 227 (1984); Adam Roberts, *The Relevance of Laws of War in the Nuclear Age*, in NUCLEAR WEAPONS: THE PEACE MOVEMENT AND THE LAW 25 (J. DEWAR et al. ed., 1986); Nicholas Grief, *The Legality of Nuclear Weapons*, in NUCLEAR WEAPONS AND INTERNATIONAL LAW 22 (ISTVAN POGANY ed., 1987); MARGARET E. GOUIN, NUCLEAR LAW: THE APPLICATION OF CANADIAN AND RELATED INTERNATIONAL PUBLIC LAW PRINCIPLES TO THE OBLIGATIONS OF CANADA IN RELATION TO NUCLEAR WEAPONS (1989); ELLIOTT L. MEYROWITZ, PROHIBITION OF NUCLEAR WEAPONS: THE RELEVANCE OF INTERNATIONAL LAW (1990); NICHOLAS GRIEF, THE WORLD COURT PROJECT ON NUCLEAR WEAPONS AND INTERNATIONAL LAW (1993).

14 See, e.g., A. Vaughan Lowe, *Shock Verdict: Nuclear War May or May Not Be Unlawful*, 55 CAMBRIDGE L.J. 415 (1996); A. S. Millet, *Les avis consultatifs de la Cour international de justice du 8 Juillet 1996*, 101 RGDIP 141 (1997); Michael J. Matheson, *The Opinions of the International Court of Justice on the Threat or Use of Nuclear Weapons*, 91 AM. J. INT'L L. 417 (1997); Michael N. Schmitt, *The International Court of Justice and the Use of Nuclear Weapons*, 7 J. LEGAL STUDIES 57 (1997); CHARLES MOXLEY, NUCLEAR WEAPONS AND INTERNATIONAL LAW IN THE POST-COLD WAR WORLD (2000); Anguel Anastassov, *Are Nuclear Weapons Illegal? The Role of Public International Law and the International Court of Justice*, 15 J. CONFLICT & SEC. L. 65, 76 (2010); Vincent Coussirat-Coustère, *Armes nucléaires et droit international: À propos des avis consultatifs du 8 juillet 1996 de la Cour internationale de justice*, 42 AFDI 337 (1996); MARIE-PIERRE LANFRANCHI, LA LICÉITÉ DE L'EMPLOI D'ARMES NUCLÉAIRES DEVANT LA COUR INTERNATIONALE DE JUSTICE: ANALYSE ET DOCUMENTS (1997); Dapo Akande, *Nuclear Weapons, Unclear Law?*, 68 BRIT. Y.B. INT'L L. 165 (1997); WILLIAM H. BOOTHBY, WEAPONS AND THE LAW OF ARMED CONFLICT 215–223 (2009); ABDULHAY SAYED, QUAND LE DROIT EST FACE À SON NÉANT: LE DROIT À L'ÉPREUVE DE L'EMPLOI DE L'ARME NUCLÉAIRE (1998); M. CHEMILLIER-GENDRAU, LA C.I.J. ENTRE POLITIQUE ET DROIT (1996); C. F. Amerasinghe, *The*

how the ICJ also did not focus much on this specific body of law,[15] and this for the relatively obvious reason that this body of law simply does not prohibit nuclear weapons.[16] Only a few legal commentators focus a significant portion of their studies on the law relating to nuclear non-proliferation per se,[17] and all of them tend to dismiss the possibility of legal resolution of disputes in this particular area, if they mention the issue at all. As the preceding paragraph mentions, a discussion of the reasons why these commentators dismiss the possibility of legal resolution in this context is reserved for Chapter 6 below. However, it is important to note here how some commentators would appear to prefer over legal resolution the stripping of the binding nature of legal norms relating to the use of force in order to allow States "the flexibility they need to deal with modern threats to their vital national security and prosperity interests,"[18] in the form of supposed nuclear proliferation. It is exactly this type of bellicose counterproliferation measure that this study hopes to avoid by presenting the alternative of legal resolution.

As a relatively minor disclaimer relating to this literature, this study does not address the global question whether nuclear weapons are legal or whether nuclear weapons should be removed from States' arsenals. Indeed, this study does not even reject the possibility that Kenneth Waltz

Legality of the Use of or Threat to Use Nuclear Weapons, 10 FINNISH Y.B. INT'L L. 5 (1999); LAURENCE BOISSONS DE CHAZOURNES and PHILIPPE SANDS (eds.), INTERNATIONAL LAW, THE INTERNATIONAL COURT OF JUSTICE AND NUCLEAR WEAPONS (1999).

15 See *Legality of the Threat or Use of Nuclear Weapons*, Advisory Opinion, 1996 ICJ Rep. 226, 247–253 (July 8) (concluding the analysis of various nuclear non-proliferation treaties with the observation that none of the treaties "amount[] to a comprehensive and universal conventional prohibition on the use, or the threat of use, of those weapons as such").

16 See Malcolm N. Shaw, *Nuclear Weapons and International Law*, in NUCLEAR WEAPONS AND INTERNATIONAL LAW 1, 9 (ISTVAN POGANY ed., 1987) (asserting that nuclear non-proliferation agreements "all proceed necessarily on the basis of the lawfulness of possession of such weapons, otherwise there would simply be no need for such treaties"); Dietrich Rauschning, *Nuclear Warfare and Weapons*, 4 ENCYCLOPEDIA OF PUBLIC INTERNATIONAL LAW 44 (1982) (concluding nothing prohibits nuclear weapons).

17 See HISAKAZU FUJITA, INTERNATIONAL REGULATION OF THE USE OF NUCLEAR WEAPONS (1988); NAGENDRA SINGH AND EDWARD MCWHINNEY, NUCLEAR WEAPONS AND CONTEMPORARY INTERNATIONAL LAW (2d rev. edn, 1989); KOLASA, *supra* note 9; DAVID B. THOMSON, A GUIDE TO THE NUCLEAR ARMS CONTROL TREATIES (2001); JOZEF GOLDBLAT, AGREEMENTS FOR ARMS CONTROL: A CRITICAL SURVEY (1982).

18 DANIEL H. JOYNER, INTERNATIONAL LAW AND THE PROLIFERATION OF WEAPONS OF MASS DESTRUCTION 371 (2009).

and others may be correct that the spread of nuclear weapons actually might stabilize the international system by establishing a nuclear deterrence to going to war in a larger number of States.[19] Instead of addressing the legality of nuclear weapons in the abstract, it must be recognized that there are many other questions relating to nuclear non-proliferation. Examples could involve questions of fact and law relating to any of the rights and obligations in the NPT that have not been overwhelmingly softened by use of such words as "undertakes" – as in "Each of the Parties to the Treaty undertakes to . . .". By focusing on the harder legal rights and obligations, this study makes a distinction between legal questions and ideally justiciable issues, as most issues arising over the interpretation of a treaty will involve legal questions but not all of them will be ideally justiciable. Chapter 6 below elaborates on this point further. This is not to say that the other legal questions are nonjusticiable or that there are any legal questions that are nonjusticiable, but rather that there are some legal questions that are more justiciable than others. The following represent a few examples from the NPT of clear rights and obligations that are ideally justiciable:

(1) Whether the NPT has been interpreted in such a way as to "affect [its] inalienable right . . . to develop research, production and use of nuclear energy for peaceful purposes without discrimination and in conformity with Articles I and II of this Treaty";[20]
(2) Whether a State party to the NPT has had its "right to participate in . . . the fullest possible exchange of equipment, materials and scientific and technological information for the peaceful uses of nuclear energy . . .";[21]
(3) Whether a State party to the NPT has properly "withdraw[n] from the Treaty" by "decid[ing] that extraordinary events, related to the subject matter of this Treaty, have jeopardized the supreme interests of its country" and by "giv[ing] notice of such withdrawal to all other Parties to the Treaty and to the United Nations Security Council three months in advance" with "a statement of the

[19] Scott D. Sagan and Kenneth N. Waltz, The Spread of Nuclear Weapons (2nd edn, 2003). See also Myres McDougal and Florentino Feliciano, Law and Minimum World Public Order 659–660 (1961) (supporting nuclear weapons).
[20] Treaty on the Non-proliferation of Nuclear Weapons (NPT), Art. IV(1), July 1, 1968, 729 U.N.T.S. 161 (extended May 11, 1995, 34 I.L.M. 959).
[21] Ibid., Art. IV(2).

extraordinary events it regards as having jeopardized its supreme interests."[22]

Other examples of valid questions could relate to the obligations in the IAEA safeguards agreements, namely:

(1) Whether the State with an IAEA safeguards agreement has "establish[ed] and maintain[s] a system of accounting for and control of all *nuclear material*," which system "enable[s] the Agency to verify, in ascertaining that there has been no diversion of nuclear material from peaceful uses to nuclear weapons or other nuclear explosive devices, findings of the State's system";[23]
(2) Whether the State with an IAEA safeguards agreement has "provided [the IAEA] with information concerning [its] nuclear material ... and the features of facilities relevant to safeguarding such material";[24]
(3) Whether the State with an IAEA safeguards agreement has "take[n] the necessary steps to ensure that Agency inspectors can effectively discharge their functions under the Agreement";[25]
(4) Whether the IAEA has required only the "minimal amount of information and data consistent with carrying out its responsibilities under the Agreement," and has arranged the "visits and activities of Agency inspectors" in such a way as to "reduce to a minimum the possible inconvenience and disturbance to the State and to the peaceful nuclear activities inspected, as well as to ensure protection of industrial secrets or any other confidential information coming to the inspectors' knowledge";[26]
(5) Whether the State with an IAEA safeguards agreement has violated any of the privileges and immunities that the agreement has provided the IAEA and its staff when it comes to their official functions;[27]
(6) Whether the State with an IAEA safeguards agreement has any nuclear material that has been consumed, diluted or properly

[22] Ibid., Art. X. See also Antonio F. Perez, *Survival of Rights under the Nuclear Non-proliferation Treaty: Withdrawal and the Continuing Right of International Atomic Energy Agency Safeguards*, 34 VA. J. INT'L L. 749 (1994) (focusing on this question).
[23] IAEA, *The Structure and Content of Agreements between the Agency and States Required in Connection with the Treaty on the Non-proliferation of Nuclear Weapons*, Art. 7, IAEA Doc. INFCIRC/153 (June 1972) (hereinafter IAEA Model Safeguards Agreement) (original emphasis).
[24] Ibid., Art. 8. [25] Ibid., Art. 9. [26] Ibid., Art. 9. [27] Ibid., Art. 10.

transferred so as to terminate the safeguarding of that nuclear material;[28] and

(7) Whether the State with an IAEA safeguards agreement has told the IAEA of any nuclear activities that require the use of safeguarded nuclear materials and has used such nuclear materials only for a peaceful activity.[29]

These are just some of the legitimate questions of a mixed legal and factual nature relating to the nuclear non-proliferation regime that require analysis by commentators and adjudicators alike in light of a host of different situations. Chapter 6.4 below, on treaty interpretation, provides examples of the ways the ICJ or an international arbitral tribunal might interpret some of these provisions, based on their interpretation of similar language in prior cases. Despite the variety and number of relevant questions that can be addressed, the entire field has been preoccupied by the red-herring issue of the legality of nuclear weapons. After all, the word "non-proliferation" acknowledges that some States can have nuclear weapons while others cannot, with the important part being that those without nuclear weapons do not become those with nuclear weapons,[30] suggesting that the legality of nuclear weapons *in general* is not particularly relevant when it comes to the class of disputes relating to nuclear *non-proliferation*. The irrelevance, in this context, of questions of the legality of nuclear weapons in general does not, however, mean that legal resolution itself is irrelevant, as this part attempts to show.

In addition to works reviewing the *Legality of Nuclear Weapons* advisory opinion, a number of works review the ICJ's 1974 *Nuclear Tests* cases decisions,[31] or otherwise assess the legality of nuclear tests,

[28] Ibid., Arts. 11–12. [29] Ibid., Arts. 14.

[30] Some commentators might see this arrangement as giving a degree of legitimacy to nuclear weapons. See Joyner, *supra* note 18, at 69; Miguel Marin Bosch, *The Nonproliferation Treaty and Its Future*, in International Law, The International Court of Justice and Nuclear Weapons 375, 383 (P. Sands and L. Boisson de Chazournes ed., 1999).

[31] See, e.g., Jozef Goldblat, French Nuclear Tests in the Atmosphere: The Question of Legality (1974); H. Thierry, *Les arrêt du 20 décembre 1974 et les relations de la France avec la C.I.J.*, 20 AFDI 286 (1974); S. Sur, *Les affaires des essais nucléaires: C.I.J. arrêt du 20 décembre 1974*, 79 RGDIP 972 (1975); J. P. Ritter, *L'affaire des essays nucléaires et la notion de jugement déclaratoire*, 1975 AFDI 278 (1975); Prudence Taylor, *Testing Times for the World Court: Judicial Process and the 1995 French Nuclear Tests Case*, 8 Colo. J. Int'l Envtl. L. & Pol'y 199 (1997); dahlitz, *supra* note 9, at 102–115 (1983); Shaw, *supra* note 16, at 12; J. Swan, *Explosive Issue in*

again mostly from the perspective of the laws of war and international environmental law.[32] However, these commentators do so without any broader, theoretical analysis of how suited legal resolution is to resolving nuclear non-proliferation disputes more generally. Julie Dahlitz provided an entire chapter on "The Adjudication of Nuclear Arms Control Agreements" in her book *Nuclear Arms Control*, which essentially is limited to reviewing the details of the *Nuclear Tests* cases and the *Hostages* case,[33] with only a brief introduction where she generalizes that "the Court's evasion of substantive issues demonstrates the limits of its genuine competence," and the one paragraph of conclusion where she fatalistically generalizes that the Court's powers on paper might diverge from its powers in practice, though she wishes these would more closely align.[34] In short, this part of this book fills a relatively large gap in the literature on the role of legal resolution of nuclear non-proliferation disputes.

In filling this gap, this part determines the viability of legal resolution of nuclear non-proliferation disputes by assessing the competence of the ICJ and international arbitral tribunals to resolve nuclear non-proliferation disputes. Legal competence deals mostly with jurisdiction and justiciability.[35] As the ICJ said of handling politically sensitive disputes in the *Border and Transborder Armed Actions* case between Nicaragua and Honduras, the two main aspects of a case that the Court must establish before it proceeds are "first, that the dispute before it is a legal

International Law: The French Nuclear Tests, 9 MELB. UNIV. L. REV. 296 (1973); Thomas M. Franck, *Word Made Law: The Decision of the I.C.J. in the Nuclear Test Cases*, 69 AM. J. INT'L L. 612 (1975); G. White, *H-Bomb Tests and the International Court*, 123 NEW L.J. 615 (1973).

32 See, e.g., Emanuel Margolis, *The Hydrogen Bomb Experiments and International Law*, 64 YALE L.J. 629 (1955); ASIAN–AFRICAN LEGAL CONSULTATIVE COMMITTEE, THE LEGALITY OF NUCLEAR TESTS (1966); MARIE FURET, EXPERIMENTATION DES ARMES NUCLÉAIRES ET DROIT INTERNATIONAL PUBLIC (1966); Peter Fliess, *The Legality of Atmospheric Nuclear Tests – Critical View of International Law in the Cold War*, 15 FLORIDA. L. REV. 21 (1962); Luke T. Lee, *The Legality of Nuclear Tests and Weapons*, 18 ÖSTERREICHISCHE ZEITSCHRIFT FÜR ÖFFENTLICHES RECHT 307 (1968).

33 See, e.g., DAHLITZ, *supra* note 9, at 102–115. Dahlitz reviews the *Hostages* case not because she sees it as involving nuclear weapons, but rather as a case that "involved the interpretation of significant contemporary treaties under stressful circumstances likely to prevail in relation to a breach of a nuclear arms control agreement." Ibid., at 102.

34 See, e.g., ibid., at 102, 112.

35 See Gowlland-Debbas, *supra* note 1, at 651 n. 47 (citing SHABTAI ROSENNE, 1 THE LAW AND PRACTICE OF THE INTERNATIONAL COURT 301–302 (1965) and essentially explaining that "competence" includes both jurisdiction and justiciability).

dispute in the sense of a dispute capable of being settled by the application of principles and rules of international law and secondly, that the court has jurisdiction to deal with it."[36] The determinations of jurisdiction and justiciability are technical matters, and both stand in the way of the ICJ and international arbitral tribunals taking up and deciding such cases.[37] These concepts also are referred to as jurisdiction *ratione personae* and jurisdiction *ratione materiae* respectively, with the first involving the question whether disputants lawfully can appear before a court or tribunal and the second involving the question whether the substance of the dispute is of a type to allow a court or tribunal to properly exercise its jurisdiction.[38] As the ICJ has spelled out for disputants, a determination of the former precedes a determination of the latter,[39] and so this study adopts the same approach with respect to its structure. As this part shows, neither jurisdiction nor justiciability poses that significant a problem for the ICJ or an international arbitral tribunal in certain situations and from a certain perspective regarding nuclear non-proliferation disputes. As the first chapter in this part shows, States often have relied on legal resolution for their politically sensitive disputes, in particular military-related disputes, and courts and tribunals often have determined that they have the appropriate tools for addressing those disputes involving those parties. These examples should go a long way towards (1) convincing States to further consent to or give effect to legal resolution in this context, (2) convincing the ICJ and international arbitral tribunals to hear and decide cases of these types when they are brought before them, and (3) convincing the sincere reader to keep a mind open to the possibility.

[36] *Border and Transborder Armed Actions (Nicaragua v. Honduras)*, Jurisdiction, 1988 ICJ Rep. 69, 91 (Dec. 20).

[37] See John G. Merrills, International Dispute Settlement 219–220 (4th edn, 2005).

[38] See generally Shabtai Rosenne, The Law and Practice of the International Court, 1920–1996 527 (3rd edn, 1997) (discussing the different types of jurisdiction); Nagendra Singh, The Role and Record of the International Court of Justice 12–13 (1989) (same); *Report of the International Law Commission on the Work of its Forty-Second Session*, U.N. GAOR, 45th Sess., Supp. 10, at 46–48, UN Doc. A/45/10 (1990) (same but in the context of the ICC); Yuval Shany, The Competing Jurisdictions of International Courts and Tribunals 21–27 (2003).

[39] See, e.g., *Application of the Convention on the Prevention and Punishment of the Crime of Genocide (Bosnia and Herzegovina v. Serbia and Montenegro)*, 2007 ICJ Rep. ¶ 132 (Feb. 26) ("Since . . . the question of a State's capacity to be a party to proceedings is a matter which precedes that of jurisdiction ratione materiae").

Before proceeding with this analysis, however, it is important at the outset to determine whether there are other reasons to avoid having the ICJ or an international arbitral tribunal get involved with a nuclear nonproliferation dispute, assuming that both prongs of jurisdiction and justiciability have been satisfied. The main reason why this question is important relates to the occasional objection of States to legal resolution *after* they unequivocally have provided their consent and after such a forum has determined the justiciability of a matter, as Jonathan Charney has observed.[40] How this happens could be a matter of these States merely changing their minds with regard to their respect for or trust in legal resolution between the time of their giving consent and that of their giving effect to that consent. Alternatively, it could be a case of States not knowing exactly the disputes that would be sent to legal resolution when they provided their consent before the dispute actually arose, and of their deciding that legal resolution no longer serves their interests now that it is clear what exactly is at stake. Another alternative could be that respondent States merely want to frustrate their opponents by frustrating efforts at legal resolution, and try to find something to which to object.[41] Such objections might be in order if the claimant State commences specious litigation as a form of protest against the political decision-making process that was going on at that time.[42] Regardless, if consent to jurisdiction can be found and if the court or tribunal is satisfied that it has the proper tools to address the issues raised through the application of law, why should the international community or anyone else paternalistically interfere with the proceedings? After all, the disputants and the court or tribunal are in the best position to make these determinations. As Rosalyn Higgins has observed, it is beyond dispute that States can rely on considerations of their vital interests, or any other considerations, when deciding to withhold or grant their consent to legal resolution.[43] Higgins went on to note with considerable astonishment how commentators in the 1960s still were arguing that

[40] See Jonathan I. Charney, *Disputes Implicating the Institutional Credibility of the Court: Problems of Non-appearance, Non-participation, and Non-performance*, in The International Court of Justice at a Crossroads 288, 291, 304 (Lori F. Damrosch ed., 1998).

[41] See Merrills, *supra* note 37, at 330.

[42] See Jan Klabbers, *Straddling Law and Politics: Judicial Review in International Law*, in Towards World Constitutionalism 809, 830 (Ronald St. John Macdonald and Douglas M. Johnston ed., 2005).

[43] See Rosalyn Higgins, *Policy Considerations and the International Judicial Process*, 17 Int'l & Comp. L.Q. 58, 66 (1968).

States could avoid legal resolution through asserting that their vital interests were involved and appealing to other similar excuses.[44] If this were the case in the 1960s, then how much more astonished should we be if these same arguments are being made roughly five decades later? States should carry the burden to take due care when exercising their sovereignty in giving their consent to legal resolution. In squarely placing this burden on States, the ICJ and international arbitral tribunal ought to give effect to unequivocal indications of State consent, making sure to base their decisions on the application of law, not on politics, as explained further in Chapter 5.3.1 below.[45]

If a State objects to the proceedings after it has unequivocally given its consent, critics might point to problems with enforcement as a reason not to rely on legal resolution of nuclear non-proliferation disputes.[46] Indeed, there always is the risk that one of the disputants will not respect the ultimate decision of the court or tribunal. However, studies have shown that State compliance with decisions arising from legal resolution is not as significant a problem as some critics might think,[47] at least not enough of a problem for the court or tribunal to let this consideration lead them to excuse disputants from the proceedings that they themselves have expressly consented to, as some commentators have been inclined to argue.[48] Some critics may point to instances in the past where the ICJ or international arbitral tribunals may have refused to take a case because it ostensibly anticipated that one of the disputants would not abide by the ultimate decision,[49] although this does

44 Ibid. (quoting Julius Stone, THE AUSTRALIAN, Sept. 27, 1966).

45 See Charney, *supra* note 40, at 291, 307–308.

46 See Dinesh Khosla, *Nuclear Weapons, Global Values and International Law*, in NUCLEAR WEAPONS AND LAW 13, 13 (ARTHUR SELWYN MILLER and MARTIN FEINRIDER ed., 1984) ("All I am suggesting is the near impossibility for the International Court of Justice, or any court, for that matter – international or national – reaching a decision that it has reason to believe will not be followed either in content or spirit by the concerned actors").

47 See generally CONSTANZE SCHULTE, COMPLIANCE WITH DECISIONS OF THE INTERNATIONAL COURT OF JUSTICE (2004) (showing that, apart from a few limited incidents in the 1970s, States generally have complied with ICJ decisions); MERRILLS, *supra* note 37, at 106; John G. Merrills, *The Means of Dispute Settlement*, in INTERNATIONAL LAW 529, 541 (MALCOLM EVANS ed., 2003); Colter Paulson, *Compliance with Final Judgments of the International Court of Justice since 1987*, 98 AM. J. INT'L. L. 434 (2004).

48 See e.g. Charney, *supra* note 40, at 305–306.

49 See e.g. W. MICHAEL REISMAN, NULLITY AND REVISION 3–4 (1971) (discussing eleven cases where the ICJ allegedly backed away from a case in which it supposedly feared that an ultimate decision would not be accepted, though it is unclear whether one

not mean that the court or tribunal necessarily will (or should) continue with this approach. Such an approach would emasculate all forms of legal resolution by allowing it to handle only the most uncontroversial matters and denying it whatever robustness States may have intended to give it through consenting to compromissory clauses in sensitive areas, including even consenting to the very creation of these courts and tribunals.[50] If, even after the disputants have given unequivocal consent to jurisdiction and the forum has determined the justiciability of the matter, a disputant does not think that the forum should proceed on account of its belief that the dispute is too significant, the forum ought to be willing to proceed notwithstanding the lack of co-operation of that disputant, as occasionally has occurred in documented cases of nonparticipation in the ICJ.[51] Otherwise, these legal fora will be tossed to and fro with the political whims and maneuvering of disputants, losing the benefits of consistency and predictability that the rule of law was supposed to bring to international relations through reliance on them.

can interpret the Court's actions as fearing non-compliance); Charney, *supra* note 40, at 305–306; DAHLITZ, *supra* note 9, at 212.

50 One must not forget that the international community intended for legal resolution to play a role in more major disputes when it created this dispute settlement regime. See Charney, *supra* note 40, at 299.

51 See generally ibid., at 288; HUGH W. A. THIRLWAY, NON-APPEARANCE BEFORE THE INTERNATIONAL COURT OF JUSTICE (1985); JEROME B. ELKIND, NON-APPEARANCE BEFORE THE INTERNATIONAL COURT OF JUSTICE: FUNCTIONAL AND COMPARATIVE ANALYSIS (1984); Gerald Fitzmaurice, *The Problem of the "Non-appearing" Defendant Government*, 51 BRIT. Y.B. INT'L L. 89, 94–121 (1980); Janusz Stanczyk, *The Equality of Parties before the International Court of Justice in Cases of Non-appearing Respondent States*, in FORTY YEARS INTERNATIONAL COURT OF JUSTICE: JURISDICTION, EQUITY AND EQUALITY 35 (A. BLOED and P. VAN DIJK ed., 1988); Geneviève Guyomar, LE DÉFAUT DES PARTIES A UN DIFFÉREND DEVANT LES JURIDICTIONS INTERNATIONALES (1960); Pierre Michel Eisemann, *Les effets de la non-comparution devant la Cour internationale de justice*, 19 AFDI 351 (1973).

4

The history of legal resolution of similarly sensitive disputes as nuclear non-proliferation disputes

American author and humorist Mark Twain observed about history, "The past does not repeat itself, but it rhymes." This chapter reviews the history of reliance on legal resolution of disputes of a similar level of sensitivity as nuclear non-proliferation disputes, with the aim of convincing the reader that if legal resolution was adequate for those disputes, it should be adequate for nuclear non-proliferation disputes. Such an argument is needed because there admittedly have not been many instances where legal resolution has been called upon to handle nuclear non-proliferation disputes or disputes involving nuclear weapons. No international court or tribunal ever has made a pronouncement on the only use of such weapons during a time of war – namely the dropping of atomic bombs on Hiroshima and Nagasaki. The Tokyo War Crimes Tribunal did not address the legality of these bombings, for the obvious reason that it was a criminal court charged with trying Japanese war criminals. However, this limited charge did not stop the Indian judge there from writing a dissenting opinion in which he asserted that these atomic bombings were equivalent to the acts that these Japanese defendants had been charged with, at a minimum.[1] In more recent times, there are the *Nuclear Tests* cases and the *Legality of the Threat or Use of Nuclear Weapons* advisory opinion of the International Court of Justice, which this chapter discusses. In addition, there is the *Hrvatska Elektroprivreda d.d. v. Slovenia* arbitration, which involves a dispute between a Croatian electric company and Slovenia over a nuclear power plant located in Slovenia that provided a significant amount of power to both countries, although that arbitration is further from being a

[1] See *Dissenting Judgment of Justice Pal*, 2 The Tokyo Judgment 982 (B. V. A. Röling and C. F. Rüter ed., 1977); Margaret E. Gouin, Nuclear Law: The Application of Canadian and Related International Public Law Principles to the Obligations of Canada in Relation to Nuclear Weapons 4 (1989) (discussing this same dissenting opinion).

nuclear non-proliferation dispute than the *Nuclear Tests* cases and the *Legality of the Threat or Use of Nuclear Weapons* advisory opinion inasmuch as that arbitration seems to treat the nuclear power plant in Slovenia the same as any other major power resource.[2] Nevertheless, these cases, especially those involving nuclear weapons, should go a long way towards discouraging critics from interpreting the null set of successful instances of legal resolution of nuclear non-proliferation disputes to mean that legal resolution patently is unsuitable for nuclear non-proliferation disputes. Indeed, just because States have not relied on legal resolution to a great extent with nuclear non-proliferation disputes and disputes involving nuclear weapons, this does not mean that legal resolution is not a viable option, as some commentators seem inclined to believe,[3] as if nothing can be done for the first time or subsequently increase in frequency. After all, the *Trail Smelter* arbitration of 1941 represents the first time States relied on legal resolution of a dispute relating to transnational pollution,[4] which arbitration would have proved wrong any critics who might have said before 1941 that legal resolution was unsuitable for political disputes relating to sensitive pollution. Critics might point out that *Trail Smelter* had the 1893 *Pacific Fur Seal* arbitration to rely on as precedent, inasmuch as that arbitration related to abuse of the environment – in that case, the high seas.[5] However, the cases discussed in this chapter arguably provide future reliance on legal resolution of a nuclear non-proliferation dispute with what the *Pacific Fur Seal* arbitration provided to *Trail Smelter*.

The limited reliance on legal resolution of actual nuclear non-proliferation disputes until this point in time does not mean that this option has not been considered in the past. Indeed, many of the sources that this study discusses concerning legal resolution of nuclear non-proliferation disputes are from the 1940s, 1950s, and 1960s, as if the debate over legal resolution of such disputes started and ended then. That actually seems to have been the case, with the United States and the Soviet Union

[2] See *Hrvatska Elektroprivreda d.d. v. Republic of Slovenia*, ICSID Case No. ARB/05/24, Decision on the Treaty Interpretation Issue, June 12, 2009.

[3] See, e.g., R. P. Anand, *Role of International Adjudication*, in 1 The Future of the International Court of Justice 9 (Leo Gross ed., 1976); Tom Ginsburg and Richard H. McAdams, *Adjudicating in Anarchy: An Expressive Theory of International Dispute Resolution*, 45 Wm and Mary L. Rev. 1229, 1327 (2004) (making this assertion in the context of the ICJ resolving armed conflict).

[4] See *Trail Smelter Case (U.S. v. Canada)*, 3 R.I.A.A. 1905 (1941).

[5] See *Pacific Fur Seal Arbitration (US v. Great Britain)*, reprinted in John Bassett Moore, 1 International Arbitration History 755–961 (1898).

debating the role of legal resolution in this context on several occasions. Inasmuch as this study attempts to reopen that general debate for an era that lacks the limitations of the Cold War, this chapter starts by laying out the history of that debate and exploring the ways in which States have relied on legal resolution of disputes of a similar level of sensitivity as nuclear non-proliferation disputes.

In terms of methodology, this chapter surveys public international arbitration cases reported by the PCA and arbitration-case digests, as well as cases of the Permanent Court of International Justice (PCIJ) and the ICJ, to find the main instances where States have relied on these fora to resolve their sensitive, military-related disputes. By "military-related dispute," this chapter means any dispute relating to the armed forces of a State.[6] While there are many disputes that are tangentially related to the military, such as border disputes that eventually might lead to armed conflict if left unresolved or contract disputes involving the military,[7] these are not seen as military-related disputes for the purposes of this chapter, nor as being otherwise sensitive enough to be included in an analogy with nuclear non-proliferation disputes. Instead, this chapter adopts a conservative approach to creating this analogy by considering as military-related disputes only those disputes that drive military action at the time that the dispute is sent to legal resolution or those that arise directly out of military action.[8] This study sees these as being the most

[6] Notably, this does not include the subject matter underlying an advisory opinion. As the ICJ noted in the *Legality of the Threat or Use of Nuclear Weapons* advisory opinion, "The purpose of the advisory function is not to settle – at least directly – disputes between States, but to offer legal advice to the organs and institutions requesting the opinion." *Legality of the Threat or Use of Nuclear Weapons*, Advisory Opinion, 1996 ICJ Rep. 226, ¶ 15 (July 8). Therefore, advisory opinions are not the focus of this study.

[7] See Christine Gray and Benedict Kingsbury, *Developments in Dispute Settlement: Inter-state Arbitration since 1945*, 63 BRIT. Y.B. OF INT'L L. 97, 108 (1992) (discussing the frequency of boundary and territorial sovereignty arbitral cases both before and after World War II). Interestingly, one of the first recorded instances of reliance on arbitration to resolve a particularly heated dispute involved the king of Kish who, in 400 B.C., defined the border between two Sumerian cities to end a dispute that could not be resolved through war. See JACKSON H. RALSTON, INTERNATIONAL ARBITRATION FROM ATHENS TO LOCARNO 153 (1929).

[8] This conservative approach is further apparent in its non-inclusion of other types of politically sensitive dispute such as those involving territorial and maritime boundaries, which are among the most common types of dispute before international courts and tribunals. See, e.g., Rama Mani, *Peaceful Settlement of Disputes and Conflict Prevention*, in THE OXFORD HANDBOOK ON THE UNITED NATIONS 300, 306 (THOMAS G. WEISS and SAM DAWS ed., 2007) (discussing how these types of dispute are the most common).

politically sensitive disputes available and those that stand the greatest chance of stalling in impasse when States rely on diplomatic forms of resolution to settle them. In such situations of impasse, legal resolution presents a valuable alternative to reach settlement.[9] Admittedly, this number of cases is not as great as those involving territorial and maritime boundary disputes, which are among the most common types of disputes.[10] Nonetheless, the examples discussed here, most of which are considered in greater detail in other portions of the analysis of this part of the book, form a significant body of analogous jurisprudence to help convince States and the international community that legal resolution might also be suitable for handling nuclear non-proliferation disputes.

4.1 Early debates between the US and the USSR over the role of legal resolution

In the 1940s, 1950s, and 1960s, the United States and the Soviet Union hotly debated the role they should give legal resolution of nuclear non-proliferation disputes. US diplomat Bernard Baruch started off the debate by proposing in June 1946 that the international community frame the legal regime surrounding atomic weapons in terms of a criminal-law approach, as opposed to a contract approach.[11] This approach basically involved the prosecution and adjudication of violations of norms by an international court or tribunal, and eventual criminal punishment of convicted violators.[12] The Soviet Union quickly rejected the US proposal, though for reasons other than its criminal-law approach to resolving disputes, which the Soviet Union apparently assented to at that time.[13]

The issue of using legal resolution to settle nuclear-weapon disputes came up again in the early 1960s when the United States and Soviet Union were negotiating the establishment of a general disarmament

[9] See Jan Klabbers, *Straddling Law and Politics: Judicial Review in International Law*, in TOWARDS WORLD CONSTITUTIONALISM 809, 830 (RONALD ST. JOHN MACDONALD and DOUGLAS M. JOHNSTON ed., 2005), at 830.

[10] See Mani, *supra* note 8, at 306.

[11] See Note, *Legal Models of Arms Control: Past, Present, and Future*, 100 HARV. L. REV. 1326, 1327 (1987) (citing Statement of the United States Policy on Control of Atomic Energy as Presented by Bernard M. Baruch, Esq., to the United Nations Atomic Energy Commission (June 14, 1946)).

[12] See ibid., at 1327–1329.

[13] See ibid., at 1327 (citing W. LAFEBER, AMERICA, RUSSIA, AND THE COLD WAR 1945–1980 42–43 (4th edn, 1980)).

treaty (which included the establishment of an International Disarmament Organization). At that time, the United States envisioned the involvement of the ICJ in resolving disputes over interpretation and application of the treaty, saying that disputes "which were not settled by negotiation or by the International Disarmament Organization would be subject to referral by any party to the dispute to the International Court of Justice, unless the parties concerned agreed on another mode of settlement."[14] In the early days of the Cold War, the Soviet Union saw international law only as the temporary rules that were selected by the Soviet Union to govern the interaction between socialist and communist States.[15] Given the limited scope and perceived subjectivity of international law, it is no surprise that the Soviet Union favored negotiation over legal resolution of any disputes that might arise,[16] which would explain the lack of provisions dealing with legal resolution in its proposal and its rejection of US proposals with their reference to legal resolution of disputes over interpretation and application.[17]

Referring to the US proposals with regard to legal resolution, the Soviet Union expressed its belief that legal resolution interferes with State sovereignty:

> But the peaceful settlement of disputes means negotiation without encroaching upon the rights and interests of any particular party; it means mutual concessions and seeking mutually acceptable settlements, without encroaching upon the sovereign rights of any State. The United States proposal emphasizes something else.[18]

Less than two months later, the Soviet Union again declared opposition to the US proposals to send disputes to the ICJ: "Free and equal negotiations between sovereign States are replaced by the capricious and despotic decision of an arbitrator."[19] Soviet lawyers tried to explain that their objections were not towards arbitration or adjudication per se, but

[14] ANDREW MARTIN, LEGAL ASPECTS OF DISARMAMENT 54 (1963) (discussing US proposals involving the ICJ with interpretation and application of the general and complete disarmament treaty that was negotiated in the early 1960s: "The Parties to the Treaty would agree that disputes concerning the interpretation or application of the Treaty which were not settled by negotiation or by the International Disarmament Organisation would be subject to referral by any party to the dispute to the International Court of Justice, unless the parties concerned agreed on another mode of settlement"); ALLAN GOTLIEB, DISARMAMENT AND INTERNATIONAL LAW: A STUDY OF THE ROLE OF LAW IN THE DISARMAMENT PROCESS 29, 100, 117 (1965).

[15] See GOTLIEB, *supra* note 14***, at 34. [16] See ibid., at 40, 96. [17] See ibid., at 110.

[18] MARTIN, *supra* note 14***, at 56 (quoting ENDC/P.V. 26, p. 29 (April 24, 1962)).

[19] GOTLIEB, *supra* note 14***, at 90 (citing ENDC/PV.56, June 14, 1962, p. 131).

rather towards the predetermination of sending a particular type of dispute to this form of resolution.[20] The Soviet Union's dislike of legal resolution extended beyond arms control and disarmament disputes to even low-level political disputes involving these superpowers or their client States.[21] Such dislike for international law and legal resolution lasted for a considerable period during the Cold War, which can explain the paucity of references to legal resolution of these kinds of disputes during that period and within a reasonable time after that period. This view of international law, however, was replaced by the belief that the rules and principles of international law had general validity because of their gradual development over time,[22] and, with this, the possibility arose for legal resolution to be mentioned in the interpretation and dispute settlement provisions of various nuclear non-proliferation agreements, as mentioned in Chapter 5.2 below. The end of the Cold War heralded an end to the dominance of bilateral nuclear non-proliferation arrangements and the start of a new multilateral era, even though bilateral arrangements continue. However, it would appear that these early debates on legal resolution between the United States and the Soviet Union have set commentators on legal resolution in this context on a particular trajectory that continues to this day – that of rejecting the possibility of legal resolution of nuclear non-proliferation disputes.

Due to the limited involvement of legal resolution with nuclear weapons in the past, as explained in the introduction to this chapter, the remainder of this chapter casts a wider net to look at how legal resolution has been used to resolve military-related matters, including cases involving the use of force, in which legal resolution has a relatively long history. Indeed, numerous commentators write on the role of legal resolution with crisis management,[23] and this study relies on and fits within that particular body of literature. These examples, set out in summary

[20] See MARTIN, *supra* note 14, at 56 (quoting Shurshalov, letter to THE TIMES, June 27, 1963). Remember that these strong feelings of the USSR against designating legal resolution as the method of resolving disputes involved disarmament and arms control matters in a hypothetical disarmed world, which portrays their distrust of legal resolution as being particularly extreme).

[21] See C. M. Dalfen, *The World Court in Idle Splendour: The Basis of State Attitudes*, 23 INT'L J. 124, 133–134 (1967) (discussing how communist states during the Cold War challenged even the availability of legal resolution of politically sensitive disputes).

[22] See GOTLIEB, *supra* note 14, at 34, 110.

[23] See SHABTAI ROSENNE, ESSAYS ON INTERNATIONAL LAW AND PRACTICE 35–63 (2007); Gregory A. Raymond, *International Adjudication and Conflict Management*, in SOVEREIGNTY AND THE GLOBAL COMMUNITY: THE QUEST FOR ORDER IN THE

fashion, obviously are not identical to nuclear non-proliferation disputes. However, they are considered closely analogous since they involve one or both of the disputants' vital interests. These examples form the foundation for the argument that legal resolution is a viable option for nuclear non-proliferation disputes, because if legal resolution was acceptable for States and the international community with these similarly sensitive disputes, it arguably should be acceptable for States and the international community currently grappling with how to handle nuclear non-proliferation disputes. At a minimum, these examples should encourage the skeptical reader to keep an open mind to the possibility.

4.2 Military-related arbitration from ancient times

The role of arbitration in resolving military-related disputes dates back to ancient Greece, if not before. Arbitration clauses were common in Greek agreements during ancient times, the implementation of which successfully helped limit armed conflict.[24] While boundary disputes were the most common subject of arbitration during those times, arbitration of military-related disputes also was relatively common, as is the case today with inter-State arbitration. Such arbitrations arose over the Achaean League's leader Aratus attacking Argos in a time of peace, as well as Athens' attack on Oropus.[25] These were not arbitrations that arose after hostilities had ceased, as happened after such wars as the American Revolutionary War and the Spanish–American War, but were

INTERNATIONAL SYSTEM 221 (HOWARD M. HENSEL ed., 2004); Richard B. Bilder, *Judicial Procedures Relating to the Use of Force*, in LAW AND FORCE IN THE NEW INTERNATIONAL ORDER 269 (LORI F. DAMROSCH and DAVID SCHEFFER ed., 1983); Dapo Akande and Sope Williams, *International Adjudication of Security Issues: What Role for the WTO?*, 43 VA. J. INT'L L. 365, 381–383 (2003); Ted L. Stein, *Contempt, Crisis, and the Court: The World Court and the Hostage Rescue Attempt*, 76 AM. J. INT'L L. 499 (1982); Andrew Coleman, *The International Court of Justice and Highly Political Matters*, 4 MELB J. INT'L L. 29 (2003); Takane Sugihara, *The Judicial Function of the International Court of Justice with Respect to Disputes Involving Highly Political Issues*, in THE INTERNATIONAL COURT OF JUSTICE: ITS FUTURE ROLE AFTER FIFTY YEARS 117, 119 (A. S. MULLER, D. RAIC, and J. M. THURANSKY ed., 1997).

24 See Stanley M. Burstein, *Arms Control in Antiquity*, in 2 ENCYCLOPEDIA OF ARMS CONTROL AND DISARMAMENT 551, 555–557 (RICHARD DEAN BURNS ed., 1993); SHEILA L. AGER, INTERSTATE ARBITRATIONS IN THE GREEK WORLD 337–90 B.C. (1996).

25 See RALSTON, *supra* note 7, at 156, 158 (citing A. RAEDER, L'ARBITRAGE INTERNATIONAL CHEZ LES HELLÈNES 248 (1912)).

arbitrations to decide the very outcome of the war. Such arbitration was characteristic of the system of peaceful settlement of disputes between alliances that was introduced in ancient Greece.[26] Such famous commentators on international law as Hugo Grotius knew of this history of arbitration with resolving war and emphasized it when promoting arbitration in more "modern" times.[27]

The Romans were considerably less enthusiastic about arbitration, with the Roman Senate instead preferring either to establish the law on the matter and assign a free community the task of adjudicating the dispute, or to send envoys to decide such matters, which decisions were subject to the Senate's ratification.[28] The inability of the parties to choose the decision-maker, the applicable law, or anything else in the process removed this method of dispute settlement from the realm of arbitration. As a result, reliance on arbitration to settle military-related disputes tapered off considerably under the Romans.[29]

Between the end of Roman times and the beginning of the Middle Ages, arbitration occasionally was used to resolve military conflicts, including such issues as the return of prisoners of war, compensation arising out of unlawful acts of war, and other issues that one might expect to be resolved through more diplomatic methods.[30] In particular, Heruli, Varnes, and Gondebaud, the kings of the Ostrogoths, invited the king of the Franks, Clovis, to give up the Franks' war with the Visigoths and let the united kings resolve the raging conflict through arbitration, to which invitation Clovis agreed.[31] During the Middle Ages, resort to arbitration primarily was not to prevent war but rather to end it, with the parties giving the arbitrators the responsibility of resolving whatever differences

[26] See RALSTON, *supra* note 7, at 156.

[27] See HUGO GROTIUS, I DE JURE BELLI AC PACIS LIBRI TRES 560–561, 562 (trans. Francis W. Kelsey, 1964); MARY ELLEN O'CONNELL, INTERNATIONAL DISPUTE RESOLUTION 7–8 (2006).

[28] See RALSTON, *supra* note 7, at 166–167 (quoting MARCUS NIEBUHR TOD, INTERNATIONAL ARBITRATION AMONG THE GREEKS 98 (1913)); RALSTON, *supra* note 7, at 167–69, 172–173 (discussing cases where the Roman Senate resolved disputes using these methods and general Roman dislike for arbitration between states).

[29] See Burstein, *supra* note 24, at 558; Hans-Jürgen Schlochauer, *Arbitration*, in 1 ENCYCLOPEDIA OF PUBLIC INTERNATIONAL LAW 215, 215–216 (RUDOLF BERNHARDT ed., 1992).

[30] See Schlochauer, *supra* note 29, at 217 (noting how there was "no clear dividing line between arbitration and diplomatic methods of settling the disputes" during that time).

[31] See RALSTON, *supra* note 7, at 174 (citing A. MERIGNHAC, TRAITÉ THÉORIQUE ET PRATIQUE DE L'ARBITRAGE INTERNATIONAL 31 (1895)).

there were that made the war continue.[32] This happened when the Count of Charolais was made the arbitrator to resolve the issues surrounding a war that was raging between the Duke of Lorraine and the Duke of Burgundy, with the count's five counselors drawing up a peace treaty and the count approving that treaty to end the war without the dukes being directly involved in the drafting.[33] Similarly, in 1334, Philip of Valois ended the conflict between the king of Bohemia, the princes of Germany, and the Duke of Brabant through this same method.[34] Perhaps most bizarrely, the arbitration award of the Duke of Burgundy of 1432 required that the eldest son of Count Redimont marry the daughter of the Duke of Anjou as a condition that was to end the war, with the arbitration award even specifying the size of the dowry.[35] After this time, and until 1794, military-related questions do not seem to have been referred to arbitration, though admittedly reliance on arbitration for resolving any type of dispute was not particularly regular during this time and until the nation-state system had fully developed and States began to see each other as legally equal and interdependent.[36]

The end of the eighteenth century saw the reintroduction of the idea of arbitration of politically sensitive disputes. Jeremy Bentham proposed in the late eighteenth century that disarmament would be the foundation for lasting peace, with an international court being established to resolve differences between States, including differences over compliance with these disarmament treaties.[37] Arbitrations under the Jay Treaty of 1794 between the United States and Great Britain mark the beginning of the contemporary arbitration system.[38] Interestingly, arbitration of disputes involving international law was the norm until the 1900s, whereas judicial settlement was the norm with disputes involving municipal law

[32] See RALSTON, *supra* note 7, at 180–181 (citing MILETA NOVACOVITCH, LES COMPROMIS ET LES ARBITRAGES INTERNATIONAUX DU XIIE AU XVE SIÈCLE 38 (1905)).

[33] See RALSTON, *supra* note 7, at 181 (citing NOVACOVITCH, *supra* note 32, at 71, 138) (mentioning how, in 1441, Francisco Sforza was the arbitrator who brought an end to a war between Venice, Florence, and Genoa on one side and the Duke of Milan on the other side).

[34] See RALSTON, *supra* note 7, at 182–183.

[35] See Manfred Lachs, *The Law and the Settlement of International Disputes*, in DISPUTE SETTLEMENT THROUGH THE UNITED NATIONS 283, 294 (K. VENKATA RAMAN ed., 1977).

[36] See RALSTON, *supra* note 7, at 178–79, 191; Schlochauer, *supra* note 29, at 218.

[37] John H. McNeill, *Commentary on Dispute Resolution Mechanisms in Arms Control Agreements*, in LAW AND FORCE IN THE NEW INTERNATIONAL ORDER 258, 259 (LORI F. DAMROSCH AND DAVID J. SCHEFFER ed., 1991).

[38] See Schlochauer, *supra* note 29, at 218; Hans von Mangoldt, *Arbitration and Conciliation Treaties*, in 1 Encyclopedia of Public International Law 230, 230–231 (RUDOLF BERNHARDT ed., 1992).

during that same time.[39] Consequently, there seem to have been many more arbitrations after 1794 than before.[40]

Parallel with the increase in inter-State arbitral proceedings was an increase in military-related arbitrations. A relatively exhaustive study of inter-State arbitration from 1794 until 1989 determined that there were 449 inter-State arbitrations during the period.[41] The most common subject for arbitration during that period appears to have been territorial and boundary disputes, which constituted approximately ninety-three such disputes, or approximately 21 percent of those arbitrations presented in Stuyt's impressive *Survey of International Arbitrations*.[42] Military-related disputes are not far behind, at approximately ninety-two arbitrations, or 21 percent.[43] Most of these military-related arbitrations – approximately forty-seven arbitrations or 10 percent of the total number of arbitrations – involved claims for reparations and indemnities following inter-State armed conflict, with approximately nineteen coming directly from the military confrontation of the First World War and four from the Second World War. In particular, the Russian Claim for Indemnities arbitration is notable, where Turkey agreed in 1879 to pay Russia indemnities from the war of 1877–1878, which it paid in 1902.[44] However, Russia demanded interest it believed it was due, which it claimed in 1910 by commencing arbitral proceedings but which the tribunal denied in 1912 because the actions of the Russian embassy in Constantinople were interpreted as Russia's renunciation of a right to interest.[45]

The next most common type of military-related arbitration involved the military seizure and detention of civilian ships during or surrounding armed conflicts, at approximately twenty-two arbitrations, or 5 percent of the total number of arbitrations. This actually was the subject of some

[39] See Gray and Kingsbury, *supra* note 7, at 102.
[40] Please note that this increase might also be a result of improved record keeping.
[41] See A. M. Stuyt, Survey of International Arbitrations 1794–1989 (3rd edn, 1990).
[42] See ibid.
[43] The non-military-related disputes involve a host of different subjects, ranging from a determination of sovereignty of a country to the resolution of private contract claims. Please note that results will vary dramatically depending on how one defines "military-related arbitration."
[44] See *Russian Claim for Interest on Indemnities (Russia v. Turkey)*, Award of the Tribunal, Nov. 11, 1912, at www.pca-cpa.org.
[45] See ibid.

of the first arbitrations between Great Britain and the United States after the signing of the Jay Treaty, and between the United States and Spain.[46] Two arbitrations involved the sinking of a civilian ship by a military ship,[47] while one case after the First World War involved the Dutch detention of a German warship.[48] To these examples can be added three relatively famous cases of arbitration: The *Manouba* arbitration, the *Carthage* arbitration, and *Norwegian Shipowners' Claims*. With the *Manouba* arbitration, Italy seized a French steamship by military force during the Italian–Turkish War of 1912, and arrested twenty-nine Turkish passengers on the ship who were suspected of being members of the Ottoman army, with the tribunal answering in the negative with regard to the question whether the seizure of the ship was justified and answering in the affirmative with regard to the question whether the arrest was lawful, and awarding damages to the French government.[49] With the *Carthage* arbitration, the Italian navy forcibly stopped a French mail steamer and detained it for four days during the Turkish–Italian War because Italy believed an airplane onboard was war contraband.[50] The arbitral tribunal concluded that, while Italy was entitled to search the ship, it was not entitled to detain the ship because there was insufficient evidence that the airplane was destined to hostile forces, and had to pay damages for the "moral and political injury" to France.[51] Finally, with the *Norwegian Shipowners' Claims* arbitration, Europeans had ordered ships to be built in the United States before the United States entered the war in 1917, but the United States requisitioned ships over 2,500 tons when it declared war, and several Norwegian owners of these ships sued for payment of indemnities.[52] The international arbitral tribunal held the United States liable for damages in requisitioning these ships because of its "discriminating use of the power of eminent domain towards citizens of a friendly nation."[53] The third most common type of military-related arbitration was over one State's military

[46] See Stuyt, *supra* note 41, at 3–5 (Stuyt Arbitration Numbers 3 and 4).
[47] See ibid., at 82, 148 (Stuyt Arbitration Numbers 81 and 148).
[48] See ibid., at 329 (Stuyt Arbitration Number 321).
[49] See the *Manouba Case (France v. Italy)*, Award of the Tribunal, May 6, 1913, at www.pca-cpa.org.
[50] See the *"Carthage" (France v. Italy)*, Award of the Tribunal, May 6, 1913, at www.pca-cpa.org.
[51] See ibid.
[52] See *Norwegian Shipowners' Claims (Norway v. US)*, Award of the Tribunal, Oct. 13, 1922, at www.pca-cpa.org.
[53] Ibid.

involvement in another State's civil war, at eight arbitrations, or approximately 2 percent.

The rest of the military-related arbitrations are somewhat more difficult to characterize. The strongest role for arbitration in resolving military-related disputes comes from this group. At one end of the spectrum, there are the cases over the purchase of military supplies, such as those between Brazil and Italy in 1896 and the Netherlands and the United States in 1938,[54] and the military service of British citizens in the Portuguese military during the liberation of Portugal that was resolved in 1842.[55] Along with this group would be the famous *Deserters of Casablanca* arbitration, where six German-national members of the French Foreign Legion who were defending Casablanca deserted their posts and received protection from the German Consulate there in 1908, but French forces forcibly took back these deserters and arrested them.[56] Attempts at diplomatic resolution failed, and so the international arbitral tribunal became involved, which ultimately concluded that, while the German Consulate was entitled to grant protection to these individuals, the French forces were wrong not to respect the actual protection the German Consulate was providing them and wrong in the force used against Moroccan soldiers at the Consulate.[57] Equally famous is the *Preferential Treatment of Claims of Blockading Powers against Venezuela* arbitration, where Germany, Italy, and the United Kingdom blockaded Venezuelan ports using military force in 1902 after Venezuela failed to make payments on various claims of these States.[58] In return for the lifting of the blockade, Venezuela agreed to recognize these claims and pay these claims back through taxes on the customs revenues of these ports. However, Venezuela started paying other creditors back before these three powers, and so a dispute arose over whether these States were entitled to preferential treatment, which the tribunal determined they did enjoy over the other creditors.

At the other end of the spectrum, there are arbitrations intended to decide the key issues surrounding the actual use of force, such as:

[54] See Stuyt, *supra* note 41, at 201, 420 (Stuyt Arbitration Numbers 196 and 406).
[55] See ibid., at 37 (Stuyt Arbitration Number 35).
[56] See *Deserters of Casablanca* arbitration (France/Germany), Award of the Tribunal, May 22, 1909, at www.pca-cpa.org.
[57] See ibid.
[58] See *Preferential Treatment of Claims of Blockading Powers against Venezuela (Germany, UK, Italy v. Venezuela)*, Award of the Tribunal, Feb. 22, 1904, at www.pca-cpa.org.

(1) the attack on the US vice-consul in Siam by Siamese soldiers in 1896;[59]
(2) the armed conflict that broke out at Wal Wal between Ethiopian forces and the invading Italian forces in 1935,[60] during which the failed arbitration hastened the eventual demise of the League of Nations;[61]
(3) the military occupation by Guatemala of Mexico that was decided in 1898 and the military conflict between Chile and Peru at the end of the nineteenth century;[62] and
(4) the sinking by French intelligence agents of Greenpeace's *Rainbow Warrior* while it was in Auckland harbour.[63]

Although not expressly mentioned in Stuyt's seemingly comprehensive study, an arbitral tribunal resolved the *Naulilaa* dispute, which arose when a guard from Portugal (initially a neutral State until it entered the First World War late in 1914) stationed in Angola killed a German soldier on the Namibian side of the frontier, and Germany retaliated with what the tribunal determined to be disproportionate force.[64] More recently, the Eritrea–Ethiopia Claims Commission was established to hear claims between these two governments arising from their 1998–2000 conflict, with claims involving such issues as the violation of international humanitarian law and the violation of international law generally.[65] It goes beyond the scope of this study to spell out the complex determination of this Claims Commission, but the overall conclusion can best be summarized by a press release from the Claims Commission that "[w]hile the compensation awarded to each Party is substantial, the Commission recognized that it is probably much less than each Party believes it is due."[66] Implementation of the

[59] See STUYT, *supra* note 41, at 210 (Stuyt Arbitration Number 205).
[60] See ibid., at 397 (Stuyt Arbitration Number 384).
[61] See R. J. OVERY, THE ORIGINS OF THE SECOND WORLD WAR 14–15 (1998).
[62] See STUYT, *supra* note 41, at 223, 397 (Stuyt Arbitration Numbers 219 and 384).
[63] See ibid., at 446–464 (Stuyt Arbitration Numbers 446–48).
[64] See *Naulilaa Case (Portugal v. FRG)*, 4 ANN. DIG. 526 (Special Arbitral Trib. 1928).
[65] See Agreement between the Government of the Federal Democratic Republic of Ethiopia and the Government of the State of Eritrea, Dec. 12, 2000, Art. 5(1), at www.pca-cpa.org (but excluding "claims arising from the cost of military operations, preparing for military operations, or the use of force, except to the extent that such claims involve violations of international humanitarian law").
[66] See Eritrea Ethiopia Claims Commission, Eritrea–Ethiopia Claims Commission Renders Final Awards on Damages, Press Release, Aug. 17, 2009, at www.pca-cpa.org.

Commission's decisions by Ethiopia and Eritrea has been slow, but one remains optimistic that this decision can act as the catalyst for a lasting peace there. The decision of the Eritrea–Ethiopia Boundary Commission, on the other hand, had a dramatic impact in terms of keeping the war from breaking out again, even though there remain some issues over implementation. History may eventually prove the Eritrea–Ethiopia Boundary Commission to be the most successful State-to-State arbitration in terms of promoting peace in the past century. Even more recent is the 2009 arbitration between the government of Sudan and the Sudan People's Liberation Movement/Army on delimiting Abyei Area, where the tribunal was asked to determine whether the Abyei Boundaries Commission was exceeding its mandate from the Comprehensive Peace Agreement of 2005 to define the boundaries of the Abyei area and to otherwise delimit the area.[67] The tribunal there determined that the commission had stayed within its mandate, except for certain aspects in the north and for not explaining itself better to the parties, but nevertheless itself demarcated many of the boundaries that the Commission earlier had set.[68] While this arbitration involves a territorial dispute, it is included here because of the fact that the dispute arises out of a peace agreement, with the real threat of a return to hostilities if the matter was not satisfactorily resolved.

Finally, there are a few examples of States relying on arbitration to resolve disputes over arms and armaments. In the *Alabama* arbitration claims between Great Britain and the United States following the American Civil War, which were successfully resolved in 1872, one of the main issues was Britain's arming of privateers.[69] In a separate dispute two years later, Nicaragua confiscated several crates of arms from a French ship, which an arbitral tribunal resolved in France's favor in 1880.[70] During the 1902 arbitration of a boundary dispute between Chile and Argentina handled by the British Government, the British foreign secretary Lord Lansdowne insisted that both sides refrain from

[67] See *In the Matter of an Arbitration before a Tribunal Constituted in Accordance with Article 5 of the Arbitration Agreement between the Government of Sudan and the Sudan People's Liberation Movement/Army on Delimiting Abyei Area*, Final Award, July 22, 2009, para. 6, *at* www.pca-cpa.org.

[68] See ibid., ¶¶ 673, 709–770.

[69] See Stuyt, *supra* note 41, at 96–97 (Stuyt Arbitration Number 94). See generally Adrian Cook, The Alabama Claims: American Politics and Anglo-American Relations 1865–1872 (1975).

[70] See Stuyt, *supra* note 41, at 118 (Stuyt Arbitration Number 115).

increasing the size of their navies until after the arbitral award had been rendered, an interim measure by which the parties abided.[71] More recently, the Iran–US Claims Tribunal has had certain claims laid before it involving the refusal of the United States to transfer to Iran military equipment the United States still had in its possession at the time of the Iranian Revolution, even though Iran allegedly had prepaid for such equipment.[72] It is important to remember that the Iran–US Claims Tribunal involves what would appear to be the largest State-to-State claims in history. Moreover, the tribunal continued to function as usual when shooting broke out between the United States and Iran in the 1980s, and it provided an important channel for communication between the two States when they had closed off virtually all other channels. In sum, the tribunal has proven to provide a robust method of resolution even in the face of extreme difficulties between the two States.

The factors that made it possible for these States to submit politically sensitive disputes to arbitration are complex and numerous; discussion of them is reserved for future research.[73] Moreover, not all of these arbitral proceedings were of a judicial nature; considerations of equity also might have been allowed, depending on whether diplomatic arbitration or judicial arbitration was involved.[74] Regardless, reliance on arbitration to resolve such sensitive military-related disputes as those mentioned above, both in ancient and in more modern times, should help reassure skeptics that arbitration can work with contemporary nuclear non-proliferation disputes.

[71] See Andrew D. Farrand, *Chile and Argentina: Entente and Naval Limitation, 1902*, in 2 ENCYCLOPEDIA OF ARMS CONTROL AND DISARMAMENT 595, 601 (RICHARD DEAN BURNS ed., 1993).

[72] See, e.g., *Iran v. United States*, Case No. B1 (Claim 4), Award No. DEC 85-B1-FT, May 18, 1989; *Iran v. United States*, Case No. B1 (Claim 4), Award No. 382-B1-FT, Aug. 31, 1988 (involving the US refusal to transfer to Iran military equipment it still had in its possession at the time of the Iranian Revolution); *Iran v. United States*, Case No. A30, Statement of Claim, Aug. 2, 1996 (involving an Iranian allegation that the United States authorized CIA covert operations inside Iran). Many of these types of inter-State claims have yet to be resolved in the Iran–US Claims Tribunal.

[73] For example, one author asserts that a large geographical separation between disputants made it possible for them to submit all kinds of disputes to arbitration before World War I. See von Mangoldt, *supra* note 38***, at 233.

[74] See Stephen M. Schwebel, *Comment: The Prospects for International Arbitration: Inter-State Disputes*, in INTERNATIONAL ARBITRATION: PAST AND PROSPECTS 101, 103 (A. H. A. SOONS ed., 1990) (distinguishing between judicial and diplomatic arbitrations).

4.3 Military-related disputes before the PCIJ and the ICJ

Before the First World War, international arbitration was the main way in which States resolved their disputes, with the tribunal being given jurisdiction through a compromissory clause in a treaty.[75] However, that changed with the introduction of the PCIJ after the First World War, which gradually decreased the importance of international arbitration.[76] At the same time, the limited provisions of the Covenant of the League of Nations to regulate war can be seen as inadequate, inasmuch as Article 12 only required States to refer "dispute[s] likely to lead to a rupture . . . either to arbitration or judicial settlement or to enquiry by the Council" and required States to refrain from resorting to war "until three months after the award by the arbitrators or the judicial decision, or the report by the Council."[77] In other words, not only did the Covenant of the League of Nations not prohibit war in certain circumstances, it expressly allowed war after a relatively brief cooling-off period of three months after the rendering of a judicial or political decision. By so doing, the Covenant directed the emphasis away from the peaceful settlement of disputes in favor of war. This emphasis in the text of the Covenant on war over the peaceful settlement of disputes reflects the general military spirit that pervaded the League of Nations and other international organizations during the interwar period, as Inis Claude has noted.[78]

Disarmament and arms control treaties after the First World War (such as the Washington and London Naval Treaties) did not include dispute settlement provisions, and so States with disputes had to rely on such mechanisms as the PCIJ and international arbitration for resolution

[75] See Louis B. Sohn, *Settlement of Disputes Relating to the Interpretation and Application of Treaties*, 150 Rec. des cours 195, 206, 209–227 (1976).

[76] See ibid., at 206 (explaining how international arbitration was at its peak before World War I, although compromissory clauses after World War II have considerably revived international arbitration); Clive Parry, *Some Considerations upon the Protection of Individuals in International Law*, 90 Rec. des cours 653, 660 (1956) (talking about the "high noon of international arbitration [having] occurred around the year 1900"). But see *Arbitration*, in International Law Anthology 323–324 (Anthony D'Amato ed., 1994) (citing Parry) (asserting that public international arbitration has stayed constant, although the increase in such investor–State arbitrations and private arbitrations have created the impression that public international arbitration is on the decline because they are handling disputes that States used to have to espouse in order to get a remedy for their citizens).

[77] See Covenant of the League of Nations, Art. 12.

[78] See Inis L. Claude, Swords into Plowshares: The Problems and Progress of International Organization 54 (4th edn, 1984).

of them, with the jurisdiction provided by *compromis* though that began to change in the late 1920s when States such as the Soviet Union began proposing quasi-adjudicative bodies for resolving disputes over specific treaties.[79] As the introduction to Part III above explained, the Soviet Union's opinion of legal resolution of matters involving politically sensitive issues shifted dramatically after the Second World War, which became apparent during the debates in the Eighteen Nation Disarmament Committee in the early 1960s between the United States and the Soviet Union over a treaty to lead to complete and general disarmament, with the United States in favor of strong dispute settlement provisions involving the ICJ and the Soviet Union strongly opposed on account of the view that arms control and disarmament disputes are too political for legal resolution.[80] However, this does not change the Soviet Union's historic role in promoting legal resolution of such politically sensitive disputes. Once the negotiations for a treaty dealing with complete and general disarmament failed, the nuclear powers and the international community moved on to partial aspects of disarmament, including a focus on non-proliferation of nuclear weapons and nuclear materials.[81] Notwithstanding this change in approach, Soviet opposition to legal resolution does not appear to have lasted long, given how it consented to compromissory clauses involving legal resolution in treaties not that long after the negotiations for this treaty fell apart. Although these compromissory clauses referred both to the ICJ and to international arbitration, international arbitration seemed to be more popular,[82] which indicates the possible revival of international arbitration from its heyday before the First World War.[83]

This section reviews the PCIJ and ICJ cases that involved military-related disputes. The review of PCIJ cases is brief, primarily because there were no military-related disputes per se. Two cases indirectly relate to the military's use of force. For example, the first case of the PCIJ – the *SS Wimbledon* case – involved a situation where the German government refused to allow a British steamship to use the Kiel Canal because it was believed to be carrying war materiel for Poland, there being a state of war between Poland and Russia, and Germany believing that its own regulations required it to remain neutral and refuse the entry of the

[79] See McNeill, *supra* note 37, at 259–260. [80] See Martin, *supra* note 14, at 57.
[81] See Jozef Goldblat, Arms Control: A Guide to Negotiations and Agreements 38 (1994).
[82] See Sohn, *supra* note 75, at 266. [83] See ibid., at 206.

Wimbledon.[84] The PCIJ determined that Germany should have allowed the ship to enter the Kiel Canal because Article 380 of the Versailles Treaty required the Kiel Canal to be "maintained free and open to the vessels of commerce and of war of all nations at peace with Germany on terms of entire equality."[85] The second example is the *Lotus* case, which perhaps is the most famous of the PCIJ. That case involved a collision between French and Turkish ships on the high seas in which eight Turkish sailors died and the Turkish ship sank.[86] When the French ship came into the Turkish port in Constantinople, the captain of the French ship was arrested and tried for involuntary manslaughter, with the French ship itself being detained.[87] France brought a claim before the PCIJ against Turkey for violating international law with the arrest of the captain and detention of the ship.[88] The PCIJ famously concluded that States can do whatever is not prohibited in international law, and since nothing prohibited Turkey's actions, they were justified under the territorial principle.[89] In both cases, the involvement of the military was indirect in terms of detaining a ship and excluding a ship from a particular area through presumably an implicit threat of military force.

From the review of PCIJ cases, one easily can see how PCIJ cases are much less politically sensitive in nature than the arbitration cases from before the First World War and ICJ cases from after the Second World War, instead focusing on technical interpretations of treaties or loan agreements, for example.[90] As explained in Chapter 6.2.1 below, the lack of military-related disputes before the PCIJ likely was due to the general limitation to legal disputes there, whereas the military-related disputes in the ICJ show how this limitation to legal disputes largely was dropped in the UN era, thus enabling legal resolution to handle such politically sensitive disputes as those involving nuclear non-proliferation matters.

The military-related disputes before the ICJ are far more informative for this study's purposes, as were the international arbitration cases discussed in the preceding section. While other commentators have reviewed the ICJ cases involving the use of force since the *Nicaragua*

84 The *SS "Wimbledon" (UK v. Germany)*, Judgment of 17 August 1923, Series A, No. 1, at 18–20.

85 Ibid., at 21–23.

86 See *Case of the SS "Lotus" (France v. Turkey)*, Judgment of 7 September 1927, Series A, No. 9, at 10.

87 See ibid., at 10–11. 88 See ibid., at 5. 89 See ibid., at 19–22, 25.

90 See Charles H. Brower, II, *The Functions and Limits of Arbitration and Judicial Settlement under Private and Public International Law*, 18 Duke J. Comp. & Int'l L. 259, 289 (2008).

case, this study is the first to cast a slightly wider net to look at all military-related disputes, not just those that involve the use of force.[91] As a result, more cases are included in this review, and go back beyond the *Nicaragua* case to even the first ICJ case. Again, such a focus on *military-related* disputes is needed in order to exclude some cases from the scope of this study, inasmuch as it is conceivable that all disputes involving a State could involve that State's vital interests, at least in its own eyes. At a minimum, as the ICJ stated in the *Hostages* case in 1980 and reconfirmed in the *Nicaragua* case in 1984, all disputes involving a sovereign State will be political "by their very nature," because of the involvement of that sovereign State.[92] Moreover, inasmuch as the ICJ is an organ of the United Nations and acts within the framework of the maintenance of international peace and security,[93] some commentators might try to include all ICJ cases within the scope of the politically sensitive.[94] Therefore, it is important to define a subset of ICJ cases for detailed review in creating a group of cases as analogous to nuclear non-proliferation disputes as possible. In total, there have been thirty-three military-related disputes before the ICJ.[95] Of those cases, two were directly related to nuclear weapons. The rest are relevant here by analogy to nuclear non-proliferation disputes.

[91] See Christine Gray, *The Use and Abuse of the International Court of Justice: Cases Concerning the Use of Force after Nicaragua*, 14 Eur. J. Int'l L. 867 (2003); Oscar Schachter, *Disputes Involving the Use of Force*, in The International Court of Justice at a Crossroads 223 (Lori F. Damrosch ed., 1987); Bilder, *supra* note 23***, at 269.

[92] *United States Diplomatic and Consular Staff in Tehran*, 1980 ICJ Rep. 3, 20 (May 24); *Military and Paramilitary Activities in and against Nicaragua*, Jurisdiction and Admissibility, 1984 ICJ Rep. 392, 433 (Nov. 26). See also Rosenne, *supra* note 23, at 38 (discussing these cases and this notion).

[93] See Vera Gowlland-Debbas, *The Relationship between the International Court of Justice and the Security Council in the Light of the Lockerbie Case*, 88 Am. J. Int'l L. 643, at 652.

[94] But see Stephen M. Schwebel, *The Performance and Prospects of the World Court*, 6 Pace Int'l L. Rev. 253, 257 (1994) (asserting that the ICJ has not had as much of an impact on international peace and security as the framers had hoped).

[95] Two additional ICJ cases involved a type of continuation of an earlier case, and so were not included in this tally of military-related disputes. See Application for Revision of the Judgment of 11 July 1996 in *Case Concerning Application of the Convention on the Prevention and Punishment of the Crime of Genocide (Preliminary Obligations) (Bosnia and Herzegovina v. Yugoslavia)*, 2003 ICJ Rep. 122 (Feb. 3); *Case Concerning Armed Activities on the Territory of the Congo (DRC v. Rwanda)*, 2002 ICJ Rep. 219 (July 10) (new application).

The thirty-three military-related cases of the ICJ can be classified into three basic categories: (1) those that involve disputes over weapons, (2) those that involve a pronouncement on the legality or illegality of a particular use of force by a State's military forces (*jus ad bellum*), and (3) those that involve a pronouncement of the legality or illegality of the way a military force used that force (*jus in bello*). The first category is the most relevant to nuclear non-proliferation disputes, and so is the first to be addressed here.

4.3.1 Nuclear-weapon-related disputes

As indicated in the introduction to this chapter, the most analogous ICJ cases to nuclear non-proliferation disputes are the 1973 *Nuclear Tests* cases and the 1996 *Legality of the Threat or Use of Nuclear Weapons* advisory opinion, for the obvious reason that they involved nuclear weapons. The *Nuclear Tests* cases began with New Zealand and Australia initiating parallel proceedings against France in May 1973, claiming that France violated their rights under international law due to the radioactive fallout from its atmospheric testing of its nuclear weapons in the South Pacific.[96] France submitted a letter to the Registrar of the Court claiming that the Court lacked jurisdiction to hear the dispute,[97] but did not participate in any other way. Without ever determining actual jurisdiction, the Court dismissed both applications in light of unilateral declarations made by the Office of the French President stating that France soon would move all of its nuclear testing underground.[98] As the Court felt these assurances met Australia's and New Zealand's objectives in bringing their claims, it declared the cases moot.[99] To be clear, the ICJ did not say that it did not have the tools to handle this type of dispute, but rather prudently dismissed the matter because it no longer presented a case or controversy upon which to

[96] See generally *Nuclear Tests (Australia v. France; NZ v. France)*, 1974 ICJ Rep. 253 (Dec. 20).

[97] Ibid. See also Don MacKay, *Nuclear Testing: New Zealand and France in the International Court of Justice*, 19 Fordham Int'l L.J. 1857, 1864–1865 (1996); Jerome B. Elkind, Non-Appearance before the International Court of Justice: Functional and Comparative Analysis (1984), at 60.

[98] See *Nuclear Tests (Australia v. France; NZ v. France)*, 1974 ICJ Rep. 253, 469–71; Elkind, *supra* note 97***, at 62.

[99] *Nuclear Tests (Australia v. France; NZ v. France)*, 1974 ICJ Rep. 253, 270–272, 475–477; Elkind, *supra* note 97***, at 62.

rule.[100] Yet the Court made it possible for New Zealand to request an examination of the situation if, in the future, the Court observes that "the basis of this Judgment were to be affected."[101]

Such underground testing continued until 1992, when a moratorium on nuclear testing was declared.[102] When President Jacques Chirac announced on June 13, 1995, that France would yet again test its nuclear weapons in the Pacific, despite the moratorium and the decision only a month earlier to indefinitely extend the Nuclear Non-Proliferation Treaty,[103] New Zealand filed a request with the ICJ to reopen its 1974 case.[104] New Zealand was careful to avoid any appearance of instituting a new proceeding, as no basis for jurisdiction over France existed at that time.[105] Instead, New Zealand sought

> a resumption of the proceedings instituted in 1973, the bases of the jurisdiction of the Court remaining the General Act for the Pacific Settlement of International Disputes of 26 September 1928, as well as France's acceptance of the Optional Clause as it stood at the time of the original Application.[106]

However, a problem that New Zealand seemed to overlook was that the Court never determined the validity of those bases of jurisdiction in the earlier case.[107] While the ICJ held out in paragraph 63 of its 1974 judgment the possibility that it could re-examine the situation of "the basis of [the] Judgment [being] affected," the Court determined in its 1995 order that the commencement of the underground nuclear tests by France was sufficiently different from the atmospheric testing at issue in 1974 to deny reopening the case under this earlier paragraph.[108]

Critics likely will point to how the ICJ has refused to rely on a unilateral declaration by Mali's head of State to make a case moot in

[100] See Nagendra Singh and Edward McWhinney, Nuclear Weapons and Contemporary International Law 296 (2nd rev. edn, 1989).

[101] *Nuclear Tests (Australia v. France; NZ v. France)*, 1974 ICJ Rep. 253, ¶ 63.

[102] See MacKay, *supra* note 97, at 1866. [103] See ibid., at 1857.

[104] See *Nuclear Tests (Australia v. France; NZ v. France)*, 1974 ICJ Rep. 253, 457; MacKay, *supra* note 97, at 1873.

[105] See *Nuclear Tests Case (NZ v. France)*, 1995 ICJ Rep. 288, 289–290 (Sept. 22).

[106] Ibid.

[107] See Prudence Taylor, *Testing Times for the World Court: Judicial Process and the 1995 French Nuclear Tests Case*, 8 Colo. J. Int'l Envtl. L. & Pol'y 199, 229 (1997).

[108] See *Request for an Examination of the Situation in Accordance with Paragraph 63 of the Court's Judgment of 20 December 1974 in the Nuclear Tests (NZ v. France)* 1995 ICJ Rep. 288, 294–295, 307 (Sept. 22).

the 1986 *Frontier Dispute* case[109] in order to show how the ICJ in the *Nuclear Tests* cases must have been engaging in a results-oriented type of analysis in order to avoid having to address that nuclear-weapon dispute.[110] However, the ICJ made a valid distinction between the *Nuclear Tests* cases and the *Frontier Dispute* case in that the ICJ in the former case satisfied itself that France actually intended to bind itself by the unilateral declaration, whereas in the latter case there was no such clear intention found on the part of Mali's head of State.[111] Besides, neither New Zealand nor Australia contested the scope of the Court's determination or asked for an interpretation,[112] suggesting that the decision at least made sense to the disputants at that time.

Turning to the other proceedings involving nuclear weapons, the ICJ received two requests for an advisory opinion in 1993 and 1995 dealing with nuclear weapons. In the *Legality of the Threat or Use of Nuclear Weapons* advisory opinion, brought in 1995, the General Assembly asked the ICJ, "Is the threat or use of nuclear weapons in any circumstance permitted under international law?"[113] The ICJ responded with the following: that the threat and use of nuclear weapons "generally [are] contrary to the rules of international law applicable in armed conflict, and in particular the principles and rules of humanitarian law," but

> in view of the current state of international law, and of the elements of fact at its disposal, the Court cannot conclude definitively whether the threat or use of nuclear weapons would be lawful or unlawful in an extreme circumstance of self-defense, in which the very survival of a state would be at stake.[114]

[109] See *Case Concerning the Frontier Dispute (Burkina Faso/Republic of Mali)*, 1986 ICJ Rep. 544, 573–574 (Dec. 22).

[110] See John Collier and Vaughan Lowe, The Settlement of Disputes in International Law: Institutions and Procedures 13 n. 26 (1999) (relying on the *Frontier Dispute* case to support their assertion that the ICJ's interpretation of the law in the *Nuclear Tests* cases was strained). See also Julie Dahlitz, Nuclear Arms Control 102 (1983) (asserting that the ICJ evaded the substantive issues in the *Nuclear Tests* cases).

[111] See *Case Concerning the Frontier Dispute (Burkina Faso/Republic of Mali)*, 1986 ICJ Rep. 544, 573–574 (Dec. 22).

[112] See MacKay, *supra* note 97, at 1872.

[113] *Legality of the Threat or Use of Nuclear Weapons*, Advisory Opinion, 1996 ICJ Rep. 226, 228 (July 8).

[114] Ibid., ¶ 105. This inconclusive decision seems to support the idea that the determination of legality has to be handled on a case-by-case basis, not in the abstract. Four judges – Judges Schwebel, Higgins, Guillaume and Oda – emphasized this point. See generally Charles Moxley, Nuclear Weapons and International Law in the

As conflicting newspaper headlines after the publication of the advisory opinion showed, many found it difficult to determine the result of this opinion.[115] Importantly, the ICJ there created a presumption of illegality of nuclear weapons, although it immediately undermined this presumption with its inconclusive response to whether nuclear weapons are legal when the extreme case of self-defense is involved.[116] This caveat is particularly problematic when one considers that it is the State using or threatening use of nuclear weapons that determines when its survival is at stake. Such broad discretion in the hands of the State using or threatening use of nuclear weapons makes it extremely difficult to scrutinize this kind of determination in a meaningful manner, as public-administration theory observes,[117] even if one assumes that the State remains under the obligations of international law.[118]

Concerning the ICJ's reference to needing more facts to reach a decision on the lawfulness in extreme circumstances of self-defense, the ICJ was not saying that it could not come up with more facts to help flesh out the issues, as Charles Moxley assumes the Court was saying when he proceeds to provide copious "unclassified and openly available" facts that the ICJ could have relied upon to conclude that the use and

Post-Cold War World 158–159 (2000) (summarizing the different opinions of the judges). Several notable commentators had been saying this for decades. See, e.g., M. S. McDougal and F. P. Feliciano, Law and Minimum World Public Order 78 (1961).

115 See Laurence Boisson de Chazournes and Philippe Sands, *Introduction*, in International Law, the International Court of Justice and Nuclear Weapons 1, 1–2 (Laurence Boisson de Chazournes and Philippe Sands ed., 1999). Regardless of the confusion, it seems a considerable stretch to characterize the advisory opinion as showing how two UN principle organs (the ICJ and the General Assembly) turned against nuclear-weapon States, as some commentators have asserted. See Miguel Marin Bosch, *The Nonproliferation Treaty and Its Future*, in International Law, The International Court of Justice and Nuclear Weapons 375, 375 (P. Sands and L. Boisson de Chazournes ed., 1999).

116 See Burns H. Weston, *Nuclear Weapons and the World Court: Ambiguity's Consensus*, 7 Transnat'l L. & Contemp. Probs. 371, 398–399 (1997).

117 See generally Michael Harmon, Responsibility as Paradox: A Critique of Rational Discourse on Government 99–125 (1995). See also Jan Klabbers, An Introduction to International Institutional Law 275–276 (2nd edn, 2009) (applying Harmon's ideas in the context of determining the responsibility of international organizations).

118 See Marcelo Kohen, *The Notion of "State Survival"*, in International Law, the International Court of Justice and Nuclear Weapons 293 (Laurence Boisson de Chazournes and Philippe Sands ed., 1999).

threatened use of nuclear weapons is illegal.[119] Rather, the lack of facts that the ICJ refers to is its way of emphasizing the problems it faced in providing a clear answer when it was not presented with a true case and controversy. As ICJ judge Shigeru Oda complained in his separate opinion to the *Legality of the Use by a State of Nuclear Weapons in Armed Conflict* advisory opinion,

> I firmly believe that the International Court of Justice should primarily function as a judicial institution to provide solutions to inter-State disputes of a contentious nature and should neither be expected to act as a legislature (although new developments in international law may well be crystallized through the jurisprudence of the Court) nor to function as an organ giving legal advice (except that the Court may give opinions on legal questions which arise within the scope of activities of the authorized international organizations) in circumstances in which there is no conflict or dispute concerning legal questions between States or between States and international organizations.[120]

This is similar to what Israel and others argued in the *Wall* advisory opinion and why the US Supreme Court does not render advisory opinions – only when there are two adverse parties in an *actual* dispute can the factual record be sufficiently developed to render a valid decision.[121] By refusing to render an answer to the General Assembly's request, the ICJ avoided this theoretical problem and maintained a degree of flexibility on the matter so that justice can be served in the future if it is faced with resolving an actual dispute.[122] In

[119] See MOXLEY, *supra* note 114, at 3, 6, 393–650 (referring to these as the "fact chapters").

[120] *Legality of the Use by a State of Nuclear Weapons in Armed Conflict*, 1996 ICJ Rep. 66, 89 (July 8) (Oda J., separate opinion).

[121] See *Legal Consequences of the Construction of a Wall in the Occupied Palestinian Territory*, Advisory Opinion, 2004 ICJ Rep. 136, 160–162 (July 9); *Simon v. Eastern Kentucky Welfare Rights Organization*, 426 U.S. 26, 37 (1976) (asserting that "no principle is more fundamental to the judiciary's proper role in our system of government than the constitutional limitation of federal-court jurisdiction to actual cases or controversies"). One can only speculate as to whether this principle common-law tradition actually played a role in the ICJ's decision-making process. After all, UN Charter and ICJ Statute draftsmen seemed to have had the civil-law tradition in mind when they created the ICJ's advisory jurisdiction. See Perez, *supra* note 25***, at 407–408 (1997).

[122] It is not that there was a gap in the law relating to nuclear weapons, as some commentators are inclined to conclude. See DANIEL H. JOYNER, INTERNATIONAL LAW AND THE PROLIFERATION OF WEAPONS OF MASS DESTRUCTION 212 (2009); MOXLEY, *supra* note 114, at 230; Daniel Bodansky, *Non Liquet and the Incompleteness of International Law*, in INTERNATIONAL LAW, THE INTERNATIONAL COURT OF JUSTICE AND NUCLEAR WEAPONS 153 (LAURENCE BOISSON DE CHAZOURNES and PHILIPPE SANDS ed., 1999); Timothy L. H. McCormack, *A* Non Liquet *on Nuclear Weapons: The ICJ Avoids the Application of General Principles of International Humanitarian Law*, 316 INT'L REV. RED CROSS 76 (1997). Instead, the ICJ meant

this regard, advisory opinions are no substitute for contentious cases in terms of presenting clear questions to the Court through the narrowing down of the question through the litigation process, especially with such important questions as those involving the legality of the threat or use of nuclear weapons. The ICJ's basis for conclusion rested largely on international humanitarian law and bodies of law other than those relating directly to nuclear weapons. Nonetheless, the ICJ still considered nuclear non-proliferation agreements in addressing the question.[123] It is not surprising that the ICJ concluded that there were no general prohibitions to be found in those nuclear-weapon treaties,[124] given how these treaties only limit certain aspects of nuclear activity, one of them – the NPT – even creating a group of nuclear-weapon States that are allowed to have nuclear weapons and the rest of them implicitly accepting that some States will possess nuclear weapons. The ICJ also noted how the treaties establishing regional nuclear-weapon-free zones allow nuclear-weapon States nuclear weapons in certain situations and that these reservations "met with no objection from the parties to the Tlatelolco or Rarotonga Treaties or from the Security Council."[125] The obviousness of the answer to the question posed might explain why the Court engaged in such a superficial analysis of these nuclear-weapon treaties when giving its advisory opinion. Alternatively, it could just be because the treaties are sufficiently clear on their face that the provisions can be allowed to speak for themselves. Regardless, the advisory opinion seems to have left all unsatisfied in one way or another,[126] as could

what it said: that there were not enough facts to reach an overarching conclusion to the question posed. Therefore, this study asserts that it was a problem with the facts (or a lack thereof), not a problem with the law, or rather that the law depended on the content of facts.

123 See *Legality of the Threat or Use of Nuclear Weapons*, Advisory Opinion, 1996 ICJ Rep. 226, 247–253 (July 8) (analyzing the Tlatelolco, Rarotonga, NPT, Antarctic, Pelindaba treaties).

124 See ibid., at 247–253. 125 Ibid., at 253.

126 See generally LAURENCE BOISSON DE CHAZOURNES and PHILIPPE SANDS (eds.), INTERNATIONAL LAW, THE INTERNATIONAL COURT OF JUSTICE AND NUCLEAR WEAPONS (1999) (most authors expressing some sort of frustration over the opinion); Richard A. Falk, *Nuclear Weapons, International Law, and the World Court: A Historic Encounter*, 91 AM. J. INT'l L. 64 (1996); Marc Perrin de Brichambaut, *Les avis consultatifs de la CIJ sur la licéité des armes nucléaires*, 42 AFDI 315 (1996); Vincent Coussirat-Coustère, *Armes nucléaires et droit international: À propos des avis de CIJ*, 42 AFDI 337 (1996); Jerome B. Elkind, *Nuclear Weapons: The World Court's Decision*, 49 REVUE HELLENIQUE DE DROIT INTERNATIONAL 401 (1996); Yves Sandoz, *Advisory Opinion of the International Court of Justice on the Legality of the Threat or Use of Nuclear Weapons*, 316 INT'L REV. RED CROSS 6 (1997); Eric David, *The Opinion of*

have been expected with such a broad question as the one posed by the General Assembly.[127]

One clear development from this advisory opinion that must not be overlooked was the Court's unanimous reaffirmation of the obligation contained in NPT Article VI, which requires States parties to "pursue negotiations in good faith on effective measures relating to cessation of the nuclear arms race at an early date and to nuclear disarmament, and on a treaty on general and complete disarmament under strict and effective international control."[128] This reaffirmation brought a measure of progress to the notion of nuclear disarmament, which had not seen progress in many years.[129] More recently, the Security Council adopted

the International Court of Justice on the Legality of the Use of Nuclear Weapons, 316 INT'L REV. RED CROSS 21 (1997); Manfred Mohr, *Advisory Opinion of the International Court of Justice on the Legality of the Use of Nuclear Weapons under International Law: A Few Thoughts on Its Strengths and Weaknesses*, 316 INT'L REV. RED CROSS 92 (1997); Louise Doswald-Beck, *International Humanitarian Law and the Advisory Opinion of the International Court of Justice on the Legality of the Threat or Use of Nuclear Weapons*, 316 INT'L REV. RED CROSS 35 (1997); Peter Weiss, *The World Court Tackles the Fate of the Earth: An Introduction to the ICJ Advisory Opinion on the Legality of the Threat and Use of Nuclear Weapons*, 7 TRANSNAT'L L. & CONTEMP. PROB. 313 (1997); Georges Abi-Saab, *The Court and the Bomb: A Case of Mutual Deterrence?*, 7 TRANSNAT'L L. & COMTEMP. PROB. 429 (1997); Hisakazu Fujita, *The Advisory Opinion of the International Court of Justice on the Legality of Nuclear Weapons*, 316 INT'L REV. RED CROSS 56 (1997); Michael J. Matheson, *The Opinions of the International Court of Justice on the Threat or Use of Nuclear Weapons*, 91 AM. J. INT'L L. 417 (1997); Peter H. F. Bekker and Judith Hippler Bello, *Legality of the Threat or Use of Nuclear Weapons Advisory Opinion*, 91 AM. J. INT'L L. 126 (1997); Martti Koskenniemi, *Faith, Identity and the Killing of the Innocent: International Lawyers and Nuclear Weapons*, 10 LEIDEN J. INT'L L. 137 (1997); Nicholas Grief, *Legality of the Threat or Use of Nuclear Weapons*, 46 INT'L & COMP. L.Q. 681 (1997); Simon Chesterman, *The ICJ Nuclear Weapons and the Law*, 44 NETH. INT'L L. REV. 149 (1997); Luigi Condorelli, *Nuclear Weapons: A Weighty Matter for the International Court of Justice* – Jura Non Novit Curia?, 316 INT'L REV. RED CROSS 9 (1997); Christopher Greenwood, *The Advisory Opinion on Nuclear Weapons and the Contribution of the International Court to International Humanitarian Law*, 316 INT'L REV. RED CROSS 65 (1997); Said Mahmoudi, *The International Court of Justice and Nuclear Weapons*, 66 NORDIC J. INT'L L. 7 (1997).

[127] See A. Vaughan Lowe, *Shock Verdict: Nuclear War May or May Not Be Unlawful*, 55 CAMBRIDGE L. J. 415 (1996).

[128] NPT, *supra* note 20, Art. VI; *Legality of the Threat or Use of Nuclear Weapons*, Advisory Opinion, 1996 ICJ Rep. 226, 263–267 (July 8).

[129] See, e.g., David A. Koplow, *Parsing Good Faith: Has the United States Violated Article VI of the Nuclear Non-proliferation Treaty*, WIS. L. REV. 301 (1993) (strongly arguing that the United States has violated its obligations under NPT Article VI).

Resolution 1887 in 2009, "[*c*]*all*[*ing*] *upon* the Parties to the NPT, pursuant to Article VI of the Treaty, to undertake to pursue negotiations in good faith on effective measures relating to nuclear arms reduction and disarmament, ... and *call*[*ing*] *on* all other States to join in this endeavour."[130] Assuming that nuclear-weapon States take this NPT Article VI obligation seriously, such an obligation significantly strengthens the nuclear non-proliferation regime inasmuch as non-nuclear-weapon States would no longer be able to point to supposedly nuclear-weapon States' noncompliance with Article VI as a reason why they should not abide by their own nuclear non-proliferation obligations.[131] Indeed, as ICJ judge Mohammed Bedjaoui observed in his declaration to the *Legality of the Threat or Use of Nuclear Weapons* advisory opinion,

> The solution arrived at in this Advisory Opinion frankly states the legal reality, while faithfully expressing and reflecting the hope, shared by all, peoples and States alike, that *nuclear disarmament will always remain the ultimate goal of all action in the field of nuclear weapons, that the goal is no longer utopian and that it is the duty of all to seek to attain it more actively than ever.*[132]

Despite such a "legal reality," serious negotiations for such a treaty and the preparation for such negotiations do not appear to have yet begun, notwithstanding the benefits that can come to both nuclear and non-nuclear States from nuclear disarmament.[133] Commentators believe that the nuclear non-proliferation regime will be considerably weakened if nuclear-weapon States do not start taking this obligation seriously.[134]

There was another question that the World Health Organization posed to the ICJ in 1993 concerning nuclear weapons, in the *Legality of the Use by a State of Nuclear Weapons in Armed Conflict* advisory opinion: "In view of the health and environmental effects, would the use of nuclear weapons by a State in war or other armed conflict be a

[130] S. C. Res 1887, UN Doc. S/RES/1887 (Sept. 24, 2009), para. 5 (original emphases).

[131] See Bosch, *supra* note 115, at 375.

[132] *Legality of the Threat or Use of Nuclear Weapons*, Advisory Opinion, 1996 ICJ Rep. 226, 263–267 (July 8) (Bedjaoui J., Declaration) (emphasis in original).

[133] See generally Hans Blix, Why Nuclear Disarmament Matters (2008) (explaining why States, even nuclear-weapon States, should want to move to nuclear disarmament); David Krieger and Carah Ong, Back to Basics: Reviving Nuclear Disarmament in the Non-proliferation Regime (2005) (same).

[134] See Thomas Graham, Jr., *International Law and the Proliferation of Nuclear Weapons*, 33 Geo. Wash. Int'l L. Rev. 49, 50 (2000).

breach of its obligations under international law including the WHO Constitution?"[135] In 1996, the ICJ ultimately refused to provide an answer to this request, instead interpreting the purposes of the WHO as contained in the WHO Constitution to conclude that the question did not sufficiently relate to the WHO's health-related purposes in accordance with the WHO Constitution.[136] In particular, the ICJ pointed out:

> International organizations are governed by the "principle of speciality," that is to say, they are invested by the States which create them with powers, the limits of which are a function of the common interests whose promotion those States entrust to them . . . In the opinion of the Court, to ascribe to the WHO the competence to address the legality of the use of nuclear weapons – even in view of their health and environmental effects – would be tantamount to disregarding the principle of speciality; for such competence could not be deemed a necessary implication of the Constitution of the Organization in the light of the purposes assigned to it by its member States.[137]

In this manner, the ICJ reins in the powers of international organizations and the doctrine of implied powers by limiting these powers and this doctrine to the purposes contained in the preambulary portions of international organizations' constitutions.[138]

This is one of the rare instances where the International Court refused to provide an advisory opinion when requested, the other instance being the *Status of Eastern Carelia* PCIJ case of 1923.[139] It is tempting to

[135] *Legality of the Use by a State of Nuclear Weapons in Armed Conflict*, Advisory Opinion, 1996 ICJ Rep. 66, 68 (July 8).

[136] See ibid., at 74–81. See generally Nicholas Rostow, *The World Health Organization, the International Court of Justice, and Nuclear Weapons*, 20 YALE J. INT'L L. 151 (1995); Martin M. Strahan, *Nuclear Weapons, the World Health Organization, and the International Court of Justice: Should an Advisory Opinion Bring Them Together?*, 2 TULSA J. COMP. & INT'L L. 395 (1995); Peter H. F. Bekker and Judith Hippler Bello, *Legality of the Use by a State of Nuclear Weapons in Armed Conflict Advisory Opinion*, 91 AM. J. INT'L L. 134 (1997).

[137] *Legality of the Use by a State of Nuclear Weapons in Armed Conflict*, Advisory Opinion, 1996 ICJ Rep. 66, 78–79 (July 8).

[138] See generally Viljam Engström, *Implied Powers of International Organizations: On the Character of a Legal Doctrine*, 14 FINNISH Y.B. INT'L L. 129 (2003); BERNARD ROUYER-HAMERAY, LES COMPÉTENCES IMPLICITES DES ORGANISATIONS INTERNATIONALES (1962); Krzysztof Skubiszewski, *Implied Powers of International Organizations*, in INTERNATIONAL LAW AT A TIME OF PERPLEXITY: ESSAYS IN HONOUR OF SHABTAI ROSENNE 855 (YORAM DINSTEIN ed., 1989).

[139] See generally *Status of Eastern Carelia*, Advisory Opinion, 1923 PCIJ Series B, No. 5 (July 23).

speculate what would have happened had the ICJ not simultaneously had the request from the General Assembly, which conveniently enabled the ICJ to answer essentially the same question that the World Health Organization had posed while at the same time being able to appear conservative when determining its advisory jurisdiction. Had there not been the General Assembly's request for an advisory opinion, the ICJ likely would have felt compelled to answer the WHO's request, notwithstanding whatever problems the request had with respect to the legality of nuclear weapons not fitting in the scope of the WHO's purposes, because the ICJ typically answers requests for advisory opinions.[140] Regardless, some commentators see the ICJ's refusal to hear the World Health Organization's request for an advisory opinion as "the court duck[ing] the issue" of the legality of nuclear weapons.[141] However, if the ICJ had been trying to avoid the issue, it would not have agreed to give an advisory opinion on essentially the same issue on the same day that it denied the World Health Organization's request.

4.3.2 ICJ cases involving the use of force

The vast majority of military-related disputes involve one State's use of force against another State – twenty-eight cases in all. The ICJ's involvement with matters relating to the use of force began early on in its history and has remained strong to this day. The *Corfu Channel* case, the ICJ's first contentious case, involved the 1947 incident where mines in Albanian waters damaged a British warship and killed British military personnel, with the question whether the sweeping for mines in Albanian waters by British warships after this initial incident violated Albania's sovereignty also being raised.[142] The ICJ concluded in 1949 that Albania could not prohibit passage through these territorial waters in times of peace and that British warships could not sweep for mines in these waters.[143]

[140] See Georges Abi-Saab, *On Discretion: Reflections on the Nature of the Consultative Function of the International Court of Justice*, in INTERNATIONAL LAW, THE INTERNATIONAL COURT OF JUSTICE AND NUCLEAR WEAPONS 36 (LAURENCE BOISSON DE CHAZOURNES and PHILIPPE SANDS ed., 1999) (discussing the death of the ICJ's discretion in choosing to give advisory opinions).

[141] See, e.g., Ginsburg and McAdams, *supra* note 3, at 1328.

[142] See Application, *Corfu Channel Case (UK v. Albania)*, ICJ Pleadings, May 22, 1947.

[143] See *Corfu Channel Case (UK v. Albania)*, Merits, 1949 ICJ Rep. 4 (Apr 9).

Six interesting cases arose in the 1950s involving the shooting down or seizure of military aircraft. In 1952, Soviet fighters attacked a US bomber flying over islands in the north of Japan, with the whereabouts of the eight crew members being unknown.[144] In 1953, Czechoslovakian fighter aircraft shot down a US military patrol aircraft over the US-controlled zone of Germany, causing injury to the pilot and damage to the US aircraft.[145] In 1954, the USSR, through the assistance of the Hungarian People's Republic, seized a US military transport plane and its four crew members that had been blown into Hungarian airspace, which led the United States to bring claims against both the USSR and the Hungarian People's Republic, entitled *Treatment in Hungary of Aircraft and Crew of United States of America.*[146] Also in 1954, Soviet fighter airplanes shot down a US patrol airplane over the Sea of Japan, killing one crew member and injuring the others.[147] Again, in 1954, two months later, Soviet fighter airplanes shot down a US bomber airplane that was flying over the northern island of Japan, again killing one crew member and injuring the other crew members.[148] In all of these cases, the United States brought a claim, and in each the ICJ determined in an order of a preliminary nature that it had no jurisdiction over the respondent State with regard to that dispute, and so dismissed the claim.[149] However, the United States presumably knew this when it brought these claims, since it did not make a colorable argument for jurisdiction, instead merely citing ICJ Statute Article 36(2), which refers to jurisdiction through an optional clause declaration, but the United States must

[144] Application, *Aerial Incident of 7 October 1952 (US v. USSR)*, ICJ Pleadings, June 2, 1955, at 10–11.

[145] See ibid., at 8–10.

[146] See Application, *Treatment in Hungary of Aircraft and Crew of United States of America (US v. USSR)*, ICJ Pleadings, March 3, 1954, at 43–44; Application, *Treatment in Hungary of Aircraft and Crew of United States of America (US v. Hungary)*, ICJ Pleadings, March 3, 1954, at 9–10.

[147] See Application, *Aerial Incident of 4 September 1954 (US v. USSR)*, ICJ Pleadings, July 25, 1958, at 8.

[148] See ibid., at 9–10.

[149] See *Aerial Incident of 4 September 1954 (US v. USSR)*, Order, 1958 ICJ Rep. 158, 160–161 (Dec. 9); *Aerial Incident of 7 November 1954 (US v. USSR)*, Order, 1959 ICJ Rep. 276, 277–278 (Oct. 7); *Treatment in Hungary of Aircraft and Crew of United States of America (US v. USSR)*, Order, 1954 ICJ Rep. 104–105 (July 12); *Treatment in Hungary of Aircraft and Crew of United States of America (US v. Hungary)*, Order, 1954 ICJ Rep. 99, 100–101 (July 12); *Aerial Incident of 7 October 1952 (US v. USSR)*, Order, 1956 ICJ Rep. 9, 11 (March 14); *Aerial Incident of 10 March 1953 (US v. Czechoslovakia)*, Order, 1956 ICJ Rep. 6, 8 (March 14).

have known that the respondent States had not made a valid declaration at that time.[150] Therefore, if anything, these cases show how States can use legal resolution both as a political tool to raise the public's awareness of a particular situation and as a form of protest.

Three other claims involved the Bulgarian shooting down of an Israeli El Al commercial airplane. In 1955, the United Kingdom, the United States and Israel all brought claims against Bulgaria for the *Aerial Incident of 27 July 1955*, which involved the same factual situation – Bulgarian fighter aircraft shooting down an Israeli El Al commercial aircraft, killing all passengers and crew members of British, American, and Israeli nationality and destroying their property.[151] Each claimant cited Bulgaria's consent to the compulsory jurisdiction of the PCIJ as the basis for why the ICJ had jurisdiction over Bulgaria,[152] but the United Kingdom and the United States later asked the ICJ to discontinue the proceedings, to which Bulgaria did not object, which led the ICJ to remove the case from its docket on August 3, 1959 and May 30, 1960, respectively.[153] The Israeli claim proceeded to the ICJ making a judgment on the preliminary objections to jurisdiction, with the ICJ concluding that it lacked jurisdiction over Bulgaria because its declaration accepting the compulsory jurisdiction of the PCIJ lapsed in 1921.[154]

Another case involving the use of force arose in 1984, when Nicaragua brought a claim against the United States entitled *Military and*

150 See Application, *Aerial Incident of 4 September 1954 (US v. USSR)*, ICJ Pleadings, July 25, 1958, at 8; Application, *Aerial Incident of 7 November 1954 (US v. USSR)*, ICJ Pleadings, June 8, 1959, at 9; Application, *Treatment in Hungary of Aircraft and Crew of United States of America (US v. USSR)*, ICJ Pleadings, March 3, 1954, at 43–44; Application, *Treatment in Hungary of Aircraft and Crew of United States of America (US v. Hungary)*, ICJ Pleadings, March 3, 1954, at 9–10; Application, *Aerial Incident of 7 October 1952 (US v. USSR)*, ICJ Pleadings, June 2, 1955, at 10–11; Application, *Aerial Incident of 10 March 1953 (US v. Czechoslovakia)*, March 29, 1955, at 8–9.

151 See Application, *Aerial Incident of 27 July 1955 (UK v. Bulgaria)*, ICJ Pleadings, Nov. 22, 1957, at 34; Application, *Aerial Incident of 27 July 1955 (US v. Bulgaria)*, ICJ Pleadings, Oct. 24, 1957, at 23–24; Application, *Aerial Incident of 27 July 1955 (UK v. Israel)*, ICJ Pleadings, Oct. 16, 1957, at 5.

152 See Application, *Aerial Incident of 27 July 1955 (US v. Bulgaria)*, ICJ Pleadings, Oct. 24, 1957, at 23–24; Application, *Aerial Incident of 27 July 1955 (UK v. Bulgaria)*, ICJ Pleadings, Nov. 22, 1957, at 36; Application, *Aerial Incident of 27 July 1955 (UK v. Israel)*, ICJ Pleadings, Oct. 16, 1957, at 5–6.

153 *Aerial Incident of 27 July 1955 (US v. Bulgaria)*, Order, 1960 ICJ Rep. 146, 147–148 (May 30); *Aerial Incident of 27 July 1955 (UK v. Bulgaria)*, Order, 1960 ICJ Rep. 264, 265 (Aug. 3).

154 See *Aerial Incident of 27 July 1955 (UK v. Israel)*, Preliminary Objections, 1959 ICJ Rep. 127, 145 (May 26).

Paramilitary Activities in and against Nicaragua for supposedly funding, equipping, and training 10,000 ex-national guardsmen in ten base camps along the border of Honduras and Nicaragua to commit attacks on Nicaragua and mine Nicaragua's ports to interfere with its commercial activities, among other harmful activities, all in violation of the UN Charter and customary international law.[155] After the ICJ determined it had jurisdiction and that the dispute was justiciable,[156] the United States stopped participating in the proceedings.[157] Nevertheless, the ICJ ultimately determined that the United States violated customary international law by intervening in the affairs of Nicaragua, using force against Nicaragua, and otherwise violating Nicaragua's sovereignty, among other things, and required the United States to stop such activities and pay reparations to Nicaragua.[158] Nicaragua brought two related cases in 1986, one with Nicaragua claiming against Costa Rica and the other against Honduras. Both of these cases were entitled *Border and Transborder Armed Actions*. Both cases arose out of the same factual situation, which involved armed bands of ex-national guardsmen that operated in Nicaragua from Costa Rica and Honduras, who had flown there after the 1979 revolution in Nicaragua. The armed bands apparently had regularly attacked government installations and military patrols, as well as killing and abducting citizens, among many other harmful activities against Nicaragua.[159] The disputants settled out of court, but not until the ICJ had determined in the *Nicaragua v. Honduras* case that it had jurisdiction both under a compromissory clause in the Pact of Bogotá and under an optional clause declaration, as well as determining that the disputes were justiciable.[160]

[155] See Application, *Military and Paramilitary Activities in and against Nicaragua (Nicaragua v. US)*, ICJ Pleadings, April 9, 1984, at 2–16.

[156] See *Military and Paramilitary Activities in and against Nicaragua (Nicaragua v. US)*, Jurisdiction and Admissibility, 1984 ICJ Rep. 392 (Nov. 26).

[157] See generally Keith Highet, *Litigation Implications of the U.S. Withdrawal from the Nicaragua Case*, 79 AM. J. INT'L L. 992 (1985); HUGH W. A. THIRLWAY, NON-APPEARANCE BEFORE THE INTERNATIONAL COURT OF JUSTICE (1985).

[158] See generally *Military and Paramilitary Activities in and against Nicaragua (Nicaragua v. US)*, 1986 ICJ Rep. 14 (June 27).

[159] See Application, *Border and Transborder Armed Actions (Nicaragua v. Honduras)*, ICJ Pleadings, July 28, 1986, at 3–5; Application, *Case Concerning Border and Transborder Armed Actions (Nicaragua v. Costa Rica)*, ICJ Pleadings, July 28, 1986, at 3–6.

[160] *Case Concerning Border and Transborder Armed Actions (Nicaragua v. Honduras)*, Jurisdiction and Admissibility, 1988 ICJ Rep. 69, 107 (Dec. 20). In the *Nicaragua v. Costa Rica* case, Nicaragua wrote a letter to the ICJ Registrar discontinuing the judicial

Another case involving the United States arose in 1987, when the United States attacked two Iranian oil platforms it believed had been used as the base for attacks on a re-flagged US oil tanker during the Iran–Iraq War.[161] The Court determined that these Iranian attacks, and the hitting of a mine by a US naval ship off the coast of Bahrain, did not constitute armed attacks by Iran that would have justified the US response as self-defense, although it did not uphold Iran's claims for reparation.[162] A year later, in 1988, Iran brought a claim against the United States for shooting down an Iranian commercial airplane with a surface-to-air missile, killing all 290 passengers and crew.[163] Iran and the United States were able to settle the dispute out of court, of which the parties informed the ICJ on February 22, 1996, at which point the ICJ removed the case from its docket without having decided jurisdiction or justiciability.[164]

In 1999, the Federal Republic of Yugoslavia brought the *Legality of Use of Force* cases, which were ten claims against NATO members – Belgium, Canada, France, Germany, Italy, the Netherlands, Portugal, Spain, the United Kingdom, and the United States – that it believed were responsible for unlawfully using force against it and its people through bombing to protect Kosovo. In particular, Yugoslavia asserted that the subject of the dispute was that each State among this group of ten

> violated its international obligation banning the use of force against another State, the obligation not to intervene in the internal affairs of another State, the obligation not to violate the sovereignty of another State, the obligation to protect the civilian population and civilian objects in wartime, the obligation to protect the environment, the obligation relating to free navigation on international rivers, the obligation regarding fundamental human rights and freedoms, the obligation not to use prohibited weapons, [and] the obligation not to deliberately inflict conditions of life calculated to cause the physical destruction of a national group.[165]

proceedings against Costa Rica on August 12, 1987, before the ICJ had been able to pronounce on the jurisdiction and justiciability of the matter. See *Case Concerning Border and Transborder Armed Actions (Nicaraga v. Costa Rica)*, Order, 1987 ICJ Rep. 182, 183 (Aug. 19).

161 See Application, *Oil Platforms (Iran v. US)*, ICJ Pleadings, Nov. 2, 1992, at 2–4.

162 See *Oil Platforms (Iran v. US)*, 2003 ICJ Rep. 161 (Nov. 6).

163 See Application, *Aerial Incident of 3 July 1988 (Iran v. US)*, ICJ Pleadings, May 17, 1988.

164 See *Aerial Incident of 3 July 1988 (Iran v. US)*, Order, 1996 ICJ Rep. 9, 10 (Feb. 22), at 4–5.

165 See Legality of the Use of Force, Application, ICJ Proceedings, April 29, 1999, at 3 (all ten applications essentially were the same, *mutatis mutandis*).

Yugoslavia crafted ten claims to reflect these different aspects of the dispute, all of which somehow related to the use of force by these States.[166] Later that same year, the ICJ dismissed the cases against the United States and Spain due to a lack of jurisdiction over these particular respondent States on account of their reservations to the compromissory clauses Yugoslavia was relying on for jurisdiction,[167] remained seized of the rest of the cases on account of the fact that they had not made a reservation to the compromissory clause excluding the Court's jurisdiction,[168] and denied provisional measures for all of them.[169] In 2004, the ICJ dismissed the rest of the cases for basically the same reason – Yugoslavia was not a member of United Nations at the time it filed its applications in 1999, which meant that it was not a member of the ICJ Statute either and could not avail itself of the Court's jurisdiction.[170]

166 See ibid., at 3–4.

167 See *Legality of Use of Force (Yugoslavia v. US)*, 1999 ICJ Rep. 916, 923–925 (June 2); *Legality of Use of Force (Yugoslavia v. Spain)*, 1999 ICJ Rep. 761, 768–771 (June 2).

168 See *Legality of Use of Force (Serbia and Montenegro v. United Kingdom)*, 1999 ICJ Rep. 826, 832–840 (June 2); *Legality of Use of Force (Serbia and Montenegro v. Portugal)*, 1999 ICJ Rep. 656, 662–672 (June 2); *Legality of Use of Force (Serbia and Montenegro v. Netherlands)*, 1999 ICJ Rep. 542, 548–558 (June 2); *Legality of Use of Force (Serbia and Montenegro v. Italy)*, 1999 ICJ Rep. 487–493 (June 2); *Legality of Use of Force (Serbia and Montenegro v. Germany)*, 1999 ICJ Rep. 422, 428–433 (June 2); *Legality of Use of Force (Serbia and Montenegro v. France)*, 1999 ICJ Rep. 363, 369–374 (June 2); *Legality of Use of Force (Serbia and Montenegro v. Canada)*, 1999 ICJ Rep. 259, 265–275 (June 2); *Legality of Use of Force (Serbia and Montenegro v. Belgium)*, 1999 ICJ Rep. 124, 130–140 (June 2).

169 See *Legality of Use of Force (Yugoslavia v. US)*, 1999 ICJ Rep. 916, 920–921, 925 (June 2); *Legality of Use of Force (Yugoslavia v. Spain)*, 1999 ICJ Rep. 761, 765–767, 774 (June 2); *Legality of Use of Force (Serbia and Montenegro v. United Kingdom)*, 1999 ICJ Rep. 826, 830–832, 840 (June 2); *Legality of Use of Force (Serbia and Montenegro v. Portugal)*, 1999 ICJ Rep. 656, 659–662, 672 (June 2); *Legality of Use of Force (Serbia and Montenegro v. Netherlands)*, 1999 ICJ Rep. 542, 546–548, 558 (June 2); *Legality of Use of Force (Serbia and Montenegro v. Italy)*, 1999 ICJ Rep. 481, 485–487, 493 (June 2); *Legality of Use of Force (Serbia and Montenegro v. Germany)*, 1999 ICJ Rep. 422, 426–428, 433 (June 2); *Legality of Use of Force (Serbia and Montenegro v. France)*, 1999 ICJ Rep. 363, 367–369, 374 (June 2); *Legality of Use of Force (Serbia and Montenegro v. Canada)*, 1999 ICJ Rep. 259, 262–265, 274 (June 2); *Legality of Use of Force (Serbia and Montenegro v. Belgium)*, 1999 ICJ Rep. 124, 128–130 (June 2).

170 See *Legality of Use of Force (Serbia and Montenegro v. United Kingdom)*, 2004 ICJ Rep. 1307, 1325–1352 (Dec. 15); *Legality of Use of Force (Serbia and Montenegro v. Portugal)*, 2004 ICJ Rep. 1160, 1178–1207 (Dec. 15); *Legality of Use of Force (Serbia and Montenegro v. Netherlands)*, 2004 ICJ Rep. 1011, 1029–1060 (Dec. 15); *Legality of Use of Force (Serbia and Montenegro v. Italy)*, 2004 ICJ Rep. 865, 884–911 (Dec. 15); *Legality of Use of Force (Serbia and Montenegro v. Germany)*, 2004 ICJ Rep. 720,

That same year, the Democratic Republic of the Congo brought claims against Burundi, Uganda, and Rwanda for the *Armed Activities on the Territory of the Congo* in the 1990s, which equated to an illegal use of force there "in flagrant violation of the United Nations Charter and of the Charter of the Organization of African Unity."[171] The DRC discontinued its claims against Burundi and Rwanda on January 15, 2001, and the ICJ removed them from its docket on January 30.[172] The ICJ, however, gave Uganda the status of an occupying power in the Ituri region of the DRC and required it to ensure that rules of international humanitarian law and international human rights law were respected, which it failed to do when it used force there, and required it to pay the DRC reparations.[173] The ICJ also concluded that the DRC had violated the Vienna Convention on Diplomatic Relations for the way it treated Ugandan diplomats and diplomatic property in the DRC, and required it to pay Uganda reparations for those injuries.[174]

Again that year, Pakistan brought a claim against India, entitled *Aerial Incident of 10 August 1999*, for shooting down a Pakistani air force plane with air-to-air missiles without warning over Pakistani air space and for sending in Indian helicopters to retrieve items from the wreckage.[175] The ICJ determined that it did not have jurisdiction over the dispute because the treaty that Pakistan asserted gave the ICJ jurisdiction did not actually provide it with jurisdiction.[176]

There were no further ICJ cases involving the use of force until 2008, when Georgia brought a claim in the ICJ against Russia for alleged violations of the International Convention on the Elimination of All Forms of Racial Discrimination (CERD) through Russia's alleged discrimination against individuals of Georgian ethnicity during hostilities between Georgia and Russia over South Ossetia and Abkhazia, among

738–765 (Dec. 15); *Legality of Use of Force (Serbia and Montenegro v. France)*, 2004 ICJ Rep. 575, 593–620 (Dec. 15); *Legality of Use of Force (Serbia and Montenegro v. Canada)*, 2004 ICJ Rep. 429, 447–475 (Dec. 15); *Legality of Use of Force (Serbia and Montenegro v. Belgium)*, 2004 ICJ Rep. 279, 298–328 (Dec. 1).

171 See Applications, *Armed Activities on the Territory of the Congo (DRC v. Burundi, DRC v. Rwanda, DRC v. Uganda)*, ICJ Proceedings, June 23, 1999.

172 See *Armed Activities on the Territory of the Congo (DRC v. Burundi, DRC v. Rwanda)*, Order, 2001 ICJ Rep. (Jan. 30).

173 See *Armed Activities on the Territory of the Congo (DRC v. Uganda)*, Judgment, 2005 ICJ Rep. 168 (Dec. 19).

174 See ibid.

175 See Application, *Aerial Incident of 10 August 1999 (Pakistan v. India)*, ICJ Pleadings, Sept. 21, 1999, at 1–2.

176 See *Aerial Incident of 10 August 1999 (Pakistan v. India)*, 2000 ICJ Rep. 12, 33 (June 21).

other alleged atrocities.[177] In October 2008, the ICJ rejected Georgia's request for provisional measures.[178] In April 2011, the ICJ upheld Russia's preliminary objection on the grounds that Georgia had not tried negotiation, as the compromissory clause in the CERD required.[179]

Even more recently, Costa Rica brought a claim currently entitled *Proceedings Instituted by the Republic of Costa Rica against the Republic of Nicaragua*, in which Costa Rica claimed on November 19, 2010, that the Nicaraguan army had invaded Costa Rican territory in relation to the building of a canal across Costa Rican territory, in violation of the UN Charter and the Charter of the Organization of American States, with the Court having jurisdiction over this dispute through Article 31 of the Pact of Bogotá.[180] The case still is at the earliest stages.

4.3.3 *ICJ cases involving international crimes by military forces*

The final category of military-related cases involves instances where a State's military forces allegedly have committed international crimes. The first such instance, the *Trial of Pakistani Prisoners of War* case, involved the 1971 war between India and Pakistan, in which India took approximately 92,000 Pakistani prisoners of war and civilian internees from Eastern Pakistan and refused to return them to Pakistan at the end of the hostilities in order to try individuals for genocide, thus allegedly violating norms of international humanitarian law.[181] Pakistan eventually asked for the proceedings to be discontinued before the Court could pronounce on jurisdiction or justiciability.[182]

177 See Application, *Application of the International Convention on the Elimination of All Forms of Racial Discrimination (Georgia v. Russian Federation)*, ICJ Proceedings, Aug. 12, 2008.

178 See *Application of the International Convention on the Elimination of All Forms of Racial Discrimination (Georgia v. Russian Federation)*, Provisional Measures, Order, 2008 ICJ Rep. 353 (Oct. 15).

179 See *Application of the International Convention on the Elimination of All Forms of Racial Discrimination (Georgia v. Russian Federation)*, Preliminary Objections, General List No. 140, April 1, 2011.

180 See Press Release, Costa Rica institutes proceedings against Nicaragua and requests the Court to indicate provisional measures, Nov. 19, 2010, at www.icj-cij.org/docket/files/150/16239.pdf.

181 See *Trial of Pakistani Prisoners of War (Pakistan v. India)*, 1973 ICJ Rep. 328 (July 13).

182 See *Trial of Pakistani Prisoners of War (Pakistan v. India)*, Order, 1973 ICJ Rep. 347, 348 (Dec. 15).

Two other cases followed approximately two decades later, both of which were entitled *Application of the Convention on the Prevention and Punishment of the Crime of Genocide* and involved the alleged genocidal activities of the military forces of the Socialist Federal Republic of Serbia against Bosnia and Croatia. In 1993, Bosnia claimed that Yugoslavia had violated the Genocide Convention by killing and displacing millions of Bosnians with military force. The disintegration of the Socialist Federal Republic of Yugoslavia caused some jurisdictional issues, but the Court determined that it had jurisdiction over the Federal Republic of Serbia under the Genocide Convention Article IX as the successor to the Socialist Federal Republic of Yugoslavia.[183] The ICJ concluded that the Federal Republic of Serbia had not committed genocide, had not conspired to commit genocide, had not incited genocide, and was not complicit in genocide, although it was in violation of its obligation to prevent genocide under the Genocide Convention for its failure to prevent the genocide in Srebrenica in July 1995, for violating a provisional measure by not preventing the atrocities at Srebrenica, and for not transferring Ratko Mladić to the ICTY for trial, but it did not require the Federal Republic of Serbia to pay any monetary compensation.[184] A related claim was brought in 1999 by Croatia, in which it claimed that military forces of Serbia and Montenegro committed genocide in Croatia.[185] Yet again, jurisdictional issues arose over whether Serbia and Montenegro was the legal successor to the Socialist Federal Republic of Serbia, with the Court again concluding that it was and that it therefore had jurisdiction over Serbia and Montenegro through the Genocide Convention.[186] The proceedings are still ongoing.

4.4 Conclusion for this chapter

Although States understandably may be reluctant to refer politically sensitive cases such as nuclear non-proliferation disputes to legal resolution, as alluded to in the introduction to this study and as explained

[183] See *Application of the Convention on the Prevention and Punishment of the Crime of Genocide (Bosnia v. Yugoslavia)*, Preliminary Objections, 1996 ICJ Rep. 585 (July 11).

[184] See *Application of the Convention on the Prevention and Punishment of the Crime of Genocide (Bosnia v. Yugoslavia)*, Merits, 2007 ICJ Rep. 91 (Feb. 26).

[185] See Application, *Application of the Convention on the Prevention and Punishment of the Crime of Genocide (Croatia v. Yugoslavia)*, ICJ Proceedings, July 2, 1999.

[186] See *Application of the Convention on the Prevention and Punishment of the Crime of Genocide (Bosnia v. Yugoslavia)*, Preliminary Objections, 2008 ICJ Rep. 412 (Nov. 18).

further in Chapters 5.3 and 6 below, the various cases discussed in this chapter that have involved sensitive, military-related disputes suggest that States are not entirely opposed to making such referrals. At a minimum, these cases show that States do not rely on legal resolution only of their easiest problems or of problems that only involve friendly States, as some commentators are inclined to believe.[187] After all, it seems unreasonable to expect enemies to voluntarily talk about how to limit their weapons if they fear war in the not-too-distant future, since they may end up needing the very arms they just restricted. If States could not rely on legal resolution of such politically sensitive disputes, the rules of international law relating to such matters would be relegated to an inferior position.[188] As John Merrills points out, "While the Charter invests the Security Council, and consequently the Permanent members, with major responsibilities in the area of peace and security, it also recognizes a role for legal procedures which the court, as the institution's legal organ, has a duty to protect."[189] If the ICJ cannot handle such sensitive matters as those military matters relating to peace and security, then it is difficult to see how the ICJ can have any meaningful role in protecting these aims of the UN Charter. Similarly, UN Charter Article 33 expressly envisions legal resolution, among other peaceful methods of dispute resolution, playing a role in resolving disputes "the continuance of which is likely to endanger the maintenance of international peace and security." Therefore, surely legal resolution cannot be limited by the political sensitivity of the dispute, or else it could not fulfill its crucial role relating to international peace and security.

In addition, these cases show that the ICJ and international arbitral tribunals do not have difficulty finding justiciability once jurisdiction has been determined. In particular, the ten *Legality of Use of Force* cases by the Federal Republic of Serbia against various NATO member States, two of the three claims in the *Armed Activities on the Territory of the*

[187] See Anna Spain, *Using International Dispute Resolution to Address the Compliance Question in International Law*, 40 GEO. J. INT'L L. 807, 858 (2009) (citing Andrew T. Guzman, *The Cost of Credibility: Explaining Resistance to Interstate Dispute Resolution Mechanisms*, 31 J. LEGAL STUD. 303 (2002)); JOHN G. MERRILLS, INTERNATIONAL DISPUTE SETTLEMENT 219–220 (4th edn, 2005); LELAND M. GOODRICH AND ANNE P. SIMONS, THE UNITED NATIONS AND THE MAINTENANCE OF INTERNATIONAL PEACE AND SECURITY 322–324 (1955); GOLDBLAT, *supra* note 81, at 5–6; Ginsburg and McAdams, *supra* note 3, at 1328.

[188] MERRILLS, *supra* note 187, at 251. [189] Ibid.

Congo, and the *Aerial Incident of 10 August 1999* all failed for lack of jurisdiction. It would appear that the claimant States there had invoked the ICJ's jurisdiction under treaties that either required too much creative interpretation to give the ICJ jurisdiction or ignored relevant reservations of respondent States. However, where jurisdiction was found through a clear compromissory clause, the Court or tribunal never had a problem finding that these military-related disputes were justiciable or arbitrable. Remember that these cases typically involved the actual use of force against States, not just the threat of the use of force, making it clear that their vital interests were involved if ever vital interests were involved in a case. Therefore, it seems reasonable to conclude from these cases that if one can find a clear compromissory clause where the respondent State expressed unequivocal consent to legal resolution, the Court or tribunal will not have a problem with hearing and deciding that particular case. As the following chapter shows, there are similarly clear compromissory clauses in nuclear non-proliferation agreements.

Some critics might try to dismiss these cases as examples of the ICJ getting involved with military-related disputes, arguing that their focus was not on the military-related elements but on broader legal issues such as State responsibility and the significance of unilateral declarations by heads of State.[190] However, the nature of the underlying incidents there must not be ignored especially when trying to create an analogy to nuclear non-proliferation disputes. Indeed, if the ICJ or an international arbitral tribunal becomes involved in resolving a nuclear non-proliferation dispute, it too will be looking at issues of treaty interpretation and possibly even State responsibility, and yet this has not been sufficient to induce previous commentators to accept (or even discuss) the possibility of legal resolution of such disputes.

[190] Guido den Dekker, The Law of Arms Control: International Supervision and Enforcement 71 (2001).

5

Jurisdiction over nuclear non-proliferation disputes

"Jurisdiction" generally means the legal power or authority to control something or someone. As George Orwell opined about control, "He who controls the present, controls the past. He who controls the past, controls the future." A court or tribunal with jurisdiction over a dispute and disputants has the unique ability to determine rights and obligations through its interpretive powers, which interpretations bind the disputants by the very nature of the judicial function. As this chapter explains, States have seen fit to give the ICJ and international arbitral tribunals jurisdiction over certain nuclear non-proliferation disputes as specified by the scope of the compromissory clauses contained in various nuclear non-proliferation agreements. States ought to invoke these jurisdictional clauses when they fear unfair treatment by the Security Council, before the Security Council takes action, inasmuch as legal resolution provides a larger measure of predictability and procedural safeguards, among other things. To be clear, this is not to say that any international courts or tribunals have express jurisdiction to review Security Council determinations. However, such review of Security Council determinations arguably already has occurred in such cases as the ICJ's *Lockerbie* case, as Thomas Franck and others have noted;[1] in the *Kadi* case (and related cases) in the European Court of First Instance and the European Court of Justice, as various scholars of international institutional law have noted;[2] and indirectly whenever any international court or tribunal interprets a

[1] See Thomas M. Franck, *The "Powers of Appreciation": Who Is the Ultimate Guardian of UN Legality?*, 86 Am. J. Int'l L. 519 (1992) (making an analogy between the ICJ's *Lockerbie* case and the US Supreme Court case *Marbury v. Madison*); see also Ken Roberts, *Second-Guessing the Security Council: The International Court of Justice and Its Powers of Judicial Review*, 7 Pace Int'l L. Rev. 281 (1995).

[2] See, for example, the forum section in volume 5 of International Organizations Law Review in 2008, which debates the impact of these cases on the ability of courts to review Security Council determinations in light of these cases.

Security Council resolution, as James Crawford and others have noted.[3] Nor is it to say that any international court or tribunal can bind the Security Council. Indeed, the Security Council easily could ignore any and all legal proceedings to determine the *intra vires* nature of the Security Council's actions, which arguably might cause more problems for the international legal order than any initial *ultra vires* act by the Security Council.[4] As explained below, the point is that the Security Council will be hard pressed to find a threat to international peace and security needed to unlock its Chapter VII powers under UN Charter Article 39 when disputants actively are already relying on *peaceful* methods of resolution, putting aside the issue of whether there is a forum that can assess whether the Security Council's actions are *ultra vires*.

When it comes to jurisdiction *rationae personae* in the international context, or simply "jurisdiction," as this study refers to it, there are two important aspects to consider: first, that the disputants have standing before the international court or tribunal, and second, that the international court or tribunal can find the disputants' consent to the forum's hearing and deciding the case before it. This chapter analyzes both aspects of jurisdiction when it comes to potential and real nuclear nonproliferation disputes and explores the reasons why States might want to give their consent to legal resolution of such disputes.

5.1 Standing before the ICJ and international arbitral tribunals

Standing, or *jus standi*, involves the ability of an entity to address itself to a court or tribunal. Standing is not necessarily the same for the ICJ as it is for international arbitral tribunals. When it comes to the ICJ, ICJ Statute Article 34(1) requires the disputants to be States.[5] In particular, international organizations, nongovernmental organizations, and individuals

[3] See James Crawford, *Marbury v. Madison at the International Level*, 36 Geo. Wash. Int'l L. Rev. 505 (2004); Jan Klabbers, *Straddling Law and Politics: Judicial Review in International Law*, in Towards World Constitutionalism 809, 819 (Ronald St. John Macdonald and Douglas M. Johnston ed., 2005) (discussing Crawford's argument, among others).

[4] See Georg Nolte, *The Limits of the Security Council's Powers and Its Functions in the International Legal System: Some Reflections*, in The Role of Law in International Politics, 315, 318 (2000); Klabbers, *supra* note 3.

[5] See Statute of the International Court of Justice, Art. 34, June 26, 1945, 59 Stat. 1055, T.S. No. 993.

cannot be a party to a dispute before the ICJ,[6] although there is less rigidity when it comes to advisory opinions and providing *amicus* briefs, inter alia.[7] In addition, it is possible for States to espouse claims of their nationals.[8] Some commentators have proposed an amendment to the ICJ Statute to give international organizations and other entities the ability to bring and defend claims in contentious cases before the ICJ,[9] although the realization of such an amendment seems a long way off.

When it comes to international arbitration, however, there is much more flexibility in terms of standing before an international arbitral tribunal. Indeed, whatever an arbitration clause in a contract or treaty provides will determine who has standing to bring a claim before the tribunal,[10] assuming that none of the procedural rules of any arbitral institution being used limit standing. All of that said, at least one of the disputants must be a State or international organization in order for the case to be considered as public international arbitration and considered for inclusion in this study, as explained in Chapter 2.2.2 above. For arbitration involving IAEA safeguards agreements, the disputants must be the IAEA and the State that is subject to

[6] It is interesting to note that the ICJ has received 1,200 requests per year from individuals in the past, with the ICJ having to tell these individuals that they lack standing to bring their claim. See Peter H. F. Bekker, *International Legal Aid Practice*, 87 AM. J. INT'L. L. 659, 663 (1993) (citing 1991–1992 ICJ Y.B. 205).

[7] See, e.g., ICJ Statute, Arts. 66(2) and 66(4) (mentioning how international organizations are allowed to make written or oral statements with an advisory opinion).

[8] See generally C. F. AMERASINGHE, DIPLOMATIC PROTECTION (2008).

[9] See, e.g., KAREL WELLENS, REMEDIES AGAINST INTERNATIONAL ORGANISATIONS 237–248 (2002); Mark Janis, *Individuals and the International Court*, in THE INTERNATIONAL COURT OF JUSTICE: ITS FUTURE ROLE AFTER FIFTY YEARS 205 (A. S. MULLER, D. RAIC, and J. M. THURANSKY ed., 1997); J. Sztucki, *International Organizations as Parties to Contentious Proceedings before the International Court of Justice*, in THE INTERNATIONAL COURT OF JUSTICE: ITS FUTURE ROLE AFTER FIFTY YEARS 141 (A. S. MULLER, D. RAIC, and J. M. THURANSKY ed., 1997); Paul C. Szasz, *Granting International Organizations* Ius Standi *in the International Court of Justice*, in THE INTERNATIONAL COURT OF JUSTICE: ITS FUTURE ROLE AFTER FIFTY YEARS 169 (A. S. MULLER, D. RAIC, and J. M. THURANSKY ed., 1997); I. Seidl-Hohenveldern, *Access of International Organizations to the International Court of Justice*, in THE INTERNATIONAL COURT OF JUSTICE: ITS FUTURE ROLE AFTER FIFTY YEARS 189 (A. S. MULLER, D. RAIC, and J. M. THURANSKY ed., 1997).

[10] See Patrick Dumberry, *The Legal Standing of Shareholders before Arbitral Tribunals: Has Any Rule of Customary International Law Crystallised?*, 3 MICH. ST. J. INT'L L. 353, 367 (2010) ("Indeed, there is no general standard on the legal standing of corporations and their access to international arbitration. The existence of this procedural right ultimately depends on the exact wording of each treaty"); Andrea K. Schneider, *Individual Rights in International Trade Organizations*, 19 U. PA. J. INT'L ECON. L. 587, 605 (1998).

that particular IAEA safeguards agreement, as opposed to two States or a State and a different international organization, as made clear in Article 22 of the Model Safeguards Agreement, as discussed in Chapter 5.2.3.2.1 below. In such a situation, this will be enough for the claimant to have standing, whether it is the IAEA or the State that is subject to that particular IAEA safeguards agreement that invoked the arbitration clause, inasmuch as that State or the IAEA both have a right of action under the safeguards agreement for breaches of that agreement. As the International Law Commission noted in its commentary to Article 43 of the Articles on Responsibility of International Organizations, which is discussed in greater depth below,

> It seems clear that the conditions for a State to invoke responsibility as an injured State cannot vary according to the fact that the responsible entity is another State or an international organization. Similarly, when an international organization owes an obligation to another international organization individually, the latter organization has to be regarded as entitled to invoke responsibility as an injured organization in case of breach.[11]

Nevertheless, disputes between two States or between a State and a different international organization over the substance of the IAEA safeguards agreement would have to be resolved using the political processes within the IAEA or perhaps using a *compromis*, given how IAEA safeguards agreements are bilateral instruments that do not appear to give rights of action to other entities, as explained below. There also is the possibility that a claimant State can transform an inter-State dispute into a dispute between a State and an international organization, assuming that the claimant State can mobilize the international organization through its political mechanisms to commence legal proceedings. For example, a State that wants to commence international arbitral proceedings under an IAEA safeguards agreement to which it is not a party can elect to exercise whatever power it might have among the thirty-five-member IAEA Board of Governors to decide to commence arbitral proceedings under the IAEA safeguards agreement with a two-thirds majority vote of those present and voting, in accordance with IAEA Statute Article VI(E).[12] However, it will be difficult for a claimant State to

[11] International Law Commission, *Report on the Work of Its Sixty-Third Session*, UN Doc. A/66/10 (2011), at 137 (hereinafter ILC 2011 Report).

[12] See Statute of the International Atomic Energy Agency, Art. VI(E), Oct. 26, 1956, 276 U.N.T.S. 3, amended Jan. 31, 1963, 471 U.N.T.S. 334 (hereinafter IAEA Statute).

transform a dispute it has with an international organization into an inter-State dispute, as the ICJ determined in the *Legality of Use of Force* cases involving Serbia and Montenegro's claims against NATO members for NATO bombings there and in the *Lockerbie* case involving Libya's claims against various Security Council members for decisions taken by the Security Council, due to the institutional veil of international organization vis-à-vis the responsibility of member States.[13] In other words, in a bilateral dispute between the United States and Iran over Iran's refusal to abide by provisions in its IAEA safeguards agreement, the United States might be able to avail itself of the compromissory clause contained in the Iran–IAEA Safeguards Agreement by lobbying members of the IAEA Board of Governors to invoke the compromissory clause. At the same time, Iran likely would not be able to commence proceedings against the United States in the ICJ under, for example, the compromissory clause of the IAEA Statute for an interpretation and application of the IAEA Statute in light of an action by the IAEA against Iran done at the behest of the United States. The same conceivably would be true if Iran were able to successfully lobby members of the IAEA Board of Governors to take action against the United States.

As noted below, there is no record of the compromissory clauses in these safeguards agreements having ever been given effect. Similarly, there is no record that indicates that a separate *compromis* has ever been agreed or given effect that would give an international arbitral tribunal jurisdiction over such a dispute. Given the confidentiality of international arbitral proceedings, this does not mean that such a proceeding never has taken place. More importantly, this does not mean that such a proceeding never can take place, as there has to be a first for all observed phenomena. Again, this study is not limited to an analysis of what *has* happened in the past, but rather aims to explore the possible benefits of using an option that has not been taken seriously before, let alone tried before.

Regardless of whether the issue involves standing before the International Court of Justice or before an international arbitral tribunal, either with a *compromis* or with a compromissory clause as the jurisdictional basis for the proceedings, the law on State responsibility over which States can invoke responsibility and bring a claim is the same.

[13] See generally CATHERINE BROLMANN, THE INSTITUTIONAL VEIL IN PUBLIC INTERNATIONAL LAW: INTERNATIONAL ORGANISATIONS AND THE LAW OF TREATIES (2007). See also ch. 4.2.2., *supra* (discussing these particular cases).

The claimant must have a direct material interest in the dispute if it is to *avoid being denied* standing, as the ICJ required of Ethiopia and Liberia in the *South West Africa* cases, where the ICJ refused to declare unlawful South Africa's actions in modern-day Namibia.[14] However, it is not necessarily enough to have a direct material interest in the dispute to actually have standing to invoke responsibility and bring a claim. A surer way for a State or an international organization to invoke responsibility is to base the claim on injury. According to Article 42 of the ILC's Articles on State Responsibility, the following is needed to invoke responsibility:

> A State is entitled as an injured State to invoke the responsibility of another State if the obligation breached is owed to:
>
> (a) That State individually; or
> (b) A group of States including that State, or the international community as a whole, and the breach of the obligation:
>   (i) Specially affects that State; or
>   (ii) Is of such a character as radically to change the position of all the other States to which the obligation is owed with respect to the further performance of the obligation.[15]

Article 43 of the Articles on the Responsibility of International Organizations is identical, apart from the addition of "or international organization" after each reference to "State" in the Articles on State Responsibility, as is common throughout the Articles on the Responsibility of International Organizations.[16] Under these provisions, injury due to a breach of international law is key to determining who can bring a claim on the international level. The ability of a State or international organization to invoke responsibility is the most obvious where the obligation was owed directly to the individual State or international organization that was injured, with that State or international organization having a specific right of action under a treaty.[17] With breaches of the IAEA safeguards agreements, the IAEA and the State that entered

[14] See *South West Africa Cases (Ethiopia v. South Africa; Liberia v. South Africa)*, Second Phase, 1966 ICJ Rep. 6, 75 (July 18). See also Barcelona Traction, *Light and Power Company, Ltd., Second Phase (Belgium v. Spain)*, 1970 ICJ Rep.3 (determining that Belgium did not have standing to sue where Spain injured a Canadian company, in the process indirectly injuring Belgian shareholders in that company).

[15] International Law Commission, *Report on the Work of Its Fifty-Third Session*, UN Doc. A/56/10 (2001), at 29 (hereinafter ILC 2001 Report).

[16] ILC 2011 Report, *supra* note 11, at 62–63.

[17] ILC 2001 Report, *supra* note 15, at 117–118.

into that particular safeguards agreement with the IAEA clearly can invoke responsibility. Since these safeguards agreements tend to be bilateral in nature, it is difficult to imagine that others will be able to invoke responsibility for a breach of these bilateral safeguards agreements.

When it comes to *multilateral* nuclear non-proliferation agreements, Article 42(b) of the Articles on State Responsibility and Article 43(b) of the Articles on the Responsibility of International Organizations dramatically open up the number of States and international organizations that can invoke responsibility and bring a claim on the international level. These provisions expressly deal with obligations owed to groups of States or to the international community as a whole, with a State or international organization being injured when these obligations are breached only if other elements exist, with subparagraphs (i) and (ii) providing those other elements.[18] Subparagraph (b) refers to a special type of obligation, which Gerald Fitzmaurice and others have referred to as interdependent obligations, which are of a higher magnitude than those of a reciprocal nature in such bilateral agreements as the IAEA safeguards agreements. Interdependent obligations, otherwise considered obligations *erga omnes partes*, must be distinguished from obligations *erga omnes*, with the former involving rights and obligations only of those States that are jointly parties to the treaty in question, and the latter involving all States, regardless of membership of the treaty in question.[19] The following five paragraphs explain the different types of obligations, with an aim to identify the nature of the obligations in multilateral nuclear non-proliferation agreements as being interdependent and to identify the impact of having such a nature on who can invoke responsibility for breaches of these obligations.

In 1958, Fitzmaurice came up with three general types of multilateral treaty obligations while drafting his reports on the law of treaties for the International Law Commission.[20] The first type was of a reciprocal

[18] See ibid., at 118–119.

[19] Gerald Fitzmaurice, *Third Report on the Law of Treaties*, UN Doc. A/CN.4/115, 2 YEARBOOK OF INT'L L. COMM'N 20, 27 (1958) (cited in JOOST PAUWELYN, A *Typology of Multilateral Treaty Obligations: Are WTO Obligations Bilateral or Collective in Nature*, 14 EURO. J. INT'L L. 907, 911 (2003)). See also generally D. N. Hutchinson, *Solidarity and Breaches of Multilateral Treaties*, 59 BRIT. Y.B. INT'L L. 152, 155 (1988).

[20] See also JOOST PAUWELYN, *The Role of Public International Law in the WTO: How Far Can We Go?*, 95 AM. J. INT'L L. 535, 549 (2001) (citing 2 Y.B. INT'L L. COMM'N 27–28, 41–45 (1958), UN Doc. A/CN.4/SER.A/1958/Add.1) (discussing these types of obligation in the context of the WTO treaty).

variety, which provided "for a mutual interchange of benefits between the parties, with rights and obligations for each involving specific treatment at the hands of and towards each of the others individually."[21] The 1961 Vienna Convention on Diplomatic Relations was the prime example. The second type of obligation, or interdependent type, involved a situation where "the participation of all the parties is a condition of the obligatory force of the treaty."[22] Disarmament and arms control treaties were the prime example there, which would include nuclear non-proliferation agreements as a subset. The last category consisted of obligations of the integral type, where the obligations are "towards all the world rather than towards particular parties" and have to be applied integrally, with the 1948 Genocide Convention being a prime example.[23] Later commentators give international humanitarian law treaties as an example of integral obligations.[24] Whether for better or for worse, the final version of the Vienna Convention on the Law of Treaties did not reflect these three types of obligations, although there are traces of these different types of obligations in at least six provisions of the VCLT – namely Articles 30, 41, 53, 58, 60, and 64.[25]

As a result of this fact, Fitzmaurice's distinctions largely have gone unnoticed within the law-of-treaties context. However, in recent years, the International Law Commission revived Fitzmaurice's distinctions during the drafting of the 2001 Articles on State Responsibility.[26] Both the ILC commentary and commentators on the Articles, such as Linos-Alexander Sicilianos, refer to these different types of obligations and share Fitzmaurice's view that disarmament and arms control agreements contain interdependent-type obligations.[27] The ILC reaches this

[21] Fitzmaurice, *supra* note 19.

[22] Fitzmaurice, *supra* note 19, at 36 (cited in Pauwelyn, *supra* note 19, at 912). See also Guido den Dekker, The Law of Arms Control: International Supervision and Enforcement 99 (2001).

[23] See Fitzmaurice, *supra* note 19, at 54–55 (cited in Pauwelyn, *supra* note 19, at 911).

[24] See Pauwelyn, *supra* note 19, at 913. [25] Ibid., at 912–915.

[26] See ILC Report 2001, *supra* note 15, at 117–119. The connection between the law of treaties and the law on State responsibility is well developed and need not be defended here. See, e.g., Pavel Sturma, *Law of Treaties Reflected in State Responsibility Rules*, 19 Thesaurus Acroasium 536 (1992); D. W. Bowett, *Treaties and State Responsibility*, in Le droit international au service de la paix, de la justice et du developpement: Melanges Michel Virally 137 (1991).

[27] See ILC Report 2001, *supra* note 15, at 119; ILC Report 2011, *supra* note 11, at 138; Linos-Alexander Sicilianos, *The Classification of Obligations and the Multilateral Dimension of the Relations of International Responsibility*, 13 Euro. J. Int'l L. 1127, 1134 (2002).

conclusion on account of the fact that these are treaties "where each parties' performance is effectively conditioned upon and requires the performance of each of the others."[28] Similarly, Sicilianos reaches this conclusion because, with disarmament and arms control agreements, "each state reduces its military power because and to the extent that the other parties do likewise."[29] Sicilianos goes on to say with regard to such interdependent obligations:

> Non-performance, or material breach, of the treaty by one of its parties would threaten the often fragile military balance brought by the agreement, by radically changing "the position of every party with respect to further performance of its obligations" (Article 60(2)(c) of the Vienna Convention). Consequently, every party to such a treaty other than the defaulting state could be regarded as an injured state, irrespective of whether it has been "specially affected" by the breach or not. The same would be true for a denuclearization treaty or "any other treaty where each party's performance is effectively conditioned upon and requires the performance of each of the others.[30]

In particular, he sees disarmament and arms control obligations as interdependent because, although they cannot be considered a bundle of bilateral relationships, they are "dominated by a sort of global reciprocity in the sense that each state disarms because the others do likewise."[31] With such obligations, one State need not be specially affected or have any other special interest apart from all of the others in order to invoke responsibility, and so each State among the group maintains the ability to invoke responsibility in reaction to a breach, as explained below.[32] In fact, breach of obligations of these types rarely leads to a specially affected State, which creates the need for a new way to determine which States can invoke responsibility.[33]

Pauwelyn takes Fitzmaurice's and Sicilianos's work and goes a step further in solidifying the classification of these multilateral obligations, although his focus is more on the obligations under the WTO Convention and international trade law. Pauwelyn goes so far as to create elaborate grids making clear the legal options for States under the various types of obligations. As Pauwelyn points out in explaining the characteristics of the interdependent nature, "Whenever one party violates its obligations [of an interdependent nature], it necessarily does

[28] ILC Report 2001, *supra* note 15, at 119. [29] Sicilianos, *supra* note 27, at 1134.
[30] Ibid. [31] Ibid., at 1135. [32] See ILC Report 2001, *supra* note 15, at 119.
[33] See ILC Report 2011, *supra* note 11, at 138.

so toward all the others and further performance would be of little use."[34] Again, he points out that "[interdependent] obligations are not purely bilateral, and the performance of one party's obligations depends on performance by all the other parties."[35] As a result, no State can withdraw from the treaty without having the whole regime unravel. With regard to disarmament and arms control treaties being of an interdependent nature, Pauwelyn agrees.[36]

To be clear, all treaties have elements of reciprocity, just as the entire area of international law is based on reciprocity.[37] The point that needs to be made here is that the obligations of disarmament and arms control treaties in general, and nuclear non-proliferation agreements in particular, are less based on obligations of a reciprocal nature than are average treaties, even though reciprocity remains relevant. Some commentators portray multilateral disarmament treaties as being essentially reciprocal in nature. For example, Fidler implies that he sees the obligations in treaties of these types as reciprocal at their heart.[38] Calderón sees acceptance of disarmament and arms control obligations by developing States as a quid-pro-quo arrangement with developed States, with the promise of economic and technological development if they play along,[39] in a way implying that these treaties contain obligations of a reciprocal nature. Daniel Joyner asserts that the NPT is an example of *traité-contrat* with reciprocal obligations because the nuclear-weapon States and the non-nuclear-weapon States are making a quid-pro-quo arrangement.[40] However, one must not lose sight of the fact that this multilateral arrangement works only if all of the member States comply with their respective obligations, and it is irrelevant that the NPT happens to create two groups with different obligations. Likewise, some human rights commentators distinguish disarmament and arms control treaties from human rights treaties in that the former are based on reciprocal duties, whereas the latter are not based on reciprocity.[41] However, multilateral

[34] Pauwelyn, *supra* note 20, at 549. [35] Ibid. [36] See ibid.

[37] See Malcolm N. Shaw, International Law 7, 1013 (5th edn, 2003).

[38] See David P. Fidler, *War, Law, and Liberal Thought: The Use of Force in the Reagan Years*, 11 Ariz. J. Int'l & Comp. Law 45, 60 (1994).

[39] See Félix Calderón, *Arms Restraint and the Avoidance of Force*, Avoidance and Settlement of Arms Control Disputes 187, 195 (Julie Dahlitz ed., 1994).

[40] See Daniel H. Joyner, International Law and the Proliferation of Weapons of Mass Destruction 9 (2009).

[41] See Ryan Goodman, *Human Rights Treaties, Invalid Reservations, and State Consent*, 96 Am. J. Int'l L. 531, 537 (2002); Julie Dahlitz, Nuclear Arms Control 47–48 (1983) (asserting that nuclear non-proliferation agreements are really bilateral issues,

disarmament and arms control treaties, including nuclear non-proliferation agreements, do not establish reciprocal obligations because the relationships between the States cannot be broken down into a bundle of bilateral relationships, but rather the promises run from one State to the collective group of States, which must collectively act to change the obligations.

Some commentators appear to agree with such an assessment. In addition to Pauwelyn and Sicilianos, noted above, Danchin asserts that reciprocity is the basis for decision-making on important issues in "various treaty-based arms control bodies" established by multilateral treaties.[42] While there may be some bilateral horse-trading involved within the international supervisory bodies, this does not change the interdependent nature of the obligations arising out of the underlying treaty that established those supervisory bodies. That said, this does not get rid of the general element of reciprocity that exists throughout international law;[43] it just means that these multilateral disarmament and arms control agreements do not fit into this particular category that Fitzmaurice established.

The discussion contained in the preceding five paragraphs on the different types of obligations in treaties and their relation to State responsibility is relevant to determining standing, as the type of obligation that has been breached determines which entities can invoke responsibility. The relevant provisions in the Articles on State Responsibility and the Articles on the Responsibility of International Organizations discussed above make clear that an injured member State of a nuclear non-proliferation agreement may be able to invoke responsibility of another member State that breaches a provision of that agreement. The central question, however, is whether there is a threshold for the amount of injury a State or international organization must suffer for it to be able to invoke responsibility. Article 31(2) of the Articles on State Responsibility indicates with its use of the word "moral" injury when defining "injury" that States need not suffer a quantifiable injury in order to invoke responsibility and claim reparations.[44] The ILC commentary

with the two States engaged in the bilateral negotiations really just allowing others to sit in on their debate).

[42] Peter G. Danchin, *U.S. Unilateralism and the International Protection of Religious Freedom: The Multilateral Alternative*, 41 Colum. J. Transnat'l L. 33, 70 n. 100 (2002).

[43] See Dekker, *supra* note 22, at 83–99 (2001).

[44] See ILC 2001 Report, *supra* note 15, at 91. See also ILC 2011 Report, supra note 11, at 60, 124 (Article 31(2) of the Articles on the Responsibility of International Organizations provides the same language, *mutatis mutandis*).

on Article 31(2) explains that this language is "intended both as inclusive, covering both material and moral damage broadly understood, and as limitative, excluding merely abstract concerns or general interests of a State which is individually unaffected by the breach."[45] The commentary is clear in recognizing that where States have an abstract concern, or where there is a harm to a general interest, States nevertheless may invoke responsibility in accordance with Article 48 of the Articles on State Responsibility, as explained below. Putting that issue aside for the moment and focusing on the injury to a group of which the claimant is a member, the ILC commentary on Article 42 of the Articles on State Responsibility explains how Article 42(b)(ii)'s limitation to injuries "of such a character as radically to change the position of all the other States to which the obligation is owed" was intended to narrow the applicability of these principles to interdependent treaties on account of the fact that "it may not be the case that just any breach of the obligation has the effect of undermining the performance of all the other States involved."[46] The ILC's commentary on the Articles on State Responsibility and the Articles on the Responsibility of International Organizations does cite cases where these issues have been addressed. Nevertheless, the ILC strongly asserts that the ability of States with interdependent obligations to invoke responsibility "has never been doubted,"[47] and presumably would be the outcome when an actual case arises. The ILC commentary does, however, suggest in a hypothetical related to Article 42 that the claim of an Antarctic Treaty State party to unclaimed territory in Antarctica, in violation of Antarctic Treaty Article 4, would meet this threshold.[48] Article 46 of the Articles on State Responsibility, entitled "Plurality of injured States," states, "Where several States are injured by the same internationally wrongful act, each injured State may separately invoke the responsibility of the State which has committed the internationally wrongful act."[49] The ILC commentary to this provision notes that Article 46 relates directly to Article 42(b)(ii) inasmuch as "all the States to which an interdependent obligation is owed within the meaning

[45] ILC 2001 Report, *supra* note 15, at 91–92.

[46] ILC 2001 Report, *supra* note 15, at 119. [47] Ibid., at 119, 123. [48] See ibid., at 119.

[49] Ibid., at 123; ILC 2011 Report, *supra* note 11, at 138 (Article 47 of the Articles on the Responsibility of International Organizations providing the same language, *mutatis mutandis*).

of article 42(b)(ii) are injured by its breach."[50] The commentary there provides a number of concrete examples where States have been able to invoke responsibility for another State's violation of an obligation that resembled an interdependent one, where the claimant State did not appear to be specially affected or injured in a direct manner. The first and most compelling example is the *SS Wimbledon* case, where Great Britain, France, Italy, and Japan brought a claim before the Permanent Court of International Justice against Germany for violating Article 380 of the Treaty of Versailles, which required, "The Kiel Canal and its approaches shall be maintained free and open to the vessels of commerce and war of all nations at peace with Germany on terms of entire equality."[51] Germany refused to allow a British steamship named *Wimbledon* and chartered by a French firm to navigate the Kiel Canal, and so these two allies of the First World War and the two others without a financial interest in the steamship brought a claim under Article 386(1) of the Treaty of Versailles, which allowed "any interested Power [to] appeal to the jurisdiction instituted for the purpose by the League of Nations."[52] The PCIJ concluded that each State could bring this claim against Germany:

> The Court has no doubt that it can take cognizance of the application instituting proceedings in the form in which it has been submitted. It will suffice to observe for the purposes of this case that each of the four Applicant Powers has a clear interest in the execution of the provisions relating to the Kiel Canal, since they all possess fleets and merchant vessels flying their respective flags. They are therefore, even though they may be unable to adduce a prejudice to any pecuniary interest, covered by the terms of Article 386(1).[53]

Another example that the commentary cites is the *Nuclear Tests* cases, in which both Australia and New Zealand claimed to be injured by France's atmospheric test of nuclear weapons on the Muraroa Atoll from 1966 to 1972, as described in Chapter 4.3.1 above. However, how France had injured Australia and New Zealand's "rights in respect of areas over

[50] ILC 2001 Report, *supra* note 15, at 123. See also ILC 2011 Report, *supra* note 11, at 143 (noting how Article 47 of the Articles on the Responsibility of International Organizations corresponds to Article 46 of the Articles on State Responsibility).

[51] The SS *Wimbledon*, 1923 P.C.I.J., Series A, No. 1, at 6; see also ILC 2001 Report, *supra* note 15, at 123.

[52] The SS *Wimbledon*, 1923 P.C.I.J., Series A, No. 1, at 6–7; see also ILC 2001 Report, *supra* note 15, at 123.

[53] The SS *Wimbledon*, 1923 P.C.I.J., Series A, No. 1, at 20; see also ILC 2001 Report, *supra* note 15, at 123.

which it has sovereignty" was not entirely clear from their applications to the ICJ.[54] These examples go a long way in demonstrating how member States of nuclear non-proliferation agreements may have the ability to invoke responsibility and bring a claim against another member State for violating a provision of the agreement.

The narrow scope of Article 42(b)(ii) may cause problems, at least in theory, for States and international organizations that want to invoke responsibility for very minor breaches of the interdependent obligations contained in a nuclear non-proliferation agreement. In practice, the distinction between major and minor breaches does not matter because of Article 48 of the Articles on State Responsibility, which is entitled "Invocation of responsibility by a State other than an injured State":

1. Any State other than an injured State is entitled to invoke the responsibility of another State in accordance with paragraph 2 if:
   (a) the obligation breached is owed to a group of States including that State, and is established for the protection of a collective interest of the group; or
   (b) the obligation breached is owed to the international community as a whole.
2. Any State entitled to invoke responsibility under paragraph 1 may claim from the responsible State:
   (a) cessation of the internationally wrongful act, and assurances and guarantees of non-repetition in accordance with article 30; and
   (b) performance of the obligation of reparation in accordance with the preceding articles, in the interest of the injured State or of the beneficiaries of the obligation breached.[55]

[54] *Nuclear Tests (Australia v. France)*, ICJ Pleadings, Vol. 1, May 8, 1973 (alluding to an uncertain threat of radiation); *Nuclear Tests (New Zealand v. France)*, ICJ Pleadings, May 9, 1973, Vol. 2, at 4; see also ILC 2001 Report, *supra* note 15, at 123–124. It is irrelevant whether France breached an express treaty provision or a customary norm, since interdependent norms can come from both sources. See ILC 2001 Report, *supra* note 15, at 126.

[55] See ILC 2001 Report, *supra* note 15, at 126. See also ILC 2011 Report, *supra* note 11, at 64, 145–146 (Article 49 of the Articles on the Responsibility of International Organizations provides the same language, *mutatis mutandis*, apart from paragraph 4, there providing the ways to invoke responsibility, instead of paragraph 2).

The ILC commentary portrays Article 48 as being complementary to Article 42,[56] which was already discussed above. Indeed, the ILC commentary makes clear that an invocation of responsibility due to injury or an invocation due to general interest does make a difference:

> Whether the States concerned do not claim compensation on their own account as distinct from a declaration of the legal situation, it may not be clear whether they are claiming as injured States or as States invoking responsibility in the common or general interest under article 48. Indeed, in such cases it may not be necessary to decide into which category they fall, provided it is clear that they fall into one or the other.[57]

The commentary goes on to explain,

> Article 48 is based on the idea that in case of breaches of specific obligations protecting the collective interests of a group of States or the interests of the international community as a whole, responsibility may be invoked by States which are not themselves injured in the sense of article 42.[58]

Collective interests are the very essence of interdependent obligations, as explained above, and are at the heart of nuclear non-proliferation agreements, inasmuch as they foster a common interest beyond that of just one State, as the commentary implies.[59] That common interest is the limitation of the spread of nuclear weapons. The ILC commentary on Article 48 of the Articles on State Responsibility makes clear that the reference to "[a]ny State" in paragraph 1 means that the other States of the interdependent obligation need not act together in order to invoke responsibility,[60] thereby removing the possibility of inadmissibility for the failure to include these other States in a claim. Article 48 was designed to respond to the situation where there "may well be . . . no State which is individually injured by the breach, yet it is highly desirable that some State or States be in a position to claim reparation, in particular restitution."[61] The ILC commentary notes that paragraph 2(b)'s requirement that the claim be made in accordance with the interests of the beneficiaries of the breached obligation "involves a measure of progressive development,"[62] again suggesting that the rest of the

56 See ILC 2001 Report, *supra* note 15, at 126.
57 ILC 2001 Report, *supra* note 15, at 123–124.
58 ILC 2001 Report, *supra* note 15, at 126. 59 See ibid., at 126–127. 60 Ibid., at 126.
61 Ibid., at 127. 62 Ibid.

provisions are *lex lata*, even though there are few tangible examples to support these provisions.

In short, these articles are useful in determining whether States will have standing to bring a claim in the International Court of Justice or in an international arbitral tribunal for a breach of a nuclear non-proliferation agreement. Articles 42, 46, and 48 of the Articles on State Responsibility make it clear that the claimant State need not be specially affected or even directly injured by the breach of an interdependent obligation. Instead, all that is needed for a State to bring a claim and invoke State responsibility is for it to show that there has been a breach of an obligation "owed to a group of States including that State" and that the obligation was "established for the protection of a collective interest of the group." Inasmuch as multilateral nuclear non-proliferation agreements involve obligations owed to a group of States and those agreements clearly are to protect the collective interest, States parties to these agreements should not have a problem in bringing claims on the international level in an effort to have the violation stopped and to receive a declaratory remedy. These provisions of the Articles on State Responsibility and the Articles on the Responsibility of International Organizations are particularly attractive in that they allow injured States and States involved with interdependent obligations to pursue reparations or cessation, as opposed to merely suspension or termination of the treaty under VCLT Article 60, with the former encouraging to a larger extent a return to compliance and a restoration of the legal order that had existed before the breach.[63]

5.2 Specific jurisdictional consent to legal resolution

In addition to standing, the ICJ or international arbitral tribunal must find specific jurisdictional consent from the States concerned. Article 36(1) of the ICJ Statute indicates how either States or the Charter must unequivocally refer disputes to it in order to have jurisdiction. States can provide their consent through a variety of ways. Commentators essentially see there being four ways for the ICJ to get jurisdiction over contentious cases: through an *ex ante* declaration based on the Optional Clause of ICJ Statute Article 36(2); through an ad hoc *compromis* (or special agreement between the disputants); through an *ante hoc* compromissory clause contained in the underlying treaty of the

[63] See ibid., at 117–119.

dispute, as alluded to in ICJ Statute Article 36(1);[64] and through *post hoc* consent with prorogated jurisdiction, which has developed through adjudicative practice.[65] International arbitral tribunals, on the other hand, are limited to finding jurisdiction through *compromis* and compromissory clauses.[66] While it might be an obvious point, it is important to emphasize here that all of these bases for jurisdiction are founded on the consent of the disputants, thus also making legal resolution based on the consent of the disputants.

In addressing these bases of jurisdiction in the context of nuclear nonproliferation disputes, this study must spend some time addressing optional-clause declarations. Sixty-six States currently have optional-clause declarations giving the ICJ jurisdiction over their disputes, often within certain limitations provided by reservations.[67] While this number of optional-clause declarations is not insignificant, it nonetheless represents a minority of States.[68] Some commentators explain that the number of optional-clause declarations has been on the decline because States dislike committing themselves beforehand to legal resolution.[69] However, if this were true, one would expect treaties with

[64] See UN Charter, Arts. 36–38. See also Jonathan I. Charney, *Compromissory Clauses and the Jurisdiction of the International Court of Justice*, 81 AM. J. INT'L L. 855 (1987) (discussing these basic ways for the ICJ to gain jurisdiction); IAN BROWNLIE, PRINCIPLES OF PUBLIC INTERNATIONAL LAW 680–690 (6th edn, 2003) (same); John G. Merrills, *The Optional Clause at Eighty*, in LIBER AMICORUM JUDGE SHIGERU ODA 435 (NISUKE ANDO et al. ed., 2002) (discussing the jurisprudence involving the optional clause); John G. Merrills, *The Optional Clause Revisited*, 64 BRIT. Y.B. INT'L L. 197 (1993) (same).

[65] See, e.g., *Corfu Channel Case (UK v. Albania)*, Preliminary Objections, 1948 ICJ Rep. 4, 27–28 (March 15). See also BROWNLIE, *supra* note 64, at 690; Sienho Yee, *Forum Prorogatum in the International Court*, 42 GERMAN Y.B. INT'L L. 147 (1999); Mohammed Bedjaoui and Fatsah Ouguergouz, *Le forum prorogatum devant la Cour internationale de justice: Les ressources d'une institution ou la face cachée du consensualisme*, 5 AF. Y.B. INT'L L. 91 (1997); Humphrey Waldock, *Forum Prorogatum or Acceptance of a Unilateral Summons to Appear before the International Court*, 2 INT'L L. Q. 377 (1948).

[66] See CHITTHARANJAN F. AMERASINGHE, JURISDICTION OF INTERNATIONAL TRIBUNALS 18–26, 549–552 (2003); Cesare P.R. Romano, *The Shift from the Consensual to the Compulsory Paradigm in International Adjudication: Elements for a Theory of Consent*, 39 N.Y.U. J. INT'L L. & POL. 791, 807–808 (2007).

[67] See International Court of Justice, Declarations Recognizing the Jurisdiction of the Court as Compulsory, at www.icj-cij.org/jurisdiction/index.php?p1=5&p2=1&p3=3 (last visited June 1, 2011).

[68] See generally C. H. M. Waldock, *Decline of the Optional Clause*, 32 British Y.B. Int'l. L. 244 (1955–1956); Charney, *supra* note 64, at 855–56; LOUIS HENKIN et al. (eds.), INTERNATIONAL LAW 811 (3rd edn, 1993).

[69] See Richard B. Bilder, *The United States and the World Court in the Post-"Cold War" ERA*, 40 CATH. U.L. REV. 251, 258 (1991) (hereinafter Bilder, *United States*).

compromissory clauses that give the ICJ and international arbitral tribunals jurisdiction also to decline, as they also involve a beforehand commitment,[70] which ostensibly has not been observed. Interestingly, of the sixty-six optional-clause declarations that have been made, none of them specifically exclude matters involving a State's vital interests (which observation is relevant to the discussion in Chapter 6 on the historical significance of "vital interests" to legal resolution), although eleven exclude matters relating to the deployment of that State's armed forces.[71] This goes against the general assertion of some commentators

[70] Some commentators assert that, if States cannot agree on a negotiated solution to a dispute and they cannot agree to send the matter to third-party settlement, then they will have to live without an authoritative resolution to the dispute. See DEKKER, *supra* note 22, at 152–153. However, this overlooks the possibility of compulsory judicial proceedings through the invocation of a compromissory clause, if one exists in an underlying treaty.

[71] See German Declaration Recognizing the Jurisdiction of the Court as Compulsory, May 1, 2008 (excluding any dispute that "relates to, arises from or is connected with the deployment of armed forces abroad, involvement in such deployments or decisions thereon"); Greek Declaration Recognizing the Jurisdiction of the Court as Compulsory, Jan. 10, 1994 (excluding "any dispute relating to defensive military action taken by the Hellenic Republic for reasons of national defence"); Honduras Declaration Recognizing the Jurisdiction of the Court as Compulsory, June 6, 1986 ("Disputes relating to facts or situations originating in armed conflicts or acts of a similar nature which may affect the territory of the Republic of Honduras, and in which it may find itself involved directly or indirectly"); Hungary Declaration Recognizing the Jurisdiction of the Court as Compulsory, Oct. 22, 1992 ("disputes relating to, or connected with, facts or situations of hostilities, war, armed conflicts, individual or collective actions taken in self-defence"); India Declaration Recognizing the Jurisdiction of the Court as Compulsory, Sept. 18, 1974 (excluding "disputes relating to or connected with facts or situations of hostilities, armed conflicts, individual or collective actions taken in self-defence, resistance to aggression"); Kenya Declaration Recognizing the Jurisdiction of the Court as Compulsory, April 19, 1965 (excluding "[d]isputes concerning any question relating to or arising out of belligerent or military occupation"); Malawi Declaration Recognizing the Jurisdiction of the Court as Compulsory, Dec. 12, 1966 (excluding "disputes concerning any question relating to or arising out of belligerent or military occupation"); Malta Declaration Recognizing the Jurisdiction of the Court as Compulsory, Dec. 6, 1966 (excluding "disputes concerning any question relating to or arising out of belligerent or military occupation"); Mauritius Declaration Recognizing the Jurisdiction of the Court as Compulsory, Sept 23, 1968 (excluding "disputes concerning any question relating to or arising out of belligerent or military occupation"); Nigeria Declaration Recognizing the Jurisdiction of the Court as Compulsory, April 30, 1998 (excluding "disputes relating to or connected with facts or situations of hostilities or armed conflict, whether internal or international in character"); Sudan Declaration Recognizing the Jurisdiction of the Court as Compulsory, Jan. 2, 1958 (excluding "disputes arising out of events occurring during any period in which the Republic of the Sudan is engaged in hostilities as a belligerent").

that legal resolution does not get involved with the most sensitive disputes because of States' careful crafting of the reservations to their optional-clause declarations.[72] Notably, none of these optional-clause declarations excludes disputes arising out of and in connection with nuclear non-proliferation matters – or even weapons, for that matter – assuming such materials have not already been deployed by armed forces or in armed conflict, taking into account the eleven exclusions mentioned above. Therefore, nuclear non-proliferation disputes conceivably can be brought under optional-clause declarations, assuming the respondent State has made such a declaration.[73] However, this study does not focus on this avenue for jurisdiction inasmuch as recalcitrant and would-be recalcitrant States in this area tend not to have made such a declaration, although many of them have obligations under compromissory clauses that give the ICJ or an international arbitral tribunal jurisdiction, and which conveniently do not require further consent by disputants before legal resolution can commence. Therefore, this study starts by looking at the compromissory clauses in nuclear non-proliferation agreements to see whether they give jurisdiction to the ICJ or to an international arbitral tribunal. Before discussing the compromissory clauses in nuclear non-proliferation agreements, however, a few words must be said about the type of consent that States provide through these compromissory clauses.

5.2.1 *Direct consent to legal resolution through compromissory clauses*

Consent in the context of international law traditionally involves the direct consent of States (expressly or implicitly) to a specific principle in

[72] See Robert Jennings, *International Courts and International Politics*, in CONTEMPORARY ISSUES IN INTERNATIONAL LAW 13, 24–25 (DAVID FREESTONE et al. ed., 2002).

[73] See Christian Tomuschat, *Article 36*, in THE STATUTE OF THE INTERNATIONAL COURT OF JUSTICE: A COMMENTARY 630, 630–631 (ANDREAS ZIMMERMANN et al. ed., 2006); Edith Brown Weiss, *Reciprocity and the Optional Clause*, in THE INTERNATIONAL COURT OF JUSTICE AT A CROSSROADS 82 (LORI F. DAMROSCH ed., 1987); Santiago Torres Bernárdez, *Reciprocity in the System of Compulsory Jurisdiction and in Other Modalities of Contentious Jurisdiction Exercised by the International Court of Justice*, in ESSAYS IN HONOUR OF JUDGE TASLIM OLAWALE ELIAS 291 (BELLO and B. A. AJIBOLA ed., 1992).

order for it to be bound by that principle. T. J. Lawrence focused on the need to protect the

> independence of states, defining independence as the right of a state to manage all its affairs, whether external or internal, without interference from other states, so long as it respects the corresponding right possessed by each full-sovereign member of the family of nations – this right of independent action is the natural result of sovereignty; it is in fact, sovereignty looked at from the point of view of other nations.[74]

Brierly talks of international law as being the sum of the rules by which States have *consented* to be bound, in addition to the implied consent that accompanies customary rules.[75] It is out of this tradition that such fundamental documents as the VCLT emerged. Indeed, most of the VCLT's provisions show the different forms in which one can find the requisite consent. In Rosenne's textual study of consent in the VCLT, he found that forty-seven out of the eighty-five articles in the VCLT explicitly or implicitly deal with consent.[76] One need only look at VCLT Article 11 to get a sense of the importance of consent under the VCLT: "The consent of a State to be bound by a treaty may be expressed by signature, exchange of instruments, constituting a treaty, ratification, acceptance, approval or accession, or by any other means if so agreed."[77] This is no different from nuclear non-proliferation agreements and their compromissory clauses, as explained below.

5.2.2 *Compromissory clauses*

Jurisdiction through compromissory clauses is known by different names, with Shihata referring to it as continued jurisdiction and

[74] T. J. Lawrence, International Law 111 (1911).

[75] See James L. Brierly, The Law of Nations: An Introduction to the International Law of Peace 52–53 (4th edn, 1949). See also L. Oppenheim, 1 International Law 11 (H. Lauterpact ed., 6th edn, 1947).

[76] See Shabtai Rosenne, *"Consent" and Related Words in the Codified Law of Treaties*, in Melanges Offerts à Charles Rousseau 229 (La Communauté Internationale ed., 1974) (leaving the following articles out of his study of consent in the VCLT: 2–6, 8, 10, 19, 21, 23, 26–33, 35, 38–41, 44–45, 52–53, 55–56, 58–61, 63–64, 66–68).

[77] VCLT, Art. 11. See also VCLT, Arts. 12–17 (going into greater depth with regard to how and where to find consent); Council of Europe, Treaty Making: Expression of Consent by States to Be Bound by a Treaty 8–12 (Council of Europe and British Institute of International and Comparative Law ed., 2001) (discussing the relevance of these provisions); T. O. Elias, The Modern Law of Treaties 18–26 (1974) (same).

Rosenne referring to it as conventional jurisdiction, while Fitzmaurice lumps it under the heading of *ante hoc* jurisdiction and Oppenheim lumps this together with jurisdiction under the optional clause as obligatory jurisdiction.[78] Regardless of the exact term, they all involve the idea that States have expressed their unequivocal consent to the jurisdiction of a court or tribunal in a provision of the underlying treaty, typically in a provision dealing with interpretation of the treaty or one dealing with settlement of disputes over that treaty.

The degree to which compromissory clauses are self-implementing is important if disputants are to avoid the need for agreement of the disputants for the dispute settlement process to begin.[79] After all, avoiding the need for further agreement between the disputants for legal resolution to proceed is the main advantage of compromissory clauses. The degree of self-implementation through the greater inclusion of details in the compromissory clause is particularly important with ad hoc international arbitration in order to avoid disagreements over the establishment of the tribunal, whereas reference to a standing body (such as the ICJ) need not have the same level of detail because of the forum's permanent nature and standing rules.[80] Nonetheless, compromissory clauses that refer to such standing bodies still need to clearly provide for the scope of the jurisdiction.[81] Given that compromissory clauses that refer to international arbitration need more details than those that refer to the ICJ, this subsection focuses mostly on those compromissory clauses that provide for international arbitration.

There are many different kinds of compromissory clauses, all with varying degrees of self-implementation. Louis Sohn divides the compromissory clauses that refer to international arbitration into varying degrees of effectiveness, with (1) the lowest level, only referring to international arbitration without designating a particular form, or

[78] See Harold J. Owen, *Compulsory Jurisdiction of the International Court of Justice: A Study of Its Acceptance by Nations*, 3 GA. L. REV. 704, 711–712 (1969) (citing 2 L. Oppenheim, International Law 58–65 (7th edn, Lauterpacht 1952); SHABTAI ROSENNE, THE INTERNATIONAL COURT OF JUSTICE: AN ESSAY IN POLITICAL AND LEGAL THEORY 273–274 (1957); Gerald Fitzmaurice, *The Law and Procedure of the International Court of Justice, 1951–1954: Questions of Jurisdiction, Competence and Procedure*, 34 BRIT. Y.B. INT'L L. 1, 70 (1959); IBRAHIM F. I. SHIHATA, THE POWER OF THE INTERNATIONAL COURT TO DETERMINE ITS OWN JURISDICTION 117 (1965)).

[79] See Louis B. Sohn, *Settlement of Disputes Relating to the Interpretation and Application of Treaties*, 150 REC. DES COURS 195, 268 (1976).

[80] See ibid., at 268–270. [81] See ibid., at 244, 259 n. 1.

leaving the details up to a later agreement between the parties; (2) a higher level, letting the disputants decide between different forms of arbitration; and (3) the highest level, providing for compulsory arbitration where all of the essential details for the tribunal's establishment are already set out in the compromissory clause itself.[82] Some commentators have asserted that the form of the arbitration agreement does not seem to be particularly important, considering the fact that the issue of form ostensibly has not arisen in any public international arbitration cases.[83] Nevertheless, it is reasonably foreseeable that many debates will arise between the parties as to how the arbitration ought to proceed if certain details are not spelled out in the relevant compromissory clause.[84] Fortunately, the compromissory clauses focused on in this section are of the highest order, and therefore should not create much debate before their implementation.

The primary concern over the self-implementation of a compromissory clause providing for international arbitration is the selection procedure of the arbitrators. Compromissory clauses that provide for international arbitration allow disputants to designate a sole arbitrator; a three-member panel where each disputant selects an arbitrator and the parties jointly select an independent third arbitrator to preside over the proceedings; two types of five-member panel where each disputant chooses one or two arbitrators and the parties jointly select one or three other arbitrators respectively; and a few other somewhat anomalous arrangements, such as where the panel consists of seven or eight members with a varying number of independent arbitrators.[85] These larger panels tend to have more elaborate rules of procedure that resemble those of a permanent judicial body and may even be designed to be permanent bodies, in which case the argument can be made that they become courts as opposed to arbitral tribunals.[86] The provisions for smaller panels also can provide details, such as requiring the independent arbitrators to be citizens of a non-disputant State and an acknowledgment that the disputants may use other agreed methods of settlement.[87] This last point, however, does not lessen the ability of one of the disputants to elect for binding arbitration. Regardless, the more details the compromissory clause can provide with regard to selection

[82] See ibid., at 268. [83] See e.g. AMERASINGHE, *supra* note 66, at 83.

[84] See JOHN G. MERRILLS, INTERNATIONAL DISPUTE SETTLEMENT 88–89 (4th edn, 2005) (discussing some debates that have arisen in prior cases, as well as asserting that arbitrators must be careful not to exceed their jurisdiction or else run the risk of having the award challenged).

[85] See Sohn, *supra* note 79, at 266–268. [86] See ibid. [87] See ibid.

and other procedures, the less chance there is that a recalcitrant State will be able to sabotage the proceedings. In particular, the recalcitrant State can sabotage the proceedings simply by refusing to appoint their arbitrator or to agree on an independent third arbitrator, assuming the compromissory clause does not foresee and pre-empt these potential problems by designating an appointing entity in the case of refusal to appoint by one of the disputants.[88] If the compromissory clause does not provide time limits to the appointment of these arbitrators, then the recalcitrant State might try to sabotage the proceedings by dragging their feet with their appointments.[89] Many compromissory clauses do not foresee and pre-empt these potential problems.[90] Fortunately, the nuclear non-proliferation agreements that are the focus of this section foresee and pre-empt these potential problems.

Not only are specific compromissory clauses important with frustrating recalcitrant States trying to sabotage the proceedings, but the structure of the panel and the procedures of that panel can have a tremendous impact on the nature of the proceedings and result. For example, disputants in a sole-arbitrator proceeding can assume that the interim and final decisions need not entirely satisfy either side, whereas a three-member panel might tend towards finding in favor of one side because the independent arbitrator will need the support of a party-appointed arbitrator in order to render a valid decision.[91] In addition, if a compromissory clause requires the panel to try to reach consensus before taking a vote, the task of the single independent arbitrator in convincing both sides of some middle-ground solution is much easier where the number of party-appointed arbitrators remains low, with the higher number of party-appointed arbitrators potentially reinforcing each other's views of the correctness of their party's position, while the higher number of independent arbitrators vis-à-vis party-appointed arbitrators will marginalize the power of the party-appointed arbitrators and allow for more of a middle-ground approach and result.[92] There is little that can be done by a single disputant about this structure once the dispute has arisen and the judicial proceedings have begun. Therefore, States ought to take considerable care during the negotiations of these treaties and their compromissory clauses, as opposed to relegating dispute settlement to the end of their priority list, lest they be faced with an unfavorable arbitral structure once a dispute arises.

[88] See ibid., at 269. [89] See ibid. [90] See ibid. [91] See ibid., at 267. [92] See ibid.

All of that said, a lack of certain details with regard to the arbitration's form does not mean the end of arbitration as a possibility. In particular, the international arbitral tribunal can decide on the procedures to be used for the proceedings, whether the compromissory clause provides this power or not. Indeed, these details can be fixed by the tribunal through a type of inherent jurisdiction provided by international law,[93] although compromissory clauses may designate which third parties can choose the procedures for the arbitration.[94] This is unlike private international arbitration, which requires numerous other elements in the consent to jurisdiction to ensure that the ultimate award is enforceable, such as a designation of the procedures to be used.[95] Nonetheless, a compromissory clause not designating the procedures or the entity to decide the procedures may not be the most efficient approach in avoiding troubles that can slow down or entirely frustrate the proceedings. Instead, the more details that can be provided in a compromissory clause, the easier it will be for the tribunal to be established and start handling the substance of the dispute. As the following subsection explains, the compromissory clauses contained in nuclear non-proliferation agreements are surprisingly detailed regarding such terms as how to form the international arbitral panel, which should minimize disputes over how to establish the tribunal once the decision to establish the tribunal as been made.

5.2.3 *Compromissory clauses in nuclear non-proliferation agreements*

This section analyzes the compromissory clauses of the IAEA Statute and seventy-eight IAEA safeguards agreements that give either the ICJ or

93 AMERASINGHE, *supra* note 66, at 21–24, 95–96; MALCOLM SHAW, INTERNATIONAL LAW 740 (6th ed, 2005); International Law Commission, Arts. 8 and 12, U.N. GAOR 13th Sess., Supp. No. 9, at 84, UN Doc. A/3859 (1958) (providing that an arbitral tribunal established by some arbitration agreement can continue to hear and decide the case even though the parties might not agree on the details of how the tribunal is to proceed).

94 See Sohn, *supra* note 79, at 269–270 (discussing the ways that compromissory clauses can designate certain entities to decide the procedures to be used for the arbitration).

95 See GARY B. BORN, INTERNATIONAL ARBITRATION AND FORUM SELECTION AGREEMENTS: PLANNING, DRAFTING AND ENFORCING 2, 37–87 (1999); PAUL D. FRIEDLAND, ARBITRATION CLAUSES FOR INTERNATIONAL CONTRACTS 39–86 (2000). That said, the parties to both kinds of dispute can enter into a compromis after the dispute has arisen in order to establish the tribunal's jurisdiction or to clarify particular arbitral procedures.

international arbitral tribunals jurisdiction over disputes arising out of or in connection with these agreements. This analysis is particularly important because commentators, surprisingly, have overlooked these compromissory clauses, either by wishing that nuclear non-proliferation agreements had these compromissory clauses or by declaring flat out that such compromissory clauses do not exist in such agreements. It would appear that only one contemporary commentator acknowledges the existence of compromissory clauses in IAEA safeguards agreements, although he relegates this observation to a footnote and seems to dismiss its importance on the ground that such clauses have not been used in practice.[96] Concerning those who longingly wish for legal resolution's involvement with nuclear non-proliferation disputes, Vejay Lalla declares, "Although international law is generally designed to prevent disputes and promote arbitration, it should play a more controlling role where there is a dispute between two parties to a nuclear non-proliferation treaty,"[97] without exploring this possibility in any way. Edwin Nazario longingly looks at the *potential* role of international arbitration in=resolving disputes over the nuclear non-proliferation regime if only States entered agreements to send such disputes to arbitration,[98] though he entirely ignores the fact that States already have entered into such arrangements through their IAEA safeguards agreements. Susan Carmody likewise talks of the merits of relying on international arbitration in resolving arms control disputes, though she surprisingly overlooks the existence of arbitration clauses in the various agreements discussed below.[99] Finally, Julie Dahlitz asserts that even if compromissory clauses existed in nuclear non-proliferation agreements, they would not have significant meaning because of the interpretation of the

[96] See DEKKER, *supra* note 22, at 134 n. 402.

[97] See Vejay Lalla, *The Effectiveness of the Comprehensive Test Ban Treaty on Nuclear Weapons Proliferation: A Review of Nuclear Non-proliferation Treaties and the Impact of the Indian and Pakistani Nuclear Tests on the Non-proliferation Regime*, 8 CARDOZO J. INT'L & COMP. L. 103, 124 (2000) (internal citations omitted).

[98] See Edwin J. Nazario, *The Potential Role of Arbitration in the Nuclear Non-proliferation Treaty Regime*, 10 AM REV. INT'L ARB. 139, 154 (1999) (proposing, inter alia, that "arbitration provisions could be set forth in advance in the Safeguards," without acknowledging that these already exist).

[99] See generally Susan Carmody, *Balancing Collective Security and National Sovereignty: Does the United Nations have the Right to Inspect North Korea's Nuclear Facilities?*, 18 FORDHAM INT'L L.J. 229 (1994) (examining legal conflicts in the non-proliferation regime that developed due to the IAEA's effort to verify North Korea's compliance with the NPT).

Hostages case that the ICJ "would not be in a position to investigate those issues [of supposed political actions by the US in Iran] unless Iran appeared to present its case."[100] In other words, she believes that States can avoid legal resolution merely by refusing to participate in a proceeding. However, compromissory clauses do not provide such an easy way out for recalcitrant States, even if pre-eminent legal experts claim the contrary; instead, if a State refuses to participate in the legal proceedings, they run the real risk of having a judgment entered against them in their absence, even though the forum likely will consider the dispute from the perspective of the absent party to ensure that the claim is well founded.[101]

In addition to these commentators, others boldly assert that nuclear non-proliferation agreements do not provide for legal resolution.[102]

[100] DAHLITZ, *supra* note 41, at 111 (asserting that the ICJ sees State participation as essential, even if it has jurisdiction).

[101] See, e.g., ICJ Statute, Art. 53(2) (asserting that when a State fails to participate in a proceeding, "The Court must, before doing so, satisfy itself, not only that it has jurisdiction in accordance with Articles 36 and 37, but also that the claim is well founded in fact and law"); Robert H. Smit and Nicholas J. Shaw, *The Center for Public Resources Rules for Non-administered Arbitration of International Disputes: A Critical and Comparative Commentary*, 8 AM. REV. INT'L ARB. 275, 311 (1997) (asserting that international arbitration does not recognize default judgment per se); LOUIS HENKIN et al. (eds.), INTERNATIONAL LAW 852 (3rd edn, 1993) (same with the ICJ). However, for more information on the actual effects of non-participation, see generally Stanimir A. Alexandrov, *Non-appearance before the International Court of Justice*, 33 COLUM. J. TRANSNAT'L L. 41 (1995); Jonathan I. Charney, *Disputes Implicating the Institutional Credibility of the Court: Problems of Non-appearance, Non-participation and Non-performance*, in THE INTERNATIONAL COURT OF JUSTICE AT A CROSSROADS 288 (LORI F. DAMROSCH ed., 1987); JEROME B. ELKIND, NON-APPEARANCE BEFORE THE INTERNATIONAL COURT OF JUSTICE: FUNCTIONAL AND COMPARATIVE ANALYSIS (1984); Janusz Stanczyk, *The Equality of Parties before the International Court of Justice in Cases of Non-appearing Respondent States*, in FORTY YEARS INTERNATIONAL COURT OF JUSTICE: JURISDICTION, EQUITY AND EQUALITY 35 (A. BLOED and P. VAN DIJK ed., 1988); HUGH W. A. THIRLWAY, NON-APPEARANCE BEFORE THE INTERNATIONAL COURT OF JUSTICE (1985).

[102] See, e.g., Hanspeter Neuhold, *Legal Aspects of Arms Control Agreements*, in LAW OF NATIONS, LAW OF INTERNATIONAL ORGANIZATIONS, WORLD'S ECONOMIC LAW 427, 448 (KARL-HEINZ BÖCKSTIEGEL et al. ed., 1988) (making this assertion with regard to arms control agreements generally, of which nuclear-weapon-related agreements are a subset); Phillip R. Trimble, *Legal Dimensions of Arms Control and Disarmament*, in 1 ENCYCLOPEDIA OF ARMS CONTROL AND DISARMAMENT 372, 372–373 (RICHARD DEAN BURNS ed., 1993). This is different from saying that arms control dispute settlement currently is done, in practice, through non-judicial procedures, as other commentators note. See DEKKER, *supra* note 22, at 71; DAHLITZ, *supra* note 41, at 17–18 (asserting that no nuclear-weapon treaties require a disputant to go to the ICJ or international arbitration).

Others implicitly assert that nuclear-non-proliferation-related agreements do not provide for legal resolution by proposing supposedly revolutionary regimes that incorporate legal resolution within their dispute settlement mechanisms.[103] Other commentators who deny the existence of compromissory clauses in these treaties read the treaties as "specify[ing] that recourse to the Court is to be by consent of the parties" and that "[t]he plain words in those treaties indicate that, unless all concerned parties agree, the Court has no jurisdiction in relation to claims arising from obligations under the treaty in question."[104] Certainly the ICJ or a tribunal would have jurisdiction if disputants entered a *compromis* to send the dispute to that forum. In many instances, a *compromis* is the only likely way for the ICJ or international arbitral tribunals to get jurisdiction over a particular dispute. For example, some commentators assert that the ICJ is the likely forum in which a breach of the North–South Joint Declaration on the Denuclearization of the Korean Peninsula or the 1994 Agreed Framework would be litigated, assuming the disputants were to enter a *compromis*.[105] However, an important distinction must be made here that a *compromis* is not required when the treaty at issue contains a compromissory clause that gives the ICJ or an international arbitral tribunal jurisdiction over the parties and the dispute. As Ian Brownlie noted about Hersch Lauterpacht's approach to international law in *The Function of Law in the International Community*, the world needs to realize that

[103] See Eric P. J. Myjer, *The Law of Arms-Control and International Supervision*, in THE UNITED NATIONS DECADE OF INTERNATIONAL LAW: REFLECTIONS ON INTERNATIONAL DISPUTES SETTLEMENT 99, 120–122 (MARCEL BRUS et al. ed., 1991); Phillip R. Trimble, *Beyond Verification: The Next Step in Arms Control*, 102 HARV. L. REV. 885, 896–901 (1989). In light of the arbitration clauses contained in other arms control and disarmament treaties discussed in Part III, *infra*, it would appear that the primary innovation that he adds is the possibility of having "nonbinding arbitration." Ibid., at 899, 901, 908. This seems to be an oxymoron in that international arbitration by definition is binding. Admittedly, States have been known to agree that a tribunal's decision will not bind them. See Christine Gray and Benedict Kingsbury, *Developments in Dispute Settlement: Inter-state Arbitration since 1945*, 63 BRIT. Y.B. OF INT'L L. 97, 98 (1992) (citing, inter alia, *Italy/US Air Services*, 16 Rep. Int'l Arb. Awards 81 (1965)). However, such an agreement would seem to remove one of the main benefits of sending a dispute to arbitration.

[104] DAHLITZ, *supra* note 41, at 111.

[105] See Matthew Liles, *Did Kim Jong-Il Break the Law? A Case Study on How North Korea Highlights the Flaws of the Non-proliferation Regime*, 33 N.C.J. INT'L L. & COM. REG. 103, 138 (2007).

international law "has more equipment than is sometimes realized,"[106] especially when it comes to trying to resolve disputes over nuclear non-proliferation agreements.

The existence of these provisions for legal resolution is not necessarily surprising, given the general trend for multilateral treaties in general to have dispute settlement provisions that refer to international adjudication, in particular international arbitration.[107] Nor is the existence of such provisions in nuclear non-proliferation agreements a new discovery. Indeed, States that negotiated and drafted these agreements obviously were aware of their existence. Moreover, some early commentators noted the existence of these clauses, primarily in the IAEA safeguards agreements,[108] although these commentators were working for the States or the international organization that were parties to these agreements,[109] so the existence of these clauses does not appear to have been widely known.

The NPT entirely lacks a provision dealing with dispute settlement. Therefore, diplomatic methods of dispute settlement are called upon to handle disputes over the NPT.[110] Without the agreement of the disputants through a *compromis* or through unilateral declarations,[111] neither

[106] See Ian Brownlie, *The Justiciability of Disputes and Issues in International Relations*, 42 British Y.B. Int'l L. 123, 124 (1967) (noting how Lauterpacht's approach in the Function of Law in the International Community (1933) was to show the world that international law "has more equipment than is sometimes realized").

[107] See Gray and Kingsbury, *supra* note 103, at 101; Louis B. Sohn, *The Role of Arbitration in Recent International Multilateral Treaties*, 23 Va. J. Int'l L. 171, 176 (1982–1983); Sohn, *supra* note 79, at 266.

[108] See Allan McKnight, Atomic Safeguards: A Study in International Verification 123–124 (1971); Paul C. Szasz, The Law and Practices of the International Atomic Energy Agency 938–945 (1970); Paul C. Szasz, *The Law of International Atomic Energy Agency Safeguards*, 3 Revue Belge de Droit Int'l 196, 226–227 (1967).

[109] For example, Szasz worked for eight years as an IAEA legal officer. See Szasz, *supra* note 108, at 1. McKnight was IAEA Inspector General from 1964 to 1968. See Mason Willrich, *Allan McKnight's Atomic Safeguards: A Study in International Verification*, 66 Am. J. Int'l L. 691, 691 (1972) (book review).

[110] See David A. Koplow, *Parsing Good Faith: Has the United States Violated Article VI of the Nuclear Non-proliferation Treaty?*, Wis. L. Rev. 301, 381–382 (1993) (listing NPT Review Conferences, the Committee on Disarmament, the LTBT Amendment Conference, and the Security Council as political fora in which disputes over the NPT might be resolved); Eric Stein, *Impact of New Weapons Technology on International Law: Selected Aspects*, 133 Rec. des cours 360–365 (1971-II) (discussing the consultative process with the NPT).

[111] Alternatively, these legal fora perhaps could gain jurisdiction through prorogated jurisdiction, although it is unlikely that a State would be careless enough in such

the ICJ nor international arbitral tribunals would have jurisdiction over NPT disputes. In particular, without North Korea's express consent to international adjudication, these legal fora will not have the jurisdiction to determine whether it properly withdrew from the NPT. Nevertheless, the nuclear non-proliferation regime is much broader than just the NPT; it definitely should include the IAEA Statute and the IAEA safeguards agreements, as explained in Chapter 2.1.1 above. It is through these other agreements of the nuclear non-proliferation regime that the ICJ and international arbitral tribunals can have the jurisdiction necessary to get involved with resolving nuclear non-proliferation disputes without the further agreement of the disputants.

5.2.3.1 IAEA Statute and dispute settlement

IAEA Statute Article XVII(A) is an extremely interesting clause for this study's purposes:

> Any question or dispute concerning the interpretation or application of this Statute which is not settled by negotiation shall be referred to the International Court of Justice in conformity with the Statute of the Court, unless the parties concerned agree on another mode of settlement.

In particular, reference to the ICJ of "[a]ny question or dispute concerning the interpretation or application of this Statute" is particularly important. However, the language "which is not settled by negotiation" must not be overlooked, inasmuch as it will be the main barrier to the ICJ having jurisdiction over such disputes. The ICJ recently determined the legal significance of this exact language in its 2011 *Application of the International Convention on the Elimination of All Forms of Racial Discrimination* judgment on preliminary objections. There, Georgia filed an application against the Russian Federation for its unlawful use of force in South Ossetia in August 2008, and claimed, inter alia, that the Russian Federation committed racial discrimination when it engaged in ethnic cleansing there in violation of the International Convention on the Elimination of All Forms of Racial Discrimination (CERD).[112] Georgia pointed to the dispute settlement clause of CERD Article 22 as providing the ICJ with jurisdiction:

sensitive disputes to act in a way to give the ICJ or an international arbitral tribunal jurisdiction.

112 See *Application of the International Convention on the Elimination of All Forms of Racial Discrimination (Georgia v. Russian Federation)*, Preliminary Objections, General List No. 140, April 1, 2011, at 1, 9–11.

> Any dispute between two or more States Parties with respect to the interpretation or application of this Convention, *which is not settled by negotiation* or by the procedures expressly provided for in this Convention, shall, at the request of any of the parties to the dispute, be referred to the International Court of Justice for decision, unless the disputants agree to another mode of settlement.[113]

The Russian Federation responded that the ICJ lacked jurisdiction because Georgia had resorted neither to negotiation nor to the special procedures provided in CERD, as CERD Article 22 required, and issued its preliminary objections in this regard.[114] Georgia insisted that the ICJ had jurisdiction in light of this provision and asserted that it had tried to settle the dispute through negotiation but it had failed, thus giving the ICJ jurisdiction over the dispute.[115] The ICJ determined that this language required the parties to affirmatively resort to negotiation or to the special procedures under CERD before the ICJ could exercise jurisdiction, which it deemed as being consistent with past decisions on the meaning of similar language.[116] The ICJ proceeded to explain that negotiation is more than mere protests and disputations – instead, one of the disputants must attempt to engage in meaningful discussions with the other disputant with the aim of resolving the dispute.[117] Moreover, the ICJ determined that the negotiations must relate to the subject matter of the treaty and the dispute.[118] Based on the facts, the ICJ concluded that Georgia had not attempted to engage in negotiations between the time the dispute arose and the filing of the application (three days).[119] In light of this case, whether disputants over the interpretation or application of a provision of the IAEA Statute have adequately attempted negotiation between the development of the dispute and the filing of the application will depend on the facts. States that invoke this compromissory clause will want to point to hard evidence showing they tried to negotiate, beyond unilateral protests. If they can provide this evidence, they can satisfy this requirement, thus making legal resolution through the ICJ compulsory.

It is important to emphasize that the negotiations need not be successful before a State can invoke a compromissory clause.[120] Indeed, if that were the case, such a reference to the ICJ in the compromissory

[113] See ibid., at 1 (citing CERD, Art. 22) (emphasis added). [114] See ibid., at 12–13, 47.
[115] See ibid., at 12–13. [116] See ibid., at 51–54. [117] See ibid., at 57.
[118] See ibid., at 59. [119] See ibid., at 59–66. [120] See ibid., at 59.

clause would be superfluous. There is the possibility that the ICJ or an international arbitral tribunal could deem negotiations to have failed after a reasonable period of time. The ICJ in the *Land and Maritime Boundary between Cameroon and Nigeria* case asserted that agreement needed to be reached within a reasonable period of time or else the negotiations were to be deemed to have failed, which then would allow the ICJ to get involved under the compromissory clause.[121] There, the time delay deemed to be unreasonable was approximately three decades, inasmuch as the negotiations over the maritime delimitation began in the 1970s and the judgment was rendered in 2002.[122] Without using so many words, Judge Manfred Lachs in his dissenting opinion in the *North Sea Continental Shelf* case involving the Federal Republic of Germany, Denmark, and the Netherlands summarized the situation by asserting that negotiations had failed when the disputants could not agree to all of the delimitations, implying a reasonable-time element to negotiations.[123] There, the time delay implied to be unreasonable was much shorter than in the *Land and Maritime Boundary between Cameroon and Nigeria* judgment, with Judge Lachs noting that the disputants had agreed on the delimitation of the coastal continental shelf in 1964 and 1965, but that the negotiations for the other parts of the boundary had failed by the time of the judgment in 1969, just four to five years after these other negotiations had succeeded. Finally, in the Separate Opinion of Judge Mohammed Bedjaoui in the *Gabcikovo-Nagymaros Project* case, Judge Bedjaoui suggested that negotiations have failed "if it has been demonstrated beyond doubt that [one State] only pretended to negotiate, whereas *its firm intention was to sabotage the seeming negotiations in order to impose at all costs a unilateral solution already decided on.*"[124] Other cases that address what a reasonable delay might be do so in an entirely different context – namely that the time limit for bringing a claim before the ICJ is deemed inadmissible as prejudicing the respondent State, not the period of time that negotiation has to be tried before a disputant can go to the ICJ or an international arbitral tribunal in

[121] See *Land and Maritime Boundary between Cameroon and Nigeria (Cameroon v. Nigeria)*, 2002 ICJ Rep. 303, 423–424 (Oct. 10).

[122] See ibid.

[123] See *North Sea Continental Shelf (FRG/Denmark, FRG/Netherlands)*, 1969 ICJ Rep.3, 218 (Feb. 20) (Lachs J., Dissenting Opinion).

[124] *Gabcikovo-Nagymaros Project (Hungary/Slovakia)*, 1997 ICJ Rep. 7, 128 (Sept. 25) (Bedjaoui J., Separate Opinion) (emphasis in original).

accordance with a compromissory clause.[125] Alternatively, there are human-rights-related cases dealing with what constitutes a reasonable delay for an accused individual to receive an adequately prompt trial.[126] Therefore, these other cases are not exactly on point here and will not be discussed. Regardless, in the types of situations mentioned above where neither side actively tries to resolve the dispute within a reasonable amount of time, and perhaps where it can be shown that one State was negotiating in bad faith, legal resolution of disputes over the IAEA Statute becomes compulsory. With such sensitive disputes as those involving nuclear non-proliferation, it is conceivable that the failure of negotiations will be relatively common. However, in light of the 2011 *Application of the International Convention on the Elimination of All Forms of Racial Discrimination* judgment on preliminary objections, affirmatively trying to resolve the dispute through negotiation is a far more reliable option than merely waiting until a reasonable time has passed in order to satisfy this requirement in a compromissory clause.[127]

Such a designation of legal resolution within the IAEA Statute is significant inasmuch as other nuclear-weapon-related treaties list the possibility of going to legal resolution merely if States so agree.[128] Moreover, such a designation is significant for this study's purposes

[125] See, e.g., *Case Concerning Certain Phosphate Lands in Naura (Nauru v. Australia)*, 1992 ICJ Rep 240, 253–254 (June 26); *Case Concerning Avena and Other Mexican Nationals (Mexico v. US)*, 2004 ICJ Rep. 12, 37–38 (March 31).

[126] See, e.g., *Ferrari v. Italy*, Grand Chamber, No. 33440/96, July 28, 1999 (unreported); *Munoz Hermoza v. Peru*, U.N. Human Rights Committee, Communication No. 203/1986, UN Doc. Supp. No. 40 (A/44/40) (1988).

[127] See *Application of the International Convention on the Elimination of All Forms of Racial Discrimination (Georgia v. Russian Federation)*, Preliminary Objections, General List No. 140, April 1, 2011, at 57–59.

[128] See, e.g., African Nuclear-Weapon-Free Zone Treaty (Pelindaba Treaty), Art. 15, April 11, 1996 (entered into force July 15, 2009) ("Any dispute arising out of the interpretation of the Treaty shall be settled by negotiation, by recourse to the Commission or another procedure agreed to by the Parties, which may include recourse to an arbitral panel or to the International Court of Justice"); Treaty on the Southeast Asia Nuclear-Weapon-Free Zone (Bangkok Treaty), Art. 21, Dec. 15, 1995 (entered into force March 27, 1997) ("Any dispute arising from the interpretation of the provision of this Treaty shall be settled by peaceful means as may be agreed upon by the States Parties to the dispute. If within one month, the parties to the dispute are unable to achieve a peaceful settlement of the dispute by negotiation, mediation, enquiry or conciliation, any of the parties concerned shall, with the prior consent of the other parties concerned, refer the dispute to arbitration or to the International Court of Justice"); The Antarctic Treaty, Art. XI(2), Dec. 1, 1959 (entered into force June 23, 1961) ("Any dispute of this character not so resolved shall, with the consent, in each case, of all parties to the dispute, be referred to the International Court of Justice for settlement"); Treaty for the

inasmuch as the IAEA Statute was the first multilateral treaty in the area of nuclear non-proliferation, established well before the NPT, which point emphasizes how the developers of the nuclear non-proliferation regime envisioned a role for legal resolution in the first legal instrument of this sensitive area of international relations.

5.2.3.2 IAEA safeguards agreements and dispute settlement

The IAEA is no stranger to arbitration clauses, as many of its contracts apparently provide for arbitration under International Chamber of Commerce (ICC) rules or an ad hoc arbitral panel of three arbitrators, which apparently is similar to the practice of other specialized agencies.[129] However, those arbitration clauses fall under the category of commercial (or private) arbitration, given the underlying commercial activities, whereas the arbitration clauses dealing with actual disputes under the interpretation or application of the agreement would fall under the category of international arbitration governed by public international law (or public international arbitration).[130] No arbitral proceedings appear to have been started under this latter type of arbitration clause. Admittedly, the general secrecy of public international arbitration could mean that arbitral proceedings have occurred under these provisions without their being made public, though it

Prohibition of Nuclear Weapons in Latin America and the Caribbean (Treaty of Tlatelolco), Art. 25, Feb. 14, 1967 (entered into force April 22, 1968) ("Unless the Parties concerned agree on another mode of peaceful settlement, any question or dispute concerning the interpretation or application of this Treaty which is not settled shall be referred to the International Court of Justice with the prior consent of the Parties to the controversy").

[129] See Relations between States and International Organizations (Second Part of the Topic: Status, Privileges and Immunities of International Organizations, Their Officials, Experts, etc.), 1985 Y.B. INT'L L. COMM'N 144, 182–84, UN Doc. A/CN.4/L.383 and Add.1–3. Please note that UN contracts normally have provisions for arbitration in case disputes arise under them, and are governed by the rules of the American Arbitration Association, the International Chamber of Commerce or the UNCITRAL Arbitration Rules. See UN Office of Legal Affairs, Implementation of the Obligation of the United Nations and Specialized Agencies to make Provision for the Settlement of Disputes of a Private Character – Practice Followed in This Respect by the Organization in Question, Letter to the Legal Counsel of the Food and Agriculture Organization of the United Nations, July 16, 1986, UN JURIDICAL Y.B. 324 (1986); see also WELLENS, *supra* note 9, at 93, 156–160 (noting that there have been arbitral proceedings involving the United Nations and private parties); see ibid., at 220 (noting that such agreements as headquarters agreements of international organizations contain arbitration clauses).

[130] Public international arbitration also can be referred to as inter-State arbitration, though the phrase "public international arbitration" is preferred here in order to include disputes between States and international organizations.

would be exceptional for such an arbitral proceeding not to publicly yield at least an award.[131] Regardless, these arbitration clauses under the IAEA safeguards agreements remain available when parties are faced with a dispute, such as allegations of noncompliance.[132]

The introduction to Part III provided a list of different issues relating to IAEA safeguards agreements that could be resolved through international arbitration, all of which involve a mix of factual and legal elements surrounding the obligations under the IAEA safeguards agreements. This section does not repeat those questions, primarily to avoid redundancy but also to downplay the substance of particular questions that legal resolution might be asked to handle, as explained towards the end of Chapter 1.3 on the methodology of this study, for the simple reason that language is ambiguous generally (in accordance with Wittgenstein's theory of linguistic meaning) and the unhierarchical methods of treaty interpretation do not aid in finding one dominant, as explained in Chapter 3.1.3 above. Instead, this section focuses on determining the contours of the jurisdiction of international arbitral tribunals under the arbitration clauses contained in IAEA safeguards agreements, with the end of determining the viability of legal resolution of disputes over IAEA safeguards agreements in general. Those readers who insist on this study explaining the way the ICJ or an international arbitral tribunal *will* interpret provisions of a nuclear non-proliferation agreement have missed or misunderstood the point that was being made in Chapter 3.1.3 above concerning the indeterminacy of the Vienna Convention on the Law of Treaties in choosing one of the many methods of interpretation to favor. This is not to say, however, that this section does not, at all, provide an idea of how legal resolution might interpret particular questions arising over these treaties. On the contrary, Chapter 5.3.3 below on the gaps in nuclear non-proliferation agreements and

[131] See Gray and Kingsbury, *supra* note 103, at 110–111.

[132] Please note that State reluctance to invoke arbitration clauses is not a phenomenon exclusively observed with disarmament and arms control disputes. See RICHARD B. BILDER, MANAGING THE RISKS OF INTERNATIONAL AGREEMENT 143–144 (1981). Indeed, there are many arbitration clauses in agreements involving the United Nations or other international organizations. See Hans-Jürgen Schlochauer, *Arbitration*, in 1 ENCYCLOPEDIA OF PUBLIC INTERNATIONAL LAW 215, 220 (RUDOLF BERNHARDT ed., 1992); Norbert Wühler, *Arbitration Clauses in Treaties*, in 1 ENCYCLOPEDIA OF PUBLIC INTERNATIONAL LAW 34, 35 (RUDOLF BERNHARDT ed., 1992). Many of these arbitration clauses ostensibly never have been invoked to resolve disputes.

Chapter 6.4 below give ample examples of how an adjudicative body such as the ICJ or an international arbitral tribunal might interpret provisions of the Nuclear Non-Proliferation Treaty from a textualist perspective, assuming disputants agreed to a *compromis* that gave this adjudicative body jurisdiction over the interpretation and application of these provisions. The point being made here is that such analysis must be viewed with the general caveat of Chapter 3.1.3 in mind.

5.2.3.2.1 Standard language IAEA safeguards agreements consistently provide for international arbitration of disputes relating to these agreements. IAEA Statute Article XI(F)(6) requires, in the context of agency projects, "Upon approving a project, the Agency shall enter into an agreement with the member or group of members submitting the project, which agreement shall . . . [m]ake appropriate provision regarding settlement of disputes."[133] Although not expressly required in the Statute, the IAEA has made it a practice to include provisions dealing with the settlement of disputes, even judicial dispute settlement mechanisms, in many of its safeguards agreements. Under Article 22 of the Model Safeguards Agreement, if the IAEA and the State are not able to settle their dispute through consultation, then either side (the IAEA through the Board of Governors) can submit the dispute to an international arbitral tribunal, whose decision will be binding on both parties.[134] It is the ability of either side to commence arbitration that makes these provisions genuine arbitration clauses, as explained at the end of this subsection.

Not only does the Model Safeguards Agreement provide for international arbitration, but all of the safeguards agreements published on the IAEA's website contain such arbitration clauses. Out of the 162 States that the IAEA reports as having a safeguards agreement in force with the IAEA, seventy-seven of those States have their safeguards agreement made public on the IAEA's website, with the former Yugoslav Republic of Macedonia accepting the conditions of a Model Safeguards Agreement in a letter in response to a letter requesting such acceptance

[133] IAEA Statute, *supra* note 12, Art. XI(F)(6).

[134] See IAEA, The Structure and Content of Agreements between the Agency and States Required in Connection with the Treaty on the Non-proliferation of Nuclear Weapons, Art. 22, IAEA Doc. INFCIRC/153 (June 1972) (hereinafter IAEA Model Safeguards Agreement). Please note that the Model Safeguards Agreement has a large exception, which is analyzed later in this section.

to the annexed model.[135] All seventy-eight of the agreements have an arbitration clause. The following is the standard language in those agreements:

> Any dispute arising out of the interpretation or application of this Agreement, except a dispute with regard to a finding by the Board under Article 19 or an action taken by the Board pursuant to such a finding, which is not settled by negotiation or another procedure agreed to by ____ and the Agency shall, at the request of either, be submitted to an arbitral tribunal composed as follows: ____ and the Agency shall each designate one arbitrator, and the two arbitrators so designated shall elect a third, who shall be the Chairman. If, within thirty days of the request for arbitration, either ____ or the Agency has not designated an arbitrator, either ____ or the Agency may request the President of the International Court of Justice to appoint an arbitrator. The same procedure shall apply if, within thirty days of the designation or appointment of the second arbitrator, the third arbitrator has not been elected. A majority of the members of the arbitral tribunal shall constitute a quorum, and all decisions shall require the concurrence of two arbitrators. The arbitral procedure shall be fixed by the tribunal. The decisions of the tribunal shall be binding on ____ and the Agency.

Fifty-four of the safeguards agreements that have been made public have the above language, including those for North Korea,[136] Iran,[137] Cuba,[138] and others that one might have expected to be different.[139] This language

[135] See IAEA, Protocol Additional to an Agreement for the Application of Safeguards in Connection with the Treaty on the Nonproliferation of Nuclear Weapons, at Art. I, IAEA Doc. INFCIRC/610/Add.1 (May 25, 2006).

[136] See IAEA, Agreement of 30 January 1992 between the Government of the Democratic People's Republic of Korea and the International Atomic Energy Agency for the Application of Safeguards in Connection with the Treaty on the Non-proliferation of Nuclear Weapons, Art. 22, IAEA Doc. INFCIRC/403 (May 1992).

[137] See IAEA, Agreement between Iran and the Agency for the Application of Safeguards in Connection with the Treaty on the Non-proliferation of Nuclear Weapons, Art. 22, IAEA Doc. INFCIRC/214 (Dec. 13, 1974).

[138] See IAEA, Agreement between the Republic of Cuba and the International Atomic Energy Agency for the Application of Safeguards in Connection with the Treaty for the Prohibition of Nuclear Weapons in Latin America and the Caribbean and the Treaty on the Non-proliferation of Nuclear Weapons, Art. 22, IAEA Doc. INFCIRC/633 (Aug. 18, 2004).

[139] Although this is mere speculation, one reason why the other eighty-five agreements are not published might be because they have a different arbitration clause or no arbitration clause. However, this is highly unlikely given the fact that the majority of safeguards agreements do not vary and such matters hardly are seen as the most pressing issues. See MARTIN HUNTER ET AL., THE FRESHFIELDS GUIDE TO ARBITRATION AND ADR ix (1st edn, 1993); Alexis C. Brown, *Presumption Meets Reality: An Exploration of*

typically is found in Article 22 within the section of the safeguards agreements entitled "Interpretation and Application of the Agreement and Settlement of Disputes," except those agreements with the United States (Article 21), the Soviet Union (Article 21), China (Article 21), the United Kingdom (Section 20), India (Section 27), and Pakistan (Section 27). Not surprisingly, the language quoted above essentially is the language that the Model Safeguards Agreement recommends, though with the recommendatory "should" replaced with the obligatory "shall" and some minor grammatical and punctuation changes.[140]

Before proceeding any further, it is necessary to analyze the two hurdles to invoking the arbitration clause. First, there is the requirement that the dispute "not [be] settled by negotiations or another procedure agreed to" by the disputants. The reader is reminded of the preceding section's analysis of when negotiations can be deemed as having failed, which essentially revolves around whether the disputants are making significant, good-faith efforts to resolve the dispute within a reasonable period of time. There are some indications that the delay need not be for very long (approximately four to five years), so the ongoing negotiations with Iran and North Korea over the past decade easily could be deemed an unreasonable delay warranting the involvement of legal resolution, although such a determination would be left to the legal forum to determine.

Second, the main hurdle involves the exception provided at the beginning of the standard text quoted above: "except a dispute with regard to a finding by the Board under Article 19 or an action taken by the Board pursuant to such a finding." The standard language of Article 19 of safeguards agreements provides:

> if the Board, upon examination of relevant information reported to it by the Director General, finds that the Agency is not able to verify that there

the Confidentiality Obligation in International Commercial Arbitration, 16 Am. U. Int'l L. Rev. 969, 990 (2001) (quoting David Fraser, *Confidentiality in Arbitration*, Address in Paris (October 12, 1998) available at http://www.bakerinfor.com/publicatoins/documents/1044_tx.html) (noting that, in the domestic context, parties "may not want to talk about the funeral while negotiating the terms of the marriage" and so arbitration clauses are "typically poorly drafted").

140 See IAEA Model Safeguards Agreement, *supra* note 134, Art. 22. Some might be tempted to criticize these provisions for lacking any mention of certain elements of arbitration such as the seat and the language of the arbitration, as one would expect with arbitration clauses in commercial contracts. However, the arbitration clauses for international arbitration between states or a state and an international organization are far less rigid in their formalities.

> has been no diversion of nuclear material required to be safeguarded under this Agreement, to nuclear weapons or other nuclear explosive devices, it may make the reports provided for in paragraph C of Article XII of the Statute of the Agency (hereinafter referred to as "the Statute") and may also take, where applicable, the other measures provided for in that paragraph. In taking such action the Board shall take account of the degree of assurance provided by the safeguards measures that have been applied and shall afford the Government of ____ every reasonable opportunity to furnish the Board with any necessary reassurance.[141]

IAEA Statute Article XII(C), which was incorporated into the standard language of Article 19 by reference, provides the Board with the ability to take two preliminary actions upon receiving a report from the IAEA director-general: (1) to call on the State "to remedy forthwith any non-compliance which it finds to have occurred," and (2) to report the situation to all IAEA members, to the UN Security Council and to the UN General Assembly.[142] If the State fails to remedy within a reasonable time, the Board may (1) curtail or suspend any assistance being provided by the IAEA or a member, (2) call for the return of materials and equipment made available to the State in question, and (3) suspend the State from the privileges and rights of membership it enjoys.[143]

Critics will read this exception and claim that, once a dispute gets sufficiently dangerous (to the point where the Security Council would be warranted in considering getting involved), the parties can no longer submit the dispute to arbitration. However, this would be an overly broad interpretation of the exception. The exception explicitly excludes only disputes over the IAEA Board's determination that it is "not able to verify that there has been no diversion of nuclear material required to be safeguarded under this Agreement," as well as disputes over the decision of the IAEA Board to call on the State to remedy its failure to provide enough information to verify that there has been no diversion, or the decision of the IAEA Board to report that particular failure to all member States, the Security Council, and the General Assembly. Notably, the exception does not exclude the Board's determination of actual breaches other than not having enough information to verify non-diversion of nuclear material, or any other disputes over the IAEA safeguards agreement that might arise. Only the Board's determination involving Iran would appear to fit within this exception, inasmuch as its determination was limited to not being able to confirm that nuclear material had not

[141] IAEA Model Safeguards Agreement, *supra* note 134, Art. 19.
[142] IAEA Statute, *supra* note 12, Art. XII(C). [143] See ibid.

been diverted.[144] For example, the Board's determination involving North Korea involved a determination of noncompliance with its IAEA safeguards agreement that was different from the IAEA not being able to confirm that nuclear material had not been diverted.[145] Therefore, the option of international arbitration would remain for such disputes under this arbitration clause, as well as for any other disputes relating to the IAEA safeguards agreement, including the other questions of law and fact posed at the introduction to this part of the book. In other words, if the dispute does not involve allegations that the IAEA cannot confirm that nuclear material has not been diverted, but rather focuses on such issues as the quality of the peaceful nuclear material as determined by the exporting and importing States – the type of difference that is likely the most common to arise under the arbitration clause[146] – then the potential claimant need not worry about the exception at all. Critics might argue that this is an overly formalistic interpretation of the exception with regard to North Korea, with the intended meaning being to exclude the possibility of arbitration once the Board gets involved. A review of the *travaux préparatoires* for this provision does not reveal such an intended meaning, although these critics very well may be correct, in which case the arbitration clause in the IAEA safeguards agreement relating to North Korea also cannot be invoked because of this exception. States could, nevertheless, enter into a *compromis*, or the ICJ or an international arbitration tribunal could find some other jurisdictional basis, thus making the rest of this study relevant in that context.

These points notwithstanding, States still might invoke the arbitration clause found in their IAEA safeguards agreements if they do so before the Board has made its determination. It is this exact situation that this study focuses on, where the situation is sufficiently serious that it potentially might endanger international peace and security in the future, but it has not yet risen to the level of actually endangering international peace and security (or worse), thereby avoiding Security Council involvement for

144 See IAEA Board of Governors, *Implementation of the NPT Safeguards Agreement in the Islamic Republic of Iran*, IAEA Doc. Gov/2006/14, ¶¶ 1, 3, 5–6 (Feb. 4, 2006).

145 *Report by the Director General on the Implementation of the Resolution Adopted by the Board on 25 February 1993 (Gov/2636) and of the Agreement between the Agency and the Democratic People's Republic of Korea for the Application of Safeguards in Connection with the Treaty on the Non-proliferation of Nuclear Weapons (INFCIRC/403)*, IAEA Doc. Gov/2645, ¶¶ 1, 2, 4 (April 1, 1993).

146 See McKnight, *supra* note 108, at 124.

the time being. In drafting its request for arbitration, the claimant State in this situation should center the claim on the IAEA inspectors' or IAEA director-general's allegations of not being able to confirm that nuclear material has not been diverted, assuming such allegations have been made, thereby avoiding this otherwise troublesome exception that focuses on the Board's determination. With a measure of anticipation and speed, potential claimants can avoid the significant legal effects of this exception and still exercise their right to arbitration. This option has long since passed for Iran, since the IAEA Board of Governors determined in 2006 that it could not confirm that Iran had not diverted nuclear materials. However, Iran retains the option of international arbitration with all other disputes involving its IAEA safeguards agreement. Moreover, there still remains the possibility of legal resolution through a *compromis* and through the compromissory clause in the IAEA Statute, as well as through the creation of a quasi-judicial subsidiary organ to handle nuclear non-proliferation disputes under the Comprehensive Test Ban Treaty, assuming Iran finally ratifies the treaty and the treaty enters into force.

Critics might point to this exception and try to exclude the possibility of legal resolution for North Korea surrounding its safeguards agreement with the IAEA. Indeed, as already explained, the Board of Governors already determined North Korea's noncompliance and referred the matter to the Security Council, at the same time mentioning, in a separate paragraph, Article 19 and its inability to confirm that nuclear material had not been diverted.[147] However, North Korea is somewhat of a special case, inasmuch as its safeguards agreement has special language. In 1977, North Korea entered into a safeguards agreement with the IAEA concerning nuclear research facilities it received from the Soviet Union and

> special fissionable and other nuclear material, including subsequent generations of special fissionable material, which is being or has been produced, processed or used within the jurisdiction of the Democratic People's Republic of Korea in or by the use of the Reactor Facility or any nuclear material referred to in this section.[148]

[147] See *Report by the Director General on the Implementation of the Resolution Adopted by the Board on 25 February 1993 (Gov/2636) and of the Agreement between the Agency and the Democratic People's Republic of Korea for the Application of Safeguards in Connection with the Treaty on the Non-proliferation of Nuclear Weapons (INFCIRC/403)*, IAEA Doc. Gov/2645, ¶¶ 1, 2, 4 (April 1, 1993).

[148] See Agreement between the International Atomic Energy Agency and the Government of the Democratic People's Republic of Korea for the Application of Safeguards to the

This agreement was not subject to termination as long as there was nuclear material from these facilities in North Korea,[149] and any material produced by this facility would be subject to safeguards in perpetuity, as the IAEA director-general had established at that time.[150] As noted above, North Korea entered into another safeguards agreement in 1993, with a caveat that it would remain in force as long as North Korea remained an NPT member. This 1993 safeguards agreement merely suspended the 1977 safeguards agreement, according to its Article 23:

> The application of Agency safeguards in [North Korea] under other safeguards agreements with the Agency shall be suspended while this Agreement is in force. If [North Korea] has received assistance from the Agency for a project, [North Korea's] undertaking in the Project Agreement not to use items which are subject thereto in such a way as to further any military purpose shall continue to apply.

Therefore, this 1977 safeguards agreement continued to exist even with the introduction of the 1993 safeguards agreement, and will govern in the absence of the 1993 safeguards agreement. These types of safeguard agreements have been referred to as the pre-NPT safeguards system.[151] However, the NPT entered into force in 1970, seven years before the conclusion of this safeguards agreement with North Korea. Therefore, it is not so much a pre-NPT safeguards system as a safeguards system that exists outside the NPT. As Mohamed Shaker explains, the post-NPT safeguards system was established as "a new system of safeguards, parallel to the existing one," which was required in order for there to be relatively uniform norms that apply to all NPT States parties.[152]

Research Reactor Facility, sec. 2, Nov. 14, 1977, IAEA Doc. INFCIRC/252, available at http://www.iaea.org/Publications/Documents/Infcircs/Others/infcirc252.pdf.

[149] See ibid.

[150] See Antonio F. Perez, *Survival of Rights under the Nuclear Non-proliferation Treaty: Withdrawal and the Continuing Right of International Atomic Energy Agency Safeguards*, 34 Va. J. Int'l L. 749, 771 n. 62 (1994) (citing IAEA Director General, *The Formulation of Certain Provisions in Agreements under the Agency's Safeguards System (1965, as provisionally extended in 1966 and 1968)*, IAEA Doc. GOV/1621 (1973)).

[151] See Perez, *supra* note 150, at 757.

[152] See Mohamed I. Shaker, 2 The Nuclear Non-proliferation Treaty: Origin and Implementation, 1959–1979 679 (1980); David Sloss, *It's Not Broken, So Don't Fix It: The International Atomic Energy Agency Safeguards System and the Nuclear Nonproliferation Treaty*, 35 Va. J. Int'l L. 841, 847–848 (1995).

Interestingly, Section 20 of the 1977 safeguards agreement of North Korea contains an arbitration clause that is not so unlike that of the 1993 safeguards agreement:

> Any dispute arising out of the interpretation or application of this Agreement which is not settled by negotiation or another procedure agreed to by the Government of the Democratic People's Republic of Korea and the Agency, shall on the request of either the Government of the Democratic People's Republic of Korea or the Agency be submitted to an arbitral tribunal composed as follows: The Government of the Democratic People's Republic of Korea and the Agency shall each designate one arbitrator, and the two arbitrators so designated shall elect a third who shall be the Chairman. If within thirty days of the request for arbitration either the Government of the Democratic People's Republic of Korea or the Agency has not designated an arbitrator, the Government of the Democratic People's Republic of Korea and the Agency may request the President of the International Court of Justice to appoint an arbitrator. The same procedure shall apply if, within thirty days of the designation or appointment of the second arbitrator, the third arbitrator has not been elected. A majority of the members of the arbitral tribunal shall constitute a quorum, and all decisions shall be made by majority vote. The arbitral procedure shall be fixed by the tribunal. The decisions of the tribunal, including all rulings concerning its constitution, procedure, jurisdiction and the division of the expenses of arbitration between the Government of the Democratic People's Republic of Korea and the Agency, shall be binding on the Government of the Democratic People's Republic of Korea and the Agency. The remuneration of the arbitrators shall be determined on the same basis as that of ad hoc judges of the International Court of Justice.

The main difference here is that arbitration is not excluded with "a finding by the Board under Article 19 or an action taken by the Board pursuant to such a finding," as the 1993 safeguards agreement excludes.[153] With this arbitration clause, it becomes possible for North Korea to arbitrate Board of Governors' decisions under this valid 1977 safeguards agreement, unlike with the 1993 safeguards agreement. While the 1977 safeguards agreement does not provide for the same special inspections as the 1993 safeguards agreement,[154] this 1977 safeguards agreement nonetheless provides relevant legal norms against which an international arbitral tribunal can assess North Korea's continuing

[153] Another substantive difference is the method for determining the remuneration of the arbitrators in the last sentence of Section 20 of the 1977 safeguards agreement.

[154] See Perez, *supra* note 150, at 771 n. 62.

nuclear activities. It will be a question of fact for the international arbitral tribunal to decide whether those facilities still operate within North Korea's alleged program to develop nuclear weapons or whether any nuclear material from those facilities is used in that program. Regardless, it would appear that the Security Council's extension in Resolution 1718 of the "terms and conditions of [the IAEA–North Korea] Safeguards Agreement" beyond North Korea's withdrawal from the NPT was unnecessary given this pre-NPT safeguards agreement. Whether under the 1977 safeguards agreement or under the 1993 safeguards agreement, North Korea enjoys the right to invoke a valid arbitration clause and send to international arbitration disputes arising out of and in connection with its safeguards agreements. North Korea might want to invoke this arbitration clause if, for example, it tires of the Security Council's coercive measures and wants a judicial determination of its rights and obligations under the safeguards agreement. Alternatively, the Security Council might want to suspend this 1977 arbitration clause if it wants to remove this option from North Korea.

It is not that the Security Council's involvement in a nuclear non-proliferation dispute necessarily precludes the possibility of legal resolution, which involvement can last for a long time inasmuch as matters tend to stay on the Security Council's agenda until removed.[155] However, it conceivably would become a problem if the Security Council decided to create obligations under its Chapter VII powers that directly conflict with the rights and obligations in these IAEA safeguards agreements (including the right to arbitration under those agreements), which would override these rights and obligations in the agreements, in accordance with UN Charter Article 103. This scenario also is relevant with the other options that give States the ability to rely on legal resolution of these types of disputes – namely through the compromissory clause in the IAEA Statute, through a *compromis*, and through the formation of a quasi-judicial subsidiary organ to handle nuclear non-proliferation

[155] See SYDNEY DAWSON BAILEY and SAM DAWS, THE PROCEDURE OF THE SECURITY COUNCIL 80–81 (1998); Provisional Rules of Procedure of the Security Council, Rule 10 (1983) ("Any item of the agenda of a meeting of the Security Council, consideration of which has not been completed at that meeting, shall, unless the Security Council otherwise decides, automatically be included in the agenda of the next meeting"). See also Georges Abi-Saab, *The Security Council Legibus Solutus? On the Legislative Forays of the Council*, in INTERNATIONAL LAW AND THE QUEST FOR ITS IMPLEMENTATION: LIBER AMICORUM VERA GOWLLAND-DEBBAS 23, 28 (LAURENCE BOISSON DE CHAZOURNES and MARCELO KOHEN ed., 2010) (noting how the Security Council determined a threat to the peace in the *Lockerbie* incident eight years after the incident had occurred, presumably because the matter remained on the Security Council's agenda for that whole time).

disputes under the Comprehensive Test Ban Treaty, the Treaty of Pelindaba, or the Treaty of Tlatelolco, as discussed later in this chapter.[156] Under UN Charter Article 103 and the ICJ's confirmation of its validity in the *Lockerbie* case, the Security Council has the ability to essentially trump treaty rights and obligations through its Chapter VII decisions,[157] which involves the suspension of these treaty rights and obligations, instead of their modification or removal, as explained in Chapter 3.1 above. In the *Lockerbie* case, Libya brought a claim in the ICJ for, inter alia, the ICJ to declare Libya in full compliance with its obligations, under Article 5 of the 1971 Montreal Convention, either to try or to extradite two Libyan nationals who allegedly were responsible for the bombing of Pan Am Flight 103 over Lockerbie, Scotland, and sought provisional measures including an injunction against the United Kingdom and the United States in forcing Libya to surrender the suspects.[158] Meanwhile, the Security Council had adopted several resolutions under its Chapter VII powers essentially suspending the "try or extradite" option of the Montreal Convention by requiring Libya to surrender the two suspects.[159] The ICJ relied heavily on these resolutions and on UN Charter Article 103 in dismissing Libya's request for provisional measures.[160] However, at the preliminary-objections stage of the proceedings, the ICJ refused to dismiss the application for want of

[156] See generally Derek Bowett, *The Impact of Security Council Decisions on Dispute Settlement Procedures*, 5 EUR. J. INT'L L. 89 (1994).

[157] UN Charter, Art. 103 ("In the event of a conflict between the obligations of the Members of the United Nations under the present Charter and their obligations under any other international agreement, their obligations under the present Charter shall prevail"); *Questions of Interpretation and Application of the 1971 Montreal Convention arising from the Aerial Incident at Lockerbie (Libya v. US)*, Order on Provisional Measures, 1992 ICJ Rep. 114, 126–127 (Order of April 14). See also Charles Cadoux, *La supériorité du droit des Nations Unies sur le droit des États membres*, 63 REVUE GÉNÉRAL DE DROIT INTERNATIONAL PUBLIC 649 (1959); Ronald St. John Macdonald, *The Charter of the United Nations and the Development of Fundamental Principles of International Law*, in CONTEMPORARY PROBLEMS OF INTERNATIONAL LAW: ESSAYS IN HONOUR OF GEORG SCHWARZENBERGER 196 (BIN CHENG and E. D. BROWN ed., 1988).

[158] See *Questions of Interpretation and Application of the 1971 Montreal Convention arising from the Aerial Incident at Lockerbie (Libya v. US)*, Order on Provisional Measures, 1992 ICJ Rep. 114, 117–118 (April 14).

[159] S.C. Res. 731, UN Doc. S/RES/731 (Jan. 21, 1992); S.C. Res. 748, UN Doc. S/RES/748 (March 31, 1992); S.C. Res. 833, UN Doc. S/RES/833 (Nov. 11, 1993).

[160] See *Questions of Interpretation and Application of the 1971 Montreal Convention arising from the Aerial Incident at Lockerbie (Libya v. US)*, Order on Provisional Measures, 1992 ICJ Rep. 114, 126–127 (April 14).

jurisdiction when the United Kingdom and the United States argued that these Chapter VII resolutions had removed the ICJ's jurisdiction, with the ICJ determining that if it "had jurisdiction on [the date that Libya filed its application], it continues to do so; the subsequent coming into existence of the above-mentioned resolutions cannot affect its jurisdiction once established."[161] Likewise, the ICJ refused to dismiss the application on inadmissibility claims by the United Kingdom and the United States that these Security Council resolutions closed off the relief Libya sought from the Montreal Convention, because "[t]he date . . . on which Libya filed its Application, is in fact the only relevant date for determining the admissibility of the Application."[162]

While the *Lockerbie* case confirms the validity of UN Charter Article 103 in allowing Security Council resolutions to trump conflicting treaty obligations, it nonetheless creates a significant caveat by refusing the Security Council the power to strip a court or tribunal of its jurisdiction over a dispute once it has been established or to render inadmissible an application that was admissible on the date the claimant filed the application. This caveat applies directly to the case of legal resolution of nuclear non-proliferation disputes. In other words, as long as a State invokes the arbitration clause in the IAEA safeguards agreement or the compromissory clause in the IAEA Statute before the Security Council acts to strip these provisions of their validity, the ICJ or international arbitral tribunal will continue to have jurisdiction over the dispute. Similarly, if the claims were admissible on the date the claimant filed the application, Security Council resolutions cannot change that, although the Security Council certainly can act without regard to any legal proceedings that might be happening, if it so chooses.

161 *Questions of Interpretation and Application of the 1971 Montreal Convention Arising from the Aerial Incident at Lockerbie (Libya v. UK)*, Preliminary Objections, 1998 ICJ Rep. 9, 23–24 (Feb. 27) (citing Nottebohm, Preliminary Objection, Judgment, 1953 ICJ Rep. 111, 122 (Nov. 18); *Right of Passage over Indian Territory (Portugal v. India)*, Preliminary Objections, Judgment, 1957 ICJ Rep.125, 142 (Nov. 26)); *Questions of Interpretation and Application of the 1971 Montreal Convention arising from the Aerial Incident at Lockerbie (Libya v. US)*, Preliminary Objections, 1998 ICJ Rep. 115, 128–129 (Feb. 27) (same).

162 *Questions of Interpretation and Application of the 1971 Montreal Convention Arising from the Aerial Incident at Lockerbie (Libya v. UK)*, Preliminary Objections, 1998 ICJ Rep. 9, 25–26 (Feb. 27); *Questions of Interpretation and Application of the 1971 Montreal Convention arising from the Aerial Incident at Lockerbie (Libya v. US)*, Preliminary Objections, 1998 ICJ Rep. 115, 130–131 (Feb. 27).

Having clarified the contours of the exception, this part of the book continues on to discuss the arbitration clauses in other safeguards agreements that derogate from the standard language quoted above, most of which do not contain the broad exception discussed here.

5.2.3.2.2 Variations on the standard language Most of the derogations from the standard language come when there are multiple States entering a safeguards agreement with the IAEA, where the number of arbitrators increases to five and the number for a quorum and for decisions increases to three. This is observed in the agreements between two multilateral groups, making up a total of nineteen States.[163]

The safeguards agreements of the five other States that have atypical agreements with the IAEA are more significant in their deviations. The India–IAEA Safeguards Agreement has four changes from the standard language provided above:

- it leaves out "except a dispute with regard to a finding by the Board under Article 19 or an action taken by the Board pursuant to such a finding";
- it replaces "at the request of either" with "on the request of either India or the Agency";
- it replaces "either ____ or the Agency may request the President of the International Court of Justice to appoint an arbitrator" with "the other party may request the President of the International Court of Justice to appoint such an arbitrator"; and
- it replaces the ending "The decisions of the tribunal shall be binding on ____ and the Agency" with "The decisions of the tribunal, including all rulings concerning its constitution, procedure, jurisdiction and the division of the expenses of arbitration between India and the Agency shall be binding on India and the Agency. The remuneration

[163] See IAEA, Agreement of 13 December 1991 between the Republic of Argentina, the Federative Republic of Brazil, the Brazilian–Argentine Agency for Accounting and Control of Nuclear Materials and the International Atomic Energy Agency for the Application of Safeguards, Art. 22, IAEA Doc. INFCIRC/435 (March 1994); IAEA, Agreement between the Kingdom of Belgium, the Kingdom of Denmark, the Federal Republic of Germany, Ireland, the Italian Republic, the Grand Duchy of Luxembourg, the Kingdom of the Netherlands, the European Atomic Energy Community and the International Atomic Energy Agency in Implementation of Article III (1) and (4) of the Treaty on the Non-proliferation of Nuclear Weapons, Art. 22, IAEA Doc. INFCIRC/193 (Sept. 14, 1973) (later adding Austria, Finland, Greece, Portugal, Spain, Sweden, Poland, Slovenia, and Slovakia).

of the arbitrators shall be determined on the same basis as that for ad hoc judges of the International Court of Justice."[164]

The first change listed here avoids the entire dilemma concerning the meaning of the exception discussed above. Interestingly, all of the safeguards agreements that contain dispute settlement provisions different from the standard text, except the USSR–IAEA Safeguards Agreement, contain this derogation from the standard language. The second change has no real significance. The third change is more restrictive because only the other can request an appointment of an arbitrator by the International Court of Justice (ICJ) president. The fourth change is more specific to meet India's specific security needs. Not surprisingly, Pakistan's agreement with the IAEA exhibited the exact same changes, *mutatis mutandis*.[165] These agreements between India and the IAEA, and Pakistan and the IAEA, reflect the language contained in the 1973 UK Agreement with the IAEA, which had all of the same changes except the last, instead replacing the last sentence with the following:

> Upon application by either Party, and if necessary to ensure that this Agreement continues to function effectively, the arbitral tribunal shall be empowered to decide upon interim measures pending a final decision on the dispute. All decisions of the tribunal, including rulings concerning its constitution, procedure, jurisdiction and the division of the expenses of arbitration between the Parties, shall be binding on both Parties. The remuneration of the arbitrators shall be determined on the same basis as that of ad hoc judges of the International Court of Justice.[166]

The USSR–IAEA Safeguards Agreement contains three deviations from the Model Agreement:

[164] IAEA, Agreement with the Government of India for the Application of Safeguards to All Nuclear Material Subject to Agency Safeguards under INFCIRC/154, Part 1 and under the Agreements between India and the IAEA Contained in Exchanges of Letters dated 1 October and 1 December 1993, Arts. 25–27, IAEA Doc. INFCIRC/433 (May 1994); IAEA, Agreement of 27 September 1988 between the IAEA and the Government of India for the Application of Safeguards in Connection with the Supply of a Nuclear Power Station from the Union of Soviet Socialist Republics, Art. 27, IAEA Doc. INFCIRC/360 (Jan. 1989).

[165] See IAEA, Agreement of 24 February 1993 between the International Atomic Energy Agency and the Government of the Islamic Republic of Pakistan for the Application of Safeguards in Connection with the Supply of a Nuclear Power Station from the People's Republic of China, Art. 27, IAEA Doc. INFCIRC/418 (March 1993).

[166] IAEA, Agreement between the Agency and the United Kingdom for the Application of Safeguards, Art. 20, IAEA Doc. INFCIRC/175 (Feb. 6, 1973).

- it takes out the following: "If, within thirty days of the request for arbitration, either ____ or the Agency has not designated an arbitrator, either ____ or the Agency may request the President of the International Court of Justice to appoint an arbitrator. The same procedure shall apply if, within thirty days of the designation or appointment of the second arbitrator, the third arbitrator has not been elected";
- it changes the end of the first sentence to "shall be settled by negotiation or other procedures agreed to by the Soviet Union and the Agency," instead of "which is not settled by negotiation or another procedure agreed to by ____ and the Agency shall . . ."; and
- it adds a full stop to emphasize the strong preference for negotiation and methods expressly agreed to by the USSR, and then goes on to say, "Where the parties agree to submit such dispute to an arbitral tribunal, it shall be composed as follows" instead of "shall, at the request of either, be submitted to an arbitral tribunal composed as follows."[167]

China's current agreement with the IAEA exhibited the exact same changes as that of the USSR, *mutatis mutandis*.[168] However, the safeguards agreement between the Republic of China and the IAEA in 1969 was more like those of India and Pakistan, in that it:

- leaves out "except a dispute with regard to a finding by the Board under Article 19 or an action taken by the Board pursuant to such a finding";
- replaces "at the request of either" with "on the request of either Party"; and
- replaces the last sentence with the following: "The decisions of the tribunal, including all rulings concerning its constitution, procedure, jurisdiction and the division of the expenses of arbitration between the Parties, shall be binding on both Parties. The remuneration of the arbitrators shall be determined on the same basis as that of ad hoc judges of the International Court of Justice."[169]

[167] IAEA, Agreement of 21 February 1985 between the Union of Soviet Socialist Republics and the Agency for the Application of Safeguards in the Union of the Soviet Socialist Republics, Art. 21, IAEA Doc. INFCIRC/327 (July 1985).

[168] See IAEA, Agreement of 20 September 1988 between the People's Republic of China and the International Atomic Energy Agency for the Application of Safeguards in China, Art. 21, IAEA Doc. INFCIRC/369 (Oct. 1989).

[169] IAEA, Text of the Safeguards Agreement between the Agency and the Republic of China, pt. VIII, § 22, IAEA Doc. INFCIRC/133 (Oct. 30, 1969).

It is important to note how this safeguards agreement did not state that only the other party could request that the ICJ president appoint an arbitrator, as both the Indian and Pakistani safeguards agreements specify. As the 1969 Chinese safeguards agreement pre-dates those of India and Pakistan by over twenty years and the UK agreement by four years, the influence of the 1969 Chinese safeguards agreement is reasonably clear.

Finally, the text of a unique, trilateral agreement between the United States, China, and the IAEA is provided here for the sake of completeness:

> Section 29 – Any dispute arising out of the interpretation or application of this Agreement which is not settled by negotiation or as may otherwise be agreed by the Parties concerned shall on the request of any Party be submitted to an arbitral tribunal composed as follows:
>
> (a) If the dispute involves only two of the Parties to this Agreement, all three Parties agreeing that the third is not concerned, the two Parties involved shall each designate one arbitrator, and the two arbitrators so designated shall elect a third, who shall be the Chairman. If within thirty days of the request for arbitration either party has not designated an arbitrator, either party to the dispute may request the President of the International Court of Justice to appoint an arbitrator. The same procedure shall apply if, within thirty days of the designation or appointment of the second arbitrator, the third arbitrator has not been elected; or
>
> (b) If the dispute involves all three Parties to this Agreement, each Party shall designate one arbitrator, and the three arbitrators so designated shall by unanimous decision elect a fourth arbitrator, who shall be the Chairman and a fifth arbitrator. If within thirty days of the request for arbitration any Party has not designated an arbitrator, any Party may request the President of the International Court of Justice to appoint the necessary number of arbitrators. The same procedure shall apply if, within thirty days of the designation or appointment of the third of the first three arbitrators, the Chairman or the fifth arbitrator has not been elected.[170]

The form of this provision is noticeably different from the others. Nonetheless, its content is largely the same. The analysis provided above of dispute settlement provisions in IAEA safeguards agreements

[170] IAEA, Text of a Safeguards Transfer Agreement Relating to a Bilateral Agreement between the Republic of China and the United States of America, sec. 29, IAEA Doc. INFCIRC/158 (March 8, 1972).

shows how deeply entrenched international arbitration is within the nuclear non-proliferation regime, at least in theory.

5.2.3.2.3 Genuine arbitration clauses Before concluding this subsection, it is important to note that all of the clauses analyzed above were designed in such a way that no *compromis* was required between the parties to a dispute for an international arbitral tribunal to be established and to eventually reach a decision.[171] Indeed, these arbitration clauses provide a considerable amount of detail as to how the international arbitral tribunal is to look and operate. Moreover, the parties to a dispute need not even agree that there is a dispute between them for an arbitration to be initiated,[172] since all of the safeguards agreements analyzed above, except the USSR–IAEA and the current China–IAEA agreements, allow *either* party to resort to arbitration for most disputes arising out of the safeguards agreement. This unilateral ability to initiate arbitration is a characteristic of a genuine arbitration clause.

As a brief aside, one commentator asserts that arbitration in the North Korea case did not happen in 1993 because the IAEA did not want it to happen.[173] However, that commentator appears to overlook the fact that the arbitration clause in that safeguards agreement (Article 22) allows *either* the State or the IAEA to initiate arbitration.[174] Admittedly, it is possible that one side to a dispute will not elect for arbitration even if they have the right to choose arbitration, perhaps based on considerations of comity or reciprocity, among other things.[175] Moreover, it is possible that one side to a dispute is pragmatic in deciding not to invoke its right to arbitration under the safeguards agreement, sensing that it would be too difficult for an arbitration to take place if the other party to the dispute were not willing to meet its obligations by appointing its arbitrator(s).[176] However, these considerations do not diminish both parties' rights to submit a dispute to arbitration, even if there are significant barriers to implementing those rights.

[171] See SZASZ, *supra* note 108, at 938–942. [172] See ibid., at 939.

[173] See Nazario, *supra* note 98, at 150.

[174] See IAEA, Agreement of 30 January 1992 between the Government of the Democratic People's Republic of Korea and the International Atomic Energy Agency for the Application of Safeguards in Connection with the Treaty on the Non-proliferation of Nuclear Weapons, Art. 22, IAEA Doc. INFCIRC/403 (May 1992).

[175] See Gray and Kingsbury, *supra* note 103, at 101; Myjer, *supra* note 103, at 112; Hans von Mangoldt, *Arbitration and Conciliation Treaties*, in 1 ENCYCLOPEDIA OF PUBLIC INTERNATIONAL LAW 230, 233 (RUDOLF BERNHARDT ed., 1992).

[176] See Wühler, *supra* note 132, at 35.

5.2.3.3 Convention on the Physical Protection of Nuclear Material

As explained in Chapter 2.1.1 above, this study focuses on the NPT, IAEA Statute, and IAEA safeguards agreements as the core of the nuclear non-proliferation regime. However, if one were to take a broader approach to nuclear non-proliferation agreements, the Convention on the Physical Protection of Nuclear Material, otherwise known as the Nuclear Materials Convention, also could be included in this review of nuclear non-proliferation agreements that contain a compromissory clause that gives jurisdiction to the ICJ or an international arbitral tribunal. This convention entered into force in 1987 and was designed to protect all types of nuclear material from illegal taking and use without interfering with States' rights to develop peaceful nuclear energy.[177] Article 17(2) of the Nuclear Materials Convention provides the arbitration clause for this multilateral treaty:

> Any dispute of this character which cannot be settled in the manner prescribed in paragraph 1 shall, at the request of any party to such dispute, be submitted to arbitration or referred to the International Court of Justice for decision. Where a dispute is submitted to arbitration, if, within six months from the date of the request, the parties to the dispute are unable to agree on the organization of the arbitration, a party may request the President of the International Court of Justice or the Secretary-General of the United Nations to appoint one or more arbitrators. In case of conflicting requests by the parties to the dispute, the request to the Secretary-General of the United Nations shall have priority.[178]

This provision of the Nuclear Materials Convention provides an equally clear arbitration clause as those contained in the IAEA safeguards agreements discussed in the preceeding subsection, perhaps even more so, given that it does not have the broad exception that the standard text of the arbitration clause in the IAEA safeguards agreements contains.

The IAEA safeguards agreements and the Nuclear Materials Convention contain express arbitration clauses that reflect member States' consent to arbitration before any disputes even have arisen.

[177] See Convention on the Physical Protection of Nuclear Material, preamble, Arts. 1–4, March 3, 1980, 1456 U.N.T.S. 101 (entered into force Feb. 8, 1987) (hereinafter Nuclear Material Convention).

[178] Ibid., Art. 17(2). For reference, paragraph 1 of Article 17 requires States with a dispute to try settling it through negotiation or another peaceful means they agree to. See ibid. Art. 17(1).

Therefore, these agreements can be considered as arbitration treaties,[179] even though their main function is not to provide for arbitration. This arrangement is interesting for two reasons. First, the arrangement is somewhat surprising given that States have been seen as agreeing to arbitration, if they agree at all, through special agreements entered into *after* a dispute has arisen.[180] Second, the existence of binding arbitration agreements in these treaties undermines the general notion that such agreements do not provide for compulsory arbitration, or for any binding form of legal resolution, for that matter.

There were 134 parties and forty-five signatories to this Convention.[181] For twenty-two of those States parties, Article 17(2) does not apply on account of reservations that were made in accordance with Article 17(3).[182] South Africa, which is not a State party yet is a signatory, has made a similar reservation.[183] El Salvador, France, and EURATOM – the sole non-State party to the Convention – entered reservations that stated that they would not be bound by the portion of Article 17(2) that deals with the International Court of Justice, with France going a step further in refusing to allow the president of the International Court of Justice to appoint an arbitrator.[184] However, this limited type of declaration does not affect the applicability of Article 17(2) as it relates to international arbitration itself. Therefore, that leaves 105 parties subject to the arbitration provision of Article 17(2).

[179] See von Mangoldt, *supra* note 175, at 230 (defining arbitration treaties as "international agreements concluded between subjects of international law in written form in order to serve the peaceful settlement of disputes through the establishment of rules . . . for a binding third-party decision by judges of the parties' own choice" that "either stipulate compulsory settlement of future disputes or institute third party jurisdiction for a given case").

[180] See, e.g., Gray and Kingsbury, *supra* note 103, at 133 (citing the Stockholm Convention on Conciliation and Arbitration within the CSCE (Stockholm, Dec. 15, 1992) available at http://www.ena.lu).

[181] See generally IAEA, *Convention on the Physical Protection of Nuclear Material, Latest Status*, IAEA Registration No. 1533, available at http://www.iaea.org/Publications/Documents/Conventions/cppnm_status.pdf (providing a summary table of all those states that have become parties to this convention).

[182] See Nuclear Material Convention, *supra* note 177, Art. 17(3); *Convention on the Physical Protection of Nuclear Material, Reservations*, IAEA Registration No. 1533 (July 6, 2007), available at http://www.iaea.org/Publications/Documents/Conventions/cppnm_reserv.pdf (hereinafter Nuclear Material Convention Reservations).

[183] See Nuclear Material Convention Reservations, *supra* note 182, at 12.

[184] See ibid., at 2–4.

While it is tempting to conclude that the forty-five signatories also are subject to this dispute settlement provision, one must note that, under Article 18(1) of the Vienna Convention on the Law of Treaties, signatories are "obliged to refrain from acts which would defeat the object and purpose of [the] treaty."[185] The question then becomes, what is the object and purpose of this treaty? As with most treaties, the Nuclear Materials Convention is silent as to its exact object and purpose. Certainly the object and purpose of the treaty cannot be the treaty itself, or else it would make the ratification process unnecessary. Indeed, while signature makes the State eligible to enter the ratification process, signature ought not to be considered as ratification in and of itself or as that State's final consent to be bound by that treaty.[186] When trying to determine the object and purpose of this treaty, it is useful to consider two of the main approaches provided in the literature in determining a treaty's object and purpose. The ILC Special Rapporteur on Reservations, Alain Pellet, has come up with numerous guidelines for dealing with reservations, one of which (Guideline 3.1.5) defines a treaty's object and purpose as "the essential provisions of the treaty, which constitute its raison d'être."[187] By contrast, Anthony Aust looks more at the results when he asserts that a signatory to a treaty should "not do anything which would affect its ability fully to comply with the treaty once it has entered into force."[188] The following paragraphs analyze the relevant case law in helping to determine whether dispute settlement provisions form part of a treaty's object and purpose.

No ICJ cases or international arbitrations appear to have answered whether a dispute settlement provision forms part of the object and purpose of the treaty containing it. A few cases come close, but they are not directly on point. In the 2004 *Legality of Use of Force* cases brought by Serbia and Montenegro against various NATO members for their use of force against the former Yugoslavia in the 1990s, Serbia and Montenegro sought to gain access to the Court based on ICJ Statute Article 35(2), which states, "The conditions under which the Court shall be open to other states shall, subject to the special provisions contained in treaties in force, be laid down by the Security Council, but in no case

[185] VCLT, Art. 18(1). [186] See Brownlie, *supra* note 64, at 582.

[187] See *Report of the International Law Commission on Its Fifty-Seventh Session* (May 2–June 3 and July 11–Aug. 5, 2005), UN GAOR, 60th Sess., Supp. No. 10, ¶ 89, UN Doc. A/CN.4/558/Add.1.

[188] Anthony Aust, Modern Treaty Law and Practice 94 (2000).

shall such conditions place the parties in a position of inequality before the Court."[189] When interpreting the phrase "treaties in force" to decide whether it was limited to treaties that already had entered into force at the point when the ICJ Statute entered into force or whether to allow later treaties to give the Court jurisdiction, the Court asked whether allowing later treaties would interfere with the object and purpose of Article 35(2),[190] not whether Article 35 formed part of the object and purpose of the ICJ Statute as a whole. Therefore, this case is not directly on point with the question at hand, nor does it help clarify how to determine a provision's object and purpose.[191]

Similarly, in the 2006 *Armed Activities on the Territory of the Congo* decision on jurisdiction and admissibility, an issue arose over Rwanda's reservation to the dispute settlement provision of the International Convention on the Elimination of All Forms of Racial Discrimination, which was the basis for jurisdiction of the DRC's claim.[192] The reservation that Rwanda provided at the time of its accession to the Convention read: "The Rwandese Republic does not consider itself as bound by article 22 of the Convention."[193] Although Rwanda showed in its Fundamental Law a willingness to "withdraw all reservations entered by Rwanda when it adhered to . . . international instruments" concerning human rights, the Court noted that Rwanda had taken no steps to withdraw its reservation in the method provided for in Article 20(3) of the Convention on Racial Discrimination, and so Rwanda "maintained that reservation."[194] As an alternative, the DRC tried to circumvent this reservation by pointing to Article 20(2) of the Convention on Racial Discrimination, which prohibits reservations that are "incompatible with the object and purpose of this Convention," with incompatibility being determined based on at least two-thirds of the member States objecting to the reservation.[195] In essence, the DRC was asking the Court whether the dispute settlement provision was part of the object and purpose of the convention, since the reservation would entirely have

[189] *Legality of Use of Force (Serbia and Montenegro v. UK)*, Preliminary Objections, 2004 ICJ Rep. 1307, 1341–1351 (Dec. 15).

[190] Ibid., at 1345–1346.

[191] Ibid., at 1346 (referring to the provision's "main thrust" without saying how it determined it).

[192] See generally *Case Concerning Armed Activities on the Territory of the Congo* (New Application: 2002) *(DRC v. Rwanda)*, Jurisdiction and Admissibility, 2006 ICJ Rep. 6 (Feb. 3).

[193] See ibid., at 34. [194] See ibid., at 34–35. [195] See ibid., at 33–35.

exempted the reserving State from the dispute settlement provision of the Convention. However, the ICJ relied on the portion of Article 20(2) that said a provision was incompatible if at least two-thirds of the member States objected to the provision, thus leaving entirely in the hands of the member States the determination of what constitutes the object and purpose of the convention.[196] The Court observed that neither two-thirds of the member States nor the DRC had objected to the reservation.[197] The Court also considered the DRC's argument for rejecting the reservation based on its conflicting with a peremptory norm, but the Court ultimately rejected that argument on the following grounds:

> the fact that a dispute concerns non-compliance with a peremptory norm of general international law cannot suffice to found the Court's jurisdiction to entertain such a dispute, and there exists no peremptory norm requiring States to consent to such jurisdiction in order to settle disputes relating to the Convention on Racial Discrimination.[198]

The Court concluded from these points that Article 22 was not an appropriate basis for finding jurisdiction.[199]

Despite the absence of useful ICJ cases and international arbitrations, the 1995 *Loizidou v. Turkey* decision on preliminary objections of the European Court of Human Rights proves to be useful in answering this question.[200] There, a Cypriot national brought a case against Turkey for refusing her access to her property in northern Cyprus, and Turkey cited as part of its preliminary objections to the case territorial restrictions it included in its declarations to the Court's jurisdiction.[201] In essence, the issue was whether Turkey's territorial restrictions of the Court's jurisdiction violated the object and purpose of the European Convention on Human Rights, thereby rendering ineffective those restrictions.[202] The Court concluded,

> Such a system, which would enable States to qualify their consent under the optional clauses, would not only seriously weaken the role of the Commission and Court in the discharge of their functions but would also diminish the effectiveness of the Convention as a constitutional instrument of European public order ("ordre public").[203]

[196] See ibid., at 35. [197] See ibid., at 34–35. [198] Ibid., at 35. [199] See ibid.
[200] See generally *Loizidou v. Turkey*, Preliminary Objections, 310 Eur. Ct. H.R. (ser. A).
[201] See ibid. ¶¶ 1, 14, 15. [202] See ibid., ¶¶ 65–89. [203] See ibid., ¶ 75.

In short, the Court considered the Convention's provisions dealing with the Court's jurisdiction to be sufficiently related to the Convention's object and purpose to refuse to allow member States to declare such restrictions.

Although the Human Rights Committee is not a court or tribunal per se, its 1994 General Comment Number 24 on the validity of member States' reservations to the International Covenant on Civil and Political Rights or its Optional Protocols is relevant to this discussion, inasmuch as it provides perhaps the clearest guide to determining the object and purpose of a treaty.[204] In paragraph 7, the Human Rights Committee identifies the object and purpose of the International Covenant on Civil and Political Rights:

> In an instrument which articulates very many civil and political rights, each of the many articles, and indeed their interplay, secures the objectives of the Covenant. The object and purpose of the Covenant is to create legally binding standards for human rights by defining certain civil and political rights and placing them in a framework of obligations which are legally binding for those States which ratify; and to provide an efficacious supervisory machinery for the obligations undertaken.[205]

The Covenant does not contain a dispute settlement provision in the sense that it gives jurisdiction to the ICJ or an international arbitral tribunal to resolve disputes or otherwise interpret or apply the Covenant for the member States.[206] Instead, Part IV of the International Covenant on Civil and Political Rights creates the Human Rights Committee as a type of supervisory mechanism, with Article 40 envisioning the Committee as gathering reports from member States on the "measures

[204] See generally UN Human Rights Committee, General Comment No. 24 (52), UN Doc. CCPR/C/21/Rev. 1/Add.6 (1994).

[205] See generally ibid., ¶ 7.

[206] It is important to note that the Covenant does not preclude the ICJ or international arbitral tribunals from getting involved. Therefore, the ICJ or an international arbitral tribunal could get involved just as the ICJ got involved with the recent dispute between Georgia and the Russian Federation over the application of the International Convention on the Elimination of All Forms of Racial Discrimination to alleged Russian attacks against ethnic Georgians in South Ossetia and Abkhazia. See generally *Application of the International Convention on the Elimination of All Forms of Racial Discrimination (Georgia v. Russian Federation)*, Preliminary Objections, General List No. 140, April 1, 2011. Interestingly, the International Convention on the Elimination of All Forms of Racial Discrimination, like the International Covenant on Civil and Political Rights, creates a committee. See International Convention on the Elimination of All Forms of Racial Discrimination, Art. 8, March 7, 1966, 660 U.N.T.S. 195.

they have adopted which give effect to the rights recognized" in the Covenant, studying these reports, and transmitting general comments "as it may consider appropriate" and the reports to member States.[207] Article 41 creates the mechanism for the Committee to "receive and consider communications to the effect that a State Party claims that another State Party is not fulfilling its obligations under the present Covenant," which resembles a dispute settlement provision.[208] The block quote above clearly shows how the Human Rights Committee considered this supervisory mechanism as forming part of the object and purpose of this Covenant. The Committee explained in paragraph 11,

> The Covenant consists not just of the specified rights, but of important supportive guarantees. These guarantees provide the necessary framework for securing the rights in the Covenant and are thus essential to its object and purpose. Some operate at the national level and some at the international level. Reservations designed to remove these guarantees are thus not acceptable.[209]

The Committee went on in that paragraph to recognize the Committee's monitoring role as being "for the better attainment of its stated objectives" and that "[r]eservations that purport to evade that essential element in the design of the Covenant, which is also directed to securing the enjoyment of the rights, are also incompatible with its object and purpose."[210] The Committee concluded paragraph 11 by asserting that "a reservation that rejects the Committee's competence to interpret the requirements of any provisions of the Covenant would also be contrary to the object and purpose of that treaty."[211]

Inasmuch as the dispute settlement provisions of the Nuclear Materials Convention – as well as the other nuclear non-proliferation agreements discussed in Chapter 5.2 above – are important in making the substantive obligations in those agreements effective, it seems logical to include such dispute settlement provisions as part of the object and purpose, at least under the logic adopted by the European Court of Human Rights in *Loizidou v. Turkey* and the Human Rights

[207] See International Covenant on Civil and Political Rights, pt. IV, G.A. Res. 2200A, 21 U. N. GAOR Supp. (No. 16), UN Doc. A/6316 (1966) (entered into force March 23, 1976).
[208] Ibid., Art. 41.
[209] See generally UN Human Rights Committee, General Comment No. 24 (52), UN Doc. CCPR/C/21/Rev. 1/Add.6 (1994), ¶ 11.
[210] See generally ibid., ¶ 11. [211] See generally ibid.

Committee in its General Comment Number 24. Again, no ICJ cases or international arbitrations appear to have applied this logic in determining whether dispute settlement provisions form part of an agreement's object and purpose, and so there arguably is room for equivocation. Nevertheless, under the logic provided above, the forty-five signatories to the Nuclear Materials Convention likely will be bound to the dispute settlement provisions, in addition to the other provisions that form the object and purpose of the Nuclear Materials Convention.

In conclusion, jurisdiction through compromissory clauses provides the greatest promise when it comes to resolving nuclear non-proliferation disputes, inasmuch as there are a considerable number of them in nuclear non-proliferation agreements. Moreover, these forms of consent to jurisdiction are particularly convenient in that any recalcitrance of a disputant becomes irrelevant on account of the fact that all States parties to the treaty already have provided their consent to jurisdiction prior to the realization of the dispute. Therefore, there is no need for any agreement on the dispute settlement mechanism or the composition of the panel, assuming the States parties designated the ICJ or international arbitration in the compromissory clause and that the compromissory clause provided these details. The fewer the details in the compromissory clause, the greater the chance a recalcitrant State will find a way to frustrate the adjudicative process. This point turns out to be academic because all of the compromissory clauses in the nuclear non-proliferation context provide ample details to get the process on its way with minimal delay.

As explained in the following section, consent to jurisdiction through a *compromis* or prorogated jurisdiction remains a possibility, although one that many would see as highly unlikely on account of the fact that agreement between the disputants is necessary. Many dispute settlement provisions in nuclear non-proliferation agreements refer to the ability of disputants to involve international arbitration or the ICJ in this manner, although this option always exists even without these dispute settlement provisions, and inclusion in the dispute settlement provision does nothing to limit the disputants' options when negotiating this *compromis*. Therefore, these dispute settlement provisions are given minimal emphasis in this study. Instead, the study emphasizes the factors that these disputants might want to consider when deciding whether to consent to the ICJ's or an international arbitral tribunal's jurisdiction. Each State's calculus in deciding whether to provide their consent will be different, and it falls far outside the limited scope of this study to speculate as to the weight each State might give each factor. Nevertheless, this study's exploration of the factors that States might consider is a helpful guide when making those calculations, inasmuch as some of the advantages of legal resolution might seem counterintuitive on their face. At a minimum, they should help States and the international community start to think about these issues in a serious manner.

5.3 Advantages and disadvantages of legal resolution

The preceding section showed how the ICJ and international arbitral tribunals can gain jurisdiction through compromissory clauses in various nuclear non-proliferation agreements. Jurisdiction through these compromissory clauses provides the greatest promise for legal resolution when it comes to resolving nuclear non-proliferation disputes, inasmuch as there are several within the nuclear non-proliferation context and they remove the need to get the consent of a recalcitrant State before the legal proceedings can commence, especially when they have sufficient details, as these do. The importance of these compromissory clauses for the proposition of greater involvement of legal resolution of nuclear non-proliferation disputes was seen as so significant as to warrant putting that analysis first in this chapter. After all, as some commentators have noted, where the Court or an international arbitral tribunal finds jurisdiction through a compromissory clause or *compromis*, this typically satisfies the forum that it can hear and decide the dispute.[212]

It must be recognized, however, that whether a disputant actually decides to give effect to these compromissory clauses depends on their calculations on whether invocation of these clauses serves their interests. Similarly, consent to jurisdiction through a *compromis* or prorogated jurisdiction remains a possibility for these fora to gain jurisdiction over nuclear non-proliferation disputes, although again whether disputants elect to pursue this option is based on their calculations of interest. Yet again, whether the international community elects to request an advisory opinion from the ICJ or establishes an adjudicative body through an international organization to decide a nuclear non-proliferation dispute depends on their calculations of interest. After all, UN Charter Articles 2(3) and 33 give States ample flexibility in choosing their preferred

[212] See Joyner, *supra* note 40, at 202, 223.

peaceful means of resolution, without any particular priority among the various means of resolution.[213] Some commentators talk about UN Charter Article 36(3) creating a "general rule" that legal disputes should be referred to the ICJ.[214] However, this would appear to be a minority view,[215] especially in light of the *Corfu Channel* ICJ case, which appears to be the only time the ICJ has relied on Article 36(3), where the ICJ interpreted Article 36(3) as supporting the point that the ICJ has jurisdiction over disputes *only* when the disputants have expressly agreed to its jurisdiction.[216] In the end, the perceived advantages and disadvantages of legal resolution are crucial to assessing its viability with nuclear non-proliferation disputes.

To be clear, this section would be remiss if it failed to point out that legal resolution might have some flaws, an analysis of which gives balance to the advocacy for legal resolution provided elsewhere in this study. Despite these advantages and disadvantages, each State's calculus in deciding whether to provide their consent to legal resolution of nuclear non-proliferation disputes will be different, and it falls far outside the limited scope of this study to speculate as to the weight each State might give each factor.

At this point, it is tempting to list the various advantages commentators have seen for legal resolution over a negotiated settlement in general: that legal resolution is dispositive and impersonal; that it allows for passing of responsibility to the court; that it is principled, impartial, orderly, and depoliticizing of disputes; and that it supports the legal system, encourages negotiation, and is relatively slow, which allows

[213] See *Fisheries Jurisdiction (Spain v. Canada)*, Jurisdiction, 1998 ICJ Rep. 436, 456 (Dec. 4). See also Merrills, *supra* note 84, at 2; David D. Caron and Galina Shinkaretskaya, *Peaceful Settlement of Disputes through the Rule of Law*, in Beyond Confrontation: International Law for the Post-Cold War Era 309 (Lori F. Damrosch et al. ed., 1995); Constantine P. Economides, *L'obligation de règlement pacifique des différends internationaux: une norme fondamentale tenue à l'écart*, in Boutros-Boutros Ghali Amicorum Discipulorumque Liber 408 (1998); Bernard H. Oxman, *Complementary Agreements and Compulsory Jurisdiction*, 95 Am. J. Int'l L. 277, 289–290 (2001).

[214] See, e.g., Christian Tomuschat, *Article 33*, in The Charter of the United Nations 583, 583–584 (Bruno Simma ed., 2nd edn, 2002); Dinah Shelton, *Form, Function, and the Powers of International Courts*, 9 Chi. J. Int'l L. 537, 558 (2009).

[215] See, e.g., Torsten Stein, *Article 36*, in The Charter of the United Nations 616, 625–627 (Bruno Simma ed, 2nd edn., 2002) (internal citations omitted).

[216] See *Corfu Channel Case (UK v. Albania)*, Preliminary Objections, 1948 ICJ Rep. 15, 18 (March 25).

disputants to buy time with the hope that tensions ease.[217] The disadvantages of legal resolution vis-à-vis a negotiated settlement would likely include the following: that legal resolution is unpredictable, all-or-nothing, superficial, inflexible, complex, costly, not as impartial as proponents assert, prone to exacerbating tensions, and slow.[218] This study is somewhat different from these earlier studies in that it compares legal resolution with Security Council resolution in the context of nuclear non-proliferation disputes, not legal resolution with negotiated settlement or legal resolution in the abstract. Therefore, this section looks at the factors that seem most relevant with this particular context in mind, as reflected in commentators' remarks on why legal resolution is inappropriate for nuclear non-proliferation disputes. As explained in the introduction to this part of the book, this review includes not only the legal literature on the nuclear non-proliferation regime, but also the legal literature on WMD as well as arms control and disarmament inasmuch as nuclear non-proliferation can be seen as a subset of these broader categories. This approach to the literature, moving out in concentric circles from that specifically on the nuclear non-proliferation regime, is felicitous here inasmuch as commentators in these outer circles tend to provide more reasons for rejecting legal resolution. These reasons presumably are relevant to understanding why the option of legal resolution has been rejected so often with nuclear non-proliferation disputes in particular and to helping anticipate the arguments of critics of this study who might maintain that legal resolution is not a viable option for nuclear non-proliferation disputes.

To begin with, this section notes that some commentators have given rather bizarre reasons for dismissing legal resolution. One commentator gives a somewhat strange reason – that judicial interpretation is problematic with such disputes because it frustrates States' efforts at reinterpreting treaties unilaterally to meet their own needs.[219] This reasoning relates to the point below dealing with the problems associated with

[217] See Bilder, *United States*, *supra* note 69, at 259; Richard B. Bilder, *International Dispute Settlement and the Role of International Adjudication*, in The International Court of Justice at a Crossroads 155, 163–167 (Lori F. Damrosch ed., 1987) (hereinafter Bilder, *Adjudication*); Richard B. Bilder, *International Third Party Dispute Settlement*, 17 Denv. J. Int'l L. & Pol'y 471, 483–486.

[218] See Bilder, *United States*, *supra* note 69, at 257–258 (in the context of discussing whether the United States should aim to give the ICJ a larger or smaller role with international relations).

[219] Dekker, *supra* note 22, at 110.

binding decisions, though it is quite a strange way of framing that issue. Indeed, one would think that frustration with such instrumentalism would be a positive reason to rely on legal resolution, not a negative one against it.[220] Another commentator strangely concluded that the ICJ was "a body of suspect reach" after the US Supreme Court determined in its *Sanchez-Llamas v. Oregon* case "that the ICJ has no *stare decisis* value," thus rendering the ICJ an inappropriate forum for deciding upon breaches of treaties relating to nuclear weapons.[221] It is entirely unclear from that article how these issues are related. Yet another set of commentators dismiss legal resolution based on an interesting, though entirely unconvincing, historical argument for why legal resolution did not have a greater role in resolving nuclear non-proliferation disputes – the focus of the majority of developing States being on other issues, such as decolonization.[222] This argument is unconvincing on account of its oversimplification of the situation in that it ignores even the possibility of States focusing on multiple issues at one time, with issues involving nuclear weapons and the possibility of nuclear war logically demanding some attention from all States, even assuming that other issues may be at the forefront at any given time. In light of the reasoning of these commentators, one might reasonably conclude that it is better that more commentators have not spent more time discussing the possibility of legal resolution of nuclear non-proliferation disputes.

This type of bizarre reasoning aside, the main reasons that commentators provide can be divided into two broad categories: first, problems of the litigation process itself; and second, problems of relying on a method of resolution that involves the application of law. These two broad categories are further divided into specific reasons, which are the focus of the remainder of this section. However, a few considerations

[220] But see PHILIP D. O'NEILL, Jr., NATIONAL SECURITY AND THE LEGAL PROCESS 233 (2008) (referring to US "reinterpretation" efforts of its obligations under Art. 5 of the ABM Treaty).

[221] Liles, *supra* note 105, at 139 (citing *Sanchez-Llamas v. Oregon*, 126 S.Ct. 2669, 2684 (2006)).

[222] See NAGENDRA SINGH and EDWARD MCWHINNEY, NUCLEAR WEAPONS AND CONTEMPORARY INTERNATIONAL LAW 292–293 (2nd rev. edn, 1989) (exploring through the other parts of the six-page chapter what sorts of question a then-future ICJ advisory opinion might be able to address and some of the factors in the *Nuclear Tests* cases in the 1970s).

are not included in this section's analysis. Complaints regarding the dispositive or authoritative nature of legal resolution are not discussed here because Chapter 2.2.2 above has already addressed this when discussing the legal approach that this study adopts on the subject of international dispute settlement.[223] The fact that there is no guarantee that disputants will comply with a decision of the ICJ, or an international arbitral tribunal,[224] is not a basis to exclude the possibility of legal resolution, as some commentators have argued.[225] This is especially true when the alternative is Security Council resolution, where non-compliance is just as real a possibility, if not more so. In addition, complaints about the cost of legal resolution are not discussed here because they seem trivial in light of the costs to the international community of the insecurity that flows from the threat of unmitigated nuclear non-proliferation disputes. Finally, the most significant perceived problem with legal resolution of nuclear non-proliferation disputes – that they are too politically sensitive – is addressed on its own in the following chapter on justiciability.

As Thomas Franck has noted, the Security Council becomes analogous to a court or tribunal "[w]hen it operates in accordance with principles of fairness" and "when it makes decisions based on a consensus among states with no partisan interest."[226] This chapter makes the key point that legal resolution is obliged to act in accordance with the principles of fairness and with no partisan interest, unlike the Security Council, as explained in Chapter 3.2.3.6 above.[227] As Robert Frost's "The Road Not Taken" concludes, this distinction should make "all the difference" in the calculations of States, one way or the other.[228]

[223] See Bilder, *Adjudication*, *supra* note 217, at 163–164.

[224] See Edwin Smith, *Commentary on Arms Control Agreements and Dynamic Obligations*, in Law and Force in the New International Order 262, 263 (Lori F. Damrosch and David J. Scheffer ed., 1991).

[225] See e.g. Dinesh Khosla, *Nuclear Weapons, Global Values and International Law*, in Nuclear Weapons and Law 13, 13 (Arthur Selwyn Miller and Martin Feinrider ed., 1984).

[226] Thomas M. Franck, Fairness in International Law and Institutions 316 (1995).

[227] See ibid. 316–317 (acknowledging these differences between the Security Council and the International Court of Justice).

[228] Robert Frost, *The Road Not Taken*, in The Poetry of Robert Frost 105 (Edward Connery Latham ed., 1969).

5.3.1 *Application of law*

Law is a necessary element to peace and security throughout the world. As Fuller notes, law creates "a sound and stable framework for [subjects'] interactions with one another."[229] As H.J. de Lange asserted in 1912,

> Only law can be the basis of good relations. The law alone can perpetuate good attitudes, prevent or satisfactorily solve disputes. Injustice, violence and anarchy lead to ruin, because there are germs of destruction in anything that is not according to the law.[230]

Director-General of the United Nations Office at Geneva Vladimir Petrovsky put it well when discussing proliferation specifically: "The creation of conditions for non-violent, evolutionary and democratic changes in the world cannot be achieved through political and diplomatic means alone."[231] Petrovsky goes on to say that those means are "most effective when they are based on a legal foundation," thus implying that a foundation in law is what is needed for nonviolent, evolutionary, and democratic changes in the world, notwithstanding any importance one might attribute to politics and diplomacy.[232] As he sees it, "Law creates norms of behaviour and serves also as a common 'language' of communication between different actors of the international scene," especially when it comes to politics.[233] As this subsection explains, basing efforts at the international settlement of nuclear non-proliferation disputes on legal resolution provides these and other benefits.

In essence, legal resolution helps with putting the rule of law over the rule of man,[234] with the former being about decision-making based on the application of law and the latter about arbitrary decision-making based on power politics. To be clear, a distinction needs to be made between decisions that have legal weight (as with Security Council Chapter VII decisions) and the making of decisions through the application of law (as with legal resolution), with the former involving the rule of man and the latter the rule of law. While both are "premised on the

229 See JAN KLABBERS, CONSTITUTIONALISM AND THE MAKING OF INTERNATIONAL LAW n. 84 (2008) (quoting LON L. FULLER, THE MORALITY OF LAW 210 (1969)).

230 H. J. de Lange, *Oorlog en Arbitrage* 2 (Ph.D. thesis, 1912), reprinted and translated in Myjers, *supra* note 103, at 99.

231 Vladimir Petrovsky, *Foreword*, in FUTURE LEGAL RESTRAINTS ON ARMS PROLIFERATION 1, 1 (JULIE DAHLITZ ed., 1996).

232 Ibid. 233 Ibid. 234 See MERRILLS, *supra* note 84, at 317–318.

same kind of quasi-judicial findings and the outcome of both affects the legal position of the states concerned,"[235] only legal resolution is required to apply law in reaching its decisions. This is what the drafters of the PCIJ Statute, such as US and UK diplomats Elihu Root and Lord Phillimore, insisted on with the PCIJ, believing that having judges decide based on what they thought was a good result would not be a good way to run the dispute settlement system.[236] Legal resolution, by definition, involves decision-making through the application of international law, hence the qualifier "legal" before "resolution." ICJ Statute Article 38(1) requires the ICJ to "decide in accordance with international law such disputes as are submitted to it," with custom indicating that the applicable law for international arbitration must be international law,[237] assuming the States do not designate another body of applicable law. What this means is that these courts and tribunals reach their decisions by *finding and applying* the positive rules and principles to which the disputants have consented when reaching a decision that is intended to resolve the dispute.[238] If the decisions of legal resolution are not based on law in the ICJ and international arbitral tribunals, then that certainly can be the basis for criticizing those decisions.[239] Putting aside the formalistic ability to criticize States' behavior that law provides,[240] the application of law in reaching decisions provides a number of benefits that often are associated with a society that is based on the rule of law, such as

[235] Vera Gowlland-Debbas, *The Relationship between the International Court of Justice and the Security Council in the Light of the Lockerbie Case*, 88 Am. J. Int'l L. 643, 661 (1994).

[236] See Mary Ellen O'Connell, International Dispute Resolution 11 (2006).

[237] See *Report of the International Law Commission to the General Assembly*, 13 UN GAOR Supp. (No. 9), UN Doc. A/3859 (1958), reprinted in 2 Y.B. Int'l L. Comm'n 78, 84 (1958), Arts. 8, 10 and 12, UN Doc. A/CN.4/117 (Art. 10 providing that the tribunal is to apply the standard sources of international law in the absence of agreement between the parties as to the applicable law); John Collier and Vaughan Lowe, The Settlement of Disputes in International Law: Institutions and Procedures 33 (1999); Mauro Rubino-Sammartano, International Arbitration Law and Practice 133–44, 157–158 (2nd edn, 2001); Malcolm N. Shaw, International Law 739 n. 143 (4th edn, 1997); Rosalyn Higgins, *The Desirability of Third-Party Adjudication: Conventional Wisdom or Continuing Truth*, in International Organization: Law in Movement 37, 39 (J. E. S. Fawcett and Rosalyn Higgins, 1974).

[238] See Jennings, *supra* note 72, at 92–93.

[239] See Merrills, *supra* note 84, at 330.

[240] See Martti Koskenniemi, *What Is International Law For?*, in International Law (Malcolm Evans ed., 3rd edn, 2010) (discussing the difference between formalism and instrumentalism).

due-process safeguards, an assumption of equality between subjects, predictability, and legitimacy, among others. This subsection explores these benefits often associated with the rule of law and legal resolution.

5.3.1.1 Impartiality of legal resolution

Some commentators classify legal resolution as being inferior because of the supposed partiality of its decision-makers and the resulting subjectivity of their decisions.[241] Such beliefs in legal resolution's partiality in modern times date back to the period just after the Second World War, when the USSR opposed ICJ involvement in the 1950s because of its supposed Western composition and bias.[242] Commentators have applied these same arguments of bias when arguing against legal resolution of nuclear non-proliferation disputes.[243] This section challenges that notion and compares the impartiality of judges and arbitrators with the impartiality of diplomats who operate the Security Council.[244]

Trust between States is an important part of all international relations. It is a fundamental paradox of the international system that States trust attempts at resolution coming from their own nation but do not trust the efforts of other nations, which leads to the importance of resolution on the international level.[245] An important aspect of resolution on the international level is the impartiality of the decision-maker. Impartiality is one of the main characteristics commentators identify as necessary for any intermediary who hopes to be successful in resolving

[241] See e.g. Bilder, *Adjudication*, *supra* note 217, at 167–68; H. W. Briggs, *Confidence, Apprehension and the International Court of Justice*, 54 AM. SOC'Y INT'L L. PROC. 25, 31 (1960); ANDREW MARTIN, LEGAL ASPECTS OF DISARMAMENT 42 (1963); C. M. Dalfen, *The World Court in Idle Splendour: The Basis of State Attitudes*, 23 INT'L J. 124, 135 (1967).

[242] See ALLAN GOTLIEB, DISARMAMENT AND INTERNATIONAL LAW: A STUDY OF THE ROLE OF LAW IN THE DISARMAMENT PROCESS 117 (1965); Owen, *supra* note 78, at 724; Dalfen, *supra* note 241, at 133.

[243] See Burns H. Weston, *Lawyers and the Search for Alternatives to Nuclear Deterrence*, 54 U. CIN. L. REV. 451, 461 (1985); Roger Fisher, *Getting to "Yes" in the Nuclear Age*, in TOWARD NUCLEAR DISARMAMENT AND GLOBAL SECURITY: A SEARCH FOR ALTERNATIVES 358 (B. WESTON ed., 1984).

[244] See Bilder, *Adjudication*, *supra* note 217, at 163; MERRILLS, *supra* note 84 (noting the relative impartiality of judges and arbitrators), at 317; Jeffrey B. Golden, *The World Court: The Qualifications of the Judges*, 14 COLUM. J.L. & SOC. PROBS. 1 (1978). But see Dalfen, *supra* note 241, at 136 (asserting that States fear the impartiality of international courts and tribunals, not their partiality).

[245] See FOREST L. GRIEVES, SUPRANATIONALISM AND INTERNATIONAL ADJUDICATION 17 (1969).

a dispute.[246] Nuclear non-proliferation issues require an added degree of trust between States parties in order for the system to work, because of the added insecurity created by the threat of such dangerous weapons as nuclear weapons,[247] combined with the added fear that States will renege on their nuclear non-proliferation promises.[248] As explained in the following paragraph, the impartiality of legal resolution can buttress that fragile trust.

Law itself is made up of pre-existing rules and principles,[249] and the fact that they are pre-existing means that they do not change (or are not supposed to change) in light of which parties come before the court or tribunal. Legal commentators see the impartiality of such application of existing international legal standards as giving legal resolution a "qualitative leap" over diplomatic methods of resolution,[250] which tends to be somewhat arbitrary and subject to abuse.[251] It is to avoid this type of arbitrariness and abuse that the rule of law was first established, as A.V. Dicey defines the rule of law, to regulate government power and to promote the notion that all are equal before the law, with adjudication playing a key part in protecting the rights of subjects.[252] Legal resolution on the international level can protect States from abuses of bias. The ICJ has emphasized its role in remaining above the arguments of the disputants, insisting that it reaches its own decisions on all

[246] See Sydney D. Bailey, *Peaceful Settlement of International Disputes*, in DISPUTE SETTLEMENT THROUGH THE UNITED NATIONS 73, 100 (K. VENKATA RAMAN ed., 1977); K. Venkata Raman, *Introduction to Part I*, in DISPUTE SETTLEMENT THROUGH THE UNITED NATIONS 53, 57 (K. VENKATA RAMAN ed., 1977).

[247] See Morris Bradley, *Conflict Dynamics and Conflict Resolution*, in THE NUCLEAR MENTALITY: A PSYCHOSOCIAL ANALYSIS OF THE ARMS RACE 49 (LYNN BARNETT and IAN LEE ed., 1989); JACQUES E. C. HYMANS, THE PHYSCHOLOGY OF NUCLEAR PROLIFERATION: IDENTITY, EMOTIONS, AND FOREIGN POLICY (2006).

[248] See Richard B. Bilder, *Nuclear Weapons and International Law*, in NUCLEAR WEAPONS AND LAW 3, 8, 10 (ARTHUR SELWYN MILLER and MARTIN FEINRIDER ed., 1984) (hereinafter Bilder, *Nuclear*).

[249] See LON FULLER, THE MORALITY OF LAW 53 (1969).

[250] See Rama Mani, *Peaceful Settlement of Disputes and Conflict Prevention*, in THE OXFORD HANDBOOK ON THE UNITED NATIONS 300, 306 (THOMAS G. WEISS and SAM DAWS ed., 2007); Higgins, *supra* note 237, at 38–39.

[251] See Simon Chesterman, *An International Rule of Law?*, 56 AM. J. COMP. L. 331 (2008); JEREMY MATAM FARRALL, UNITED NATIONS SANCTIONS AND THE RULE OF LAW 27, 29 (2007).

[252] See Chesterman, *supra* note 251, at n. 25 (quoting A. V. Dicey, Lectures Introductory to the Study of the Law of the Constitution 171–72, 177–78, 208); FARRALL, *supra* note 251, at 35.

matters and does not rely solely on the assertions of the parties as to the existence of a dispute or the content of a particular law, for example.[253] One need only look as far as the examples of how the ICJ fully considers the case from the perspective of the absent party to a dispute, as required by ICJ Statute Article 53(2), to know to what extent the ICJ tries to be objective,[254] almost to the point of putting the participating State at a disadvantage.[255]

At the same time, one need only look as far as the fact that all five permanent members of the Security Council are nuclear-weapon States under the NPT to get a distinct hint at the potential bias of the Security Council when handling nuclear non-proliferation disputes, all of which have a vested interest in maintaining the status quo that favors themselves.[256] The Security Council is made up of States, and given the interdependent nature of the safeguards system, most States on the Security Council will have an interest in the resolution of nuclear non-proliferation disputes. The International Court of Justice and international arbitral tribunals, on the other hand, are made up of men and women acting in their private capacities, thereby giving them a large measure of independence in their judicial activities.[257] One need only look as far as the significant number of times that judges have voted against their State of citizenship when they believed that the State was wrong concerning the law to see their degree of impartiality, with even the Soviet judge voting against the Soviet Union and the US judge voting against the United States on several of the issues in the *Interhandel* case,

[253] See *Military and Paramilitary Activities in and against Nicaragua (Nicaragua v. US)*, Judgment, 1986 ICJ Rep. 14, 97 (June 27).

[254] See Statute of the International Court of Justice, *supra* note 5, Art. 53 ("The Court must, before doing so, satisfy itself, not only that it has jurisdiction in accordance with Articles 36 and 37, but also that the claim is well founded in fact and law").

[255] See Collier and Lowe, *supra* note 237, at 180–81; Gerald Fitzmaurice, *The Problem of the "Non-appearing" Defendant Government*, 51 Brit. Y.B. Int'l L. 89, 94–99, 109 (1980); Ian Sinclair, *Some Procedural Aspects of Recent International Litigation*, 30 Int'l & Comp. L. Q. 338, 349–350 (1981).

[256] See Ian Johnstone, *Legislation and Adjudication in the UN Security Council: Bringing down the Deliberative Deficit*, 102 Am. J. Int'l L. 275, 291 (2008).

[257] See, e.g., Ruth Mackenzie, *International Courts and Tribunals and the Independence of the International Judge*, 44 Harv. Int'l L.J. 271 (2003); Edith Brown Weiss, *Judicial Independence and Impartiality: A Preliminary Inquiry*, in The International Court of Justice at a Crossroads 123 (Lori F. Damrosch ed., 1987); Gilbert Guillaume, *De l'indépendance des membres de la Cour internationale de justice*, in Boutros Boutros-Ghali Amicorum Discipulorumque Liber 475 (1998).

which took place at the height of the Cold War in 1959.[258] Various ethics rules require all international arbitrators to be impartial, including those who are appointed by one of the disputants.[259] For example, the International Bar Association's Rules of Ethics for International Arbitrators states that international arbitrators need to be impartial, with the International Bar Association's Guidelines on Conflicts of Interest in International Arbitration requiring the international arbitrator to be impartial "at the time of accepting an appointment to serve and shall remain so during the entire arbitration proceeding until the final award has been rendered or the proceeding has otherwise finally terminated."[260] Likewise, with the ICJ, fifteen States have a national on the bench,[261] and a disputant without a national on the bench can appoint an ad hoc judge for the duration of the case, in accordance with ICJ Statute Article 31.[262] Similar to arbitrators, all ICJ judges are required to be impartial, with ICJ Statute Articles 2, 17(2), and 20 requiring the ICJ judge to be independent and of "high moral character,"

[258] See Arthur Larson, *The Role of Law in Building Peace*, in PREVENTING WORLD WAR III: SOME PROPOSALS 332, 337–338 (QUINCY WRIGHT et al. ed., 1962) (noting that ICJ judges had voted twenty-four times against their States of citizenship in 103 votes, as of 1962, and noting the observation in the Interhandel case); *Interhandel (US v. Switzerland)*, Preliminary Objections, 1959 ICJ Rep. 6 (March 21). But see Eric A. Posner and Miguel F. P. de Figueiredo, *Is the International Court of Justice Biased*, 34 J. LEGAL STUD. 599 (2005) (asserting that ICJ judges are biased in favor of the States that appointed them).

[259] See generally Yuval Shany, *Squaring the Circle? Independence and Impartiality of Party-Appointed Adjudicators in International Legal Proceedings*, 30 LOY. L.A. INT'L & COMP. L. REV. 473 (2008).

[260] See International Bar Association, Rules of Ethics for International Arbitrators, Introductory Note (1987); International Bar Association, Guidelines on Conflicts of Interest in International Arbitration 4–12 (2004). See also Susan D. Franck, Men of Affairs? *The Role of International Arbitrators*, 12 ILSA J. INT'L & COMP. L. 499, 516–518 (discussing the ways that international arbitrators are required to be impartial); Catherine A. Rogers, *Regulating International Arbitrator: A Functional Approach to Developing Standards of Conduct*, 41 STAN. J. INT'L L. 53, 59–60 (2005) (same); Murray L. Smith, *Impartiality of the Party-Appointed Arbitrator*, 6 ARB. INT'L 320 (1990). But see David J. Branson, *American Party-Appointed Arbitrators: Not the Three Monkeys*, 30 DAYTON L. REV. 1, 3–4 (2004) (saying it is impossible for party-appointed arbitrators to remain impartial while still being sympathetic to the case of their appointer, as some States expect of their appointed arbitrator).

[261] See ICJ Statute, Art. 3.

[262] See ICJ Statute, Art. 31; Stephen M. Schwebel, *National Judges and Judges Ad Hoc of the International Court of Justice*, 48 INT'L & COMP. L.Q. 889 (1999); Daniel D. Nsereko, *The International Court, Impartiality and Judges Ad Hoc*, 13 INDIAN J. INT'L L. 207 (1973).

to be devoid of conflicts of interest regarding the dispute before them, and to make "a solemn declaration in open court that he will exercise his powers impartially and conscientiously"; Article 31(6) expressly applies these obligations to ad hoc judges.[263] Therefore, these judges and arbitrators are in a very different position than are decision-makers in the Security Council. Such a requirement for these judicial decision-makers to be impartial makes their decisions far more objective and impartial than those of political bodies such as the Security Council.[264] Nevertheless, a political element is bound to remain in the ICJ inasmuch as its judges are nominated by national groups of the Permanent Court of Arbitration and are elected by the General Assembly and the Security Council, in accordance with ICJ Statute Chapter I.[265] Moreover, in the end, it is the Security Council that may have to enforce judicial decisions on the international level, under UN Charter Article 94, which might have a trickle-down effect on the thought processes of international judges. However, inasmuch as judicial decisions are enforced without having to resort to Security Council enforcement measures under Article 94,[266] this supposed trickle-down effect likely has a negligible impact.

[263] ICJ Statute, Arts. 2, 17(2), 20, 31(6). See also Georges Abi-Saab, *Ensuring the Best Bench: Ways of Selecting Judges*, in INCREASING THE EFFECTIVENESS OF THE INTERNATIONAL COURT OF JUSTICE: PROCEEDINGS OF THE ICJ/UNITAR COLLOQUIUM TO CELEBRATE THE 50TH ANNIVERSARY OF THE COURT 188 (CONNIE PECK and ROY S. LEE ed., 1997); Kenneth J. Keith, *International Court of Justice: Reflections on the Electoral Process*, 9 CHINESE J. INT'L L. 49 (2010).

[264] See International Bar Association, Rules of Ethics for International Arbitrators, Arts. 1, 3–5, available at http://www.ibanet.org/images/downloads/pubs/Ethics_arbitrators.pdf (requiring impartiality and neutrality of international arbitrators, among other positive qualities); see also American Arbitration Association, Commercial Arbitration Rules and Mediation Procedures, Rules 12, 17, 18, at http://www.adr.org/sp.asp?id=22440 (last modified Sept. 1, 2007) (referring to the possibility that party-appointed arbitrators could be "non-neutral" should the parties agree to such partiality, and accepting this apparent lack of neutrality). In reality, there likely is a mix of advocacy and impartiality of party-appointed arbitrators, regardless of which rules govern in the arbitration. After all, as the Soviets complained in the 1940s, no one truly is neutral. See LINCOLN P. BLOOMFIELD et al., KHRUSHCHEV AND THE ARMS RACE: SOVIET INTERESTS IN ARMS CONTROL AND DISARMAMENT 1954–1964 11 (1966).

[265] ICJ Statute, Ch. I. See also Roberto Lavalle, *Nationality as a Factor in the Election of the Members of the International Court of Justice, with Particular Reference to Occasional Elections*, 29 RUVUE BELGE DE DROIT INTERNATIONAL 625 (1996); Adam M. Smith, *"Judicial Nationalism" in International Law: National Identity and Judicial Autonomy at the ICJ*, Bepress Legal Series Working Paper 428, November 22, 2004, at law.bepress.com/expresso/eps/428.

[266] See Colter Paulson, *Compliance with Final Judgments of the International Court of Justice Since 1987*, 98 AM. J. INT'L L. 434 (2004).

In addition to the supposed impartiality of judges and arbitrators, it is tempting to point to the rules of evidence with international adjudication as an advantage vis-à-vis the Security Council. However, much to the surprise of nonspecialists in the area of international adjudication, there essentially are no formal rules on the admissibility of evidence in international adjudication,[267] not even a best-evidence rule,[268] presumably in order to preserve a maximum amount of flexibility for the court or tribunal to admit any evidence that helps it determine the truth. The notion of "best evidence" has its roots in English cases from the early 1700s, with elaboration on the principle by Chief Baron Gilbert in 1756, which commentators typically quote to explain the principle:

> The first and most signal rule in relation to evidence is this, that a man must have the utmost evidence that the nature of the fact is capable of . . . the true meaning of which is that no evidence shall be brought which *ex natura rei* supposes still a greater evidence behind in the party's own possession or power.[269]

The principle and its related rules form the foundation for most exclusionary rules relating to evidence, such as the exclusion of hearsay and secondary evidence, and the requirement for proof of attested documents other than by attesting witnesses and proof of consent other than by calling the consenting party, inter alia.[270] In short, the principle requires "introduction of the most accurate and convincing evidence available to the proponent,"[271] as is reflected in Rule 1002 of the Federal Rules of Evidence. All other evidence will be inadmissible as insufficient to prove the fact at issue.[272] One might expect the ICJ and international arbitration to have adopted the best-evidence principle, or at least some variation of it. However, this does not appear to be the case, with which

[267] See Chittharanjan F. Amerasinghe, Evidence in International Litigation 37 (2005).

[268] See ibid., at 204–208; Anna Riddell and Brendan Plant, Evidence before the International Court of Justice 410 (2009); Mojtaba Kazazi, Burden of Proof and Related Issues: A Study on Evidence before International Tribunals 217–219 (1996).

[269] Baron Gilbert, The Law of Evidence 4 (1st edn, 1756). See also Hodge M. Malek (ed.), Phipson on Evidence ¶ 7.41 (17th edn, 2010) (quoting this paragraph).

[270] See Malek, *supra* note 269, ¶ 7.41; Cynthia de Silva, *California's Best Evidence Rule Repeal: Toward a Greater Appreciation for Secondary Evidence*, 30 McGeorge L. Rev. 646, 649–650 (1999).

[271] Malek, *supra* note 269, ¶ 7.41.

[272] See ibid.; Dale A. Nance, *The Best Evidence Principle*, 73 Iowa L. Rev. 227 (1988).

critics of legal resolution might have a problem. ICJ judge Gerald Fitzmaurice discussed the best-evidence rule in his separate opinion in the second phase of the *Barcelona Traction* case, which involved Belgium's failure to produce "trust deeds" at issue in that case:

> Of course the Trust Deeds would, if produced, constitute what is known in Common Law parlance as the "best" evidence, and unless they could be shown to have been lost or destroyed, it is unlikely that a municipal court would admit secondary evidence of their contents. International tribunals are not tied by such firm rules, however, many of which are not appropriate to litigation between governments.[273]

In addition, in the merits phase of the ICJ *Corfu Channel* case, the International Court of Justice indicated that other forms of proof are acceptable where direct evidence is unavailable.[274] Both of these cases suggest that there is no best-evidence rule in international adjudication. Regardless, this does not mean that disputants cannot challenge their opponent's evidence; on the contrary, this is a major part of the presentation of evidence within legal resolution.[275]

Even though legal resolution lacks clear evidentiary rules, there seem to be various general principles of law that nevertheless guide international courts and tribunals in determining the weight they are to give certain types of evidence. For example, the ICJ explained in the *Armed Activities on the Territory of the Congo (Democratic Republic of the Congo v. Uganda)* what types of evidence it would favor or handle with caution when it was presented with a report prepared by the Ugandan government concerning an alleged use of force by Uganda at Kitona in 1998:

> The Court will treat with caution evidentiary materials specially prepared for this case and also materials emanating from a single source. It will *prefer* contemporaneous evidence from persons with direct knowledge. It will give particular attention to reliable evidence acknowledging facts or conduct unfavourable to the State represented by the person making them. The Court will also give weight to evidence that has not, even before this litigation, been challenged by impartial persons for the correctness of what it contains. The Court moreover notes that evidence obtained by examination of persons directly involved, and who were

[273] *Case Concerning the Barcelona Traction, Light and Power Company, Limited (New Application: 1962) (Belgium v. Spain)*, Second Phase, 1970 ICJ Rep. 3, 99 (Feb. 5).

[274] See the *Corfu Channel* case, 1949 ICJ Rep. 4, 18 (April 9). See also AMERASINGHE, *supra* note 267, at 206 (qutoing from the *Corfu Channel* case).

[275] See AMERASINGHE, *supra* note 267, at 205; KAZAZI, *supra* note 268, at 219.

> subsequently cross-examined by judges skilled in examination and experienced in assessing large amounts of factual information, some of it of a technical nature, merits special attention. The Court thus will give appropriate consideration to the Report of the Porter Commission, which gathered evidence in this manner. The Court further notes that, since its publication, there has been no challenge to the credibility of this Report, which has been accepted by both Parties.[276]

Weighing all of the evidence in this manner and considering the challenges to this evidence by the Democratic Republic of the Congo, the Court concluded that Uganda had not been involved in the use of force at Kitona.[277]

By using the court or tribunal's procedures for challenging evidence, disputants can help the court or tribunal determine the weight that it should give the evidence and whether to require original evidence or to allow secondary evidence, thereby having a measure of influence over the outcome of the case.[278] While the ICJ and international arbitral tribunals might not have the same clear rules of evidence that certain national courts enjoy, the procedures for challenging evidence in these international fora help give legal resolution a distinct advantage over the assessment-of-evidence processes in political bodies such as the Security Council and the IAEA. Indeed, one of the main reasons that North Korea gives for its claim that the IAEA is biased against it is that the IAEA based its decision of noncompliance in 1993 on secret intelligence that North Korea was not able to properly challenge.[279] North Korea also would consider Security Council decisions biased against it on the same grounds, inasmuch as the Security Council is known to rely often on secret intelligence of member States that other States cannot easily challenge.[280] For example, concerning Iraq's alleged WMD programs in 2002, there was no meaningful examination of the evidence that US Secretary of State Colin Powell presented to the Security Council during

[276] *Armed Activities on the Territory of the Congo (DRC v. Uganda)*, 2005 ICJ Rep. 168, 201 (Dec. 19) (citing *Military and Paramilitary Activities in and against Nicaragua (Nicaragua v. US)*, Merits, Judgment, 1986 ICJ Rep. 14, 41 (June 27)) (emphasis added).

[277] See *Armed Activities on the Territory of the Congo (DRC v. Uganda)*, 2005 ICJ Rep. 168, 201–205 (Dec. 19).

[278] See Amerasinghe, *supra* note 267, at 205 (quoting Dissenting Opinion of Richard M. Mosk to Final Award in *Ultrasystems Incorp. v. Iran*, Final Award No. 89-84-3 (Dec. 7, 1983)).

[279] See Nazario, *supra* note 98, at 146.

[280] See Joyner, *supra* note 40, at 55 (citing www.dni.gov/press_releases/20071203_release.pdf).

a special meeting on February 5, 2003, in which for over an hour he presented the US case for invading Iraq to other foreign ministers, who then merely read their prepared speeches after Secretary Powell had finished his presentation, as already noted in Chapter 3.2.3.6 above.[281] Where such sensitive topics as WMD proliferation and the possibility of invading another State that allegedly possesses such weapons are involved, one would hope that the standard of proof would be sufficiently high in order to avoid reliance on shoddy evidence to make such a key determination. Perhaps clear and convincing evidence would be the most appropriate standard where military action is threatened, while nonmilitary sanctions might be authorized on a lesser standard, such as preponderance of the evidence.[282] Possible reliance on classified information provided by national intelligence services further exacerbates the hypothetical problem of the Security Council's meeting evidentiary standards.[283] To be clear, the Security Council is not obliged to meet the evidentiary standards that exist with legal resolution. However, assuming that the Security Council has an interest in having target States comply with its decisions, the Security Council might think about whether improving the procedural safeguards for target States could improve this compliance. This does not invert means and ends, but rather recognizes that the means might impact the ends – namely the target State's co-operation.

Perhaps the Security Council would want to establish some procedural rules for admitting evidence under its powers provided by UN Charter Article 30 (for example, allowing evidence from treaty bodies, but requiring certain corroboration of evidence provided by national intelligence networks),[284] at least where military actions are being proposed. In addition, a procedure of advocacy might also be useful in such cases, where one State acts as impartial prosecutor and the other as defense counsel, with the target State having a *right* to participate in the

[281] See Harald Müller, *Dealing with WMD Crises: The Role of the United Nations in Compliance Politics*, in ARMS CONTROL AFTER IRAQ: NORMATIVE AND OPERATIONAL CHALLENGES 114, 128 (WAHEGURU PAL SINGH SIDHU and RAMESH THAKUR ed., 2006).

[282] See Karel Wellens, *The U.N. Security Council and New Threats to the Peace: Back to the Future*, 8 J. CONFLICT & SECURITY. L. 15, 23 (2003).

[283] See, e.g., SIMON CHESTERMAN, SHARED SECRETS: INTELLIGENCE AND COLLECTIVE SECURITY 47–54 (2006) (discussing intelligence sharing in determining the extent of weapons proliferation in Iraq).

[284] See Müller, *supra* note 281, at 133. See UN Charter, Art. 30 ("The Security Council shall adopt its own rules of procedure, including the method of selecting its President").

deliberations.[285] The Security Council might also want to place considerable emphasis on determining a target State's intent, much like a criminal judge or jury would be asked to do, which could be done by calling in an expert group to assess the evidence and by calling neighboring States as witnesses.[286] With all of this information, the Security Council would be in a far better position to craft its response specifically to the intents of the target State and the magnitude of the threat.

All of this is not to say that legal resolution is not vulnerable to criticism concerning the quality of evidence it relies on in reaching a decision. Indeed, the ICJ occasionally has been criticized for its reliance on weak, or even illegally gathered, evidence when reaching its decisions.[287] There is, of course, the *Legality of the Threat or Use of Nuclear Weapons* advisory opinion, where the ICJ determined that "in view of . . . the [limited] elements of fact at its disposal, the Court cannot conclude definitively whether the threat or use of nuclear weapons would be lawful or unlawful in an extreme circumstance of self-defense, in which the very survival of a state would be at stake."[288] As explained in Chapter 4.3.1 above, this advisory opinion was not so much about the quality of the evidence as it was about the absence of a true case and controversy. The issue of the quality of evidence instead arose in various other ICJ cases, including the *Nicaragua* case, where there were problems in "tracing material proof of the identity of the perpetrator" and the acts were "shrouded in secrecy,"[289] and in the *Application of the Convention on*

[285] See Müller, *supra* note 281, at 133. [286] Ibid., at 121, 133–134.

[287] See, e.g., Andrea Gattini, *Evidentiary Issues in the ICJ's Genocide Judgment*, 5 J. Int'l Crim. Justice 889 (2007); Andrew B. Loewenstein and Stephen A. Kostas, *Divergent Approaches to Determining Responsibility for Genocide*, 5 J. Int'l Crim. Justice 839 (2007); Vojin Dimitrijevic and Marko Milanovic, *The Strange Story of the Bosnian Genocide Case*, 21 Leiden J. Int'l L. 65 (2008); W. Michael Reisman and Eric E. Freedman, *The Plaintiff's Dilemma: Illegally Obtained Evidence and Admissibility in International Adjudication*, 76 Am. J. Int'l L. 737 (1982).

[288] *Legality of the Threat or Use of Nuclear Weapons*, Advisory Opinion, 1996 ICJ Rep.226, 266 (July 8). This inconclusive decision seems to support the idea that the determination of legality has to be handled on a case-by-case basis, not in the abstract. Four judges – Judges Schwebel, Higgins, Guillaume, and Oda – emphasized this point. See generally Charles Moxley, Nuclear Weapons and International Law in the Post-Cold War World 158–159 (2000) (summarizing the different opinions of the judges). Several notable commentators had been saying this for decades. See, e.g., M. S. McDougal and F. P. Feliciano, Law and Minimum World Public Order 78 (1961).

[289] *Military and Paramilitary Activities in and against Nicaragua (Nicaragua v. US)*, 1986 ICJ Rep.14, 38–39 (June 27). See generally Keith Highet, *Evidence, the Court and the Nicaragua Case*, 81 Am. J. Int'l L. 1 (1987).

the Prevention and Punishment of the Crime of Genocide case, where Serbia redacted large portions of the relevant documents it provided as "military secrets."[290] The strength of the ICJ's evidentiary determinations in its *Armed Activities on the Territory of the Congo* case between the Democratic Republic of the Congo and Uganda, some of which were alluded to above, also have been challenged by ICJ judges and commentators alike. In particular, Judge Parra-Aranguren criticized the majority in his separate opinion for basing a particularly important conclusion on tenuous facts – that a Ugandan general's appointment of a "governor" over Kibali-Ituri definitively established Uganda as an occupying force there.[291] Similarly, commentators have taken issue with the Court's untenable position that the "legal and factual circumstances for the exercise of a right of self-defence by Uganda against the DRC were not present," based simply on the facts that were presented to the Court.[292] In defense of the Court, the disputants alleged so many facts of unclear validity concerning so many different uses of force that any factual determination by the Court likely would have raised criticism from someone.

When it comes to illegally gathered evidence, the ICJ seems willing to accept that evidence, and a rule to exclude such evidence is not seen as being needed, presumably on account of the difficulty of gathering evidence in general due to a lack of coercive powers with such matters.[293] Regardless, from a relative perspective vis-à-vis the Security Council and the IAEA, legal resolution arguably offers greater opportunities for disputants to challenge evidence and greater care in determining the weight to be given to evidence. Such an advantage, in addition to the impartiality of judges and arbitrators, might make legal resolution a somewhat attractive option for parties to nuclear non-proliferation disputes.

[290] See *Application of the Convention on the Prevention and Punishment of the Crime of Genocide (Bosnia and Herzegovina v. Serbia and Montenegro)*, General List No. 91, Feb. 26, 2007, at 75–76.

[291] See *Armed Activities on the Territory of the Congo (DRC v. Uganda)*, 2005 ICJ Rep. 168, 300 (Dec. 19) (separate opinion J. Parra-Aranguren) (quoting 2005 ICJ Rep., at 230).

[292] See Theresa Reinold, *State Weakness, Irregular Warfare, and the Right to Self-Defense Post-9/11*, 105 Am. J. Int'l L. 244, 259–260 (2011) (quoting *Armed Activities on the Territory of the Congo (DRC v. Uganda)*, 2005 ICJ Rep. 168, 223 (Dec. 19).

[293] See generally Hugh Thirlway, *Dilemma or Chimera? Admissibility of Illegally Obtained Evidence in International Adjudication*, 78 Am. J. Int'l L. 622, 639–641 (1984).

5.3.1.2 Greater control through procedural safeguards

The loss (or perceived loss) of control of disputants over their nuclear non-proliferation dispute is one of the main criticisms of legal resolution in this context. The retention of control seems of paramount importance to governments in resolving their politically sensitive disputes, as opposed to businesses, which are more willing to give up control in favor of decisive decisions by impartial tribunals.[294] The question remains why control is such an important factor with these types of disputes, to the point that commentators dismiss even the possibility with little or no consideration. It cannot merely be because disputants do not know the outcome beforehand and lose control over that outcome, because that is the case with all types of disputes that are sent to international adjudication.[295] What makes nuclear non-proliferation disputes so different? The answer likely boils down to an issue of trust, as discussed in the preceding subsection. In this regard, these subsections are related. This subsection focuses on the way in which the procedural due-process safeguards of legal resolution provide a measure of control over the proceedings, at least compared to those in the Security Council.

It is important to note at the outset how States that are the target of Security Council Chapter VII decisions do not enjoy any control over the process and the result, contrary to the assertion by some commentators that "the accused party always has a possibility to demonstrate its innocence."[296] Indeed, they lose virtually all control over the process and result, assuming the disputants are not members of the Security Council. The main danger in getting a political body such as the Security Council involved with nuclear non-proliferation disputes is that it lacks the procedural rules and legal competence to reach objective, reliable decisions.[297] Indeed, the Security Council makes its decisions concerning the maintenance of international peace and security with politics in mind, not law or law enforcement.[298] This is the case even if some commentators happen to characterize the Security Council as a court

[294] See Collier and Lowe, *supra* note 237, at 8.

[295] See Dekker, *supra* note 22, at 110.

[296] Jozef Goldblat, Arms Control: A Guide to Negotiations and Agreements 234 (1994).

[297] See Sohn, *supra* note 42, at 264–265.

[298] See Gowlland-Debbas, *supra* note 235, at 654; Nigel D. White, Keeping the Peace: The United Nations and the Maintenance of International Peace and Security 33 (1993); Johnstone, *supra* note 256, at 299.

or arbitrator.[299] Admittedly, the Security Council has been known to include in its Chapter VII resolutions legal determinations of breach of international law, almost as if the pronounced breach somehow determines that there is a threat to international peace and security, thereby making Chapter VII applicable.[300] If it can be said that the Security Council is acting like a court when acting in this manner, it certainly does not act like a very good court, inasmuch as it fails to give the disputants before it the most basic procedural rights, such as the opportunity to be heard, and has other problems associated with its opaque assessment of evidence and weighing of legal claims.[301] While these types of rights typically are protected in the domestic setting under a State's constitution, similar rights also exist on the international level, as the European Court of Justice concluded in its *Kadi* decision.[302] Critics might claim that the Security Council's responding to situations quickly, without any concern for the rights or interests of the target State, would nevertheless lead to reliable decisions. That might, indeed, be the case. However, whatever reliability that decision might enjoy arguably would be outweighed by the decreased chance of the co-operation of the target State in a process that disadvantages it from the start. As the introduction to this study noted, the target State's compliance with the ultimate decision (of either the Security Council, the International Court of Justice or some other body) might be influenced by the procedures followed in reaching that decision. That is the underlying theme of this study.

Security Council proceedings lack not only transparency, but also fairness in that they do not allow the target States to participate in a meaningful way.[303] While the Security Council is to meet in public,

[299] See, e.g., Johnstone, *supra* note 256, at 282; DEKKER, *supra* note 22, at 110 (2001); Keith Harper, *Does the United Nations Security Council Have the Competence to Act as Court and Legislature?*, 27 NYU INT'L L. & POL'Y 103, 108–127 (1994) (discussing the various ways that the Security Council has acted like a court in making legal determinations); MARTIN, *supra* note 241, at 53 (referring to the Security Council as the arbitrator of disputes, but this apparently is not to say that the Security Council applies law in reaching its decisions).

[300] See JOYNER, *supra* note 40, at 178–79; Johnstone, *supra* note 256, at 282.

[301] Johnstone, *supra* note 256, at 300.

[302] See Joined Cases C-402/05 P and C-415/05 P, *Kadi and Al Barakaat v. Council of the European Union and EC Commission*, 3 C.M.L.R. 41 (2008).

[303] This likely would not be the case if a target State was a member of the Security Council at the time of the debates. Indeed, it is not impossible that Iran and North Korea could become members of the Security Council, thereby including them in the Security Council's decision-making process. After all, Iran was a member of the Security

informal consultations generally are held in private, and it is there that the lion's share of actual decision-making occurs.[304] Concerning the Security Council's meetings, UN Charter Article 31 provides nonmembers of the Security Council with the possibility to "participate, without vote, in the discussion of any question brought before the Security Council," and Article 32 similarly provides such States the possibility to "participate, without vote, in the discussion relating to the dispute."[305] There are two barriers to these provisions providing adequate protection for target States: first, such States must be *invited* by the Security Council; second, the Security Council is free to refer to the questions and disputes under its consideration under Articles 31 and 32 as "issues," "concerns," "matters," or any other euphemism that would relieve the Security Council of having to decide whether to extend an invitation, or instead to assert that the *party* to the dispute is not a State at all.[306] Assuming, *arguendo*, that such States are liberally granted the ability to participate actively in Security Council debates, they neither have the right to a reasoned decision from the Security Council that can stand up to scrutiny nor the possibility of appeal,[307] among other standard due-process safeguards. This would be the case even if such recalcitrant States

Council in 1955 and 1956, though this was well before the Islamic Revolution in Iran in 1979. Nonetheless, sometimes States that do not enjoy the support of Western States are elected to the Security Council by the General Assembly under UN Charter Article 23, such as Syria, which was a member in 2002 and 2003.

[304] See Bailey and Daws, *supra* note 159, at 53–54, 60–75.

[305] UN Charter, Arts. 31–32.

[306] But see Rudolf Dolzer, *Article 31*, in The Charter of the United Nations: A Commentary 495, 497, 500–501 (Bruno Simma ed., 1995) (asserting that a party to a dispute has the right to participate under Article 31, though he conflates permissive and obligatory language by relying on Rule 37 of the Provisional Rules of Procedure for support of that right, a rule that merely states that non-members may be invited to participate by the Security Council, thus putting himself on a "weak legal foundation" as opposed to the other way around).

[307] See *Case Concerning Questions of Interpretation and Application of 1971 Montreal Convention Arising from the Aerial Incident at Lockerbie, Request for the Indication of Provisional Measures (Libya v. US)*, 1992 ICJ 114, 125–126 (April 14); see also Frederic L. Kirgis, Jr., *The Security Council's First Fifty Years*, 89 Am. J. Int'l L. 506, 527 (1995) (claiming that no judicial review is available, so the Security Council is left alone to decide how far to stretch the United Nation's "purposes and principles"; please note that this was written before the *Lockerbie* case). But see John Dugard, *Judicial Review of Sanctions*, in United Nations Sanctions and International Law 83, 87 (Vera Gowlland-Debbas ed., 2001) (citing ICJ and ICTY review as examples); Thomas M. Franck, *The "Powers of Appreciation": Who Is the Ultimate Guardian of U.N. Legality*, 86 Am. J. Int'l L. 519, 521–522 (1992) (comparing the *Lockerbie* case with the US Supreme Court case *Marbury v. Madison*, and suggesting how *Lockerbie* might also be used to establish judicial review on the international level).

as Iran and North Korea were members of the Security Council. While it would be unreasonable to expect the Security Council to provide all the procedural safeguards that are provided in the domestic legal setting, the Security Council should provide at least a minimum amount of procedural fairness,[308] which arguably would include the opportunity to be heard, among the other rights discussed in this section. Such procedural fairness could increase the chances of the target States co-operating with the end result. Critics might see the Security Council's lack of transparency as an advantage in that it can respond to matters quickly and not open itself up to scrutiny by the media and others when it refuses to explain its decisions. However, as explained in the introduction to this study, international dispute settlement is not all about expediency, especially with these types of politically sensitive disputes, or else tossing a coin to resolve matters might be the preferred method. Instead, one must not overlook the possibility that resolution of disputes of these kinds depends on the target State's acceptance of the ultimate decision. The chances of that happening increase with greater participation in the process and other procedural safeguards.

There is some evidence that States are not liberally granted the ability to participate actively in Security Council debates. For example, India complained of not being allowed to participate in the debates before the Security Council adopted Resolution 1172 that condemned it for its nuclear tests in 1998[309] – even though the Security Council has, at times, been exceedingly generous in letting States participate in certain debates.[310] Even if a State is invited to participate, there is no guarantee that it will be allowed an opportunity to be heard before the Security Council votes on a resolution that may create significant obligations for that State. For example, Iran complained in 2006 that the president of the Security Council did not allow it to address the Council before the vote on Resolution 1696, which, inter alia, demanded that Iran "suspend all

[308] Johnstone, *supra* note 256, at 294.

[309] Letter dated 4 June 1998 from the Permanent Representative of India to the United Nations Addressed to the President of the Security Council, para. 2, UN Doc. S/1998/464 (India complaining during the debates leading up to the adoption of Resolution 1172 that the Security Council "disregarded [Article 31] by not giving India an opportunity to participate in the discussions on this draft," thus showing how the Security Council "is neither open nor transparent").

[310] See, e.g., Newton R. Bowles, The Diplomacy of Hope: The United Nations since the Cold War 164 (2004) (noting that "[t]he number of extra-Council states attending rose to over 60 in February" for the debates over whether to establish a new mandate to use force against Iraq).

enrichment-related and reprocessing activities, including research and development, to be verified by the IAEA,"[311] even though it had requested such an opportunity on several occasions, thus reflecting "the degree of the Council's transparency and fairness that it has adopted a presidential statement and a resolution without even allowing the views of the concerned party to be heard."[312] It is absolutely crucial that target States of Security Council actions in the nuclear non-proliferation realm have the opportunity to defend themselves and their interests,[313] given the political sensitivity of these matters for the target States inasmuch as nuclear non-proliferation norms relate to that State's vital interests (or perceived vital interests). This opportunity to defend themselves obviously must be provided *before* the Security Council votes in order for such participation to have real meaning. Without such meaningful participation, it is difficult to imagine any State taking seriously the ultimate decision of the Security Council on such matters, regardless of the State's relative strength.

Some commentators believe that the Security Council might enjoy greater State compliance with its decisions if they are seen as being more just,[314] perhaps through improvements to its procedures, such as measures to facilitate broader participation in Security Council deliberation, including publication and circulation of drafts of its resolutions for comment, having more open debates to facilitate inclusive consultations, providing better reasoned justifications for its decisions, and allowing for (even encouraging) independent review of its decisions, perhaps through the ICJ.[315] Such changes would emphasize the theory of deliberative democracy and the ideas of Habermas's communicative theory

[311] S.C. Res. 1696, ¶ 2, UN Doc. S/RES/1696 (July 31, 2006).

[312] Security Council, Official Records, 61st Year, 5500th Meeting, at 2, 7, UN Doc. S/PV.5500 (July 31, 2006) (Iran complaining that the president of the Security Council did not allow it to address the Council before the vote for Resolution 1696, even though it had requested such an opportunity on several occasions).

[313] See Müller, *supra* note 281, at 123.

[314] See Johnstone, *supra* note 256, at 277. See generally IAN JOHNSTONE, *Discursive Power in the UN Security Council*, 21 J. INT'L L. & INT'L REL 73 (2006); IAN JOHNSTONE, THE POWER OF DELIBERATION: INTERNATIONAL LAW, POLITICS AND ORGANIZATIONS (2011); Ian Johnstone, *Security Council Deliberations: The Power of the Better Argument*, 14 EUR. J. INT'L L. 437 (2003); Ian Johnstone, *Legal Argumentation in International Decision-Making*, in THE FAULTLINES OF LEGITIMACY 175 (HILARY CHARLESWORTH and JEAN-MARC COICAUD ed., 2009).

[315] See Johnstone, *supra* note 256, at 276, 302–307.

mentioned in Chapter 5.3.2 below,[316] even if they do not lead to more accurate decisions being made by the Security Council in terms of upholding international law.[317] However, all of these options are unlikely to be realized, given the veto of permanent members of the Security Council and the apparent preference for the status quo in general.

Critics reasonably could argue that the Security Council is becoming more conscious of due-process considerations. For example, the Security Council demonstrated its understanding of the significance of due process when it established the ICTY and International Criminal Tribunal for Rwanda (ICTR) as subsidiary bodies and gave accused individuals such rights as the right to be present for the trial,[318] in accordance with Article 14(3)(d) of the International Covenant on Civil and Political Rights.[319] Although Security Council Resolutions 1373 and 1526 dealing with counterterrorism measures after the September 11, 2001 attacks showed serious deficiencies in terms of due process, in that they required States to adopt sanctions "without delay" against suspected terrorists,[320] among other measures, this gradually has been improved. Such an improvement is likely due to the pressure that European Union (EU) member States and Switzerland placed on the Security Council to establish a delisting process for those who found themselves on the lists of terrorists maintained by the 1267 Committee;[321] a delisting procedure was not included in Resolution 1526 but eventually was included in

[316] Ibid., at 278–79; JÜRGEN HABERMAS, BETWEEN FACTS AND NORMS: CONTRIBUTIONS TO A DISCOURSE THEORY OF LAW AND DEMOCRACY (trans. William Rehg, 1998); Thomas Risse, *Let's Argue!: Communicative Action in World Politics*, 54 INT'L ORG. 1 (2000).

[317] See Johnstone, *supra* note 256, at 280–281.

[318] See S.C. Res. 827,¶ 2, UN Doc. S/RES/827 (May 27, 1993) (incorporating by reference Report of the Secretary-General Pursuant to Paragraph 2 of Security Council Resolution 808 (1993), UN Doc. S/25704 (May 3, 1993), Annex Art. 21(4)(d)); S.C. Res. 955, Art. 20(4)(d), UN Doc. S/RES/955/Annex (Nov. 8, 1994).

[319] See, e.g., International Covenant on Civil and Political Rights, G.A. Res. 2200A (XXI), Annex, Art. 14(3)(d), UN Doc. A/6316 (Dec. 16, 1966).

[320] S.C. Res. 1373, ¶ 1(c), UN Doc. S/RES/1373 (Sept. 28, 2001) ("Freeze without delay funds" (emphasis added)); S.C. Res. 1526, ¶ 1(a), UN Doc. S/RES/1526 (Jan. 30, 2004) (essentially the same language as S.C. Res. 1373).

[321] See Security Council, Official Records, 59th Year, 4892nd Meeting, at 23–24, 28 UN Doc. S/PV.4892 (Jan. 14, 2004) (statements of Richard Ryan, Permanent Representative of Ireland to the United Nations, on behalf of the EU, and Pierre Helg, Deputy Permanent Representative of Switzerland to the United Nations).

Resolution 1730.[322] Despite this evidence of being conscious of due-process safeguards, alleged violations of nuclear non-proliferation norms by such States as Iran and North Korea are not likely to inspire the Security Council to go out of its way to protect the due-process rights of target States, as was the case with *individuals* before the international criminal tribunals or on Security Council Committee terrorist lists.

Legal resolution, on the other hand, provides disputants with many procedural safeguards. Indeed, legal resolution can be distinguished from other forms of dispute settlement by the due-process aspects it incorporates into its proceedings.[323] At first glance, it might appear that international adjudicative proceedings are no better than Security Council proceedings in terms of due-process safeguards. After all, it is not as though international arbitral proceedings are public. However, the parties to the dispute before a tribunal will be included in those proceedings, whereas the parties to the matter before the Security Council will have no vested right to access the formal and informal meetings unless they are Security Council members, which is a significant deficiency of Security Council resolution. Although international arbitral proceedings generally are not made public without the consent of the parties

[322] See S.C. Res. 1730, ¶¶ 1–2 and annex, UN Doc. S/RES/1730/Annex (Dec. 19, 2006); S.C. Res. 1526, UN Doc. S/RES/1526 (Jan. 30, 2004). These procedures appear to have been modeled after the delisting procedures established by the Resolution 1267 Committee in November 2006 where the entity on the list can petition its government of residence or citizenship to review the case, which then approaches the government that initially put that entity on the list to consider the justifications for removal; either government can request that the Committee remove the requesting entity, which can be removed by consensus of the Committee members or by a decision of the Security Council. See Security Council Committee Established Pursuant to Resolution 1267 (1999) Concerning Al-Qaida and the Taliban and Associated Individuals and Entities, Guidelines of the Committee for the Conduct of its Work, at 7 (Nov. 29, 2006), available at http://www.un.org/Docs/sc/committees/1267/1267_guidelines.pdf. However, Resolution 1730 adds the possibility of entities on these lists to submit delisting requests through the U.N. Secretariat. See S.C. Res. 1730, annex ¶ 1, UN Doc. S/RES/1730/Annex (Dec. 19, 2006).

[323] See JULIAN D. M. LEW et al., COMPARATIVE INTERNATIONAL COMMERCIAL ARBITRATION ¶¶ 28–80 (2003); ROBERT B. AHDIEH, *Between Dialogue and Decree: International Review of National Courts*, 79 N.Y.U. L. REV. 2029, 2124 n. 451 (2004) (distinguishing international due-process norms from international norms of due process). See generally Matti Kurkela, *Due Process in Arbitration: A Finnish Perspective*, 21 J. INT'L ARB. 221 (2004) (distinguishing arbitration from other alternative dispute resolution methods, in part, through a discussion of its provision of due process). It is important to note that the due-process standards that a party can expect in an international arbitral proceeding are international standards of due process and not those typically provided by domestic legislation.

involved, the parties do have the benefit of having a reasoned decision by the international arbitral tribunal,[324] which adds tremendous transparency to the process generally. With regard to the other benefits of legal resolution as a result of due-process safeguards, while decisions are binding, this does not mean that they cannot be appealed or interpreted by an enforcing or annulment court,[325] or by a disputant requesting the ICJ to construe the meaning or scope of a judgment under ICJ Statute Article 60.[326] In addition, one must not overlook the significant benefits of legal resolution in its principles of equality of parties, the requirement of proper notice, and the opportunity to present one's case, all of which derive from international adjudication's wholehearted commitment to party consent.[327] All of these due-process safeguards should make legal resolution a particularly attractive option for disputants over nuclear non-proliferation issues, especially when the alternatives are Security Council resolution or war.

5.3.1.3 Predictability through the rule of law

Some commentators claim that legal resolution leads to unpredictable results, from either bias, chance, or incompetence, among other possible

[324] See MERRILLS, *supra* note 84, at 252–253.

[325] Ibid., at 95–100. In addition, there is the possibility that the winning party to an arbitration tries to enforce the award under the New York Convention (even though the New York Convention does not particularly apply to inter-State arbitrations). See William W. Park, *Safeguarding Procedural Integrity in International Arbitration*, 63 TUL. L. REV. 647, 664–667 (1989) (citing, inter alia, *Dallal v. Bank Mellat*, 1 All E.R. 239 (1986) (where a UK court recognized an Iran–US Claims Tribunal award even though it was not covered by the New York Convention per se)). If this happens, the enforcing state will get a chance to look at the decision, though in the limited context of the five reasons provided under the New York Convention for refusing to recognize and enforce an award. See Convention on the Recognition and Enforcement of Foreign Arbitral Awards, Art. V, June 10, 1958, 330 U.N.T.S. 38.

[326] ICJ Statute, Art. 60 ("In the event of dispute as to the meaning or scope of the judgment, the Court shall construe it upon the request of any party").

[327] See Smit and Shaw, *supra* note 101, at 277; S. I. Strong, *Intervention and Joinder As of Right in International Arbitration: An Infringement of Individual Contract Rights or a Proper Equitable Measure?*, 31 VAND. J. TRANSNAT'L L. 915, 987 (1998); Frank-Bernd Weigand, *Introduction*, in PRACTITIONER'S HANDBOOK ON INTERNATIONAL ARBITRATION 1, 77–79 (FRANK-BERND WEIGAND ed., 2002); Joel R. Junker, *The Public Policy Defense to Recognition and Enforcement of Foreign Arbitral Awards*, 7 CAL. W. INT'L L.J. 228, 231 (1977) (noting how procedural due-process safeguards, such as proper notice and the opportunity to be heard, are crucial for international arbitration to maintain its credibility).

factors.[328] Such an observation has been made of legal resolution of nuclear non-proliferation disputes.[329] This might be true in terms of commentators and disputants giving various factors in a dispute different legal weight than the decision-makers ultimately give. It is this kind of unpredictability that makes both sides to a dispute think they can win, thereby leading them to continue with the litigation process instead of settling the dispute out of court, and is to be expected. However, what both sides share is the expectation of the process that will be used to reach that decision.[330] This is what should make, and does make, legal resolution so attractive to disputants and potential disputants.

The problematic type of unpredictability is where the factors to be considered by the decision-makers are unknown and likely unknowable. As explained in the introduction to this section, legal resolution's application of law in reaching a decision makes it far more predictable than methods of resolution that are not based on law. The predictability of legal resolution comes from the fact that law, by definition, is known, or at least knowable.[331] In other words, States can know of the rules and principles that the ICJ or international arbitral tribunal will apply in resolving any dispute even before that dispute has been placed before these fora for adjudication by simply engaging in honest analysis of the law. Such predictability ultimately leads to consistency between disputes involving similar legal issues and facts, which predictability and consistency are the essence of the rule of law.[332]

5.3.1.3.1 Defining "consistency" Consistency in decision-making is one of the main benefits of the application of law by the ICJ and international arbitral tribunals. Commentators on legal resolution,[333] like

[328] See Bilder, *Nuclear*, *supra* note 248, at 167; R. Anand, Compulsory Jurisdiction of the International Court of Justice 189 (1961).

[329] See Nazario, *supra* note 98, at 145–146.

[330] See Raman, *supra* note 246, at 56.

[331] See Fuller, *supra* note 249, at 24 (describing the requirement that law must be knowable); Joseph Raz, The Authority of Law 210–229 (1979). See also Margaret Jane Radin, *Reconsidering the Rule of Law*, 69 B.U. L. Rev. 781, 784 (1989) (discussing knowability of the law).

[332] See, e.g., Brian Tamanaha, On the Rule of Law 122 (2004).

[333] See, e.g., Susan D. Franck, *The Legitimacy Crisis in Investment Treaty Arbitration: Privatizing Public International Law through Inconsistent Decisions*, 73 Fordham L. Rev. 1521 (2005) (hereinafter Franck, *Legitimacy*); Andrea J. Menaker, *Benefiting from Experience, in the United States' Most Recent Investment Agreements*, 12 U.C. Davis J. Int'l L. & Pol'y 121, 122 (2005); Abul F. M. Maniruzzaman, *The Lex Mercatoria and International Contracts: A Challenge for International Commercial Arbitration?*,

commentators on domestic adjudication,[334] tend merely to assume that consistency is intrinsically good and inconsistency bad, without much explanation. David Gerber also noted this characteristic of most discussions of consistency:

> Claims for consistency in the application of laws are typically based on the following proposition: Inconsistency in the application of law is intuitively wrong. The last two words in this statement point to the core of the problem of analyzing consistency. The adverb "intuitively" locates the issue in assumptions. Intuition derives from values and associations that are merely assumed, often with little or no awareness of their influence or their consequences. The other key word is "wrong". This is normally the language of morality and ethics. It may in some contexts influence legal decisions, but in most modern legal systems it is understood to be distinct from law, having different functions and different referents. Together, these two aspects of the issue of inconsistent application of law reveal the need to rethink the basis for analyzing the consistency issue. They demonstrate that those policies may often rest on foundations that are inappropriate to the legal and political context in which such policies are applied.[335]

There is the general notion within common law systems that it is better for a "rule of law to be settled than that it be settled right,"[336] which somewhat extreme notion seems to have been carried over into the literature on legal resolution. This might be the type of foolish consistency that the American author Ralph Waldo Emerson referred to as "the hobgoblin of little minds." The following paragraphs explore why meaningful consistency is important to international dispute settlement.

14 Am. U. Int'l L. Rev. 657, 733 (1999) ("A global institutional control mechanism should be established to standardize international arbitral practice and jurisprudence and to help develop a consistent body of arbitral lex mercatoria"). But see Tai-Heng Cheng, *Precedent and Control in Investment Treaty Arbitration*, 30 Fordham Int'l L. J. 1014, 1014 (2007) (going into depth about how precedent operates alongside what he refers to as control).

334 See, e.g., Michael G. Schwartz and Amy Yip-Kikugawa, *Sunshine Beauty Supplies, Inc. v. United States District Court: Mandatory Venue and Motions to Confirm or Vacate under the Federal Arbitration Act*, 32 U.S.F.L. Rev. 629, 652 (1998).

335 See David J. Gerber, *Consistent Application of Competition Laws across System Borders: Rethinking the Issues*, in Parallel and Conflicting Enforcement of Law 167, 167 (Torbjörn Andersson ed., 2005).

336 Susan D. Franck, *The Nature and Enforcement of Investor Rights under Investment Treaties: Do Investment Treaties Have a Bright Future*, 12 U.C. Davis J. Int'l L. & Pol'y 47, 66–67 (2005) (hereinafter Franck, *Nature*) (quoting *Burnet v. Coronado Oil and Gas Co.*, 285 U.S. 393, 406 (1932) (dissenting opinion of Judge Brandeis)).

Before this, however, a definition of consistency must be provided. This subsection adopts the plain-language definition of consistency – "agreement of the parts or elements of a thing with each other."[337] More than just uniform results, this subsection also is interested in uniform procedural rules and the application of those rules. Gerber provides a somewhat useful distinction between procedural consistency and outcome consistency, which provides a useful framework for thinking about this general topic.[338] By procedural consistency, or what is referred to as internal consistency, this subsection means a host of different things dealing with the mechanics of the process: that procedural rules of legal resolution must be made consistent with current practices and with the procedural wishes of the parties,[339] and that the proceedings must be consistent with those rules in order to produce a fair and predictable process for the parties, which will give the parties greater confidence in legal resolution as a method of resolving disputes.[340] By outcome consistency, or external consistency, this subsection means that similarly situated individuals receive a similar resolution of their disputes, regardless of the precise rules or decision-makers involved in the proceedings. Where differences exist between cases, these differences may lead a tribunal to reach different outcomes. Such differences in outcome do not necessarily disrupt consistency as long as the logic behind the two cases remains consistent. This nonuniformity of outcomes is an important aspect of consistency because rarely, if ever, are two disputes

337 "Consistency," OXFORD ENGLISH DICTIONARY (2nd edn, 1989, online version March 2011).

338 See Gerber, *supra* note 335, at 169. Since Gerber is talking about consistency in the enforcement of competition laws, his distinctions are not entirely parallel to the context here, though his thinking is nonetheless helpful in understanding what is at stake.

339 See Henry S. Noyes, *If You (Re)Build It, They Will Come: Contracts To Remake The Rules Of Litigation In Arbitration's Image*, 30 HARV. J.L. & PUB. POL'Y 579, 642–643 (2007) (pointing out how the parties to an arbitration generally can choose to waive such things as oral hearings and rules of evidence, as well as to limit discovery, as long as it is consistent with the arbitration provider's policies).

340 See W. Michael Reisman, *The Breakdown of the Control Mechanism in ICSID Arbitration*, DUKE L.J. 739, 787 (1989); Stephen Hayford and Ralph Peeples, *Commercial Arbitration in Evolution: An Assessment and Call for Dialogue*, 10 OHIO ST. J. ON DISP. RESOL. 343, 349 (1995) (discussing the need for predictability). According to some commentators, procedural safeguards in arbitration are considerably consistent, so much so that they deem arbitration appropriate for resolving such sensitive claims as discrimination within the domestic context. See Jacob E. Tyler, *Mandatory Arbitration of Discrimination Claims under Collective Bargaining Agreements: The Effect of Wright: Wright v. Universal Marine Service Corp., 119 S. Ct. 391 (1998)*, 4 HARV. NEGOTIATION L. REV. 253, 266 (1999).

completely identical. The same presumably can be said about nuclear non-proliferation disputes. It is interesting to note how some commentators directly link consistency between outcomes and the quality of those decisions,[341] which is not necessarily the case considering that a one-page decision in a multimillion-dollar case that comes to the same conclusion as a fifty-page decision is not necessarily a high-quality decision.

Although these are distinct aspects of consistency, they obviously are interlinked. In noting that it is difficult to compare outcomes on account of the various ways of measuring outcomes, Gerber also notes the link between procedure and outcomes – the internal and the external, if you will:

> one can ask whether the outcomes of two court proceedings are consistent when on a given set of facts they both require payment of compensation in the same amount. At one level, yes, but differences in procedural systems . . . may lead to very significant differences in the consequences of the specified orders.[342]

Not only is the relationship between procedures and outcomes complex in the context of studying consistency, there also might be a considerable amount of consistency that occurs through mere chance,[343] so it is particularly difficult to analyze consistency in such a decentralized system as legal resolution.

These paragraphs have provided a basic framework for how to think of consistency in the context of legal resolution. The following section focuses on outcome consistency and some of the main goals that this type of consistency serves.

5.3.1.3.2 Goals of consistency Conceivably there are many goals that consistency serves. The first, and likely ultimate, goal for consistency would appear to be systemic in nature – namely to help perpetuate legal resolution as a valid method of international dispute settlement. The

[341] See also Michael Straubel, *Enhancing the Performance of the Doping Court: How the Court of Arbitration for Sport Can Do Its Job Better*, 36 Loy. U. Chi. L.J. 1203, 1253–1254 (2005) ("Creating a single supplementary of law, such as Swiss law, would make CAS and AAA-CAS decisions more consistent, and thus improve the quality of the decisions, the efficiency of the arbitration process, and protect the fairness of the process").

[342] Gerber, *supra* note 335, at 169 n. 2.

[343] See, e.g., John Y. Gotanda, *Awarding Interest in International Arbitration*, 90 Am. J. Int'l. L. 40, 54 (1996).

causal link would appear to be as follows: consistency increases predictability, which strengthens legal resolution's perceived fairness, which increases users' confidence in the process for settling disputes, and thereby perpetuates the method of resolution.[344] Inconsistency, on the other hand, is a problem because it affects predictability,[345] which in turn impacts potential users' perceptions of fairness and undermines their confidence in the process, thus making it less likely that parties to a transaction will agree beforehand to rely on legal resolution to settle their future disputes or after a dispute has arisen. All the links in this causal chain can be seen as goals in and of themselves, with a host of functional advantages flowing from each. Other goals seem to be able to be fit within these three broader goals leading up to the perpetuation of legal resolution as a valid method of resolving disputes. The remainder of this subsection discusses each in order.

5.3.1.3.2.1 *Predictability* Consistent decision-making through legal resolution, coupled with systematic reporting of those decisions, can lead to predictability.[346] Much in the same way commentators assume the merits of consistency, commentators also assume the merits of predictability.[347] Some commentators even lump consistency and predictability together when talking about legal resolution on the systemic level.[348] Predictability is distinct in that it is the "ability to anticipate future decisions based upon previous determinations such that individuals can plan for the consequences – legal or otherwise – of their actions,"[349] with consistency being one of the elements that makes this possible. Although Susan Franck sees reliability as different from predictability, where reliability is "the ability to depend upon previous

[344] See generally Reisman, *supra* note 333, at 787. Another step also might be added in the causal chain – that the perpetuation of such peaceful means for settling disputes helps avoid armed conflict over these same underlying disputes.

[345] See Franck, *Legitimacy*, *supra* note 333, at 1522 n. 2 (without explaining why predictability is such a problem to the regime).

[346] See Alan Redfern and Martin Hunter, Law and Practice of International Commercial Arbitration 92 (1986). The reporting element falls under transparency, and is discussed more in the section on fairness.

[347] See Matthew Saunders, *Bilateral Investment Treaties Oil the Wheels of Commerce: An Increase in BITs in Recent Years Is Helping to Encourage and Protect International Business, IBA in the News*, June 23, 2004, at http://www.lexisnexis.com/publisher/EndUser?Action=UserDisplayFullDocument&orgId=1746&topicId=26635&docId=l:214719388&start=24.html.

[348] See Gotanda, *supra* note 343, at 55–56.

[349] Franck, *Nature*, *supra* note 336, at 63 n. 62.

determination and know with some certainty that one's conduct conforms to articulated rules and standards,"[350] this subsection sees these as essentially the same.

Predictability in decision-making is the essence of the rule of law.[351] However, what exact benefits does predictability provide to legal resolution, apart from making the rule of law possible (which is no small benefit)? Indeed, predictability of legal resolution provides numerous potential benefits. From the parties' perspective, predictability can help establish a guide for disputants so that they know which arguments to make in their effort to win a case, which guide can also have a preventive role in helping actors know how to behave in order to avoid legal disputes in the future.[352] For example, the OECD concluded in 2005 that international arbitral awards impact the future actions of States that find themselves as defendants in investor–State arbitrations.[353] From the international court or tribunal's perspective, having a consistent line of cases on a particular issue has the potential to make its job considerably easier, inasmuch as uniform practice makes it more obvious which legal rules to apply to particular facts in the case and which not to apply. Such ease in decision-making makes the process more efficient in that the court or tribunal does not need to rethink issues resolved in the prior decisions being followed, which, in turn, could cut the costs and time of legal resolution. Still, there need not be absolute consistency in decisions on a particular issue in order for the court or tribunal to follow prior decisions, as some commentators imply,[354] since following just one other case is still following precedent, even when the bulk of the prior decisions on a particular issue say something entirely different. Therefore, following a prior decision does not necessarily make the decision-making process any easier, since the court or tribunal still has to decide which other case to follow, assuming there are multiple options available to it.

[350] Ibid. [351] See FULLER, *supra* note 249, at 33, 38.

[352] See Sara Needleman Kline, *Sexual Harassment, Wrongful Discharge, and Employer Liability: The Employer's Dilemma*, 43 AM. U.L. REV. 191, 228 (1993).

[353] See Franck, *Nature*, *supra* note 336, at 57 (citing OECD, *Transparency and Third Party Participation in Investor-State Dispute Settlement Procedures: Statement by the OECD Investment Committee*, June 11, 2005, http://www.oecd.org/dataoecd/25/3/34786913.pdf).

[354] See Lynn Katzler, *Should Mandatory Written Opinions Be Required in All Securities Arbitrations? The Practical and Legal Implications to the Securities Industry*, 45 AM. U. L. REV. 152, 196 (1995).

5.3.1.3.2.2 *Fairness* Fairness is the next link in the causal chain. Thomas Franck's work in this area has been particularly influential. In Franck's prolific career of over fifty years as an international-law scholar,[355] he perhaps will be best known for pushing the discourse from whether international law is law and whether international law is effective to whether international law is fair through his 1995 book *Fairness in International Law and Institutions.*[356] Resembling in a way the fairness spoken of by Immanuel Kant, John Rawls, and other philosophers related to the notion of justice as fairness,[357] Franck breaks fairness down into, first, procedural fairness based on whether a community uses the right process in reaching a decision, and, second, substantive fairness based on whether the result is just in the eyes of that community in accordance with notions of distributive justice.[358] With regard to procedural fairness, Franck explains:

> humanity wants reassurance that the emerging legal system is capable of ensuring both stability and progressive change ... They expect that decisions about distributive and other entitlements will be made by those duly authorized, in accordance with procedures which protect against corrupt, arbitrary, or idiosyncratic decision-making or decision-executing. The fairness of international law, as of any other legal system, will be judged ... by the extent to which the rules are made and applied in accordance with what the participants perceive as right process ... Legitimacy thus expresses the preference for order, which may or may not be conducive to change. Nevertheless, it is a key factor in fairness, for it accommodates a deeply felt popular belief that for a system of rules to be fair, it must be firmly rooted in a framework of formal requirements about how rules are made, interpreted, and applied.[359]

[355] See, e.g., David Kennedy, *Tom Franck and the Manhattan School*, 35 N.Y.U. J. INT'L L. & POL. 397, 397 (2003) (praising how prolific Franck was during his career: "A twenty-seven page list of publications. A book every 17.8 months for 43 years. Or 6.34 publications a year – one every 8.2 weeks – for more than four decades").

[356] See FRANCK, *supra* note 226, at 6; see generally ibid. Those who praise Franck's work in this area include the following: ASIL, *Awards Announced at ASIL Annual Member Business Meeting in March*, ASIL Newsletter, 1996 (announcing the book received an ASIL Certificate of Merit); Francis Fukuyama, Book Review, FOR. AFF., May/June 1996, at 135 (praising the book); Rosalyn Higgins, *Thomas M. Franck (1931–2009)*, 103 AM. J. INT'L L. 502, 507 (2009) (same); *International Law and Justice in the Twenty-First Century: The Enduring Contributions of Thomas M. Franck*, 35 N.Y.U. J. INT'L L. & POL. 291 (2003) (same).

[357] See generally JOHN RAWLS, A THEORY OF JUSTICE (1972).

[358] See FRANCK, *supra* note 226, at 7–8. [359] See ibid.

Franck's ideas of procedural fairness are related to his concept of the legitimacy pull of international law.[360] This study fits into these debates perpetuated by Franck. Another Franck, this time Susan Franck, mentions that consistency adds to clarity, which arguably fits under fairness (and transparency), inasmuch as clarity is the "ability to ascertain and understand both the scope of a law and its application."[361] Commentators consider consistency as an indicator of legitimacy (or fairness).[362] Indeed, through consistency, parties to international adjudicative proceedings will know roughly what to expect, which increases the legitimacy of the process.[363]

Fairness often is considered a vague, somewhat subjective notion that commonly is cited by the powerless.[364] *Black's Law Dictionary* defines "fair" as: "Having the qualities of impartiality and honesty; free from prejudice, favoritism, and self-interest. Just; equitable; even-handed; equal, as between conflicting interests."[365] In order to know if a process is fair – or impartial and honest, inter alia – it is important for the process to be transparent so that the process can be assessed according to these factors. Indeed, transparency makes it possible for the parties, as well as possibly interested third parties, to assess for themselves the outcome of the process, thus making the outcome more palatable if adverse to their interests.[366] Providing reasoned decisions and the publication of those decisions are the most important factors in improving the transparency of the international adjudicative process. Nonetheless, consistency can be seen as playing an important secondary role in transparency and fairness inasmuch as it reassures observers that the decisions under inspection are not reached arbitrarily. Interestingly, commentators occasionally lump consistency and transparency together under the same

[360] See Thomas M. Franck, *Legitimacy in the International System*, 82 Am. J. Int'l L. 705, 711–712 (1988); Thomas M. Franck, The Power of Legitimacy Among Nations 50–66 (1990).

[361] See Franck, *Nature*, *supra* note 336, at 63.

[362] See Franck, *Legitimacy*, *supra* note 333, at 1584.

[363] See Cindy G. Buys, *The Tensions between Confidentiality and Transparency in International Arbitration*, 14 Am. Rev. Int'l Arb. 121, 136 (2003).

[364] See, e.g., Ronald Sokol, *Do We Really Need Lawyers?*, Int'l Herald Tribune 7 (March 10, 2006).

[365] Black's Law Dictionary 535 (5th edn, 1979).

[366] See Weixia Gu, *Confidentiality Revisited: Blessing or Curse in International Commercial Arbitration?*, 15 Am. Rev. Int'l Arb. 607, 631 (2004).

general notion.[367] That said, the blind following of past decisions can be considered as arbitrary in itself, for who is to say that those past decisions are worthy of being followed in new (and different) situations? Therefore, the causal link between consistency and transparency is not entirely persuasive. On the contrary, transparency can lead to consistency in that decision-makers and parties alike can know how international courts and tribunals have resolved certain issues in past and present cases, which in turn improves the perceived fairness of the process inasmuch as it allays fears of arbitrariness and informs parties as to what to expect.[368]

Returning to fairness itself, the essence of fairness in this context would seem to be to treat similarly situated individuals similarly, as this means treating the parties evenhandedly and equally between different cases. Indeed, there is the general belief that failure to treat like cases alike "is arbitrary, and consequently unjust or unfair."[369] Such equal treatment is a fundamental aspect of legal resolution,[370] not to mention a crucial element of the rule of law.[371] In the end, a legal system that does not have consistent decisions is bound not to last because "[i]t shocks the sense of rule of law or fairness."[372] Moreover, legal resolution is based on the notion of giving effect to the intentions of the parties. Fairness is the factor that both parties likely expected more than anything else before beginning the adjudicative process; without consistency, therefore, expectations undoubtedly are upset and fairness denigrated,[373] thus making the parties reluctant to rely on it with future disputes.

5.3.1.3.2.3 *Confidence in legal resolution* Consistency is important in helping States have greater confidence in legal resolution, inasmuch as

[367] See e.g. Richard H. Kreindler, *"Arbitral Forum Shopping": Observations on Recent Developments in International Commercial and Investment Arbitration*, 16 AM. REV. INT'L ARB. 157, 172 (2005).

[368] See Buys, *supra* note 363, at 136.

[369] See Franck, *Nature*, *supra* note 336, at 65 (citing, inter alia, Frederick Schauer, *Precedent*, 39 STAN. L. REV. 571, 595–596 (1987)).

[370] See Strong, *supra* note 327, at 987; Smit and Shaw, *supra* note 263, at 277.

[371] See Franck, *supra* note 260, 510–511 n. 47.

[372] See Franck, *Nature*, *supra* note 336, at 66. See also Ian Laird and Rebecca Askew, *Finality versus Consistency: Does Investor-State Arbitration Need an Appellate System*, 7 J. APP. PRAC. & PROCESS 285, 294 (2005) (asserting that investor-State arbitration might not last if certain States, including the United States, are not convinced of its overall fairness).

[373] See Thomas J. Stipanowich, *Arbitration and the Multiparty Dispute: The Search for Workable Solutions*, 72 IOWA L. REV. 473, 502 (1987).

disputants may see it as a hostile environment.[374] In addition to this general environment, inconsistencies often are seen as signaling error or structural flaws within an international dispute settlement regime, which leads to a loss of confidence in that regime.[375] After all, major inconsistencies bring "the law into disrepute," as well as legal resolution into disrepute.[376] Insofar as inconsistency hinders the development of international adjudicative rules and principles, then both are brought into disrepute at the same time.[377]

Predictability, fairness, and confidence in the international adjudication regime are three of the main goals of consistency. Again, commentators may focus on different aspects of any of these, such as clarity or reliability, which this subsection fits under fairness, and may even say that consistency is an end in and of itself. Regardless, there is much agreement in the literature that consistency is needed in order for the international legal system to maintain its viability. Where legal resolution is faced with a hard case, such as with nuclear non-proliferation disputes, such consistency, predictability, and overall fairness are particularly helpful with respect to the disputants' accepting the ultimate decision, even if it goes against their interests.[378] Of course, this is not to say that Security Council actions do not enjoy their own form of legitimacy, namely that provided through collective action.[379] However, when it comes to legitimacy through predictability and procedure, the Security Council arguably comes up short,[380] at least when compared to legal resolution.

374 See Jonathan I. Charney, *Disputes Implicating the Institutional Credibility of the Court: Problems of Non-appearance, Non-participation, and Non-performance*, in THE INTERNATIONAL COURT OF JUSTICE AT A CROSSROADS 288, 305 (LORI F. DAMROSCH ed., 1987).

375 See Franck, *Nature*, *supra* note 336, at 64.

376 See ibid. (citing Matthew Rushton, *Clifford Chance Entangled in Bitter Lauder Arbitrations*, Legal Business, Oct. 2001, at 108).

377 See Maniruzzaman, *supra* note 333, at 733.

378 See Robert Jennings, *Presentation on the Contributions of the Court to the Resolution of International Tensions*, Proceedings of the ICJ/UNITAR Colloquium to Celebrate the 50th Anniversary of the Court, reprinted in CONNIE PECK and ROY S. LEE (eds.), INCREASING THE EFFECTIVENESS OF THE INTERNATIONAL COURT OF JUSTICE 78, 83–84 (1997).

379 See David D. Caron, *The Legitimacy of the Collective Authority of the Security Council*, 87 AM. J. INT'L L. 552 (1993).

380 See David M. Malone, *The Security Council in the 1990s: Inconsistent, Improvisational, Indispensable?*, in NEW MILLENNIUM, NEW PERSPECTIVES: THE UNITED NATIONS, SECURITY AND GOVERNANCE 21 (RAMESH THAKUR and EDWARD NEWMAN ed., 2000). Please note, though, that other international organizations

This section has explored the various benefits of relying on a dispute settlement mechanism that applies law in reaching its decision, which benefits include impartiality, greater control through procedural safeguards, and predictability through the rule of law. These benefits are particularly significant when compared with Security Council resolution, and should go a long way in convincing States and the international community to give legal resolution further consideration. However, legal resolution is not without its flaws in this context, one of which is the focus of the following subsection.

5.3.1.4 Potential conflicts of interest

Chapter 5.3.1.1 above emphasized the impartiality of ICJ judges and international arbitrators in advocating legal resolution of nuclear nonproliferation disputes. Despite all of the guidelines and provisions in the ICJ Statute requiring impartiality and the general expectation that these decision-makers are impartial, observers cannot forget that fifteen States have a national on the bench of the ICJ (in accordance with ICJ Statute Article 3) and a disputant without a national on the bench can appoint an ad hoc judge for the duration of the case (in accordance with ICJ Statute Article 31). Likewise, disputants involved with international arbitration typically directly appoint at least one-third of the arbitrators. Notwithstanding all of the guidelines and requirements of impartiality, a review of ICJ cases and international arbitral proceedings shows that there are quite a few instances where impartiality is questionable, even if an actual conflict does not exist.

The ICJ's most troublesome conflict appears to be when a former counsel or legal adviser in a case before the ICJ becomes an ICJ judge in that very case.[381] When it comes to international arbitration, there are more examples of potential conflicts of interest. In particular, there are

enjoy a somewhat greater degree of predictability when it comes to their procedures and due process safeguards with investigations. See generally CHRIS DE COOKER (ed.), ACCOUNTABILITY, INVESTIGATION AND DUE PROCESS IN INTERNATIONAL ORGANIZATIONS (2005).

381 See, e.g., *Armed Activities on the Territory of the Congo (Democratic Republic of the Congo v. Rwanda)* (New Application), 2006 ICJ Rep. 6 (Feb. 3) (the ad hoc judge designated by Congo was counsel for Congo in the same case); *Barcelona Traction, Light and Power Company, Limited (Belgium v. Spain)* (New Application), 1970 ICJ Rep. 3 (Feb. 5) (the ad hoc judge designated by Spain was counsel for Spain in the same case); *South West Africa (Ethiopia v. South Africa; Liberia v. South Africa)*, 1966 ICJ Rep. 6 (July 18) (the ad hoc judge designated by Liberia was an agent for Liberia in the same case); *Rights of Nationals in the United States of America in Morocco (France v. US)*, 1952 ICJ Rep. 176 (Aug. 27) (the national judges of the case had previously been

four phenomena that might give the appearance of conflict, even if an actual conflict does not exist:

(1) co-counsels in one case become counsel and arbitrator in another, which was simultaneous with or close in time to the earlier arbitration;[382]
(2) co-arbitrators in one case become counsel and arbitrator in another, which was simultaneous with or close in time to the earlier arbitration;[383]
(3) an arbitrator and a counsel switched roles in one arbitration, which was simultaneous with or close in time to another;[384] and
(4) counsel in a later arbitration refers to precedents established in an earlier arbitration in which they acted as arbitrator.[385]

legal adviser to the Foreign Ministry at a diplomatic level before the case reached the ICJ); *Fisheries (UK v. Norway)*, 1951 ICJ Rep. 116 (Dec. 18) (the national judge of one of the parties sat as an ICJ judge despite having been a member of the Norwegian Supreme Court and had ruled in that case on the compatibility of the baseline with Norwegian law). See also ANDREAS ZIMMERMANN et al. (eds.), THE STATUTE OF THE INTERNATIONAL COURT OF JUSTICE: A COMMENTARY 346–348 (2006) (noting as examples the *Asylum* case, the *Right of Passage over Indian Territory* case, the *North Sea Continental Shelf* case, and the *Anglo-Iranian Oil Co.* case).

382 See, e.g., *Universal Compression International Holdings, S.L.U. v. Bolivarian Republic of Venezuela*, ICSID Case No. ARB/10/9, Decision on the Proposal for the Disqualification of Two Members of the Arbitral Tribunal, May 20, 2011 (Venezuela challenged Guido Santiago Tawil's appointment as arbitrator because he and the claimant's counsel had been co-counsel together on a recent arbitration).

383 For example, Mohammed Chemloul and Emmanuel Gaillard were co-arbitrators in the *Victor Pey Casado v. Chile* arbitration, and at the same time, Emmanuel Gaillard served as arbitrator and Chemloul as counsel for the *Consortium Groupement v. Algeria* arbitration and the *LESI v. Algeria* arbitration. See, e.g., *Víctor Pey Casado and President Allende Foundation v. Republic of Chile*, ICSID Case No. ARB/98/2, Registered April 20, 1998; *Consortium Groupement L.E.S.I. - DIPENTA v. People's Democratic Republic of Algeria*, ICSID Case No. ARB/03/8, Award, Jan. 10, 2005; *LESI S.p.A. and Astaldi S.p.A. v. People's Democratic Republic of Algeria*, ICSID Case No. ARB/05/3, Award, Nov. 12, 2008.

384 For example, Schwebel was counsel and Paulsson was arbitrator in *Industria Nacional de Alimentos v. Peru*. See *Industria Nacional de Alimentos S.A. and Indalsa Perú S.A. (formerly Empresas Lucchetti S.A. and Lucchetti Perú S.A.) v. Republic of Peru*, ICSID Case No. ARB/03/4, Award, Feb. 7, 2005. Those roles switched during the same time for the *Hussein Nuaman Soufraki v. United Arab Emirates* arbitration. See *Hussein Nuaman Soufraki v. United Arab Emirates*, ICSID Case No. ARB/02/7, Award, July 7, 2004. Shortly after the end of *Industria Nacional de Alimentos*, their roles again switched in the *Helna International Hotels v. Egypt* arbitration, so that Paulsson served as counsel and Schwebel as arbitrator. See *Helnan International Hotels A/S v. Arab Republic of Egypt*, ICSID Case No. ARB/05/19, Award, July 3, 2008.

385 For example, Stephen Schwebel was an arbitrator in the *Mondev International v. United States* arbitration, which tribunal was constituted on 12 Jan. 2000 and rendered its award on 11 Oct. 2002. See *Mondev International Ltd. v. United States*, ICSID Case No.

It is important to note that just because counsel and arbitrators have these types of relationships in international arbitral proceedings it does not necessarily follow that there is an actual conflict of interests. Instead, these relationships are mentioned simply as examples of cases where an observer might take issue due to the *potential* for conflict to exist.

The fears of bias and potential bias associated with the observations made above could influence the opinion of States and commentators that legal resolution is not appropriate to nuclear non-proliferation disputes, as discussed at the beginning of Part III above. However, if disputants are aware of these risks and remain vigilant in looking for these problems at all stages of the proceedings, they will be able to raise challenges, as has happened in international arbitral proceedings and in ICJ proceedings in the past,[386] thereby having the chance to correct whatever problems might arise. Whether the reader *believes* that problems of these sorts can be corrected through challenges of these types is a separate matter – one that will leave critics of this study doubting, notwithstanding the perceived advantages of legal resolution that come from the application

ARB(AF)/99/2, Award, Oct. 11, 2002. At the same time, Schwebel was counsel in the *Fireman's Fund Insurance Co. v. Mexico* arbitration, in which the award cites the *Mondev* award as precedent. See *Fireman's Fund Insurance Company v. United Mexican States*, ICSID Case No. ARB(AF)/02/1, Award, July 17, 2006, ¶ 176 (referring to *Mondev International Ltd. v. United States of America*, ICSID Case No. ARB(AF)/99/2, Award, Oct. 12, 2002). The same happened with the *PSEG v. Turkey* tribunal referring to the *Mondev* award as precedent, with Schwebel serving as counsel in the *PSEG* arbitration. See *PSEG Global Inc. and Konya Ilgin Elektrik Üretim ve Ticaret Limited Sirketi v. Republic of Turkey*, ICSID Case No. ARB/02/5, Award, Jan. 19, 2007, ¶ 232 (referring to *Mondev International Ltd. v. United States of America*, ICSID Case No. ARB(AF)/99/2, Award, Oct. 12, 2002). Please note that the *PSEG* arbitration started in the same year that the *Mondev* arbitration ended. It is unknown who brought up the *Mondev* precedent in both of these subsequent arbitrations, although critics might speculate.

386 See, e.g., *Free Zones of Upper Savoy and the District of Gex (France v. Switzerland)*, 1929 P.C.I.J. (ser. A) No. 22 (Aug. 19); *Legal Consequences of the Construction of a Wall in the Occupied Palestinian Territory*, Advisory Opinion, Order, 2004 ICJ Rep.3, 4–6 (Jan 30) (Israel challenging Judge Elaraby's participation in the case due to his involvement as a legal adviser to the Egyptian government in the Tenth Emergency Special Session of the General Assembly, which dealt with these same issues of the case, but the Court determined that his involvement in the General Assembly did not warrant his exclusion from the case); *Duke Energy International Peru Investments No. 1 Ltd v. Republic of Peru*, ICSID Case No. ARB/03/28, Aug. 18. 2008 (challenging arbitrator Guido Santiago Tawil); *Participaciones Inversiones Portuarias SARL v. Gabonese Republic*, ICSID Case No. ARB/08/17, Decision on Proposal for Disqualification of an Arbitrator, Nov. 12, 2009 (challenging arbitrator Fadlallah for his involvement in another arbitration against the Gabonese Repubic, which challenge was dismissed).

of law, which has been the focus of this section, or the litigation process, which is the focus of the next.

5.3.2 *The litigation process*

This section explores a number of other important benefits to the disputants and the international community of the litigation process, primary among which is the back-and-forth between the disputants.

5.3.2.1 Showing good faith through legal resolution

Some commentators see States as not taking the litigation process seriously, instead bringing claims before the ICJ or commencing international arbitral proceedings merely as a form of protest against or harassment of the respondent State.[387] Indeed, States sometimes bring claims to the ICJ knowing that the latter would dismiss the case for not having jurisdiction, but still do so in order to bring publicity to the matter, such as the United States did against the Soviet Union for downing US planes in the 1950s.[388] Presumably this would be one fear of States relying on legal resolution of their nuclear non-proliferation disputes. However, such efforts at harassment arguably are not that common, for the simple reason that a State's precious reputation might be damaged if they engaged in harassment.

As constructivist theory posits, reputation might be the main driving force behind why States comply with international law, or rather why they try to be seen as complying with international law.[389] If States are seen as bad actors within the international community, they may lose cooperation opportunities, which can be quite costly.[390] Over time, and in general, States mold their behavior and identity to be seen as complying

[387] See Jan Klabbers, *Straddling Law and Politics: Judicial Review in International Law*, in Towards World Constitutionalism 809, 830 (Ronald St. John Macdonald and Douglas M. Johnston ed., 2005) (citing Tim Koopmans, Courts and Political Institutions 262 (2003)); Bilder, *Adjudication*, *supra* note 217, at 172; Smith, *supra* note 224, at 262–263 (worrying that a court or tribunal's involvement in resolving a nuclear non-proliferation dispute will encourage the "political pursuit of claims of non-compliance even though the claims may have little practical relevance to strategic reality").

[388] See Bilder, *Adjudication*, *supra* note 217, at 172.

[389] See Andrew T. Guzman, How International Law Works 9, 71–117 (2008) (saying that cost-and-benefit analysis determines whether States stress about being seen as complying).

[390] See Eric A. Posner, The Perils of Global Legalism ix (2009).

with international law.[391] Anthony Arend gives as an example that non-nuclear-weapon States under the NPT will see themselves as such, and therefore will not bother to develop a nuclear-weapon program because such actions would be against their perceptions of their own identity.[392] Indeed, it would appear that perceptions and image are particularly important with such sensitive matters as those involving arms control and disarmament,[393] which would include nuclear non-proliferation matters.

States can enjoy several improvements in their image and position by relying on legal resolution. Reliance on legal resolution shows a strong commitment to the obligations under UN Charter Article 2(3) to the peaceful resolution of disputes. Indeed, reliance on legal resolution of disputes is a symbol of civilization and ordered behavior,[394] showing the international community that one is a peace-loving State. As precommitment theory postulates, by exercising self-restraint and limiting their future options by agreeing to legal resolution through compromissory clauses and by giving effect to those agreements, States can improve their future welfare by such measures since they may come to enjoy greater support from other States.[395] Conversely, States that threaten use of nuclear weapons in an aggressive manner risk having the international community form a coalition against them, which works together to ostracize that State.[396] From a psychological perspective, States that rely on legal resolution and the back-and-forth litigation process can gain a measure of satisfaction from showing the world that they take their obligations under UN Charter Article 2(3) seriously by resolving difficult disputes peacefully, as opposed to relying on war or the threat of war.[397] In addition, reliance on legal resolution shows a genuine belief in one's argument, inasmuch as States show that they are willing to defend

[391] See ANTHONY CLARK AREND, LEGAL RULES AND INTERNATIONAL SOCIETY 124–137 (1999).

[392] Ibid., at 136. [393] See generally DANIEL FREI, PERCEIVED IMAGES (1986).

[394] See Bilder, *United States*, *supra* note 69, at 260.

[395] See Steven R. Ratner, *Precommitment Theory and International Law: Starting a Conversation*, 81 TEX. L. REV. 2055, 2057–2060 (2003) (citing, inter alia, THOMAS C. SCHELLING, THE STRATEGY OF CONFLICT 21–52 (1960)).

[396] See DAHLITZ, *supra* note 41, at 36–37.

[397] See E. ALLAN LIND AND TOM R. TYLER, THE SOCIAL PSYCHOLOGY OF PROCEDURAL JUSTICE 26–40 (1988); Robert G. Bone, *The Role of the Judge in the Twenty-First Century: Securing the Normative Foundations of Litigation Reform*, 86 B.U.L. REV. 1155, 1160–1161 (2006).

themselves in open court with legal persuasion.[398] Admittedly, States with a tendency or an inclination not to comply with nuclear non-proliferation obligations likely will have a mindset different from the one mentioned here. Nevertheless, if these would-be noncompliant States were to experiment with compliance, they might find that it also serves their interests by, for example, decreasing the political costs of interacting with other States in the international arena. These potential benefits to relying on legal resolution, however, pale in comparison to the possibility of reliance on legal resolution slowing the Security Council's interference in the situation with its Chapter VII powers, inasmuch as it is difficult for the Security Council to claim that the situation threatens international peace and security when the disputants actively are pursuing peaceful methods of resolution on their own. Thucydides noted many centuries ago that Archidamus, king of Sparta, declared that one could not attack an enemy who was willing to be held accountable for his actions by legal resolution – there, an arbitral tribunal.[399] Arguably, reliance on legal resolution lessens, if it does not entirely remove, the threat to international peace and security because it shows that options other than war still remain and that the disputants are willing to pursue these options. Without such an immediate threat, the Security Council should not interfere in the matter under its Chapter VII powers,[400] assuming that the Security Council takes the language of the UN Charter seriously. As UN Charter Article 39 requires, the Security Council must find the existence of a "threat to the peace, breach of the peace, or act of aggression" before taking measures under Articles 41 and 42 of Chapter VII. The ICTY Appeals Chamber reaffirmed this point in the *Tadić* case.[401] Removing the threat to the peace should forestall the Security Council's Chapter VII actions, if not by removing

[398] See Bilder, *supra* note 217, at 165; Richard B. Bilder, *Judicial Procedures Relating to the Use of Force*, 31 VA. J. INT'L L. 249, 268 (1991).

[399] See JACKSON H. RALSTON, INTERNATIONAL ARBITRATION FROM ATHENS TO LOCARNO 155 (1929) (citing A. MÉRIGNHAC, TRAITÉ THÉORIQUE ET PRATIQUE DE L'ARBITRAGE INTERNATIONAL (1895)); Stanley M. Burstein, *Arms Control in Antiquity*, in 2 ENCYCLOPEDIA OF ARMS CONTROL AND DISARMAMENT 551, 555–556 (RICHARD DEAN BURNS ed., 1993) (noting how a state's refusal of a Greek offer to arbitrate a dispute in ancient times would be seen as undermining that state's cause).

[400] See Dieter Fleck, *Current Legal and Policy Issues*, in FUTURE LEGAL RESTRAINTS ON ARMS PROLIFERATION 21, 36 (JULIE DAHLITZ ed., 1996).

[401] *Prosecutor v. Tadić*, Case No. IT-94-I-AR72, Decision on the Defence Motion for Interlocutory Appeal on Jurisdiction, ¶ 29 (Oct. 2, 1995).

its ability to unlock its powers under Articles 41 and 42 by not finding a threat to the peace or breach of the peace, then by there being insufficient public support to warrant further coercive measures. For States that find themselves within the crosshairs of Security Council Chapter VII actions in response to alleged noncompliance with nuclear non-proliferation agreements, taking the initiative to start the litigation process is one option available to them in a situation in which they might otherwise see themselves as powerless to defend themselves. Even if the Security Council gets involved after the disputants have turned to legal resolution as a peaceful method of resolution, the unilateral sending of a dispute to legal resolution should reduce overall tensions, inasmuch as it shows to the counterparty and the international community alike a willingness to rely on peaceful methods of resolution.[402]

Admittedly, there might be little desire by the international community to protect the sovereignty of recalcitrant States that have acted in such a way as to provoke their being targeted by Security Council Chapter VII actions. Nonetheless, the international community arguably has a collective interest in ensuring that the Security Council continues to operate within the parameters established by the UN Charter, in particular Article 39, lest the Security Council act in an *ultra vires* manner.

5.3.2.2 Expediency through legal resolution

Commentators claim that legal resolution might be too slow and time-consuming for certain politically sensitive disputes,[403] with others identifying nuclear non-proliferation disputes as such disputes.[404] Nuclear non-proliferation disputes pose such significant risks to international peace and security that speed of responsiveness to a situation is important. Indeed, while it may take years and even decades to develop the capacity to make weapon-grade nuclear material, it might not take that long to actually weaponize the nuclear material. Therefore, speed in handling a dispute once it arises is paramount when trying to resolve a nuclear non-proliferation dispute before the situation gets out of hand.

Commentators generally see reliance on legal resolution as injecting urgency into an issue, although presumably nuclear non-proliferation

[402] See Bailey, *supra* note 246, at 114.

[403] Jennings, *supra* note 378, at 85; Tom Ginsburg and Richard H. McAdams, *Adjudicating in Anarchy: An Expressive Theory of International Dispute Resolution*, 45 Wm and Mary L. Rev. 1229, 1327 (2004); Bilder, *Adjudication*, *supra* note 217, at 170.

[404] See Nazario, *supra* note 98, at 145–146.

disputes do not lack in urgency on their own account.[405] What legal resolution lends to nuclear non-proliferation disputes is the ability to resolve matters in a relatively timely fashion through its role in crisis management.[406] One of the key tools of legal resolution that helps in achieving this is what Shabtai Rosenne refers to as incidental jurisdiction, which allows these fora to take whatever measures are necessary for the proceedings to continue without interruption once the forum is seized of the matter and has prima facie jurisdiction over both the person and the matter.[407] ICJ Statute Article 41 provides the ICJ with these particular powers as "circumstances so require," whereas these powers in the context of international arbitration tend to be implied based on the doctrine of functional necessity.[408] As the ICJ explained about incidental proceedings in the *Land, Island and Maritime Frontier Dispute* case, "Incidental proceedings by definition must be those which are incidental to a case which is already before the Court or Chamber. An incidental proceeding cannot be one which transforms the case into a different case with different parties."[409] These necessary measures typically take the form of orders for provisional measures, which do not prejudice the disputants' position on the merits and do not require the consent of the parties,[410] two aspects that are important when it comes to cases

[405] See COLLIER and LOWE, *supra* note 237, at 8–9.

[406] See SHABTAI ROSENNE, ESSAYS ON INTERNATIONAL LAW AND PRACTICE 35–63 (2007) (discussing the ICJ's role in crisis management through its use of provisional measures and its ability to determine its own jurisdiction with such crises as those in Yugoslavia, the DRC, and Iran).

[407] See SHABTAI ROSENNE, 2 THE LAW AND PRACTICE OF THE INTERNATIONAL COURT 1920–2005 578 (4th edn, 2006); SHABTAI ROSENNE, PROVISIONAL MEASURES IN INTERNATIONAL LAW 9–12 (2005) (hereinafter ROSENNE, PROVISIONAL); Vratislav Pechota, *The Future of the Law Governing the International Arbitral Process: Unification and Beyond*, 3 AM REV INT'L ARB 17 (1992) (discussing provisional measures specifically in international arbitration). For more information on provisional measures in legal resolution, see, e.g., JERZY SZTUCKI, INTERIM MEASURES IN THE HAGUE COURT (1983); John G. Merrils, *Interim Measures of Protection in the Recent Jurisprudence of the International Court of Justice*, 44 INT'L & COMP. L.Q. 90 (1995); AMERASINGHE, *supra* note 66, at 314–383.

[408] See generally Lawrence Collins, *Provisional and Protective Measures in International Litigation*, 111 REC. DES COURS 9 (1992); William Wang, *International Arbitration: The Need for Uniform Interim Measures of Relief*, 28 BROOK. J. INT'L L. 1059, 1061–1062 (2003).

[409] *Land, Island and Maritime Frontier Dispute (El Salvador/Hondorus; Nicaragua Intervening)*, Application to Intervene, Judgment, 1990 ICJ Rep. 92, 134 (Sept. 13). See also ROSENNE, PROVISIONAL, *supra* note 407, at 9 (quoting this ICJ case).

[410] See ROSENNE, PROVISIONAL, *supra* note 407, at 9.

involving a State's vital interests. These orders, nevertheless, can be binding, as the ICJ determined in the *LaGrand* case, which involved the ICJ's granting provisional measures to require the respondent State to stay execution of certain foreign individuals on death row in its prisons.[411] An order of provisional measures involves the forum's urgent attempt to avoid irreparable harm to the subject matter of the dispute before a judgment can be rendered.[412] The ICJ repeatedly has required "irreparable prejudice . . . to rights which are the subject of dispute . . ." before granting provisional measures.[413] As this language would indicate, the ICJ has granted measures of these types in only a limited number of instances, typically where a decision on the matter absolutely could not be put off until the end, as with the capital sentences in the *Breard*, *LaGrand*, and *Avena* cases,[414] and as with the use or threat of force in the *Nicaragua* case, the *Armed Activities in the Territory of the Congo* case between the DRC and Uganda in 2000, and the *Application of the International Convention on the Elimination of All Forms of Racial Discrimination* case between Georgia and the Russian Federation in 2008.[415] In the end, the determination depends upon the facts, so it is

[411] See *LaGrand Case (Germany v. US)*, 2001 ICJ Rep. 446, 501–504 (June 27).

[412] See generally ROSENNE, PROVISIONAL, *supra* note 407; Mita Manouvel, *Métamorphose de l'article 41 du Statut de la CIJ*, 106 RGDIP 103 (2002); David E. Wagoner, *Interim Relief in International Arbitration: Enforcement Is a Substantial Problem*, 51 DISP. RESOLUTION J. 68 (1996); John G. Merrills, *Interim Measures of Protection in the Recent Jurisprudence of the International Court of Justice*, 44 INT'L & COMP. L.Q. 90 (1995); D. W. Greig, *The Balancing of Interests and the Granting of Interim Protection by the International Court*, 11 AUSTRALIAN Y.B. INT'L L. 108 (1991); Hugh Thirlway, *The Indication of Provisional Measures by the International Court of Justice*, in INTERIM MEASURES INDICATED BY INTERNATIONAL COURTS 1 (RUDOLF BERNHARDT ed., 1994); Neil E. McDonell, *The Availability of Provisional Relief in International Arbitration*, 22 COLUM. J. TRANSNAT'L L. 273 (1984); JERZY SZTUCKI, INTERIM MEASURES IN THE HAGUE COURT (1983); JEROME B. ELKIND, INTERIM PROTECTION: A FUNCTIONAL APPROACH (1981).

[413] See, e.g., *LaGrand Case (Germany v. US)*, Provisional Measures, Order, 1999 ICJ Rep. 9, 15 (March 3); *Vienna Convention on Consular Relations (Paraguay v. US)*, Provisional Measures, Order, 1998 ICJ Rep. 248, 257 (April 9); Application of the Convention on the Prevention and Punishment of the Crime of Genocide, Provisional Measures, Order, 1993 ICJ Rep.3, 19 (April 8); *Nuclear Tests (Australia v. France)*, Provisional Measures, Order, 1973 ICJ Rep. 99, 103 (June 22).

[414] See *Vienna Convention on Consular Relations (Paraguay v. US)*, Provisional Measures, Order, 1998 ICJ Rep. 248, 257 (1998); *LaGrand Case (Germany v. US)*, Provisional Measures, Order, 1999 ICJ Rep. 9, 15 (March 3); *Avena and Other Mexican Nationals (Mexico v. US)*, Provisional Measures, Order, 2003 ICJ Rep. 77, 91 (Feb. 5).

[415] See *Military and Paramilitary Activities in and against Nicaragua*, Provisional Measures, Order, 1984 ICJ Rep. 169, 186–187 (May 1984); *Armed Activities in the*

difficult to generalize as to the situations in which these fora order provisional measures. International arbitral tribunals show less focus on irreparable harm per se, instead enjoying greater discretion in ordering such interim measures which "it deems necessary to preserve the respective rights of either party."[416] The power to impose provisional measures gives these legal fora tremendous discretion in making sure that the adjudicative process is not frustrated and thus can proceed to conclusion, much like the contempt powers in domestic common-law jurisdictions.[417] If the situation over any nuclear non-proliferation dispute becomes sufficiently urgent to the point where irreparable harm is likely to be caused, it is reasonably foreseeable that the ICJ or an international arbitral tribunal would grant an order of provisional measures.

Admittedly, law and the back-and-forth between disputants involved in the litigation process will take time, inasmuch as States need time to prepare their submissions.[418] However, legal resolution is not as slow as some commentators claim. As the ICJ showed in the *Hostages* case, the ICJ can expedite a claim and a decision in order to respond to emergency situations, handing down an interim order for Iran to return the hostages only two weeks after the United States brought the claim before the ICJ.[419] Even where a claim is not expedited in such a special manner, legal resolution seems to operate faster than its competitors. As Humphrey Waldock noted, the duration of legal proceedings can last between one and four years, although difficult negotiations, such as those involving nuclear non-proliferation matters, typically last much longer than that and may even drag out indefinitely without any progress

Territory of the Congo (DRC/Uganda), Provisional Measures, Order, 2000 ICJ Rep. 111, 127 (July 1); *Application of the International Convention on the Elimination of All Forms of Racial Discrimination, Provisional Measures*, Order, 2008 ICJ Rep. 353, 392–396 (Oct. 15).

416 Permanent Court of Arbitration Optional Rules for Arbitrating Disputes between Two States, Art. 26(1), available at www.pca-cpa.org/upload/files/2STATENG.pdf (last visited June 6, 2011); see also UNCITRAL Arbitration Rules (as revised in 2010), Art. 26(1), available at www.uncitral.org/uncitral/en/uncitral_texts/arbitration/2010 Arbitration_rules.html (last visited June 6, 2011) (listing in a non-exhaustive manner various reasons for an arbitral tribunal to order interim measures).

417 See Ted L. Stein, *Contempt, Crisis, and the Court: The World Court and the Hostage Rescue Attempt*, 76 Am. J. Int'l L. 499, 507 (1982).

418 See Higgins, *supra* note 237, at 45; Alain Pellet, Commentary on the Contributions of the Court to the Resolution of International Tensions, Proceedings of the ICJ/UNITAR Colloquium to Celebrate the 50th Anniversary of the Court, reprinted in Connie Peck and Roy S. Lee (eds.), Increasing the Effectiveness of the International Court of Justice 91, 92 (1997).

419 See Dahlitz, *supra* note 41, at 110.

having been made.[420] This would appear to be the case with the nuclear non-proliferation disputes involving Iran and North Korea.

5.3.2.3 Revealing the heart of the dispute

Not only does the litigation process lead the parties to better understand themselves and their opponent, it helps the ICJ or international arbitral tribunal better understand the nub of the dispute. Through the litigation process, States are able to narrow down the real dispute for the forum and to winnow out facts that are not relevant to the heart of the issue, so that the forum does not waste time and energy addressing side issues and extraneous differences of opinion. Furthermore, when addressing the heart of the matter, the forum will have greater information with which to make their decision inasmuch as the disputants have been able to address their arguments to this matter. This increase in information increases the accuracy of the result in terms of what the disputants' legal obligations were, thereby helping to protect the integrity of the law itself.[421] These benefits of the litigation process are addressed further in the following chapter, so this subsection can be kept brief.

5.3.2.4 Improper shifting of burdens

It is important to note at least one disadvantage of the back-and-forth between the disputants during the litigation process in order to bring more balance to the analysis. The disadvantage that this subsection focuses on is the potential for the ICJ or an international arbitral tribunal to adopt inferences that shift the burden of proof between the disputants in an unpredictable manner. One example is the ICJ's somewhat obscure practice concerning positive inferences in favor of disputants who lose key documents. Two cases can be used to illustrate how such a positive inference has worked in the past in terms of shifting burdens between the disputants. First, in the *Military and Paramilitary Activities* case between Nicaragua and the United States, in which Nicaragua brought a claim against the United States for assisting rebels and mining a port in Nicaragua, the United States claimed that the ICJ did not have jurisdiction because, among other things, the court (actually its predecessor, the PCIJ) never received Nicaragua's unilateral declaration accepting the court's jurisdiction, and therefore the court had no jurisdiction over

[420] See Francis Vallat, *Foreword*, in HUMPHREY WALDOCK, INTERNATIONAL DISPUTES: THE LEGAL ASPECTS I (1972), at vii, xvi.

[421] See Bone, *supra* note 397, at 1162–1163.

the United States either.[422] In response, Nicaragua claimed without any evidence that the ratified declaration must have been lost at sea during the Second World War, which excuse the ICJ blindly accepted in allowing the claim to proceed, over strong US objections.[423]

Second, in the *Land, Island and Maritime Frontier Dispute* case between El Salvador and Honduras, El Salvador and Honduras disagreed over the legal status of islands and maritime spaces within and outside the Gulf of Fonseca. In trying to settle ownership of those spaces, Honduras referred to a 1742 title that a fire supposedly had destroyed and produced a 1766 survey of the land and post-independence republican titles that mentioned the 1742 title, while El Salvador produced to the court an actual (though later) title.[424] In giving Honduras the benefit of the doubt and finding in its favor, the court surprisingly based its decision on this unproduced 1742 title, notwithstanding the enormous debates over its content and validity.[425]

In both cases, the Court was willing to draw certain inferences from questionable evidence, thereby shifting the burden of proof to the other disputant to show that that evidence was in fact incorrect. In both cases, that other disputant was not in a position to have access to the type of information to show that that evidence was incorrect because they had not been involved in the initial activity at issue. This is not to say that the ICJ or an international arbitral tribunal would make similar inferences with a nuclear non-proliferation dispute. Nevertheless, given the political sensitivity and secrecy surrounding attempts at nuclear proliferation, the ICJ or an international arbitral tribunal might have to rely on circumstantial evidence and various inferences made from that evidence to reach its conclusions. Disputants will need to be aware of the possible dangers of the creative use of inferences and be prepared, with the help of competent counsel, to urge the forum to limit itself to conservative inferences made from the available evidence, thereby keeping the burden of proof on the claimant until that burden has been properly satisfied.

This and the preceding subsection focused on the myriad reasons why a State might, and might not, want to give its consent to legal resolution, regardless of whether that consent is given before the dispute arises

422 See *Military and Paramilitary Activities in and against Nicaragua (Nicaragua v. United States)*, Jurisdiction and Admissibility, 1984 ICJ Rep. 392, 399–400 (Nov. 24).

423 See ibid.

424 See *Land, Island and Maritime Frontier Dispute (El Salvador/Honduras)*, Judgment, 1992 ICJ Rep. 351, 459–465 (Sept. 11).

425 See ibid., at 466.

through negotiating and ratifying a treaty with a compromissory clause that gives the ICJ or international arbitral tribunal jurisdiction, or after a dispute arises through a *compromis* or through participating in the litigation. These same factors come into play when a disputant is deciding whether to give effect to that compromissory clause once the dispute has arisen. The international community will consider these same factors when deciding whether to involve legal resolution, either through a request for an ICJ advisory opinion or through the creation of an adjudicative body by an international organization. In short, legal resolution of nuclear non-proliferation disputes has the potential to put legal considerations above political considerations, which adds a large measure of predictability and legitimacy to the resolution of disputes of these types, which in turn can help with the international system's stability. Admittedly, critics of legal resolution always are willing to find a problem with the process,[426] but the analysis provided above suggests at a minimum that not all is bad about legal resolution.

5.3.3 Gaps in nuclear non-proliferation agreements

Before proceeding to the chapter on justiciability, however, this final subsection of this chapter addresses a perceived problem with legal resolution of nuclear non-proliferation disputes that centers on a mischaracterization of the underlying law, not on legal resolution itself, and so was not included in the two preceding subsections on the advantages and disadvantages of the litigation process and the application of law. Some commentators assert that inadequacies in the law frustrate efforts at legal resolution in trying to answer legal questions posed by the disputants.[427] Commentators in the context of this study also make this argument. As Jack Beard has asserted, indeterminate language in arms control agreements, which create ambiguities and gaps in the law, can combine with other negative aspects of the law (such as a relative lack of transparency) to create an especially "unstable environment for cooperation."[428] It is for this reason that this study focuses on legal resolution of disputes involving harder norms such as those involving

[426] See Merrills, *supra* note 84, at 330.

[427] See Rosalyn Higgins, *Policy Considerations and the International Judicial Process*, 17 Int'l & Comp. L.Q. 58, 66–68 (1968).

[428] Jack M. Beard, *The Shortcomings of Indeterminacy in Arms Control Regimes*, 101 Am. J. Int'l L. 271, 286 (2007).

rights and obligations, as explained in the introduction to Part III and in Chapter 6.4 below. To be clear, not all provisions in nuclear non-proliferation agreements constitute soft norms, as some commentators imply when they conclude that legal resolution has not and should not get involved with this regime.[429] This subsection posits that nuclear non-proliferation agreements do not have the level of ambiguities and gaps that these commentators claim.

It is tempting to provide here a review of all of the nuclear non-proliferation agreements with an eye towards identifying *all* of their potential gaps and ambiguities. A review of some of the perceived gaps and ambiguities will suffice for this study's purposes. In analyzing these perceived gaps and ambiguities, it is important to remember that legal resolution and legal analysis of treaties are not about finding abstract meaning, which is difficult according to Wittgenstein's theory of linguistic meaning.[430] Rather, legal resolution is about choosing between competing meanings presented by the disputants through the litigation process.[431] As Dworkin's theory of just adjudication posits, the judge or arbitrator is to make this choice between interpretations in the best possible manner in furthering the requirements of judicial integrity.[432] Critics might claim that Dworkin's theory of just adjudication is too broad a tool to lead to a reliable interpretation of such critically important treaty provisions as those in nuclear non-proliferation agreements. However, as noted above in Chapter 5.2.3.1, the whole point of Chapter 3.1.3 on the indeterminative nature of the Vienna Convention on the Law of Treaties in interpreting treaties, in combination with Wittgenstein's theory of linguistic meaning, is that it seems unwise to insist on any one narrow tool of interpretation over competing tools. The mere fact that a choice between interpretations has to be made does not necessarily make the process inherently subjective, as some commentators are inclined to conclude.[433] Again, impartiality of the decision-maker and the procedural safeguards that legal resolution adopts (as explained in sections 5.3.1.1 and 5.3.1.2 above) are key in making the

[429] See Dahlitz, *supra* note 41, at 126–27, 175; Liles, *supra* note 105, at 139–140.
[430] See Ludwig Wittgenstein, Zettel 5 (1967). [431] See Posner, *supra* note 390, at ix.
[432] See Ronald Dworkin, Law's Empire 243 (1986).
[433] See Paul Martin, *Chavez, the Organization of American States, and Democracy in International Law*, 46 Alberta L. Rev. 933, 941 (2009); Karen Knop, *Reflections on Thomas Franck, Race and Nationalism (1960): "General Principles of Law" and Situated Generality*, 35 N.Y.U.J. Int'l L. & Pol. 437, 446–447 (2003).

operation objective,[434] or at least far less subjective than when, for example, a political body such as the Security Council intervenes where some of the members might have a stake in the matter. Admittedly, impartiality of a court or tribunal does not necessarily guarantee objectivity.[435] Indeed, policy considerations might come into play when choosing between alternative interpretations and rules. However, it is the relative improvement in objectivity – what Franck calls "a subjective determination on the basis of the greatest possible openness, sensitivity and reciprocity"[436] – that should make legal resolution far more attractive an option to the target State and international community than reliance on political resolution of the dispute. Given the ambiguity of language and the variety of tools for interpreting language, it would be futile to go through all of the nuclear non-proliferation agreements and give an "authoritative" interpretation or determination of "gaps." Instead, this subsection reviews some of the supposed loopholes that commentators have identified and assesses from a textualist perspective whether they are as problematic for legal resolution as these commentators claim. When commentators talk of "ambiguities" and "gaps," they tend to talk about those areas that are not covered by the treaty (at least on its face) that they thought should have been covered, or provisions that States subsequently have tried to interpret in order to protect interests that they think are not protected by the treaty (at least on its face).[437] Neither situation necessarily leads to an actual ambiguity or gap within the treaty itself. The fact that a State has a unique interpretation of the treaty which it declares after it has signed the treaty does not mean that the treaty itself contains an ambiguity or gap. States can sign a treaty agreeing that pink is pink and green is green, but then issue a unilateral declaration that they interpret pink as green and green as pink, but that does not change the underlying agreement or its relative clarity.

This is the case with the core treaties in the nuclear non-proliferation regime. From the beginning, avoidance of loopholes has been a priority of drafters of nuclear non-proliferation agreements. In 1965, the General Assembly asked the Conference of the Eighteen Nation Committee on

[434] See THOMAS M. FRANCK, THE STRUCTURE OF IMPARTIALITY: EXAMINING THE RIDDLE OF ONE LAW IN A FRAGMENTED WORLD 82–87 (1968); Knop, *supra* note 433, at 446.

[435] See Knop, *supra* note 433, at 446–447.

[436] THOMAS M. FRANCK, THE STRUCTURE OF IMPARTIALITY: EXAMINING THE RIDDLE OF ONE LAW IN A FRAGMENTED WORLD 307 (1968).

[437] See GOLDBLAT, *supra* note 296, at 116, 149–152.

Disarmament to take care when drafting the NPT not to create loopholes by leaving gaps or ambiguities that might encourage nuclear proliferation.[438] In order to do this, there conceivably are two basic strategies that can be pursued: (1) to be exhaustive in anticipating the potential loopholes and address them adequately so that they no longer exist, or (2) to work in broader principles. It is difficult to anticipate all potential ambiguities inasmuch as language itself can be indeterminate. Therefore, it is no surprise that the Conference and other drafting committees have chosen to work in broader principles. While these broader principles might not specify exactly all of the situations that are prohibited or allowed, this does not mean that these principles are not justiciable or clear.[439] If someone adopted the Atkins rule of no carbohydrates in their diet, would they be following a principle that was any less clear than one that attempted to list all of the carbohydrate-containing foods that are prohibited? Indeed, it is clearer to adopt the broader principle, because they then would not be tempted to play the game of finding carbohydrate-containing foods that were not included in the list because the maker of the list did not have the time or knowledge to be exhaustive when listing all the carbohydrate-containing foods in the world. The same is true of recalcitrant States that may try to exploit to their own benefit any perceived gaps in a list.[440] Some commentators on arms control and disarmament see rules as the only type of norm that is "formulated so specifically and clearly, that they describe a particular type of behaviour and explicitly or implicitly lay down who is obliged to engage in that behaviour and who is the beneficiary of it."[441] However, this study values the use of principles over the use of rules, inasmuch as the former better avoid the creation of loopholes, and especially given that nuclear-weapon technology and systems change so quickly that the flexibility of principles is particularly needed. As Martti Koskenniemi has noted, flexibility in adjudicating nuclear-weapon-related matters is important in order to preserve options for the decision-maker when

[438] For a discussion of this General Assembly resolution, see JOYNER, *supra* note 40, at 6.

[439] GOLDBLAT, *supra* note 296 (asserting that less precision in a definition reflects an impasse that could not be overcome in the negotiations).

[440] David S. Gualtieri et al., *Advancing the Law of Weapons Control: Comparative Approaches to Strengthen Nuclear Non-proliferation*, 16 MICH. J. INT'L L. 1029, 1102 (1995).

[441] DEKKER, *supra* note 22, at 91.

trying to reach the proper solution to a very complex situation, as typically will be the case in life-or-death struggles of States.[442]

Regardless of the presence of principles in nuclear non-proliferation agreements, the precise rules contained therein also are amenable to adjudication. Rules can be divided into rules of conduct and rules of result.[443] While arms control and disarmament treaties are seen as containing many rules of conduct,[444] there also are many rules of result, such as the basic one of the NPT that non-nuclear-weapon States do not acquire nuclear weapons. Some commentators point to NPT Article VI that requires States to "undertake[] to pursue negotiations in good faith on effective measures relating to cessation of the nuclear arms race at an early date and to nuclear disarmament, and on a treaty on general and complete disarmament under strict and effective international control" as an example of a rule that defies a clear classification as one or the other.[445] However, the ICJ clarified the nature of this obligation in its *Legality of the Threat or Use of Nuclear Weapons* advisory opinion as "an obligation to achieve a precise result – nuclear disarmament in all its aspects – by adopting a particular course of conduct, namely, the pursuit of negotiations on the matter in good faith."[446] Regardless, it is the distinction between positive and negative obligations that makes it easier to review the actions of States in accordance with the treaty inasmuch as States have less discretion concerning positive obligations.[447] While there are several negative obligations, such as the one just mentioned, there are plenty of positive obligations that easily can be assessed by a court or tribunal, such as the obligation in Article III(1) to submit to IAEA safeguards, including the requirement in safeguards agreements to "establish and maintain a system of accounting for and control of all nuclear material subject to safeguards under the Agreement."[448] Given these points and given the inherent ambiguity in language, disputes over nuclear non-proliferation agreements seem no less suitable for

[442] See Martti Koskenniemi, *The Silence of Law/The Voice of Justice*, in INTERNATIONAL LAW, THE INTERNATIONAL COURT OF JUSTICE AND NUCLEAR WEAPONS 509 (LAURENCE BOISSON DE CHAZOURNES and PHILIPPE SANDS ed., 1999).

[443] See DEKKER, *supra* note 22, at 97. [444] See ibid., at 97. [445] Ibid., at 98.

[446] See *Legality of the Threat or Use of Nuclear Weapons*, Advisory Opinion, 1996 ICJ Rep. 226, 264 (July 8).

[447] See DEKKER, *supra* note 22, at 97.

[448] *The Structure and Content of Agreements between the Agency and States Required in Connection with the Treaty of the Non-proliferation of Nuclear Weapons*, IAEA Doc. INFCIRC/153, ¶ 7 (1972). See also some of the other questions relating to positive obligations listed in the introduction to Part III.

resolution through legal methods than disputes over treaties in other areas. Indeed, while specific numbers of weapons to be destroyed by a certain time might make adjudication easier with other arms control treaties,[449] the absolute and positive prohibition of acquiring nuclear weapons for non-nuclear-weapon States is sufficiently clear not to require these other elements that commentators see as necessary for other arms control treaties with a less absolute nature. To be clear, this study does not claim that there are no loopholes in these nuclear non-proliferation agreements, although it does claim that the loopholes in these agreements are no more problematic than the loopholes in other treaties, given the inherent ambiguity in language and the variety of interpretive tools that exist.

Admittedly, there are some references in these treaties to agreements that were to be reached in the future, the contents of which were impossible to know at the time the NPT entered into force, thus demonstrating a clear ambiguity or gap in the primary treaty.[450] Indeed, NPT Article V refers to non-nuclear-weapon States being "able to obtain such benefits [from any peaceful applications of nuclear explosions], pursuant to a special international agreement or agreements, through an appropriate international body with adequate representation of non-nuclear-weapon States."[451] However, the mystery of which international body this would be did not last long, with the IAEA requesting that it be that body in 1969, the General Assembly agreeing in 1970, and the IAEA Board of Governors adopting guidelines in 1972 for the IAEA to carry out those specific obligations under the NPT.[452] Therefore, these inchoate obligations became not much of an ambiguity or gap, even though they had been at the time the NPT entered into force. These inchoate provisions aside, nuclear-weapon treaties are not overly ambiguous to the point that the ICJ and international arbitral tribunals cannot interpret them and resolve disputes involving their interpretation. Rather, these supposed ambiguities represent legal principles, which are part of the law and are just as amenable to interpretation through the application of law as legal rules.

[449] See Dekker, *supra* note 22, at 97.

[450] See Göran Lysén, The International Regulation of Armaments: The Law of Disarmament 84 (1990).

[451] NPT, Art. V.

[452] See Donald W. Greig, *The Interpretation of Treaties and Article IV.2 of the Nuclear Non-proliferation Treaty*, 6 Aust. Y.B. Int'l L. 77, 106 (1974).

As this subsection has shown, the gaps that commentators see between the treaties making up the nuclear non-proliferation regime are not as significant as those commentators assert. First, some commentators mistakenly envision a gap when no such gap exists. Philip O'Neill sees a significant gap in the NPT in that the NPT "parties are allowed to create their own indigenous facilities without being in violation since only 'transfer' rather than 'development' of nuclear technology is regulated."[453] O'Neill goes on to explain that this gap was "inserted into the NPT by inadvertence rather than by design, as the assumption was made that the requisite know-how was confined to the nuclear-weapon states (NWS)."[454] However, NPT Article II clearly states that non-nuclear-weapon States cannot "manufacture or otherwise acquire nuclear weapons or other nuclear explosive devices." Therefore, O'Neill envisions a gap in the NPT that simply does not exist. Similarly, in the debate over whether the IAEA can inspect undeclared facilities, commentators who say that the IAEA lacks such powers because of some ambiguities in the NPT seem to intentionally ignore the language of NPT Article III(1),[455] which declares in the last sentence, "The safeguards required by this Article shall be applied on all source or special fissionable material in all peaceful nuclear activities within the territory of such State, under its jurisdiction, or carried out under its control anywhere." As Jessica Eve Stern notes, the focus in Article III(1) is on the materials, wherever they can be found within the State's jurisdiction, not merely its facilities.[456] Nor is the reference in Article III(1) to "peaceful nuclear activities" somehow a limitation on the IAEA's ability to inspect only certain nuclear facilities, as George Bunn asserts it is.[457] While the pre-NPT safeguards agreements did not allow the IAEA to conduct special inspections, this changed with this provision of the NPT.[458] Finally, Dahlitz points to an alleged loophole in NPT Article III(2) that prohibits

[453] O'Neill, *supra* note 220, at 196. [454] Ibid.

[455] See Sloss, *supra* note 152, at 850.

[456] See Jessica Eve Stern, *Co-operative Security and the CWC: A Comparison of the Chemical and Nuclear Weapons Non-proliferation Regimes*, Contemp. Security Pol'y, Dec. 1994, at 30, 35–36 (cited in Sloss, *supra* note 152, at 850).

[457] See George Bunn, *Does the NPT Require Its Non-nuclear-Weapon Parties to Permit Inspection by the IAEA of Nuclear Activities That Have Not Been Reported to the IAEA?*, in A New Nuclear Triad: The Non-proliferation of Nuclear Weapons, International Verification and the International Atomic Energy Agency 44, 45–47 (David Fischer et al. ed., 1992) (cited in Sloss, *supra* note 152, at 850).

[458] See Perez, *supra* note 150, at 771.

non-nuclear-weapon States from providing other non-nuclear-weapon States with "special fissionable material [and] equipment or material especially designed or prepared for the processing, use or production of special fissionable material, to any non-nuclear-weapon State for peaceful purposes. . . ."[459] She emphasizes the phrase "for peaceful purposes," asserting that States can provide and receive this equipment and material if the purpose is for a non-peaceful (i.e. military) purpose.[460] This view not only makes a mockery of the purpose of the NPT, but it also ignores the language in Article II that non-nuclear-weapon States are "not to seek or receive any assistance in the manufacture of nuclear weapons or other nuclear explosive devices," which arguably covers the so-called loophole she envisions in Article III(2).

Other commentators artificially create an "ambiguity" in nuclear non-proliferation agreements. For example, Daniel Joyner points out that NPT Article II does not say whether "manufacture" there includes the development of "design information regarding nuclear explosive devices,"[461] which is correct. Nor do regional nuclear-weapon-free zones such as under the Treaty of Tlatelolco prohibit transit of nuclear weapons in aircraft and ships, as Goldblat points out.[462] However, must a treaty list absolutely all possible permutations of an allowance or a prohibition for the treaty to not have any gaps? What about the *Lotus* principle – that States are allowed to do whatever is not prohibited by international law? Commentators who artificially create these "ambiguities" seem to forget about this principle, thus requiring a treaty to exhaustively spell out all that is allowed and prohibited under a treaty. Indeed, the prohibition to "manufacture or otherwise acquire nuclear weapons or other nuclear explosive devices" seems clear enough using the plain-language meaning of the words provided in that sentence. For example, the plain-language meaning of "manufacture" is "to make a product out of raw material."[463] However, "otherwise acquire" would seem to limit "manufacture" to the more advanced stages of owning a nuclear weapon or nuclear explosive device. Therefore, a reasonable reading of that provision would not prohibit designs of such devices. Similarly, Joyner and others cite NPT Article II's prohibition of

[459] DAHLITZ, *supra* note 41, at 175. [460] Ibid.

[461] JOYNER, *supra* note 40, at 16–17. See also LYSÉN, *supra* note 450, at 160.

[462] See GOLDBLAT, *supra* note 296, at 150.

[463] "Manufacture," OXFORD ENGLISH DICTIONARY (3rd edn, 2000, online version, March 2011).

non-nuclear-weapon States to "receive the transfer from any transferor whatsoever of nuclear weapons or other nuclear explosive devices or of control over such weapons or explosive devices directly, or indirectly," and notes that it is unclear whether the United States physically locating its nuclear weapons in the territory of NATO non-nuclear-weapon allies is a violation.[464] Joyner observes that the United States maintains both physical possession and operational control over these weapons, although he notes that NATO strategic policy allows the US president to authorize the deployment of these weapons by NATO allies in times of general war, under the overall command of the NATO supreme allied commander.[465] However, this situation is not a transfer of nuclear weapons, according to the plain-language meaning of "transfer" – "to convey or take from one place, person, etc. to another."[466] A situation in which NATO allies might be able take physical control over these nuclear weapons is problematic in light of NPT Article II, with the transfer of physical control seeming to violate that provision. However, until that actually takes place, plans to allow such transfer are not prohibited by the NPT, in the same way that the design of nuclear weapons and nuclear explosive devices is not a violation of Article II. These stretched scenarios do not show gaps in the nuclear non-proliferation regime so much as show what the legal limits are of its provisions.

Again, some might see ambiguity in NPT Article IV by asking how inalienable are the rights of NPT members to "develop research, production and use of nuclear energy for peaceful purposes without discrimination," as the NPT provides.[467] Some see this as a major inconsistency of the NPT in prohibiting non-nuclear-weapon States from developing nuclear weapons but allowing them to develop nuclear energy for peaceful purposes.[468] It is unclear what is so inconsistent

[464] See Joyner, *supra* note 40, at 13–14. See also Singh and McWhinney, *supra* note 222, at 242.

[465] See Joyner, *supra* note 40, at 13–14.

[466] "Transfer," Oxford English Dictionary (2nd edn, 1989, online version, March 2011).

[467] Alice Slater, *The "Inalienable Right" to Peaceful Nuclear Power: A Recipe for Chaos*, in At the Nuclear Precipice: Catastrophe or Transformation? 57 (Richard Falk and David Krieger ed., 2008) (analyzing perceived paradoxes with inalienability in this context); Greig, *supra* note 452, at 77.

[468] See Lysén, *supra* note 450, at 160; Giorgio Franceschini, *Assessing the Nuclear Non-proliferation Regime: What Are the Loopholes? What Are the Challenges?*, in Europe Facing Nuclear Weapons Challenges 155, 170–173 (Grégory Boutherin ed., 2008) (calling the ability of non-nuclear-weapon States to develop

about this as to classify it as an ambiguity or a gap. Indeed, it simply is what is prohibited and what is allowed in the treaty, with the key point being that efforts at producing nuclear energy cannot be diverted away from their peaceful purposes. Indeed, the ability to separate the peaceful use of nuclear energy from the military use is the fundamental premise of the entire nuclear non-proliferation regime – the Grand Bargain of the nuclear non-proliferation regime.

The entire nuclear non-proliferation movement and regime centers on providing non-nuclear-weapon States with technology for producing nuclear energy for peaceful purposes – that was the goal behind the Atoms for Peace initiative in 1953, the creation of the IAEA in 1957, and the adoption of the NPT in 1968.[469] In return, as part of the Grand Bargain of the NPT, non-nuclear-weapon States were to relinquish nuclear-weapon ambitions and submit to safeguards measures. By removing the major benefits to States of the ability to develop their nuclear energy capacities for peaceful purposes, the Grand Bargain would stop being so grand for non-nuclear-weapon States. Iran claims that all of its recent involvement with nuclear energy research is for peaceful purposes, while the West questions Iran's motivation for, among other things, the reason that it has an abundance of oil and natural gas, which removes the need for nuclear energy there.[470] The West's logic seems clear and understandable,[471] although it nonetheless seems quite discriminatory – just because Iran has oil and natural gas should not mean that it somehow loses its "inalienable right" mentioned in Article IV.[472] One must not forget that even uranium enrichment, when declared, is not a violation of the NPT per se, even if other States want such enrichment efforts to stop.[473]

While there are problems in the application of the NPT's norms, these problems do not result from any ambiguity in the NPT, unless one is willing to accept the type of untenable interpretation method that

nuclear energy for peaceful purposes the "largest loophole in the non-proliferation regime").

469 See Namira Negm, Transfer of Nuclear Technology under International Law: Case Study of Iraq, Iran and Israel 1, 14–38 (2009) (discussing the benefits of nuclear energy used for peaceful purposes).

470 See Joyner, *supra* note 40, at 50–51.

471 See Albert Wohlstetter et al., Swords from Plowshares: The Military Potential of Civilian Nuclear Energy (1977) (seeing the main problem of the regime as the ease in diverting nuclear energy for peaceful purposes to weapon-related purposes); Matthew Kroenig, Exporting the Bomb: Technology Transfer and the Spread of Nuclear Weapons (2010) (same).

472 See Joyner, *supra* note 40, at 53.

473 See ibid., at 52–53.

renders "inalienable" as meaning something other than "inalienable." Such an argument seems as reasonable as an argument that the reference to "nuclear weapons" and "other nuclear explosive devices" is too unclear. Admittedly, the drafters should have included a definition of these terms, similar to the one provided in Article 5 of the Treaty of Tlatelolco, as discussed in Chapter 2.1.2 above:

> any device which is capable of releasing nuclear energy in an uncontrolled manner and which has a group of characteristics that are appropriate for use for warlike purposes. An instrument that may be used for the transport or propulsion of the device is not included in this definition if it is separable from the device and not an indivisible part thereof.

Nonetheless, is it really that difficult to know what a nuclear explosive device is? After all, either a weapon or device "derives its destructive power from the release of nuclear energy" or it does not, as the plain-language meaning of the term "nuclear" provides.[474] How nitpicky should we be over such common-sense terms? Indeed, as explained below, there are considerable benefits to not being too specific in these treaties, primary among which is avoiding recalcitrant States' exploiting perceived loopholes.

Again, much frustration has been exhibited by non-nuclear-weapon States over the apparent lack of progress by nuclear-weapon States in reaching nuclear disarmament, not to mention general and complete disarmament. NPT Article VI requires States parties to "undertake[] to pursue negotiations in good faith on effective measures relating to cessation of the nuclear arms race at an early date and to nuclear disarmament, and on a treaty on general and complete disarmament under strict and effective international control." Some commentators point to the ambiguity of this provision in the phrases "to pursue negotiations" and "at an early date,"[475] although these phrases make it clear that this provision requires no particular result, but only that States *try* to negotiate in good faith towards these ends. Admittedly, "good faith" is a legal principle, the determination of which could be justiciable.[476] However, according to Article VI, negotiations are allowed to go slow and still be done in good faith, so it will be difficult to point to other measurable indicators to show a violation of this requirement. The 2000 NPT Review Conference made clear that good faith requires thirteen

[474] Lesley Brown (ed.), The New Shorter Oxford English Dictionary on Historical Principles 1951 (5th edn, 1993).
[475] See Joyner, *supra* note 40, at 57. [476] Ibid., at 57–58.

practical steps towards implementing Article VI, including the ratification of the CTBT and the continued negotiation of the Fissile Materials Cutoff Treaty, but the 2005 NPT Review Conference stepped back from including many of these practical steps under the definition of "good faith" in this context.[477] In short, the intent of the negotiating parties to the NPT seems entirely clear in this regard in not binding the parties to a particular result, and any perceived ambiguity will not be in the treaty itself but in the ultimate outcome of such a weak obligation. In light of such weak obligations, it is difficult to accept an argument that non-nuclear-weapon States could reasonably rely on this lack of significant progress as a legal justification to claim that the NPT obligations on non-nuclear-weapon States are null and void, as Joyner claims.[478]

Admittedly, the withdrawal provisions of many of the nuclear non-proliferation agreements cause some problems. PTBT Article IV on withdrawal provides, "Each Party shall in exercising its national sovereignty have the right to withdraw from the Treaty if it decides that extraordinary events, related to the subject matter of this Treaty, have jeopardized the supreme interests of its country." While Andrew Martin hoped in 1963 that this language would not prove to be the model for withdrawal provisions in future nuclear non-proliferation agreements,[479] this hope was dashed in 1970 with the entry into force of NPT Article X and most other non-proliferation agreements. In particular, the ability of a State to determine for itself what constitutes an extraordinary event goes against the legal maxim that one should not act as judge in one's own case.[480] However, this provision is clear in allowing such self-determination. In short, a less-than-ideal provision does not constitute a gap or ambiguity in that provision. What constitutes an "extraordinary event" or "supreme interests" might be unclear, and commentators and world opinion might try to objectively define such key terms as "extraordinary" and "supreme interests" here.[481] Indeed, "extraordinary" here could mean a breach of the PTBT or a test by a nonmember, for example.[482] However, the fact that the defining of these phrases falls into the hands of the withdrawing State to decide means that it ultimately does not matter what the exact definition might be, which undoubtedly was the intent of the drafters, most notably the Soviet Union.[483]

[477] Ibid., at 60. [478] See ibid., at 66–67. [479] See MARTIN, *supra* note 241, at 80.
[480] See ibid., at 79. [481] See, e.g., LYSÉN, *supra* note 450, at 176–181.
[482] See GOLDBLAT, *supra* note 296, at 42. [483] See MARTIN, *supra* note 241, at 79.

Finally, some commentators see gaps in application of the law as gaps in the treaty itself. In particular, they emphasize the point that not all States are members and that the treaty does not cover all possible individuals and entities, and characterize this as a fundamental gap in the treaty. The Council on Foreign Relations and others see gaps in the NPT (and by extension the IAEA Statute and IAEA safeguards agreements) as meaning that there are nonmembers and that some entities are not covered by treaty, such as non-State actors.[484] However, these are not gaps in the treaty but rather gaps in its applicability. Complete universality of a treaty would be too much for anyone to expect from any treaty, inasmuch as no treaties have all States as members except the Geneva Conventions. Not even the UN Charter enjoys universality, with the Cook Islands, the Holy See, and Niue still nonmembers of that regime.

The problem with the nuclear non-proliferation regime ultimately might be the fact that there are some States who refuse to become or remain a party.[485] However, that does not necessarily equate with an inadequacy of the treaties making up the nuclear non-proliferation regime. There are ways to encourage recalcitrant States to join the regime. For example, Barry Kellman argues that members of the NPT and IAEA safeguards system could have easier access to the argument of self-defense than nonmembers when using force against another State to destroy their nuclear capabilities.[486] However, a nonmember would find it much more difficult to justify the same attack,[487] even though the right to self-defense ostensibly is an inherent right of States, as alluded to in UN Charter Article 51, thereby constituting an infringement of nonmembers' rights in an effort to shift their incentive structure to becoming members. Other suggestions may be far more respectful of State sovereignty and try to incentivize nonmembers by giving them reasons to trust that they can commit to denuclearization, such as creating greater security assurances from nuclear States and the creation of nuclear-weapon-free zones in key regions of the world.[488] However, most of these new incentives do not come in the form of amending the NPT or other key instruments, as these tend to be seen as sacrosanct.

[484] See Council on Foreign Relations, *Issue Brief: The Global Nuclear Nonproliferation Regime*, www.cfr.org/publication/18984/; O'Neill, *supra* note 220, at 196; Singh and McWhinney, *supra* note 222, at 245; Bilder, *Nuclear*, *supra* note 248, at 5.

[485] See Fleck, *supra* note 400, at 25; Joyner, *supra* note 40, at 68.

[486] See Barry Kellman, *International Consensus and States Non-parties*, in Future Legal Restraints on Arms Proliferation 151, 172–173 (Julie Dahlitz ed., 1996).

[487] See ibid.

[488] See Petrovsky, *supra* note 231, at 5–6.

Again, this study does not see the problem with imperfect application as being a result of some ambiguity of the nuclear non-proliferation regime, as some commentators seem inclined to argue.

In sum, although commentators might see provisions of nuclear non-proliferation agreements as being "vague" or undesirable, these should not be translated into seeing nothing but gaps in the law. While some commentators see lawyers as being good at detecting ambiguities in treaties,[489] lawyers in the context of the nuclear non-proliferation regime seem good at manufacturing ambiguities, or rather calling provisions they think are less than ideal "ambiguous." Such less-than-ideal language need not be a negative of the regime, because, as explained above concerning the distinction between rules and principles, principles have a perceived advantage in avoiding loopholes. Regardless, legal commentators should avoid seeking to, as Michael Reisman refers to it, "narcotize ourselves into an imagined bliss by transforming only in our own minds preference into prescription."[490]

5.4 Conclusion for this chapter

This chapter has laid out the various ways in which compromissory clauses provide the ICJ and international arbitral tribunals with jurisdiction over nuclear non-proliferation disputes. This chapter also explored some of the key factors that States might consider when deciding whether to consent to a treaty containing a compromissory clause giving these fora jurisdiction or to a *compromis* that similarly gives these fora jurisdiction, or otherwise to participate in the proceedings, thus giving the forum prorogated jurisdiction. The international community might also consider these same factors when deciding whether to work through the UN General Assembly to request an advisory opinion from the ICJ on a legal question relating to a nuclear non-proliferation issue, to create a quasi-judicial body through the plenary organ of an international organ to handle a nuclear non-proliferation dispute, or otherwise to encourage the resolution of nuclear non-proliferation disputes through legal resolution.

As the following chapter on justiciability explains, justiciability likely will not be that significant a barrier inasmuch as treaty interpretation

[489] See Martin, *supra* note 241, at 6.

[490] W. Michael Reisman, *Deterrence and International Law*, in Nuclear Weapons and Law 129 (Arthur Selwyn Miller and Martin Feinrider ed., 1984).

and application lie at the heart of most nuclear non-proliferation disputes, which is a distinctly legal operation. In other words, clear consent to the jurisdiction of the ICJ or an international arbitral tribunal essentially will be enough for the tribunal eventually to decide on the merits. After all, it presumably will be difficult for these fora to justify their existence if they refuse to handle the disputes that States voluntarily give them to resolve. Therefore, developing the will of States to invoke legal resolution contained in compromissory clauses and to join treaties with such compromissory clauses is even more important than the analysis of whether legal resolution has the tools to resolve these disputes, which is why this chapter was placed before the following one concerning justiciability. Nevertheless, in developing States' will to rely on legal resolution, justiciability is relevant inasmuch as the question whether a forum has the tools to handle a dispute will influence a State's willingness to consent to that forum's jurisdiction. Therefore, justiciability simultaneously (and paradoxically) is important and unimportant.

6

Justiciability of nuclear non-proliferation disputes

Former prime minister of Pakistan Benazir Bhutto proved the eternal optimist when she affirmed, "All our problems, all our disputes, all our disagreements can be resolved quickly to mutual satisfaction if we address the question." While this study does not necessarily share her overall optimism, it nevertheless shares her belief in the central importance of disputants "addressing the question." Under a derivative form of Habermas's communicative theory (as alluded to in the preceding chapter), disputants become better able to understand one another as they prepare submissions and otherwise participate in the litigation process, inasmuch as it helps clarify strengths and weaknesses on both sides and helps focus the disputants on the nub of the dispute, as uncontested issues fall away after each round of submissions and disputants further hone their points. From this constructivist perspective, which is similar to Harold Lasswell's theory of communication,[1] law and legal processes actually are forms of communication that foster collaborative efforts at reaching greater understanding. At the same time as this communication is going on, a legal forum naturally becomes capable of resolving even the most politically sensitive dispute as the disputants transform the dispute into a legal one by framing the issues in legal terms, as this chapter posits under the process approach to justiciability. Under this approach, not only can the ICJ or an international arbitral tribunal find it has the tools necessary to resolve a dispute, but the disputants improve their ability to "address the question" while gaining in mutual understanding through that process. In short, the process associated with legal resolution may be the very thing that disputants need to make progress, *especially* with such complex, politically sensitive disputes as those involving nuclear non-proliferation.

[1] See generally Harold Lasswell, *The Structure and Function of Communication in Society*, in THE COMMUNICATION OF IDEAS 37 (LYMAN BRYSON ed., 1948).

The preceding chapter focused on some of the reasons critics might give for why legal resolution cannot handle nuclear non-proliferation disputes. This chapter focuses on presumably the main reason why legal resolution has not been seen as a viable option – the belief that such disputes are too politically sensitive to be given to a third party to reach a decision that would bind them.[2] Such a criticism is not limited to nuclear non-proliferation disputes and weapon-related disputes but is levied against legal resolution of all disputes that are important for international relations.[3] The essence of this argument involves justiciability, or arbitrability, as the case may be,[4] and the question whether legal resolution can handle a dispute that has political elements to it.

These questions are addressed from two perspectives. First, critics might claim that these disputes involve a State's vital interests (or national security interests), with the belief that a State will not relinquish control over such matters to third parties in such situations because of issues with State sovereignty and general distrust.[5] In this regard, the section in Chapter 5.3 on control and trust with legal resolution and

[2] See GUIDO DEN DEKKER, THE LAW OF ARMS CONTROL 71 (2001); ANDREW MARTIN, LEGAL ASPECTS OF DISARMAMENT 1, 52–59 (1963); DANIEL H. JOYNER, INTERNATIONAL LAW AND THE PROLIFERATION OF WEAPONS OF MASS DESTRUCTION 200–201, 216 (2009); JULIE DAHLITZ, NUCLEAR ARMS CONTROL 91 (1983); Harry H. Almond Jr., *Deterrence and a Policy-Oriented Perspective on the Legality of Nuclear Weapons*, in NUCLEAR WEAPONS AND LAW 57, 59 (ARTHUR SELWYN MILLER and MARTIN FEINRIDER ed., 1984); *Military and Paramilitary Activities in and against Nicaragua (Nicaragua v. US)*, 1986 ICJ Rep. 14, 168 (June 27) (Judge Lachs asserting in his separate opinion that disputes involving disarmament and issues of the balance of power would be types of substance that might not be suitable for legal resolution on account of their high political sensitivity, though without distinguishing nuclear non-proliferation disputes from other disarmament disputes).

[3] See LELAND M. GOODRICH AND ANNE P. SIMONS, THE UNITED NATIONS AND THE MAINTENANCE OF INTERNATIONAL PEACE AND SECURITY 322 (1955).

[4] Commentators often see justiciability and arbitrability as interchangeable, as Judge Huber asserted in the arbitration British Claims in the Spanish Zone of Morocco. See JOHN COLLIER and VAUGHAN LOWE, THE SETTLEMENT OF DISPUTES IN INTERNATIONAL LAW: INSTITUTIONS AND PROCEDURES 14 (1999) (citing *British Claims in the Spanish Zone of Morocco*, 2 UNRIAA 615 (1925)). Some see international arbitral tribunals as not paying much attention to arbitrability if jurisdiction clearly exists for the tribunal. However, a relatively recent tribunal indicates that arbitrability is of crucial importance. See *SGS Société Générale de Surveillance S.A. v. Republic of the Philippines*, Decision on Objections to Jurisdiction, Jan. 29, 2004, para. 154.

[5] See Hans von Mangoldt, *Arbitration and Conciliation Treaties*, in 1 ENCYCLOPEDIA OF PUBLIC INTERNATIONAL LAW 230, 233 (RUDOLF BERNHARDT ed., 1992); Joanne K. Lelewer, *International Commercial Arbitration as a Model for Resolving Treaty Disputes*, 21 N.Y.U. J. INT'L L. & POL. 379, 401 (1989); DEKKER, *supra* note 2, at 71, 110.

nuclear non-proliferation disputes is relevant here, which is why those sections preceded this chapter. As this chapter posits, the UN era and the dispute settlement provisions entered into during the UN era seem to have heralded the end of the notion of vital interests acting as a formal barrier to a court or tribunal's hearing and deciding a matter.

Second, critics might frame the issue in terms of the political elements that exist alongside the legal ones in such nuclear non-proliferation disputes to argue that legal resolution cannot handle such mixed disputes on account of these political elements.[6] Indeed, some commentators assert that the involvement of politics in a dispute can actually end up destroying a court or tribunal.[7] However, as this chapter shows, legal resolution has no problem in handling disputes of a mixed legal–political nature. Assuming, *arguendo*, that there are some elements that are too political for a court or tribunal to handle, the dispute easily can be fragmented into its respective elements, with the more legal ones being sent to legal resolution, thereby leaving a simpler overall dispute for resolution through more diplomatic channels. As a result, the ICJ and international arbitral tribunals should be seen as having the tools to hear and decide nuclear non-proliferation disputes, thereby overcoming the question of justiciability.

This chapter is divided into several sections. Chapter 6.1 provides a transition between this and the previous chapters by defining justiciability and explaining its similarities with jurisdiction. This transition not only helps avoid confusion between the two, but more importantly it sets up this chapter's sub-thesis that jurisdiction largely will trump justiciability when it comes to disputes that involve compromissory clauses. Chapter 6.2 reviews the historic importance of justiciability of legal resolution, especially the time when the involvement of a State's "vital interests" was a major limitation. Chapter 6.3 analyzes justiciability when a court or tribunal is faced with the task of treaty interpretation, since it is foreseen that nuclear non-proliferation disputes primarily will involve the interpretation of treaties. Chapter 6.4 explores how the ICJ or an international arbitral tribunal would interpret two nuclear non-proliferation agreement provisions, with the recent case in mind of China selling nuclear reactors to Pakistan for two

6 See Adrian Fisher, *Arms Control and Disarmament in International Law*, 50 VA. L. REV. 1200, 1219 (1964); ALLAN GOTLIEB, DISARMAMENT AND INTERNATIONAL LAW: A STUDY OF THE ROLE OF LAW IN THE DISARMAMENT PROCESS 30 (1965).

7 See JEAN ALLAIN, A CENTURY OF INTERNATIONAL ADJUDICATION: THE RULE OF LAW AND ITS LIMITS 2 (2000) (discussing the rise and fall of the 1907 Central American Court of Justice).

nuclear power plants there. Assuming, *arguendo*, that justiciability is not obvious to the forum faced with this task, Chapter 6.5 analyzes and evaluates the basic approaches that the ICJ and international arbitral tribunals have taken to justiciability and asserts that one of those ways seems to be the preferred approach – the approach where all disputes placed before a court or tribunal become justiciable based on the process these fora apply to the dispute in attempting to resolve it. Again, assuming, *arguendo*, that the reader is not persuaded that this process approach is the appropriate way for determining justiciability, perhaps because of its functional orientation, Chapter 6.6 explores the possibility of fragmenting disputes into their constituent elements, sending the more legal elements to legal resolution and leaving the simplified remainder for political resolution. In short, this chapter concludes that justiciability and arbitrability are not likely to be significant barriers to legal resolution's playing a role in resolving nuclear non-proliferation disputes, assuming that the forum finds the requisite jurisdiction to handle the matter.

6.1 Basics of justiciability

This chapter begins with definitions. It is difficult to define "justiciability" without also defining "dispute." The standard definition of "dispute" in the international-law context comes from the Permanent Court of International Justice, which explained in *obiter dicta* of its *Mavrommatis Palestine Concessions* case that a "dispute" is "a disagreement on a point of law or fact, or a conflict of legal views or interests between two persons."[8] The ICJ often quotes this definition when

[8] *Mavrommatis Palestine Concessions (Greece v. UK)*, 1924 P.C.I.J. (ser. A) No. 2, at 11 (Aug. 30). See Robert Jennings, *Reflections on the Term "Dispute"*, in Essays in Honour of Wang Tieya 401, 402 (R. St. J. Macdonald ed., 1993) (hereinafter Jennings, *Reflections*) (arguing that this is *obiter dicta* because the PCIJ had jurisdiction over all disputes between the Mandatory and members of the League of Nations under Article 26 of the Mandate for Palestine, not just legal disputes); Nii Lante Wallace-Bruce, The Settlement of International Disputes: The Contribution of Australia and New Zealand 5 (1998). It is important to note here that the definition of "dispute" in the judicial context is distinct from "dispute" under UN Charter Articles 1(1) and 2(3) and Chapter VI, which determines when the UN Charter mechanisms for peaceful dispute settlement are to come into action. UN Charter Article 1(1) specifies that one of the main principles of the UN Charter is "to bring about by peaceful means, and in conformity with the principles of justice and international law, adjustment or settlement of *international disputes* or situations which might lead to a breach of the peace." If nothing else, the last portion of that provision establishes that not all disagreements rise to the level of an international dispute within the meaning of the UN Charter,

deciding whether there is a dispute for preliminary purposes.[9] The determination is an objective one for the Court to make,[10] with the requirement that a claim by one party is directly opposed by the other party.[11] This type of dispute also must exist at the time that the application was filed with the Court.[12] This definition also is considered as the definition for "legal dispute," or rather a dispute that a court or tribunal is able to resolve by applying rules of law,[13] thus indirectly requiring all

since there also can be situations or conflicts that cause problems for international peace and security similar to those international disputes cause, as was alluded to in Chapter 4 above. One point that should not be overlooked in the last portion of Article 1(1) is that these situations and conflicts that fall short of an international dispute nevertheless enter the Charter's definition of "dispute" once it is deemed that they "might lead to a breach of the peace." In short, since disputes, situations and conflicts all can give rise to either UN Charter Chapter VI or Chapter VII measures, it is not crucial to distinguish between these for the purposes of this section on justiciability.

9 See, e.g., *Case Concerning Application of the International Convention on the Elimination of All Forms of Racial Discrimination (Georgia v. Russian Fedaration)*, Preliminary Objections, ICJ General List No. 140, April 1, 2011, at 16; *Avena and Other Mexican Nationals (Mexico v. US)*, 2003 ICJ Rep. 77, 88 (Feb. 5); *East Timor (Portugal v. Australia)*, 1995 ICJ Rep. 90, 99 (June 30); *Case Concerning the Continental Shelf (Tunisia v. Libya)*, 1985 ICJ Rep. 192, 192 (Dec. 10); *Aegean Sea Continental Shelf (Greece v. Turkey)*, Jurisdiction, 1978 ICJ Rep. 3, 13 (Dec. 19); *Northern Cameroons (Cameroon v. UK)*, Preliminary Objections, 1963 ICJ Rep. 15, 27 (Dec. 2).

10 *Case Concerning Application of the International Convention on the Elimination of All Forms of Racial Discrimination (Georgia v. Russian Fedartation)*, Preliminary Objections, ICJ General List No. 140, April 1, 2011, at 16 (citing the following case); *Interpretation of Peace Treaties with Bulgaria, Hungary and Romania, First Phase*, Advisory Opinion, 1950 ICJ Rep. 65, 74 (March 30).

11 *Case Concerning Application of the International Convention on the Elimination of All Forms of Racial Discrimination (Georgia v. Russian Federation)*, Preliminary Objections, ICJ General List No. 140, April 1, 2011, at 16 (citing the following cases); *South West Africa Cases (Ethiopia v. South Africa; Liberia v. South Africa)*, Preliminary Objections, 1962 ICJ Rep. 319, 328 (Dec. 21); *Armed Activities on the Territory of the Congo (New Application: 2002) (DRC v. Rwanda)*, Jurisdiction and Admissibility, Judgment, 2006 ICJ Rep. 6, 40 (Feb. 3).

12 *Case Concerning Application of the International Convention on the Elimination of All Forms of Racial Discrimination (Georgia v. Russian Federation)*, Preliminary Objections, ICJ General List No. 140, April 1, 2011, at 16 (citing the following cases); *Questions of Interpretation and Application of the 1971 Montreal Convention Arising from the Aerial Incident at Lockerbie (Libya v. UK)*, Preliminary Objections, 1998 ICJ Rep. 9, 25–26 (Feb. 27); *Questions of Interpretation and Application of the 1971 Montreal Convention Arising from the Aerial Incident at Lockerbie (Libya v. US)*, Preliminary Objections, 1998 ICJ Rep. 115, 130–131 (Feb. 27).

13 See Collier and Lowe, *supra* note 4, at 10; Edward Gordon, *"Legal Disputes" under Article 36(2) of the Statute*, in The International Court of Justice at a Crossroads 183 (Lori F. Damrosch ed., 1987).

disputes before the ICJ to be legal in nature, or at least so the argument goes. In other words, it is through this definition that the "legal" qualifier has invaded other forms of ICJ jurisdiction, even though the provisions of the ICJ Statute relating to these other forms of jurisdiction do not expressly limit the ICJ to "legal" disputes, as explained in Chapter 6.2 below. This is the source of considerable theoretical confusion when deciding the justiciability of certain disputes, presumably including nuclear non-proliferation disputes.

Even though the definition of "dispute" provided by the *Mavrommatis Palestine Concessions* case often has been cited in ICJ cases, the definition seems to have some shortcomings. Most criticize it for being underdeveloped. Nii Wallace-Bruce calls it "deceptively simple, giving no guidance at all on its application."[14] Use of the word "simple" here does not seem that fitting, since it can have positive connotations – something that he does not see in the definition. As Robert Jennings asserts, there is nothing simple about this definition – it is not a definition at all but rather "an unexplained, even unacknowledged, decision to understand 'dispute' in this context as meaning a particular kind of dispute which kind is now usually called a 'legal dispute' (or 'différend d'ordre juridique')."[15] This assessment appears entirely correct, although the PCIJ's and ICJ's approach is quite predictable, given that courts and tribunals obviously feel most comfortable when handling legal disputes inasmuch as they are best at applying law.[16]

In the end, as Vera Gowlland-Debbas observes, "There appears to be little agreement on the meaning of the terms *legal* or *justiciable disputes*,"[17] and this definition provided in the *Mavrommatis Palestine Concessions* case certainly does not help at all. Apart from providing the basic terms in which to discuss justiciability, the relatively vague wording of this definition provides little guidance without reference to other case

[14] Wallace-Bruce, *supra* note 8, at 3.

[15] See Jennings, *Reflections*, *supra* note 8, at 402.

[16] See Robert Jennings, *Commentary on the Contributions of the Court to the Resolution of International Tensions, Proceedings of the ICJ/UNITAR Colloquium to Celebrate the 50th Anniversary of the Court*, reprinted in Increasing the Effectiveness of the International Court of Justice 92, 92–93 (Connie Peck and Roy S. Lee ed., 1997) (hereinafter Jennings, *Commentary*).

[17] Vera Gowlland-Debbas, *The Relationship between the International Court of Justice and the Security Council in the Light of the Lockerbie Case*, 88 Am. J. Int'l L. 643, 649 (1994).

law to flesh out the criteria for justiciability. The problem is that the ICJ has not provided clear standards for justiciability, nor has it found nonjusticiability in any cases other than the rare one that involved only a purely political dispute – the *Haya de la Torre* case.[18] Therefore, disputants and commentators are somewhat left to their own devices in creating ways to formulate justiciability. Chapter 6.5 below discusses two of those approaches to determining justiciability – the substantive approach and the process approach. Despite the reference to "law" and "legal views or interests" in the definition contained in the *Mavrommatis Palestine Concessions* case, this should not be interpreted as meaning that international courts and tribunals can only hear purely legal disputes. This point is reflected in the definition's reference to points of "fact" and conflicts over "interests between two persons," which is further discussed in Chapter 6.5 below.

Putting aside formal definitions for a moment, determining justiciability seems to be a policy question for the international court or tribunal. As the ICJ stated in its *Nicaragua* case, justiciability essentially is a policy question of whether the Court should exercise "prudential discretion in the interest of the integrity of the judicial function" and refuse to hear and decide on the dispute that it otherwise has the authority to hear and decide.[19] After all, States do not enjoy a *right* to the ICJ or international arbitral tribunal's taking up their dispute, even if they have provided these fora with their unequivocal consent to jurisdiction.[20] The overarching issue explored in this section is whether the ICJ and international arbitral tribunals should exercise this "prudential discretion" and refrain from handling nuclear non-proliferation disputes. In exploring this overarching question, this section looks at legal resolution more from the perspective of the judge or arbitrator, whereas the preceding chapter on jurisdiction looked at legal resolution more from the perspective of the disputants. This difference in perspective of justiciability and jurisdiction is a key distinction to keep in mind throughout this chapter.

[18] See generally *Haya de la Torre (Colombia/Peru)*, 1951 ICJ Rep. 71 (June 13).

[19] *Case Concerning Military and Paramilitary Activities in and against Nicaragua (Nicaragua v. US)*, 1984 ICJ Rep. 392, 429–430 (Nov. 26) (the US characterizing justiciability in this manner, with the ICJ seeming to accept this characterization).

[20] See Collier and Lowe, *supra* note 4, at 4.

6.1.1 How justiciability relates to jurisdiction

Despite this difference between jurisdiction and justiciability, these two concepts are closely connected. On a somewhat superficial level, a court or tribunal's formal determination of justiciability typically follows after it has determined jurisdiction, so a forum might not have to address justiciability if the claim fails for lack of jurisdiction. As with jurisdiction, justiciability typically is challenged by the respondent of a claim, which often uses the broader political context of the dispute as a way of trying to avoid having to defend its actions before a binding third-party process.[21] Moreover, on a more substantive level, jurisdiction and justiciability are related in that a State likely will not consent to legal resolution contained in a compromissory clause or give effect to that consent unless that method of resolution is considered suitable for resolving the anticipated disputes that will arise out of that treaty, since no State wants to waste resources or run the risk of being bound by a decision that was reached through an inappropriate method. Moreover, in a way, if disputants have consented to the Court's jurisdiction, then the dispute is legal by definition inasmuch as the Court is bound to apply international law when deciding that dispute,[22] thus making jurisdiction the only important element when determining the suitability of international adjudication in handling a particular dispute. Chapter 6.5.2 below returns to this point when discussing the process approach to determining justiciability.

In practice, the ICJ considers jurisdiction and justiciability separately,[23] and so this study does as well. Nonetheless, one might rightly question whether such separate analysis is necessary, especially where jurisdiction is provided through a compromissory clause or *compromis*, as raised in Chapter 6.5.2 below. Putting that possibility to the side for the time being, the key difference between jurisdiction and justiciability is who makes the

[21] See John G. Merrills, *The Role and Limits of International Adjudication*, in INTERNATIONAL LAW AND THE INTERNATIONAL SYSTEM 169, 174 (WILLIAM E. BUTLER ed., 1987). However, please note that Italy filed an application in the *Monetary Gold* case and then immediately challenged the court's jurisdiction over that very dispute. See *Monetary Gold Removed from Rome in 1943 (Italy v. France, UK, US)*, Preliminary Question, 1954 ICJ Rep. 19, 24 (June 15); JEROME B. ELKIND, NON-APPEARANCE BEFORE THE INTERNATIONAL COURT OF JUSTICE: FUNCTIONAL AND COMPARATIVE ANALYSIS 41–43 (1984).

[22] See Gowlland-Debbas, *supra* note 17, at 651; von Mangoldt, *supra* note 5, at 507 n. 387.

[23] See Gowlland-Debbas, *supra* note 17, at 651; Gordon, *supra* note 13, at 190.

decision. The decision to place a dispute or a class of disputes before a court or tribunal is for States to make through the signing and ratification of a treaty that contains such a compromissory clause, for example. Such a decision, and the court or tribunal's finding of that decision, are crucial to the court or tribunal's actually hearing and deciding on a particular dispute.[24] Whether the forum has jurisdiction is a technical question of fact that depends on the consent of the disputants and the scope of that consent. Again, Chapter 5.2 above analyzed how some States already have given their consent to legal resolution through their consenting to compromissory clauses in nuclear non-proliferation agreements. However, while State consent to legal resolution is a necessary condition for such a proceeding to take place, it is not a sufficient condition, at least in theory. In other words, even if disputants have consented to legal resolution of their nuclear non-proliferation disputes (or any other dispute, for that matter), there still is another hurdle to clear – a determination of justiciability or arbitrability. Unlike with jurisdiction, this question of justiciability is for the court or tribunal to decide. The review of cases provided in Chapter 6.2 below where justiciability issues have been raised shows that respondent States often raise this issue. The fact that only one case has been dismissed due to non-justiciability and the lack of a clear standard on what constitutes justiciable and nonjusticiable suggests that legal resolution remains flexible in deciding this issue. It is because of this flexibility of justiciability that this study believes that legal resolution may handle a nuclear non-proliferation dispute in the future, as thinking on these issues evolves over time. Apart from helping that thinking evolve, the purpose of this study is to show that there are few, if any, technical barriers to the ICJ's or an international arbitral tribunal's handling of nuclear non-proliferation disputes.

6.1.2 How justiciability differs from admissibility

Some commentators who write on justiciability focus solely on the political nature of the dispute as the basis for a determination of justiciability (or rather nonjusticiability), without mentioning any other aspects of justiciability.[25] However, justiciability can be quite a broad concept, going beyond merely a court or tribunal's determination of the

[24] See JOHN G. MERRILLS, INTERNATIONAL DISPUTE SETTLEMENT 219–220 (4th edn, 2005).

[25] See, e.g., J. L. SIMPSON AND HAZEL FOX, INTERNATIONAL ARBITRATION: LAW AND PRACTICE 43–44 (1959).

legal or political nature of a dispute before it. Merrills included within his list of factors for determining nonjusticiability the political nature of the dispute, failure to include a necessary third party, interference with a political means of settlement, and existence of a hypothetical question at the heart of the claim.[26] Brownlie similarly listed these factors along with a few others, such as the failure to exhaust local remedies and incomplete formulation of the issues.[27] Amerasinghe avoids using the word "justiciability," instead preferring to talk about admissibility, which includes such preliminary matters as the nationality of the claims and the exhaustion of local remedies, and competence, which includes such preliminary matters as mootness and the presence of a dispute,[28] with competence here being the closest to what other commentators refer to as justiciability. A defect with any one of these aspects of justiciability or a combination thereof can act as the basis for the Court to exercise its discretion and refuse to proceed to the merits of the case, notwithstanding a finding of jurisdiction.[29] Moreover, as Brownlie has noted,[30] these different aspects of justiciability can act in combination to push the Court or tribunal to exercise its discretion to dismiss a claim for being nonjusticiable where any single factor might not be sufficient for such an action. Nevertheless, this study focuses on the political nature of a dispute as determining nonjusticiability, mainly because this presumably will be the most significant criticism against legal resolution's being allowed to handle nuclear non-proliferation disputes.

[26] See Merrills, *supra* note 21, at 171–180.

[27] See Ian Brownlie, *The Justiciability of Disputes and Issues in International Relations*, 42 British Y.B. Int'l L. 123, 124–136 (1967).

[28] See Chittharanjan F. Amerasinghe, Jurisdiction of International Tribunals 18–26, 202–204, 241–285 (2003).

[29] See Brownlie, *supra* note 27, at 123–136 (1967) (making it seem that justiciability and admissibility are the same, though alluding to them being different at the beginning); Ian Brownlie, Principles of Public International Law 681 (6th edn, 2003); Marcella David, *Passport to Justice: Internationalizing the Political Question Doctrine for Application in the World Court*, 40 Harv. Int'l L.J. 81, 128 (1999) (noting that justiciability and admissibility are equivalent); Arthur Eyffinger, The International Court of Justice 1946–1996 138–139 (1996); Natalie S. Klein, *Multilateral Disputes and the Doctrine of Necessary Partie in the East Timor Case*, 21 Yale J. Int'l L. 305 (1996); *Oil Platforms (Iran v. US)*, 2003 ICJ Rep. 161, 177 (Nov. 6) ("Objections to admissibility normally take the form of an assertion that, even if the Court has jurisdiction and the facts stated by the applicant State are assumed to be correct, nonetheless there are reasons why the Court should not proceed to an examination of the merits").

[30] See Brownlie, *supra* note 27, at 142.

6.1.3 *Justiciability and optional clause declarations*

When it comes to nuclear non-proliferation disputes where the forum has jurisdiction through a compromissory clause, justiciability seems relatively unimportant, at least from a textualist perspective when interpreting the ICJ Statute. The main reason is because justiciability is most relevant to matters where the ICJ's jurisdiction comes through an optional clause declaration and in other situations where the ICJ Statute requires a "legal" dispute for it to have jurisdiction over the matter.[31] As ICJ Statute Article 36(2) provides,

> The states parties to the present Statute may at any time declare that they recognize as compulsory ipso facto and without special agreement, in relation to any other state accepting the same obligation, the jurisdiction of the Court in all *legal disputes* concerning: a. the interpretation of a treaty; b. any question of international law; c. the existence of any fact which, if established, would constitute a breach of an international obligation; d. the nature or extent of the reparation to be made for the breach of an international obligation.[32]

Advisory opinions also care about justiciability inasmuch as UN Charter Article 96 makes clear that the General Assembly, other UN organs, and specialized agencies can request advisory opinions only for *legal* questions. ICJ Statute Article 65 also states, "The Court may give an advisory opinion on any *legal* question at the request of whatever body may be authorized by or in accordance with the Charter of the United Nations to make such a request."[33] As the ICJ stated in the *Reservations to the Convention on the Prevention and Punishment of the Crime of Genocide* advisory opinion, requests for an opinion "should not, in principle, be refused,"[34] so justiciability is perhaps less important than with cases involving optional clause declarations. None of the other ways for the ICJ to have jurisdiction over contentious disputes mentioned in Chapter 5.2 expressly limits the disputes to legal ones.[35] In particular, ICJ Statute Article 36(1) provides, with regard to compromissory clauses and

[31] See Gordon, *supra* note 13, at 183; WALLACE-BRUCE, *supra* note 8, at 19–20, 25.
[32] ICJ Statute, Art. 36(2) (emphasis added).
[33] Ibid., Art. 65. See also WALLACE-BRUCE, *supra* note 8, at 25.
[34] See *Reservations to the Convention on the Prevention and Punishment of the Crime of Genocide*, Advisory Opinion, 1951 ICJ Rep. 15, 19 (May 28).
[35] See GÖRAN LYSÉN, THE INTERNATIONAL REGULATION OF ARMAMENTS: THE LAW OF DISARMAMENT 197 (1990) (making this same observation).

compromis, that the ICJ has jurisdiction over "*all cases* which the parties refer to it and all matters specially provided for in the Charter of the United Nations or in treaties and conventions in force."[36]

One may ask why there is a difference in the importance of justiciability between the different types of jurisdiction. As discussed later in Chapter 6.3, compromissory clauses typically (at least the ones at issue in this study) involve only the interpretation and application of the treaties containing the compromissory clause, which necessarily involves a legal dispute, thereby removing the question of justiciability altogether. Moreover, some commentators see the difference between jurisdiction through an optional clause declaration and the rest as lying in the belief that it would be inappropriate for the Court to abstain from rendering a decision in a case where the disputants have provided their consent to the forum's jurisdiction for that case.[37] However, even where an optional clause declaration is involved, the disputants unequivocally have provided their consent, so some other factor likely is at play. The more likely reason for the difference lies in the different *quality* of consent that States provide through these various forms of consent. Indeed, legal resolution would seem most appropriate where the consent of the parties to that particular dispute is explicit and specific, which is the case except with jurisdiction based on an optional clause declaration and advisory opinions where the consent conceivably is somewhat removed from the immediate dispute and from that exact type of dispute.[38] Critics might assert that the Court is careful to avoid settling disputes between States when it relies on its advisory jurisdiction, thereby making the ICJ's objectives there entirely different from its objectives in contentious cases. Indeed, the ICJ expressly has adopted the notion that States should not abuse its advisory jurisdiction and resolve actual disputes, as it first articulated in the *Eastern Carelia* advisory opinion,[39] and later

[36] ICJ Statute, Art. 36(1) (emphasis added).

[37] See Jonathan I. Charney, *Disputes Implicating the Institutional Credibility of the Court: Problems of Non-appearance, Non-participation, and Non-performance*, in The International Court of Justice at a Crossroads 288, 306 (Lori F. Damrosch ed., 1987).

[38] See Wallace-Bruce, *supra* note 8, at 25 (mentioning that "the contemporary trend appears to be for the ICJ to skirt the issue of justiciability, and to find cases or issues admissible rather than adhere to a strict application of a rule" with everything except jurisdiction through optional-clause declarations and advisory jurisdiction).

[39] See *Status of Eastern Carelia*, Advisory Opinion, 1923 P.C.I.J. (ser. B) No. 5, at 27–28 (July 23).

confirmed in its 1975 *Western Sahara* and 1989 *Mazilu* advisory opinions.[40] Nonetheless, such a backdoor approach to getting ICJ involvement with a particular dispute seems to happen in practice, as with the 2004 *Wall* advisory opinion, where Palestine actually cosponsored the resolution for the advisory opinion.[41] Moreover, the decision on its face was binding on Israel and on all other States, despite the widely held belief that advisory opinions are non-binding.[42] Indeed, the court explicitly required Israel to halt construction and dismantle the finished portions, pay damages to those affected by Israel's actions, return the land taken or used by the wall, respect the claims of Palestinians to self-determination, ensure access to the holy sites, and discontinue all violations of international humanitarian law and other international obligations,[43] none of which reflect "advisory" language. As the date for oral hearings drew closer, some of the media heralded it as Palestine's day in court.[44] Others saw this clearly as an Israel–Palestine dispute, with commentators explaining what Israel argued and how Palestine replied,

[40] See *Applicability of Article VI, Section 22, of the Convention on the Privileges and Immunities of the United Nations*, Advisory Opinion, 1989 ICJ Rep. 177, ¶ 38 (Dec. 15); *Western Sahara*, Advisory Opinion, 1975 ICJ Rep. 12, ¶¶ 28–30 (Oct. 16). See also ROSALYN HIGGINS, PROBLEMS AND PROCESS: INTERNATIONAL LAW AND HOW WE USE IT 200–201 (1994).

[41] See *Legal Consequences of the Construction of a Wall in the Occupied Palestinian Territory*, Advisory Opinion, 2004 ICJ Rep. 136 (July 9); Legal Consequences of the Construction of a Wall in the Occupied Palestinian Territory, Order, 2003 ICJ Rep. 428 (Dec. 19) (noting how the General Assembly "has granted Palestine a special status of observer and that the latter is co-sponsor of the draft resolution requesting the advisory opinion"). In his separate opinion to the *Legality of the Use by a State of Nuclear Weapons in Armed Conflict* advisory opinion (requested by the World Health Organization), ICJ Judge Shigeru Oda implies the ICJ should handle requests for advisory opinions where there is some sort of conflict or dispute, as opposed to where "there is no conflict or dispute concerning legal questions between States or between States and international organizations." *Legality of the Use by a State of Nuclear Weapons in Armed Conflict*, 1996 ICJ Rep. 66, 89 (July 8) (Oda J., separate opinion).

[42] See, e.g., Dietmar W. Prager, *The Proliferation of International Judicial Organs: The Role of the International Court of Justice*, in PROLIFERATION OF INTERNATIONAL ORGANIZATIONS: LEGAL ISSUES 279, 291 (NIELS M. BLOKKER and HENRY G. SCHERMERS ed., 2001). See also Roberto Ago, *"Binding" Advisory Opinions of the International Court of Justice*, 85 AM. J. INT' L. 439 (1991).

[43] See *Legal Consequences of the Construction of a Wall in the Occupied Palestinian Territory*, Advisory Opinion, 2004 ICJ Rep. 136, 188–89, 197–198 (July 9).

[44] See, e.g., Mustafa Barghouthi, *An Issue of World Peace*, MORNING STAR, Feb. 20, 2004, at 8.

and vice versa.[45] At least one scholar implies that Israel's and Palestine's submissions in the *Wall* advisory opinion are party submissions,[46] suggesting that he views this advisory opinion as a contentious case with actual parties. Some would dismiss these views as mischaracterizations based on confusion over the nature of advisory opinions by the lay media, instead maintaining that there can be no dispute or parties, and that those involved are only interested entities that have relevant information to aid the court in making its decision on an abstract legal question. However, the media's observations uncover the flaws inherent in such formalism, and to conclude otherwise would improperly put form over substance. Regardless of the reasons for the difference in the importance of justiciability between the different types of jurisdiction, on the face of the ICJ Statute it would appear that determining the nature of the dispute only relates to where compulsory jurisdiction is involved, and States can avoid the Court or tribunal's analysis of justiciability if they provide their jurisdictional consent through some other means.

This does not change the fact that legal resolution had been limited to *legal* questions in many situations before the Second World War, which the following section discusses. During that time, even if the questions posed were legal, legal resolution could not deal with those questions if they related to a State's vital interests. It must be noted, however, that that changed after the Second World War, with the textual limitation to legal questions and the exclusion of vital-interest issues being largely removed with the UN Charter and the ICJ Statute. This point is made at the end of the following section. Finally, assuming, *arguendo*, that justiciability is important for disputes other than just those involving jurisdiction through an optional clause declaration, the following section explores how the ICJ has handled justiciability of politically sensitive disputes and how it should handle justiciability of such disputes in the future.

[45] See, e.g., Ian Black, *Conflict over Israel's "Apartheid Wall" Hits The Hague*, MANCHESTER GUARDIAN WEEKLY, Feb. 26–March 3, 2004, at 2; Marda Dunsky, *Build Bridges, Not Walls*, CHI. TRIB., Feb. 22, 2004, at C4.

[46] See Colin B. Picker, *Reputational Fallacies in International Law: A Comparative Review of United States and Canadian Trade Actions*, 30 Brook. J. Int'l L. 67, 75 n. 22 (2004).

6.2 History of justiciability

6.2.1 *Justiciability before 1945*

The notion of legal resolution not being suitable for disputes that involve a State's vital interests has a long history within the discourse of international-law theory. Vattel appears to have made the first reference to suitability of legal resolution of such disputes in 1758: "Arbitration is a very reasonable means, and one that is entirely in accord with the natural law, of terminating every dispute which does not directly affect the safety of the State."[47] Vattel also noted that, with disputes between States, it is important to distinguish between "essential rights and less important rights," the former not being handled by international adjudication.[48] Although Vattel did not use the term "justiciable" or "justiciability," nor did he mention adjudication by international courts, for the obvious reason that none existed at the time, his comments capture the essence of the concept being discussed in this section. The essence of the idea is that legal resolution cannot handle matters involving a State's vital interests in order to give the State ultimate control over the outcome of these sensitive matters.[49] To be clear, it is not about there being no legal standards that govern such matters for a court or tribunal to apply in addressing the matter, as some commentators assert,[50] similar to the antiquated idea of *inter arma silent leges*, or "in time of war, laws are silent." After all, it is no mystery that there are well-developed bodies of law that currently regulate the decision to use force and how to use that force, and the same is true of the methods and means of warfare. As the United States implicitly acknowledged during the preliminary stages of the *Nicaragua* case, the use-of-force issues in that case were regulated by law, but they should still be

[47] Emmerich de Vattel, Law of Nations, or Principles of Natural Law Applied to the Conduct and Affairs of Nations and of Sovereigns 224 (1916, trans. Charles Fenwick, 1964).
[48] Ibid., at 225.
[49] See Gowlland-Debbas, *supra* note 17, at 649; Hersch Lauterpacht, The Function of Law in the International Community 4–7 (1933).
[50] See Dapo Akande and Sope Williams, *International Adjudication of Security Issues: What Role for the WTO?*, 43 Va. J. Int'l L. 365, 381–382 (2003); William W. Burke-White and Andreas von Staden, *Investment Protection in Extraordinary Times: The Interpretation and Application of Non-precluded Measures Provisions in Bilateral Investment Treaties*, 48 Va. J. Int'l L. 307, 376 (2008).

deemed nonjusticiable.[51] As explained in the following section, there are ample laws that regulate the vital interests that are involved with the disputes in question here – nuclear non-proliferation disputes. What is important, however, is whether legal resolution should nevertheless be prohibited from handling such sensitive matters out of concerns over sovereignty. This idea turns out to be an antiquated one as well.

Returning to the history of justiciability, the concept of vital interests hindering attempts at legal resolution did not come into full focus until after the judicialization of international arbitration with the *Alabama* case and the subsequent interest in international arbitration to solve essentially all the world's ills.[52] The *Alabama* arbitrations in the eighteenth century started the judicialization of arbitration, as well as the pro-arbitration movement. This movement in favor of inter-State arbitration culminated in the First Hague Conference in 1899 and the Hague Convention for the Pacific Settlement of International Disputes, which essentially established the norm requiring the peaceful settlement of disputes.[53] At this First Hague Conference, arbitration and disarmament were seen as the new models for international legal activism.[54] The

[51] See *Military and Paramilitary Activities in and against Nicaragua (Nicaragua v. US)*, Jurisdiction and Admissibility, 1984 ICJ Rep. 392, 431–436 (Nov. 26) (the laws that apply are various provisions of the UN Charter, primary among which is Article 51 on self-defense).

[52] See LAUTERPACHT, *supra* note 49, at 9 (noting how one disputant asserted that the *Alabama* arbitration involved individuals' claims and therefore was not one of "high policy" and importance).

[53] See Ion Diaconu, *Peaceful Settlement of Disputes between States: History and Prospects*, in THE STRUCTURE AND PROCESS OF INTERNATIONAL LAW: ESSAYS IN LEGAL PHILOSOPHY DOCTRINE AND THEORY 1095, 1096 (R. ST. J. MACDONALD and DOUGLAS M. JOHNSTON ed., 1983); MARY ELLEN O'CONNELL, INTERNATIONAL DISPUTE RESOLUTION 7 (2006).

[54] See David Kennedy, *International Law and the Nineteenth Century: History of an Illusion*, 17 QUINNIPIAC L. REV. 99, 129–130 (1997); Jeremy Rabkin, *The Politics of the Geneva Conventions: Disturbing Background to the ICC Debate*, 44 VA. J. INT'L L. 169, 179 (2003). Some commentators have asserted that this was largely due to Russia's belief that these two mechanisms would help frustrate Japan's territorial aspirations in China, since Russia aspired to have this territory for itself. See LILLIAN L. RANDOLPH, THIRD-PARTY SETTLEMENT OF DISPUTES IN THEORY AND PRACTICE 176 (1973). But see MAURICE BERTRAND, THE UNITED NATIONS: PAST, PRESENT AND FUTURE 17 (1994) (asserting that Tsar Nicholas II suggested multilateral disarmament at the First Hague Conference in order to avoid having to try to reduce its reinforcement of Austria's artillery to the requested levels through bilateral negotiations). Not surprisingly, Russia chose to downplay disarmament and even the limitation of arms at the 1907 Second Hague Conference after its 1905 defeat by Japan. See SYLVESTER JOHN HEMLEBEN, PLANS FOR WORLD PEACE THROUGH SIX CENTURIES 131 (1943).

Hague Convention was the first codification of the legal–political distinction in the context of international dispute settlement:

> In questions of a legal nature, and especially in the interpretation or application of international conventions, arbitration is recognized by the signatory Powers as the most effective, and at the same time the most equitable, means of settling disputes which diplomacy has failed to settle. Consequently, it would be desirable that, in disputes about the above-mentioned questions, the contracting Powers should, if the case arose, have recourse to arbitration, in so far as circumstances permit.[55]

It is interesting to note that the Draft Regulations for International Arbitral Procedure of 1873 talked about how arbitration was not for "non-legal disputes whose nature does not admit of a judgement according to the rules of law."[56] However, these draft regulations never entered into force, and so the 1899 Hague Convention is the first example of codification of this idea. Article 38 of the 1907 Hague Convention for the Pacific Settlement of International Disputes repeated this provision of the 1899 Hague Convention for the Pacific Settlement of International Disputes. These provisions unequivocally identified certain questions as being distinct from others and identified legal resolution (in particular arbitration, because court-based resolution on the international level did not exist yet[57]) as the most appropriate method of dispute settlement for legal questions. Of particular importance here is the idea that the interpretation and application of treaties have a uniquely legal nature to them, an idea that is repeated in numerous treaties. Most notable for this discussion of the history of justiciability, these treaties did not create any binding obligations on their States parties, such as prohibiting States from sending their disputes of a mixed nature to legal resolution or otherwise prohibiting international arbitral tribunals from handling disputes of a mixed nature.

Instead of through multilateral agreements,[58] a stricter limitation of legal resolution to *legal* disputes arose through various bilateral

[55] Please note that the Draft Regulations for International Arbitral Procedure of 1873 talked about how arbitration was not for "non-legal disputes whose nature does not admit of a judgement according to the rules of law." LAUTERPACHT, *supra* note 49, at 9–10. However, these draft regulations never entered into force, and so the 1899 Hague Convention is the first example of codification.

[56] Ibid. [57] See COLLIER and LOWE, *supra* note 4, at 38.

[58] See, e.g., Protocol for the Pacific Settlement of International Disputes, Opened for Signature at Geneva on October 2, 1924, reprinted in MAX HABICHT, POST-WAR TREATIES FOR THE PACIFIC SETTLEMENT OF INTERNATIONAL DISPUTES 929 (1931) (failing to

arbitration treaties from between the Second Hague Conference in 1907 and the end of the First World War. Fearing that they would lose control over the resolution of politically sensitive disputes, States developed the concept of limiting legal resolution to *legal* disputes and codified this concept in bilateral arbitration treaties in order to claw back a measure of control over dispute settlement in these sensitive areas.[59] However, by doing so, these vital-interest provisions of arbitration treaties essentially emasculated the treaties.[60] These arbitration treaties might still be in effect, but the vital-interests provisions do not hinder international arbitration's handling such matters because international arbitral tribunals easily can base their jurisdiction on other treaties that provide the requisite jurisdiction. Regardless, at the time of agreeing to those bilateral arbitration treaties, such provisions that returned a measure of control to the States likely were needed if arbitration was to continue to flourish at that time, which compromise is not unlike the way in which the political-question doctrine in the United States was used to limit the judiciary in exchange for the expansion of its powers through judicial review.[61] This type of clawback is notably different from the situation under the Hague Conventions, which merely identified legal resolution as the most effective and equitable way to settle *legal* disputes after the failure of diplomatic efforts at resolution. However, it did not prohibit legal resolution of politically sensitive disputes.

The Legal Section of the League of Nations provided in 1927 a comprehensive study of the eighty-five treaties for the pacific settlement

qualify any references to "disputes" with "legal"); General Act for the Pacific Settlement of International Disputes Adopted by the Ninth Assembly of the League of Nations on September 26, 1928, Arts. 17–21, 39, reprinted in MAX HABICHT, POST-WAR TREATIES FOR THE PACIFIC SETTLEMENT OF INTERNATIONAL DISPUTES 929 (1931) (not qualifying "disputes" as "legal," and providing States with the ability to avoid legal resolution in accordance with reservations they make to future treaties, although not mentioning "vital interests," "independence," "honour," or anything similar).

59 See Andrew Coleman, *The International Court of Justice and Highly Political Matters*, 4 MELB J. INT'L L. 29, 32–33 (2003); Rosalyn Higgins, *Policy Considerations and the International Judicial Process*, 17 INT'L & COMP. L.Q. 58, 63 (1968) (hereinafter Higgins, *Policy Considerations*) (asserting that "it was felt that obligatory arbitration could better be commended to governments if it were made clear that 'political' issues were beyond the scope of the tribunal").

60 See MARTIN, *supra* note 2, at 80.

61 See THOMAS M. FRANCK, POLITICAL QUESTIONS/JUDICIAL ANSWERS: DOES THE RULE OF LAW APPLY TO FOREIGN AFFAIRS? 12 (1992) (asserting that US Supreme Court Chief Justice Marshall developed the political-question doctrine as a trade-off for judicial review – a limitation in exchange for an expansion of powers).

of disputes that had been agreed until that point.[62] Of these, thirty-three were arbitration treaties and thirty-four were treaties of arbitration and conciliation, making a total of sixty-seven treaties that related to international arbitration in some way.[63] These treaties allow international arbitration either for all disputes (fourteen treaties), for all disputes with certain reservations (sixteen treaties), for disputes of a certain kind (three treaties), or for disputes of a certain kind with certain reservations (thirty-four treaties).[64] It is within the reservations and within the definitions of which disputes arbitration can handle that disputes involving a State's vital interests, independence, and matters of honor were excluded from the purview of international arbitration.

Starting with the designation of certain types of disputes in thirty-seven treaties, the main distinction – involving twenty-four treaties – was to require the disputes to be legal or in relation to the disputants' "respective rights," which can be seen as being equivalent to requiring the dispute to be legal.[65] Twelve other treaties required the dispute to be a type of dispute that generally was considered as being suitable for submission to arbitration, which also can be seen as being equivalent to requiring the dispute to be legal. The relevant categories were as follows:

(a) the interpretation of a treaty;
(b) any questions of international law;
(c) the existence of any fact which, if established, would constitute a breach of an international obligation; and
(d) the nature or extent of the reparation to be made for a breach of an international obligation.[66]

Finally, one treaty, the Treaty of Arbitration and Conciliation of December 3, 1921, between Germany and Switzerland, excluded from

[62] See Legal Section of the Secretariat of the League of Nations, Arbitration and Security: Systematic Survey of the Arbitration Conventions and Treaties of Mutual Security Deposited with the League of Nations 19 (1927).

[63] See ibid. (citations to the exact treaties omitted).

[64] See ibid., at 20.

[65] See ibid., at 22. Please note that the editors seem to have mistakenly included two treaties in this review that should not be there – their Treaty Nos. 1567 and 1618, which are treaties with limitations based on reservations.

[66] Ibid. Again, please note that the editors seem to have mistakenly included a treaty in this review that should not have been there – their Treaty No. 1224, which was a conciliation treaty. See ibid., at 453.

arbitration disputes that were "mainly political."[67] Therefore, in total, all thirty-seven bilateral arbitration treaties required, in some way or another, disputes to be legal disputes in order for legal resolution to handle them. This constitutes the only limitation, outside reservations, on the types of disputes that arbitration could handle.

Shifting the focus to reservations, of the fifty bilateral arbitration treaties that contained certain reservations to the types of disputes that arbitration could handle, twenty-four contained a reservation concerning the disputants' vital interests or independence. The standard language for this reservation seems to be from Article 1 of the Treaty between France and the United Kingdom of October 14, 1903:

> Differences which may arise of a legal nature or relating to the interpretation of treaties existing between the two Contracting Parties and which it may not have been possible to settle by diplomacy, shall be referred to the Permanent Court of Arbitration established at The Hague by the Convention of the 29th of July, 1899, provided, nevertheless, *that they do not affect the vital interests, the independence, or the honour* of the two Contracting States, and do not concern the interests of third Parties.[68]

By using the word "nevertheless," this type of reservation excludes from the Court's jurisdiction legal disputes that "affect the vital interests, the independence, or the honour" of the States. Therefore, the fact that a dispute might be a "legal" one does not save it from being excluded. For all but four of these twenty-four, "honour" is included with "vital interests" and "independence." All four of these treaties that lack a reference to honor are treaties of arbitration and conciliation.[69] While the literature fails to explain the reason for leaving "honor" off this list in these arbitration and conciliation treaties, one commonality is that they all involved Germany as a party. However, Germany agreed to similar treaties at around this same time that included a reference to "honor," so it would appear that the explanation for the anomaly cannot be as simple as the involvement of Germany in concluding the treaty. Other reservations in the bilateral arbitration treaties from this time involved such matters as the interests of third States, the involvement of previous disputes, disputes involving territorial integrity or territorial status,

[67] Ibid., at 23 (citing Treaty of Arbitration and Conciliation of December 3, 1921, between Germany and Switzerland, Art. 4(2)).

[68] Ibid., at 91 (reproducing the Treaty between France and the United Kingdom of October 14, 1903) (emphasis added).

[69] Ibid., at 23 (citing Germany and Switzerland, Dec. 3, 1921; Germany and Sweden, Aug. 29, 1924; Germany and Finland, March 14, 1925; Germany and Estonia, Aug. 10, 1925).

disputes arising out of the War of 1914, questions affecting internal legislation, and questions affecting the jurisdiction of the national courts,[70] all of which are sufficiently different in nature from the reservation dealing with vital interests to be excluded from this section's analysis. Surprisingly, with regard to "vital interests," "independence," and "honor," none of the twenty-four bilateral arbitration treaties that refer to them defines them in any way. Nor do any judicial cases from this time appear to struggle with defining any of these terms. Instead, these vague terms seem to have had a chilling effect on arbitration as a whole, with the conclusion of the bulk of these bilateral arbitration treaties coinciding with the shift from international arbitration to international adjudication before the PCIJ.

Despite all of these bilateral arbitration treaties and their limitation of legal resolution to *legal* disputes that also did not affect a State's vital interests and similar factors, other treaties during this same time were stepping away from this limitation. Examples, which are discussed below, include the Covenant of the League of Nations and the PCIJ Statute. The creation of the PCIJ essentially pushed inter-State arbitration (and the PCA) into hibernation,[71] with the PCIJ picking up where international arbitration had left off. The appeal of the PCIJ (and later the ICJ) was its institutional nature and its accompanying prestige, among other factors.[72] Concerning justiciability, the PCIJ had a much less clear limitation on handling only legal disputes.

The Covenant of the League of Nations dramatically improved the prospects for legal resolution compared to the Hague Conventions, because it *required* legal resolution – in particular, arbitration under Articles 12, 13 and 15 – if a conflict broke out.[73] While Article 13 of the original Covenant mentioned only arbitration, this was amended in 1924 to include judicial settlement by the Permanent Court of International Justice. Article 13 *required* members to submit to arbitration or judicial settlement "any dispute [that] shall arise between them which they recognise to be *suitable for submission* to arbitration or judicial settlement and which cannot be satisfactorily settled by diplomacy."[74] This provision essentially introduced the idea of the limitation of legal resolution to *legal* disputes on the multilateral level, although regional

[70] See ibid., at 23–26. [71] See Lysén, *supra* note 35, at 195–196.
[72] See Collier and Lowe, *supra* note 4, at 38.
[73] See Diaconu, *supra* note 53, at 1097.
[74] See Covenant of the League of Nations, Art. 13 (emphasis added).

dispute settlement treaties quickly followed suit.[75] Article 13 went on to describe the types of disputes that would be suitable for resolution through arbitration or judicial settlement, though in an inclusive manner:

> Disputes as to the interpretation of a treaty, as to any question of international law, as to the existence of any fact which if established would constitute a breach of any international obligation, or as to the extent and nature of the reparation to be made for any such breach, are declared to be among those which are generally suitable for submission to arbitration or judicial settlement.[76]

This list provided a measure of guidance to disputants of what would be considered a justiciable dispute. By providing this list, the drafters seemed to acknowledge the prior difficulties for tribunals of distinguishing between justiciable claims and nonjusticiable ones and attempted to remedy the problem. However, its nonexclusive nature meant that it only partially ameliorated the situation, leaving disputants to argue and tribunals to determine what was and what was not a legal dispute.[77] Similar to the Covenant, PCIJ Statute Article 36 also referred to

> classes of *legal* disputes concerning: (a) the interpretation of a treaty; (b) any question of international law; (c) the existence of any fact which, if established, would constitute a breach of an international obligation; (d) the nature or extent of the reparation to be made for the breach of an international obligation.[78]

There has been some debate over whether this language in the Covenant and the PCIJ Statute impacted a State's ability to rely on the involvement of its vital interests to escape the application of law in that particular situation. For Leland Goodrich and Anne Simons writing in 1955, this language was seen as leading to States that submitted to the compulsory jurisdiction of the PCIJ losing the ability to determine which disputes were suitable for submission to judicial settlement.[79] However, Brierly focused in 1944 on the numerous qualifications by States of their consent to the PCIJ's compulsory jurisdiction to explain how the exclusion from

[75] See Diaconu, *supra* note 53, at 1098.

[76] Covenant of the League of Nations, Art. 13.

[77] See Robert Jennings, *International Courts and International Politics*, in Contemporary Issues in International Law 13, 15 (David Freestone et al. ed., 2002) (hereinafter Jennings, *International Courts*).

[78] PCIJ Statute, Art. 36 (emphasis added).

[79] See Goodrich and Simons, *supra* note 3, at 320–321.

legal resolution of disputes that involved a State's vital interests remained throughout the interwar period.[80] Brierly went on to question whether law would play a greater role in the future with "the great issues of international politics," presumably those involving disputants' vital interests – a question that he saw as "surely one of the greatest of the open questions of the future."[81]

In actuality, however, the Covenant of the League of Nations and the PCIJ Statute were not as committed to limiting legal resolution to *legal* disputes as bilateral arbitration treaties were and as commentators have asserted. With regard to the Covenant, even though Covenant Article 13 talks about certain disputes being *suitable* for legal resolution, as mentioned above, Covenant Article 14 unequivocally declares that the PCIJ "shall be competent to hear and determine *any* dispute of an international character which the parties thereto submit to it."[82] Similarly, Article 36 of the PCIJ Statute and its reference to "legal disputes" expressly applied only to situations where the disputants had given the PCIJ jurisdiction through signature and ratification of the Protocol, with the entirety of Article 36 reading as follows:

> The jurisdiction of the Court comprises all cases which the parties refer to it and all matters specially provided for in treaties and conventions in force. The Members of the League of Nations and the States mentioned in the Annex to the Covenant may, either when signing or ratifying the Protocol to which the present Statute is adjoined, or at a later moment, declare that they recognize as compulsory ipso facto and without special agreement, in relation to any other Member or State accepting the same obligation, the jurisdiction of the Court in all or any of the classes of legal disputes concerning:
>
> (a) the interpretation of a treaty;
> (b) any question of international law;
> (c) the existence of any fact which, if established, would constitute a breach of an international obligation;
> (d) the nature or extent of the reparation to be made for the breach of an international obligation.
>
> The declaration referred to above may be made unconditionally or on condition of reciprocity on the part of several or certain Members or States, or for a certain time. In the event of a dispute as to whether the

[80] See James L. Brierly, *Vital Interests and the Law*, 21 BRITISH Y.B. INT'L L. 51, 51 (1944).
[81] Ibid. [82] Covenant of the League of Nations, Art. 14 (emphasis added).

> Court has jurisdiction, the matter shall be settled by the decision of the Court.

Similar to Article 14 of the Covenant quoted above, the first sentence of Article 36 of the PCIJ Statute made clear that the Court had jurisdiction over "all cases which the parties refer to it and all matters specially provided for in treaties and conventions in force," suggesting that the later limitation to legal disputes did not apply to instances where the Court had jurisdiction through compromissory clauses or through *compromis*. However, it was not until the UN Charter and the ICJ Statute after the Second World War that it became perfectly clear that justiciability was of limited importance to situations involving such types of jurisdiction.

This subsection has explained that, under the old system where legal resolution was precluded from addressing disputes that involved a State's vital interests, legal resolution essentially was stopped from resolving disputes that could not be resolved through political means. As E. H. Carr wrote in 1939, "The exclusion . . . of disputes affecting 'vital interests,' 'independence,' or 'national honour' meant the exclusion of precisely those matters on which political agreement could not be attained."[83] This arrangement essentially created a gap such that the international rule of law could not be applied where a State's vital interests were concerned. International lawyers after the First World War seem to have had the goal of creating an international order that put the international rule of law at the foundation of international dispute settlement.[84] This was reflected in the PCIJ Statute, but the ability of courts and tribunals to handle politically sensitive disputes could have been clearer. As Carr explained in 1939, "The majority of international disputes which have in the past been settled by arbitration or by some other legal procedure have been either pecuniary claims or disputes about national frontiers in remote and sparsely inhabited regions."[85] As Carr went on to note, this largely was due to the perceived limitation of legal resolution before this time not to look at matters involving a

[83] E. H. Carr, The Twenty Years' Crisis 1919–1939 196 (1939).

[84] See Antony Anghie, *Colonialism and the Birth of International Institutions: Sovereignty, Economy, and the Mandate System of the League of Nations*, 34 N.Y.U. J. Int'l L. & Pol. 513, 528–529 (2002) (citing, inter alia, Nathaniel Berman, *A Perilous Ambivalence: Nationalist Desire, Legal Autonomy and the Limits of the Interwar Framework*, 33 Harv. Int'l L.J. 353 (1992)) (noting also how the initiative towards judicial resolution of disputes began with the Hague Peace Conferences).

[85] Carr, *supra* note 83, at 196.

State's vital interests.[86] However, this limitation would no longer exist after the Second World War, as explained in the following subsection.

6.2.2 *Justiciability after 1945*

Throughout the period from the end of the First World War to the end of the Second, legal scholars debated the dominance of law or politics in international society. The key thinkers in this debate included Hans Morgenthau and Carl Schmitt, who argued for the dominance of politics,[87] and Hans Kelsen and Hersch Lauterpacht, who argued for the dominance of law.[88] The debate ignited in the realm of international dispute settlement in 1931, with the *Customs Regime between Germany and Austria* PCIJ advisory opinion provoking strong feelings on both sides, where the PCIJ handled what many considered to be an entirely political matter.[89] It was in response to this case that Lauterpacht wrote his 1933 classic of public international law *The Function of Law in the International Community*, in which he thoroughly developed the idea that all international disputes can be formulated in legal terms and addressed through legal methods of dispute resolution – namely international arbitration and resolution through an international court of law, then the Permanent Court of International Justice.[90] The Chilean international lawyer Alejandro Alvarez responded to this debate with what he referred to as an American-style approach of pragmatism to international law that urged viewing disputes and their potential solutions through a lens where legal and political considerations were fused, with the goal of using this blend to bring about a particular social result.[91] It is no surprise, given the outcome of the Second World War and the central role the United States played in establishing the postwar international order, that the UN Charter's provisions on international

[86] Ibid.

[87] See, e.g., Hans J. Morgenthau, *Positivism, Functionalism and International Law*, 34 AM. J. INT'L L. 260 (1940); CARL SCHMITT, LEGALITY AND LEGITIMACY (1932) (trans. Jeffrey Seitzer, 2004).

[88] See, e.g., HANS KELSEN, PRINCIPLES OF INTERNATIONAL LAW (R. W. TUCKER ed., 9th rev. edn, 1966); HANS KELSEN, PEACE THROUGH LAW (1944); HANS KELSEN, GENERAL THEORY OF LAW AND STATE (1945); LAUTERPACHT, *supra* note 49.

[89] See Customs Regime between Germany and Austria, PCIJ, Ser. A./B., No. 41, 1931.

[90] See generally LAUTERPACHT, *supra* note 49.

[91] See Alejandro Alvarez, *The New International Law*, 15 TRANSACTIONS OF THE GROTIUS SOCIETY 35–47 (1930) (cited in Anghie, *supra* note 84, at 542–43).

dispute settlement reflected this brand of American pragmatism through its focus on the end result – namely the *peaceful* resolution of disputes.

As explained in the preceding section, the Covenant of the League of Nations, the PCIJ Statute, and the arbitration treaties before 1945 listed types of disputes that were considered particularly suitable for legal resolution. The ICJ Statute provides an identical list to that of the PCIJ Statute, with ICJ Statute Article 36(2) stating:

> The states parties to the present Statute may at any time declare that they recognize as compulsory ipso facto and without special agreement, in relation to any other state accepting the same obligation, the jurisdiction of the Court in all legal disputes concerning:
>
> a. the interpretation of a treaty;
> b. any question of international law;
> c. the existence of any fact which, if established, would constitute a breach of an international obligation;
> d. the nature or extent of the reparation to be made for the breach of an international obligation.

The rest of ICJ Statute Article 36 reflects the same language and structure of the other parts of PCIJ Statute Article 36.

In both the PCIJ Statute and the ICJ Statute, the limitation to legal disputes exists for cases where the Court has jurisdiction through declarations under PCIJ Statute Article 36 and ICJ Statute Article 36(2), which often are referred to as optional clause declarations. In fact, both are relatively clear in acknowledging that the court can handle "*all* cases which the parties refer to it and all matters specifically provided for in treaties and conventions in force," with the ICJ Statute inserting "in the Charter of the United Nations" before "in treaties." Both of these instruments implicitly mean that justiciability is of limited importance when the jurisdictional basis is anything other than through an optional clause declaration. This point is emphasized for the ICJ in the fact that the ICJ Statute uses the word "dispute" on six occasions,[92] though without ever

[92] See ICJ Statute, Art. 4(2) (referring to "Article 44 of the Convention of The Hague of 1907 for the pacific settlement of international disputes"); Art. 36(2) ("The states parties to the present Statute may at any time declare that they recognize as compulsory ipso facto and without special agreement, in relation to any other state accepting the same obligation, the jurisdiction of the Court in all legal disputes"); Art. 36(6) ("In the event of a dispute as to whether the Court has jurisdiction, the matter shall be settled by the decision of the Court"); Art. 38(1) (The Court, whose function is to decide in accordance with international law such disputes as are submitted to it, shall apply"); Art. 40(1) ("In either case the subject of the dispute and the parties shall be indicated"); Art. 60 ("In the

defining the term, suggesting that the framers neither wanted to limit the ICJ's jurisdiction to only certain kinds of disputes nor wanted to tell States what kinds of disputes they could send to the ICJ. This point is emphasized in the context of the PCIJ Statute in Article 1, which acts like a type of preamble: "This Court [the Permanent Court of International Justice] shall be in addition to the Court of Arbitration organized by the Conventions of The Hague of 1899 and 1907, and to the special Tribunals of Arbitration to which States are always at liberty to submit their disputes for settlement." The general reference to "disputes" at the end of that provision would suggest an acknowledgment that international arbitration is at a minimum capable of handling disputes of a mixed nature. Justiciability also is important where the ICJ's advisory jurisdiction is involved, as ICJ Statute Article 65(1) makes clear with its reference to "legal question": "The Court may give an advisory opinion on any legal question at the request of whatever body may be authorized by or in accordance with the Charter of the United Nations to make such a request."[93] This same point is articulated in UN Charter Article 96, as explained below. Where justiciability might be important for these jurisdictional bases other than optional-clause declarations is where a State tries to intervene in a proceeding, as provided in ICJ Statute Article 62(1) with its reference to "legal nature": "Should a state consider that it has an interest of a legal nature which may be affected by the decision in the case, it may submit a request to the Court to be permitted to intervene." Apart from these instances where the qualifier "legal" was inserted, the ICJ Statute does not limit the ICJ to handling legal disputes where it relies on its other forms of jurisdiction.[94]

Moreover, in both the PCIJ Statute and the ICJ Statute, the interpretation of treaties is seen as clearly involving legal disputes, whereas Article 13 of the Covenant of the League of Nations sees these issues only as "*generally* suitable for submission to arbitration or judicial settlement."[95] The following subsection goes into greater depth about whether treaty interpretation *always* involves a legal dispute and is therefore justiciable per se, assuming it is not enough to dismiss

event of dispute as to the meaning or scope of the judgment, the Court shall construe it upon the request of any party").

93 Please note, though, that the PCIJ Statute does not expressly limit the Court's advisory jurisdiction to legal questions.

94 But see Coleman, *supra* note 59, at 33 (not making this distinction when he broadly declares that "Article 36 of the Statute of the ICJ restricts the jurisdiction of the Court to legal questions").

95 Covenant of the League of Nations, Art. 13 (emphasis added).

justiciability simply because it involves jurisdiction through a compromissory clause or *compromis*. The remainder of this subsection, however, focuses on the main difference between justiciability before and after the Second World War – namely the pragmatic perspective on international dispute settlement reflected in the UN Charter.

The main difference between before and after the Second World War stems from the shift in perspective from a more idealistic view of international dispute settlement to a more practical one. A relatively dramatic change in this realm seemed necessary for the obvious reason that the old way had failed to avoid the Second World War. The provisions dealing with international dispute settlement, primarily Article 2(3) and Chapter VI of the UN Charter, are the obvious starting point. A review of these provisions shows a clear desire on the part of the drafters to promote a particular social result – namely the *peaceful* settlement of disputes – over a perceived ideal concerning the way that disputes were to be handled, as had been observed in the past.

UN Charter Articles 2(3) and 33 are the main places where this result-oriented approach is reflected. Article 2(3) states that one of the main principles of the UN Charter system involves the following: "All Members shall settle their international disputes by peaceful means in such a manner that international peace and security, and justice, are not endangered." The key parts here are the obvious emphases on "peaceful means" and that "international peace and security, and justice, are not endangered," as well as the obligatory language "shall settle." It is this last phrase that distinguishes Article 2(3) from Article 33; the former requires States to settle their disputes peacefully, whereas the latter only requires States to *seek* to resolve their disputes peacefully. Some commentators would read "seek" into Article 2(3),[96] but this is incorrect; the obligation is to *find* a peaceful solution, not merely to seek a peaceful solution. Article 2(3) is not a negative obligation only, as some commentators assert when focusing on the last part of Article 2(3) "that Member nations not settle disputes by means that might endanger international peace,"[97] but rather the emphasis must be placed on the first part – that states "shall settle their international disputes by peaceful means." This

[96] Rama Mani, *Peaceful Settlement of Disputes and Conflict Prevention*, in THE OXFORD HANDBOOK ON THE UNITED NATIONS 300, 316 (THOMAS G. WEISS and SAM DAWS ed., 2007); Richard B. Bilder, *An Overview of International Dispute Settlement*, 1 EMORY J. INT'L DIS. RESOL. 1, pt. III (1986) (hereinafter Bilder, *Overview*).

[97] Bilder, *Overview*, *supra* note 96, at 1.

language of Article 2(3) contains an obligation of results, not of conduct. If States are not able to do so, then these States have an obligation to refer the matter to the Security Council, according to Article 37(1). It is this requirement to find a peaceful solution that sets the UN Charter apart from its predecessors. For example, the 1899 Hague Convention for the Pacific Settlement of International Disputes referred to States making their "best efforts" at finding a peaceful settlement of international disputes "as far as possible,"[98] and the 1907 Hague Convention for the Pacific Settlement of International Disputes referred to the member States resolving to "promote by all the efforts in their power" the peaceful settlement of disputes, and "[w]ith a view to obviating as far as possible recourse to force in the relations between States . . . use their best efforts to ensure the pacific settlement of international differences."[99] The norm created by these instruments essentially amounted to a recommendation,[100] whereas the UN Charter creates an obligation to resolve disputes peacefully.

UN Charter Article 33 can be seen as a more detailed extension of Article 2(3) inasmuch as it lays out some of the ways to avoid endangering international peace and security, as was mentioned in Article 2(3). However, it would be incorrect to claim that Article 33 is "very precise about the ways and means by which all member states must seek the peaceful settlement of disputes," as some commentators assert.[101] Chapter 2.2.2 provided an analysis of Article 33. Without repeating that analysis, this paragraph must highlight some of the relevant language for the argument being discussed here. Article 33(1) refers to the need for parties to resolve through peaceful means "*any dispute*, the continuance of which is likely to endanger the maintenance of international peace and security."[102] Article 33(1) proceeds to inclusively, not exclusively, list the peaceful means of resolution: "negotiation, enquiry, mediation, conciliation, arbitration, judicial settlement, resort to regional agencies or arrangements, or other peaceful means of their own choice." On its face, Article 33(1) clearly emphasizes at the end that the list of methods of international dispute settlement are some

[98] 1899 Hague Convention (I), preamb. ¶ 2, Art. 1,

[99] 1907 Hague Convention for the Pacific Settlement of International Disputes, preamb. ¶ 3, Art. 1, Art. 38, available at www.pca-cpa.org/upload/files/1907ENG.pdf.

[100] See Diaconu, *supra* note 53, at 1096.

[101] Mani, *supra* note 96, at 304, 307 (mentioning "other peaceful means," although he does not acknowledge that the parties can rely on methods not enumerated in Art. 33).

[102] UN Charter, Art. 33 (emphasis added).

"peaceful means" for avoiding endangering international peace and security, with the emphasis on "peaceful means." Moreover, such flexibility in terms of which peaceful means are to be used suggests an emphasis on the results. As Article 33(1) expressly lists arbitration and judicial settlement among the ways to resolve "any dispute," it would appear that the framers clearly had abandoned any lingering notion from the heyday of bilateral arbitration treaties that only "legal" disputes could be handled by these methods of resolution.

Admittedly there are several provisions in the UN Charter that refer to "legal" disputes, in addition to those already mentioned in the ICJ Statute, as discussed in the above paragraphs.[103] Indeed, UN Charter Article 36(3) refers to the idea that "legal disputes should as a general rule be referred by the parties to the International Court of Justice in accordance with the provisions of the Statute of the Court." However, this does not mean that *only* legal disputes should be referred to the ICJ, so this should not be seen as a limitation on the ICJ itself. Moreover, UN Charter Article 96 refers to "legal questions" on two occasions with regard to the ICJ's advisory jurisdiction:

(a) The General Assembly or the Security Council may request the International Court of Justice to give an advisory opinion on any legal question.
(b) Other organs of the United Nations and specialized agencies, which may at any time be so authorized by the General Assembly, may also request advisory opinions of the Court on legal questions arising within the scope of their activities.

Again, neither reference to "legal questions" limits the ICJ's powers. If anything, Article 96 limits the abilities of requesters of advisory opinions in the types of questions they can ask. Obviously this will indirectly limit the ICJ when it comes to its advisory opinions because the ICJ is to answer the questions posed. The point being made here merely is that nothing under either provision stops the ICJ from answering questions that have a strong political element to them.[104]

[103] The UN Charter and the ICJ Statute were designed to be read together, which is made clear by the UN Charter including the ICJ Statute as an annex and UN Charter Article 92 indicating that the ICJ Statute is "an integral part of the present Charter."

[104] See Hermann Mosler, *Article 96*, in THE CHARTER OF THE UNITED NATIONS: A COMMENTARY 1008, 1013–1014 (BRUNO SIMMA ed., 1994).

The UN Charter's willingness to allow legal resolution to handle all types of disputes is not entirely a break from the agreements from before the Second World War. The change, nonetheless, is crucial in terms of emphasizing the pragmatic approach now adopted in the UN era, focusing on the *result* of peaceful dispute settlement. ICJ judges have noted the general shift in approach to justiciability between the pre-UN and UN eras. For example, Judge Manfred Lachs in his separate opinion in the *Nicaragua* case, where he defends the notion of nonjusticiability of politically sensitive disputes, acknowledges that the practice before the UN era was different concerning justiciability and vital interests: "in the last century and the beginning of the present, those [disputes] concerning 'vital interests' of States, or their 'honour', were viewed as political, and thus not subject to third-party settlement" – implying that things had changed since then.[105] Nonetheless, some commentators still prefer to ignore or downplay these changes in order to emphasize how the involvement of a disputant's vital interests categorically disqualifies legal resolution as an option.[106] It is this general attitude that this chapter seeks to correct.

To be clear, these changes did not mean that the ICJ and international arbitral tribunals had become free to hear and decide entirely nonlegal issues, such as purely economic, religious, and sporting matters. Instead, it means that the ICJ does not always have to undertake a meaningful analysis of justiciability that is separate from an analysis of its jurisdiction in cases where it has jurisdiction in a way other than via an optional clause declaration, though the option remained open where the ICJ wanted to refuse to hear and decide a matter for some reason. This change likely had two related effects. First, where jurisdiction through an optional-clause declaration was not involved, disputes that contained stronger nonlegal elements could be heard and decided as long as jurisdiction was found. Second, this pushed the involvement of a disputant's vital interests in a dispute towards influencing whether a State consented to legal resolution through a compromissory clause or *compromis*, not whether the forum should refuse to hear and decide notwithstanding a finding that it had jurisdiction.[107] Higgins has

105 *Military and Paramilitary Activities in and against Nicaragua (Nicaragua v. US)*, Merits, 1986 ICJ Rep. 14, 168.

106 See, e.g., Coleman, *supra* note 59, at 33 (broadly declaring that "Article 36 of the Statute of the ICJ restricts the jurisdiction of the Court to legal questions").

107 See Richard Falk, *Appraisals of the ICJ's Decision: Nicaragua v. United States (Merits)*, 81 Am. J. Int'l. L. 106 (1987).

observed that vital interests certainly should play a role when States are deciding to consent to a forum's jurisdiction, though it is anachronistic to use the argument of vital interests to allow States to undo their consent and avoid legal resolution altogether.[108] In short, one might have a basis to see justiciability as a type of vestigial remnant of olden times in the body of law relating to international dispute settlement. This is not to say that justiciability has no use, just as the appendix is believed to serve certain functions that are still being explored, though perhaps not the same crucial functions associated with the digestion of grasses as for our ancient predecessors. Likewise, justiciability represents a convenient escape hatch for courts and tribunals to avoid having to deal with troublesome disputes (either for jurisprudential or other reasons). However, when critics assert the unsuitability or nonjusticiability of a particular type of dispute based on its relevance to a disputant's vital interests,[109] even though legal resolution has jurisdiction over these disputes, they essentially are returning to a time when these types of arguments mattered far more. As Lauterpacht asserted, "[T]here is no fixed limit to the possibilities of judicial settlement; that all conflicts in the sphere of international politics can be reduced to contests of a legal nature; and that the only decisive test of the justiciability of the dispute is the willingness of the disputants to submit the conflict to the arbitrament of law."[110] In this manner, justiciability and jurisdiction seem to merge into the same concept, and everything hinges upon finding the consent of the disputants to legal resolution of that dispute.

This subsection has addressed the shift in importance of justiciability between the pre-UN and UN eras from being an all-important principle during the heyday of the bilateral arbitration treaties, to one of limited importance starting with the PCIJ Statute, and then of even less importance under the UN Charter. The following subsection makes an argument in the alternative that, assuming *arguendo* that justiciability still is as crucial a principle for all types of jurisdictional bases, the tasks that the ICJ and international arbitral tribunals will be required to perform regarding nuclear non-proliferation disputes are legal in nature and so

[108] See Rosalyn Higgins, *The Desirability of Third-Party Adjudication: Conventional Wisdom or Continuing Truth?*, in INTERNATIONAL ORGANIZATION: LAW IN MOVEMENT 37, 66 (J. E. S. FAWCETT and ROSALYN HIGGINS, 1974) (hereinafter Higgins, *Desirability*).

[109] See Akande and Williams, *supra* note 50, at 381–82; Burke-White and von Staden, *supra* note 50, at 376.

[110] LAUTERPACHT, *supra* note 49, at 164.

finding justiciability should not be a problem for the Court and international arbitral tribunals.

6.3 Treaty interpretation as a legal dispute

This section briefly tries to anticipate the types of questions the ICJ or international arbitral tribunal will be faced with when handling a nuclear non-proliferation dispute in order to see if it might have an impact on the forum's determination of justiciability. In particular, this section sees nuclear non-proliferation norms as being contained mostly, if not exclusively, in treaties, with any disputes over these norms centering on a dispute over the interpretation of a treaty. The treaties mentioned in Chapter 2.1.1 that make up the nuclear non-proliferation regime show that this area of law is not *in statu nascendi*,[111] and act as a key indication of the legalization of norms relating to nuclear material and nuclear weapons. As arms control and disarmament law expert Göran Lysén explains, "The international regulation of armaments, namely the law of disarmament, has developed gradually with the conclusion of treaties between States. Accordingly, this field of law consists of treaty-made law."[112] Other experts in this area seem to agree.[113] In particular, David Fidler asserts that treaties provide "the most prominent and direct use of

[111] See A. Bolintineanu, *International Law and Disarmament*, 21 Revue roumaine d'études internationales 21, 22 (1987).

[112] Göran Lysén, *The Adequacy of the Law of Treaties Regarding Arms Control Agreements*, in Avoidance and Settlement of Arms Control Disputes 123, 123 (Julie Dahlitz ed., 1994).

[113] See Richard L. Williamson Jr., *Hard Law, Soft Law, and Non-law in Multilateral Arms Control: Some Compliance Hypotheses*, 4 Chi. J. Int'l L. 59, 62–63 (2003) (asserting customary disarmament and arms control law does not exist); Jean-Pierre Cot and Pascal Boniface, *Le contrôle de l'armement et le désarmement*, in 2 Droit international 865, 867–868 (Mohammed Bedjaoui ed., 1991); Dieter Fleck, *Current Legal and Policy Issues*, Future Legal Restraints on Arms Proliferation 21, 33 (Julie Dahlitz ed., 1996); Eric P. J. Myjer, *The Settlement of Disputes under the Chemical Weapons Convention and the Case of the Confidentiality Commission*, in The Convention on the Prohibition and Elimination of Chemical Weapons: A Breakthrough in Multilateral Disarmament 537, 550 (Daniel Bardonnet ed., 1995). But see Julie Dahlitz, *The Role of Customary Law in Arms Limitations*, in The International Law of Arms Control and Disarmament 157 (Julie Dahlitz and Detlev Dicke ed., 1991) (emphasizing the importance of customary international law in this area).

international law" in this general area.[114] Commentators call this type of focus on treaties to regulate weapons the "arms control approach."[115] It makes sense that customary international law and other sources of international law do not play a greater role in the formation of disarmament or arms control law, especially with regard to nuclear weapons and nuclear materials, because the sensitivity of this subject matter makes written obligations preferable to unwritten ones so that there is less ambiguity. If there are non-treaty norms that directly regulate the proliferation of arms, including nuclear weapons, they are of limited importance.[116] Inasmuch as a treaty norm or obligation touches upon the likely activities in question, it is possible to tie in the need for treaty interpretation to make it a justiciable dispute.[117] As a result of their perceived emphasis on treaties in the area of arms control and disarmament, which includes nuclear non-proliferation, disputes that arise there likely can be framed in terms of treaty-based rights and obligations, thus making justiciability a relatively easy issue to handle.

Commentators often recognize treaty interpretation and application as among the most common activities of legal resolution and the most obvious type of legal dispute that is justiciable.[118] As Jennings asserts, treaty interpretation and application are "the most obvious example of a legal, or justiciable dispute."[119] Examples abound of treaties stating as much. The 1899 and 1907 Hague Conventions for the Pacific Settlement of International Disputes state as much in indicating when it is appropriate to move to international adjudication: "In questions of a legal nature, and especially in the interpretation or application of international conventions."[120] Similarly, Article 13 of the Covenant of the League of Nations identified "legal disputes," or disputes that were "generally suitable for submission to arbitration or judicial settlement," as such matters as "the interpretation of a treaty, . . . any question of international law, . . . the existence of any fact which, if established, would constitute a breach of any international obligation, or . . . the

[114] David P. Fidler, *International Law and Weapons of Mass Destruction: End of the Arms Control Approach*, 14 Duke J. Comp. & Int'l L. 39, 41 (2004).

[115] Ibid., at 42. [116] See Fleck, *supra* note 113, at 33.

[117] See Brownlie, *supra* note 27, at 138.

[118] See Mani, *supra* note 96, at 306; Gowlland-Debbas, *supra* note 17, at 649–650.

[119] Jennings, *International Courts*, *supra* note 77, at 13–14. See also Jennings, *Commentary*, *supra* note 16, at 92–93.

[120] 1899 Hague Convention, Art. 16; 1907 Hague Convention, Art. 38.

extent and nature of the reparation to be made for any such breach."[121] Numerous ICJ cases support this view, such as its determination in its *Hostages* case where it found that a dispute over the interpretation and application of a multilateral convention is one "which by its very nature falls within international jurisdiction."[122] In the *Certain Expenses* advisory opinion, the ICJ refused to "attribute a political character to a request which invites it to undertake an essentially judicial task, namely, the interpretation of a treaty provision."[123] On at least two occasions, in the *Admission of a State to the United Nations* advisory opinion and in the *Competence of the General Assembly for the Admission of a State to the United Nations* advisory opinion, the ICJ has stated that treaty interpretation in particular is a judicial task, and even went so far as to assert that one cannot classify such judicial tasks as having a political nature.[124] Both the ICJ and international arbitration have a long history of interpreting treaties, even politically sensitive treaties in politically sensitive situations.[125] The interpretation and application of treaties is seen as one of the seven main categories of disputes that the ICJ is asked to handle.[126] These views on the ability of legal resolution to interpret treaties do not necessarily make cases involving treaty interpretation entirely legal disputes. However, where the dispute is limited to treaty interpretation and application, then the dispute would be legal in nature.

Some commentators assert that issues of interpretation of a treaty may be political even though they involve an operation involving a treaty.[127] Surely, at the heart of the obligations contained in nuclear non-proliferation agreements are political decisions inasmuch as

[121] Covenant of the League of Nations, Art. 13.

[122] *United States Diplomatic and Consular Staff in Tehran (US v. Iran)*, Provisional Measures, Order, 1979 ICJ Rep. 7, 16 (Dec. 15).

[123] *Certain Expenses of the United Nations (Art. 17, para. 2 of the Charter)*, Advisory Opinion, 1962 ICJ Rep. 151, 155 (July 20).

[124] See *Conditions of Admission of a State to the United Nations (Article 4 of the Charter)*, Advisory Opinion, 1948 ICJ Rep. 57, 61 (May 28); *Competence of the General Assembly for the Admission of a State to the United Nations*, Advisory Opinion, 1950 ICJ Rep. 4, 6–7 (March 3); Gowlland-Debbas, *supra* note 17, at 652 (citing these cases and making this point).

[125] See John G. Merrills, *The Contribution of the Permanent Court of Arbitration to International Law and to the Settlement of Disputes by Peaceful Means*, in THE PERMANENT COURT OF ARBITRATION: INTERNATIONAL ARBITRATION AND DISPUTE RESOLUTION 3, 10 (P. HAMILTON et al. ed., 1999).

[126] See Mani, *supra* note 96, at 306.

[127] See Oscar Schachter, *International Law in Theory and Practice*, 178 REC. DES COURS 13, 211–215 (1982); Charney, *supra* note 37, at 291, 307–308.

political entities are involved, thus intertwining the legal and the political. Moreover, the decisions of courts and tribunals interpreting these treaties may be political inasmuch as they impact political entities and even people.[128] Disarmament and arms control obligations and decisions certainly are no exception.[129] However, by States codifying these decisions in treaty form, these political decisions are given legal effect and are given a distinctly legal character.[130] Therefore, lawyers are not only helpful in drafting treaties,[131] they also are helpful once treaties have been concluded and the exact obligations under these treaties come into question. In fact, the codification of a political arrangement into a treaty shifts the issues from being political to being legal in nature, simply by their inclusion in a treaty or regulation by a treaty,[132] thus giving lawyers a crucial role in determining the extent of these obligations. In particular, regarding interpreting treaties, it becomes possible to isolate legal matters from political ones because the treaty already has done that,[133] which is where the lawyers can come in handy. Even though nuclear non-proliferation disputes are surrounded by politically sensitive factors, such as national security and the survival of States, this does not change the fact that these materials are regulated by treaties and the legal rules and principles that they contain. Because of this, nuclear non-proliferation disputes are going to tend to be legal disputes, with disputes over treaties themselves being legal disputes per se.[134]

Critics might argue that this section's focus on treaty interpretation with nuclear non-proliferation disputes conveniently tries to avoid the relatively difficult task of determining the exact extent to which politically sensitive disputes are justiciable by focusing on the most justiciable of disputes. Indeed, this section has argued that the task of interpreting a treaty is legal per se, and therefore the Court or tribunal need not spend much time considering the justiciability of such matters. The following section gives examples of provisions from nuclear non-proliferation

[128] See Cristobal Orrego, *Natural Law under Other Names:* De Nominibus non est Disputandum, 52 AM. J. JURIS. 77, 86 (2007).

[129] See GOTLIEB, *supra* note 6, at 30; Fisher, *supra* note 6, at 1219; MARTIN, *supra* note 2, at 1.

[130] See GOTLIEB, *supra* note 6, at 120.

[131] See MARTIN, *supra* note 2, at 1.

[132] See Christopher J. Borgen, *Resolving Treaty Conflicts*, 37 GEO. WASH. INT'L L. *Rev.* 573, 573–574 (2005); MARTIN, *supra* note 2, at 1.

[133] See MARTIN, *supra* note 2, at 4–5.

[134] See GOTLIEB, *supra* note 6, at 120.

agreements that the Court or an international arbitral tribunal can interpret.

6.4 Treaty interpretation of nuclear non-proliferation agreements

This section looks at two of the provisions in nuclear non-proliferation agreements that the introduction to Part III listed as potential issues in which the ICJ or an international arbitral tribunal might be able to get involved – NPT Article IV(1) and NPT Article IV(2). To remind the reader, Article IV(1) protects a member State's "inalienable right . . . to develop research, production and use of nuclear energy for peaceful purposes without discrimination and in conformity with Articles I and II of this Treaty,"[135] and Article IV(2) protects a member State's "right to participate in . . . the fullest possible exchange of equipment, materials and scientific and technological information for the peaceful uses of nuclear energy."[136] Article IV(2) is analyzed from the perspective of a contemporary nuclear non-proliferation dispute that the Security Council has not become involved with using its Chapter VII powers – namely China's providing Pakistan with two nuclear reactors and providing other assistance to Pakistan with those two nuclear power plants. The fact that China is involved with that dispute suggests that the Security Council will not get involved with that dispute, since China holds a veto within the Security Council. The lack of Security Council involvement means that this provision has not been suspended in that situation by the creation of a conflicting obligation by the Security Council. As the NPT does not provide a compromissory clause that can act as the jurisdictional basis for the ICJ or an international arbitral tribunal, it will be assumed that these fora can find jurisdiction through some other means in order to address the issue of interpretation of these sample provisions.

To be clear, the purpose of this section is not to determine definitively how the ICJ or an international arbitral tribunal would interpret these provisions. Chapter 3.1.3 above notes the myriad ways the ICJ or an international arbitral tribunal might interpret these provisions, and a review of how each method of interpretation might lead to a different

[135] Treaty on the Non-proliferation of Nuclear Weapons (NPT), Art. IV(1), July 1, 1968, 729 U.N.T.S. 161 (extended May 11, 1995, 34 I.L.M. 959).

[136] Ibid., Art. IV(2).

outcome falls outside the scope of this study. Instead, this section's purpose is to show that the ICJ or an international arbitral tribunal *can* interpret these provisions, simply based on the ways in which international courts and tribunals have interpreted similar language in past cases. The past cases cited here do not involve nuclear non-proliferation disputes or agreements, and so the applicability of these observations to the context of interpreting actual provisions of nuclear non-proliferation agreements will have to be done through analogy. Such arguments by analogy are appropriate here inasmuch as analogies have been made during legal resolution in the past.[137]

Before proceeding with this analysis, two disclaimers are in order. First, in interpreting these provisions, this section adopts a textualist approach, which starts with the face of the provision before moving out from there as ambiguities are encountered.[138] The ICJ occasionally has adopted this approach when it has emphasized the ordinary meaning of the text over evidence of the meaning that exists outside the text,[139] and seems like a conservative approach to take when interpreting a treaty provision. Second, the observations made in this section about the situation involving China are based on the information available in newspapers and other sources that are publicly accessible. It must be recognized that these sources are not always entirely reliable. An attempt has been made to independently confirm these reports, without notable success. However, since these reports ostensibly have not been denied by the respective States or the international community as a whole, it is relatively safe to assume that there is at least some merit to these sources. Those with contrary evidence are invited to make such information publicly available.

[137] See, e.g., *Case Concerning the Arrest Warrant of 11 April 2000 (DRC v. Belgium)*, 2000 ICJ Rep. 121, 145–146 (Feb. 14) (Van den Wyndaert, J., dissenting) (noting how the ICJ adopted an "analogy with immunities for diplomatic agents and Heads of State"); Jedediah Purdy and Kimberly Fielding, *Sovereigns, Trustees, Guardians: Private-Law Concepts and the Limits of Legitimate State Power*, 70 LAW & CONTEMP. PROB. 165, 201 (2007) (noting the relevance of various analogies in the *South West Africa* case of the ICJ).

[138] See Francis G. Jacobs, *Varieties of Approach to Treaty Interpretation: With Special Reference to the Draft Convention on the Law of Treaties before the Vienna Diplomatic Conference*, 18 INT'L & COMP. L.Q. 318, 319 (1969).

[139] See *Competence of the General Assembly for the Admission of a State to the United Nations*, Advisory Opinion, 1950 ICJ Rep. 4, 8 (March 3); *Constitution of the Maritime Safety Committee of the Inter-governmental Maritime Consultative Organization*, Advisory Opinion, 1960 ICJ Rep. 150, 159–160 (June 8); SS *Lotus*, 1927 P.C.I.J. (ser. A) No. 10, at 16 (Sept. 7).

The analysis of this section begins with NPT Article IV(1):

> Nothing in this Treaty shall be interpreted as affecting the inalienable right of all the Parties to the Treaty to develop research, production and use of nuclear energy for peaceful purposes without discrimination and in conformity with Articles I and II of this Treaty.[140]

Each of the six elements of this provision will be analyzed here, again not to show definitively how the ICJ or an international arbitral tribunal would interpret this provision, but rather to show that the ICJ or an international arbitral tribunal could interpret this provision, based on the fact that they have interpreted similar language in past cases.

Starting with "inalienable right," when this phrase has come up in ICJ decisions, it typically has been within the context of a people's inalienable right to self-determination. In most instances, the Court does not address the exact meaning of the phrase. For example, the *Namibia* advisory opinion, its separate opinions, and its dissenting opinions make references to the inalienable right to self-determination (at times referred to as a "sacred trust"), but without providing a definition.[141] However, in the 1995 *East Timor* case between Portugal and Australia, the Court directly addressed the scope of the right of the people of East Timor to self-determination. There, the Court described this right as being "one of the essential principles of contemporary international law," considering "irreproachable" an argument that this right, "as it evolved from the Charter and from United Nations practice, has an *erga omnes* character."[142] In terms of legal effect, the involvement of an inalienable right seems to transform a dispute over these types of rights beyond a bilateral one to one where other States have a legal interest in ensuring that the right is respected. The ICJ mentioned in the *Wall* advisory opinion that that dispute was not just a bilateral dispute between Israel and Palestine because the United Nations and the

[140] Treaty on the Non-proliferation of Nuclear Weapons, Art. IV(1), July 1, 1968, 729 U.N. T.S. 161 (extended May 11, 1995, 34 I.L.M. 959).

[141] See, e.g., *Legal Consequences for States of the Continued Presence of South Africa in Namibia (South West Africa) Notwithstanding Security Council Resolution 276 (1970)*, Advisory Opinion, 1971 ICJ Rep. 16 (June 21). The ICJ discussed in the *Military and Paramilitary Activities in and against Nicaragua* case between Nicaragua and the United States the "inherent" right of States to "individual and collective self-defence" under UN Charter Art. 51, although a connection between this term and "inalienable" was not made. See *Military and Paramilitary Activities in and against Nicaragua (Nicaragua v. US)*, 1986 ICJ Rep. 14 (June 27).

[142] *East Timor (Portugal v. Australia)*, 1995 ICJ Rep. 90, 102 (June 30).

international community had taken many steps to "realiz[e] the inalienable rights of the Palestinian people" to self-determination, through the UN's adoption of various resolutions, and the creation of various bodies to help with realizing those rights.[143] The United Nations has adopted such resolutions not only in the context of Palestine but also where self-determination was involved for other peoples. For example, Security Council Resolutions 384 and 389 called on "all States to respect the territorial integrity of East Timor as well as the inalienable right of its people to self-determination," as the ICJ noted in the *East Timor* case.[144] Such a transformative power of such inalienable rights presumably would help with the standing issue to enable a wider number of States to bring a claim for violating that right, as noted in Chapter 5.1 above.

Second, when it comes to "research," in the *Brazilian Loans* case, the PCIJ roughly equated "researches" with "obtain[ing] knowledge."[145] In the 1999 *Difference Relating to Immunity from Legal Process of a Special Rapporteur of the Commission on Human Rights* advisory opinion, the ICJ was careful to distinguish between the different tasks of Special Rapporteur Cumaraswamy on his research mission to Malaysia, noting how research is different from monitoring and reporting.[146]

Third, when it comes to "nuclear energy," the ICJ or an international arbitral tribunal has not defined this phrase. However, as noted in Chapter 2.1.2 above, the ICJ has provided a definition of "nuclear weapons" in the *Legality of the Threat or Use of Nuclear Weapons* advisory opinion: "explosive devices whose energy results from the fusion or fission of the atom."[147] A definition for "nuclear energy" can be derived from this definition of "nuclear weapons" by simply eliminating the portion relating to weapons, which would leave "energy result[ing] from the fusion or fission of an atom," which would seem like a somewhat conservative approach to defining "nuclear energy."

[143] *Legal Consequences of the Construction of a Wall in the Occupied Palestinian Territory*, 2004 ICJ Rep. 136, 158–159 (July 9).

[144] *East Timor (Portugal v. Australia)*, 1995 ICJ Rep. 90, 96, 103 (June 30).

[145] *The Payment in Gold of Brazilian Federal Loans Contracted in France (Brazil/France)*, 1929 PCIJ, ser. A, No. 21, at 124 (July 12) (in that context, the research was concerning the content of municipal law).

[146] See *Difference Relating to Immunity from Legal Process of a Special Rapporteur of the Commission on Human Rights*, Advisory Opinion, 1999 ICJ Rep. 62, 83 (April 29).

[147] *Legality of the Threat or Use of Nuclear Weapons*, Advisory Opinion, 1996 ICJ Rep. 226, 243 (July 8).

Fourth, when it comes to "for peaceful purposes," the 1998 *Fisheries Jurisdiction* case is particularly helpful. There, the ICJ interpreted the phrase "for peaceful purposes" contained in Article 88 of the 1982 United Nations Convention on the Law of the Sea, which simply states, "The high seas shall be reserved for peaceful purposes."[148] The ICJ interpreted this phrase "for peaceful purposes" as meaning that this is a "maritime area . . . where no State is entitled to use force in order to enforce measures of conservation and management of living resources against vessels in that area flying the flag of another State."[149] Adjusting this interpretation so that it applies *mutatis mutandis* here, "for peaceful purposes" would involve the lack of the use of force or the lack of an intent to use force with that nuclear energy.

Fifth, regarding "without discrimination," the ICJ in the 1996 preliminary objections phase of the *Application of the Convention on the Prevention and Punishment of the Crime of Genocide* case equated "without discrimination" with "without distinction" in the context of interpreting paragraph 7 of the Declaration on Principles of International law and its protection of equal rights and self-determination of peoples.[150] In the 1986 *Military and Paramilitary Activities in and against Nicaragua* case, the ICJ determined that the US support of the Contras in Nicaragua violated the principle of nonintervention.[151] In reaching this decision, the ICJ interpreted the US legislation concerning its limitation to humanitarian assistance in giving aid to the Contras in Nicaragua, noting how a fundamental principle, humanitarian assistance, is "bring[ing] assistance without discrimination to the wounded on the battlefield."[152] The ICJ went on to take an extreme interpretation of "without discrimination" by noting how it prohibited discrimination "of any kind" – in that context, without distinguishing between "all in need in Nicaragua, not merely . . . the *contras* and their dependents."[153]

Sixth, regarding the "in conformity with" phrase, the ICJ has had to interpret that on a number of occasions. The instance that this section

148 United Nations Convention on the Law of the Sea, Art. 88, Dec. 10, 1982, 1833 U.N.T.S. 397.

149 *Fisheries Jurisdiction Case (Spain v. Canada)*, Jurisdiction, 1998 ICJ Rep. 432, 729–730 (Dec. 4).

150 *Application of the Convention on the Prevention and Punishment of the Crime of Genocide (Bosnia and Herzegovina v. Yugoslavia)*, Preliminary Objections, 1996 ICJ 595, 742 (July 11).

151 *Military and Paramilitary Activities in and against Nicaragua*, 1986 ICJ Rep. 14, 124 (June 27).

152 Ibid., at 124–125. 153 Ibid., at 125.

focuses on is the 1998 *Fisheries Jurisdiction* case, where the ICJ had to interpret the scope of a reservation of Canada to the Court's jurisdiction that excluded "disputes arising out of or concerning conservation and management measures taken by Canada with respect to vessels fishing in the NAFO Regulatory Area, as defined in the Convention on Future Multilateral Co-operation in the Northwest Atlantic Fisheries, 1978, and the enforcement of such measures."[154] Spain tried to limit the phrase "conservation and management measures" by means of "in conformity with international law," as noted in the agreed minutes from the amendments adopted on May 25, 1994, to Canada's Coastal Fisheries Protection Act.[155] In rejecting Spain's argument, the ICJ distinguished between internal and external types of conformity, with internal types involving "a matter of definition," not a "question of legality."[156] Inasmuch as Article IV(1) requires conformity with an internal provision of the NPT, this language might be seen as clarifying the definition of the terms in that provision. In other words, this element re-emphasizes the point that the research, production, and use of nuclear energy have to be for peaceful purposes, not for nuclear weapons or other nuclear explosive devices, as prohibited in NPT Articles I and II.

The analysis of NPT Article IV(2) is shorter inasmuch as it contains some of the same words as Article IV(1), such as the reference to peaceful uses of nuclear energy. The main phrase that the ICJ or an international arbitral tribunal would have to interpret would be "the fullest possible" phrase. In a dispute between the European Communities and the United States over a US definitive safeguard measure on European imports of wheat gluten, both the United States and the European Communities appealed to the WTO Appellate Body various issues of law and legal interpretations of the Panel Report in the 2000 case *Definitive Safeguard Measures on Imports of Wheat Gluten from the European Communities*.[157] The United States appealed the Panel's determination that it had not provided notice to the Committee on Safeguards "immediately," as Article 12.1 of the Agreement on Safeguards required, because, according to the United States, "it was sufficiently prompt as to allow Members concerned to review the notification and to exercise fully

154 *Fisheries Jurisdiction Case (Spain v. Canada)*, Jurisdiction, 1998 ICJ Rep. 432, 439 (Dec. 4).

155 Ibid., at 445. 156 Ibid., at 460.

157 See WTO Appellate Body Report, *United States – Definitive Safeguard Measures on Imports of Wheat Gluten from the European Communities*, WT/DS166/AB/R, ¶ 1 (Dec. 22, 2000).

their rights under the *Agreement on Safeguards*."[158] The United States actually had given notice sixteen days after it had initiated a safeguards investigation.[159] The European Communities argued that the United States had "failed to notify each event listed in Article 12.1 of the *Agreement on Safeguards* in a timely manner." In resolving this issue, the Appellate Body defined "immediate" as the amount of notification that "allows the Committee on Safeguards, and Members, the *fullest possible period* to reflect upon and react to an ongoing safeguard investigation."[160] The Appellate Body went on to expressly disagree with the US position that "immediate" does not mean that the Committee on Safeguards and the WTO membership has "sufficient time to review that notification." This case shows how the WTO Appellate Body used "fullest possible" in a rather extreme manner, without defining the word "possible" or otherwise explaining whether a reasonable delay would be allowed. In a declaration in the *Nuclear Tests* case, ICJ judge Jimenez de Arechaga qualified "fullest possible" as "within the limits of time and of materials available for that purpose" when the Court was deciding whether to grant provisional measures:

> This [urgent] situation [involving a decision on provisional measures] places upon each Member of the Court the duty to make, at this stage, an appreciation of whether – in the light of the grounds invoked and of the other materials before him – the Court will possess jurisdiction to entertain the merits of the dispute. From a subjective point of view, such an appreciation or estimation cannot be fairly described as a mere preliminary or even cursory examination of the jurisdictional issue: on the contrary, one must be satisfied that this basic question of the Court's jurisdiction has received the fullest possible attention which one is able to give to it within the limits of time and of materials available for that purpose.[161]

Judge ad hoc Elihu Lauterpacht quoted this same material in his separate opinion for the provisional measures order in the *Application of the Convention on the Prevention and Punishment of the Crime of Genocide* case to find in favor of allowing the provisional measures requested.[162] This qualification of "fullest possible" suggests that a decision-maker

158 Ibid., ¶ 110. 159 See ibid., ¶ 109. 160 Ibid., ¶ 106 (emphasis in original).

161 *Nuclear Tests Case (Australia v. France)*, 1973 ICJ Rep. 99, 107 (Jimenez de Arechaga J., declaration, June 22); *(New Zealand v. France)*, 1973 ICJ Rep. 135, 143 (June 22).

162 See *Application of the Convention on the Prevention and Punishment of the Crime of Genocide (Bosnia and Herzegovina v. Yugoslavia)*, Provisional Measures, 1993 ICJ Rep. 325, 411 (Sept. 13).

faced with interpreting this phrase might read in a reasonableness element, thus shaving off a bit of the extremeness of the phrase.

Turning to the case involving China, the Group of 77 (or G-77) developing countries, which formed in 1964 to help in co-ordinating the negotiation of the Nuclear Non-Proliferation Treaty and now numbers 130 countries, along with China, began pushing the IAEA in March 2011 to increase the amount of assistance given to developing the nuclear energy programs of the G-77 countries.[163] The G-77 asked the IAEA to facilitate that assistance through the "sharing [of] science and exchanging [of] information about the management of the nuclear knowledge, capacity-building and defining safety standards."[164] Shortly after this request, the IAEA Board of Governors unanimously gave China approval to provide Pakistan with two nuclear power plants, the Chasnupp-3 and C-4 plants, with China providing the nuclear reactors for these plants, in addition to providing other assistance.[165] Just a month later, in April 2011, China purchased from US company Westinghouse Electric Co. the plans for the next generation of nuclear power plants, thus establishing China as a strong exporter of nuclear power plants.[166] Some Western commentators have been skeptical about China providing Pakistan these nuclear power plants, fearing safety problems inasmuch as Pakistan might be prone to violence and has not subjected itself to full IAEA safeguards, as well as fearing that China might be trying to aid Pakistan's nuclear-weapon program.[167] China continues to encourage the IAEA and the rest of the international community to promote further the peaceful use of nuclear energy, primarily through "nuclear infrastructure building, drawing up nuclear energy policies, establishing regulatory system, fostering safety culture, and training highly-qualified

[163] See *G-77 Seeks IAEA Assistance to Member States' Nuclear Programs*, FARS News Agency, March 8, 2011.

[164] Ibid.

[165] See *IAEA Approves Pakistan Chasnupp-3 and C-4 Nuclear plants*, Rupee News, March 9, 2011; IAEA nod to China, *Pak Pact for Two New Nuclear Reactors*, Press Trust of India, March 9, 2011.

[166] See Lou Kilzer, *Westinghouse Surrendered Next-Generation Nuclear Plant Specs*, PITTSBURGH TRIBUNE REV., April 4, 2011; *Nuclear China Question*, UNITED NEWS OF INDIA, May 3, 2011.

[167] See, e.g., Steven Jiang, *Pakistan Cements China Ties Amid Tension with U.S.*, CNN.COM, May 17, 2011; Mark Hibbs, *Condoleezza Rice and Germany on the Sino-Pakistan Deal*, STATES NEWS SERVICE, July 17, 2011; *The China Challenge: A Strategic Vision for U.S.-India Relations*, STATES NEWS SERVICE, July 18, 2011.

personnel," with the IAEA apparently praising China's efforts in this area.[168]

Still, in the face of challenges to the legality of the China–Pakistan nuclear power plant deal and its other efforts to promote the peaceful use of nuclear energy, China could seek a declaration from an international court or tribunal that deals of this sort are protected by its right under NPT Article IV(2) "to participate in the fullest possible exchange of equipment, materials and scientific and technological information for the peaceful uses of nuclear energy." Legal resolution likely would become a more attractive option if the criticism increased in intensity over time.

Despite the general arguments in Chapter 6.3 above on the inherent justiciability of interpreting treaties and the examples here that show that the ICJ and international arbitral tribunals can interpret provisions in nuclear non-proliferation agreements, the following section makes another argument in the alternative, assuming, *arguendo*, that not all cases involving treaty interpretation are legal disputes or that some nuclear non-proliferation disputes are not treaty based, it is not difficult for the Court or tribunal to satisfy itself that the dispute placed before it is justiciable inasmuch as it can transform disputes into legal ones through the litigation process.

6.5 Handling mixed disputes

Disputes these days can be relatively complex, involving a variety of types of issues identified under the banner of one overarching dispute or conflict.[169] The more obvious kinds of issues are those of a political, economic, social, and legal nature.[170] International courts and arbitral tribunals obviously can handle legal issues, because that is their main task in applying law, although they have been known to handle political and economic issues as well.[171] However, the many instances where the ICJ has handled mixed legal–political disputes establishes beyond doubt that legal resolution can handle such disputes of a mixed nature.[172]

[168] See *China Asks IAEA to Play Key Role in Promoting Peaceful Use of Nuclear Energy*, Xinhua, Sept. 20, 2011.

[169] See Manfred Lachs, *The Law and the Settlement of International Disputes*, in Dispute Settlement through the United Nations 283, 286–287 (K. Venkata Raman ed., 1977).

[170] See Higgins, *Desirability*, *supra* note 108, at 41–42.

[171] See ibid.

[172] See Louis B. Sohn, *The Role of Arbitration in Recent International Multilateral Treaties*, in Resolving Transnational Disputes through International

While it might be a stretch to say that legal resolution necessarily is at its best with politically sensitive disputes,[173] since a court or tribunal of law obviously has the tools to handle more legal disputes, as the name implies, still these fora consistently have been willing and able to handle mixed disputes. Chapter 4 above provided examples of where these fora have handled such mixed disputes. This section mentions the instances where these fora and commentators have explained why they feel legal resolution can handle such mixed disputes.

Apart from the largely theoretical possibility of uniquely political or uniquely legal disputes, as discussed below, the vast majority of disputes fall into this mixed category.[174] Just as the involvement of treaties tends to legalize international disputes, the involvement of States – inherently political entities – in disputes tends to politicize them.[175] No matter how distinctly legal these disputes might be (such as those involving treaty interpretation, as explained in the preceding section), the disputes mainly are important for the politics involved.[176] All disputes involving a State are bound to have some strong political elements and consequences to them, given that States themselves are political entities.[177] As the ICJ determined in the *US Diplomatic and Consular Staff in Tehran* case, all legal questions derive from a political context,[178] thus implying that there will be political elements to all questions before international

ARBITRATION 21, 27 (THOMAS E. CARBONNEAU ed., 1984); Robert Jennings, *Presentation on the Contributions of the Court to the Resolution of International Tensions*, Proceedings of the ICJ/UNITAR Colloquium to Celebrate the 50th Anniversary of the Court, reprinted in INCREASING THE EFFECTIVENESS OF THE INTERNATIONAL COURT OF JUSTICE 78, 79 (CONNIE PECK and ROY S. LEE ed., 1997) (hereinafter Jennings, *Presentation*) (asserting that the ICJ and arbitral tribunals can handle disputes of a mixed legal-political nature, and even "grave political disputes and situations").

173 See James A. R. Nafziger, *Political Dispute Resolution by the World Court, with Reference to United States Courts*, 26 DENV. J. INT'L L. & POL'Y 775, 776–777 (1998) ("[T]he Court is at its best when it is resolving political disputes").

174 See Jennings, *International Courts*, *supra* note 77, at 15.

175 See SHABTAI ROSENNE, ESSAYS ON INTERNATIONAL LAW AND PRACTICE 38 (2007) (citing *United States Diplomatic and Consular Staff in Tehran* case, ICJ Rep. 1980 3, 20; *Military and Paramilitary Activities in and against Nicaragua (Jurisdiction and Admissibility)* case, ICJ Rep. 1984 392, 433) (viewing the ICJ as saying, in the *Hostages* case and the *Nicaragua* case, that all disputes involving States will be political); Edward Gordon, *Discretion to Decline to Exercise Jurisdiction*, 81 AM. J. INT'L. L. 129, 133 (1987).

176 See Jennings, *International Courts*, *supra* note 77, at 13, 19.

177 See Merrills, *supra* note 21, at 171–172.

178 See *US Diplomatic and Consular Staff in Tehran (US v. Iran)*, Judgment, 1980 ICJ Rep. 3, 18–20 (May 24).

courts and tribunals. It is not enough to rely on the involvement of some political elements or political consequences to conclude that those disputes are nonjusticiable. Otherwise, international courts and tribunals where States have *jus standi* will cease to exist on account of the fact that all of the disputes before them are political to some degree and presumably would be disqualified. Moreover, there would have been no point in establishing these courts and tribunals in the first place if they could not have heard and decided any of these inter-State disputes that were their *raison d'être*. Finally, since both the ICJ and international arbitral tribunals have the ability to decide cases *ex aequo et bono* with the consent of the disputants,[179] or rather without the application of law, these fora at least must be able to think and decide in nonlegal terms and handle nonlegal elements that are incidental to the legal elements.

This is a sentiment that has been repeated in international adjudication jurisprudence. Commentators have provided a string of quotes from PCIJ and ICJ cases since the First World War where either of these courts has declared and explained that it can handle mixed disputes,[180] including the *Lockerbie* case, the *Hostages* case,[181] the *Aegean Sea Continental Shelf* case,[182] and the *Nicaragua* case,[183] to name only a few. Indeed, as the ICJ acknowledged in the *Nicaragua* case, since the ICJ's first contentious case (the *Corfu Channel* case) "the Court has never shied away from a case brought before it merely because it had political implications

[179] See ICJ Statute, Art. 38(2); UNCITRAL Arbitration Rules, Art. 33 (1976). See generally Charles de Visscher, De l'équité dans le règlement arbitral ou judiciaire des litiges de droit international public (1972); Prosper Weil, *L'équité dans la jurisprudence de la Cour internationale de justice: Un mystère en voie de disparition?*, in Fifty Years of the International Court of Justice: Essays in Honour of Sir Robert Jennings 121 (Vaughan Lowe and Malgosia Fitzmaurice ed., 1996).

[180] See, e.g., Coleman, *supra* note 59, at 43 (providing essentially strings of quotations); Takane Sugihara, *The Judicial Function of the International Court of Justice with Respect to Disputes Involving Highly Political Issues*, in The International Court of Justice 117 (Sam Muller et al. ed., 1997) (same); Rosenne, *supra* note 175, at 38–39 (when saying that legal resolution can handle legal questions in a broader political context, quoting *Interpretation of the Agreement of 25 March 1951 between the WHO and Egypt*, Advisory Opinion, 1980 ICJ Rep. 73, 87 (Dec. 20); *Legality of the Threat or Use of Nuclear Weapons*, Advisory Opinion, 1996 ICJ Rep. 226, 234 (July 8)).

[181] See *US Diplomatic and Consular Staff in Tehran (US v. Iran)*, 1980 ICJ Rep. 3, 19 (May 28).

[182] See *Aegean Sea Continental Shelf Case (Greece v. Turkey)*, 1978 ICJ Rep. 12, 27 (Dec. 19).

[183] See *Military and Paramilitary Activities in and against Nicaragua (Nicaragua v. US)*, Jurisdiction, 1984 ICJ Rep. 392 (Nov. 26).

or because it involved serious elements of the use of force."[184] The cases following the *Corfu Channel* case indeed suggest that the ICJ has never since shied away from cases with strong political implications. A few of the declarations that might be mentioned here are the following. According to the ICJ, the 1980 *Hostages* case was the first time when a party – there Iran – had argued that the political aspects of a dispute should lead the Court to decline to resolve the legal issues placed before it, with the Court asserting that it had the ability to answer the legal questions of such a mixed-nature dispute.[185] In 1984, the ICJ again was faced with this same argument in the *Nicaragua* case, although this time from the United States, and the ICJ again rejected the argument.[186] In the 1988 *Border and Transborder Armed Actions* case, the ICJ again declared that it did not care whether there were political aspects to a dispute brought before it when determining jurisdiction and justiciability,[187] indicating that the existence of political elements in a dispute does not remove justiciability. In 1992, Libya argued that the *Lockerbie* dispute was entirely legal inasmuch as it merely involved interpretation of the Montreal Convention, and so it was appropriate to have the ICJ handle the dispute as opposed to the Security Council,[188] although the ICJ nonetheless refused to proceed with the case. Finally, all of the military-related disputes that legal resolution has handled over the years, which are discussed in Chapter 4 above, also support this point and essentially place it beyond challenge.

Similar conclusions can be found in advisory opinions as well. In the *Legality of the Threat or Use of Nuclear Weapons* advisory opinion, quoting the 1973 *Application for Review of Judgment No. 158 of the United Nations Administrative Tribunal* advisory opinion, the ICJ stated,

> The question put to the Court by the General Assembly is indeed a legal one, since the Court is asked to rule on the compatibility of the threat or

[184] Ibid., at 435.

[185] *US Diplomatic and Consular Staff in Tehran (US v. Iran)*, 1980 ICJ Rep. 3, 20–22 (May 28).

[186] *Military and Paramilitary Activities in and against Nicaragua (Nicaragua v. US)*, Jurisdiction, 1984 ICJ Rep. 392, 435 (Nov. 26).

[187] See *Border and Transborder Armed Actions (Nicaragua v. Honduras)*, Jurisdiction, 1988 ICJ Rep. 69, ¶ 52 (Dec. 20).

[188] See *Questions of Interpretation and Application of the 1971 Montreal Convention Arising from the Aerial Incident at Lockerbie (Libya v. US)*, Preliminary Objections, 1988 ICJ Rep. 115 (Feb. 22).

> use of nuclear weapons with the relevant principles and rules of international law . . . The fact that this question also has political aspects, as, in the nature of things, is the case with so many questions which arise in international life, does not suffice to deprive it of its character as a "legal question" and to "deprive the Court of a competence expressly conferred on it by its Statute."[189]

Other advisory opinions exhibit similarly strong political aspects, and yet the ICJ has not shied away from providing an opinion based on the political aspects of the question posed. The ICJ in the *Legality of the Use by a State of Nuclear Weapons in Armed Conflict* (WHO request for an advisory opinion) declared, "The political nature of the motives which may be said to have inspired the request and the political implications that the opinion given might have are of no relevance to the establishment of its jurisdiction to give such an opinion."[190] Moreover, the 1950 *Second Admissions* advisory opinion and the 1962 *Certain Expenses* advisory opinion also emphasize this point that the existence of political aspects of a dispute cannot strip an otherwise legal dispute of its legal nature, or rather strip the ICJ of its jurisdiction.[191]

In a way, with such politically sensitive disputes as those involving States, nonlegal factors are bound to creep in during any adjudication process, and probably should be allowed to creep in so that the dispute and its solution are kept realistic and applicable. Indeed, apart from when advisory opinions are involved, legal questions in contentious cases have to be addressed along with their accompanying facts, as is reflected in the case-and-controversy doctrine.[192] Moreover, assuming that the classification of the dispute is not agreed by the parties at the commencement of a dispute, it is not as though the nature of a dispute is static, but it can change over the course of the dispute, depending on the

189 *Legality of the Threat or Use of Nuclear Weapons*, Advisory Opinion, 1996 ICJ Rep. 226, 233–234 (July 8).

190 *Legality of the Use by a State of Nuclear Weapons in Armed Conflict*, Advisory Opinion, 1996 ICJ Rep. 66, 72–73 (July 8).

191 See generally *Competence of the General Assembly for the Admission of a State to the United Nations*, Advisory Opinion, 1950 ICJ Rep. 4 (March 3); *Certain Expenses of the United Nations (Article 17, paragraph 2, of the Charter)*, Advisory Opinion, 1962 ICJ Rep. 151 (July 20); see also Higgins, *Desirability*, *supra* note 108, at 43 (discussing this point and various ICJ advisory opinions, including these opinions).

192 See Richard B. Bilder, *The Fact/Law Distinction in Int'l Adjudication*, in FACT-FINDING BEFORE INTERNATIONAL TRIBUNALS 124 (RICHARD B. LILLICH ed., 1992).

perceptions and arguments of the disputants.[193] These perceptions and arguments can depend on a number of factors, one of which is internal political considerations.[194]

Arguments that the ICJ cannot handle mixed disputes seem to be limited to those made by respondents and dissenting judges, such as the joint dissenting opinion of ICJ judges Spender and Fitzmaurice in the 1962 *South-West Africa* case,[195] and Judge Manfred Lachs's dissenting opinion in the 1986 *Nicaragua* case.[196] A minority of commentators assert that legal resolution cannot resolve complex disputes, contrary to what the ICJ has said on many occasions.[197] While dissenting opinions have a role with the progressive development of international law, or international law *de lege ferenda*, they cannot be seen as declarative of international law per se, or international law *de lege lata*. Therefore, these opinions must be severely discounted in terms of creating international law.

There is only one ICJ case where the Court concluded that the dispute was nonjusticiable based on the legal–political dimensions to the case – the 1951 decision in *Haya de la Torre*, where the ICJ was asked to choose "amongst the various courses by which [Colombia's granting of asylum to Haya de la Torre] may be terminated,"[198] an asylum that the ICJ had determined was illegal in a case less than a year earlier.[199] The ICJ dismissed the submission because the Court determined that a "choice amongst [the options] could not be based on legal considerations, but only on considerations of practicability or of political expediency; it is not part of the Court's judicial function to make such a choice."[200] There, it was not the existence of political elements per se in the dispute that made it nonjusticiable, but rather the absolute *absence* of legal

[193] See Merrills, *supra* note 24, at 313. [194] See ibid., at 314.

[195] See *South West Africa Case (Ethiopia v. South Africa; Liberia v. South Africa)*, Preliminary Objections, 1962 ICJ Rep. 465, 466–467 (Dec. 21). See also Brownlie, *supra* note 27, at 132–133 (discussing this case).

[196] See *Military and Paramilitary Activities in and against Nicaragua (Nicaragua v. US)*, Merits, 1986 ICJ Rep. 14, 168 (June 27) (Lachs J., dissenting opinion).

[197] See Edwin J. Nazario, *The Potential Role of Arbitration in the Nuclear Non-proliferation Treaty Regime*, 10 Am. Rev. Int'l Arb. 139, 145 (1999).

[198] See *Haya de la Torre Case (Colombia/Peru)*, Judgment, 1951 ICJ Rep. 71, 79 (June 13).

[199] See *Asylum Case (Colombia/Peru)*, Judgment, 1950 ICJ Rep. 266, 288 (Nov. 20).

[200] *Haya de la Torre Case (Colombia/Peru)*, Judgment, 1951 ICJ Rep. 71, 79, 83 (June 13).

elements.[201] Another example of an entirely political dispute might include one over how to change a law,[202] not just how to implement a law, as in the *Haya de la Torre* case. Such disputes squarely belong to resolution not in the adjudicative arena, but in the political arena,[203] which decisions are made by diplomats and politicians, not judges and arbitrators.[204] Indeed, *Haya de la Torre* involved an exceptional situation that will rarely be repeated, given the relative ease in finding a legal question associated with a dispute on account of the general proliferation of treaty law and its relevance to most, if not all, inter-State relations and activities.[205] The *Haya de la Torre* case shows that entirely political, or rather entirely nonlegal, disputes stand a chance of being deemed non-justiciable in practice, whereas the chance of other mixed disputes being so deemed seems to be possible only in theory. However, it must be noted that this chance need not be particularly great, given how there are instances of the Court finding justiciable what some commentators have considered entirely political disputes – namely the *Customs Regime between Germany and Austria* advisory opinion by the PCIJ.[206]

This section has so far shown how legal resolution has seen itself as being able to handle disputes of a mixed legal–political nature. The remainder of this section assumes, *arguendo*, that legal resolution cannot handle the political elements of a mixed dispute, contrary to what the Court already has acknowledged, and proposes two ways for legal resolution to proceed nevertheless in handling such disputes. First, disputes can be transformed into legal ones through the litigation process. Second, overall disputes can be fragmented into their constituent elements, with the more legal parts being sent to international adjudication and the remaining simplified dispute being sent to more political methods of resolution.

201 Therefore, the assertion of William Burke-White and Andreas von Staden appears correct that international courts and tribunals "have never recognized the political nature of a question as a legal bar to the exercise of their jurisdiction and have regularly pronounced on cases concerned with national security issues" – Burke-White and von Staden, *supra* note 50, at 377 – even though they fail to identify the *Haya de la Torre* case as a potential exception and why it is not an exception.

202 See Jennings, *Presentation*, *supra* note 172, at 78.

203 See WALLACE-BRUCE, *supra* note 8, at 18.

204 See Jan Klabbers, *Constitutionalism Lite*, 2 INT'L ORG. L. REV. 56 (2005).

205 See Higgins, *Desirability*, *supra* note 108, at 43.

206 Please note, though, that this study does not see this advisory opinion as being entirely political inasmuch as it involved a legal question – namely the interpretation of Article 88 of the Treaty of St. Germain of September 10, 1919, "to abstain from any act which might directly or indirectly or by any means whatever compromise her independence."

6.5.1 *Substantive approach to justiciability*

When it comes to actually determining justiciability, the *Mavrommatis* definition seems to have very little importance. Rather, there are two basic approaches that courts and commentators take after dutifully citing the above definition – the substantive approach, which relies on the substance of the dispute to determine justiciability, and the process approach, which looks at the process to which the dispute has been submitted by the disputants. The remainder of this section posits not only that legal resolution can handle disputes of a mixed political–legal nature, but that political elements actually can be transformed into legal ones by States submitting them to the litigation process. Before talking about the transformative powers of legal resolution, this subsection discusses the substantive approach to determining justiciability.

The essence of the substantive approach to determining justiciability is that the material of a dispute should be allowed to determine which mechanisms are used to resolve the dispute.[207] This substantive approach grounds itself in the law–politics distinction and the belief that courts and tribunals can distinguish between the two, in addition to the belief that the nature of some disputes makes them unsuitable for legal resolution. Such an approach to determining justiciability has a long history. Charles de Visscher referred to these approaches to determining justiciability as the politician's approach and the lawyer's approach.[208] Likewise, different members of a panel during the 1924 annual meeting of the American Society of International Law focusing on the "Distinction between Legal and Political Questions" took these different approaches to determining justiciability, which Steven Ratner identified in 2006.[209]

Neither the Court nor an international arbitral tribunal has spelled out exactly what types of substance are justiciable or nonjusticiable. As a result, commentators are left to develop their own lists. There are only a few types of issues that clearly fall into one or the other under this

[207] See MERRILLS, *supra* note 24, at 313.

[208] See CHARLES DE VISSCHER, THÉORIES ET RÉALITÉS EN DROIT INTERNATIONAL PUBLIC 396 (1953).

[209] See Steven R. Ratner, *Land Feuds and Their Solutions: Finding International Law beyond the Tribunal Chamber*, 100 AM. J. INT'L L. 808, 813 (2006) (quoting Charles G. Fenwick, *Remarks in the Distinction between Legal and Political Questions*, 18 AM. SOC'Y INT'L L. PROC. 44, 44 (1924), and Edwin M. Borchard, *Remarks in the Distinction between Legal and Political Questions*, 18 AM. SOC'Y INT'L L. PROC. 50, 53 (1924)).

approach. As explained in the preceding section, a dispute over treaty interpretation is perhaps the clearest example of a justiciable dispute. Another candidate for inclusion on the list of justiciable disputes would be territorial disputes, although there is a considerable amount of debate over this.[210] For example, Anthony D'Amato asserted that legal resolution is good for resolving border disputes but not for matters that involve the "central interests of the state,"[211] but this could be seen as contradictory if one thought that all border disputes are central to the State's interests.

As for the types of disputes that clearly are nonjusticiable based on their political sensitivity and connection with a disputant's vital interests, commentators are bound to disagree over where to draw the line between two such nebulous groups as political matters of low to normal sensitivity and those of sufficiently high sensitivity to justify the avoidance of the application of law to that dispute. A judgment that may strike one reader as admirably "legal" in its premises and conclusions may appear to another to be riddled with a whole range of extralegal elements. While in each case the analysis may seem to be entirely "objective in character," its outcome will necessarily depend upon the analyst's own preconceptions, some of which may be "objective" and others "subjective," according to the stance of the critic.[212] This study would distinguish between justiciable and nonjusticiable disputes based on whether or not firm legal rights and obligations are involved, as explained in the introduction to Part III above. However, with the process approach to justiciability, there is no need to rely on such a distinction, as explained in the following section.

6.5.2 *Process approach to justiciability*

The second approach to justiciability, or the lawyer's approach, focuses on the process used in trying to resolve the dispute. This subsection

210 See Ratner, *supra* note 209, at 813–814; Borchard, *supra* note 209; James L. Brierly, *The Judicial Settlement of International Disputes*, 4 J. BRIT. INST. INT'L AFF. 227, 240 (1925).

211 *Arbitration*, in INTERNATIONAL LAW ANTHOLOGY 324 (ANTHONY D'AMATO ed., 1994).

212 See generally Elihu Lauterpacht, *The Juridical and the Meta-juridical in International Law*, in THEORY OF INTERNATIONAL LAW AT THE THRESHOLD OF THE 21ST CENTURY 215 (JERZY MAKARCZYK ed., 1996).

looks at this process approach in determining justiciability. Here, it is not the substance of the dispute that is of central importance.[213] In short, if one assumes, *arguendo*, that the political elements of a dispute over the interpretation of a nuclear safeguards-system agreement can make the dispute chiefly political, this approach enables the court or tribunal to turn such political questions into legal questions. This approach essentially is that if an issue can be briefed and responded to through memorials and countermemorials in a court or tribunal of law, then the issue can be considered a legal dispute and justiciable, or rather will become a legal dispute through this litigation process, if it is not already.

The roots of this approach can be traced to Hersch Lauterpacht and his assertion that all disputes can be framed in legal terms and resolved through international adjudication. In particular, Lauterpacht saw all disputes in the realm of international relations as being disputes of a legal nature, with the only determining factor being whether the parties are willing to submit the dispute to international adjudication.[214] Not surprisingly, Lauterpacht defined political, or nonlegal, disputes as those that States are unwilling to submit to international adjudication.[215] In particular, Lauterpacht posited that once an issue has been placed before a court or tribunal, that forum *must* be able to resolve the dispute through the application of law because of the principle of international law that prohibits *non liquet*. Hans Kelsen seems to share this approach to justiciability, focusing on the nature of the norms that are applied in trying to resolve the dispute instead of the nature of the dispute at hand:

> The legal or political character of a dispute does not depend, as the traditional doctrine seems to assume, on the nature of the dispute, that is to say, on the subject matter to which the dispute refers, but on the nature of the norms to be applied in the settlement of the dispute. A

[213] Nevertheless, the substance of the dispute is important because it determines *what* law must be applied when resolving the dispute.

[214] See LAUTERPACHT, *supra* note 49, at 164. Some more recent commentators share this view that all disputes have a legal element that can be resolved through the application of law. See Elisabeth Zoller, *Commentary on the Contributions of the Court to the Resolution of International Tensions*, Proceedings of the ICJ/UNITAR Colloquium to Celebrate the 50th Anniversary of the Court, reprinted in INCREASING THE EFFECTIVENESS OF THE INTERNATIONAL COURT OF JUSTICE 86, 88 (CONNIE PECK and ROY S. LEE ed., 1997).

[215] See LAUTERPACHT, supra note 49, at 164.

> dispute is a legal dispute if it is to be settled by the application of legal norms, that is to say, by the application of existing law.[216]

In other words, a dispute is settled by the application of *legal* norms when it is submitted to an international court or international arbitral tribunal for resolution, whereas it is settled by the application of political norms when it is submitted to more political fora.[217]

Lauterpacht's and Kelsen's approaches to justiciability share some similarities. Lauterpacht's approach does not necessarily see the legal process as transforming the dispute into a legal one, but rather remains as rooted in the law–politics distinction as his predecessors, even though his opinion is that there is no type of dispute that law cannot handle. In this regard, Lauterpacht's approach is merely a variant of Kelsen's, which emphasized the principle of law over politics, at least partially as an effort to protect against the erosion of law.[218] Still, Lauterpacht took a far more extreme approach, with his missionary-like faith in law as the panacea to any conceivable dispute placed before a court or tribunal. In a later publication, Lauterpacht seemed to step back from his relatively extreme position, explaining that a court or tribunal very well could determine that there are gaps in the law when it is exercising its advisory jurisdiction because States are not depending on the forum for an answer, unlike disputants with contentious cases.[219] Lauterpacht's and Kelsen's pragmatic approach to determining justiciabilty based on the forum to which the dispute was submitted essentially removed justiciability determinations from international proceedings and placed them squarely with States, in particular the claimant. Such an approach represents a break from convention, eventually leading to the development of a new process-based approach to determining justiciability that was developed by Higgins and Jennings, as explained below.

Rosalyn Higgins was the first to develop to its full extent this process-based approach to justiciability, which she explained as follows:

[216] Hans Kelsen, Principles of International Law 56 (R. W. Tucker ed., 9th rev. edn, 1966); see also Gowlland-Debbas, *supra* note 17, at 652–653 (quoting Kelsen and discussing this matter).

[217] See David Kennedy, *Theses about International Law Discourse*, 23 German Y.B. Int'l. L. 353, 372–374 (1980).

[218] See Anghie, *supra* note 84, at 543 n. 94 (noting how they shared this basic view of international disputes).

[219] See Hersch Lauterpacht, The Development of International Law by the International Court 177 (1996).

> *the terms "political dispute" and "legal dispute" refer to the decision making process which is to be employed in respect of them, and not to the nature of the dispute itself.* A dispute is a "legal" dispute if it is to be resolved by authoritative legal decision, no matter what the component elements of that dispute. In other words, there is little reality in any definition of a political, or legal, question; what is relevant is the distinction between a political *method* and a legal *method* of solving disputes.[220]

That Higgins picked up on and developed this approach to international dispute settlement is not surprising, given her connection to Yale and the New Haven School of Legal Science, with its emphasis on international law (and even all law) as a decision-making *process*, not merely the application of rules under legal positivism.[221] One of the main lessons that Higgins appears to have come away with from her stint at Yale is an understanding of the fundamentally different views of British lawyers and American lawyers with regard to the nature of legal resolution, with the former seeing courts as applying neutral rules and the latter taking a more holistic approach to dispute settlement where "the assessment of 'extra-legal' considerations *is part of the legal process*, just as is reference to the accumulation of past decisions and current norms."[222] While the result is not unlike Alvarez's fusion of law and politics referred to at the beginning of Chapter 6.2.2 above, Higgins was unique in focusing on the decision-making process as the force that fused them together. By focusing on the decision-making process, Higgins emphasizes that "[t]here are no events which are inherently beyond authoritative decision-making," including nuclear-weapon disputes.[223]

Robert Jennings, Lauterpacht's successor as Whewell Professor of International Law at Cambridge, generally saw all disputes as having the potential to become legal ones through the lawyering process. This process approach conveniently avoids the sticky *non liquet* issue or even stickier distinction between law and politics, which seems to have been

220 Higgins, *Policy Considerations*, *supra* note 59, at 74 (emphasis in original; internal citations omitted).

221 See, e.g., Myres McDougal, *Some Basic Theoretical Concepts about International Law: A Policy-Oriented Framework of Enquiry*, 4 J. Conflict Res. 337 (1960). Higgins received her JSD from Yale Law School in 1962, under the direction of McDougal. See Rosalyn C. Higgins, *McDougal as Teacher, Mentor and Friend*, 108 Yale L.J. 957 (1999).

222 Higgins, *Policy Considerations*, *supra* note 59, at 58, 60, 62 (emphasis in original).

223 Ibid., at 70 (1968) (emphasis in original).

the reason behind developing this new approach.[224] Jennings went beyond Lauterpacht's *non liquet* argument in explaining what exactly it was about the process that had the potential for turning all disputes into legal ones. Jennings emphasized the litigation process itself:

> Cases brought before a court of law, whether a standing court or one appointed ad hoc, invariably have a pleadings procedure by which the matter is indeed "reduced" to a specific issue, or a series of such specific issues, upon which the parties are in conflict concerning the applicable law, or the facts, or both. Everyone with experience of drawing such pleadings knows that the drafting of the submissions will be the moment of truth for some arguments which, before the imposition of this discipline, had seemed cogent.[225]

In other words, it is the adversarial process, where counsel for the parties package, and further refine, the problems into finite issues of fact and law for the court or tribunal to decide after considering written and oral submissions from the parties, that transforms disputes into legal ones.[226]

In this regard, Jennings reached a similar conclusion as Higgins in that law and politics in a way become fused through the legal process, though his was a more practical explanation, compared to Higgins's more theoretical one. According to Jennings, it is specifically the mechanics of the briefing process and the opportunity of rebuttal that can transform questions into legal ones. Rules of legal resolution generally allow for the parties to provide submissions and respond to the other's arguments.[227] Through this briefing process, disputants' pleadings are to be submissions that the Court is to decide upon, which submissions are to take into account what the other side already has submitted.[228] This refining of arguments over time into discrete issues for the court to

[224] See ibid., at 64 (pointing out that, while the PCIJ and ICJ Statutes shifted the burden of deciding between the legal and the political when it comes to compulsory jurisdiction, this task became no easier because these statutes provided no guidance for making this determination).

[225] Jennings, *International Courts*, *supra* note 77, at 16.

[226] See Jennings, *Reflections*, *supra* note 8, at 403, 405; Jennings, *International Courts*, *supra* note 77, at 15–16; Jennings, *Presentation*, *supra* note 172, at 80.

[227] See ICJ Rules of Court, April 14, 1978, Art. 45 (entered into force July 1, 1978) (authorizing the submission of a memorial by the applicant, a countermemorial from the respondent, a reply by the applicant, and another response by the respondent).

[228] See Jennings, *International Courts*, *supra* note 77, at 16 (quoting Rules of the ICJ Art. 46(4); citing *Continental Shelf Boundary (Tunisia/Libya)*, 1984 ICJ Rep. 18 (Feb. 24), where both parties had to adjust their arguments at the countermemorial stage where unforeseen arguments had been made at the initial stage).

decide ensures that disputes placed before the court become legal, if they were not so to begin with.[229] Once the adjudicative process has started, it is difficult to stop,[230] and so the end result tends to be a legal solution to whatever problem is placed before the court. At the same time, a legal dispute handled through nonlegal methods of resolution can turn into a nonlegal dispute.[231] In other words, one would expect politicians to start horse-trading if they were given a legal issue to resolve, not to decide the issues based on the application of law, thus turning it into a political issue even though it originated as a legal one (such as treaty interpretation).

The exception where the court or tribunal might refuse to transform an issue to a legal one is where the nonlegal issues obviously overpower the legal ones or where legal issues do not exist at all,[232] as with the *Haya de la Torre* case discussed in the introductory portion of this chapter. In other words, legal resolution is not always appropriate to all disputes, and the litigation process cannot transform absolutely all aspects of a dispute into legal ones.[233] However, as the PCIJ showed in the *Customs Union* advisory opinion, even in these situations it is up to the court or tribunal whether the issue is justiciable. The ICJ emphasized in its 1950 *Interpretation of Peace Treaties* case its power to decide whether a matter before it involves a dispute that it can handle, even if one or both parties deny the existence of a dispute.[234] Assuming, *arguendo*, that more political aspects to an overall dispute cannot be transformed into legal ones through the adjudicative process, the following section explores whether overall disputes can be fragmented into their constituent elements, with legal resolution being given the more legal aspects of the

[229] Admittedly, this assumes a measure of legal competence on the part of States' counsel in crafting submissions, as well as a measure of good faith towards the process. Questioning the legal skills of States' counsel and States' commitment to the obligation to act in good faith goes outside the scope of this study, and so these assumptions are taken as a given.

[230] See Hugh W. A. Thirlway, *Commentary on the Contributions of the Court to the Resolution of International Tensions*, Proceedings of the ICJ/UNITAR Colloquium to Celebrate the 50th Anniversary of the Court, reprinted in INCREASING THE EFFECTIVENESS OF THE INTERNATIONAL COURT OF JUSTICE 96, 96–98 (CONNIE PECK and ROY S. LEE ed., 1997).

[231] See Lachs, *supra* note 169, at 286–287.

[232] See Higgins, *Desirability*, *supra* note 108, at 42.

[233] See ibid., at 48; COLLIER and LOWE, *supra* note 4, at 5; MERRILLS, *supra* note 24, at 313.

[234] See *Interpretation of Peace Treaties with Bulgaria, Hungary and Romania*, Advisory Opinion, 1950 ICJ Rep. 65 (March 30).

overall dispute, leaving the remaining simplified dispute for political resolution.

Before delving into that analysis, however, it is important to identify who is responsible for the transformation – the disputants or the forum. Admittedly, Jennings seems to contradict himself on this point. At one stage, Jennings asserts that the transformation of disputes into legal ones falls outside the disputants' control, which obviously would make States cautious in resorting to legal resolution.[235] However, it is not the court or tribunal that is responsible for transforming the dispute into a legal one, but rather the disputants, as they are the ones who actually narrow down their arguments into distinct questions of law and fact in their submissions, as Jennings himself acknowledges. The fact that the target audience is a group of individuals charged with applying law in reaching its decision certainly will influence the general approach that the disputants take in framing the questions of law and fact, but the disputants ultimately are the ones who must voluntarily undertake this task for the transformation to occur. It is this tendency to induce disputants to legalize the issues, and not the forum's quasi-coercive legalization of the issues, that may deter disputants from resorting to legal resolution. States, by consenting to legal resolution, either beforehand or after the dispute has arisen, essentially have acknowledged their willingness to couch the issues of their dispute in legal terms, thereby making it possible for courts and tribunals to address the problems placed before them. At the point when the court or tribunal gets involved, the disputants already have decided that it can be made into a legal dispute, thus in a way absolving the forum of the need to decide on that particular matter. Therefore, justiciability would become subsumed under jurisdiction.

6.5.3 *Reasons to favor the process approach*

There are numerous reasons to favor the process approach. International adjudication jurisprudence seems to support this process-based approach to justiciability. This should not be surprising, given that the 1978 ICJ Rules of Court, as amended in 2005, seem to give preference to the process approach. In particular, provisions such as Article 38(1) suggest that a dispute only exists (from the perspective of the ICJ) after

[235] See Jennings, *International Courts*, *supra* note 77, at 19.

it has been explained in submissions to the Court.[236] The ICJ affirmed this approach in its *East Timor* case when it focused on the submissions of the disputants in determining who the actual disputants were and what was the actual dispute.[237] Other cases also support this approach. In the *Hostages* case, the ICJ implied that the litigation process can transform nonlegal issues into legal ones when it encouraged Iran to submit as a defense or counterclaim its allegedly nonlegal arguments involving the "more than 25 years of continual interference by the United States in the internal affairs of Iran, the shameless exploitation of our country, and numerous crimes perpetrated against the Iranian people, contrary to and in conflict with all international and humanitarian norms," if Iran thought that these arguments were relevant to the dispute before the Court.[238] Iran did not take the ICJ's suggestion on this point, and so the ICJ determined that it could not rely on Iran's arguments concerning the political nature of the dispute for the following reasons:

> [L]egal disputes between sovereign States by their very nature are likely to occur in political contexts, and often form only one element in a wider and long-standing political dispute between the States concerned. Yet never has the view been put forward before that, because a legal dispute submitted to the Court is only one aspect of a political dispute, the Court should decline to resolve for the parties the legal questions at issue between them. Nor can any basis for such a view of the Court's functions or jurisdiction be found in the Charter or the Statute of the Court; if the Court were, contrary to its settled jurisprudence, to adopt such a view, it would impose a far-reaching and unwarranted restriction upon the role of the Court in the peaceful solution of international disputes.[239]

These are just two examples of how the ICJ has shown an inclination to support the process approach.

Moreover, the process approach would appear to be the majority approach among commentators in deciding whether a disagreement is

236 See ICJ Rules of Court (1978, amendments entering into force in 2005), Art. 38(1) ("When proceedings before the Court are instituted by means of an application addressed as specified in Article 40, paragraph 1, of the Statute, the application shall indicate the party making it, the State against which the claim is brought, and the subject of the dispute").

237 See *East Timor (Portugal v. Australia)*, Judgment, 1995 ICJ Rep. 90, 99–100 (June 30).

238 *United States Diplomatic and Consular Staff in Tehran (US v. Iran)*, 1980 ICJ Rep. 3, 19 (May 24). See also Merrills, *supra* note 21, at 173 (discussing this portion of the case).

239 *United States Diplomatic and Consular Staff in Tehran*, 1980 ICJ Rep. 3, 20 (May 24).

a legal dispute and thereby justiciable. Numerous other commentators appear to join Higgins and Jennings in favoring the process approach. John Merrills would appear to agree with this approach when he focuses on procedure: "A dispute may be defined as a specific disagreement concerning a matter of fact, law or policy in which a claim or assertion of one party is met with refusal, counter-claim or denial by another."[240] Richard Bilder echoes this procedural definition of "dispute" by pointing out that the disagreement must be specific and "involve conflicting claims or assertions," or, in other words, "one party must actually assert or manifest what it wants or believes itself entitled to with respect to the other, and the other party must manifest its refusal or its conflicting claim."[241] It is not enough for a State to feel injured by another entity for there to be a dispute, for, as Bilder says, "until that sense of grievance is formulated into a specific claim or assertion which is resisted by the other, there is no 'dispute' between them."[242] O'Connell similarly focuses on the procedure when defining the dispute – "The disagreement must rise to the level of inviting a counterclaim or denial."[243] For Collier and Lowe, a diplomatic dispute can shift to a legal one simply by either party using legal words in reference to aspects of the dispute (for example, by alleging "tortious liability" or "theft," which are distinctly legal terms), and a direct response by the target State is not necessary for it to be become a legal dispute,[244] which is simpler than the procedures already discussed in this paragraph because it assumes that this sort of procedure will follow.

The belief that disputes or aspects of disputes can become legal ones through the simple act of submitting them to legal resolution reflects a somewhat skeptical view of justiciability issues generally. Such skepticism, however, is not uncommon among commentators. Hersch Lauterpacht saw States as tending to challenge international claims based on perceived inadequacies of justiciability simply in order to get out of having to defend themselves before an international court or tribunal.[245] In particular, these skeptics may question the integrity of justiciability determinations, seeing the concept as an analytical black

[240] MERRILLS, *supra* note 24, at 1.
[241] Bilder, *Overview*, *supra* note 96, at 4. The quote goes on to say "Such a manifestation may be through statements, diplomatic notes, specific actions or otherwise," so the exchange need not be in a court of law.
[242] Ibid. [243] O'CONNELL, *supra* note 53, at 4.
[244] See COLLIER and LOWE, *supra* note 4, at 3–4.
[245] See LAUTERPACHT, *supra* note 49, at 164.

box without clear legal standards that gives the ICJ and international arbitral tribunals a convenient escape hatch for getting out of having to deal with unpleasant disputes, for whatever reason. As a result, some commentators see a trend in the ICJ's avoiding justiciability determinations, simply saying that the dispute is justiciable without applying any clear rules to making that determination.[246] This study sees the first type of skepticism as involving an obvious point, since it would seem almost expected to challenge a claim on all preliminary grounds, perhaps out of a fear that failure to do so would lead to malpractice claims if a winning argument were to be left out. It is the second type of skepticism that is far more interesting. However, this study goes in the opposite direction to these other skeptics in saying that justiciability is not an escape hatch but rather a black hole, sucking all types of disputes into the gravitic pull of justiciability.

As ICJ jurisprudence seems to support both the substantive and the process approaches to some degree, deciding which one is the better approach in the context of resolving nuclear non-proliferation disputes may depend on a balance of their perceived strengths and weaknesses. In the end, this study favors the process approach primarily because of two perceived weaknesses of the substantive approach. First, the substantive approach seems inherently flawed because any list will become outdated. After all, international law and international relations are dynamic, and no static list can hope to remain current for a significant period of time.[247] A related flaw with the substantive approach is that no list can be sufficiently nuanced to be an adequate guide to determining justiciability, since the real situation a court or tribunal is faced with usually will be complex. Jennings refers to this type of exercise of listing what kinds of disputes are best suited to legal resolution as "the blind alleys of the old learning about the supposed differences between legal and political disputes."[248] If the international system is anything, it is dynamic. It is no mystery that treaties have the power to legalize otherwise political matters. Some see this as the main "civilizing purpose" of international law – to turn political passions into dry, legal technicalities, thus defusing potentially troublesome situations.[249] An example of a legalized political matter is Article 15(1) of the European Convention

[246] See Wallace-Bruce, *supra* note 8, at 25.
[247] See Collier and Lowe, *supra* note 4, at 14–16.
[248] Jennings, *Presentation*, *supra* note 172, at 85.
[249] See Jennings, *International Courts*, *supra* note 77, at 26.

on Human Rights, which allows for derogation from particular human rights "[i]n time of war or other public emergency threatening the life of the nation."[250] In the context of nuclear-weapon-related law and disputes, one of the most obvious political matters that has been transformed into a legal one through its incorporation into a treaty is Article X(1) of the Nuclear Non-Proliferation Treaty, which affirms the right of a member to withdraw from the treaty "if it decides that extraordinary events, related to the subject matter of this Treaty, have jeopardized the supreme interests of its country." States intend to legalize politically sensitive matters when they negotiate, sign, and ratify treaties that deal with such matters. Placing emphasis on the perceived political nature of the dispute or its perceived political impact over its legal nature through its incorporation into a treaty would inappropriately undermine the intent of the member States to that treaty. A State that argues otherwise can be seen as exhibiting a degree of bad faith inasmuch as it ignores its legal obligations. While legalization through a treaty is not the same as legalization through process, as some commentators seem to imply,[251] it nonetheless undermines the substantive approach to justiciability by showing how political disputes are not static.

Second, the substantive approach is flawed because it is too easy for States to be able to escape legal resolution by merely claiming the involvement of national security or vital interests with a dispute. It seems repugnant to allow States to use the involvement of their vital interests in a dispute to escape the application of law against them. If the subject matter of a treaty touches upon the vital interests of a State, then that State should have withheld its consent to that treaty to begin with. Once the treaty has entered into force vis-à-vis that State and a dispute has arisen over its provisions, however, the time is far past for that State to claim that its vital interests are involved in order to escape having a court or tribunal pronounce on those matters. Otherwise, the law would not have the binding effect that is the general point of law. At a minimum, there should be an objective determination of whether this invoking of vital interests is correct.

Still, the process approach to justiciability admittedly is not without its own perceived flaws. This subsection mentions three such potential flaws. First, the substantive approach to determining justiciability might encourage States to designate legal resolution in compromissory

[250] See Brownlie, *supra* note 27, at 138.
[251] See Jennings, *International Courts*, *supra* note 77, at 19.

clauses and fully participate in proceedings if they know that the court or tribunal will be limited to the disputes involving low politics.[252] However, it arguably is more important to give effect to compromissory clauses in high-politics contexts where States obviously have consented to the jurisdiction of courts and tribunals. Otherwise, States have less incentive to be careful when providing their jurisdictional consent in such high-politics contexts.

Second, the process approach does little, if anything, to limit the application of law in virtually all circumstances where jurisdiction is found. However, this is not necessarily a negative characteristic. On the contrary, removing the need for a finding on justiciability and placing all of the emphasis on jurisdiction not only simplifies the proceedings for the court or tribunal but appropriately places the burden on disputants to be more careful when giving their consent to the jurisdiction of those fora. A State can avoid a forum's jurisdiction by refusing to give its consent to jurisdiction, by making a reservation that withholds its consent in certain situations and by acting in a way that does not imply consent to jurisdiction. If a State fails to take adequate steps to protect its supposedly "vital interests" in these ways, it is difficult to explain why the forum should even entertain the argument that it should refuse to hear and decide on the dispute on the grounds of the alleged involvement of a disputant's *vital* interests. After all, as the proverb goes, "Actions speak louder than words."

6.6 Fragmentation of disputes as an alternative

Assuming, *arguendo*, that legal resolution cannot handle disputes that contain a political aspect, the question arises whether the forum can separate the bigger dispute into its constituent disputes and handle those smaller disputes on their merits without getting bogged down with the broader issues. Such an arrangement is known as fragmentation or fractionation of international disputes.[253] This approach to international dispute settlement is seen as requiring a genuine desire of disputants to

[252] See Gowlland-Debbas, *supra* note 17, at 649 (citing LAUTERPACHT, *supra* note 49, at 4–7).

[253] See ROGER FISHER, INTERNATIONAL CONFLICT AND BEHAVIORAL SCIENCE 91–109 (1964); Sydney D. Bailey, *Peaceful Settlement of International Disputes*, in DISPUTE SETTLEMENT THROUGH THE UNITED NATIONS 73, 97–98, 101 (K. VENKATA RAMAN ed., 1977).

change the situation,[254] which should not be taken as a given. Indeed, it is possible that one disputant might prefer continued conflict to losing a dispute.[255] However, where the outbreak of war is being threatened over a particular dispute, it seems reasonable to assume that States that are acting in good faith will want to act in such a way as to avoid war, especially if the possibility of nuclear war is involved.

One way to divide the overall dispute into smaller ones would be to divide the legal and political elements, handle the legal elements with legal resolution, and reserve the political elements for more political methods of resolution. To be clear, it is not that the fragments that legal resolution would handle would somehow involve so-called low politics, with politics being left to handle the high-politics issues. Instead, legal resolution would handle the *legal* aspects of a high-politics dispute, which can be just as "high" as those elements left for more political forms of resolution. This, of course, assumes an ability to distinguish between legal and political elements in a dispute, which might be quite difficult, as commentators have asserted, on account of the view that legal and political elements become intertwined in international relations.[256] However, it does not mean that legal resolution is not competent to distinguish legal elements from political ones; on the contrary, legal resolution has been known to be able to make such distinctions.[257] For example, the ICJ in the *Nicaragua* case makes an important distinction when it explains in the merits phase its determination of justiciability – that the questions posed to it by Nicaragua did not lead it to get involved in handling a political or military matter per se, which it considered would not be appropriate for a court or tribunal to handle, but rather legal aspects of such disputes.[258]

The ICJ in the *Lockerbie* case essentially concluded that no conflicts are strictly legal or political, and so the ICJ and Security Council both could act in a complementary manner when attempting to resolve the

254 See Bailey, *supra* note 253, at 97–98.

255 See Tom Ginsburg and Richard H. McAdams, *Adjudicating in Anarchy: An Expressive Theory of International Dispute Resolution*, 45 Wm and Mary L. Rev. 1229, 1327 (2004).

256 See Charney, *supra* note 37, at 305 (pointing out how "many have made unsuccessful attempts to differentiate between political and legal matters").

257 See Zoller, *supra* note 214, at 88.

258 See *Military and Paramilitary Activities in and against Nicaragua (Nicaragua v. US)*, Merits, 1986 ICJ Rep. 14, 26–27 (June 27).

complex conflicts placed before them.[259] However, this does not mean that there are no inherently legal or political tasks that make up part of an overall dispute. On the contrary, the fact that the ICJ and Security Council simultaneously could be involved in resolving an overall dispute in a complementary manner underlines the point that there are inherently legal and political components to one overall dispute, which conceivably can be fragmented from one another and resolved separately. The ICJ acknowledged in its *Hostages* case the possibility of making the distinction between political and legal elements, fragmenting a legal aspect of an otherwise politically sensitive dispute, and sending that legal fragment to international adjudication:

> Yet never has the view been put forward before that, because a legal dispute submitted to the Court is only one aspect of a political dispute, the Court should decline to resolve for the parties the legal questions at issue between them. Nor can any basis for such a view of the Court's functions or jurisdictions be found in the Charter or the Statute of the Court; if the Court were, contrary to its settled jurisprudence, to adopt such a view, it would impose a far-reaching and unwarranted restriction upon the role of the Court in the peaceful solution of international disputes.[260]

Thus not only is fragmentation of disputes a possibility, it may also be a necessary step for the Court or international arbitral tribunal to take in order to fulfill its role in finding a peaceful solution to an international dispute placed before it. In particular, international adjudication can defuse tension and avoid war by helping the parties focus down on the nub of their differences through the back-and-forth of the litigation process.[261] This is to say nothing of the potential long-run benefits of the Court's or tribunal's clarifying the meaning of the treaties being interpreted for future disputants.[262]

A few prominent commentators, such as Manfred Lachs and Shabtai Rosenne, have seen the benefits of fragmenting disputes into separate issues for separate resolution in this manner.[263] As Mohamed

[259] See *Questions of Interpretation and Application of the 1971 Montreal Convention Arising from the Aerial Incident at Lockerbie (Libya v. US)*, Order on Provisional Measures, 1992 ICJ Rep. 114, 134 (April 14).

[260] *United States Diplomatic and Consular Staff in Tehran*, 1980 ICJ Rep. 3, 20 (May 24). Chapter 6.4.3 above already provided this quote. This section provides the quote again for the sake of the convenience of the reader.

[261] See Ginsburg and McAdams, *supra* note 255, at 1328–1329.

[262] Ibid.

[263] See Lachs, *supra* note 169, at 294–95; ROSENNE, *supra* note 175, at 38.

Shahabuddeen has noted, the ICJ does not try to resolve all of the aspects of a conflict placed before it but rather is content with addressing only the legal parts.[264] However, as Lachs frames it, the challenge is to sell this approach to States, which tend to see issues of a larger dispute as being too integrated to be broken apart and handled separately.[265] It might be easy to see all points of disagreement as somehow feeding into the broader issue of (hostile) relations between disputants. Nevertheless, if any task can be seen as distinct, it should be treaty interpretation, as was explained in Chapter 6.3 above. As explained in Chapter 2.2.2 above, the international-relations approach to conflict resolution thinks in terms of overarching conflicts, whereas the international-law approach to dispute settlement focuses on the disputes making up an overarching conflict. In short, the distinction between "disputes" and "conflicts" is that the latter involves outright hostility, whereas the former is more of a disagreement, even though such disagreements can lead to serious strains on international relations and international peace.[266] Such hostility influences the way the matter is resolved, with resolution of the overall conflict being difficult, compared to resolving disputes. As Collier and Lowe suggest, disputes can be resolved, while the best one might hope for with unfocused conflicts is their management, not their resolution.[267] It is possible, and even probable, that the process of legal resolution of a dispute will lead to an outcome that actually does not make the overall conflict disappear.[268] Charles de Visscher asserts that this is a main reason why States do not rely more on legal resolution for politically sensitive disputes – "not because it would be impossible for the judge to decide them, but because his decision would not satisfy the grievances out of which such conflicts spring."[269] Admittedly it would be naive to expect

[264] See Mohamed Shahabuddeen, *The World Court at the Turn of the Century*, in THE INTERNATIONAL COURT OF JUSTICE: ITS FUTURE ROLE AFTER FIFTY YEARS 3, 23 (A. S. MULLER, D. RAIC, and J. M. THURANSKY ed., 1997).

[265] See Lachs, *supra* note 169, at 294–295. See also Schachter, *supra* note 127, at 211–215.

[266] See Bailey, *supra* note 253, at 81. [267] See COLLIER and LOWE, *supra* note 4, at 1.

[268] See MERRILLS, *supra* note 24, at 219–220; Pieter H. Kooijmans, *International Arbitration in Historical Perspective: Past and Present (Comments on a Paper by Professor L. B. Sohn)*, in INTERNATIONAL ARBITRATION: PAST AND PROSPECTS 23, 26 (A. H. A. SOONS ed., 1990).

[269] Charles De Visscher, THEORY AND REALITY IN PUBLIC INTERNATIONAL LAW 331–332 (1957). See also Merrills, *supra* note 21, at 174 (asserting that the failure of legal resolution to resolve all issues, both legal and nonlegal, might make the ultimate decision less acceptable to certain parties).

international adjudication to dispose of such deeply rooted problems in the international system.

That does not mean, however, that attempts at legal resolution of politically sensitive disputes lack merit, or that disputants and the international community should be frozen in inaction if they cannot come up with a single solution at a single time – the silver bullet, so to speak – to make the entire conflict disappear. While the international-relations approach to dispute resolution might be ideal in that it continues beyond the binding decision to look at whether States actually implement the decision,[270] its insistence on never losing sight of the overall conflict hobbles its ability to promote gradual resolution of the conflict, thereby making it somewhat impractical vis-à-vis the legal approach. As Manfred Lachs has noted, with complex conflicts, some issues need not be touched from the very beginning: "it may be necessary sometimes to leave several of the issues [of a conflict] untouched, extract the most urgent and drastic one and approach it with the object of arriving at a solution."[271] Such a piecemeal approach is the essence of the legal approach to international dispute settlement and the essence of fragmentation.

As explained in Chapter 2.2.2 above, from the legal perspective the dispute need not go away for it to be considered settled, since the establishment of new rules and principles that govern the activities of the States concerned is sufficient, which rules and principles can be provided by a binding decision of an international court or tribunal.[272] In this sense, international disputes are not much different from domestic ones, where domestic judgments often are not complied with, but rather become the starting point for negotiations, though this does not make these domestic decisions any less binding.[273] While the outcome of a particular international dispute settlement mechanism might be binding (as with arbitration, adjudication before international courts, and decisions by the Security Council), this does not necessarily mean that

[270] See Bilder, *Overview*, *supra* note 96, pt. VII. [271] Lachs, *supra* note 169, at 288.

[272] See ibid., at 286; Bilder, *Overview*, *supra* note 96, pt. VII.

[273] See Collier and Lowe, *supra* note 4, at 5 (asserting that "something like 80 per cent of English court judgments are neither complied with voluntarily, nor enforced in their entirety," and concluding that "[t]he [domestic] judgment becomes merely one further stage in the dispute settlement process; and the dispute is usually finally resolved by a negotiated settlement based on the judgment").

the outcome will lead to complete resolution of the dispute. The greater degree to which a decision is binding, the greater the corresponding chance of the actual disappearance of the disagreement at the conclusion of the process, although there is no guarantee of this.[274] Legal resolution, nevertheless, is binding because of its creation of new rules and principles, and it may not even expect resolution of the overall conflict. The essence of this difference is that the international-relations approach places too high expectations on the mechanism of adjudication, thus leading to a type of fatalism that seems counterproductive to finding helpful solutions to real problems. Fragmentation of the conflict does not diminish the importance of making crucial political decisions, just as legal determinations concerning State succession with the former Yugoslavia in the 1990s could not have taken the place of the need for political decisions on the bigger issues.[275] However, it simplifies the situation so that the diplomats can focus on the political issues and not spend energy on legal issues, which they can defer to the court or tribunal's determination. Such simplification of the overall conflict into bite-sized issues makes it more likely for progress to be made in piecemeal fashion so that momentum can gather towards tackling bigger and bigger issues, as opposed to getting frustrated by trying to handle the entire dispute in one go without the help of positive momentum.

The piecemeal approach of legal resolution can make the resolution of the overall conflict easier by removing small elements from the negotiating table, thereby leaving the disputants to a conflict with fewer issues to address.[276] Indeed, while the parties to a conflict might not like the outcome of a legal proceeding, it becomes considerably more difficult for those States to continue debating that particular matter without losing the appearance of acting in good faith. For example, it would become difficult for either North Korea or the international community to question whether North Korea properly withdrew from the NPT once an arbitral tribunal or the ICJ had pronounced on the matter, regardless of the substance of that decision. This arguably would let these parties move past this issue to the other issues that might remain. In this manner, legal resolution of these disputes has the potential to have a positive impact on the

[274] See MERRILLS, *supra* note 24, at 311.
[275] See Jennings, *Presentation*, *supra* note 172, at 78.
[276] See MERRILLS, *supra* note 24, at 219–20; Jennings, *International Courts*, *supra* note 77, at 19.

resolution of the overall conflict, though such an impact is by no means guaranteed. Indeed, whether the debate proceeds to the actual heart of the conflict depends on whether resolution of that issue entirely relieves the tensions between the parties or whether it leads to a further refining of the conflict. Such a discussion of recursive self-similarity ventures into the realm of fractal mathematics and philosophy,[277] which goes far beyond the scope of this study. What is relatively clear, however, is that the disputants need to be willing to depoliticize the matter if they hope eventually to resolve it.[278] Allowing legal resolution to gradually depoliticize the overall conflict by handling politically sensitive matters within the confines of its relatively objective rules and procedures is one strategy for tackling the overall conflict, and arguably one worth trying, especially if the best alternative is impasse and the worst alternative is armed hostilities.

6.6.1 *Examples of fragmentation*

Good results have come from adopting a fragmented approach to resolving complex disputes in the past, as opposed to trying to resolve an entire conflict in one fell swoop. A main example is the agreement between the United States and the United Kingdom in 1794 (or the Jay Treaty), which established an international arbitration tribunal to handle persistent disputes that the Treaty of Peace of 1783 between these same States failed to address, such as outstanding claims for damages to ships owned by both sides.[279] Most interestingly for the purpose of this study, this 1794 agreement was very unpopular at the time of its conclusion and entry into force because it did not address many more political issues that existed then between the two States, such as various boundary disputes along the US–Canadian border, instead preferring to handle the overall situation in a piecemeal fashion.[280] The arbitration commissions from the Jay Treaty provided 536 awards between 1799 and 1804, with the border issues not being resolved until the Webster–Ashburton

[277] See generally JOHN BRIGGS, FRACTALS: THE PATTERNS OF CHAOS (1994).

[278] See R. P. Anand, *Role of International Adjudication*, in THE FUTURE OF THE INTERNATIONAL COURT OF JUSTICE 1, 1 (L. GROSS ed., 1976).

[279] See John M. Raymond and Barbara J. Frischholz, *Lawyers Who Established International Law in the United States, 1776–1914*, 76 AM. J. INT'L. L. 802, 809 (1982).

[280] See ibid., at 809–810.

Treaty of 1842 and the 1909 Treaty between the United States and United Kingdom, mainly because of the difficulties in demilitarizing the border between the United States and Canada.[281] This is an excellent example of how not to let the most politically sensitive issues of an overall dispute frustrate the resolution of simpler disputes within the whole.

More recently, the *Hostages* case and the *North Sea Continental Shelf* cases are examples in that these cases had an ameliorative effect on the underlying animosity between the parties.[282] In particular, the *Hostages* case is an important example, where Iran argued that the US legal claims must be seen in their larger political and historical context, which argument the ICJ rejected because Iran had not distilled the issues into ones that the court could answer, and because the fact that legal claims are part of a bigger problem does not preclude the ICJ from deciding on the matters properly before it.[283] The same is true with the *Nicaragua* case, though there it was the United States that was arguing for the Court to reject the claim in light of the broader political context, which argument the Court rejected.[284] Andrew Coleman focuses on the *Frontier Dispute* case between Burkina Faso and Mali and the *Territorial Dispute between Libya and Chad* to make the same point, noting that the ICJ's decision in the former led to an OAU cease-fire agreement that the parties observed, and the ICJ's decision in the latter led to a peace agreement, deployment of peacekeepers, and Libya's volunteering to remove its troops from the disputed area.[285]

Besides these specific examples, there is evidence coming from the basic approach to international dispute settlement in the UN era that supports the idea of fragmentation of a dispute into its constituent elements. Indeed, such an approach is supported by the general willingness of States and the international community to allow efforts at legal resolution at the same time as efforts at political resolution, as was observed with the Security Council and the International Court of Justice simultaneously acting in such situations as the *Hostages* case and the *Lockerbie* case, and as was observed with the Contadora peace process and the ICJ simultaneously acting in the *Nicaragua* case.[286] While the *Lockerbie* case demonstrates how political

[281] See ibid., at 810–811. [282] See Jennings, *International Courts*, *supra* note 77, at 19.

[283] See Jennings, *Reflections*, *supra* note 8, at 404; Zoller, *supra* note 214, at 88.

[284] See Merrills, *supra* note 24, at 219–220.

[285] See Coleman, *supra* note 59, at 62 (citing *Frontier Dispute (Burkina Faso v. Mali)*, Provisional Measures, 1986 ICJ Rep. 3 (Dec. 22); *Territorial Dispute (Libya/Chad)*, Judgment, 1994 ICJ Rep. 6 (Feb. 3)).

[286] See Collier and Lowe, *supra* note 4, at 15–16.

attempts at reaching resolution may alter a State's rights and the adjudication process, it is important to note how the political efforts at resolution did not themselves stop the judicial process.[287]

6.6.2 *Criticism of fragmentation*

Critics may raise certain arguments in response to this idea of fragmenting these politically sensitive disputes. To begin, critics might have two problems with these examples supporting the fragmentation approach to handling overarching disputes. First, critics might claim that it is difficult to accept the conclusion that the overarching conflict between the disputants would have remained had it not been for the ICJ's resolution of these disputes. The difficulty with this reasoning is that it involves counterfactual analysis, which is a problem in itself in that it relies on a "fanciful and unknowable state of affairs" on account of it never having existed.[288] ICJ resolution of these disputes might have or might not have played a part in helping the underlying conflict between these disputants disappear; commentators can speculate, but we never will know.

Second, and more specific to the *Hostages* case, it is difficult to accept an assertion that the conflict between Iran and the United States disappeared after the *Hostages* case and the release of the hostages.[289] Certainly, armed hostilities have not broken out between the two since the taking of the hostages in 1978, which is commendable, but perhaps that is not for a lack of trying. Moreover, extreme tension between the two has remained in the intervening three decades, as is reflected in the lack of formal diplomatic relations or even contact outside the Iran–US Claims Tribunal. While the Tribunal clearly has served its purpose in promoting jaw-jaw over war-war, to borrow the words of Churchill,[290] the overall conflict nevertheless remains, which likely impacts the treatment of Iran by the international community with regard to its nuclear non-proliferation obligations. Despite these flaws in the reasoning, it

[287] See ibid.

[288] See Wex S. Malone, *Ruminations on Cause-in-Fact*, 9 Stan. L. Rev. 60, 67 (1956).

[289] See Collier and Lowe, *supra* note 4, at 1 (seeing "feelings of hostility" existing beyond any of the constituent disputes of a conflict and beyond all of the disputes combined, and asserting that Iran and the United States would have general hostility towards each other regardless of what happened to the hostages and other disputes between them).

[290] See Respectfully Quoted: A Dictionary of Quotations 359 (Suzy Platt ed., 1989), available at www.bartleby.com/73/1914.html (last visited June 4, 2011).

does make intuitive sense that an overall conflict becomes simplified and easier to resolve when some of its constituent disputes are removed.

Some critics may dismiss the legal approach adopted here as a vain attempt to justify the relevance of – and thus the study of – law in this area.[291] Indeed, if the overall conflict is ignored when focusing on its constituent disputes, critics might see States, when reaching their decisions, as eventually pushing law and the fora that apply the law off to the side as irrelevant, as happened to the 1907 Central American Court of Justice. However, the relatively unstudied history of legal resolution of nuclear non-proliferation disputes, combined with the relatively unstudied ways in which States already have consented to legal resolution through compromissory clauses in nuclear non-proliferation agreements, suggest that there might be more to the legal approach in this context than previously has been mentioned.

Other critics will point to the perceived danger of this approach of disregarding the morality of the law or the morality of the outcome of the law's application through international adjudication. For example, the law and legal resolution ultimately might allow North Korea to withdraw from the NPT and its safeguards agreement, thereby freeing it from the bulk of the strictures of the nuclear non-proliferation regime and endangering the world with further nuclear proliferation – results that international-relations scholars, not to mention the average citizen of the world, likely will have difficulty accepting. These clearly are valid concerns, and this study should not be read in any way as defending nuclear proliferation or the actions of would-be proliferators. However, these concerns are better addressed in a study of international relations that focuses on the politics surrounding the negotiations for nuclear non-proliferation agreements, which is when those strictures were being established. If States do not like what the nuclear non-proliferation agreements provide, then they should have lobbied harder during the negotiating phase of these agreements. The law and the legal approach take over where those political negotiations end, with rule-of-law considerations taking precedence over the law's ultimate impact on international relations.

Admittedly, this approach is somewhat formalistic and positivistic, which critics might claim is dangerous when the stakes are so high, as

[291] See Gerry Simpson, *On the Magic Mountain: Teaching Public International Law*, 10 Eur. J. Int'l L. 70, 73–76 (1999) (discussing how discussions over international law often have to make the case for its relevance); Jennings, Presentation, *supra* note 172, at 79.

with nuclear non-proliferation disputes. However, the instrumentalism that some States and commentators might be inclined to use when interpreting international law to reach a desired "moral" outcome – namely keeping the NPT- and IAEA-related obligations in place against Iran and North Korea – might be equally dangerous inasmuch as these target States perceive such instrumentalist interpretations as infringing on their rights, thereby fostering a fortress (us-versus-them) mentality within those States and an entire rejection of law by those States, which cannot be seen as a desirable result. Such instrumentalism might be the reason why States such as Iran and North Korea oppose sending such disputes to legal resolution to begin with, where they might perceive that the majority of decision-makers will not be predisposed to agreeing with them. Indeed, from the perspective of a State such as Iran or North Korea, it is difficult to see legal resolution as anything more than Inis Claude's "collective legitimization" or Oliver Lissitzyn's "emotional satisfaction" of the international community in participating in the legal process against those target States.[292] Nonetheless, compared to being the target of coercive measures, either in the form of a Security Council decision under Chapter VII or in the form of armed hostilities, one would expect that a rational State would be willing to consider taking its chances with such a forum if it meant even the possibility of avoiding such unpleasant measures being taken against them.

6.7 Conclusion for this chapter

This chapter on justiciability has provided an extensive definition of the principle and a comparison with other potential barriers to legal resolution's handling of nuclear non-proliferation disputes, as well as setting out the history of the principle in relation to "vital interests," offering an explanation of why justiciability is of limited importance with disputes where the forum has jurisdiction based on something other an optional clause declaration, and giving an exhaustive analysis of how and why legal resolution can handle politically sensitive disputes such as nuclear non-proliferation disputes. The ICJ and international arbitral

[292] See C. M. Dalfen, *The World Court in Idle Splendour: The Basis of State Attitudes*, 23 *Int'l J.* 124, 137 (1967); Inis L. Claude Jr., *Collective Legitimization as a Political Function of the United Nations*, 20 Int'l Org. 367 (1966); Oliver J. Lissitzyn, The International Court of Justice: Its Role in the Maintenance of International Peace and Security (1978).

tribunals have the tools to handle nuclear non-proliferation disputes because these fora have said that they can handle politically sensitive disputes of a mixed legal–political nature, because the litigation process transforms disputes of a more political orientation into a sufficiently legal dispute for legal resolution to handle, and because fragmentation of politically sensitive disputes enables legal resolution to be given the more legal elements of a politically sensitive dispute. In the end, justiciability should not be a problem for the ICJ or an international arbitral tribunal if faced with a nuclear non-proliferation dispute, assuming that the question posed to the forum is not along the lines of what was asked in *Haya de la Torre* case, such as how a State should implement a particular law. Barring this extreme, legal resolution should be deemed suitable for nuclear non-proliferation disputes as long as a basis for jurisdiction has been found. Chapter 6 has provided an extensive analysis of the situations where legal fora might find the requisite jurisdiction to hear and decide a nuclear non-proliferation dispute. Combined with the review in Chapter 4 of all of the military-related cases where States have involved legal resolution in the settlement of those disputes, all of these factors should help convince a State or the international community to give legal resolution of nuclear non-proliferation disputes further consideration, especially when war and coercive Security Council resolution are the alternatives.

PART IV

Conclusion

7

Conclusion

A proverb admonishes that great things start with small beginnings. This study has presented the possibility of legal resolution of nuclear non-proliferation disputes. Such disputes are so politically sensitive and enduring that critics might be tempted to quote John Stuart Mill when belittling the possible benefits of legal resolution of such disputes: "Against a great evil, a small remedy does not produce a small result; it produces no result at all." However, without the benefit of hindsight, it is impossible to gauge the significance of paths taken or paths not taken. Without the aid of a crystal ball, how can one say which options bring small results and which ones bring big results? With such intractable disputes as those involving nuclear non-proliferation, is not any path to possible improvement worth exploring? And where the possibility of war, even nuclear war,[1] becomes more likely over such disputes, the more willing we should become to consider more "bizarre" options for resolution.[2]

Admittedly, legal resolution is not the panacea to all of the world's problems. Nor will these particular problems be handed to lawyers with the "military, scientific, strategic, and political problems neatly solved," with the only remaining issue being a finite legal question.[3] This study does not envision legal resolution of nuclear non-proliferation disputes as leading to a neat and tidy settlement of the whole matter with

[1] See B.V.A. Röling, *International Law, Nuclear Weapons, Arms Control and Disarmament*, in NUCLEAR WEAPONS AND LAW 181, 183 (ARTHUR SELWYN MILLER and MARTIN FEINRIDER ed., 1984) (asserting that modern instances of war have the potential to become nuclear war).

[2] Richard B. Bilder, *Nuclear Weapons and International Law*, in NUCLEAR WEAPONS AND LAW 3, 11 (ARTHUR SELWYN MILLER and MARTIN FEINRIDER ed., 1984) ("If nuclear war becomes thinkable, even the most bizarre schemes for trying to avoid it may also become thinkable").

[3] Adrian Fisher, *Arms Control and Disarmament in International Law*, 50 VA. L. REV. 1200, 1219 (1964); ALLAN GOTLIEB, DISARMAMENT AND INTERNATIONAL LAW: A STUDY OF THE ROLE OF LAW IN THE DISARMAMENT PROCESS 30 (1965).

absolutely no subsequent disputes arising, just as Shabtai Rosenne acknowledges with all crisis situations where legal resolution gets involved.[4] All of that said, it is believed that legal resolution may be an option worth exploring. It is not an all-or-nothing, binary decision between diplomatic resolution or legal resolution, as some commentators frame the issue,[5] but rather one about the availability of options. As ICJ judge Mohammed Bedjaoui pointed out in his separate opinion in the *Gabcikovo-Nagymaros Project* case,

> It is no secret that when States undertake negotiations, they often envisage, in a spirit of caution and realism, other solutions should the negotiations fail. A prudent State always approaches the negotiating table with one or more substitute solutions up its sleeve in case of failure.[6]

Indeed, States should not fear the proliferation of available dispute settlement mechanisms, but rather cherish the availability of options.[7] In the same spirit of caution and realism that Bedjaoui mentioned, this study represents the first step in developing the option of legal resolution of nuclear non-proliferation disputes.

In taking this first step, the substantive portion of this study began with Part II setting out the problems associated with Security Council involvement under Chapter VII in order to understand better the benefits of relying on legal resolution of such disputes. In particular, in its surprisingly long history of dealing with nuclear non-proliferation matters, the Security Council's imposition of nuclear non-proliferation obligations on States like India, Iran, Iraq, Israel, and Pakistan through its Chapter VII decisions is seen as potentially causing problems in at least five ways:

- by requiring States to join nuclear non-proliferation agreements;
- by requiring States to abide by certain nuclear non-proliferation agreements that are not already binding on those States;

4 See SHABTAI ROSENNE, ESSAYS ON INTERNATIONAL LAW AND PRACTICE 38 (2007).

5 See, e.g., T. Treves, *Diplomatic Settlement or Adjudication? Advantages and Drawbacks*, in RÈGLEMENT PACIFIQUE DES DIFFÉRENDS ENTRE ÉTATS: PERSPECTIVES UNIVERSELLE ET EUROPÉENNE 17 (LUCIUS CAFLISCH ed., 1998).

6 *Gabcikovo-Nagymaros Project Case (Hungary/Slovakia)*, 1997 ICJ Rep. 7, 128 (Sept. 25) (J. Bedjaoui, Separate Opinion) (emphasis in original).

7 See generally Gerhard Hafner, *Should One Fear the Proliferation of Mechanisms for the Peaceful Settlement of Disputes?*, in THE PEACEFUL SETTLEMENT OF DISPUTES BETWEEN STATES: UNIVERSAL AND EUROPEAN PERSPECTIVES 25 (LUCIUS CAFLISCH ed., 1998).

- by requiring States to abide by obligations that resemble modified nuclear non-proliferation agreement provisions;
- by requiring States to abide by certain nuclear non-proliferation obligations not contained in treaties; and
- by recalling pre-existing nuclear non-proliferation agreement obligations on States, thereby incorporating them into the UN law framework and modifying the nature of those obligations in doing so, since a State cannot withdraw from a Security Council resolution, for example.

Again, it presumably is within the Security Council's discretion to suspend treaty rights and obligations and to impose other obligations. However, this does not mean that the Security Council should impose these types of obligations or that the situation will not deteriorate because of the imposition of such obligations. This study invites the international community and commentators to consider whether legal resolution might not have its advantages vis-à-vis Security Council involvement under Chapter VII.

As Part III set out, legal resolution is a method of international dispute settlement that is friendlier to the target State in terms of better respecting its sovereignty by requiring its direct consent to legal resolution and through the use of better procedural mechanisms. States should provide that consent to legal resolution or give effect to that consent because of, inter alia,

- the relative impartiality of legal resolution,
- the greater control States enjoy through procedural safeguards,
- the greater predictability States enjoy through the rule of law,
- the ability to show good faith through participation in legal resolution, and
- the ability to resolve the dispute in a relatively efficient manner.

With a measure of political will from target States, as well as from the international community, legal resolution can be given a larger role in resolving such politically sensitive disputes as those involving nuclear non-proliferation through special agreements and other avenues for jurisdiction.

However, it must not be overlooked that States already have given the ICJ and international arbitral tribunals jurisdiction over certain nuclear non-proliferation disputes through compromissory clauses contained in nuclear non-proliferation agreements, such as the IAEA Statute, the IAEA safeguards agreements, and the Convention on the Physical Protection of Nuclear Material. These examples go a long way towards refuting the assertions of classical realists like E. H. Carr and Hans Morgenthau that legal resolution cannot handle disputes involving a State's vital interests.[8] If States have involved legal resolution of disputes in the interpretation and application of these politically sensitive treaties, then surely States must see legal resolution as being capable of handling such disputes. Critics might respond that States did not know what they were doing when they agreed to legal resolution in those treaties or that they did not mean to involve legal resolution in such matters, but this improperly ignores both the central tenet of realism that States are rational actors and the clear language of those treaties. In disputes over the interpretation or application of these agreements, the stage appears set for legal resolution to play a greater role even without the consent of the disputants after the dispute has arisen. Instead, the main requirement simply seems to be for one of the disputants to invoke the compromissory clause. When the ICJ or an international arbitral tribunal is faced with a nuclear non-proliferation dispute that it has jurisdiction over, the fear might be that the court or tribunal will reject the claim because of its political sensitivity. However, as these fora have demonstrated on numerous occasions, legal resolution can handle disputes that have a strong political element to them. Even if, *arguendo*, it is believed that legal resolution should refrain from handling legal disputes with such a strong political element, there is the option of fragmenting the dispute into its more legal and more political elements and then sending the more legal elements to legal resolution, thereby leaving for diplomatic forms of resolution a simpler dispute than before. Regardless, assuming the ICJ or international arbitral tribunal can find jurisdiction over a nuclear non-proliferation dispute, justiciability should not be a technical barrier to these fora hearing and deciding the matter.

As Martin Luther King Jr. declared, "Peace is not merely a distant goal that we seek, but a means by which we arrive at that goal." By having *all* methods of peaceful dispute settlement available for resolving all types of disputes – here, including legal resolution as a possibility with nuclear non-proliferation disputes – the ultimate goal of international peace and security stands the greatest chance of being maintained. To reject *ab initio* any method of peaceful dispute settlement of such important disputes is to flirt with disaster.

[8] See, e.g., E. H. CARR, THE TWENTY YEARS CRISIS 1919–1939 196 (1939); Hans J. Morgenthau, *Positivism, Functionalism, and International Law*, 34 AM. J. INT'L L. 260 (1940).

BIBLIOGRAPHY

I. Books and treatises

Ager, Sheila L., *Interstate Arbitrations in the Greek World 337–90 B.C.* (1996).
Allain, Jean, A *Century of International Adjudication: The Rule of Law and Its Limits* (2000).
Alland, Denis, *Droit international public* (2000).
Allison, Graham T., *Nuclear Terrorism: The Ultimate Preventable Catastrophe* (2004).
Alvarez, José E., *International Organizations as Law-Makers* (2005).
Amerasinghe, C. F., *Diplomatic Protection* (2008).
Amerasinghe, Chittharanjan F., *Evidence in International Litigation* (2005).
Amerasinghe, Chittharanjan F., *Jurisdiction of International Tribunals* (2003).
Amerasinghe, Chittharanjan F., *Principles of the Institutional Law of International Organizations* (2nd edn 2005).
Amr, Mohamed Sameh M., *The Role of the International Court of Justice as the Principle Judicial Organ of the United Nations* (2003).
Arbour, J.-Maurice, *Droit international public* (3rd edn 1997).
Arend, Anthony Clark, *Legal Rules and International Society* (1999).
Asian–African Legal Consultative Committee, *The Legality of Nuclear Tests* (1966).
Anand, R., *Compulsory Jurisdiction of the International Court of Justice* (1961).
Asamoah, Obed Y., *The Legal Significance of the Declarations of the General Assembly of the United Nations* (1966).
Asculai, Ephraim, *Verification Revisited: The Nuclear Case* (2002).
Aust, Anthony, *Modern Treaty Law and Practice* (2000).
Baehr, Peter R., and Leon Gordenker, *The United Nations in the 1990s* (1994).
Bahmanyar, Mir, *Afghanistan Cave Complexes 1979–2004: Mountain Strongholds of the Mujahideen, Taliban & Al Qaeda* (2004).
Bailey, Kathleen C., *Doomsday Weapons in the Hands of Many: The Arms Control Challenge of the 90s* (1991).
Bailey, Sydney Dawson and Sam Daws, *The Procedure of the Security Council* (1998).

Beck, Jasper, *Rogue Regime: Kim Jong Il and the Looming Threat of North Korea* (2005).

Bedjaoui, Mohammed, *The New World Order and the Security Council: Testing the Legality of Its Acts* (1994).

Bekker, Peter H. F., *The Legal Position of Intergovernmental Organizations: A Functional Necessity Analysis of Their Legal Status and Immunities* (1994).

Bellany, Ian, *Curbing the Spread of Nuclear Weapons* (2005).

Bentham, Jeremy, *Of Laws in General (The Collected Works of Jeremy Bentham: Principles of Legislation)* (H. L. A. Hart ed., 1970).

Bertrand, Maurice, *The United Nations: Past, Present and Future* (1994).

Bilder, Richard B., *Managing the Risks of International Agreement* (1981).

Blix, Hans, *Disarming Iraq* (2004).

Blix, Hans, *Why Nuclear Disarmament Matters* (2008).

Bloomfield, Lincoln P. et al., *Khrushchev and the Arms Race: Soviet Interests in Arms Control and Disarmament 1954–1964* (1966).

Boissons de Chazournes, Laurence and Philippe Sands (eds.), *International Law, the International Court of Justice and Nuclear Weapons* (1999).

Boothby, William H., *Weapons and the Law of Armed Conflict* (2009).

Born, Gary B., *International Arbitration and Forum Selection Agreements: Planning, Drafting and Enforcing* (1999).

Bos, Maarten, *A Methodology of International Law* (1984).

Bowles, Newton R., *The Diplomacy of Hope: The United Nations since the Cold War* (2004).

Boyd, Andrew, *Fifteen Men on a Powder Keg: A History of the UN Security Council* (1971).

Brierly, James L., *The Law of Nations: An Introduction to the International Law of Peace* (4th edn, 1949).

Brolmann, Catherine, *The Institutional Veil in Public International Law: International Organisations and the Law of Treaties* (2007).

Broms, Bengt, *The Doctrine of Equality of States as Applied in International Organizations* (1959).

Brownlie, Ian, *Principles of Public International Law* (6th edn, 2003).

Burton, Steven J., *Judging in Good Faith* (1992).

Carr, E. H., *The Twenty Years' Crisis 1919–1939* (1939).

Castañeda, Jorge, *Legal Effects of United Nations Resolutions* (trans. Alba Amoia, 1969).

Chayes, Abram, *Arms Control Agreements* (1985).

Chemillier-Gendrau, M., *La C.I.J. entre politique et droit* (1996).

Cheng, Patrick Low Kim, *Successfully Negotiating in Asia* (2010).

Chesterman, Simon, *Shared Secrets: Intelligence and Collective Security* (2006).

Clark, Grenville, and Louis B. Sohn, *Peace through Disarmament and Charter Revision* (1953).

Claude, Inis L., *Swords into Plowshares: The Problems and Progress of International Organization* (4th edn, 1984).
Collier, John and Vaughan Lowe, *The Settlement of Disputes in International Law: Institutions and Procedures* (1999).
Combacau, Jean, *Le pouvoir de sanction de l'O.N.U.* (1974).
Combacau, Jean and Serge Sur, *Droit international public* (6th edn, 2004).
Cook, Adrian, *The Alabama Claims: American Politics and Anglo-American Relations 1865–1872* (1975).
Cooker, Chris de (ed.), *Accountability, Investigation and Due Process in International Organizations* (2005).
Corten, Olivier, *L'utilisation du "raisonnable" par le juge international: Discours juridique, raison et contradictions* (1997).
Council of Europe et al. (eds.), *Treaty Making: Expression of Consent by States to Be Bound by a Treaty* (2001).
Courlander, Harold, *Shaping Our Times: What the United Nations is and Does* (1960).
Coyle, David Cushman, *The United Nations and How It Works* (1969).
Dahlitz, Julie, *Nuclear Arms Control* (1983).
Damrosch, Lori F. (ed.), *Multilateral Disputes, The International Court of Justice at a Crossroads* (1987).
Decaux, Emmanuel, *Droit international public* (5th edn, 2006).
Dekker, Guido den, *The Law of Arms Control: International Supervision and Enforcement* (2001).
Dinh, Nguyen Quoc, Patrick Daillier, and Alain Pellet, *Droit international public* (7th edn, 2002).
Douglass, Joseph D., Jr., *Why the Soviets Violate Arms Control Treaties* (1988).
Dugard, John et al., *International Law: A South African Perspective* (3rd edn, 2005).
Dupuy, Pierre-Marie, *Droit international public* (6th edn, 2002).
Dupuy, T. and G. Hammerman (ed.), *A Documentary History of Arms Control and Disarmament* (1973).
Dworkin, Ronald, *Law's Empire* (1986).
Eichelberger, Clark M., *UN: The First Twenty Years* (1965).
ElBaradei, Mohamed, *The Age of Deception: Nuclear Diplomacy in Treacherous Times* (2011).
Elias, T. O., *The Modern Law of Treaties* (1974).
Elkind, Jerome B., *Interim Protection: A Functional Approach* (1981).
Elkind, Jerome B., *Non-appearance before the International Court of Justice: Functional and Comparative Analysis* (1984).
Elsen, Theodoor J. H., *Litispendence between the International Court of Justice and the Security Council* (1986).
Emanuelli, Claude, *Droit international public* (2nd edn, 2004).

Epstein, William and Bernard T. Feld (eds.), *New Directions in Disarmament* (1974).

Eyffinger, Arthur, *The International Court of Justice 1946–1996* (1996).

Falk, Richard and David Krieger (eds.), *At the Nuclear Precipice: Catastrophe or Transformation?* (2008).

Falk, Richard et al., *Nuclear Weapons and International Law* (1981).

Farrall, Jeremy Matam, *United Nations Sanctions and the Rule of Law* (2007).

Ferguson, Charles D., *Preventing Catastrophic Nuclear Terrorism* (2006).

Ferencz, Benjamin B., *New Legal Foundations for Global Survival: Security through the Security Council* (1994).

Fischer, David, *History of the International Atomic Energy Agency: The First Forty Years* (1997).

Fisher, Roger, *International Conflict and Behavioral Science* (1964).

Fitzmaurice, Malgosia and Olufemi Elias, *Contemporary Issues in the Law of Treaties* (2005).

Fontes, Lisa Aronson, *Interviewing Clients across Cultures: A Practitioner's Guide* (2009).

Franck, Thomas M., *Fairness in International Law and Institutions* (1995).

Franck, Thomas M., *Political Questions/Judicial Answers: Does the Rule of Law Apply to Foreign Affairs?* (1992).

Franck, Thomas M., *The Power of Legitimacy among Nations* (1990).

Franck, Thomas M., *Recourse to Force: State Action against Threats and Armed Attacks* (2002).

Franck, Thomas M., *The Structure of Impartiality: Examining the Riddle of One Law in a Fragmented World* (1968).

Frei, Daniel, *Perceived Images* (1986).

Friedland, Paul D., *Arbitration Clauses for International Contracts* (2000).

Fujita, Hisakazu, *International Regulation of the Use of Nuclear Weapons* (1988).

Fuller, Lon, *The Morality of Law* (1969).

Furet, Marie, *Experimentation des armes nucléaires et droit international public* (1966).

Galtung, Johan, *There Are Alternatives! Four Roads to Peace and Security* (1984).

Gardiner, Richard, *Treaty Interpretation* (2008).

Gardner, Gary T., *Nuclear Nonproliferation: A Primer* (1994).

Gareis, Sven Bernhard and Johannes Varwick, *The United Nations: An Introduction* (2005, Lindsay P. Cohn trans., first published 2003).

Glaser, Stefan, *L'arme nucléaire à la lumière du droit international* (1964).

Goldberg, Andrew C. et al. (eds.), *Avoiding the Brink: Theory and Practice in Crisis Management* (1990).

Goldblat, Jozef, *Agreements for Arms Control: A Critical Survey* (1982).

Goldblat, Jozef, *Arms Control: A Guide to Negotiations and Agreements* (1994).

Goldblat, Jozef, *French Nuclear Tests in the Atmosphere: The Question of Legality* (1974).
Gompert, David C. et al. (eds.), *Nuclear Weapons and World Politics: Alternatives for the Future* (1974).
Goodman, Lisl Marburg and Lee Ann Hoff, *Omnicide: The Nuclear Dilemma* (1990).
Goodrich, Leland M. and Anne P. Simons, *The United Nations and the Maintenance of International Peace and Security* (1955).
Goodrich, Leland M. et al., *Charter of the United Nations: Commentary and Documents* (1969).
Gotlieb, Allan, *Disarmament and International Law: A Study of the Role of Law in the Disarmament Process* (1965).
Gouin, Margaret E., *Nuclear Law: The Application of Canadian and Related International Public Law Principles to the Obligations of Canada in Relation to Nuclear Weapons* (1989).
Gowlland-Debbas, Vera, *Collective Responses to Illegal Acts in International Law: United Nations Action in the Question of Southern Rhodesia* (1990).
Graham, Thomas, Jr. and Damien J. LaVera, *Cornerstones of Security: Arms Control Treaties in the Nuclear Era* (2003).
Gray, Christine, *International Law and the Use of Force* (2nd edn, 2004).
Greenspan, Morris, *The Modern Law of Land Warfare* (1959).
Grief, Nicholas, *The World Court Project on Nuclear Weapons and International Law* (1993).
Grieves, Forest L., *Supranationalism and International Adjudication* (1969).
Gross, Ernest A., *The United Nations: Structure for Peace* (1962).
Gross, Leo, 1 *Essays on International Law and Organization* (1984).
Grotius, Hugo, 1 *De Jure Belli ac Pacis Libri Tres* (trans. Francis W. Kelsey, 1964).
Guyomar, Geneviève, *Le défaut des parties à un différend devant les juridictions internationales* (1960).
Guzman, Andrew T., *How International Law Works* (2008).
Habermas, Jürgen, *Between Facts and Norms: Contributions to a Discourse Theory of Law and Democracy* (1998).
Habermas, Jürgen, *Communication and the Evolution of Society* (1979).
Hampsch, George H., *Preventing Nuclear Genocide* (1988).
Harmon, Michael, *Responsibility as Paradox: A Critique of Rational Discourse on Government* (1995).
Hemleben, Sylvester John, *Plans for World Peace through Six Centuries* (1943).
Henkin, Louis et al. (eds.), *International Law* (3rd edn, 1993).
Higgins, Rosalyn, *Problems and Process: International Law and How We Use It* (1994).
Hilaire, Max, *United Nations Law and the Security Council* (2005).
Hiscocks, Richard, *The Security Council: A Study in Adolescence* (1974).

Hunter, Martin et al., *The Freshfields Guide to Arbitration and ADR* (1st edn, 1993).

Hymans, Jacques E. C., *The Physchology of Nuclear Proliferation: Identity, Emotions, and Foreign Policy* (2006).

Ikenberry, G. John, *After Victory: Institutions, Strategic Restraint, and the Rebuilding of Order after Major Wars* (2001).

Jenks, C. Wilfred, *The Prospects of International Arbitration* (1964).

Johnstone, Ian, *The Power of Deliberation: International Law, Politics and Organizations* (2011).

Joyner, Daniel H., *International Law and the Proliferation of Weapons of Mass Destruction* (2009).

Joyner, Daniel H., *Interpreting the Nuclear Non-proliferation Treaty* (2011).

Kaczorowska, Alina, *Public International Law* (4th edn, 2010).

Kaufmann, Johan, *United Nations Decision Making* (1980).

Kay, David A., *The New Nations in the United Nations* (1970).

Kazazi, Mojtaba, *Burden of Proof and Related Issues: A Study on Evidence before International Tribunals* (1996).

Kelsen, Hans, *General Theory of Law and State* (1945).

Kelsen, Hans, *Introduction to the Problems of Legal Theory* (trans. Bonnie Litschewski Paulson and Stanley Paulson, 1992) (1932).

Kelsen, Hans, *Law and Peace in International Relations* (1952).

Kelsen, Hans, *The Law of the United Nations: A Critical Analysis of Its Fundamental Problems* (1950).

Kelsen, Hans, *Peace through Law* (1944).

Kelsen, Hans, *Principles of International Law* (R. W. Tucker ed., 9th rev. edn, 1966).

Kelsen, Hans, *Pure Theory of Law* (trans. Max Knight, 1967).

Kennedy, Robert F., *Thirteen Days: A Memoir of the Cuban Missile Crisis* (2nd edn, 1971).

Khan, Saira, *Iran and Nuclear Weapons: Protracted Conflict and Proliferation* (2010).

Kissinger, Henry, *Diplomacy* (1995).

Klabbers, Jan, *Constitutionalism and the Making of International Law* (2008).

Klabbers, Jan, *An Introduction to International Institutional Law* (2nd edn, 2009).

Kolasa, Jan, *Disarmament and Arms Control Agreements: A Study on Procedural and Institutional Law* (1995).

Kolb, Robert, *Interprétation et création du droit international: Esquisse d'une herméneutique juridique moderne pour le droit international public* (2006).

Koopmans, Tim, *Courts and Political Institutions* (2003).

Koskenniemi, Martti, *From Apology to Utopia: The Structure of International Legal Argument* (2006).

Krieger, David and Carah Ong, *Back to Basics: Reviving Nuclear Disarmament in the Non-proliferation Regime* (2005).

Kroenig, Matthew, *Exporting the Bomb: Technology Transfer and the Spread of Nuclear Weapons* (2010).

Lafeber, W., *America, Russia, and the Cold War 1945–1980* (4th edn, 1980).

Lanfranchi, Marie-Pierre, *La licéité de l'emploi d'armes nucléaires devant la Court internationale de justice: Analyse et documents* (1997).

Levi, Michael A., *On Nuclear Terrorism* (2007).

Levi, Michael A., and Michael E. O'Hanlon, *The Future of Arms Control* (2005).

Lew, Julian D. M. et al., *Comparative International Commercial Arbitration* (2003).

Luard, Evan, 1 *A History of the United Nations* (1982).

Laurenti, Jeffrey and Carl Robichaud (eds.), *Breaking the Nuclear Impasse: New Prospects for Security against Weapons Threats* (2007).

Lauterpacht, Hersch, (ed.), *L. Oppenheim, 1 International Law* (6th edn, 1947).

Lauterpacht, Hersch, *The Development of International Law by the International Court* (1958).

Lauterpacht, Hersch, *The Function of Law in the International Community* (1933).

Lawrence, T. J., *International Law* (1911).

Lebow, Richard Ned, *Nuclear Crisis Management: A Dangerous Illusion* (1987).

Legal Section of the Secretariat of the League of Nations, *Arbitration and Security: Systematic Survey of the Arbitration Conventions and Treaties of Mutual Security Deposited with the League of Nations* (1927).

Lieberman, Joseph I., *The Scorpion and the Tarantula: The Struggle to Control Atomic Weapons 1945–1949* (1970).

Lind, E. Allan and Tom R. Tyler, *The Social Psychology of Procedural Justice* (1988).

Lindell, Ulf, *Modern Multilateral Negotiation: The Consensus Rule and Its Implications in International Conferences* (1988).

Lissitzyn, Oliver J., *The International Court of Justice: Its Role in the Maintenance of International Peace and Security* (1951).

Luck, Edward C., *The UN Security Council: Practice and Promise* (2006).

Lysén, Göran, *The International Regulation of Armaments: The Law of Disarmament* (1990).

McCauley, Martin, *Russia, America and the Cold War, 1949–1991* (2nd edn, 2004).

McCormack, Timothy L. H., *Self-Defense in International Law: The Israeli Raid on the Iraqi Nuclear Reactor* (1997).

McDougal, M. S. and F. P. Feliciano, *Law and Minimum World Public Order* (1961).

McKnight, Allan, *Atomic Safeguards: A Study in International Verification* (1971).

McNamara, Robert S., *Argument without End: In Search of Answers to the Vietnam Tragedy* (1999).

McWhinney, Edward, *Judicial Settlement of International Disputes: Jurisdiction, Justiciability and Judicial Law-Making on the Contemporary International Court* (1991).

Martin, Andrew, *Legal Aspects of Disarmament* (1963).
Marton, Kati, *A Death in Jerusalem* (1994).
Merignhac, A., *Traité théorique et pratique de l'arbitrage international* (1895).
Merrills, John G., *International Dispute Settlement* (4th edn, 2005).
Meyrowitz, Elliott L., *Prohibition of Nuclear Weapons: The Relevance of International Law* (1990).
Mingst, Karen A., *The United Nations in the Post-Cold War Era* (2000).
Moore, John Norton et al. (eds.), *National Security Law* (1990).
Morgenthau, Hans J., *Politics among Nations* (1949).
Moxley, Charles, *Nuclear Weapons and International Law in the Post-Cold War World* (2000).
Naidu, M. V., *Collective Security and the United Nations* (1975).
Negm, Namira, *Transfer of Nuclear Technology under International Law: Case Study of Iraq, Iran and Israel* (2009).
Noel-Baker, Philip, *The Arms Race: A Programme for World Disarmament* (1958).
Novacovitch, Mileta, *Les compromis et les arbitrages internationaux du xiie au xve siècle* (1905).
O'Brien, John, *International Law* (2001).
O'Connell, Mary Ellen, *International Dispute Resolution* (2006).
O'Neill, Philip D., Jr., *National Security and the Legal Process* (2008).
Orakhelashvili, Alexander, *The Interpretation of Acts and Rules in Public International Law* (2008).
Österdahl, Inger, *Threat to the Peace: The Interpretation by the Security Council of Article 39 of the UN Charter* (1998).
Overy, R. J., *The Origins of the Second World War* (1998).
Patterson, Charles, *The Oxford 50th Anniversary Book of the United Nations* (1995).
Peaslee, Amos J., *United Nations Government* (1945).
Pilat, Joseph F., *Atoms for Peace: A Future after Fifty Years?* (2007).
Pollack, Kenneth M., *The Threatening Storm: The Case for Invading Iraq* (2002).
Posner, Eric A., *The Perils of Global Legalism* (2009).
Potter, William C. and Gaukhar Mukhatzhanova (eds.), *Forecasting Nuclear Proliferation in the 21st Century: The Role of Theory* (2010).
Poulose, T. T., *The Future of Nuclear Arms Control* (1987).
Raeder, A., *L'arbitrage international chez les hellènes* (1912).
Ralston, Jackson H., *International Arbitration from Athens to Locarno* (1929).
Randolph, Lillian L., *Third-Party Settlement of Disputes in Theory and Practice* (1973).
Ranjeva, Raymond and Charles Cadoux, *Droit international public* (1992).
Rawls, John, *A Theory of Justice* (1972).
Raz, Joseph, *The Authority of Law* (1979).

Redfern, Alan and Martin Hunter, *Law and Practice of International Commercial Arbitration* (1986).
Reisman, W. Michael, *Nullity and Revision* (1971).
Richard, Henry and Edouard Descamps, *Arbitration: Two Views* (1971).
Riddell, Anna and Brendan Plant, *Evidence before the International Court of Justice* (2009).
Righter, Rosemary, *Utopia Lost: The United Nations and World Order* (1995).
Roderick, Hilliard and Ulla Magnusson (eds.), *Avoiding Inadvertent War: Crisis Management* (1983).
Roling B. V. A. and O. Sukovic, *The Law of War and Dubious Weapons* (1976).
Ronen, Yaël, *The Iran Nuclear Issue* (2010).
Rosenne, Shabtai, *Essays on International Law and Practice* (2007).
Rosenne, Shabtai, *The International Court of Justice: An Essay in Political and Legal Theory* (1957).
Rosenne, Shabtai, *The Law and Practice of the International Court* (1965).
Rosenne, Shabtai, *The Law and Practice of the International Court 1920–2005* (4th edn, 2006).
Rosenne, Shabtai, *Provisional Measures in International Law* (2005).
Ross, Alf, *The United Nations: Peace and Progress* (1966).
Ross, Thomas, *Just Stories: How the Law Embodies Racism and Bias* (1996).
Rouyer-Hameray, Bernard, *Les compétences implicites des organisations internationales* (1962).
Rubino-Sammartano, Mauro, *International Arbitration Law and Practice* (2nd edn, 2001).
Russel, R. B. and J. E. Muther, *A History of the United Nations Charter* (1958).
Russell, Bertrand, *Has Man a Future?* (1961).
Ruzié, David, *Droit international public* (19th edn, 2008).
Sato, Tetsuo, *Evolving Constitutions of International Organizations: A Critical Analysis of the Interpretative Framework of the Constituent Instruments of International Organizations* (1996).
Sayed, Abdulhay, *Quand le droit est face à son néant: Le droit à l'épreuve de l'emploi de l'arme nucléaire* (1998).
Scheinman, Lawrence, *The International Atomic Energy Agency and World Nuclear Order* (1987).
Schelling, Thomas C., *The Strategy of Conflict* (1960).
Schermers, Henry G. and Niels M. Blokker, *International Institutional Law* (3rd rev. edn, 2003).
Schmitt, Carl, *Legality and Legitimacy* (1932) (trans. Jeffrey Seitzer, 2004).
Schoff, James L. et al., *Nuclear Matters in North Korea: Building a Multilateral Response for Future Stability in Northeast Asia* (2008).
Schulte, Constanze, *Compliance with Decisions of the International Court of Justice* (2004).

Schwarzenberger, Georg, *The Legality of Nuclear Weapons* (1958).

Schweigman, David, *The Authority of the Security Council under Chapter VII of the UN Charter: Legal Limits and the Role of the International Court of Justice* (2001).

Shaker, Mohamed I., *The Nuclear Non-proliferation Treaty: Origin and Implementation, 1959–1979* (1980).

Shaw, Malcolm, *International Law* (6th edn, 2005).

Shihata, Ibrahim F. I., *The Power of the International Court to Determine Its Own Jurisdiction* (1965).

Simma, Bruno (ed.), *The Charter of the United Nations: A Commentary* (1994).

Simpson, Gerry, *Great Powers and Outlaw States: Unequal Sovereigns in the International Legal Order* (2004).

Simpson, John L. and Hazel Fox, *International Arbitration: Law and Practice* (1959).

Singh, Nagendra, *The Role and Record of the International Court of Justice* (1989).

Singh, Nagendra and Edward McWhinney, *Nuclear Weapons and Contemporary International Law* (2nd rev. edn, 1989).

Sohn, Louis B., *Adjudication and Enforcement in Arms Control* (1960).

Sohn, Louis B., *Cases on United Nations Law* (1956).

Sonnenfeld, Renata, *Resolutions of the United Nations Security Council* 7 (Tomasz Dobrowolski trans., 1988).

Spaight, J., *The Atomic Problem* (1948).

Squassoni, Sharon A. et al., *Proliferation Control Regimes: Background and Status* (2002).

Sutterlin, James S., *The United Nations and the Maintenance of International Security: A Challenge to Be Met* (2003).

Szasz, Paul C., *The Law and Practices of the International Atomic Energy Agency* (1970).

Sztucki, Jerzy, *Interim Measures in the Hague Court* (1983).

Tamanaha, Brian, *On the Rule of Law* (2004).

Tavares de Sá, Hernane, *The Play within the Play: The Inside Story of the UN* (1966).

Teixeira, Pascal, *The Security Council at the Dawn of the Twenty-First Century* (2003).

Teubner, Gunther, *Law as an Autopoietic System* (trans. Anne Bankowska and Ruth Adler, 1993).

Thakur, Ramesh, *The United Nations, Peace and Security: From Collective Security to the Responsibility to Protect* (2006).

Thee, M. (ed.), *Armaments and Disarmament in the Nuclear Age* (1976).

Thirlway, Hugh W. A., *Non-appearance before the International Court of Justice* (1985).

Thomson, David B., *A Guide to the Nuclear Arms Control Treaties* (2001).

Tod, Marcus Niebuhr, *International Arbitration among the Greeks* (1913).
United Nations, *Everyone's United Nations* (10th edn, 1986).
United Nations, *The United Nations at Forty: A Foundation to Build on* (1985).
Vattel, Emmerich de, *Law of Nations, or Principles of Natural Law Applied to the Conduct and Affairs of Nations and of Sovereigns* (1916, trans. Charles Fenwick, 1964).
Visscher, Charles de, *De l'équité dans le règlement arbitral ou judiciaire des litiges de droit international public* (1972).
Visscher, Charles de, *Théories et réalités en droit international public* (1953).
Wallace-Bruce, Nii Lante, *The Settlement of International Disputes: The Contribution of Australia and New Zealand* (1998).
Walton, Richard E. and Robert B. McKersie, *A Behavioral Theory of Labor Negotiation* (1965).
Weston, Burns H. (ed.), *Toward Nuclear Disarmament and Global Security: A Search for Alternatives* (1984).
Weber, Max, *On Law in Economy and Society* (G. Roth and C. Wittich ed., 1968).
Wellens, Karel, *Remedies against International Organisations* (2002).
Wet, Erika de, *The Chapter VII Powers of the United Nations Security Council* (2004).
White, Nigel D., *Keeping the Peace: The United Nations and the Maintenance of International Peace and Security* (1993).
Whittaker, David J., *United Nations in the Contemporary World* (1997).
Wilcox, Francis O. and Carl M. Marcy, *Proposals for Changes in the United Nations* (1955).
Wittgenstein, Ludwig, *Tractatus Logico - Philosophicus* (trans. C. K. Ogden, 1992) (1922).
Wittner, Lawrence S., *One World or None: A History of the World Nuclear Disarmament Movement through 1953* (1993).
Wohlstetter, Albert et al., *Swords from Plowshares: The Military Potential of Civilian Nuclear Energy* (1977).
Wolff, Christian, *The Law of Nations Treated According to a Scientific Method* (1749, trans. Joseph D. Drake, 1934).
Wright, Quincy, *International Law and the United Nations* (1960).
Yemin, Edward, *Legislative Powers in the United Nations and Specialized Agencies* (1969).

II. Articles and book chapters

Abbott, Kenneth W. and Duncan Snidal, Why States Act through Formal International Organizations, 42 *J. Conflict Res.* 3 (1998).
Abbott, Kenneth W. et al., The Concept of Legalization, 54 *Int'l Org.* 401 (2000).

Abi-Saab, Georges, The Court and the Bomb: A Case of Mutual Deterrence?, 7 *Transnat'l L. & Comtemp. Probs.* 429 (1997).

Abi-Saab, Georges, De l'évolution de la Cour internationale: Réflexions sur quelques tendances récentes, 96 *RGDIP* 273 (1992).

Abi-Saab, Georges, Ensuring the Best Bench: Ways of Selecting Judges, in *Increasing the Effectiveness of the International Court of Justice: Proceedings of the ICJ/UNITAR Colloquium to Celebrate the 50th Anniversary of the Court* 188 (Connie Peck and Roy S. Lee ed., 1997).

Abi-Saab, Georges, The International Court as a World Court, in *Fifty Years of the International Court of Justice: Essays in Honour of Sir Robert Jennings* 3 (Vaughan Lowe and Malgosia Fitzmaurice ed., 1996).

Abi-Saab, Georges, On Discretion: Reflections on the Nature of the Consultative Function of the International Court of Justice, in *International Law, International Court of Justice and Nuclear Weapons* 36 (Laurence Boisson de Chazournes and Philippe Sands ed., 1999).

Abi-Saab, Georges, The Security Council Legibus Solutus? On the Legislative Forays of the Council, in *International Law and the Quest for Its Implementation: Liber Amicorum Vera Gowlland-Debbas* 23 (Laurence Boisson de Chazournes and Marcelo Kohen ed., 2010).

Acevedo, Domingo E., Disputes under Consideration by the UN Security Council or Regional Bodies, in *The International Court of Justice at a Crossroads* 242 (Lori F. Damrosch ed., 1987).

Acton, James M., The Problem with Nuclear Mind Reading, *Survival* 119, (February 2009).

Ago, Roberto, "Binding" Advisory Opinions of the International Court of Justice, 85 *Am. J. Int' L.* 439 (1991).

Ahdieh, Robert B., Between Dialogue and Decree: International Review of National Courts, 79 *N.Y.U. L. Rev.* 2029 (2004).

Akande, Dapo, The International Court of Justice and the Security Council: Is There Room for Judicial Control of Decisions of the Political Organs of the United Nations?, 46 *Int'l & Comp. L.Q.* 309 (1997).

Akande, Dapo, Nuclear Weapons, Unclear Law?, 68 *Brit. YB Int'l L.* 165 (1997).

Akande, Dapo and Sope Williams, International Adjudication of Security Issues: What Role for the WTO?, 43 *Va. J. Int'l L.* 365 (2003).

Akehurst, Michael, Equity and General Principles of Law, 25 *Int'l & Comp. L.Q.* 801 (1976).

Alexandrov, Stanimir A., Non-appearance before the International Court of Justice, 33 *Colum. J. Transnat'l L.* 41 (1995).

Almond, Harry H., Jr., Deterrence and a Policy-Oriented Perspective on the Legality of Nuclear Weapons, in *Nuclear Weapons and Law* 57 (Arthur Selwyn Miller and Martin Feinrider ed., 1984).

Alvarez, Alejandro, The New International Law, 15 *Transactions of the Grotius Society* 35 (1930).

Alvarez, Jose, Judging the Security Council, 90 *Am. J. Int'l L.* 1 (1996).

Amerasinghe, C. F., The Legality of the Use of or Threat to Use Nuclear Weapons, 10 *Finnish Y.B. Int'l L.* 5 (1999).

Anand, R. P., Role of International Adjudication, in 1 *The Future of the International Court of Justice* 9 (Leo Gross ed., 1976).

Anastassov, Anguel, Are Nuclear Weapons Illegal? The Role of Public International Law and the International Court of Justice, 15 *J. Conflict & Sec. L.* 65, 76 (2010).

Andemicael, Berhanykun, Nuclear Verification in North Korea and Iran, in *Swords into Plowshares: Building Peace through the United Nations* 123 (Roy S. Lee ed., 2006).

Angehr, Mark, The International Court of Justice's Advisory Jurisdiction and the Review of Security Council and General Assembly Resolutions, 103 *Nw. Univ. L. Rev.* 1007 (2009).

Angelet, Nicolas, International Law Limits to the Security Council, in *United Nations Sanctions and International Law* 71 (Vera Gowlland-Debbas ed., 2001).

Angelet, Nicholas, Protest against Security Council Decisions, in *International Law: Theory and Practice: Essays in Honour of Eric Suy* 277 (Karel Wellens ed., 1998).

Anghie, Antony, Colonialism and the Birth of International Institutions: Sovereignty, Economy, and the Mandate System of the League of Nations, 34 *N.Y.U. J. Int'l L. & Pol.* 513 (2002).

Arsanjani, Mahnoush H., Claims against International Organizations: Quis Custodiet Ipsos Custodes, 7 *Yale J. World Public Order* 131 (1981).

Azaran, Amir, NPT, Where Art Thou? The Nonproliferation Treaty and Bargaining: Iran as a Case Study, 6 *Chi. J. Int'l L.* 415 (2005).

Bailey, Sydney D., Peaceful Settlement of International Disputes, in *Dispute Settlement through the United Nations* 73 (K. Venkata Raman ed., 1977).

Bajema, Natasha and Mary Beth Nikitin, Assessing Nuclear Maturity: Determining Which States Should Have Access to What Nuclear Technology, 28 *Fletcher F. World Aff.* 157 (2004).

Barnett, Randy E., Consenting to Form Contracts, 71 *Fordham L. Rev.* 627 (2002).

Beard, Jack M., The Shortcomings of Indeterminacy in Arms Control Regimes, 101 *Am. J. Int'l L.* 271 (2007).

Bederman, David J., Counterintuiting Countermeasures, 96 *Am. J. Int'l L.* 817 (2002).

Bedjaoui, Mohammed and Fatsah Ouguergouz, Le forum prorogatum devant la Cour internationale de justice: Les ressources d'une institution ou la face cachée du consensualisme, 5 *Af. Y.B. Int'l L.* 91 (1997).

Bekker, Peter H. F., International Legal Aid Practice, 87 *Am. J. Int'l. L.* 659 (1993).

Bekker, Peter H. F. and Judith Hippler Bello, Legality of the Threat or Use of Nuclear Weapons Advisory Opinion, 91 *Am. J. Int'l L.* 126 (1997).

Bekker, Peter H. F. and Judith Hippler Bello, Legality of the Use by a State of Nuclear Weapons in Armed Conflict Advisory Opinion, 91 *Am. J. Int'l L.* 134 (1997).

Beres, Louis René, Israel, Iran and Preemption: Choosing the Least Unattractive Option under International Law, 14 *Dick. J. Int'l L.* 187 (1996).

Berman, Nathaniel, A Perilous Ambivalence: Nationalist Desire, Legal Autonomy and the Limits of the Interwar Framework, 33 *Harv. Int'l L.J.* 353 (1992).

Bernhardt, Rudolf, Article 103, in *The Charter of the United Nations: A Commentary* 1292 (Bruno Simma ed., 2002).

Bilder, Richard, Adjudication: International Arbitration Tribunals and Courts, in *Peacemaking in International Conflict: Methods and Techniques* 155 (I. William Zartman and J. Lewis Rasmussen ed., 1997).

Bilder, Richard, Distinguishing Human Rights and Humanitarian Law: The Issue of Nuclear Weapons, 31 *Am. Univ. L. Rev.* 959 (1982).

Bilder, Richard B., The Fact/Law Distinction in International Adjudication, in *Fact-Finding before International Tribunals* 124 (Richard B. Lillich ed., 1992).

Bilder, Richard B., International Dispute Settlement and the Role of International Adjudication, in *The International Court of Justice at a Crossroads* 155 (Lori F. Damrosch ed., 1987).

Bilder, Richard B., International Third Party Dispute Settlement, 17 *Denv. J. Int'l L. & Pol'y* 471 (1989).

Bilder, Richard B., Judicial Procedures Relating to the Use of Force, in *Law and Force in the New International Order* 269 (Lori F. Damrosch and David Scheffer ed., 1983).

Bilder, Richard B., Judicial Procedures Relating to the Use of Force, 31 *Va. J. Int'l L.* 249 (1991).

Bilder, Richard B., An Overview of International Dispute Settlement, 1 *Emory J. Int'l Disp. Resol.* 1 (1986).

Bilder, Richard B., The United States and the World Court in the Post-"Cold War" Era, 40 *Cath. U.L. Rev.* 251 (1991).

Blix, Hans, The Principles of Peaceful Settlement of Disputes, in *The Legal Principles Governing Friendly Relations and Co-operation among States* 44 (Mohammed K. Nawaz et al. ed., 1966).

Blix, Hans, The Role of the IAEA in the Development of International Law, 58 *Nordic J. Int'l L.* 231 (1989).

Böckstiegel, Karl-Heinz, States in the International Arbitral Process, in *Contemporary Problems in International Arbitration* 40 (Julian D. M. Lew ed., 1986).

Bodansky, Daniel, Non Liquet and the Incompleteness of International Law, in *International Law, International Court of Justice and Nuclear Weapons* 153 (Laurence Boisson de Chazournes and Philippe Sands ed., 1999).

Boisson de Chazournes, Laurence and Philippe Sands, Introduction, in *International Law, the International Court of Justice and Nuclear Weapons* 1 (Laurence Boisson de Chazournes and Philippe Sands ed., 1999).

Bolintineanu, A., International Law and Disarmament, 21 *Revue roumaine d'études internationales* 21 (1987).

Bone, Robert G., The Role of the Judge in the Twenty-First Century: Securing the Normative Foundations of Litigation Reform, 86 *B.U.L. Rev.* 1155 (2006).

Bongiorno, Carla, A Culture of Impunity: Applying International Human Rights Law to the United Nations in East Timor, 33 *Colum. Hum. Rts. L. Rev.* 623 (2002).

Borchard, Edwin M., Remarks in the Distinction Between Legal and Political Questions, 18 *Am. Soc'y Int'l L. Proc.* 50 (1924).

Borgen, Christopher J., Resolving Treaty Conflicts, 37 *Geo. Wash. Int'l L. Rev.* 573 (2005).

Bosch, Miguel Marin, The Non-proliferation Treaty and Its Future, in *International Law, International Court of Justice and Nuclear Weapons* 375 (Laurence Boisson de Chazournes and Philippe Sands ed., 1999).

Bothe, Michael, Les limites des pouvoirs du Conseil de sécurité, in *The Development of the Role of the Security Council* 67 (Rene-Jean Dupuy ed., 1993).

Bourantonis, Dimitris and Marios Evriviades, New Directions in Disarmament, in *The United Nations in the New World Order: The World Organization at Fifty* 154 (Dimitris Bourantonis and Jarrod Wiener ed., 1995).

Bowett, Derek, The Impact of Security Council Decisions on Dispute Settlement Procedures, 5 *Eur. J. Int'l L.* 89 (1994).

Bowett, Derek, Treaties and State Responsibility, in *Le droit international au service de la paix, de la justice et du développement: Mélanges Michel Virally* 137 (1991).

Bradley, Morris, Conflict Dynamics and Conflict Resolution, in *The Nuclear Mentality: A Psychosocial Analysis of the Arms Race* 49 (Lynn Barnett and Ian Lee ed., 1989).

Branson, David J., American Party-Appointed Arbitrators: Not the Three Monkeys, 30 *Dayton L. Rev.* 1 (2004).

Brenner, Michael J., Renewing the Non-proliferation Regime: A Multilateral Approach, in *Arms Control: The Multilateral Alternative* 145 (Edward C. Luck ed., 1983).

Brenner, Susan W. and Marc D. Goodman, In Defense of Cyberterrorizm: An Argument for Anticipating Cyber-Attacks, *U. Ill. J.L. Tech. & Pol'y* 1 (2002).

Bretton, P., Le problème des "méthodes et moyens de guerre ou de combat" dans les Protocoles additionnels aux Conventions de Genève du 12 août 1949, 82 *RGDIP* 32 (1978).

Brierly, James L., The Judicial Settlement of International Disputes, 4 *J. Brit. Inst. Int'l Aff.* 227 (1925).

Brierly, James L., Vital Interests and the Law, 21 *British Y.B. Int'l L.* 51 (1944).

Briggs, H. W., Confidence, Apprehension and the International Court of Justice, 54 *Am. Soc'y Int'l L. Proc.* 25 (1960).

Bright, Fred, Nuclear Weapons as a Lawful Means of Warfare, 30 *Mil. L. Rev.* 1 (1965).

Brilmayer, Lea, Transforming International Politics: An American Role for the Post Cold War World, 64 *U. Cin. L. Rev.* 119 (1995).

Brower, Charles H., II, The Functions and Limits of Arbitration and Judicial Settlement under Private and Public International Law, 18 *Duke J. Comp. & Int'l L.* 259 (2008).

Brown, Alexis C., Presumption Meets Reality: An Exploration of the Confidentiality Obligation in International Commercial Arbitration, 16 *Am. U. Int'l L. Rev.* 969 (2001).

Brownlie, Ian, The Justiciability of Disputes and Issues in International Relations, 42 *British Y.B. Int'l L.* 123 (1967).

Brownlie, Ian, Some Legal Aspects of the Use of Nuclear Weapons, 14 *Int'l & Comp. L.Q.* 437 (1965).

Bruning, R. C., The United Nations' Military Staff Committee: Future or Failure?, 43 *Revue de droit penal militaire et de droit de la guerre* 35 (1974).

Bryde, Brun-Otto and August Reinisch, Article 47, in *The Charter of the United Nations: A Commentary* 769 (Bruno Simma ed., 2002).

Bunn, George, Does the NPT Require Its Non-nuclear-Weapon Parties to Permit Inspection by the IAEA of Nuclear Activities That Have Not Been Reported to the IAEA?, in *A New Nuclear Triad: The Non-proliferation of Nuclear Weapons, International Verification and the International Atomic Energy Agency* 44 (David Fischer et al. ed., 1992).

Bunn, George, The Nuclear Nonproliferation Treaty: History and Current Problems, *Arms Control Today* 1 (Dec. 2003).

Bugnion, Francois, The International Committee of the Red Cross and Nuclear Weapons: From Hiroshima to the Dawn of the 21st Century, 859 *Int'l Rev. Red Cross* 511 (2005).

Burke-White, William W. and Andreas von Staden, Investment Protection in Extraordinary Times: The Interpretation and Application of Non-precluded Measures Provisions in Bilateral Investment Treaties, 48 *Va. J. Int'l L.* 307 (2008).

Burstein, Stanley M., Arms Control in Antiquity, in 2 *Encyclopedia of Arms Control and Disarmament* 551 (Richard Dean Burns ed., 1993).

Burton, John, The Analysis of Conflict by Casework, 21 *Y.B. World Aff.* 20 (1967).

Butler, Richard, The Evolving Role of the UN and Disarmament, in *The Future of Disarmament* 176 (United Nations ed., 1998).

Butler, Rohan, Peace Settlement of Versailles 1918–1933, in 12 *The New Cambridge Modern History* 220 (C. L. Mowat ed., 2nd edn, 1968).

Buys, Cindy G., The Tensions between Confidentiality and Transparency in International Arbitration, 14 *Am. Rev. Int'l Arb.* 121 (2003).

Byers, Michael, Agreeing To Disagree: Security Council Resolution 1441 and International Ambiguity, 10 *Global Governance* 165 (2004).

Cadoux, Charles, La supériorité du droit des Nations Unies sur le droit des États membres, 63 *Revue général de droit international public* 649 (1959).

Calamita, N. Jansen, Sanctions, Countermeasures, and the Iranian Nuclear Issue, 42 *Vand. J. Transnat'l L.* 1393 (2009).

Calderón, Félix, Arms Restraint and the Avoidance of Force, in *Avoidance and Settlement of Arms Control Disputes* 187 (Julie Dahlitz ed., 1994).

Carle, Christophe, Arms Control in Reluctant Installments: Iraq and North Korea, Arms Control and Disarmament Cluster 1999–2000, Occasional Paper Series No. 9, 3 (2000).

Condron, Sean M., Justification for Unilateral Action in Response to the Iraqi Threat: A Critical Analysis of Operation Desert Fox, 161 *Mil. L. Rev.* 115 (1999).

Cardenas, Emilio J., The United Nations Security Council's Quest for Effectiveness, 25 *Mich. J. Int'l L.* 1341 (2004).

Carlson, Geoffrey S., An Offer They Can't Refuse? The Security Council Tells North Korea to Re-sign the Nuclear Non-proliferation Treaty, 46 *Colum. J. Transnat'l L.* 420 (2008).

Carmody, Susan, Balancing Collective Security and National Sovereignty: Does the United Nations Have the Right to Inspect North Korea's Nuclear Facilities?, 18 *Fordham Int'l L. J.* 229 (1994).

Caron, David D. and Galina Shinkaretskaya, Peaceful Settlement of Disputes through the Rule of Law, in *Beyond Confrontation: International Law for the Post-Cold War Era* 309 (Lori F. Damrosch et al. ed., 1995).

Carvalho-Soto, Perla, Mexican Perspectives on Nuclear Disarmament, 31 *Case W. Res. J. Int'l L.* 647 (1999).

Charlesworth, Hilary, International Law: A Discipline of Crisis, 65 *Modern L. Rev.* 377 (2002).

Charlier, R. E., Questions juridiques soulevées par l'évolution de la science atomique, 91 *Rec. des cours* 354 (1957).

Charney, Jonathan I., Compromissory Clauses and the Jurisdiction of the International Court of Justice, 81 *Am. J. Int'l L.* 855 (1987).

Charney, Jonathan I., Disputes Implicating the Institutional Credibility of the Court: Problems of Non-appearance, Non-participation, and Non-performance, in *The International Court of Justice at a Crossroads* 288 (Lori F. Damrosch ed., 1998).

Charney, Jonathan I., International Lawmaking: Article 38 of the ICJ Statute Reconsidered, in *New Trends in International Lawmaking: International "Legislation" in the Public Interest* 171 (Jost Delbrück ed., 1997).

Chayes, Antonia Handler and Abram Chayes, From Law Enforcement to Dispute Settlement: A New Approach to Arms Control Verification and Compliance, 14 *Int'l Sec.* 147 (1990).

Cheever, Daniel S., The UN and Disarmament, 19 *Int'l Org.* 463 (1965).

Cheng, Tai-Heng, Precedent and Control in Investment Treaty Arbitration, 30 *Fordham Int'l L.J.* 1014 (2007).

Chesterman, Simon, The ICJ Nuclear Weapons and the Law, 44 *Neth. Int'l L. Rev.* 149 (1997).

Chesterman, Simon, An International Rule of Law?, 56 *Am. J. Comp. L.* 331 (2008).

Chesterman, Simon, UNaccountable? The United Nations, Emergency Powers, and the Rule of Law, 42 *Vand. J. Transnat'l L.* 1509 (2009).

Ciobanu, Dan, Litispendence between the International Court of Justice and the Political Organs of the United Nations, in *The Future of the International Court of Justice* 209 (Leo Gross ed., 1976).

Clark, Roger S., The Laws of Armed Conflict and the Use or Threat of Use of Nuclear Weapons, 7 *Crim. L.F.* 265 (1996).

Claude, Inis L., Collective Legitimization as a Political Function of the United Nations, 20 *Int'l Org.* 367 (1966).

Claude, Inis L., Management of Power in the Changing United Nations, 15 *Int'l Org.* 229 (1961).

Coleman, Andrew, The International Court of Justice and Highly Political Matters, 4 *Melb J. Int'l L.* 29 (2003).

Collins, Lawrence, Provisional and Protective Measures in International Litigation, 111 *Rec. des cours* 9 (1992).

Condorelli, Luigi, Nuclear Weapons: A Weighty Matter for the International Court of Justice – Jura Non Novit Curia?, 316 *Int'l Rev. Red Cross* 9 (1997).

Coombs, Cody, Blue Morning-Glories in the Sky: Correcting Sanctions to Enforce Nuclear Nonproliferation in Iran, 19 *Ind. Int'l & Comp. L. Rev.* 419 (2009).

Cot, Jean-Pierre and Pascal Boniface, Le Contrôle de l'armement et le désarmement, in 2 *Droit international* 865 (Mohammed Bedjaoui ed., 1991).

Courteix, Simone, La contrôle de la prolifération des armes nucléaires, 28 *McGill L. J.* 591 (1983).

Cousineau, Helen, The Nuclear Non-proliferation Treaty and Global Non-proliferation Regime: A U.S. Policy Agenda, 12 *B.U. Int'l L.J.* 407 (1994).

Coussirat-Coustère, Vincent, Armes nucléaires et droit international: À propos des avis consultatifs du 8 Juillet 1996 de la Cour internationale de justice, 42 *AFDI* 337 (1996).

Crawford, James, Marbury v. Madison at the International Level, 36 *GW Int'l L. Rev.* 505 (2004).

Crawford, James, The Relationship between Sanctions and Countermeasures, in *United Nations Sanctions and International Law* 57 (Vera Gowlland-Debbas ed., 2001).

Crook, John R., Continuing U.S. and Multilateral Efforts to Curb Iran's Nuclear Program, 102 *Am. J. Int'l L.* 187 (2008).

Cumings, Bruce, Nuclear Imbalance of Terror: The American Surveillance Regime and North Korea's Nuclear Programme, in *The Nuclear Non-proliferation Regime* 207 (Raju G. C. Thomas ed., 1998).

Cummings, Edward, The Role of Humanitarian Law, 9 *Brooklyn J. Int'l L.* 269 (1983).

Dahinden, Erwin, The Future of Arms Control Law: Towards a New Regulatory Approach and New Regulatory Techniques, 10 *J. Conflict & Security L.* 263 (2005).

Dahlitz, Julie, Security Council Powers and Possibilities, in *Avoidance and Settlement of Arms Control Disputes* 57 (Julie Dahlitz ed., 1994).

Dahlitz, Julie, The Role of Customary Law in Arms Limitations, in *The International Law of Arms Control and Disarmament* 157 (Julie Dahlitz and Detlev Dicke ed., 1991).

Dalfen, C. M., The World Court in Idle Splendour: The Basis of State Attitudes, 23 *Int'l J.* 124 (1967).

Dallmeyer, Dorinda G., The Future Role of the United Nations in Disarmament: Learning from the Iraq Experience, in *Adapting the United Nations to a Postmodern Era: Lessons Learned* 129 (W. Andy Knight ed., 2001).

D'Amato, Anthony, Arbitration, in *International Law Anthology* 323 (Anthony D'Amato ed., 1994).

D'Amato, Anthony, Good Faith, in *Encyclopedia of Public International Law* 599 (Rudolf Bernhardt ed., 1992).

D'Amato, Anthony, Israel's Air Strike upon the Iraqi Nuclear Reactor, 77 *Am. J. Int'l L.* 584 (1983).

Damrosch, Lori F., Enforcing International Law through Non-forcible Measures, 269 *Rec. des cours* 191 (1997).

Danchin, Peter G., U.S. Unilateralism and the International Protection of Religious Freedom: The Multilateral Alternative, 41 *Colum. J. Transnat'l L.* 33 (2002).

Dantiki, Sumon, Power through Process: An Administrative Law Framework for United Nations Legislative Resolutions, 40 *Geo. J. Int'l L.* 655 (2009).

David, Eric, À propos de certaines justifications théoroiques à l'emploi de l'arme nucléaire, in *Studies and Essays on International Humanitarian Law and Red Cross Principles in Honour of Jean Pictet* 325 (Christophe Swinarski ed., 1984).

David, Eric, The Opinion of the International Court of Justice on the Legality of the Use of Nuclear Weapons, 316 *Int'l Rev. Red Cross* 21 (1997).

David, Marcella, Passport to Justice: Internationalizing the Political Question Doctrine for Application in the World Court, 40 *Harv. Int'l L.J.* 81 (1999).

Davis, Zachary S., The NPT: Coping with the Best and Worst Cases, in *The Nuclaer Non-proliferation Regime* 140 (Raju G. C. Thomas ed., 1998).

Dekker, Guido den, The Effectiveness of International Supervision in Arms Control Law, 9 *J. Conflict & Security L.* 315 (2004).

Delbrück, Jost, Arms Control, in *United Nations: Law, Politics and Practice* 39 (Rüdiger Wolfrum ed., 1995).

Delbrück, Jost, Article 25, in *The Charter of the United Nations: A Commentary* 452 (Bruno Simma ed., 2002).

Delbrück, Jost, Collective Self-Defence, in *Encyclopedia of Public International Law* 646 (1992).

de Silva, Cynthia, California's Best Evidence Rule Repeal: Toward a Greater Appreciation for Secondary Evidence, 30 *McGeorge L. Rev.* 646 (1999).

Diaconu, Ion, Peaceful Settlement of Disputes between States: History and Prospects, in *The Structure and Process of International Law: Essays in Legal Philosophy Doctrine and Theory* 1095 (R. St. J. Macdonald and Douglas M. Johnston ed., 1983).

Dimitrijevic, Vojin and Marko Milanovic, The Strange Story of the Bosnian Genocide Case, 21 *Leiden J. Int'l L.* 65 (2008).

Doehring, Karl, Unlawful Resolutions of the Security Council and Their Legal Consequences, 1 *Max Planck Y.B. UN L.* 91 (1997).

Dolzer, Rudolf, Article 31, in *The Charter of the United Nations: A Commentary* 573 (Bruno Simma ed., 2002).

Dolzer, Rudolf, Article 32, in *The Charter of the United Nations: A Commentary* 580 (Bruno Simma ed., 2002).

Doswald-Beck, Louise, International Humanitarian Law and the Advisory Opinion of the International Court of Justice on the Legality of the Threat or Use of Nuclear Weapons, 316 *Int'l Rev. Red Cross* 35 (1997).

Duarte, Sergio, Nuclear Weapons and the Rule of Law, 33 *Fordham Int'l L.J.* 573 (2010).

Duffy, Gloria, Arms Control Treaty Compliance, in 1 *Encyclopedia of Arms Control and Disarmament* 279 (Richard Dean Burns ed., 1993).

Dugard, John, Judicial Review of Sanctions, in *United Nations Sanctions and International Law* 83 (Vera Gowlland-Debbas ed., 2001).

Dumberry, Patrick, The Legal Standing of Shareholders before Arbitral Tribunals: Has Any Rule of Customary International Law Crystallised?, 3 *Mich. St. J. Int'l L.* 353 (2010).

Dunn, Lewis A., The Collapse of the NPT: What If?, in *Beyond 1995: The Future of the NPT Regime* 27 (Joseph F. Pilat and Robert E. Pendley ed., 1990).

Dunsky, Marda, Build Bridges, Not Walls, *Chi. Trib.* C4 (Feb. 22, 2004).

Dupuy, Pierre-Marie, The Danger of Fragmentation or Unification of the International Legal System and the International Court of Justice, 31 *N.Y.U. J. Int'l L. & Pol.* 791 (1999).

Dupuy, Pierre-Marie, The Place and Role of Unilateralism in Contemporary International Law, 11 *Eur. J. Int'l L.* 19 (2000).

Economides, Constantine P., L'obligation de règlement pacifique des différends internationaux: Une norme fondamentale tenue à l'écart, in *Boutros-Boutros Ghali Amicorum Discipulorumque Liber* 408 (1998).

Edwards, D.M., International Legal Aspects of Safeguards and the Non-proliferation of Nuclear Weapons, 33 *Int'l & Comp. L.Q.* 1 (1984).

Eisemann, Pierre Michel, Les effets de la non-comparution devant la Cour internationale de justice, 19 *AFDI* 351 (1973).

Eizenstat, Stuart E., U.S. Relations with the European Union and the Changing Europe, 9 *Emory Int'l L. Rev.* 1 (1995).

Ekeus, Rolf, The Iraqi Experience and the Future of Nuclear Nonproliferation *Wash. Q.* 67 (Autumn 1992).

Elkind, Jerome B., Nuclear Weapons: The World Court's Decision, 49 *Revue Hellenique de Droit International* 401 (1996).

Engström, Viljam, Implied Powers of International Organizations: On the Character of a Legal Doctrine, 14 *Finnish Y.B. Int'l L.* 129 (2003).

Euler, A., Légalité ou illégalité des armes nucléaires, 2 *Rec. de la Société internationale de droit pénal militaire et de droit de la guerre* 93 (1963).

Falk, Richard, Appraisals of the ICJ's Decision: Nicaragua v. United States (Merits), 81 *Am. J. Int'l. L.* 106 (1987).

Falk, Richard A., Nuclear Weapons, International Law, and the World Court: A Historic Encounter, 91 *Am. J. Int'l L.* 64 (1996).

Falk, Richard A., The Shimoda Case: A Legal Appraisal of the Atomic Attacks upon Hiroshima and Nagasaki 59 *Am. J. Int'l L.* 759 (1965).

Falk, Richard, Toward a Legal Regime for Nuclear Weapons, in *Nuclear Weapons and Law* 107 (Arthur Selwyn Miller and Martin Feinrider ed., 1984).

Farrand, Andrew D., Chile and Argentina: Entente and Naval Limitation, 1902, in 2 *Encyclopedia of Arms Control and Disarmament* 595 (Richard Dean Burns ed., 1993).

Fassbender, Bardo, The UN Security Council and International Terrorism, in *Enforcing International Law Norms against Terrorism* 83 (Andrea Bianchi ed., 2004).

Fassbender, Bardo, The United Nations Charter as Constitution of the International Community, 36 *Colum. J. Transnat'l L.* 529 (1998).

Fenwick, Charles G., Remarks in the Distinction between Legal and Political Questions, 18 *Am. Soc'y Int'l L. Proc.* 44 (1924).

Feiveson, Harold A. and Theodore B. Taylor, Alternative Strategies for International Control of Nuclear Power, in *Nuclear Proliferation:*

Motivations, Capabilities, and Strategies for Control 123 (Ted Greenwood et al. ed., 1974).

Feuerie, Loie, Informal Consultation: A Mechanism in Security Council Decision-Making 18 *NYU J. Int'l L & Pol.* 267 (1985).

Fidler, David P., International Law and Weapons of Mass Destruction: End of the Arms Control Approach, 14 *Duke J. Comp. & Int'l L.* 39 (2004).

Fidler, David P., War, Law, and Liberal Thought: The Use of Force in the Reagan Years, 11 *Ariz. J. Int'l & Comp. Law* 45 (1994).

Findlay, Trevor, Lessons of UNSCOM and UNMOVIC for WMD Non-proliferation, Arms Control and Disarmament, in *Arms Control after Iraq: Normative and Operational Challenges* 140 (Waheguru Pal Singh Sidhu and Ramesh Thakur ed., 2006).

Finlay, Lorraine, Between a Rock and a Hard Place: The Kadi Decision and Judicial Review of Security Council Resolutions, 18 *Tulane J. Int'l & Comp. L.* 477 (2009).

Fisher, Adrian, Arms Control and Disarmament in International Law, 50 *Va. L. Rev.* 1200 (1964).

Fisher, Roger, Getting to "Yes" in the Nuclear Age, in *Toward Nuclear Disarmament and Global Security: A Search for Alternatives* 358 (B. Weston 1984).

Fitzmaurice, Gerald, The Law and Procedure of the International Court of Justice ed., 1951–1954: Questions of Jurisdiction, Competence and Procedure 34 *Brit. YB. Int'l L.* 1 (1959).

Fitzmaurice, Gerald, The Problem of the "Non-appearing" Defendant Government 51 *Brit. Y.B. Int'l L.* 89 (1980).

Fitzmaurice, Gerald, Vae Victis or Woe to the Negotiators! Your Treaty or Our "Interpretation" of It?, in *The Law of Treaties* 281 (Scott Davidson ed., 2004).

Fleck, Dieter, Current Legal and Policy Issues, in *Future Legal Restraints on Arms Proliferation* 21 (Julie Dahlitz ed., 1996).

Fliess, Peter, The Legality of Atmospheric Nuclear Tests: Critical View of International Law in the Cold War, 15 *Florida. L. Rev.* 21 (1962).

Fombad, Charles Manga, Consultation and Negotiation in the Pacific Settlement of International Disputes, 1 *Af. J. Int'l & Comp. L.* 707 (1989).

Ford, Christopher A., The Nonproliferation Bestiary: A Typology and Analysis of Nonproliferation Regimes, 39 *N.Y.U. J. Int'l L. & Pol.* 937 (2007).

Forsyth, Murray, Hobbes's Contractarianism: A Comparative Analysis, in *The Social Contract from Hobbes to Rawls* 35 (David Boucher and Paul Kelly ed., 1994).

Forsythe, David P., Humanitarian Mediation by the International Committee of the Red Cross, in *International Mediation in Theory and in Practice* 233 (Saadia Touval and William Zartman ed., 1985).

Fox, Hazel, States and the Undertaking to Arbitrate, 37 *Int'l & Comp. L.Q.* 1 (1988).

Franceschini, Giorgio, Assessing the Nuclear Non-proliferation Regime: What are the Loopholes? What are the Challenges?, in *Europe Facing Nuclear Weapons Challenges* 155 (Grégory Boutherin ed., 2008).

Franck, Susan D., The Legitimacy Crisis in Investment Treaty Arbitration: Privatizing Public International Law through Inconsistent Decisions, 73 *Fordham L. Rev.* 1521 (2005).

Franck, Susan D., Men of Affairs? The Role of International Arbitrators, 12 *ILSA J. Int'l & Comp. L.* 499 (2006).

Franck, Susan D., The Nature and Enforcement of Investor Rights under Investment Treaties: Do Investment Treaties Have a Bright Future, 12 *U.C. Davis J. Int'l L. & Pol'y* 47 (2005).

Franck, Susan D., The Role of International Arbitrators, 12 *ILSA J. Int'l & Comp. L.* 499 (2006).

Franck, Thomas M., Legitimacy in the International System, 82 *Am. J. Int'l L.* 705 (1988).

Franck, Thomas M., The "Powers of Appreciation": Who Is the Ultimate Guardian of UN Legality?, 86 *Am. J. Int'l L.* 519 (1992).

Franck, Thomas M., Word Made Law: The Decision of the I.C.J. in the Nuclear Test Cases, 69 *Am. J. Int'l L.* 612 (1975).

Frost, Robert, The Road Not Taken, in *The Poetry of Robert Frost* 105 (Edward Connery Latham ed., 1969).

Frowein, Jochen Abr. and Nico Krisch, Article 40, in *The Charter of the United Nations: A Commentary* 729 (Bruno Simma ed., 2002).

Frowein, Jochen Abr. and Nico Krisch, Article 41, in *The Charter of the United Nations: A Commentary* 735 (Bruno Simma ed., 2002).

Frowein, Jochen Abr. and Nico Krisch, Article 42, in *The Charter of the United Nations: A Commentary* 748 (Bruno Simma ed., 2002).

Frowein, Jochen Abr., Unilateral Interpretation of Security Council Resolutions: A Threat to Collective Security?, in *Liber amicorum Gunther Jaenicke* 97 (Volkmar Gotz et al. ed., 1998).

Fujita, Hisakazu, The Advisory Opinion of the International Court of Justice on the Legality of Nuclear Weapons, 316 *Int'l Rev. Red Cross* 56 (1997).

Fujita, Hisakazu, The Role of Transparency in the Avoidance and Settlement of Arms Control Disputes, in *Avoidance and Settlement of Arms Control Disputes* 87 (Julie Dahlitz ed., 1994).

Fukatsu, Eiichi, Coercion and the Theory of Sanctions in International Law, in *The Structure and Process of International Law: Essays in Legal Philosophy Doctrine and Theory* 1187 (R. St. J. Macdonald and Douglas M. Johnston ed., 1983).

Gaja, Gorgio, Use of Force Made or Authorized by the United Nations, in *The United Nations at Age Fifty* 39 (Christian Tomuschat 1995).

Garrison, M. Scott, Sovereignty of Aves Island: An Argument against Compulsory, Standardized Arbitration of Maritime Boundary Disputes Subject to Review by the International Court of Justice, 38 *U. Miami Inter-Am. L. Rev.* 185 (2006).

Garvey, Jack I., To Fix the Nuclear Non-proliferation Regime: Avoid State Classification, 21 *Fla. J. Int'l L.* 371 (2009).

Gattini, Andrea, Evidentiary Issues in the ICJ's Genocide Judgment, 5 *J. Int'l Crim. Justice* 889 (2007).

Gerard, Ralph W., Truth Detection, in *Preventing World War III: Some Proposals* 52 (Quincy Wright et al. ed., 1962).

Gerber, David J., Consistent Application of Competition Laws across System Borders: Rethinking the Issues, in *Parallel and Conflicting Enforcement of Law* 167 (Torbjörn Andersson ed., 2005).

Gerstenberg, Oliver, Denationalization and the Very Idea of Democratic Constitutionalism: The Case of the European Community, 14 *Ratio Juris* 298 (2001).

Ginsburg, Tom and Richard H. McAdams, Adjudicating in Anarchy: An Expressive Theory of International Dispute Resolution, 45 *Wm and Mary L. Rev.* 1229 (2004).

Goldblat, Jozef, The Role of the United Nations in Arms Control: An Assessment, in *The United Nations and the Maintenance of International Peace and Security* 369 (UN Institute for Training & Research ed., 1987).

Golden, Jeffrey B., The World Court: The Qualifications of the Judges, 14 *Colum. J.L. & Soc. Probs.* 1 (1978).

Gomez, Marshal Costa, Nuclear Arms and the Danger of an Atomic War, in 2 *Towards a Nuclear Weapon-Free and Non-violent World* (V. Narasimha Rao 1990).

Goodman, Ryan, Human Rights Treaties, Invalid Reservations, and State Consent, 96 *Am. J. Int'l L.* 531 (2002).

Goodwin, Geoffrey, The General Assembly of the United Nations, in *The Evolution of International Organizations* 42 (Evan Luard ed., 1966).

Gordon, Edward, Discretion to Decline to Exercise Jurisdiction, 81 *Am. J. Int'l L.* 129 (1987).

Gordon, Edward, *"Legal Disputes" under Article 36(2) of the Statute, in The International Court of Justice at a Crossroads* 183 (Lori F. Damrosch ed., 1987).

Gorkovskiy, Evgeniy, The Evolving Role of the UN and Disarmament, in *The Future of Disarmament* 176 (United Nations ed., 1998).

Gotanda, John Y., Awarding Interest in International Arbitration, 90 *Am. J. Int'l L.* 40 (1996).

Gowlland-Debbas, Vera, The Limits of Unilateral Enforcement of Community Objectives in the Framework of UN Peace Maintenance, 11 *Eur. J. Int'l L.* 361 (2000).

Gowlland-Debbas, Vera, The Relationship between the International Court of Justice and the Security Council in the Light of the Lockerbie Case, 88 *Am. J. Int'l L.* 643 (1994).

Gowlland-Debbas, Vera, Security Council Enforcement Action and Issues of State Responsibility, 43 *Int'l Comp. L.Q.* 55 (1994).

Grad, Frank P., Consequences of Nuclear Weapons Use as Viewed by an Environmental Lawyer, in *Nuclear Weapons and Law* 387 (Arthur Selwyn Miller and Martin Feinrider ed., 1984).

Graham, Thomas, Jr., International Law and the Proliferation of Nuclear Weapons, 33 *Geo. Wash. Int'l L. Rev.* 49 (2000).

Grant, John P., Beyond the Montreal Convention, 36 *Case W. Res. J. Int'l L.* 453 (2004).

Gray, Christine, The Use and Abuse of the International Court of Justice: Cases Concerning the Use of Force after Nicaragua, 14 *Eur. J. Int'l L.* 867 (2003).

Gray, Christine and Benedict Kingsbury, Developments in Dispute Settlement: Inter-state Arbitration since 1945, 63 *Brit. Y.B. of Int'l L.* 97 (1992).

Greenwood, Christopher, New World Order or Old? The Invasion of Kuwait and the Rule of Law, 55 *Modern L. Rev.* 153 (1992).

Greenwood, Christopher, The Advisory Opinion on Nuclear Weapons and the Contribution of the International Court to International Humanitarian Law, 316 *Int'l Rev. Red Cross* 65 (1997).

Greig, Donald W., The Balancing of Interests and the Granting of Interim Protection by the International Court, 11 *Australian YB Int'l L.* 108 (1991).

Greig, Donald W., The Interpretation of Treaties and Article IV.2 of the Nuclear Non-proliferation Treaty, 6 *Aust. YB Int'l L.* 77 (1974).

Grieco, Joseph, Anarchy and the Limits of Cooperation: A Realist Critique of the Newest Liberal Institutionalism, 42 *Int'l Org.* 485 (1988).

Grief, Nicholas, The Legality of Nuclear Weapons, in *Nuclear Weapons and International Law* 22 (Istvan Pogany ed., 1987).

Grief, Nicholas, Legality of the Threat or Use of Nuclear Weapons, 46 *Int'l & Comp. L.Q.* 681 (1997).

Griffiths, John, What Is Legal Pluralism?, 19 *J. Legal Pluralism & Unofficial L.* 1 (1986).

Groom, A. J. R. and Jean-François Guilhaudis, UNSSODS: The Quest for Structure and Norms, in *Global Issues in the United Nations' Framework* 116 (Paul Taylor and A. J. R. Groom ed., 1989).

Grossman, Claudio, Supervision within the International Atomic Energy Agency, in *Supervisory Mechanisms in International Economic Organizations* 489 (P. van Dijk ed., 1984).

Grotto, Andrew, Why Do States That Oppose Nuclear Proliferation Resist New Nonproliferation Obligations? Three Logics of Nonproliferation Decision-Making, 18 *Cardozo J. Int'l & Comp. L.* 1 (2010).

Gu, Weixia, Confidentiality Revisited: Blessing or Curse in International Commercial Arbitration?, 15 *Am. Rev. Int'l Arb.* 607 (2004).

Gualtieri, David. S. et al., *Advancing the Law of Weapons Control: Comparative Approaches to Strengthen Nuclear Non-proliferation,* 16 *Mich. J. Int'l L.* 1029 (1995).

Guba, Egon G. and Yvonna S. Lincoln, Paradigmatic Controversies, Contradictions, and Emerging Influences, in *The Sage Handbook of Qualitative Research* 191 (Norman K. Denzin and Yvonna S. Lincoln ed., 3rd edn, 2005).

Guillaume, Gilbert, De l'indépendance des membres de la Cour internationale de justice, in *Boutros Boutros-Ghali Amicorum Discipulorumque Liber* 475 (1998).

Gutherie, Peter, Security Council Sanctions and the Protection of Individual Rights, 60 *NYU Annual Survey of American Law* 491 (2004).

Guzman, Andrew T., The Cost of Credibility: Explaining Resistance to Interstate Dispute Resolution Mechanisms, 31 *J. Legal Stud.* 303 (2002).

Hafner, Gerhard, Should one Fear the Proliferation of Mechanisms for the Peaceful Settlement of Disputes?, in *The Peaceful Settlement of Disputes between States: Universal and European Perspectives* 25 (Lucius Caflisch ed., 1998).

Haggard, Stephan and Beth A. Simmons, Theories of International Regimes, 41 *Int'l Org.* 491 (1987).

Hailbronner, Kay and Eckart Klein, Article 11, in *The Charter of the United Nations: A Commentary* 276 (Bruno Simma ed., 2002).

Hampson, Françoise and Hilaire McCoubrey, Evidence in Cases Involving Proliferation Issues, in *Future Legal Restraints on Arms Proliferation* 273 (Julie Dahlitz ed., 1996).

Happold, Matthew, Security Council Resolution 1373 and the Constitution of the United Nations, 16 *Leiden J. Int'l L.* 593 (2003).

Harper, Keith, Does the United Nations Security Council Have the Competence to Act as Court and Legislature?, 27 *N.Y.U. Int'l L. & Pol'y* 103 (1994).

Hayford, Stephen and Ralph Peeples, Commercial Arbitration in Evolution: An Assessment and Call for Dialogue, 10 *Ohio St. J. on Disp. Resol.* 343 (1995).

Hewitson, Patricia, Nonproliferation and Reduction of Nuclear Weapons: Risks of Weakening the Multilateral Nuclear Nonproliferation Norm, 21 *Berkeley J. Int'l L.* 405 (2003).

Heydte, F. von der, Le problème que pose l'existence des armes de destruction massive et la distinction entre les objectifs militaries et non militaries en general, 52(2) *Annuaire de l'Institut de droit international* 88 (1967).

Hilf, Meinhard and Daniel-Erasmus Khan, Article 22, in *The Charter of the United Nations: A Commentary* 420 (Bruno Simma ed., 2002).

Higgins, Rosalyn, The Desirability of Third-Party Adjudication: Conventional Wisdom or Continuing Truth?, in *International Organization: Law in Movement* 37 (J. E. S. Fawcett and Rosalyn Higgins ed., 1974).

Higgins, Rosalyn, Policy Considerations and the International Judicial Process, 17 *Int'l & Comp. L.Q.* 58 (1968).

Higgins, Rosalyn, Thomas M. Franck (1931–2009), 103 *Am. J. Int'l L.* 502 (2009).

Higgins, Rosalyn C., McDougal as Teacher, Mentor and Friend, 108 *Yale L.J.* 957 (1999).

Highet, Keith, Evidence, the Court and the Nicaragua Case, 81 *Am. J. Int'l L.* 1 (1987).

Highet, Keith, Litigation Implications of the U.S. Withdrawal from the Nicaragua Case, 79 *Am. J. Int'l L.* 992 (1985).

Hossain, Kamrul, Legality of Security Council Action: Does the ICJ Move to Take up the Challenge of Judicial Review?, 5 *Rev. Int'l L. & Pol* 133 (2009).

Howard, Michael, The United Nations and International Security, in *United Nations Divided World* 33 (Adam Roberts and Benedict Kingsbury ed., 1991).

Hutcheson, Joseph C., Jr., The Judgment Intuitive: The Function of the "Hunch" in Judicial Decision, 14 *Cornell L.Q.* 274 (1929).

Hutchinson, D. N., Solidarity and Breaches of Multilateral Treaties, 59 *Brit. Y.B. Int'l L.* 152 (1988).

Ikeberry, G. John, America's Imperial Ambition, *For. Aff.* 56 (Oct./Sept. 2002).

Jacobs, Francis G., Varieties of Approach to Treaty Interpretation: With Special Reference to the Draft Convention on the Law of Treaties before the Vienna Diplomatic Conference, 18 *Int'l & Comp. L.Q.* 318 (1969).

Janis, Mark, Individuals and the International Court, in *The International Court of Justice: Its Future Role after Fifty Years* 205 (A. Sam Muller et al. ed., 1997).

Japloner, Clemens, Kelsen and His Circle: The Viennese Years, 9 *Eur. J. Int'l L.* 368 (1998).

Jasentuliyana, Nandasiri, Effective Arms Control Law, in *The International Law of Arms Control and Disarmament* 172 (Julie Dahlitz and Detlev Dicke ed., 1991).

Jennings, Robert, Commentary on the Contributions of the Court to the Resolution of International Tensions, Proceedings of the ICJ/UNITAR Colloquium to Celebrate the 50th Anniversary of the Court, reprinted in *Increasing the Effectiveness of the International Court of Justice* 92 (Connie Peck and Roy S. Lee ed., 1997).

Jennings, Robert, International Courts and International Politics, in *Contemporary Issues in International Law* 13 (David Freestone et al. ed., 2002).

Jennings, Robert, Presentation on the Contributions of the Court to the Resolution of International Tensions, Proceedings of the ICJ/UNITAR Colloquium to Celebrate the 50th Anniversary of the Court, reprinted in *Increasing the Effectiveness of the International Court of Justice* 78 (Connie Peck and Roy S. Lee ed., 1997).

Jennings, Robert, Reflections on the Term *"Dispute"*, in *Essays in Honour of Wang Tieya* 401 (R. St. J. Macdonald ed., 1993).

Jennings, Robert, The Role of the International Court of Justice 68 *Brit. Y.B. Int'l L.* 1 (1997).

Jennings, Robert Y., The Differences between Conducting a Case in the ICJ and in an ad hoc Tribunal: An Inside View, in *Liber Amicorum Judge Shigeru Oda* 893 (N. Ando et al. ed., 2002).

Jibril, Nejib, The Binding Dilemma: From Bakassi to Badme – Making States Comply with Territorial Decisions of International Judicial Bodies, 19 *Am. U. Int'l L. Rev.* 633 (2004).

Jonas, David S., Variations on Non-nuclear: May the "Final Four" Join the Nuclear Nonproliferation Treaty as Non-nuclear Weapon States while Retaining Their Nuclear Weapons?, 2005 *Mich. St. L. Rev.* 417 (2005).

Jonas, David S. and Christopher Swift, Reformulating the Nuclear Nonproliferation Regime: Al-Qaeda, Global Terrorism, and the Rogue State Paradigm, 13 *UCLA J. Int'l L. & For. Aff.* 337 (2008).

Johnson, D. H. N., International Arbitration Back in Favour?, 34 *Y.B. World Aff.* 305 (1980).

Johnstone, Ian, Discursive Power in the UN Security Council, 21 *J. Int'l L. & Int'l Rel* 73 (2006).

Johnstone, Ian, Legal Argumentation in International Decision-Making, in *The Faultlines of Legitimacy* 175 (Hilary Charlesworth and Jean-Marc Coicaud ed., 2009).

Johnstone, Ian, Legislation and Adjudication in the UN Security Council: Bringing down the Deliberative Deficit, 102 *Am. J. Int'l L.* 275 (2008).

Johnstone, Ian, The Security Council as Legislature, in *The UN Security Council and the Politics of International Authority* 80 (Bruce Cronin and Ian Hurd ed., 2008).

Johnstone, Ian, Security Council Deliberations: The Power of the Better Argument, 14 *Eur. J. Int'l L.* 437 (2003).

Joyner, Christopher C., Collective Sanctions as Peaceful Coercion: Lessons from the United Nations Experience, 16 *Austl. Y.B. Int'l L.* 241 (1995).

Junker, Joel R., The Public Policy Defense to Recognition and Enforcement of Foreign Arbitral Awards, 7 *Cal. W. Int'l L.J.* 228 (1977).

Kalshoven, Frits, Arms, Armament and International Law, 191 *Rec. des Cours* 183 (1985-II).

Kanwar, Vik, Two Crises of Confidence: Securing Non-proliferation and the Rule of Law through Security Council Resolutions, 35 *Ohio N.U.L. Rev.* 171 (2009).

Katzler, Lynn, Should Mandatory Written Opinions Be Required in All Securities Arbitrations? The Practical and Legal Implications to the Securities Industry, 45 *Am. U.L. Rev.* 152 (1995).

Kaufmann-Kohler, Gabrielle, When Arbitrators Facilitate Settlement: Amiable Imposition or Actual Solution?, 25 *Arb. Int'l* 187 (2009).

Keeley, James F., Compliance and the Non-proliferation Treaty: Developments in Safeguards and Supply Controls, in *Treaty Compliance: Some Concerns and Remedies* 21 (Canadian Council on International Law ed., 1998).

Kellman, Barry, International Consensus and States Non-parties, in *Future Legal Restraints on Arms Proliferation* 151 (Julie Dahlitz ed., 1996).

Kellman, Barry and David S. Gualtieri, Barricading the Nuclear Window: A Legal Regime to Curtain Nuclear Smuggling, *U. Ill. L. Rev.* 667 (1996).

Kelsen, Hans, Sanctions in International Law under the Charter of the United Nations, 31 *Iowa L. Rev.* 499 (1946).

Kennedy, David, International Law and the Nineteenth Century: History of an Illusion, 17 *Quinnipiac L. Rev.* 99 (1997).

Kennedy, David, Theses about International Law Discourse, 23 *German Y.B. Int'l L.* 353 (1980).

Kennedy, David, Tom Franck and the Manhattan School, 35 *N.Y.U. J. Int'l L. & Pol.* 397 (2003).

Kennedy, David W., A New World Order: Yesterday, Today, and Tomorrow, 4 *Transnat'l L. & Contemp. Probs.* 329 (1994).

Kennedy, John F., Commencement Address at American University (June 10, 1963), in *"Let the Word Go Forth": The Speeches, Statements, and Writings of John F. Kennedy 1947–1963* 282 (1988).

Khosla, Dinesh, Nuclear Weapons, Global Values and International Law, in *Nuclear Weapons and Law* 13 (Arthur Selwyn Miller and Martin Feinrider ed., 1984).

Kirgis, Frederic L., Jr., The Security Council's First Fifty Years, 89 *Am. J. Int'l L.* 506 (1995).

Kittrie, Orde F., Averting Catastrophe: Why the Nuclear Nonproliferation Treaty Is Losing Its Deterrence Capacity and How to Restore It, 28 *Mich. J. Int'l L.* 337 (2007).

Klabbers, Jan, Constitutionalism Lite, 2 *Int'l Org. L. Rev.* 56 (2005).

Klabbers, Jan, The Life and Times of the Law of International Organizations, 70 *Nordic J. Int'l L.* 287 (2001).

Klabbers, Jan, Straddling Law and Politics: Judicial Review in International Law, in *Towards World Constitutionalism* 809 (Ronald St. John Macdonald and Douglas M. Johnston ed., 2005).

Klein, Natalie S., Multilateral Disputes and the Doctrine of Necessary Parties in the East Timor Case, 21 *Yale J. Int'l L.* 305 (1996).

Kline, Sara Needleman, Sexual Harassment, Wrongful Discharge, and Employer Liability: The Employer's Dilemma, 43 *Am. U.L. Rev.* 191 (1993).

Knop, Karen, Reflections on Thomas Franck, Race and Nationalism (1960): "General Principles of Law" and Situated Generality, 35 *N.Y.U.J. Int'l L. & Pol.* 437 (2003).

Kohen, Marcelo, The Notion of "State Survival", in *International Law, International Court of Justice and Nuclear Weapons* 293 (Laurence Boisson de Chazournes and Philippe Sands ed., 1999).

Kono, Tsutsomu, Role in Addressing WMD Issues: Assessment and Outlook, in *Arms Control after Iraq: Normative and Operational Challenges* 83 (Waheguru Pal Singh Sidhu and Ramesh Thakur ed., 2006).

Kooijmans, Pieter H., International Arbitration in Historical Perspective: Past and Present (Comments on a Paper by Professor L.B. Sohn), in *International Arbitration: Past and Prospects* 23 (A. H. A. Soons 1990).

Koplow, David A., The Jurisprudence of Non-proliferation: Taking International Law Seriously, 2 *Transnat'l L & Contemp. Probs.* 357 (1992).

Koplow, David A., Parsing Good Faith: Has the United States Violated Article VI of the Nuclear Non-proliferation Treaty?, *Wis. L. Rev.* 301 (1993).

Koppel, Glenn S., Reflections on the "Chimera" of a Uniform Code of State Civil Procedure: The Virtue of Vision in Procedural Reform, 58 *DePaul L. Rev.* 971 (2009).

Korkeakivi, Antti, Consequences of "Higher" International Law: Evaluating Crimes of State and Erga Omnes, 2 *J. Int'l Legal Stud.* 81 (1996).

Koskenniemi, Martti, Faith, Identity and the Killing of the Innocent: International Lawyers and Nuclear Weapons, 10 *Leiden J. Int'l L.* 137 (1997).

Koskenniemi, Martti, The Politics of International Law, 1 *Eur. J. Int'l L.* 4 (1990).

Koskenniemi, Martti, The Silence of Law/The Voice of Justice, in *International Law, the International Court of Justice and Nuclear Weapons* 509 (Laurence Boisson de Chazournes and Philippe Sands ed., 1999).

Koskenniemi, Martti, What Is International Law For?, in *International Law* 89 (Malcolm Evans ed., 3rd edn, 2010).

Krasner, Stephen D., *Structural Causes and Regime Consequences: Regimes as Intervening Variables*, in International Regimes 1 (Stephen D. Krasner ed., 1983).

Kreindler, Richard H., "Arbitral Forum Shopping": Observations on Recent Developments in International Commercial and Investment Arbitration, 16 *Am. Rev. Int'l Arb.* 157 (2005).

Kristjansdottir, Edda, The Legality of the Threat or Use of Nuclear Weapons under Current International Law: The Arguments behind the World Court's Advisory Opinion, 30 *N.Y.U. J. Int'l L. & Pol.* 291 (1998).

Kuhner, Timothy K., Human Rights Treaties in U.S. Law: The Status Quo, Its Underlying Bases, and Pathways for Change, 13 *Duke J. Comp. & Int'l L.* 419 (2003).

Kuhner, Timothy K., The Status of Victims in the Enforcement of International Criminal Law, 6 *Or. Rev. Int'l L.* 95 (2004).

Kurkela, Matti, Due Process in Arbitration: A Finnish Perspective, 21 *J. Int'l Arb.* 221 (2004).

Lachs, Manfred, The Law and the Settlement of International Disputes, in *Dispute Settlement through the United Nations* 283 (K. Venkata Raman ed., 1977).

Lachs, Manfred, Some Thoughts on the Role of Good Faith in International Law, in *Declarations on Principles: A Quest for Universal Peace* 47 (Robert J. Akkerman et al. ed., 1977).

Laird, Ian and Rebecca Askew, Finality versus Consistency: Does Investor–State Arbitration Need an Appellate System, 7 *J. App. Prac. & Process* 285 (2005).

Lalive, Pierre, Transnational (or Truly International) Public Policy and International Arbitration, in *Comparative Arbitration Practice and Public Policy in Arbitration* 257 (Pieter Sanders ed., 1987).

Lalla, Vejay, The Effectiveness of the Comprehensive Test Ban Treaty on Nuclear Weapons Proliferation: A Review of Nuclear Non-proliferation Treaties and the Impact of the Indian and Pakistani Nuclear Tests on the Non-proliferation Regime, 8 *Cardozo J. Int'l & Comp. L.* 103 (2000).

Larson, Arthur, The Role of Law in Building Peace, in *Preventing World War III: Some Proposals* 332 (Quincy Wright et al. ed., 1962).

Laudy, Mark, The Vatican Mediation of the Beagle Channel Dispute, in *Words over War: Mediation and Arbitration to Prevent Deadly Conflict* 293 (Melanie C. Greenberg et al. ed., 2000).

Lavalle, Roberto, Nationality as a Factor in the Election of the Members of the International Court of Justice, with Particular Reference to Occasional Elections, 29 *Revue belge de droit international* 625 (1996).

Leben, Charles, Hans Kelsen and the Advancement of International Law, 9 *Eur. J. Int'l L.* 287 (1998).

Lee, Eric Yong-Joong, The Six-Party Talks and the North Korean Nuclear Dispute Resolution under the IAEA Safeguards Regime, 5 *Asian–Pacific L. & Pol'y J.* 101 (2004).

Lee, Luke T., The Legality of Nuclear Tests and Weapons, 18 *Österreichische Zeitschrift für öffentliches Recht* 307 (1968).

Legal Models of Arms Control: Past, Present, and Future, 100 *Harv. L. Rev.* 1326 (1987).

Leitner, Matthew, The First Cold War: The Battle for Europe, speech at the Graduate Institute of International Studies, May 8, 2006 (on file with the author).

Lelewer, Joanne K., International Commercial Arbitration as a Model for Resolving Treaty Disputes, 21 *N.Y.U. J. Int'l L. & Pol.* 379, 401 (1989).

Lewis, Patricia, Why We Got It Wrong: Attempting to Unravel the Truth of Bioweapons in Iraq, in *Arms Control after Iraq: Normative and Operational Challenges* 160 (Waheguru Pal Singh Sidhu and Ramesh Thakur ed., 2006).

Lewis, William H. and Christopher C. Joyner, Proliferation of Unconventional Weapons: The Case for Coercive Arms Control, 10 *Comp. Strategy* 299 (1991).

Liles, Matthew, Did Kim Jong-Il Break the Law? A Case Study on How North Korea Highlights the Flaws of the Non-proliferation Regime, 33 *N.C. J. Int'l L. & Com. Reg.* 103 (2007).

Lobel, Jules and Michael Ratner, Bypassing the Security Council: Ambiguous Authorizations to Use Force, Cease-Fires and the Iraqi Inspection Regime, 93 *Am. J. Int'l L.* 124 (1999).

Lodgaard, Sverre, Iran's Uncertain Nuclear Ambitions, in *Nuclear Proliferation and International Security* 96 (Morten Bremer Mærli and Sverre Lodgaard ed., 2007).

Loewenstein, Andrew B. and Stephen A. Kostas, Divergent Approaches to Determining Responsibility for Genocide, 5 *J. Int'l Crim. Justice* 839 (2007).

Lowe, A. Vaughan, Shock Verdict: Nuclear War May or May Not Be Unlawful, 55 *Cambridge L. J.* 415 (1996).

Luhmann, Niklas, Quod Omnes Tangit: Remarks on Jürgen Habermas's Legal Theory, 17 *Cardozo L. Rev.* 883 (1996).

Lund, Matthew, The Eighty Percent and Twenty Percent Solutions to Nuclear Proliferation, *BYU L. Rev.* 741 (2009).

Lysén, Göran, The Adequacy of the Law of Treaties Regarding Arms Control Agreements, in *Avoidance and Settlement of Arms Control Disputes* 123 (Julie Dahlitz ed., 1994).

McCormack, Timothy L. H., A Non Liquet on Nuclear Weapons: The ICJ avoids the Application of General Principles of International Humanitarian Law, 316 *Int'l Rev. Red Cross* 76 (1997).

Macdonald, Ronald St. John, The Charter of the United Nations and the Development of Fundamental Principles of International Law, in *Contemporary Problems of International Law: Essays in Honour of Georg Schwarzenberger* 196 (Bin Cheng and E. D. Brown ed., 1988).

McDonell, Neil E., The Availability of Provisional Relief in International Arbitration, 22 *Colum. J. Transnat'l L.* 273 (1984).

McDougal, Myres, Some Basic Theoretical Concepts about International Law: A Policy-Oriented Framework of Enquiry, 4 *J. Conflict Res.* 337 (1960).

MacKay, Don, Nuclear Testing: New Zealand and France in the International Court of Justice, 19 *Fordham Int'l L.J.* 1857 (1996).

Mackenzie, Ruth, International Courts and Tribunals and the Independence of the International Judge, 44 *Harv. Int'l L.J.* 271 (2003).

McLaughlin, Gerald T., Remembering the Bay of Pigs: Using Letters of Credit to Facilitate the Resolution of International Disputes, 32 *Ga. J. Int'l & Comp. L.* 743 (2004).

McNeill, John H., Commentary on Dispute Resolution Mechanisms in Arms Control Agreements, in *Law and Force in the New International Order* 258 (Lori Fisler D. and David J. Scheffer ed., 1991).

McNiel, Dale E., The NAFTA Panel Decision on Canadian Tariff-Rate Quotas: Imagining a Tariffying Bargain, 22 *Yale J. Int'l L.* 345 (1997).

Mahmoudi, Said, The International Court of Justice and Nuclear Weapons, 66 *Nordic J. Int'l L.* 7 (1997).
Makarczyk, Jerzy, The International Court of Justice on the Implied Powers of International Organizations, in *Essays in International Law in Honour of Judge Manfred Lachs* 501 (Jerzy Makarczyk ed., 1984).
Mallison, W. Thomas, The Laws of War and Juridical Control of Weapons of Mass Destruction in General and Limited War, 36 *Geo. Wash. L. Rev.* 308 (1968).
Mallison, W. Thomas and Sally V. Mallison, The Israeli Aerial Attack of June 7, 1981, upon the Iraqi Nuclear Reactor: Aggression or Self-Defense?, 15 *Vand. J. Transnat'l L.* 417 (1982).
Malone, David M., The Security Council in the 1990s: Inconsistent, Improvisational, Indispensable?, in *New Millennium, New Perspectives: The United Nations, Security and Governance* 21 (Ramesh Thakur and Edward Newman ed., 2000).
Malone, Wex S., Ruminations on Cause-in-Fact, 9 *Stan. L. Rev.* 60 (1956).
Mani, Rama, Peaceful Settlement of Disputes and Conflict Prevention, in *The Oxford Handbook on the United Nations* 300 (Thomas G. Weiss and Sam Daws ed., 2007).
Maniruzzaman, Abul F. M., The Lex Mercatoria and International Contracts: A Challenge for International Commercial Arbitration?, 14 *Am. U. Int'l L. Rev.* 657 (1999).
Manouvel, Mita, Métamorphose de l'article 41 du Statut de la CIJ, 106 *RGDIP* 103 (2002).
Margolish, Emanuel, The Hydrogen Bomb Experiments and International Law, 64 *Yale L. J.* 629 (1955).
Mark, J. Carson, Consequences of Nuclear War, in *The Dangers of Nuclear War* 7 (Franklyn Griffiths and John C. Polanyi ed., 1979).
Martenczuk, Bernd, The Security Council, the International Court and Judicial Review, 10 *Eur. J. Int'l L.* 517 (1999).
Martin, Paul, Chavez, the Organization of American States, and Democracy in International Law, 46 *Alberta L. Rev.* 933 (2009).
Matheson, Michael J., The Opinions of the International Court of Justice on the Threat or Use of Nuclear Weapons, 91 *Am. J. Int'l L.* 417 (1997).
Meise, Gary J., Securing the Strength of the Renewed NPT: China, the Linchpin "Middle Kingdom", 30 *Vand. J. Transnat'l L.* 539 (1997).
Meltzer, Joshua, State Sovereignty and the Legitimacy of the WTO, 26 *U. Pa. J. Int'l Econ. L.* 693 (2005).
Menaker, Andrea J., Benefiting from Experience, in the United States' Most Recent Investment Agreements, 12 *U.C. Davis J. Int'l L. & Pol'y* 121 (2005).
Merrills, John G., The Contribution of the Permanent Court of Arbitration to International Law and to the Settlement of Disputes by Peaceful Means, in *The*

Permanent Court of Arbitration: International Arbitration and Dispute Resolution 3 (P. Hamilton et al. ed., 1999).

Merrills, John G., Interim Measures of Protection in the Recent Jurisprudence of the International Court of Justice, 44 *Int'l & Comp. L.Q.* 90 (1995).

Merrills, John G., The Means of Dispute Settlement, in *International Law* 529 (Malcolm Evans ed., 2003).

Merrills, John G., The Optional Clause at Eighty, in *Liber Amicorum Judge Shigeru Oda* 435 (Nisuke Ando et al. ed., 2002).

Merrills, John G., The Optional Clause Revisited, 64 *Brit. Y.B. Int'l L.* 197 (1993).

Merrills, John G., The Role and Limits of International Adjudication, in *International Law and the International System* 169 (William E. Butler ed., 1987).

Meyrowitz, Elliott L., The Laws of War and Nuclear Weapons, in *Nuclear Weapons and Law* 19 (Arthur Selwyn Miller and Martin Feinrider ed., 1984).

Meyrowitz, Henri, Les juristes devant l'arme nucléaire, 1963 *RGDIP* 820 (1963).

Meyrowitz, Henri, La stratégie nucléaire et le Protocole additionnel aux Conventions de Genève de 1949, 83 *RGDIP* 905 (1979).

Mian, Ajmal, The Challenge of Nuclear Proliferation Control in South Asia, in *Future Legal Restraints on Arms Proliferation* 187 (Julie Dahlitz ed., 1996).

Miller, Steven E., Proliferation Gamesmanship: Iran and the Politics of Nuclear Confrontation, 57 *Syracuse L. Rev.* 551 (2007).

Millet, A. S., Les avis consultatifs de la Cour international de Justice du 8 Juillet 1996, 101 *RGDIP* 141 (1997).

Mohr, Manfred, Advisory Opinion of the International Court of Justice on the Legality of the Use of Nuclear Weapons under International Law: A Few Thoughts on Its Strengths and Weaknesses, 316 *Int'l Rev. Red Cross* 92 (1997).

Moore, John Norton, Nuclear Weapons and the Law: Enhancing Strategic Stability, in *Nuclear Weapons and Law* 51 (Arthur Selwyn Miller and Martin Feinrider ed., 1984).

Morgenthau, Hans J., Positivism, Functionalism and International Law, 34 *Am. J. Int'l L.* 260 (1940).

Morriss, David M., From War to Peace: A Study of Cease-Fire Agreements and the Evolving Role of the United Nations, 36 *Va. J. Int'l L.* 801 (1996).

Mosk, Richard M., Lessons from the Hague: An Update on the Iran–United States Claims Tribunal, 14 *Pepp. L. Rev.* 814 (1987).

Mosler, Hermann, Article 96, in The Charter of the United Nations: A Commentary 1008 (Bruno Simma ed., 1994).

Müller, Harald, Dealing with WMD Crises: The Role of the United Nations in Compliance Politics, in *Arms Control after Iraq: Normative and Operational Challenges* 114 (Waheguru Pal Singh Sidhu and Ramesh Thakur ed., 2006).

Murphy, John F., Force and Arms, in 1 *United Nations Legal Order* 247 (Oscar Schachter and Christopher Joyner ed., 1995).

Myjer, Eric P. J., The Law of Arms-Control and International Supervision, in *The United Nations Decade of International Law: Reflections on International Disputes Settlement* 99 (Marcel Brus et al. ed., 1991).

Myjer, Eric P. J., The Settlement of Disputes under the Chemical Weapons Convention and the Case of the Confidentiality Commission, in *The Convention on the Prohibition and Elimination of Chemical Weapons: A Breakthrough in Multilateral Disarmament* 537 (Daniel Bardonnet ed., 1995).

Nafziger, James A. R., Political Dispute Resolution by the World Court, with Reference to United States Courts, 26 *Denv. J. Int'l L. & Pol'y* 775 (1998).

Nance, Dale A., The Best Evidence Principle, 73 *Iowa L. Rev.* 227 (1988).

Nanda, Ved, Nuclear Weapons and the Right to Peace under International Law, 9 *Brooklyn J. Int'l L.* 283 (1983).

Nazario, Edwin J., The Potential Role of Arbitration in the Nuclear Non-proliferation Treaty Regime, 10 *Am. Rev. Int'l Arb.* 139 (1999).

Netanel, Neil Weinstock, Cyberspace Self-Governance: A Skeptical View from Liberal Democratic Theory, 88 *Cal. L. Rev.* 395 (2000).

Neuhold, Hanspeter, Legal Aspects of Arms Control Agreements, in Law of Nations, Law of International Organizations, World's Economic Law 427 (Karl-Heinz Böckstiegel et al. ed., 1988).

Nolte, Georg, Lawmaking through the UN Security Council: A Comment on Erika de Wet's Contribution, in *Developments of International Law in Treaty Making* 237 (Rüdiger Wolfrum and Volker Röben ed., 2005).

Nolte, Georg, The Limits of the Security Council's Powers and Its Functions in the International Legal System: Some Reflections, in *The Role of Law in International Politics* 315 (Michael Byers ed., 2000).

Noyes, Henry S., If You (Re)Build It, They Will Come: Contracts to Remake the Rules of Litigation in Arbitration's Image, 30 *Harv. J.L. & Pub. Pol'y* 579 (2007).

Nozick, Robert, Coercion, in Philosophy, Science, and Method: Essays in Honor of Ernest Nagel 440 (Sidney Morgenbesser et al. ed., 1969).

Nsereko, Daniel D., The International Court, Impartiality and Judges ad hoc, 13 *Indian J. Int'l L.* 207 (1973).

Obama, Barack, Renewing American Leadership, *For. Aff.* 8 (July/Aug. 2007).

Oellers-Frahm, Karin, Article 41, in *The Statute of the International Court of Justice: A Commentary* 923 (Andreas Zimmermann et al. ed., 2006).

Orrego, Cristobal, Natural Law under Other Names: De Nominibus non est Disputandum, 52 *Am. J. Juris.* 77 (2007).

Onuma, Hideharu, The ICJ: An Emperor without Clothes? International Conflict Resolution, Article 38 of the ICJ Statute and the Sources of International Law, in *Liber Amicorum Judge Shigeru Oda* 191 (Nisuke Ando et al. ed., 2002).

Oosthuizen, Gabriël, Playing the Devil's Advocate: The UN Security Council Is Unbound by Law, 12 *Leiden J. Int'l L.* 549 (1999).

Owen, Harold J., Compulsory Jurisdiction of the International Court of Justice: A Study of Its Acceptance by Nations, 3 *Ga. L. Rev.* 704 (1969).

Oxman, Bernard H., Complementary Agreements and Compulsory Jurisdiction, 95 *Am. J. Int'l L.* 277 (2001).

Oyuela, Miguel E. Estrada, The Tlatelolco Treaty (1967), in *Verification of Current Disarmament and Arms Limitation Agreements: Ways, Means and Practices* 149 (Serge Sur ed., 1991).

Ozaki, Shigeyoshi, International Law and Coercion, 27 *Japanese Annual of Int'l L.* 12 (1984).

Pallieri, G. Balladore, Le droit interne des organisations internationales, 127 *Rec. des cours* 1 (1969-II).

Panofsky, Wolfgang, Barriers to Negotiated Arms Control, in *Barriers to Conflict Resolution* 310 (Kenneth J. Arrow et al. ed., 1995).

Park, William W., Safeguarding Procedural Integrity in International Arbitration, 63 *Tul. L. Rev.* 647 (1989).

Parry, Clive, Some Considerations upon the Protection of Individuals in International Law, 90 *Rec. des Cours* 653 (1956).

Paulson, Colter, Compliance with Final Judgments of the International Court of Justice since 1987, 98 *Am. J. Int'l. L.* 434 (2004).

Paulsson, Jan, Avoiding Unintended Consequences, in *Appeals Mechanism in International Investment Disputes* 241 (Karl P. Sauvant and Michael Chiswick-Patterson ed., 2008).

Paulus, Andreas, Article 29, in *The Charter of the United Nations: A Commentary* 539 (Bruno Simma ed., 2002).

Pauwelyn, Joost, The Role of Public International Law in the WTO: How Far Can We Go?, 95 *Am. J. Int'l L.* 535 (2001).

Pauwelyn, Joost, A Typology of Multilateral Treaty Obligations: Are WTO Obligations Bilateral or Collective in Nature?, 14 *Euro. J. Int'l L.* 907 (2003).

Pechota, Vratislav, The Future of the Law Governing the International Arbitral Process: Unification and Beyond, 3 *Am. Rev. Int'l Arb.* 17 (1992).

Pellet, Alain, Commentary on the Contributions of the Court to the Resolution of International Tensions, Proceedings of the ICJ/UNITAR Colloquium to Celebrate the 50th Anniversary of the Court, reprinted in *Increasing the Effectiveness of the International Court of Justice* 91 (Connie Peck and Roy S. Lee ed., 1997).

Pélopidas, Benoît, Comparative and Prospective Looks at the EU Non-proliferation Policy, in *Europe Facing Nuclear Weapons Challenges* 181 (Grégory Boutherin ed., 2008).

Perez, Antonio F., Survival of Rights under the Nuclear Non-proliferation Treaty: Withdrawal and the Continuing Right of International Atomic Energy Agency Safeguards, 34 *Va. J. Int'l L.* 749 (1994).

Pernice, Ingolf, The Treaty of Lisbon: Multilevel Constitutionalism in Action, 15 *Colum. J. Eur. L.* 349 (2009).

Perrin de Brichambaut, Marc, Les avis consultatifs de la CIJ sur la licéité des armes nucléaires, 42 *AFDI* 315 (1996).

Petersmann, Ernst-Ulrich, The Dispute Settlement System of the World Trade Organization and the Evolution of the GATT Dispute Settlement System since 1948, 31 *Common Mkt. L. Rev.* 1157 (1994).

Petrovsky, Vladimir, Foreword, in *Future Legal Restraints on Arms Proliferation* 1 (Julie Dahlitz ed., 1996).

Picker, Colin B., Reputational Fallacies in International Law: A Comparative Review of United States and Canadian Trade Actions, 30 *Brook. J. Int'l L.* 67 (2004).

Pilat, Joseph F. and Charles W. Nakhleh, A Treaty Reborn? The NPT after Extension, in *The Nuclear Non-proliferation Regime* 41 (Raju G. C. Thomas ed., 1998).

Posner, Eric A. and Miguel F. P. de Figueiredo, Is the International Court of Justice Biased, 34 *J. Legal Stud.* 599 (2005).

Posner, Eric A. and John C. Yoo, Judicial Independence in International Tribunals, 93 *Cal. L. Rev.* 1 (2005).

Prager, Dietmar W., The Proliferation of International Judicial Organs: The Role of the International Court of Justice, in *Proliferation of International Organizations: Legal Issues* 279 (Niels M. Blokker and Henry G. Schermers ed., 2001).

Printer, Norman G., Jr., Establishing an International Criminal Tribunal for Iraq: The Time Is Now, 36 *UWLA L. Rev.* 27 (2005).

Puissochet, Jean-Pierre, The Court of Justice and International Action by the European Community: The Example of the Embargo against the Former Yugoslavia, 20 *Fordham Int'l L.J.* 1557 (1997).

Purdy, Jedediah and Kimberly Fielding, Sovereigns, Trustees, Guardians: Private-Law Concepts and the Limits of Legitimate State Power, 70 *Law & Contemp. Prob.* 165 (2007).

Rabkin, Jeremy, The Politics of the Geneva Conventions: Disturbing Background to the ICC Debate, 44 *Va. J. Int'l L.* 169 (2003).

Radin, Margaret Jane, Reconsidering the Rule of Law, 69 *B.U.L. Rev.* 781 (1989).

Raines, Erik, North Korea: Analyzing the "New" Nuclear Threat, 12 *Cardozo J. Int'l & Comp. L.* 349 (2004).

Raman, K. Venkata, Introduction to Part I, in *Dispute Settlement through the United Nations* 53 (K. Venkata Raman ed., 1977).

Randelzhofer, Albrecht, Article 51, in *The Charter of the United Nations: A Commentary* 788 (Bruno Simma ed., 2002).

Ratner, Steven R., Land Feuds and Their Solutions: Finding International Law beyond the Tribunal Chamber, 100 *Am. J. Int'l L.* 808 (2006).

Ratner, Steven R., Precommitment Theory and International Law: Starting a Conversation, 81 *Tex. L. Rev.* 2055 (2003).

Rauf, Tariq and Jan Lodding, UNSCR 1540 and the Role of the IAEA, in *Global Non-proliferation and Counter-Terrorism: The Impact of UNSCR 1540* 86 (Olivia Bosch and Peter Van Ham ed., 2007).

Rauschning, Dietrich, Nuclear Warfare and Weapons, 4 *Encyclopedia of Public International Law* 44 (1982).

Raymond, Gregory A., International Adjudication and Conflict Management, in *Sovereignty and the Global Community: The Quest for Order in the International System* 221 (Howard M. Hensel ed., 2004).

Raymond, John M. and Barbara J. Frischholz, Lawyers Who Established International Law in the United States, 1776–1914, 76 *Am. J. Int'l. L.* 802 (1982).

Raz, Joseph, The Relevance of Coherence, 72 *B.U.L. Rev.* 273 (1992).

Reichert, Douglas D., Problems with Parallel and Duplicate Proceedings: The Litispendence Principle and International Arbitration, 8 *Arb. Int'l* 237 (1992).

Reinisch, August, Developing Human Rights and Humanitarian Law Accountability of the Security Council for the Imposition of Economic Sanctions, 95 *Am. J. Int'l L.* 851 (2001).

Reisman, W. Michael, The Breakdown of the Control Mechanism in ICSID Arbitration, 1989 *Duke L.J.* 739 (1989).

Reisman, W. Michael, Deterrence and International Law, in *Nuclear Weapons and Law* 129 (Arthur Selwyn Miller and Martin Feinrider ed., 1984).

Reisman, W. Michael and Eric E. Freedman, The Plaintiff's Dilemma: Illegally Obtained Evidence and Admissibility in International Adjudication, 76 *Am. J. Int'l L.* 737 (1982).

Rhinelander, John B., Limitations and Safeguards in Arms Control Agreements, in *Law and Force in the New International Order* 247 (Lori F. Damrosch and David J. Scheffer ed., 1991).

Risse, Thomas, Let's Argue! Communicative Action in World Politics, 54 *Int'l Org.* 1 (2000).

Ritter, J. P., L'affaire des essays nucléaires et la notion de jugement déclaratoire, 1975 *AFDI* 278 (1975).

Roberts, Adam, The Relevance of Laws of War in the Nuclear Age, in *Nuclear Weapons: The Peace Movement and the Law* 25 (J. Dewar et al. ed., 1986).

Roberts, Adam and Benedict Kingsbury, The UN's Roles in a Divided World, in *United Nations Divided World* 1 (Adam Roberts and Benedict Kingsbury ed., 1991).

Roberts, Guy B., The Counterproliferation Self-Help Paradigm: A Legal Regime for Enforcing the Norm Prohibiting the Proliferation of Weapons of Mass Destruction, 27 *Denv. J. Int'l L. & Pol'y* 483 (1999).

Roberts, Ken, Second-Guessing the Security Council: The International Court of Justice and Its Powers of Judicial Review, 7 *Pace Int'l L. Rev.* 281 (1995).

Rogers, Catherine A., Regulating International Arbitrator: A Functional Approach to Developing Standards of Conduct, 41 *Stan. J. Int'l L.* 53 (2005).

Röling, B. V. A., International Law, Nuclear Weapons, Arms Control and Disarmament, in *Nuclear Weapons and Law* 181 (Arthur Selwyn Miller and Martin Feinrider ed., 1984).

Romano, Cesare P. R., The Proliferation of International Judicial Bodies: The Pieces of the Puzzle, 31 *NYU J. Int'l L. & Pol.* 709 (1999).

Romano, Cesare P. R., The Shift from the Consensual to the Compulsory Paradigm in International Adjudication: Elements for a Theory of Consent, 39 *N.Y.U. J. Int'l L. & Pol.* 791 (2007).

Rosand, Eric, The Security Council as "Global Legislator": Ultra Vires or Ultra Innovative?, 28 *Fordham Int'l L.J.* 542 (2005).

Rosand, Eric, Security Council Resolution 1373, the Counter-terrorism Committee, and the Fight against Terrorism, 97 *Am. J. Int'l L.* 333 (2003).

Rosenne, Shabtai, "Consent" and Related Words in the Codified Law of Treaties, in *Mélanges offerts à Charles Rousseau* 229 (La Communauté Internationale ed., 1974).

Rostow, Nicholas, The World Health Organization, the International Court of Justice, and Nuclear Weapons, 20 *Yale J. Int'l L.* 151 (1995).

Rubin, Alfred P., Secession and Self-Determination: A Legal, Moral, and Political Analysis, 36 *Stan. J. Int'l L.* 253 (2000).

Sabahi, Babback, The ICJ's Authority to Invalidate Security Council Decisions under Chapter VII: Legal Romanticism or the Rule of Law?, 17 *N.Y. Int'l L. Rev.* 1 (2004).

Sajoo, Amynmohamed, Human Rights Perspectives on the Arms Race, 28 *McGill L. Rev.* 628 (1982).

Sandoz, Yves, Advisory Opinion of the International Court of Justice on the Legality of the Threat or Use of Nuclear Weapons, 316 *Int'l Rev. Red Cross* 6 (1997).

Schachter, Oscar, Disputes Involving the Use of Force, in *The International Court of Justice at a Crossroads* 223 (Lori F. Damrosch ed., 1987).

Schachter, Oscar, International Law in Theory and Practice, 178 *Rec. des Cours* 13 (1982).

Schauer, Frederick, Precedent, 39 *Stan. L. Rev.* 571 (1987).

Schill, Stephan W., System-Building in Investment Treaty Arbitration and Lawmaking, 12 *German L.J.* 1083 (2011).

Schlochauer, Hans-Jürgen, Arbitration, in 1 *Encyclopedia of Public International Law* 215 (Rudolf Bernhardt ed., 1992).

Schmitt, Michael N., The International Court of Justice and the Use of Nuclear Weapons, 7 *J. Legal Studies* 57 (1997).

Schneider, Andrea K., Individual Rights in International Trade Organizations, 19 *U. Pa. J. Int'l Econ. L.* 587 (1998).

Schneider, Jan, The Gulf of Maine Case: The Nature of an Equitable Result, 79 *Am. J. Int'l L.* 539 (1985).

Schütz, Hans-Joachim, Article 26, in *The Charter of the United Nations: A Commentary* 464 (Bruno Simma ed., 2002).

Schwartz, Michael G. and Amy Yip-Kikugawa, Sunshine Beauty Supplies, Inc. v. United States District Court: Mandatory Venue and Motions to Confirm or Vacate under the Federal Arbitration Act, 32 *U.S.F.L. Rev.* 629 (1998).

Schwebel, Stephen M., Comment, The Prospects for International Arbitration: Inter-State Disputes, in *International Arbitration: Past and Prospects* 101 (A. H. A. Soons ed., 1990).

Schwebel, Stephen M., National Judges and Judges Ad Hoc of the International Court of Justice, 48 *Int'l & Comp. L.Q.* 889 (1999).

Schwebel, Stephen M., The Performance and Prospects of the World Court, 6 *Pace Int'l L. Rev.* 253 (1994).

Seidl-Hohenveldern, I., Access of International Organizations to the International Court of Justice, in *The International Court of Justice: Its Future Role after Fifty Years* 189 (A. S. Muller, D. Raic and J. M. Thuransky ed., 1997).

Sena, Pasquale De and Maria Vitucci, The European Courts and the Security Council: Between Dedoublement Fonctionnel and Balancing of Values, 20 *Eur. J. Int'l L.* 193 (2009).

Shahabuddeen, Mohamed, The World Court at the Turn of the Century, in *The International Court of Justice: Its Future Role after Fifty Years* 3 (A. S. Muller et al. ed., 1997).

Shahshahani, Sepehr, Politics under the Cover of Law: Can International Law Help Resolve the Iran Nuclear Crisis?, 25 *B.U. Int'l L.J.* 369 (2007).

Shany, Yuval, Squaring the Circle? Independence and Impartiality of Party-Appointed Adjudicators in International Legal Proceedings, 30 *Loy. L.A. Int'l & Comp. L. Rev.* 473 (2008).

Shaw, Malcolm, The Beagle Channel Arbitration Award, 6 *Int'l Relations* 415 (1978).

Shaw, Malcolm N., Nuclear Weapons and International Law, in *Nuclear Weapons and International Law* 1 (Istvan Pogany ed., 1987).

Shaw, Malcolm N., The Security Council and the International Court of Justice: Judicial Drift and Judicial Function, in *The International Court of Justice: Its Future Role after Fifty Years* 219 (A. S. Muller et al. ed., 1997).

Shelton, Dinah, Form, Function, and the Powers of International Courts, 9 *Chi. J. Int'l L.* 537 (2009).

Shelton, Dinah, International Law and "Relative Normativity", in *International Law* 145 (Malcolm D. Evans ed., 2003).

Shraga, Daphna, U.N. Peacekeeping Operations: Applicability of International Humanitarian Law and Responsibility for Operations-Related Damage, 94 *Am. J. Int'l L.* 406 (2000).

Sicilianos, Linos-Alexander, The Classification of Obligations and the Multilateral Dimension of the Relations of International Responsibility, 13 *Euro. J. Int'l L.* 1127 (2002).

Simpson, Gerry, On the Magic Mountain: Teaching Public International Law, 10 *Eur. J. Int'l L.* 70 (1999).

Sinclair, Ian, Some Procedural Aspects of Recent International Litigation, 30 *Int'l & Comp. L.Q.* 338 (1981).

Sinclair, Ian, State Crimes Implementation Problems: Who Reacts?, in *International Crimes of State* 256 (Joseph H. H. Weiler et al. ed., 1989).

Sinclair, Ian M., Vienna Conference on the Law of Treaties, 19 *Int'l & Comp. L.Q.* 47 (1970).

Skubiszewski, Krzysztof, Implied Powers of International Organizations, in *International Law at a Time of Perplexity: Essays in Honour of Shabtai Rosenne* 855 (Yoram Dinstein ed., 1989).

Slater, Alice, The "Inalienable Right" to Peaceful Nuclear Power: A Recipe for Chaos, in *At the Nuclear Precipice: Catastrophe or Transformation?* 57 (Richard Falk and David Krieger ed., 2008).

Sloan, Blaine, The United Nations Charter as a Constitution, 1 *Pace Y.B. Int'l L.* 61 (1989).

Sloss, David, It's Not Broken, So Don't Fix It: The International Atomic Energy Agency Safeguards System and the Nuclear Nonproliferation Treaty, 35 *Va. J. Int'l L.* 841 (1995).

Smit, Robert H. and Nicholas J. Shaw, The Center for Public Resources Rules for Non-administered Arbitration of International Disputes: A Critical and Comparative Commentary, 8 *Am. Rev. Int'l Arb.* 275 (1997).

Smith, Edwin, Commentary on Arms Control Agreements and Dynamic Obligations, in *Law and Force in the New International Order* 262 (Lori F. Damrosch and David J. Scheffer ed., 1991).

Smith, Murray L., Impartiality of the Party-Appointed Arbitrator, 6 *Arb. Int'l* 320 (1990).

Sohn, Louis B., The Future of Dispute Settlement, in *The Structure and Process of International Law* 1121 (R. St. J. Macdonald and Douglas M. Johnston ed., 1986).

Sohn, Louis B., The Role of Arbitration in Recent International Multilateral Treaties, 23 *Va. J. Int'l L.* 171 (1982–1983).

Sohn, Louis B., Settlement of Disputes Relating to the Interpretation and Application of Treaties, 150 *Rec. des Cours* 195 (1976).

Sokol, Ronald, Do We Really Need Lawyers?, *Int'l Herald Tribune* 7 (Mar. 10, 2006).

Spain, Anna, Using International Dispute Resolution to Address the Compliance Question in International Law, 40 *Geo. J. Int'l L.* 807 (2009).

Spies, Michael, Iran and the Limits of the Nuclear Non-proliferation Regime, 22 *Am. U. Int'l L. Rev.* 401 (2007).

Stanczyk, Janusz, The Equality of Parties before the International Court of Justice in Cases of Non-appearing Respondent States, in *Forty Years International*

Court of Justice: Jurisdiction, Equity and Equality 35 (A. Bloed and P. van Dijk ed., 1988).
Stein, Eric, Impact of New Weapons Technology on International Law: Selected Aspects, 133 *Rec. des Cours* 13 (1971-II).
Stein, Ted L., Contempt, Crisis, and the Court: The World Court and the Hostage Rescue Attempt, 76 *Am. J. Int'l L.* 499 (1982).
Stein, Torsten, Article 36, in *The Charter of the United Nations* 616 (Bruno Simma ed., 2nd edn, 2002).
Stern, Jessica Eve, Co-operative Security and the CWC: A Comparison of the Chemical and Nuclear Weapons Non-proliferation Regimes, *Contemp. Security Pol'y* 30 (Dec. 1994).
Stipanowich, Thomas J., Arbitration and the Multiparty Dispute: The Search for Workable Solutions, 72 *Iowa L. Rev.* 473 (1987).
Stowell, Ellery, The Law of War and the Atomic Bomb, 39 *Am. J. Int'l L.* 784 (1945).
Strahan, Martin M., Nuclear Weapons, the World Health Organization, and the International Court of Justice: Should an Advisory Opinion Bring Them Together?, 2 *Tulsa J. Comp. & Int'l L.* 395 (1995).
Straubel, Michael, Enhancing the Performance of the Doping Court: How the Court of Arbitration for Sport Can Do Its Job Better, 36 *Loy. U. Chi. L.J.* 1203 (2005).
Strong, S. I., Intervention and Joinder as of Right in International Arbitration: An Infringement of Individual Contract Rights or a Proper Equitable Measure?, 31 *Vand. J. Transnat'l L.* 915 (1998).
Sturma, Pavel, Law of Treaties Reflected in State Responsibility Rules, 19 *Thesaurus Acroasium* 536 (1992).
Sugihara, Takane, The Judicial Function of the International Court of Justice with Respect to Disputes Involving Highly Political Issues, in *The International Court of Justice* 117 (Sam Muller et al. ed., 1997).
Sulemna, Arsalan M., Bargaining in the Shadow of Violence: The NPT, IAEA, and Nuclear Non-proliferation Negotiations, 26 *Berkeley J. Int'l L.* 206 (2008).
Sultan, Allen N., Judicial Autonomy under International Law, 21 *Dayton L. Rev.* 585 (1996).
Summary of Discussion, in *The International Law of Arms Control and Disarmament* 219 (Julie Dahlitz and Detlev Dicke ed., 1991).
Sur, Serge, Les affaires des essais nucléaires: C.I.J. arrêt du 20 décembre 1974, 79 *RGDIP* 972 (1975).
Swaine, Edward T., Unsigning, 55 *Stan. L. Rev.* 2061 (2003).
Swan, J., Explosive Issue in International Law: The French Nuclear Tests, 9 *Melb. Univ. L. Rev.* 296 (1973).
Szasz, Paul C., Granting International Organizations Ius Standi in the International Court of Justice, in *The International Court of Justice: Its Future Role after Fifty Years* 169 (A. S. Muller et al. ed., 1997).

Szasz, Paul C., The Law of International Atomic Energy Agency Safeguards, 3 *Revue Belge de Droit Int'l* 196 (1967).

Szasz, Paul C., The Security Council Starts Legislating, 96 *Am. J. Int'l L.* 901 (2002).

Sztucki, J., International Organizations as Parties to Contentious Proceedings before the International Court of Justice?, in *The International Court of Justice: Its Future Role after Fifty Years* 141 (A. S. Muller et al. ed., 1997).

Talmon, Stefan, The Security Council as World Legislature, 99 *Am. J. Int'l L.* 175 (2005).

Taylor, Prudence, Testing Times for the World Court: Judicial Process and the 1995 French Nuclear Tests Case, 8 *Colo. J. Int'l Envtl. L. & Pol'y* 199 (1997).

Teixeira de Silva, Pascal, Weapons of Mass Destruction: The Iraqi Case, in *The UN Security Council: From the Cold War to the 21st Century* 205 (David Malone ed., 2004).

Thierry, H., Les arrêts du 20 décembre 1974 et les relations de la France avec la C.I. J., 20 *AFDI* 286 (1974).

Thirlway, Hugh, Dilemma or Chimera? Admissibility of Illegally Obtained Evidence in International Adjudication, 78 *Am. J. Int'l L.* 622 (1984).

Thirlway, Hugh, The Indication of Provisional Measures by the International Court of Justice, in *Interim Measures Indicated by International Courts* 1 (Rudolf Bernhardt ed., 1994).

Thirlway, Hugh, The Law and Procedure of the International Court of Justice 1960–1989, 67 *British Y.B. Int'l L.* 27 (1996).

Thomas, Elbert D., Atomic Bombs in International Society, 39 *Am. J. Int'l L.* 736 (1945).

Thomas, Elbert D., Atomic Warfare and International Law, 40 *Am. J. Int'l L.* 84 (1946).

Thompson, Alexander, Coercion through IOs: The Security Council and the Logic of Information Transmission, 60 *Int'l Org.* 1 (2006).

Tomuschat, Christian, Article 33, in *The Charter of the United Nations: A Commentary* 583 (Bruno Simma ed., 2002).

Tomuschat, Christian, Article 36, in *The Statute of the International Court of Justice: A Commentary* 630 (Andreas Zimmermann et al. ed., 2006).

Tomuschat, Christian, Obligations Arising for States without or against their Will, 241 *Rec. des Cours* 195 (1993-IV).

Trachtman, Joel P., The Jurisdiction of the World Trade Organization: Remarks by Joel P. Trachtman, 98 *ASIL Proc.* 139 (2004).

Treves, T., Diplomatic Settlement or Adjudication? Advantages and Drawbacks, in *Règlement pacifique des différends entre États: Perspectives universelle et européenne* 17 (Lucius Caflisch ed., 1998).

Trimble, Phillip R., Beyond Verification: The Next Step in Arms Control, 102 *Harv. L. Rev.* 885 (1989).

Trimble, Phillip R., Legal Dimensions of Arms Control and Disarmament, in 1 *Encyclopedia of Arms Control and Disarmament* 372 (Richard Dean Burns ed., 1993).

Tsipis, Kosta, Foreword, in C. Moxley, *Nuclear Weapons and International Law in the Post-Cold War World* i (2000).

Tyler, Jacob E., Mandatory Arbitration of Discrimination Claims under Collective Bargaining Agreements: The Effect of Wright: Wright v. Universal Marine Service Corp., 119 S. Ct. 391 (1998), 4 *Harv. Negotiation L. Rev.* 253 (1999).

Vallat, Francis, Foreword, in Humphrey Waldock, *International Disputes: The Legal Aspects* i (1972).

Vaziri, Haleh, Iran's Nuclear Quest: Motivations and Consequences, in *The Nuclear Non-proliferation Regime* 310 (Raju G. C. Thomas ed., 1998).

Virally, Michel, La notion de function dans la théorie de l'organisation internationale, in *Mélanges offerts à Charles Rousseau: la communauté internationale* 277 (1974).

Visscher, Charles de, Reflections on the Present Prospects of International Adjudication, 50 *Am. J. Int'l L.* 467 (1956).

Wagoner, David E., Interim Relief in International Arbitration: Enforcement Is a Substantial Problem, 51 *Disp. Resolution J.* 68 (1996).

Waldock, C. H. M., Decline of the Optional Clause, 32 *British Y.B. Int'l L.* 244 (1955–56).

Waldock, C. H. M., Forum Prorogatum or Acceptance of a Unilateral Summons to Appear before the International Court, 2 *Int'l L.Q.* 377 (1948).

Waldron, Jeremy, John Locke: Social Contract versus Political Anthropology, in *The Social Contract from Hobbes to Rawls* 51 (David Boucher and Paul Kelly ed., 1994).

Wall, Andru E., The Legal Case for Invading Iraq and Toppling Hussein, 32 *Isr. Y. B. Hum. Rts.* 165 (2002).

Wang, William, International Arbitration: The Need For Uniform Interim Measures of Relief, 28 *Brook. J. Int'l L.* 1059 (2003).

Ware, Alyn, Rule of Force or Rule of Law? Legal Responses to Nuclear Threats from Terrorism, Proliferation, and War, 2 *Seattle J. Soc. Just.* 243 (2004).

Washington, Monica J., The Practice of Peer Review in the International Nuclear Safety Regime, 72 *N.Y.U.L. Rev.* 430 (1997).

Wastler, Benjamin, Having Its Yellowcake and Eating It Too: How the NSG Waiver for India Threatens to Undermine the Nuclear Nonproliferation Regime, 33 *B.C. Int'l & Comp. L. Rev.* 201 (2010).

Watson, Geoffrey, Constitutionalism, Judicial Review and the World Court, 34 *Harv. Int'l L.J.* 1 (1993).

Wautele, Patrick, Gravieres Rhenanes, 3 *Colum. J. Eur. L.* 465 (1998).

Waxman, Matthew C., The Use of Force against States that Might Have Weapons of Mass Destruction, 31 *Mich. J. Int'l L.* 1 (2009).

Weigand, Frank-Bernd, Introduction, in *Practitioner's Handbook on International Arbitration* 1 (Frank-Bernd Weigand ed., 2002).

Weil, Prosper, L'équité dans la jurisprudence de la cour internationale de justice: Un mystère en voie de disparition?, in *Fifty Years of the International Court of Justice: Essays in Honour of Sir Robert Jennings* 121 (Vaughan Lowe and Malgosia Fitzmaurice ed., 1996).

Weiner, Allen S., The Use of Force and Contemporary Security Threats: Old Medicine for New Ills?, 59 *Stan. L. Rev.* 415 (2006).

Weiss, Edith Brown, Judicial Independence and Impartiality: A Preliminary Inquiry, in *The International Court of Justice at a Crossroads* 123 (Lori F. Damrosch ed., 1987).

Weiss, Edith Brown, Reciprocity and the Optional Clause, in *The International Court of Justice at a Crossroads* 82 (Lori F. Damrosch ed., 1987).

Weiss, Peter, Nuclear War in the Courts, in *Nuclear Weapons, the Peace Movement and the Law* 178 (John Dwar et al. ed., 1986).

Weiss, Peter, The World Court Tackles the Fate of the Earth: An Introduction to the ICJ Advisory Opinion on the Legality of the Threat and Use of Nuclear Weapons, 7 *Transnat'l L. & Contemp. Prob.* 313 (1997).

Weiszäcker, Richard von, All Depends on Member States, in *Paix, développement, démocratie: Boutros Boutros-Ghali Amicorum Discipulorumque Liber* 827 (Georges Abi-Saab et al. ed., 1999).

Wellens, Karel, The UN Security Council and New Threats to the Peace: Back to the Future, 8 *J. Conflict & Security. L.* 15 (2003).

Weston, Burns H., Law and Alternative Security: Toward a Nuclear Weapons-Free World, 75 *Iowa L. Rev.* 1077 (1990).

Weston, Burns H., Lawyers and the Search for Alternatives to Nuclear Deterrence, 54 *U. Cin. L. Rev.* 451 (1985).

Weston, Burns H., Nuclear Weapons and International Law: Prolegomenon to General Illegality, 4 *N.Y. L. Sch'l J. Int'l & Comp. L.* 227 (1984).

Weston, Burns H., Nuclear Weapons and the World Court: Ambiguity's Consensus, 7 *Transnat'l L. & Contemp. Prob.* 371 (1997).

Weston, Burns H., Nuclear Weapons versus International Law: A Contextual Reassessment, in *Nuclear Weapons and Law* 133 (Arthur Selwyn Miller and Martin Feinrider ed., 1984).

White, G., H-Bomb Tests and the International Court, 123 *New L.J.* 615 (1973).

Williamson, Richard L., Jr., Hard Law, Soft Law, and Non-law in Multilateral Arms Control: Some Compliance Hypotheses, 4 *Chi. J. Int'l L.* 59 (2003).

Williamson, Richard L., Jr., Law and the H-Bomb: Strengthening the Nonproliferation Regime to Impede Advanced Proliferation, 28 *Cornell Int'l L.J.* 71 (1995).

Winters, Raven, Preventing Repeat Offenders: North Korea's Withdrawal and the Need for Revisions to the Nuclear Non-proliferation Treaty, 38 *Vand. J. Transnat'l L.* 1499 (2005).

Wood, Michael C., The Interpretation of Security Council Resolutions, 2 *Max Planck Y.B. UNL.* 73 (1998).

Woodliffe, John, Nuclear Weapons and Non-proliferation: The Legal Aspects, in *Nuclear Weapons and International Law* 84 (Istvan Pogany ed., 1987).

Wright, Quincy, Arbitration as a Symbol of Internationalism, in *International Trade Arbitration* 3 (M. Domke ed., 1958).

Wühler, Norbert, Arbitration Clauses in Treaties, in 1 *Encyclopedia of Public International Law* 34 (Rudolf Bernhardt ed., 1992).

Yee, Sienho, Forum Prorogatum in the International Court, 42 *German Y.B. Int'l L.* 147 (1999).

Young, Reuven, Defining Terrorism: The Evolution of Terrorism as a Legal Concept in International Law and Its Influence on Definitions in Domestic Legislation, 29 *B.C. Int'l & Comp. L. Rev.* 23 (2006).

Zimmermann, Andreas and Tobias Thienel, Article 60, in *The Statute of the International Court of Justice: A Commentary* 1275 (Andreas Zimmermann et al. ed., 2006).

INDEX

For additional information about specific countries, please check relevant opinions, cases, and arbitration under the entries "advisory opinions," "case law," and "international arbitration cases."